Language, Truth, and Religious Belief

AMERICAN ACADEMY OF RELIGION
TEXTS AND TRANSLATIONS SERIES

Edited by

Terry Godlove
Hofstra University

Number 19
LANGUAGE, TRUTH, AND
RELIGIOUS BELIEF

edited by
Nancy K. Frankenberry
Hans H. Penner

Language, Truth, and Religious Belief

Studies in Twentieth-Century Theory and Method in Religion

edited by
Nancy K. Frankenberry
Hans H. Penner

Scholars Press
Atlanta, Georgia

Language, Truth, and Religious Belief

Studies in Twentieth-Century Theory and Method in Religion

Edited by
Nancy K. Frankenberry
Hans H. Penner

Library of Congress Cataloging in Publication Data

Language, truth, and religious belief : studies in twentieth-century theory and method in religion / edited by Nancy K. Frankenberry, Hans H. Penner.

p. cm. — (Texts and translations series ; no. 19)
Includes bibliographical references.
ISBN 0-7885-0540-8 (pbk. : alk. paper)
1. Religion—Philosophy. 2. Religion—Methodology.
I. Frankenberry, Nancy, 1947– II. Penner, Hans H., 1934–
III. Series: Texts and translations series (American Academy of Religion) ; no. 19.
BL51.L354 1999
210—dc21 99-12982
CIP

Printed in the United States of America
on acid-free paper

Contents

PREFACE

This book originated as the Senior Year Course at Dartmouth, team-taught by the editors in 1996. Coming from two different areas of specialization—philosophy of religion, and history and anthropology of religion—we shared an interest in methodological and theoretical questions, along with a distaste for eclectic courses that canvas a wide variety of conflicting methods and theories. What could we agree on as the crucial issues and most important readings? What did we have in common intellectually, and what could we agree we wanted Religion majors to know about the study of religion? Slightly pared down for publication, this volume is the result of that surprisingly fruitful and stimulating collaboration.

Having thought about and argued over each of these essays for as long as we have, we want to offer them to other readers along with three bold claims: (1) These readings are among the most important and influential papers or chapters that have been written in English on the topics of language, truth, and religious belief in the twentieth century. (2) The authors represented in these pages, including those we criticize, are likely to remain intellectually provocative and rewarding to engage for quite some time. (3) Any one interested in the study of religion today should know this material, and be able to critically evaluate much of it.

Neither a simple survey nor an exhaustive inventory, the volume is one that can be used by scholars of religion at all levels. Professional colleagues in several disciplines should find here a novel integration of material to prompt reconsideration of familiar terrain. General readers, interested in religion but unaware of developments in the academic study of religion, will find that wrestling with the ideas presented here will take them well beyond the cultural clichés that abound in the media. Graduate students in religious studies who are willing to put these authors in critical conversation with each other will wind up encountering *all* of the major issues in the study of religion today, and advanced undergraduates, like our own, will study formative intellectual legacies that even now they are learning to surpass.

We owe thanks first and foremost to our students, especially those in the Senior Year Course in Spring, 1996, who responded so ably to these readings. We are grateful to our colleagues in the Department of Religion who have discussed "theories and methods" with us over the years, some of them at such distance from the work gathered in this volume that they have been our best critics.

For her invaluable assistance in preparing this manuscript for publication, we are grateful to Jennifer Walker-Johnson. For stepping in at a crucial point, we thank Ross Wilken. For dedicated and professional academic assistance and office management, we are grateful to Sandra Curtis and Stephanie Nelson on a daily basis.

We are happy to acknowledge the advice and encouragement of Terry F. Godlove, Jr., Hofstra University, editor of the AAR Texts and Translations Series. Rex Matthews and Leigh Andersen of Scholars Press guided these pages to print. This book is dedicated to all those Dartmouth Religion majors, past, present, and future, whose inquiring minds make teaching a continuing education for us.

Nancy K. Frankenberry
Hans H. Penner

Acknowledgments and References to Reprinted Articles

Ayer, Alfred J. 1935a. Critique of Ethics and Philosophy. *Language, Truth and Logic,* 102–120. New York: Dover Publications. Reprinted by permission of the publisher.

—— 1935b. The Self and the Common World. *Language, Truth and Logic,* 120–133. New York: Dover Publications. Reprinted by permission of the publisher.

Davidson, Donald. 1984. On the Very Idea of a Conceptual Scheme. *Inquiries into Truth and Interpretation,* 183–198. Oxford: Oxford University Press. Reprinted by permission of the publisher.

—— 1989. The Myth of the Subjective. In Michael Krausz (ed.), *Relativism: Interpretation and Confrontation,* 159–171. Notre Dame: University of Notre Dame Press. Reprinted by permission of the publisher.

Edwards, Paul. 1965. Professor Tillich's Confusions. *Mind,* Vol. LXXIV, No. 294, 192–214. Reprinted by permission of Oxford University Press and the author.

Frankenberry, Nancy. Pragmatism, Truth, and the Disenchantment of Subjectivity. Printed with permission of the author.

Frankenberry, Nancy and Hans H. Penner. Geertz's Longlasting Moods, Motivations, and Metaphysical Conceptions. Printed with permission of the authors.

Geertz, Clifford. 1966. Religion as a Cultural System. In Michael Banton (ed.), *Anthropological Approaches to the Study of Religion,* 1–42. London: Routledge. Reprinted by permission of the publisher and author.

Godlove, Terry. 1984. In What Sense Are Religions Conceptual Frameworks? *Journal of the American Academy of Religion,* Vol. LII/2, 289–305. Reprinted by permission of the publisher and author.

Horton, Robin. 1976. Professor Winch on Safari. *European Journal of Sociology*, Vol. XVII, No. 1, 157–180. Reprinted by permission of the Journal.

Klemke, E. D. 1960. Are Religious Statements Meaningful? *Journal of Religion*, Vol. XL, 27–39. Reprinted by permission of the University of Chicago Press and the author.

Malcolm, Norman. 1977. The Groundlessness of Belief. In Stuart C. Brown (ed.), *Reason and Religion*, 143–157. Cornell: Cornell University Press. Reprinted by permission of the publisher and author.

Penner, Hans H. 1989. Functional Explanations of Religion. *Impasse and Resolution: A Critique of the Study of Religion*, 103–123. New York: Peter Lang Publisher. Reprinted by permission of the publisher and author.

Penner, Hans H. 1995. Why Does Semantics Matter to the Study of Religion? *Method and Theory in the Study of Religion*, Vol. 7-3, 221–249. Reprinted by permission of the publisher and author.

Rorty, Richard. 1986. Pragmatism, Davidson and Truth. In Ernest LePore (ed.), *Truth and Interpretation: Perspectives on the Philosophy of Donald Davidson*, 333–355. Oxford: Blackwell Publishers. Reprinted by permission of the publisher.

Spiro, Melford E. 1966. Religion: Problems of Definition and Explanation. In Michael Banton (ed.), *Anthropological Approaches to the Study of Religion*, 85–122. London: Routledge. Reprinted by permission of the publisher.

Tillich, Paul. 1951. Truth and Verification. *Systematic Theology*, 100–103. Chicago: University of Chicago Press. Reprinted by permission of the publisher.

—— 1951b. The Actuality of God. *Systematic Theology*, 235–252. Chicago: University of Chicago Press. Reprinted by permission of the publisher.

—— 1957. Symbols of Faith. *The Dynamics of Faith*, 41–54. New York: Harper Collins. Reprinted by permission of Harper Collins Publishers, Inc.

Winch, Peter. 1964. Understanding a Primitive Society. *American Philosophical Quarterly*, Vol. I, 307–324. Reprinted by permission of the Journal.

Wittgenstein, Ludwig. 1966. Lectures on Religious Belief. Oxford: Basil Blackwell. In Cyril Barrett (ed.), *L. Wittgenstein: Lectures and Conversations on Aesthetics, Psychology and Religious Belief,* translated/edited by Barrett, C., 54–72. Berkeley: University of California Press, 1967. Reprinted by permission of the University of California Press.

Introduction

Hans H. Penner
Nancy K. Frankenberry

Why is religion widely regarded as subjective? Or as symbolic? Or as expressive and non-rational? Why is faith frequently said to be the only mode of grasping its meaning? Why is religion often regarded as a worldview, bestowing ultimate meaning or indicating the answers to life's deep problems? Why is religion often equated with "what one does with one's own solitude" or what is reserved for a private sphere? Why is religion regularly opposed to science? Where do these beliefs come from and how are they to be evaluated? As we hope to show in this volume, these assumptions are the product of very powerful but problematic theories of the relations between language, truth, and religious belief. Far from being inescapable either logically or historically, these assumptions are quite modern and can be traced to distinct methods and theories that have been used in the analysis of religion and religious beliefs throughout the twentieth century.

This book brings together influential authors and essays of the "received tradition" in the philosophy of religion and the anthropology of religion, together with new work in semantic theory that has crucial consequences for an explanation of religion. In the first three parts, we have selected classic examples of methods or theories that constitute the received tradition: positivism, functionalism, and relativism. Despite the prevalence and popularity of these three "isms," they stand in need of critical analysis. In Part IV we present readings that represent a new point of departure for religious studies. It is too soon to give a definitive name to this new orientation, although "holism" and "neopragmatism" and "antifoundationalism" are its most common philosophical expressions today. We are less interested in adding but one more "ism" than in allowing these authors to speak for themselves (for ourselves) in terms of the ideas they command. If these ideas turn out to converge on a significant theoretical and methodological revolution in the study of religion in the twenty-first century, it will be one in which appeals to subjectivity, to private states of consciousness, to worldviews, to faith, and to the satisfaction of human needs will make little sense.

Our root assumption is that the turn to holistic theory and linguistics in the twentieth century has transformed the way in which we think of "meaning" and "truth." This transformation has consequences for traditional issues concerning "religious belief." In particular, the breakdown of the received tradition has inspired interest in theories of language that have helped us to understand the inadequacy, incoherence, or fallacy of positivism, functionalism, and relativism. Although different in purpose and type, all three have circulated with insistent regularity in twentieth century thought, often determining the very premises of debates concerning religious language, meaning, belief and practice.

Positivism accepts the tenets of Humean empiricism according to which all knowledge is of two kinds. Either a statement is analytically true by definition and its denial a contradiction ("All widows are women") or it is synthetic (empirical) and subject to verification through sense experience ("Jane is a widow"). According to the verification principle, only those statements that can be empirically verified are factually meaningful. First employed as a club with which to beat down religious and metaphysical "nonsense," the verification principle eventually waned as it became clear that it amounted only to a fragile tautology: assertions not testable in certain approved ways are not testable in those approved ways.

The spirit of positivism yet lingers, however, and its theory of meaning is still assumed even among scholars of religion. In crucial ways, both E. D. Klemke and Paul Tillich in Part I embrace A. J. Ayer's Bulldozer and simply re-label as "absolute presuppositions" or "symbolic language," respectively, the very same ground ploughed by Ayer as "pseudo-synthetic." Readers inclined to accept the verification principle of meaning will need to show how they would construct a second whole theory of meaning for the domain of religion. On the other hand, readers who find Paul Edwards' criticism of Tillichese devastating should also notice that his interpretation of religion assumes that the principle of verification makes sense.

Functionalism has for many decades been the primary theory of much social science. It has, indeed, become the common sense view of how religion is best explained: it functions to satisfy certain needs. Functionalist arguments focus attention on the putative needs and interests served by particular beliefs, whether they be the needs and interests of discrete individuals, groups, classes, institutions, structures, or systems. Thus it is said that religious beliefs function variously to satisfy complex biological, psychological, and social needs of humans, as well as a grand need for Meaning (Melford Spiro, Edmund Leach, Clifford Geertz).

Functionalist arguments are offered as causal explanations for the existence of particular beliefs, practices and institutions on the assumption that the function constitutes the cause of the belief or practice or institution. For example, religion is said to exist or persist because it serves as a cause of social maintenance or the reduction of anxiety in an individual. The function of religion is also explained as providing a framework for meaning, and securing answers to deep moral and existential questions.

Glossed over in such arguments is the question we (the editors) regard as most important: what are the truth conditions of these putative functions? In other words, are the religious beliefs, frameworks, concerns, and answers *true*? Functionalists have answered this question in three different ways. The first answer, ever since E. B. Tylor, tells us that taken literally as answers to empirical questions religious beliefs are false. The second response, ever since Durkheim, asserts that all religions are true, in the sense that they function to maintain or integrate social systems. The third response, ever since Freud, states that religious beliefs and frameworks of meaning are neither true nor false. They are symbolic of hidden meanings that must be deciphered or decoded. All three of these responses to the question of meaning entail an attempt to reduce the question of meaning and truth to a type of causal explanation.

Over the course of sustained criticism, functionalist explanations have gone through many revisions without, however, achieving satisfactory formulation. Chapter 8 presents a detailed argument against the *logic* of functionalism, showing that the addition of "latent" functions, "functional equivalents," or "classes of functions," does not save the theory from logical fallacies or trivial conclusions.

Of the three dominant received traditions, relativism has so far proved to be the most resilient. Whether in the form of conceptual, linguistic, cultural, epistemological, or moral relativism, the thesis holds that what is true or false is determined in and by the various conceptual frameworks, languages, cultural systems, epistemes, or moral paradigms one either acquiesces in or adopts. Notoriously, these frameworks differ, and inevitably lead to the conclusion that there are different truths relative to different religious worldviews. Thus there can be no valid test of the truth of one worldview from within another worldview because they are incommensurable; that is to say, translation between worldviews or paradigms is impossible. This maxim lurks behind the popular notion that in order to understand Buddhism, for example, one must become a Buddhist. The problem, of course, is that given the impasse of incommensurablity, no one ever can tell us just how this is to be done.

The critique of positivism was completed by the 1960s in the philosophy of science, but its lingering influence continues in the study of religion up to the present day. The critique of functionalism in the social sciences was well-known by roughly the same time, but still remains either unknown or unheeded in religious studies today. The critique of relativism has barely been broached in the human sciences as a whole, and in the study of religion has become confused with "pluralism." Just as the two versions of positivist meaning ("religious beliefs are false" or "religious belief is neither true nor false") help to set the stage for functionalist explanations ("it persists because certain needs cause it to persist"), functionalism in turn feeds into relativism ("different cognitive systems respond to the same needs").

We emphasize that the intellectual traditions encompassed in this book are at once very narrow and very large. Unlike eclectic anthologies of every known "method and theory," the readings brought together here are narrowly focused on major Anglo-American methods and theories by which religion has been studied in the twentieth century. At the same time, we find that these received traditions have exerted a very large influence and cast a long shadow across many disciplines in addition to religious studies. Our two fields, philosophy of religion (Frankenberry) and anthropology of religion (Penner), show significant overlap methodologically and theoretically. A unique feature of this book is that it draws upon both specializations in collecting some of the most representative authors and essays in the philosophy and anthropology of religion.

In the introductions to each section we sketch the kind of critical analysis we want readers of this volume to undertake in greater detail. In strategic locations within each section, we include readings that offer a critical or constructive perspective on the other essays. For example, in Part II, the concluding essay (Penner) offers an argument against the theory presupposed in the previous essays. In Part III, the first two essays (Davidson) frame the way in which readers can interpret the remaining essays. (In fact, Davidson's essays deserve to be read carefully several times, and used as a critical tool for evaluating *all* of the readings in Parts I, and II, and III.) Points of view are often combative. Not everything goes. Even in Part IV, subtle debates appear among authors who share in common a theory of holism.

We conceive this anthology as having three primary aims. First, we want to introduce and invite criticism of the received tradition of theory in the study of religion. Second, we hope that readers engaged in the academic study of religion will recognize the legacy of these three impasses in most of what they currently read about religion, religious belief, symbolism, and practice. Third, we are proposing an alternative approach to the study of religion, truth, and meaning. Found in several of the cognitive sciences, this alternative is based upon the holistic principle that no single element, unit, or symbol has its own intrinsic properties, values or meanings. If this principle is true, then it follows that the inherent rationality of a linguistic, cultural or religious system consists in the relations that constitute the various elements of the system. Therefore, a phoneme, a word, a belief, or an act has no intrinsic meaning in itself, but only in relation to words, sentences, belief systems, and other actions. Finally, a holistic theory of religion entails that the domain of mental events, for example, cannot be explained independently of the social environment in which they are located. The reason for this is not because mental events are not states of the brain and the nervous system—they may well be that—but because such reductions would violate the first two principles of holism: that meaning is constituted by relations and no single element, unit, or symbol has its own intrinsic properties, values, or meaning; and that rationality is understood in terms of the coherence of relations in a system of beliefs or events.

On this account, any causal explanation of beliefs and desires that accounts for them as need-fulfilling, or as computational states of the brain, cannot be correct. Beliefs, desires, and other propositional attitudes such as hope and fear cannot be explained by a theoretical reduction either to their causal antecedents or to their consequences.

The essays in Part IV present holistic theory and the application of some of its principles to the academic study of religion.

We can expect dramatic intellectual repercussions to follow from repudiation of the three long-entrenched mistakes of positivism, functionalism, and relativism, and the adoption of holism. If we are right, a new and more exciting set of challenges beckons to scholars of religion in the 21st century.

Part I

The Legacy of Logical Positivism for the Study of Religion

INTRODUCTION TO PART I

How do we know whether a statement is true? The most clear-cut answer to that question given in twentieth century philosophy appeared in the movement known as logical positivism. Starting in Vienna and flourishing in England and North America in the 1930's and 1940's, logical positivism treated the word "true" as a stamp to be placed on statements that could be inspected and certified either as "factual states of affairs" or as tautologies. When metaphysicians or theologians assert "God is Being-Itself" they are making a cognitive claim, that is, a claim to know something is true. Positivists thought they could show that statements of this kind were incapable of being true and that, therefore, theologians who write these sentences cannot be making genuine cognitive claims. Classically formulated in A. J. Ayer's *Language, Truth, and Logic,* logical positivism held that religious beliefs, having no factual meaning, serve merely to express the attitudes, intentions, or emotions of the speaker. Thus, not only religious discourse, but also ethics and aesthetics, belonged in a non-cognitive dustbin and could be swept into an expressivist theory of language.

According to Ayer, only two classes of statements do have a capacity for being true: the analytic and the synthetic. A statement is cognitively meaningful if it is analytic or genuinely synthetic. A statement is factually (or empirically) meaningful, if and only if, it is genuinely synthetic. Pseudo-synthetic statements are incapable of being either true or false and therefore are considered cognitively and factually meaningless. A special type of meaning was assigned to the pseudo-synthetic: emotive meaning.

The issue of verification that arises with this proposal has been in many ways one of the most important intellectual issues of the twentieth century with its reverence for scientific thinking and mathematical exactitude. Verification concerns the possibility of checking on the truth or falsity of supposedly synthetic statements by means of observations. A statement such as "God loves the world" appears to be as synthetic as the statement "hydrogen atoms have one electron." Religious believers who make statements of the first sort seem to be providing factual information about the world. Unlike scientists, however, they do not specify observations that would verify the truth of their claims, and they frequently hold their convictions immune to falsification.

Two crucial assumptions characterized logical positivism and contributed to its demise: first, that any proposition that is not a literal proposition is meaningless; and second, that the test of literal meaning is verification by sense experience. On this basis, religious propositions were in jeopardy but so too were many other propositions that positivists had no desire to challenge, such as "All bodies falling from a state of rest will accelerate at a rate of 32 feet per second." In the end, the most serious weakness of logical positivism was its inability to state the semantic status of the verification principle of looking for some actual or possible state of affairs which will confirm or disconfirm a statement. The theory that the materials for meaning arise from observation is a theory that is not itself subject to verification by observation. Is it then meaningless?

Neither the positivists nor their analytic successors ever came up with a viable version of verifiability. The various versions of verification and falsification that succeeded in eliminating religious and metaphysical statements also eliminated key scientific statements along with them. Finally, the confirmation criterion kept scientific statements in but allowed for the legitimacy of religious and metaphysical statements as well. If the verification and falsification criteria of meaning were too restrictive, the confirmation criterion was too permissive.

Today logical positivism is flawed and flogged, but not yet dead. As both a method and a theory (of meaning), it forms an implicit set of background assumptions, nowhere more so than in debates about religious belief. It is the problematic against which Norman Malcolm, for example, devises his Wittgensteinian strategy of separating science and religion as different language games whose framework principles are themselves groundless (Chapter 12).

The legacy of logical positivism is apparent in the way many theorists of religion over-emphasize the very features the positivists pulverized, namely, the personal, the subjective, the non-cognitive, the emotive, and the imaginative. Existentialists in particular have valorized these as the special domain of "the religious," parallel to positivism's privileging of "the observation of facts." The legacy can also be found in the continuing debate about whether rituals are rational or non-rational, cognitive or expressive.

In one of the most interesting twists to the verificationist theory, some interpreters have agreed that religious statements if taken literally are either false or meaningless, but they have held that religious language still has a valid *use*. This has led to the development of various theological proposals according to which religious language is to be understood as expressive (Klemke) or as symbolic (Tillich).

E. D. Klemke's essay is indicative of how a number of religious thinkers have tried to meet A. J. Ayer's challenge. Klemke's answer, in "Are Religious Statements Meaningful?" is that while religious statements may have no meaning as sentences, they have meaning as absolute presuppositions, i.e., as suppositions that are neither true nor false, proved nor disproved. They can only be believed or accepted on faith. Unfortunately for Klemke's position, a religious absolute presupposition turns out to have meaning only *for a particular person,* and thus this line of defense quickly reduces to subjectivism. On the issue of the truth or falsity of absolute presuppositions, Klemke can only say that "one cannot know and does not ask."

The appeal of such a position to theologians can be seen in Paul Tillich's development of an existentialist theology and ontological framework of meaning. Tillich is concerned with the meaning of existence rather than with the meaning of statements and propositions. He recommends "experiential" rather than experimental verification. In "Symbols of Faith" Tillich develops the view that the language of faith is the language of symbol and myth, not of literal meaning. This selection and the one on "Truth and Verification" can be read as though directly addressed to A. J. Ayer. So significant was the verification challenge and empiricist criteria of "literal meaning" that theologians like Tillich, if they were to show how religious beliefs could be "true," had to defend some other, higher, level of "truth" than that staked out by logical positivism. Thus, the truth of faith is had in symbols, and experiential verification is deemed "truer to life, though less exact and definite." Aside from the obvious difficulties with Tillich's notion that verification occurs "within the totality of a life-process," his account of symbolic language raises two questions that go unanswered in his system: (1) why do people continue to use symbolic language if they understand it to be symbolic or metaphorical or figurative? and (2) if they do not understand the language of faith symbolically or metaphorically, how is it the case that they fail to grasp the meaning of their own natural language?

The critic Paul Edwards charges Tillich with offering only a "bombastic redescription of empirical facts." Edwards confronts Tillich with the following dilemma: he must either admit that his ontological language about being and non-being amounts to nothing more than a statement of fact about various matters, or he must show the "extra" meaning that is involved in the ontological statement—an effort that Edwards regards as doomed to failure.

Defending Tillich, one could note that it is not "empirical facts" that he bombastically redescribes. His ultimate concern, as he makes clear, is not with empirical facts but with the presuppositions of being and truth which make it possible to experience empirical facts at all. It would perhaps be more fair to say that Tillich's system presents a "bombastic redescription of human experience."

In evaluating Edwards's essay, readers should take into account three questions. First, does Tillich intend to offer non-symbolic translations of religious statements, as Edwards assumes? Second, are there meaningful, irreducible symbolic statements? Third, what is the defense of Edwards own semantic principle which states that a symbolic or metaphorical statement is meaningful only if its cognitive content is expressible by some "literal statement"?

In the end we have two principal criticisms of Tillich's rendering of language, truth, and the logic of religious belief. The first pertains to his understanding of symbolic meaning and the second to his use of a two-level theory of truth. It is very hard to see how the ontological statements about God in terms of being-itself can perform the job of explanation and interpretation when they too are said to be symbolic. Do not symbolic statements stand as much in need of translation as the theological statements about God they purport to interpret? To the extent that a depth of meaning is thought to inhere in religious symbols, a means of extracting it is needed. Once that means is discovered, however, and the code is cracked, the hidden meaning disclosed, it seems that religious symbols are thereby converted to ordinary language and meaning, rendering the symbols irrelevant. In fact, in most instances, once the symbols are decoded the gods have surprisingly little or nothing to say.

A parallel criticism can be made of the two-level theory of truth. By emphasizing a second kind of truth, over and above that of the analytic and the synthetic regarded as true by positivism, twentieth century theologians hoped to consign some valid, but limited, truths to a lower level and to salvage religious truths for a higher level accessible to the "subjective" or "existential" participant. But the contrast between two fundamental modes of truth inevitably divided into "objective" truth and "subjective" truth with no way of reconciling the two. Even more problematically, the hierarchical ordering of higher and lower types of truth left the religious level impervious to criticisms from the so-called lower level. Under a variety of formats, the topic of "truth" in religion came to be associated with "faith" and "commitment" apart from propositional utterances. But to the extent that the truths grasped by faith could be linguistically stated, they were not immune to questions about their truth-conditions, and to the extent that they had truth-conditions, they were on a logical par with the "lower" level.

Laboring under the threat of existential meaninglessness, the theological imagination turned repeatedly to the category of "faith." But everywhere that we find the recommendation to adopt religious beliefs solely on the basis of faith, we also find tacit consent to the positivist picture of knowledge as consisting of two halves, an empirical given and a theoretical structure. Since most beliefs that persons assented to as "religious" were not, in any direct way, about observations based in experience, and were not put forward as purely analytic propositions, all avenues seemed exhausted and religious recourse could only be made by leaps of decision that went against the odds. Faith, as stressed by "theological positivists," was *not* knowledge and was therefore associated with risk and doubt. The ideal of persisting in spite of the evidence became integral to the modern understanding of religious belief. In this way, for the last two hundred years both sceptics and believers could join in agreement that faith is indeed a subjective passion that lacks any rational justification.

1

Language, Truth and Logic

A. J. Ayer

I. The Elimination of Metaphysics

The traditional disputes of philosophers are, for the most part, as unwarranted as they are unfruitful. The surest way to end them is to establish beyond question what should be the purpose and method of a philosophical enquiry. And this is by no means so difficult a task as the history of philosophy would lead one to suppose. For if there are any questions which science leaves it to philosophy to answer, a straightforward process of elimination must lead to their discovery.

We may begin by criticising the metaphysical thesis that philosophy affords us knowledge of a reality transcending the world of science and common sense. Later on, when we come to define metaphysics and account for its existence, we shall find that it is possible to be a metaphysician without believing in a transcendent reality; for we shall see that many metaphysical utterances are due to the commission of logical errors, rather than to a conscious desire on the part of their authors to go beyond the limits of experience. But it is convenient for us to take the case of those who believe that it is possible to have knowledge of a transcendent reality as a starting-point for our discussion. The arguments which we use to refute them will subsequently be found to apply to the whole of metaphysics.

One way of attacking a metaphysician who claimed to have knowledge of a reality which transcended the phenomenal world would be to enquire from what premises his propositions were deduced. Must he not begin, as other men do, with the evidence of his senses? And if so, what valid process of reasoning can possibly lead him to the conception of a transcendent reality? Surely from empirical premises nothing whatsoever concerning the properties, or even the existence, of anything super-empirical can legitimately be inferred. But this objection would be met by a denial on the part of the metaphysician that his assertions were ultimately based on the evidence of his senses. He would say that he was endowed with a faculty of intellectual intuition which enabled him to know facts that could not be known through sense-experience. And even if it could be shown that he was relying on empirical premises, and that his venture into a nonempirical world was therefore logically unjustified, it would not follow that the assertions which he made concerning this nonempirical world could not be true. For the fact that a conclusion does not follow from its putative premise is not sufficient to show that it is false. Consequently one cannot overthrow a system of transcendent metaphysics merely by criticising the way in which it comes into being. What is required is rather a criticism of the nature of the actual statements which comprise it. And this is the line of argument which we shall, in fact, pursue. For we shall maintain that no statement which refers to a "reality" transcending the limits of all possible sense-experience can possibly have any literal significance; from which it must follow that the labours of those who have striven to describe such a reality have all been devoted to the production of nonsense.

It may be suggested that this is a proposition which has already been proved by Kant. But although Kant also condemned transcendent metaphysics, he did so on different grounds. For he said that the human understanding was so constituted that it lost itself in contradictions when it ventured out beyond the limits of possible experience and attempted to deal with things in themselves. And thus he made the impossibility of a transcendent metaphysic not, as we do, a matter of logic, but a matter of fact. He asserted, not that our minds could not conceivably have had the power of penetrating beyond the phenomenal world, but merely that they were in fact devoid of it. And this leads the critic to ask how, if it is possible to know only what lies within the bounds of sense-experience, the author can be justified in asserting that real things do exist beyond, and how he can tell what are the boundaries beyond which the human understanding may not venture, unless he succeeds in passing them himself. As Wittgenstein says, "in order to draw a limit to thinking, we should have to think both sides of this limit,"[1] a truth to which Bradley gives a special twist in maintaining that the man who is ready to prove that metaphysics is impossible is a brother metaphysician with a rival theory of his own.[2]

Whatever force these objections may have against the Kantian doctrine, they have none whatsoever against the thesis that I am about to set forth. It cannot here be said that the author is himself overstepping the barrier he maintains to be impassable. For the fruitlessness of attempting to transcend the limits of possible sense-experience will be deduced, not from a psychological hypothesis concerning the actual constitution of the human mind, but from the rule which determines the literal significance of language. Our charge against the metaphysician is not that he attempts to employ the understanding in a field where it cannot profitably venture, but that he produces sentences which fail to conform to the conditions under which alone a sentence can be literally significant. Nor are we ourselves obliged to talk nonsense in order to show that all sentences of a certain type are necessarily devoid of literal significance. We need only formulate the criterion which enables us to test whether a sentence expresses a genuine proposition about a matter of fact, and then point out that the sentences under consideration fail to satisfy it. And this we shall now proceed to do. We shall first of all formulate the criterion in somewhat vague terms, and then give the explanations which are necessary to render it precise.

The criterion which we use to test the genuineness of apparent statements of fact is the criterion of verifiability. We say that a sentence is factually significant to any given person, if, and only if, he knows how to verify the proposition which it purports to express—that is, if he knows what observations would lead him, under certain conditions, to accept the proposition as being true, or reject it as being false. If, on the other hand, the putative proposition is of such a character that the assumption of its truth, or falsehood, is consistent with any assumption whatsoever concerning the nature of his future experience, then, as far as he is concerned, it is, if not a tautology, a mere pseudo-proposition. The sentence expressing it may be emotionally significant to him; but it is not literally significant. And with regard to questions the procedure is the same. We enquire in

---

1 *Tractatus Logico-Philosophicus*, Preface.

2 Bradley, *Appearance and Reality*, 2nd ed., p.1.

every case what observations would lead us to answer the question, one way or the other; and, if none can be discovered, we must conclude that the sentence under consideration does not, as far as we are concerned, express a genuine question, however strongly its grammatical appearance may suggest that it does.

As the adoption of this procedure is an essential factor in the argument of this book, it needs to be examined in detail.

In the first place, it is necessary to draw a distinction between practical verifiability, and verifiability in principle. Plainly we all understand, in many cases believe, propositions which we have not in fact taken steps to verify. Many of these are propositions which we could verify if we took enough trouble. But there remain a number of significant propositions, concerning matters of fact, which we could not verify even if we chose; simply because we lack the practical means of placing ourselves in the situation where the relevant observations could be made. A simple and familiar example of such a proposition is the proposition that there are mountains on the farther side of the moon.[3] No rocket has yet been invented which would enable me to go and look at the farther side of the moon, so that I am unable to decide the matter by actual observation. But I do know what observations would decide it for me, if, as is theoretically conceivable, I were once in a position to make them. And therefore I say that the proposition is verifiable in principle, if not in practice, and is accordingly significant. On the other hand, such a metaphysical pseudo-proposition as "the Absolute enters into, but is itself incapable of, evolution and progress,"[4] is not even in principle verifiable. For one cannot conceive of an observation which would enable one to determine whether the Absolute did, or did not, enter into evolution and progress. Of course it is possible that the author of such a remark is using English words in a way in which they are not commonly used by English-speaking people, and that he does, in fact, intend to assert something which could be empirically verified. But until he makes us understand how the proposition that he wishes to express would be verified, he fails to communicate anything to us. And if he admits, as I think the author of the remark in question would have admitted, that his words were not intended to express

---

[3] This example has been used by Professor Schlick to illustrate the same point.

[4] A remark taken at random from *Appearance and Reality*, by F.H. Bradley.

either a tautology or a proposition which was capable, at least in principle, of being verified, then it follows that he has made an utterance which has no literal significance even for himself.

A further distinction which we must make is the distinction between the "strong" and the "weak" sense of the term "verifiable." A proposition is said to be verifiable, in the strong sense of the term, if, and only if, its truth could be conclusively established in experience. But it is verifiable, in the weak sense, if it is possible for experience to render it probable. In which sense are we using the term when we say that a putative proposition is genuine only if it is verifiable?

It seems to me that if we adopt conclusive verifiability as our criterion of significance, as some positivists have proposed,[5] our argument will prove too much. Consider, for example, the case of general propositions of law—such propositions, namely, as "arsenic is poisonous"; "men are mortal"; "a body tends to expand when it is heated." It is of the very nature of these propositions that their truth cannot be established with certainty by any finite series of observations. But if it is recognised that such general propositions of law are designed to cover an infinite number of cases, then it must be admitted that they cannot, even in principle, be verified conclusively. And then, if we adopt conclusive verifiability as our criterion of significance, we are logically obliged to treat these general propositions of law in the same fashion as we treat the statements of the metaphysician.

In face of this difficulty, some positivists[6] have adopted the heroic course of saying that these general propositions are indeed pieces of nonsense, albeit an essentially important type of nonsense. But here the introduction of the term "important" is simply an attempt to hedge. It serves only to mark the authors' recognition that their view is somewhat too paradoxical, without in any way removing the paradox. Besides, the difficulty is not confined to the case of general propositions of law, though it is there revealed most plainly. It is hardly less obvious in the case of propositions about the remote past. For it must surely be admitted that, however strong the

---

[5] E.g. M. Schlick, "Positivismus und Realismus," *Erkenntnis*, Vol. I, 1930. F. Waismann, "Logische Analyse des Warscheinlichkeitsbegriffs," *Erkenntnis*, Vol. I, 1930.

[6] E.g. M. Schlick, "Die Kausalität in der gegenwärtigen Physik," *Naturwissenschaft*, Vol. 19, 1931.

evidence in favour of historical statements may be, their truth can never become more than highly probable. And to maintain that they also constituted an important, or unimportant, type of nonsense would be unplausible, to say the very least. Indeed, it will be our contention that no proposition, other than a tautology, can possibly be anything more than a probable hypothesis. And if this is correct, the principle that a sentence can be factually significant only if it expresses what is conclusively verifiable is self-stultifying as a criterion of significance. For it leads to the conclusion that it is impossible to make a significant statement of fact at all.

Nor can we accept the suggestion that a sentence should be allowed to be factually significant if, and only if, it expresses something which is definitely confutable by experience.[7] Those who adopt this course assume that, although no finite series of observations is ever sufficient to establish the truth of a hypothesis beyond all possibility of doubt, there are crucial cases in which a single observation, or series of observations, can definitely confute it. But, as we shall show later on, this assumption is false. A hypothesis cannot be conclusively confuted any more than it can be conclusively verified. For when we take the occurrence of certain observations as proof that a given hypothesis is false, we presuppose the existence of certain conditions. And though, in any given case, it may be extremely improbable that this assumption is false, it is not logically impossible. We shall see that there need be no self-contradiction in holding that some of the relevant circumstances are other than we have taken them to be, and consequently that the hypothesis has not really broken down. And if it is not the case that any hypothesis can be definitely confuted, we cannot hold that the genuineness of a proposition depends on the possibility of its definite confutation.

Accordingly, we fall back on the weaker sense of verification. We say that the question that must be asked about any putative statement of fact is not, would any observations make its truth or falsehood logically certain? but simply, would any observations be relevant to the determination of its truth or falsehood? And it is only if a negative answer is given to this second question that we conclude that the statement under consideration is nonsensical.

To make our position clearer, we may formulate it in another way. Let us call a proposition which records an actual or possible

---

[7] This has been proposed by Karl Popper in his *Logik der Forschung*.

observation an experiential proposition. Then we may say that it is the mark of a genuine factual proposition, not that it should be equivalent to an experiential proposition, or any finite number of experiential propositions, but simply that some experiential propositions can be deduced from it in conjunction with certain other premises without being deducible from those other premises alone.[8]

This criterion seems liberal enough. In contrast to the principle of conclusive verifiability, it clearly does not deny significance to general propositions or to propositions about the past. Let us see what kinds of assertion it rules out.

A good example of the kind of utterance that is condemned by our criterion as being not even false but nonsensical would be the assertion that the world of sense-experience was altogether unreal. It must, of course, be admitted that our senses do sometimes deceive us. We may, as the result of having certain sensations, expect certain other sensations to be obtainable which are, in fact, not obtainable. But, in all such cases, it is further sense-experience that informs us of the mistakes that arise out of sense-experience. We say that the senses sometimes deceive us, just because the expectations to which our sense-experiences give rise do not always accord with what we subsequently experience. That is, we rely on our senses to substantiate or confute the judgements which are based on our sensations. And therefore the fact that our perceptual judgements are sometimes found to be erroneous has not the slightest tendency to show that the world of sense-experience is unreal. And, indeed, it is plain that no conceivable observation, or series of observations, could have any tendency to show that the world revealed to us by sense-experience was unreal. Consequently, anyone who condemns the sensible world as a world of mere appearance, as opposed to reality, is saying something which, according to our criterion of significance, is literally nonsensical.

An example of a controversy which the application of our criterion obliges us to condemn as fictitious is provided by those who dispute concerning the number of substances that there are in the world. For it is admitted both by monists, who maintain that reality is one substance, and by pluralists, who maintain that reality is many, that it is impossible to imagine any empirical situation which would

---

[8] This is an over-simplified statement, which is not literally correct. I give what I believe to be the correct formulation in the Introduction.

be relevant to the solution of their dispute. But if we are told that no possible observation could give any probability either to the assertion that reality was one substance or to the assertion that it was many, then we must conclude that neither assertion is significant. We shall see later on[9] that there are genuine logical and empirical questions involved in the dispute between monists and pluralists. But the metaphysical question concerning "substance" is ruled out by our criterion as spurious.

A similar treatment must be accorded to the controversy between realists and idealists, in its metaphysical aspect. A simple illustration, which I have made use of in a similar argument elsewhere,[10] will help to demonstrate this. Let us suppose that a picture is discovered and the suggestion made that it was painted by Goya. There is a definite procedure for dealing with such a question. The experts examine the picture to see in what way it resembles the accredited works of Goya, and to see if it bears any marks which are characteristic of a forgery; they look up contemporary records for evidence of the existence of such a picture and so on. In the end, they may still disagree, but each one knows what empirical evidence would go to confirm or discredit his opinion. Suppose, now, that these men have studied philosophy and some of them proceed to maintain that this picture is a set of ideas in the perceiver's mind, or in God's mind, others that it is objectively real. What possible experience could any of them have which would be relevant to the solution of this dispute one way or the other? In the ordinary sense of the term "real," in which it is opposed to "illusory," the reality of the picture is not in doubt. The disputants have satisfied themselves that the picture is real, in this sense, by obtaining a correlated series of sensations of sight and sensations of touch. Is there any similar process by which they could discover whether the picture was real, in the sense in which the term "real" is opposed to "ideal"? Clearly there is none. But, if that is so, the problem is fictitious according to our criterion. This does not mean that the realist-idealist controversy may be dismissed without further ado. For it can legitimately be regarded as a dispute concerning the analysis of existential propositions, and so as involving a logical problem which, as we shall see,

---

[9] In Chapter VIII.

[10] Vide "Demonstration of the Impossibility of Metaphysics," *Mind*, 1934, p. 339.

can be definitively solved.[11] What we have just shown is that the question at issue between idealists and realists becomes fictitious when, as is often the case, it is given a metaphysical interpretation.

There is no need for us to give further examples of the operation of our criterion of significance. For our object is merely to show that philosophy, as a genuine branch of knowledge, must be distinguished from metaphysics. We are not now concerned with the historical question how much of what has traditionally passed for philosophy is actually metaphysical. We shall, however, point out later on that the majority of the "great philosophers" of the past were not essentially metaphysicians, and thus reassure those who would otherwise be prevented from adopting our criterion by considerations of piety.

As to the validity of the verification principle, in the form in which we have stated it, a demonstration will be given in the course of this book. For it will be shown that all propositions which have factual content are empirical hypotheses; and that the function of an empirical hypothesis is to provide a rule for the anticipation of experience.[12] And this means that every empirical hypothesis must be relevant to some actual, or possible, experience, so that a statement which is not relevant to any experience is not an empirical hypothesis, and accordingly has no factual content. But this is precisely what the principle of verifiability asserts.

It should be mentioned here that the fact that the utterances of the metaphysician are nonsensical does not follow simply from the fact that they are devoid of factual content. It follows from that fact, together with the fact that they are not *a priori* propositions. And in assuming that they are not *a priori* propositions, we are once again anticipating the conclusions of a later chapter in this book.[13] For it will be shown there that *a priori* propositions, which have always been attractive to philosophers on account of their certainty, owe this certainty to the fact that they are tautologies. We may accordingly define a metaphysical sentence as a sentence which purports to express a genuine proposition, but does, in fact, express neither a tautology nor an empirical hypothesis. And as tautologies and empirical hypotheses form the entire class of significant propositions,

---

[11] Vide Chapter VIII.

[12] Vide Chapter V.

[13] Chapter IV.

we are justified in concluding that all metaphysical assertions are nonsensical. Our next task is to show how they come to be made.

The use of the term "substance," to which we have already referred, provides us with a good example of the way in which metaphysics mostly comes to be written. It happens to be the case that we cannot, in our language, refer to the sensible properties of a thing without introducing a word or phrase which appears to stand for the thing itself as opposed to anything which may be said about it. And, as a result of this, those who are infected by the primitive superstition that to every name a single real entity must correspond assume that it is necessary to distinguish logically between the thing itself and any, or all, of its sensible properties. And so they employ the term "substance" to refer to the thing itself. But from the fact that we happen to employ a single word to refer to a thing, and make that word the grammatical subject of the sentences in which we refer to the sensible appearances of the thing, it does not by any means follow that the thing itself is a "simple entity," or that it cannot be defined in terms of the totality of its appearances. It is true that in talking of "its" appearances we appear to distinguish the thing from the appearances, but that is simply an accident of linguistic usage. Logical analysis shows that what makes these "appearances" the "appearances of" the same thing is not their relationship to an entity other than themselves, but their relationship to one another. The metaphysician fails to see this because he is misled by a superficial grammatical feature of his language.

A simpler and clearer instance of the way in which a consideration of grammar leads to metaphysics is the case of the metaphysical concept of Being. The origin of our temptation to raise questions about Being, which no conceivable experience would enable us to answer, lies in the fact that, in our language, sentences which express existential propositions and sentences which express attributive propositions may be of the same grammatical form. For instance, the sentences "Martyrs exist" and "Martyrs suffer" both consist of a noun followed by an intransitive verb and the fact that they have grammatically the same appearance leads one to assume that they are of the same logical type. It is seen that in the proposition "Martyrs suffer," the members of a certain species are credited with a certain attribute, and it is sometimes assumed that the same thing is true of such a proposition as "Martyrs exist." If this were actually the case, it would, indeed, be as legitimate to speculate about the Being of martyrs as it is to speculate about their suffering. But, as Kant pointed out,[14] existence is not an attribute. For, when we ascribe an attribute to a thing, we covertly assert that it exists: so that if existence were itself an attribute, it would follow that all positive existential propositions were tautologies, and all negative existential propositions self-contradictory; and this is not the case.[15] So that those who raise questions about Being which are based on the assumption that existence is an attribute are guilty of following grammar beyond the boundaries of sense.

A similar mistake has been made in connection with such propositions as "Unicorns are fictitious." Here again the fact that there is a superficial grammatical resemblance between the English sentences "Dogs are faithful" and "Unicorns are fictitious," and between the corresponding sentences in other languages, creates the assumption that they are of the same logical type. Dogs must exist in order to have the property of being faithful, and so it is held that unless unicorns in some way existed they could not have the property of being fictitious. But, as it is plainly self-contradictory to say that fictitious objects exist, the device is adopted of saying that they are real in some non-empirical sense—that they have a mode of real being which is different from the mode of being of existent things. But since there is no way of testing whether an object is real in this sense, as there is for testing whether it is real in the ordinary sense, the assertion that fictitious objects have a special non-empirical mode of real being is devoid of all literal significance. It comes to be made as a result of the assumption that being fictitious is an attribute. And this is a fallacy of the same order as the fallacy of supposing that existence is an attribute, and it can be exposed in the same way.

In general, the postulation of real non-existent entities results from the superstition, just now referred to, that, to every word or phrase that can be the grammatical subject of a sentence, there must somewhere be a real entity corresponding. For as there is no place in the empirical world for many of these "entities," a special non-empirical world is invoked to house them. To this error must be attributed, not only the utterances of a Heidegger, who bases his

---

[14] Vide *The Critique of Pure Reason*, "Transcendental Dialectic," Book II, Chapter iii, section 4.

[15] This argument is well stated by John Wisdom, *Interpretation and Analysis*, pp. 62, 63.

metaphysics on the assumption that "Nothing" is a name which is used to denote something peculiarly mysterious,[16] but also the prevalence of such problems as those concerning the reality of propositions and universals whose senselessness, though less obvious, is no less complete.

These few examples afford a sufficient indication of the way in which most metaphysical assertions come to be formulated. They show how easy it is to write sentences which are literally nonsensical without seeing that they are nonsensical. And thus we see that the view that a number of the traditional "problems of philosophy" are metaphysical, and consequently fictitious, does not involve any incredible assumptions about the psychology of philosophers.

Among those who recognise that if philosophy is to be accounted a genuine branch of knowledge it must be defined in such a way as to distinguish it from metaphysics, it is fashionable to speak of the metaphysician as a kind of misplaced poet. As his statements have no literal meaning, they are not subject to any criteria of truth or falsehood: but they may still serve to express, or arouse, emotion, and thus be subject to ethical or aesthetic standards. And it is suggested that they may have considerable value, as means of moral inspiration, or even as works of art. In this way, an attempt is made to compensate the metaphysician for his extrusion from philosophy.[17]

I am afraid that this compensation is hardly in accordance with his deserts. The view that the metaphysician is to be reckoned among the poets appears to rest on the assumption that both talk nonsense. But this assumption is false. In the vast majority of cases the sentences which are produced by poets do have literal meaning. The difference between the man who uses language scientifically and the man who uses it emotively is not that the one produces sentences which are incapable of arousing emotion, and the other sentences which have no sense, but that the one is primarily concerned with the expression of true propositions, the other with the creation of a work of art. Thus, if a work of science contains true and important propositions, its value as a work of science will hardly be diminished

---

[16] Vide *Was ist Metaphysik*, by Heidegger: criticised by Rudolf Carnap in his "*Überwindung der Metaphysik durch logische Analyse der Sprache*," *Erkenntnis*, Vol. II, 1932.

[17] For a discussion of this point, see also C. A. Mace, "Representation and Expression," *Analysis*, Vol. I, No. 3; and "Metaphysics and Emotive Language," *Analysis*, Vol. II, Nos. 1 and 2.

by the fact that they are inelegantly expressed. And similarly, a work of art is not necessarily the worse for the fact that all the propositions comprising it are literally false. But to say that many literary works are largely composed of falsehoods, is not to say that they are composed of pseudo-propositions. It is, in fact, very rare for a literary artist to produce sentences which have no literal meaning. And where this does occur, the sentences are carefully chosen for their rhythm and balance. If the author writes nonsense, it is because he considers it most suitable for bringing about the effects for which his writing is designed.

The metaphysician, on the other hand, does not intend to write nonsense. He lapses into it through being deceived by grammar, or through committing errors of reasoning, such as that which leads to the view that the sensible world is unreal. But it is not the mark of a poet simply to make mistakes of this sort. There are some, indeed, who would see in the fact that the metaphysician's utterances are senseless a reason against the view that they have aesthetic value. And, without going so far as this, we may safely say that it does not constitute a reason for it.

It is true, however, that although the greater part of metaphysics is merely the embodiment of humdrum errors, there remain a number of metaphysical passages which are the work of genuine mystical feeling; and they may more plausibly be held to have moral or aesthetic value. But, as far as we are concerned, the distinction between the kind of metaphysics that is produced by a philosopher who has been duped by grammar, and the kind that is produced by a mystic who is trying to express the inexpressible, is of no great importance: what is important to us is to realise that even the utterances of the metaphysician who is attempting to expound a vision are literally senseless; so that henceforth we may pursue our philosophical researches with as little regard for them as for the more inglorious kind of metaphysics which comes from a failure to understand the workings of our language.

II. Critique of Ethics and Theology

There is still one objection to be met before we can claim to have justified our view that all synthetic propositions are empirical hypotheses. This objection is based on the common supposition that our speculative knowledge is of two distinct kinds—that which relates to questions of empirical fact, and that which relates to questions of value. It will be said that "statements of value" are genuine synthetic propositions, but that they cannot with any show of justice be represented as hypotheses which are used to predict the course of our sensations, and accordingly, that the existence of ethics and aesthetics as branches of speculative knowledge presents an insuperable objection to our radical empiricist thesis.

In face of this objection, it is our business to give an account of "judgements of value" which is both satisfactory in itself and consistent with our general empiricist principles. We shall set ourselves to show that in so far as statements of value are significant, they are ordinary "scientific" statements; and that in so far as they are not scientific, they are not in the literal sense significant, but are simply expressions of emotion which can be neither true nor false. In maintaining this view, we may confine ourselves for the present to the case of ethical statements. What is said about them will be found to apply, *mutatis mutandis,* to the case of aesthetic statements also.[18]

The ordinary system of ethics, as elaborated in the works of ethical philosophers, is very far from being a homogeneous whole. Not only is it apt to contain pieces of metaphysics, and analyses of non-ethical concepts: its actual ethical contents are themselves of very different kinds. We may divide them, indeed, into four main classes. There are, first of all, propositions which express definitions of ethical terms, or judgements about the legitimacy or possibility of certain definitions. Secondly, there are propositions describing the phenomena of moral experience, and their causes. Thirdly, there are exhortations to moral virtue. And, lastly, there are actual ethical judgements. It is unfortunately the case that the distinction between these four classes, plain as it is, is commonly ignored by ethical philosophers; with the result that it is often very difficult to tell from their works what it is that they are seeking to discover or prove.

In fact, it is easy to see that only the first of our four classes, namely that which comprises the propositions relating to the definitions of ethical terms, can be said to constitute ethical philosophy. The propositions which describe the phenomena of moral experience, and their causes, must be assigned to the science of psychology, or sociology. The exhortations to moral virtue are not

---

[18] The argument that follows should be read in conjunction with the Introduction, pp. 20–22.

propositions at all, but ejaculations or commands which are designed to provoke the reader to action of a certain sort. Accordingly, they do not belong to any branch of philosophy or science. As for the expressions of ethical judgements, we have not yet determined how they should be classified. But inasmuch as they are certainly neither definitions nor comments upon definitions, nor quotations, we may say decisively that they do not belong to ethical philosophy. A strictly philosophical treatise on ethics should therefore make no ethical pronouncements. But it should, by giving an analysis of ethical terms, show what is the category to which all such pronouncements belong. And this is what we are now about to do.

A question which is often discussed by ethical philosophers is whether it is possible to find definitions which would reduce all ethical terms to one or two fundamental terms. But this question, though it undeniably belongs to ethical philosophy, is not relevant to our present enquiry. We are not now concerned to discover which term, within the sphere of ethical terms, is to be taken as fundamental; whether, for example, "good" can be defined in terms of "right" or "right" in terms of "good," or both in terms of "value." What we are interested in is the possibility of reducing the whole sphere of ethical terms to non-ethical terms. We are enquiring whether statements of ethical value can be translated into statements of empirical fact.

That they can be so translated is the contention of those ethical philosophers who are commonly called subjectivists, and of those who are known as utilitarians. For the utilitarian defines the rightness of actions, and the goodness of ends, in terms of the pleasure, or happiness, or satisfaction, to which they give rise; the subjectivist, in terms of the feelings of approval which a certain person, or group of people, has towards them. Each of these types of definition makes moral judgements into a sub-class of psychological or sociological judgements; and for this reason they are very attractive to us. For, if either was correct, it would follow that ethical assertions were not generically different from the factual assertions which are ordinarily contrasted with them and the account which we have already given of empirical hypotheses would apply to them also.

Nevertheless we shall not adopt either a subjectivist or a utilitarian analysis of ethical terms. We reject the subjectivist view that to call an action right, or a thing good, is to say that it is generally approved of, because it is not self-contradictory to assert that some actions which are generally approved of are not right, or that some things which are generally approved of are not good. And we reject the alternative subjectivist view that a man who asserts that a certain action is right, or that a certain thing is good, is saying that he himself approves of it, on the ground that a man who confessed that he sometimes approved of what was bad or wrong would not be contradicting himself. And a similar argument is fatal to utilitarianism. We cannot agree that to call an action right is to say that of all the actions possible in the circumstances it would cause, or be likely to cause, the greatest happiness, or the greatest balance of pleasure over pain, or the greatest balance of satisfied over unsatisfied desire, because we find that it is not self-contradictory to say that it is sometimes wrong to perform the action which would actually or probably cause the greatest happiness, or the greatest balance of pleasure over pain, or of satisfied over unsatisfied desire. And since it is not self-contradictory to say that some pleasant things are not good, or that some bad things are desired, it cannot be the case that the sentence "*x* is good" is equivalent to "*x* is pleasant," or to "*x* is desired." And to every other variant of utilitarianism with which I am acquainted the same objection can be made. And therefore we should, I think, conclude that the validity of ethical judgements is not determined by the felicific tendencies of actions, any more than by the nature of people's feelings; but that it must be regarded as "absolute" or "intrinsic," and not empirically calculable.

If we say this, we are not, of course, denying that it is possible to invent a language in which all ethical symbols are definable in non-ethical terms, or even that it is desirable to invent such a language and adopt it in place of our own; what we are denying is that the suggested reduction of ethical to non-ethical statements is consistent with the conventions of our actual language. That is, we reject utilitarianism and subjectivism, not as proposals to replace our existing ethical notions by new ones, but as analyses of our existing ethical notions. Our contention is simply that, in our language, sentences which contain normative ethical symbols are not equivalent to sentences which express psychological propositions, or indeed empirical propositions of any kind.

It is advisable here to make it plain that it is only normative ethical symbols, and not descriptive ethical symbols, that are held by us to be indefinable in factual terms. There is a danger of confusing these two types of symbols, because they are commonly constituted by signs of the same sensible form. Thus a complex sign of the form "x is wrong" may constitute a sentence which expresses a moral judgement concerning a certain type of conduct, or it may constitute a sentence which states that a certain type of conduct is repugnant to the moral sense of a particular society. In the latter case, the symbol "wrong" is a descriptive ethical symbol, and the sentence in which it occurs expresses an ordinary sociological proposition; in the former case, the symbol "wrong" is a normative ethical symbol, and the sentence in which it occurs does not, we maintain, express an empirical proposition at all. It is only with normative ethics that we are at present concerned; so that whenever ethical symbols are used in the course of this argument without qualification, they are always to be interpreted as symbols of the normative type.

In admitting that normative ethical concepts are irreducible to empirical concepts, we seem to be leaving the way clear for the absolutist view of ethics—that is, the view that statements of value are not controlled by observation, as ordinary empirical propositions are, but only by a mysterious "intellectual intuition." A feature of this theory, which is seldom recognized by its advocates, is that it makes statements of value unverifiable. For it is notorious that what seems intuitively certain to one person may seem doubtful, or even false, to another. So that unless it is possible to provide some criterion by which one may decide between conflicting intuitions, a mere appeal to intuition is worthless as a test of a proposition's validity. But in the case of moral judgements, no such criterion can be given. Some moralists claim to settle the matter by saying that they "know" that their own moral judgements are correct. But such an assertion is of purely psychological interest, and has not the slightest tendency to prove the validity of any moral judgement. For dissentient moralists may equally well "know" that their ethical views are correct. And, as far as subjective certainty goes, there will be nothing to choose between them. When such differences of opinion arise in connection with an ordinary empirical proposition, one may attempt to resolve them by referring to, or actually carrying out, some relevant empirical test. But with regard to ethical statements, there is, on the "absolutist" or 'intuitionist" theory, no relevant empirical test. We are therefore justified in saying that on this theory ethical statements are held to be unverifiable. They are, of course, also held to be genuine synthetic propositions.

Considering the use which we have made of the principle that a synthetic proposition is significant only if it is empirically verifiable, it is clear that the acceptance of an "absolutist" theory of ethics would undermine the whole of our main argument. And as we have already rejected the "naturalistic" theories which are commonly supposed to provide the only alternative to "absolutism" in ethics, we seem to have reached a difficult position. We shall meet the difficulty by showing that the correct treatment of ethical statements is afforded by a third theory, which is wholly compatible with our radical empiricism.

We begin by admitting that the fundamental ethical concepts are unanalysable, inasmuch as there is no criterion by which one can test the validity of the judgements in which they occur. So far, we are in agreement with the absolutists. But, unlike the absolutists, we are able to give an explanation of this fact about ethical concepts. We say that the reason why they are unanalysable is that they are mere pseudo-concepts. The presence of an ethical symbol in a proposition adds nothing to its factual content. Thus if I say to someone, "You acted wrongly in stealing that money," I am not stating anything more than if I had simply said, "You stole that money." In adding that this action is wrong I am not making any further statement about it. I am simply evincing my moral disapproval of it. It is as if I had said, "You stole that money," in a peculiar tone of horror, or written it with the addition of some special exclamation marks. The tone, or the exclamation marks, adds nothing to the literal meaning of the sentence. It merely serves to show that the expression of it is attended by certain feelings in the speaker.

If now I generalise my previous statement and say, "Stealing money is wrong," I produce a sentence which has no factual meaning—that is, expresses no proposition which can be either true or false. It is as if I had written "Stealing money!!"—where the shape and thickness of the exclamation marks show, by a suitable convention, that a special sort of moral disapproval is the feeling which is being expressed. It is clear that there is nothing said here which can be true or false. Another man may disagree with me about the wrongness of stealing, in the sense that he may not have the same feelings about stealing as I have, and he may quarrel with me on account of my moral sentiments. But he cannot, strictly speaking, contradict me. For in saying that a certain type of action is right or wrong, I am not making any factual statement, not even a statement about my own state of mind. I am merely expressing certain moral sentiments. And the man who is ostensibly contradicting me is merely expressing his moral sentiments. So that there is plainly no sense in asking which of us is in the right. For neither of us is asserting a genuine proposition.

What we have just been saying about the symbol "wrong" applies to all normative ethical symbols. Sometimes they occur in sentences which record ordinary empirical facts besides expressing ethical feeling about those facts: sometimes they occur in sentences which simply express ethical feeling about a certain type of action, or situation, without making any statement of fact. But in every case in which one would commonly be said to be making an ethical judgement, the function of the relevant ethical word is purely "emotive." It is used to express feeling about certain objects, but not to make any assertion about them.

It is worth mentioning that ethical terms do not serve only to express feeling. They are calculated also to arouse feeling, and so to stimulate action. Indeed some of them are used in such a way as to give the sentences in which they occur the effect of commands. Thus the sentence "It is your duty to tell the truth" may be regarded both as the expression of a certain sort of ethical feeling about truthfulness and as the expression of the command "Tell the truth." The sentence "You ought to tell the truth" also involves the command "Tell the truth," but here the tone of the command is less emphatic. In the sentence "It is good to tell the truth" the command has become little more than a suggestion. And thus the "meaning" of the word "good," in its ethical usage is differentiated from that of the word "duty" or the word "ought." In fact we may define the meaning of the various ethical words in terms both of the different feelings they are ordinarily taken to express, and also the different responses which they are calculated to provoke.

We can now see why it is impossible to find a criterion for determining the validity of ethical judgements. It is not because they have an "absolute" validity which is mysteriously independent of ordinary sense-experience, but because they have no objective validity whatsoever. If a sentence makes no statement at all, there is obviously no sense in asking whether what it says is true or false. And we have seen that sentences which simply express moral judgements do not say anything. They are pure expressions of feeling and as such do not come under the category of truth and falsehood.

They are unverifiable for the same reason as a cry of pain or a word of command is unverifiable—because they do not express genuine propositions.

Thus, although our theory of ethics might fairly be said to be radically subjectivist, it differs in a very important respect from the orthodox subjectivist theory. For the orthodox subjectivist does not deny, as we do, that the sentences of a moralizer express genuine propositions. All he denies is that they express propositions of a unique non-empirical character. His own view is that they express propositions about the speaker's feelings. If this were so, ethical judgements clearly would be capable of being true or false. They would be true if the speaker had the relevant feelings, and false if he had not. And this is a matter which is, in principle, empirically verifiable. Furthermore they could be significantly contradicted. For if I say, "Tolerance is a virtue," and someone answers, "You don't approve of it," he would, on the ordinary subjectivist theory, be contradicting me. On our theory, he would not be contradicting me, because, in saying that tolerance was a virtue, I should not be making any statement about my own feelings or about anything else. I should simply be evincing my feelings, which is not at all the same thing as saying that I have them.

The distinction between the expression of feeling and the assertion of feeling is complicated by the fact that the assertion that one has a certain feeling often accompanies the expression of that feeling, and is then, indeed, a factor in the expression of that feeling. Thus I may simultaneously express boredom and say that I am bored, and in that case my utterance of the words, "I am bored," is one of the circumstances which make it true to say that I am expressing or evincing boredom. But I can express boredom without actually saying that I am bored. I can express it by my tone and gestures, while making a statement about something wholly unconnected with it, or by an ejaculation, or without uttering any words at all. So that even if the assertion that one has a certain feeling always involves the expression of that feeling, the expression of a feeling assuredly does not always involve the assertion that one has it. And this is the important point to grasp in considering the distinction between our theory and the ordinary subjectivist theory. For whereas the subjectivist holds that ethical statements actually assert the existence of certain feelings, we hold that ethical statements are expressions and excitants of feeling which do not necessarily involve any assertions.

We have already remarked that the main objection to the ordinary subjectivist theory is that the validity of ethical judgements is not determined by the nature of their author's feelings. And this is an objection which our theory escapes. For it does not imply that the existence of any feelings is a necessary and sufficient condition of the validity of an ethical judgement. It implies, on the contrary, that ethical judgements have no validity.

There is, however, a celebrated argument against subjectivist theories which our theory does not escape. It has been pointed out by Moore that if ethical statements were simply statements about the speaker's feelings, it would be impossible to argue about questions of value.[19] To take a typical example: if a man said that thrift was a virtue, and another replied that it was a vice, they would not, on this theory, be disputing with one another. One would be saying that he approved of thrift, and the other that *he* didn't; and there is no reason why both these statements should not be true. Now Moore held it to be obvious that we do dispute about questions of value, and accordingly concluded that the particular form of subjectivism which he was discussing was false.

It is plain that the conclusion that it is impossible to dispute about questions of value follows from our theory also. For as we hold that such sentences as "Thrift is a virtue" and "Thrift is a vice" do not express propositions at all, we clearly cannot hold that they express incompatible propositions. We must therefore admit that if Moore's argument really refutes the ordinary subjectivist theory, it also refutes ours. But, in fact, we deny that it does refute even the ordinary subjectivist theory. For we hold that one really never does dispute about questions of value.

This may seem, at first sight, to be a very paradoxical assertion. For we certainly do engage in disputes which are ordinarily regarded as disputes about questions of value. But, in all such cases, we find, if we consider the matter closely, that the dispute is not really about a question of value, but about a question of fact. When someone disagrees with us about the moral value of a certain action or type of action, we do admittedly resort to argument in order to win him over to our way of thinking. But we do not attempt to show by our arguments that he has the "wrong" ethical feeling towards a situation whose nature he has correctly apprehended. What we attempt to

---

[19] Cf. *Philosophical Studies*, "The Nature of Moral Philosophy."

show is that he is mistaken about the facts of the case. We argue that he has misconceived the agent's motive; or that he has misjudged the effects of the action, or its probable effects in view of the agent's knowledge; or that he has failed to take into account the special circumstances in which the agent was placed. Or else we employ more general arguments about the effects which actions of a certain type tend to produce, or the qualities which are usually manifested in their performance. We do this in the hope that we have only to get our opponent to agree with us about the nature of the empirical facts for him to adopt the same moral attitude towards them as we do. And as the people with whom we argue have generally received tbe same moral education as ourselves, and live in the same social order, our expectation is usually justified. But if our opponent happens to have undergone a different process of moral "conditioning" from ourselves, so that, even when he acknowledges all the facts, he still disagrees with us about the moral value of the actions under discussion, then we abandon the attempt to convince him by argument. We say that it is impossible to argue with him because he has a distorted or undeveloped moral sense; which signifies merely that he employs a different set of values from our own. We feel that our own system of values is superior, and therefore speak in such derogatory terms of his. But we cannot bring forward any arguments to show that our system is superior. For our judgement that it is so is itself a judgement of value, and accordingly outside the scope of argument. It is because argument fails us when we come to deal with pure questions of value, as distinct from questions of fact, that we finally resort to mere abuse.

In short, we find that argument is possible on moral questions only if some system of values is presupposed. If our opponent concurs with us in expressing moral disapproval of all actions of a given type *t*, then we may get him to condemn a particular action A, by bringing forward arguments to show that A is of type *t*. For the question whether A does or does not belong to that type is a plain question of fact. Given that a man has certain moral principles, we argue that he must, in order to be consistent, react morally to certain things in a certain way. What we do not and cannot argue about is the validity of these moral principles. We merely praise or condemn them in the light of our own feelings.

If anyone doubts the accuracy of this account of moral disputes, let him try to construct even an imaginary argument on a question of value which does not reduce itself to an argument about a question of logic or about an empirical matter of fact. I am confident that he will not succeed in producing a single example. And if that is the case, he must allow that its involving the impossibility of purely ethical arguments is not, as Moore thought, a ground of objection to our theory, but rather a point in favour of it.

Having upheld our theory against the only criticism which appeared to threaten it, we may now use it to define the nature of all ethical enquiries. We find that ethical philosophy consists simply in saying that ethical concepts are pseudo-concepts and therefore unanalysable. The further task of describing the different feelings that the different ethical terms are used to express and the different reactions that they customarily provoke, is a task for the psychologist. There cannot be such a thing as ethical science, if by ethical science one means the elaboration of a true system of morals. For we have seen that, as ethical judgements are mere expressions of feeling, there can be no way of determining the validity of any ethical system, and, indeed, no sense in asking whether any such system is true. All that one may legitimately enquire in this connection is, What are the moral habits of a given person or group of people, and what causes them to have precisely those habits and feelings? And this enquiry falls wholly within the scope of the existing social sciences.

It appears, then, that ethics, as a branch of knowledge, is nothing more than a department of psychology and sociology. And in case anyone thinks that we are overlooking the existence of casuistry, we may remark that casuistry is not a science, but is a purely analytical investigation of the structure of a given moral system. In other words, it is an exercise in formal logic.

When one comes to pursue the psychological enquiries which constitute ethical science, one is immediately enabled to account for the Kantian and hedonistic theories of morals. For one finds that one of the chief causes of moral behaviour is fear, both conscious and unconscious, of a god's displeasure, and fear of the enmity of society. And this, indeed, is the reason why moral precepts present themselves to some people as "categorical" commands. And one finds, also, that the moral code of a society is partly determined by the beliefs of that society concerning the conditions of its own happiness—or, in other words, that a society tends to encourage or discourage a given type of conduct by the use of moral sanctions according as it appears to promote or detract from the contentment of the society as a whole. And this is the reason why altruism is recommended in most moral codes and egotism condemned. It is from the observation of this connection between morality and happiness that hedonistic or eudaemonistic theories of morals ultimately spring, just as the moral theory of Kant is based on the fact, previously explained, that moral precepts have for some people the force of inexorable commands. As each of these theories ignores the fact which lies at the root of the other, both may be criticized as being one-sided; but this is not the main objection to either of them. Their essential defect is that they treat propositions which refer to the causes and attributes of our ethical feelings as if they were definitions of ethical concepts. And thus they fail to recognise that ethical concepts are pseudo-concepts and consequently indefinable.

As we have already said, our conclusions about the nature of ethics apply to aesthetics also. Aesthetic terms are used in exactly the same way as ethical terms. Such aesthetic words as "beautiful" and "hideous" are employed, as ethical words are employed, not to make statements of fact, but simply to express certain feelings and evoke a certain response. It follows, as in ethics, that there is no sense in attributing objective validity to aesthetic judgements, and no possibility of arguing about questions of value in aesthetics, but only about questions of fact. A scientific treatment of asthetics would show us what in general were the causes of aesthetic feeling, why various societies produced and admired the works of art they did, why taste varies as it does within a given society, and so forth. And these are ordinary psychological or sociological questions. They have, of course, little or nothing to do with aesthetic criticism as we understand it. But that is because the purpose of aesthetic criticism is not so much to give knowledge as to communicate emotion. The critic, by calling attention to certain features of the work under review, and expressing his own feelings about them, endeavours to make us share his attitude towards the work as a whole. The only relevant propositions that he formulates are propositions describing the nature of the work. And these are plain records of fact. We conclude, therefore, that there is nothing in aesthetics, any more than there is in ethics, to justify the view that it embodies a unique type of knowledge.

It should now be clear that the only information which we can legitimately derive from the study of our aesthetic and moral experiences is information about our own mental and physical make-up. We take note of these experiences as providing data for our psychological and sociological generalisations. And this is the only way in which they serve to increase our knowledge. It follows that any attempt to make our use of ethical and aesthetic concepts the basis of a metaphysical theory concerning the existence of a world of values, as distinct from the world of facts, involves a false analysis of these concepts. Our own analysis has shown that the phenomena of moral experience cannot fairly be used to support any rationalist or metaphysical doctrine whatsoever. In particular, they cannot, as Kant hoped, be used to establish the existence of a transcendent god.

This mention of God brings us to the question of the possibility of religious knowledge. We shall see that this possibility has already been ruled out by our treatment of metaphysics. But, as this is a point of considerable interest, we may be permitted to discuss it at some length.

It is now generally admitted, at any rate by philosophers, that the existence of a being having the attributes which define the god of any non-animistic religion cannot be demonstratively proved. To see that this is so, we have only to ask ourselves what are the premises from which the existence of such a god could be deduced. If the conclusion that a god exists is to be demonstratively certain, then these premises must be certain; for, as the conclusion of a deductive argument is already contained in the premises, any uncertainty there may be about the truth of the premises is necessarily shared by it. But we know that no empirical proposition can ever be anything more than probable. It is only *a priori* propositions that are logically certain. But we cannot deduce the existence of a god from an *a priori* proposition. For we know that the reason why a *priori* propositions are certain is that they are tautologies. And from a set of tautologies nothing but a further tautology can be validly deduced. It follows that there is no possibility of demonstrating the existence of a god.

What is not so generally recognised is that there can be no way of proving that the existence of a god, such as the God of Christianity, is even probable. Yet this also is easily shown. For if the existence of such a god were probable, then the proposition that he existed would be an empirical hypothesis. And in that case it would be possible to deduce from it, and other empirical hypotheses, certain experiential propositions which were not deducible from those other hypotheses alone. But in fact this is not possible. It is sometimes claimed, indeed, that the existence of a certain sort of regularity in nature constitutes sufficient evidence for the existence of a god. But if the sentence "God exists" entails no more than that certain types of phenomena occur in certain sequences, then to assert the existence of a god will be simply equivalent to asserting that there is the requisite regularity in nature; and no religious man would admit that this was all he intended to assert in asserting the existence of a god. He would say that in talking about God, he was talking about a transcendent being who might be known through certain empirical manifestations, but certainly could not be defined in terms of those manifestations. But in that case the term "god" is a metaphysical term. And if "god" is a metaphysical term, then it cannot be even probable that a god exists. For to say that "God exists" is to make a metaphysical utterance which cannot be either true or false. And by the same criterion, no sentence which purports to describe the nature of a transcendent god can possess any literal significance.

It is important not to confuse this view of religious assertions with the view that is adopted by atheists, or agnostics.[20] For it is characteristic of an agnostic to hold that the existence of a god is a possibility in which there is no good reason either to believe or disbelieve; and it is characteristic of an atheist to hold that it is at least probable that no god exists. And our view that all utterances about the nature of God are nonsensical, so far from being identical with, or even lending any support to, either of these familiar contentions, is actually incompatible with them. For if the assertion that there is a god is nonsensical, then the atheist's assertion that there is no god is equally nonsensical, since it is only a significant proposition that can be significantly contradicted. As for the agnostic, although he refrains from saying either that there is or that there is not a god, he does not deny that the question whether a transcendent god exists is a genuine question. He does not deny that the two sentences "There is a transcendent god" and "There is no transcendent god" express propositions one of which is actually true and the other false. All he says is that we have no means of telling which of them is true, and therefore ought not to commit ourselves to either. But we have seen that the sentences in question do not express propositions at all. And this means that agnosticism also is ruled out.

---

[20] This point was suggested to me by Professor H. H. Price.

Thus we offer the theist the same comfort as we gave to the moralist. His assertions cannot possibly be valid, but they cannot be invalid either. As he says nothing at all about the world, he cannot justly be accused of saying anything false, or anything for which he has insufficient grounds. It is only when the theist claims that in asserting the existence of a transcendent god he is expressing a genuine proposition that we are entitled to disagree with him.

It is to be remarked that in cases where deities are identified with natural objects, assertions concerning them may be allowed to be significant. If, for example, a man tells me that the occurrence of thunder is alone both necessary and sufficient to establish the truth of the proposition that Jehovah is angry, I may conclude that, in his usage of words, the sentence "Jehovah is angry" is equivalent to "It is thundering." But in sophisticated religions, though they may be to some extent based on men's awe of natural process which they cannot sufficiently understand, the "person" who is supposed to control the empirical world is not himself located in it; he is held to be superior to the empirical world, and so outside it, and he is endowed with super-empirical attributes. But the notion of a person whose essential attributes are nonempirical is not an intelligible notion at all. We may have a word which is used, as if it named this "person," but, unless the sentences in which it occurs express propositions which are empirically verifiable, it cannot be said to symbolize anything. And this is the case with regard to the word "god," in the usage in which it is intended to refer to a transcendent object. The mere existence of the noun is enough to foster the illusion that there is a real, or at any rate a possible entity corresponding to it. It is only when we enquire what God's attributes are that we discover that "God," in this usage, is not a genuine name.

It is common to find belief in a transcendent god conjoined with belief in an after-life. But, in the form which it usually takes, the content of this belief is not a genuine hypothesis. To say that men do not ever die, or that the state of death is merely a state of prolonged insensibility, is indeed to express a significant proposition, though all the available evidence goes to show that it is false. But to say that there is something imperceptible inside a man, which is his soul or his real self, and that it goes on living after he is dead, is to make a metaphysical assertion which has no more factual content than the assertion that there is a transcendent god.

It is worth mentioning that, according to the account which we have given of religious assertions, there is no logical ground for antagonism between religion and natural science. As far as the question of truth or falsehood is concerned, there is no opposition between the natural scientist and the theist who believes in a transcendent god. For since the religious utterances of the theist are not genuine propositions at all, they cannot stand in any logical relation to the propositions of science. Such antagonism as there is between religion and science appears to consist in the fact that science takes away one of the motives which make men religious. For it is acknowledged that one of the ultimate sources of religious feeling lies in the inability of men to determine their own destiny; and science tends to destroy the feeling of awe with which men regard an alien world, by making them believe that they can understand and anticipate the course of natural phenomena, and even to some extent control it. The fact that it has recently become fashionable for physicists themselves to be sympathetic towards religion is a point in favour of this hypothesis. For this sympathy towards religion marks the physicists' own lack of confidence in the validity of their hypotheses, which is a reaction on their part from the anti-religious dogmatism of nineteenth-century scientists, and a natural outcome of the crisis through which physics has just passed.

It is not within the scope of this enquiry to enter more deeply into the causes of religious feeling, or to discuss the probability of the continuance of religious belief. We are concerned only to answer those questions which arise out of our discussion of the possibility of religious knowledge. The point which we wish to establish is that there cannot be any transcendent truths of religion. For the sentences which the theist uses to express such "truths" are not literally significant.

An interesting feature of this conclusion is that it accords with what many theists are accustomed to say themselves. For we are often told that the nature of God is a mystery which transcends the human understanding. But to say that something transcends the human understanding is to say that it is unintelligible. And what is unintelligible cannot significantly be described. Again we are told that God is not an object of reason but an object of faith. This may be nothing more than an admission that the existence of God must be taken on trust since it cannot be proved. But it may also be an assertion that God is the object of a purely mystical intuition, and cannot therefore be defined in terms which are unintelligible to the reason. And I think there are many theists who would assert this. But if one allows that it is impossible to define God in intelligible terms then one is allowing that it is impossible for a sentence both to be significant and to be about God. If a mystic admits that the object of his vision is something which cannot be described, then he must also admit that he is bound to talk nonsense when he describes it.

For his part, the mystic may protest that his intuition does reveal truths to him, even though he cannot explain to others what these truths are; and that we who do not possess this faculty of intuition can have no ground for denying that it is a cognitive faculty. For we can hardly maintain *a priori* that there are no ways of discovering true propositions except those which we ourselves employ. The answer is that we set no limit to the number of ways in which one may come to formulate a true proposition. We do not in any way deny that a synthetic truth may be discovered by purely intuitive methods as well as by the rational method of induction. But we do say that every synthetic proposition, however it may have been arrived at, must be subject to the test of actual experience. We do not deny *a priori* that the mystic is able to discover truths by his own special methods. We wait to hear what are the propositions which embody his discoveries in order to see whether they are verified or confuted by our empirical observations. But the mystic, so far from producing propositions which are empirically verified, is unable to produce any intelligible propositions at all. And therefore we say that his intuition has not revealed to him any facts. It is no use his saying that he has apprehended facts but is unable to express them. For we know that if he really had acquired any information he would be able to express it. He would be able to indicate in some way or other how the genuineness of his discovery might be empirically determined. The fact that he cannot reveal what he knows or even himself devise an empirical test to validate his knowledge shows that his state of mystical intuition is not a genuinely cognitive state. So that in describing his vision the mystic does not give us any information about the external world; he merely gives us indirect information about the condition of his own mind.

These considerations dispose of the argument from religious experience, which many philosophers still regard as a valid argument in favour of the existence of a god. They say that it is logically possible for men to be immediately acquainted with God, as they are immediately acquainted with a sense-content, and that there is no reason why one should be prepared to believe a man when he says that he is seeing a yellow patch, and refuse to believe him when he says that he is seeing God. The answer to this is that if the man who asserts that he is seeing God is merely asserting that he is experiencing a peculiar kind of sense-content, then we do not for a moment deny that his assertion may be true. But, ordinarily, the man who says that he is seeing God is saying not merely that he is experiencing a religious emotion, but also that there exists a transcendent being who is the object of this emotion just as the man who says that he sees a yellow patch is ordinarily saying not merely that his visual sense-field contains a yellow sense-content, but also that there exists a yellow object to which the sense-content belongs. And it is not irrational to be prepared to believe a man when he asserts the existence of a yellow object, and to refuse to believe him when he asserts the existence of a transcendent god. For whereas the sentence "There exists here a yellow-coloured material thing" expresses a genuine synthetic proposition which could be empirically verified, the sentence "There exists a transcendent god" has, as we have seen, no literal significance.

We conclude, therefore, that the argument from religious experience is altogether fallacious. The fact that people have religious experiences is interesting from the psychological point of view, but it does not in any way imply that there is such a thing as religious knowledge, any more than our having moral experiences implies that there is such a thing as moral knowledge. The theist, like the moralist, may believe that his experiences are cognitive experiences, but, unless he can formulate his "knowledge" in propositions that are empirically verifiable, we may be sure that he is deceiving himself. It follows that those philosophers who fill their books with assertions that they intuitively "know" this or that moral or religious "truth" are merely providing material for the psycho-analyst. For no act of intuition can be said to reveal a truth about any matter of fact unless it issues in verifiable propositions. And all such propositions are to be incorporated in the system of empirical propositions which constitutes science.

III. The Self and the Common World

It is customary for the authors of epistemological treatises to assume that our empirical knowledge must have a basis of certainty, and that there must therefore be objects whose existence is logically indubitable. And they believe, for the most part, that it is their business, not merely to describe these objects, which they regard as being immediately "given" to us, but also to provide a logical proof of the existence of objects which are not so "given." For they think that without such a proof the greater part of our so-called empirical knowledge will lack the certification which it logically requires.

To those who have followed the argument of this book it will, however, be clear that these familiar assumptions are mistaken. For we have seen that our claims to empirical knowledge are not susceptible of a logical, but only of a pragmatic, justification. It is futile, and therefore illegitimate, to demand an *a priori* proof of the existence of objects which are not immediately "given." For unless they are metaphysical objects, the occurrence of certain sense-experiences will itself constitute the only proof of their existence which is requisite or obtainable; and the question whether the appropriate sense-experiences do or do not occur in the relevant circumstances is one that must be decided in actual practice, and not by any *a priori* argumentation. We have already applied these considerations to the so-called problem of perception, and we shall shortly be applying them also to the traditional "problems" of our knowledge of our own existence, and of the existence of other people. In the case of the problem of perception, we found that in order to avoid metaphysics we were obliged to adopt a phenomenalist standpoint, and we shall find that the same treatment must be accorded to the other problems to which we have just now referred.

We have seen, furthermore, that there are no objects whose existence is indubitable. For, since existence is not a predicate, to assert that an object exists is always to assert a synthetic proposition; and it has been shown that no synthetic propositions are logically sacrosanct. All of them, including the propositions which describe the content of our sensations, are hypotheses which, however great their probability, we may eventually find it expedient to abandon. And this means that our empirical knowledge cannot have a basis of logical certainty. It follows, indeed, from the definition of a synthetic proposition that it cannot be either proved or disproved by formal logic. The man who denies such a proposition may be acting irrationally, by contemporary standards of rationality, but he is not necessarily contradicting himself. And we know that the only propositions that are certain are those which cannot be denied without self-contradiction, inasmuch as they are tautologies.

It must not be thought that in denying that our empirical knowledge has a basis of certainty we are denying that any objects are really "given." For to say that an object is immediately "given" is to say merely that it is the content of a sense-experience, and we are very far from maintaining that our sense-experiences have no real content, or even that their content is in any way indescribable. All that we are maintaining in this connection is that any description of the content of any sense-experience is an empirical hypothesis of whose validity there can be no guarantee. And this is by no means equivalent to maintaining that no such hypothesis can actually be valid. We shall not, indeed, attempt to formulate any such hypotheses ourselves, because the discussion of psychological questions is out of place in a philosophical enquiry; and we have already made it clear that our empiricism is not logically dependent on an atomistic psychology, such as Hume and Mach adopted, but is compatible with any theory whatsoever concerning the actual characteristics of our sensory fields. For the empiricist doctrine to which we are committed is a logical doctrine concerning the distinction between analytic propositions, synthetic propositions, and metaphysical verbiage; and as such it has no bearing on any psychological question of fact.

It is not possible, however, to set aside all the questions which philosophers have raised in connection with the "given" as being psychological in character, and so outside the scope of this enquiry. In particular, it is impossible to deal in this way with the question whether sense-contents are mental or physical, or with the question whether they are in any sense private to a single self, or with the question whether they can exist without being experienced. For none of these three questions is capable of being solved by an empirical test. They must, if they are soluble at all, be soluble *a priori.* And as they are all questions which have given rise to much dispute among philosophers, we shall in fact attempt to provide for each of them a definitive a *priori* solution.

To begin with, we must make it clear that we do not accept the realist analysis of our sensations in terms of subject, act, and object. For neither the existence of the substance which is supposed to perform the so-called act of sensing nor the existence of the act itself, as an entity distinct from the sense-contents on which it is supposed to be directed, is in the least capable of being verified. We do not deny, indeed, that a given sense-content can legitimately be said to be experienced by a particular subject but we shall see that this relation of being experienced by a particular subject is to be analyzed in terms of the relationship of sense-contents to one another, and not in terms of a substantial ego and its mysterious acts. Accordingly, we define a sense-content not as the object, but as a part of a sense-experience. And from this it follows that the existence of a sense-content always entails the existence of a sense-experience.

It is necessary, at this point, to remark that when one says that a sense-experience, or a sense-content, exists, one is making a different type of statement from that which one makes when one says that a material thing exists. For the existence of a material thing is defined in terms of the actual and possible occurrence of the sense-contents which constitute it as a logical construction, and one cannot significantly speak of a sense-experience, which is a whole composed of sense-contents, or of a sense-content itself as if it were a logical construction out of sense-contents. And in fact when we say that a given sense-content or sense-experience exists, we are saying no more than that it occurs. And, accordingly, it seems advisable always to speak of the "occurrence" of sense-contents and sense-experiences in preference to speaking of their "existence," and so to avoid the danger of treating sense-contents as if they were material things.

The answer to the question whether sense-contents are mental or physical is that they are neither; or rather, that the distinction between what is mental and what is physical does not apply to sense-contents. It applies only to objects which are logical constructions out of them. But what differentiates one such logical construction from another is the fact that it is constituted by different sense-contents or by sense-contents differently related. So that when we distinguish a given mental object from a given physical object, or a mental object from another mental object, or a physical object from another physical object, we are in every case distinguishing between different logical constructions whose elements cannot themselves be said to be either mental or physical. It is, indeed, not impossible for a sense-content to be an element both of a mental and of a physical object; but it is necessary that some of the elements, or some of the relations, should be different in the two logical constructions. And it may be advisable here to repeat that, when we refer to an object as a logical construction out of certain sense-contents, we are not saying that it is actually constructed out of those sense-contents, or that the sense-contents are in any way parts of it, but are merely expressing, in a convenient, if somewhat misleading, fashion, the syntactical fact that all sentences referring to it are translatable into sentences referring to them.

The fact that the distinction between mind and matter applies only to logical constructions and that all distinctions between logical constructions are reducible to distinctions between sense-contents, proves that the difference between the entire class of mental objects and the entire class of physical objects is not in any sense more fundamental than the difference between any two sub-classes of mental objects, or the difference between any two sub-classes of physical objects. Actually, the distinguishing feature the objects belonging to the category of "one's own mental states" is the fact that they are mainly constituted by "introspective" sense-contents and by sense-contents which are elements of one's own body; and the distinguishing feature of the objects belonging to the category of "the mental states of others" is the fact the they are mainly constituted by sense-contents which are element of other living bodies; and what makes one unite these two classes of objects to form the single class of mental objects is the fact the there is a high degree of qualitative similarity between many of the sense-contents which are elements of other living bodies and many of the elements of one's own. But we are not now concerned with the provision of an exact definition of "mentality." We are interested only in making it plain that the distinction between mind and matter, applying as it does to logical constructions out of sense-contents, cannot apply to sense-contents themselves. For a distinction between logical constructions which is constituted by the fact that there are certain distinctions between their elements is clearly of a different type from any distinction that can obtain between the elements.

It should be clear, also, that there is no philosophical problem concerning the relationship of mind and matter, other than the linguistic problems of defining certain symbols which denote logical constructions in terms of symbols which denote sense-contents. The problems with which philosophers have vexed themselves in the past, concerning the possibility of bridging the "gulf" between mind and matter in knowledge or in action, are all fictitious problems arising out of the senseless metaphysical conception of mind and matter, or minds and material things, as substances. Being freed from metaphysics, we see that there can be no *a priori* objections to the existence either of causal or of epistemological connections between minds and material things. For, roughly speaking, all that we are saying when we say that the mental state of a person A at a time *t* is a state of awareness of a material thing X, is that the sense-experience which is the element of A occurring at time *t* contains a sense-content which is an element of X, and also certain images which define A's expectation of the occurrence in suitable circumstances of certain further elements of X, and that this expectation is correct: and what we are saying when we assert that a mental object M and a physical object X are causally connected is that, in certain conditions, the occurrence of a certain sort of sense-content, which is an element of X, is a reliable sign of the occurrence of a certain sort of sense-content, which is an element of X, or vice-versa. And the question whether any propositions of these kinds are true or not is clearly an empirical question. It cannot be decided, as metaphysicians have attempted to decide it, *a priori.*

We turn now to consider the question of the subjectivity of sense-contents—that is, to consider whether it is or is not logically possible for a sense-content to occur in the sense-history of more than a single self. And in order to decide this question we must proceed to give an analysis of the notion of a self.

The problem which now confronts us is analogous to the problem of perception with which we have already dealt. We know that a self, if it is not to be treated as a metaphysical entity, must be held to be a logical construction out of sense-experiences. It is, in fact, a logical construction out of the sense-experiences which constitute the actual and possible sense-history of a self. And, accordingly, if we ask what is the nature of the self, we are asking what is the relationship that must obtain between for them to belong to the sense-history of the same self. And the answer to this question is that for any two sense-experiences to belong to the sense-history of the same self it is necessary and sufficient that they should contain organic sense-contents which are elements of the same body.[21] But, as it is logically impossible for any organic sense-content to be an element of more

[21] This is not the only criterion. Vide *The Foundations of Empirical Knowledge*, pp. 142–4.

than one body, the relation of "belonging to the sense-history of the same self" turns out to be a symmetrical and transitive relation.[22] And, from the fact that the relation of belonging to the sense-history of the same self is symmetrical and transitive, it follows necessarily that the series of sense-experiences which constitute the sense-histories of different selves cannot have any members in common. And this is tantamount to saying that it is logically impossible for a sense-experience to belong to the sense-history of more than a single self. But if all sense-experiences are subjective, then, all sense-contents are subjective. For it is necessary by definition for a sense-content to be contained in a single sense-experience.

To many people, the account of the self, on which this conclusion depends, will no doubt appear paradoxical. For it is still fashionable to regard the self as a substance. But, when one comes to enquire into the nature of this substance, one finds that it is an entirely unobservable entity. It may be suggested that it is revealed in self-consciousness but this is not the case. For all that is involved in self-consciousness is the ability of a self to remember some of its earlier states. And to say that a self A is able to remember some of its earlier states is to say merely that some of the sense-experiences which constitute A contain memory images which correspond to sense-contents which have previously occurred in the sense-history of A.[23] And thus we find that the possibility of self-consciousness in no way involves the existence of a substantive ego. But if the substantive ego is not revealed in self-consciousness, it is not revealed anywhere. The existence of such an entity is completely unverifiable. And accordingly, we must conclude that the assumption of its existence is no less metaphysical than Locke's discredited assumption of the existence of a material substratum. For it is clearly no more significant to assert that an "unobservable somewhat" underlies the sensations which are the sole empirical manifestations of the self than it is to assert that an "unobservable somewhat" underlies the sensations which are the sole empirical manifestations of a material thing. The considerations which make it necessary, as Berkeley saw, to give a phenomenalist account of material things, make it necessary also, as Berkeley did not see, to give a phenomenalist account of the self.

---

[22] For a definition of a symmetrical transitive relation, see Chapter III, p. 66.

[23] Cf. Bertrand Russell, *Analysis of Mind*, Lecture IX.

Our reasoning on this point, as on so many others, is in conformity with Hume's. He, too, rejected the notion of a substantive ego on the ground that no such entity was observable. For, he said, whenever he entered most intimately into what he called himself, he always stumbled on some particular perception or other—of heat or cold, light or shade, love or hatred, pain or pleasure. He never could catch himself at any time without a perception, and never could observe anything but the perception. And this led him to assert that a self was "nothing but a bundle or collection of different perceptions."[24] But, having asserted this, he found himself unable to discover the principle on which innumerable distinct perceptions among which it was impossible to perceive any "real connection" were united to form a single self. He saw that the memory must be regarded not as producing, but rather as discovering, personal identity—or, in other words, that, whereas self-consciousness has to be defined in terms of memory, self-identity cannot be; for the number of my perceptions which I can remember at any time always falls far short of the number of those which have actually occurred in my history, and those which I cannot remember are no less constitutive of my self than those which I can. But having, on this ground, rejected the claim of memory to be the unifying principle of the self, Hume was obliged to confess that he did not know what was the connection between perceptions in virtue of which they formed a single self.[25] And this confession has often been taken by rationalist authors as evidence that it is impossible for a consistent empiricist to give a satisfactory account of the self.

For our part, we have shown that this charge against empiricism is unfounded. For we have solved Hume's problem by defining personal identity in terms of bodily identity, and bodily identity is to be defined in terms of the resemblance and continuity of sense-contents. And this procedure is justified by the fact that whereas it is permissible, in our language, to speak of a man as surviving a complete loss of memory, or a complete change of character, it is self-contradictory to speak of a man as surviving the annihilation of his body[26] for that which is supposed to survive by those who look forward to a "life after death" is not the empirical self, but a meta-

---

[24] *Treatise of Human Nature,* Book 1, Part IV, section vi.

[25] *Treatise of Human Nature,* Appendix.

[26] This is not true if one adopts a psychological criterion of personal identity.

physical entity—the soul. And this metaphysical entity, concerning which no genuine hypothesis can be formulated, has no logical connection whatsoever with the self.

It must, however, be remarked that, although we have vindicated Hume's contention that it is necessary to give a phenomenalist account of the nature of the self, our actual definition of the self is not a mere restatement of his. For we do not hold, as he apparently did, that the self is an aggregate of sense-experiences, that the sense-experiences which constitute a particular self are in any sense parts of it. What we hold is that the self is reducible to sense-experiences, in the sense that to say anything about the self is always to say something about sense-experiences and our definition of personal identity is intended to show how this reduction could be made.

In thus combining a thoroughgoing phenomenalism with the admission that all sense-experiences, and the sense-contents which form part of them, are private to a single self, we are pursuing a course to which the following objection is likely to be raised. It will be said that anyone who maintains both that all empirical knowledge resolves itself on analysis into knowledge of the relationships of sense-contents, and also that the whole of a man's sense-history is private to himself, is logically obliged to be a solipsist—that is, to hold that no other people besides himself exist, or at any rate that there is no good reason to suppose that any other people beside himself exist. For it follows from his premises, so it will be argued, that the sense-experiences of another person cannot possibly form part of his own experience, and consequently that he cannot have the slightest ground for believing in their occurrence; and, in that case, if people are nothing but logical constructions out of their sense-experiences, he cannot have the slightest ground for believing in the existence of any other people. And it will be said that even if such a solipsistic doctrine cannot be shown to be self-contradictory, it is nevertheless known to be false.[27]

I propose to meet this objection, not by denying that solipsism is known to be false, but by denying that it is a necessary consequence of our epistemology. I am, indeed, prepared to admit that if the personality of others was something that I could not possibly observe, then I should have no reason to believe in the existence of anyone else. And in admitting this I am conceding a point which

---

[27] Cf. L. S. Stebbing, *Logical Positivism and Analysis.*

would not, I think, be conceded by the majority of those philosophers who hold, as we do, that a sense-content cannot belong to the sense-history of more than a single self. They would maintain, on the contrary, that, although one cannot in any sense observe the existence of other people, one can nevertheless infer their existence with a high degree of probability from one's own experiences. They would say that my observation of a body whose behavior resembled the behavior of my own body entitled me to think it probable that that body was related to a self which I could not observe, in the same way as my body was related to my own observable self. And in saying this, they would be attempting to answer not the psychological question, What causes me to believe in the existence of other people? but the logical question, What good reason have I for believing in the existence of other people? So that their view cannot be refuted, as is sometimes supposed, by an argument which shows that infants come by their belief in the existence of other people intuitively, and not through a process of inference. For although my belief in a certain proposition may in fact be causally dependent on my apprehension of the evidence which makes the belief rational, it is not necessary that it should be. It is not self contradictory to say that beliefs for which there are rational grounds are frequently arrived at by irrational means.

The correct way to refute this view that I can use an argument from analogy, based on the fact that there is a perceptible resemblance between the behavior of other bodies and that of my own, to justify a belief in the existence of other people whose experiences I could not conceivably observe, is to point out that no argument can render probable a completely unverifiable hypothesis. I can legitimately use an argument from analogy to establish the probable existence of an object which has never in fact manifested itself in my experience, provided that the object is such that it could conceivably be manifested in my experience. If this condition is not fulfilled, then, as far as I am concerned, the object is a metaphysical object, and the assertion that it exists and has certain properties is a metaphysical assertion. And, since a metaphysical assertion is senseless, no argument can possibly render it probable. But, on the view which we are discussing, I must regard other people as metaphysical objects; for it is assumed that their experiences are completely inaccessible to my observation.

The conclusion to be drawn from this is not that the existence of other people is for me a metaphysical, and so fictitious, hypothesis, but that the assumption that other people's experiences are completely inaccessible to my observation is false; just as the conclusion to be drawn from the fact that Locke's notion of a material substratum is metaphysical is not that all the assertions which we make about material things are nonsensical, but that Locke's analysis of the concept of a material thing is false. And just as I must define material things and my own self in terms of their empirical manifestations, so I must define other people in terms of their empirical manifestations—that is, in terms of the behavior of their bodies, and ultimately in terms of sense-contents. The assumption that "behind" these sense-contents there are entities which are not even in principle accessible to my observation can have no more significance for me than the admittedly metaphysical assumption that such entities "underlie" the sense-contents which constitute material things for me, or my own self. And thus I find that I have as good a reason to believe in the existence of other people as I have to believe in the existence of material things. For in each case my hypothesis is verified by the occurrence in my sense-history of the appropriate series of sense-contents.[28]

It must not be thought that this reduction of other people's experiences to one's own in any way involves a denial of their reality. Each of us must define the experiences of the others in terms of what he can at least in principle observe, but this does not mean that each of us must regard all the others as so many robots. On the contrary, the distinction between a conscious man and an unconscious machine resolves itself into a distinction between different types of perceptible behavior. The only ground I can have for asserting that an object which appears to be a conscious being is not really a conscious being, but only a dummy or a machine, is that it fails to satisfy one of the empirical tests by which the presence or absence of consciousness is determined. If I know that an object behaves in every way as a conscious being must, by definition, behave, then I know that it is really conscious. And this is an analytical proposition. For when I assert that an object is conscious I am asserting no more than that it

---

[28] Cf. Rudolf Carnap, "Scheinprobleme in der Philosophie: das Fremdpsychische und der Realismusstreit," and "Psychologie in physikalische Sprache," *Erkenninis*, Vol. III, 1932.

would, in response to any conceivable test, exhibit the empirical manifestations of consciousness. I am not making a metaphysical postulate concerning the occurrence of events which I could not, even in principle, observe. It appears, then, that the fact that a man's sense-experiences are private to himself, inasmuch as each of them contains an organic sense-content which belongs to his body and to no other, is perfectly compatible with his having good reason to believe in the existence of other men. For, if he is to avoid metaphysics, he must define the existence of other men in terms of the actual and hypothetical occurrence of certain sense-contents, and then the fact that the requisite sense-contents do occur in his sense-history gives him a good reason for believing that there are other conscious beings besides himself. And thus we see that the philosophical problem of "our knowledge of other people" is not the insoluble, and, indeed, fictitious, problem of establishing by argument the existence of entities which are altogether unobservable, but is simply the problem of indicating the way in which a certain type of hypothesis is empirically verified.[29]

It must be made clear, finally, that our phenomenalism is compatible not merely with the fact that each of us has good reason to believe that there exist a number of conscious beings of the same kind as himself, but also with the fact that each of us has good reason to believe that these beings communicate with one another and with him, and inhabit a common world. For it might appear, at first sight, as if the view that all synthetic propositions ultimately referred to sense-contents, coupled with the view that no sense-content could belong to the sense-history of more than one person, implied that no one could have any good reason to believe that a synthetic proposition ever had the same literal meaning for any other person as it had for himself. That is, it might be thought that if each person's experiences were private to himself, no one could have good reason to believe that any other person's experiences were qualitatively the same as his own, and consequently that no one could have good reason to believe that the propositions which he understood, referring as they did to the contents of his own sense-experiences,

[29] This question is referred to in the Introduction, pp. 19–20.

were ever understood in the same way by anybody else.[30] But this reasoning would be fallacious. It does not follow from the fact that each man's experiences are private to himself that no one ever has good reason to believe that another man's experiences are qualitatively the same as his own. For we define the qualitative identity and difference of two people's sense-experiences in terms of the similarity and dissimilarity of their reactions to empirical tests. To determine, for instance, whether two people have the same color sense we observe whether they classify all the color expanses with which they are confronted in the same way; and, when we say that a man is color-blind, what we are asserting is that he classifies certain color expanses in a different way from that in which they would be classified by the majority of people. It may be objected that the fact that two people classify color expanses in the same way proves only that their color worlds have the same structure, and not that they have the same content; that it is possible for another man to assent to every proposition which I make about colors on the basis of entirely different color sensations, although, since the difference is systematic, neither of us is ever in a position to detect it. But the answer to this is that each of us has to define the content of another man's sense-experiences in terms of what he can himself observe. If he regards the experiences of others as essentially unobservable entities, whose nature has somehow to be inferred from the subjects' perceptible behavior, then, as we have seen, even the proposition that there are other conscious beings becomes for him a metaphysical hypothesis. Accordingly, it is a mistake to draw a distinction between the structure and the content of people's sensations—such as that the structure alone is accessible to the observation of others, the content inaccessible. For if the contents of other people's sensations really were inaccessible to my observation, then I could never say anything about them. But, in fact, I do make significant statements about them; and that is because I define them, and the relations between them, in terms of what I can myself observe.

In the same way, each of us has good reason to suppose that other people understand him, and that he understands them, because he observes that his utterances have the effect on their actions which

---

[30] This argument is used by Professor L. S. Stebbing in her article on "Communication and Verification," *Supplementary Proceedings of the Aristotelian Society*, 1934.

he regards as appropriate, and that they also regard as appropriate the effect which their utterances have on his actions; and mutual understanding is defined in terms of such harmony of behavior. And, since to assert that two people inhabit a common world is to assert that they are capable, at least in principle, of understanding one another, it follows that each of us, although his sense-experiences are private to himself, has good reason to believe that he and other conscious beings inhabit a common world. For each of us observes the behavior, on the part of himself and others, which constitutes the requisite understanding. And there is nothing in our epistemology which involves a denial of this fact.

2

Are Religious Statements Meaningful?

E. D. Klemke

During the past twenty or so years, there has taken place, in philosophical circles, a severe questioning of the meaningfulness of religious statements. The philosophical position known as logical positivism, or as some now prefer, logical empiricism, achieved notorious fame by its thesis: Religious statements (along with metaphysical, ethical, and aesthetic propositions) are meaningless.[1] It has been profoundly shocking to me to note that theologians (with few exceptions, primarily in England) have almost completely ignored this discussion. And, I truly believe, at their peril. For, whether or not the discussion has yielded an adequate solution of the problems, it has not been irrelevant. On the contrary, it has extreme relevance for the theologian or the philosopher of religion. And I do not see how a serious attempt at theology, or philosophy of religion, can fail to take cognizance of the philosophical controversy. I say this even though I am fully aware that the movement is not quite as vigorous as it once was[2] and that it has been somewhat superseded (in England, at least) by what is loosely referred to as Oxford

---

[1] The reader who is unacquainted with this philosophical "movement" will find an especially vivid (though not necessarily the most capable) summary in A. J. Ayer, *Language, Truth, and Logic* (2d ed.; New York: Dover, 1946). See also Feigl and Sellars, *Readings in Philosophical Analysis* (New York: Appleton-Century-Crofts, 1949); or Richard von Mises, *Positivism* (Cambridge: Harvard University Press, 1951.)

[2] It is, nevertheless, still alive, in spite of the protests of its adversaries. For a more popular presentation, with excellent bibliographies at the end of each chapter, see John Hospers, *An Introduction to Philosophical Analysis* (New York: Prentice-Hall, Inc., 1953).

analysis.[3] The latter, in my opinion, often obscures many issues, instead of clarifying them. I shall not, however, attempt to demonstrate that here.[4]

My topic, then, is the status of religious statements. Are they meaningful or not? Why? Or, since there is not merely one kind, which of them are meaningful and which (if any) meaningless? My "program" is as follows: In Section I, I shall schematically classify the various types of religious statements, or sentences which purport to be statements, in contrast with sentences which, clearly, are not statements. As we shall see, of those sentences which purport to be statements, some among them are problematical and peculiar. The problem of meaningfulness arises in connection with these. In Section II, I shall state the views of philosophical analysts who have maintained the these problematical sentences are meaningless, and I shall attempt to show why the conclusion was reached. (I shall here ignore the refinements which individual philosophers have made on this doctrine, as they are not important for our purposes. Before turning to an attempted resolution of the problem (or, if you will, an "answer" to the analysts), I shall, in Section III, present R. G. Collingwood's doctrine of absolute presuppositions. Finally, in Section IV, I shall use Collingwood's doctrine, though not his specific views concerning it, to suggest a possible answer as to the status of religious assertions of the problematical type.

First, some definitions are needed. By "religious sentences" I mean: (*a*) sentences which are found within the Christian faith (omitting from consideration here other religions); (*b*) all kinds of such sentences, not merely those which refer to the deity or those which are creedal utterances, etc. By "statement" I mean an indicative sentence which expresses an assertion, which is intended to be

---

[3] See, e.g., John Urmson, *Philosophical Analysis* (London: Oxford University Press, 1956), Part III. A more popular treatment is given in Ryle *et al.*, *Revolution in Philosophy* (London: Macmillan & Co., Ltd., 1957). See also A. G. N. Flew (ed.), *Logic and Language* ("First and Second Series" (Oxford: Basil Blackwell, 1955); Flew (ed.), *Essays in Conceptual Analysis* (London: Macmillan & Co., Ltd., 1956). The "sacred book" of the movement is Ludwig Wittgenstein, *Philosophical Investigations* (Oxford: Basil Blackwell, 1953).

[4] An excellent critique may be found in Gustav Bergmann, "The Revolt against Logical Atomism," *Philosophical Quarterly*, Vol. VII, No. 29; Vol. VIII, No. 30. An even better one may be found in Arthur Pap, *Semantics and Necessary Truth* (New Haven: Yale University Press, 1958), Part Two.

literally interpreted, and which may be appropriately labeled either "true" or "false." By "apparent statement" I mean an indicative sentence which obviously has poetical, rather than literal, intent. By "non-statement" I mean a sentence or phrase which expresses an ejaculation, exhortation, etc. I add to these, in a tenuous position, another category, "pseudo-statement," which I shall define in the sequel. In my initial discussion pseudo-statements will be included within the class of statements. But, as we shall see, I believe that they must form a separate class, since they lack the characteristics which actual statements possess.

By a "literal" statement I mean one which is either: *(a)* a logical truth (and, thus, analytic or tautological) or *(b)* an empirical assertion which is capable of verification in the broad sense. By "verification in the broad sense" I mean the finding of some actual or possible state of affairs which will confirm or disconfirm the statement. I shall elaborate these points in later parts of the paper.

So much for preliminaries. I turn now to a rough schematic classification of the various kinds of religious sentences. Whether or not my specific classification is complete is beside the point. For whatever scheme is used, certain sentences will still be peculiar. And here is where the problem of meaningfulness arises.

I.

1. There are, of course, many kinds of religious sentences which are *non-statements*. Some of these are: (A) Commands or exhortations: "Thou shalt not take the name of the Lord thy God in vain" or "Love one another. " (B) Prayers: "Lord, have mercy unto me." (C) Blessings: "Grace to you and peace from God our Father and the Lord Jesus Christ." (D) Questions: "Whence cometh my help?" (E) Ejaculations: "Woe is me, wretched man that I am!" etc.

Since none of the above utterances (and others like them) are statements, as no assertions are made in them, it would be inappropriate to apply tests for truth or falsity, or to attempt verification of them. We may, therefore, pass by them.

2. Many religious sentences seem to be statements but are only *apparent statements*. Some examples are: "The Lord is my shepherd" or "Faith moves mountains." I presume that I do not have to argue the case. I believe that most religious persons would deny that these sentences are to be literally interpreted. Sentences of this type seem to

assert something, yet not in the same sense in which "Jones is my auto mechanic" or "The Smith Company moves houses" do. In seeking to understand sentences of the above sort, we realize that we must not be too literal, that these are figurative expressions, etc. For example, faith has never been known to move structures such as Mount Everest, but "genuine" faith has been known (it is often said) to perform wonders somewhat similar. Perhaps, indeed, it moves psychical or "spiritual" mountains. And so on, with respect to other apparent statements.

3. I turn now to the class of (actual) *statements.* I distinguish at least five types of religious sentences which *have been held* to be actual statements. As I have already indicated, sentences of the fifth type are problematic.

(1) Many religious statements are *descriptions.* There are, e.g., statements which describe the actions, character, or beliefs of certain religious individuals or groups. Some instances are: "Many Christians pray," or "X believes the assertions of the Apostles' Creed," etc. As no particular problems arise in connection with such statements, I move on to the next.

(2) Certain religious statements may be called *explanations.* Some examples are: "The lack of rain in X is due to the people's sinfulness" (where X is a specified region or country); or "Britain's military failure of 1916 occurred because farmers planted potatoes on Sunday,"[5] etc. Undoubtedly, assertions of this crude kind are seldom made today by sophisticated Christians. However, statements of this sort are often encountered. It is possible to test these explanatory hypotheses for validity. Sufficient tests might lead one to believe that there is or is not a connection between, say, the people's sinfulness and rainfall, or between Sunday planting and military failures. To be sure, we may not obtain certainty. This, however, is not the point. As Hume (and others) have emphasized, matter-of-fact statements are never certain.

(3) Some religious statements are *historical statements.* We might (roughly) divide them into two (or more) groups. *(a)* Some historical statements cause no further problems with respect to verification than those which are found in the case of non-religious historical assertions. Instances of these might be: "Jesus was born in Bethle-

---

[5] Bertrand Russell, *Unpopular Essays* (New York: Simon & Schuster, 1950), p. 75.

hem," "The apostle Paul was imprisoned," etc. Admittedly, the evidence is scanty. But so is it, in a sense, with respect to judgments about, say, Socrates. And, of course, statements of this kind are also only probable. But, at least, one would know what to look for as evidence by which to assess some "degree" of probability. *(b)* Other historical statements (within Christianity) are more difficult to confirm. Examples are: "Jesus healed paralytics instantaneously," or "Jesus arose from the dead, " etc. Perhaps, in practice, such sentences cannot be verified. But they are certainly not unverifiable in principle. Again, one would know what to look for if one had been there at the time of the supposed resurrection, or the healings. (I pass over the spiritual interpretation of the resurrection.)

(4) Certain religious statements might be called "autobiographical statements," or, perhaps, "testimonies." Examples of these are: "I am persuaded that nothing can separate us from the love of Christ," or "I am convinced that Christ died for me," etc. Sentences of this kind are somewhat similar to both historical statements and descriptions. But they are more limited than either of those kinds of statements are. They characterize certain attitudes, passions, concerns, and convictions of various individuals. They are not "emotive" utterances, however, since it is possible to confirm the statements. One could find some state of affairs in the world, e.g., the asserter's beliefs or actions, which provides confirmation of the statements.

(5) I turn, finally, to the last type of religious sentences which have, traditionally, been held to be statements. Our main problem arises in connection with these. Perhaps some examples will reveal the difficulty: "God exists," "God created the world," "God is triune," "Jesus is the Son of God" (or "Jesus is divine"), "God loves us," "God has given men free will," "The Holy Spirit descended upon them," "There is a life after the death of the body," etc.

Sentences such as these purport to be statements. Most religious people who utter such sentences would believe them not to be disguised exhortations, ejaculations, etc. Nor would they be content to say that they are only apparent statements. (Some religious people, of course, would.) And, since they are not descriptive, explanatory, historical, or autobiographical statements, they must form a separate class by themselves. What should they be called? Let us withhold a label for the time being.

More important than a name is the status which such sentences possess. Surely sentences of type (5) are not statements, according to the criteria to which all other statements are subjected. Consider: Actual statements, remember, are those which are confirmable (or disconfirmable) by some state of affairs which warrants the truth (or falsity) of the statements. Sentences of type (5) are not so confirmable—or, even, disconfirmable (as will be shown in Section II). Thus, if they are held to be actual statements, then "statement" will mean something different, in this case, from what it normally does. Hence one is faced with a decision. Either: *(a)* the sentences in (5) are not statements; or *(b)* our usual definition of "statement" is not correct. The religious man hesitates to assert *(a)*. Yet, if *(b)* is espoused, then "statement" will now have two meanings: (i) a normal one which has been given clarity, consistency, and adequacy by the tools of logical and philosophical analysis; and (ii) a peculiar religious meaning which denies the characterizations possessed by the usual one. But if one must resort to this maneuver, then some sentences will be statements by the religious criterion but (at the same time) non-statements by the normal criterion. But, now, what sense does it make to still use the word "statement" for such sentences? Are we not "trying to have our cake and eat it too"?

II.

A view which has gained rather wide acceptance in recent years among philosophical analysts runs as follows:

(A) Sentences of type (5) are not confirmable.

(1) Rational demonstration does not prove them.

(2) Religious experience does not confirm them.

(3) They are unverifiable in principle.

(B) Sentences of type (5) are not falsifiable.

(C) The resort to revelation, faith, etc., fails to provide a third alternative.

Hence: Since only verifiable (or falsifiable) sentences are meaningful, sentences of type (5) are cognitively meaningless.[6]

---

[6] This position is discussed in Ayer's book (see footnote 1). Many contributors to a recent volume of essays also argue for it. See A. Flew and A. Macintyre (eds.), *New Essays in Philosophical Theology* (New York: Macmillan Co., 1955).

The view deserves a fair run for its money. I shall act as its advocate, by giving content to the above structure. The philosophical analyst argues as follows:

(A) Sentences of type (5) are not confirmable. Take the sentence "God exists." (That is, he exists actually, and not merely for thought.) Obviously, as far as grammar is concerned, this is a proper statement. However, grammar is not the only criterion by which to judge whether or not a sentence is meaningful. "Happiness travels at the speed of 60 miles per hour," is grammatically proper. Yet it has no clear meaning. In a similar way, it is appropriate to ask whether "God exists" has any meaning. And, of course, if it is the case that "God exists" is meaningless, then "God does not exist" is equally meaningless—as Ayer has shown.[7] One cannot, therefore, escape the problem by professing atheism, for, if the affirmation of a sentence is absurd, then the denial is equally absurd.

(1) Rational demonstration does not prove sentences of type (5) to be true. Sufficient labors have been spent upon the traditional arguments for the existence of God to show that they are not valid. Even theologians and philosophers of religion have admitted this.[8] A few fallacies in reasoning might be mentioned. The sentence "God exists" is held, in the ontological argument and in variants of the cosmological argument, to be logically necessary; but no existential proposition can be logically necessary. And the argument from analogy, which occurs in the teleological argument, is shaky, since arguments from analogy never bridge the leap from the finite evidence to the infinite existent.

One might object that although these particular arguments, and all variants of them, are invalid, the conclusion may, nevertheless, be true. Very well, what other means shall we attempt in order to discover whether or not "God exists" is true?

(2) Let us try the religious experience claim. Some religious people profess to have knowledge of the existence of God upon the basis of direct experience of God. They say that our knowledge of God rests upon the revelation of his personal presence, or that our knowledge of God comes through a direct, personal encounter or

---

[7] Ayer, *op. cit.*, chap. vi.

[8] I shall not rehash old arguments. If the reader is unconvinced, I refer him to H. J. Paton, *The Modern Predicament* (New York: Macmillan Co., 1955), chaps. xii-xiv.

confrontation with him. It must be noticed that people who talk this way do not simply assert that they had an unusual experience. They claim to have had an experience of God.

But this procedure is incapable of establishing what it hopes to establish. Just as the assertion that God exists cannot be shown to be warrantable by means of rational demonstration, so it cannot be shown to be warrantable by the religious experience claim. For all that the sentence "I have had an experience of God" can certify is that I have had certain feelings, sensations, etc. It cannot confirm the further assertion that God exists. The method of religious experience can, thus, give one a feeling or "inner assurance" that God exists or may exist, but it cannot confirm that God does, in fact, exist. In order for the assertion "God exists" to be warrantable, it would have to be intersubjectively testable. Yet the possibility of such testability is precisely what proponents of the religious experience claim deny. They maintain that the way of knowing God through religious experience is unique. They say that one cannot know what the experience of God is until one has had it. And apparently only a few are privileged to have it.

Thus, the religious experience method never answers the question: "How can you know when anyone has had an experience of God?" There are certain tests by which I can know, with a high degree of probability, as to whether or not I have had, say, an experience of flying in an airplane. But what tests can be devised by which I can know whether or not I have had an experience of God? The proponents of the religious experience claim are silent here. In place of tests they posit the notion of an "immediacy" of knowledge which is supposed to carry its own guaranty of confirmation. But, surely, many people who claim to have had genuine experiences of something or other have been wrong! Therefore, the religious-experience method cannot confirm the assertion, "I have had direct experiences of God, and God exists." The most which it can confirm is the assertion, "I have had some kind of peculiar experience, by which it seems to me that God exists," and this is something very different from the first sentence.

Other methods which have been used in the attempt to confirm the sentence "God exists" (the moral arguments, etc.) bring us no nearer to a satisfactory conclusion. Our purpose here is not to give an exhaustive treatment of the alternatives with respect to the single sentence "God exists" but to indicate the kinds of problems which one encounters with sentences of type (5). It may be objected that we have unfairly selected the most difficult sentence of this group. However, the other sentences of this type presuppose the sentence "God exists" and would be meaningless if this one were no statement at all. In fact, many of the others include the assertion of God's existence when attributing qualities or actions to God. Thus, in actual practice, religious people think of the sentence "God loves us" as expressing both "God exists" and "He loves us. " Hence the problems reappear.

(3) The primary difficulty with sentences of type (5) arises not merely because such assertions are unverifiable *in practice;* rather, it lies in the fact that such sentences are not even verifiable *in principle.* There is no conceivable way by which one could test such sentences. If a sentence refers to God, e.g., we not only face the problem that we cannot find some actual state of affairs by which to confirm it. We are further handicapped by the fact that we could not conceive of any possible method of verification. To take an example now famous in philosophical literature, the sentence "There are mountains on the other side of the moon" is, at present, unverifiable in practice. *Yet, if we could some day reach the moon and survive,* we would, at least, know what to look for in order to confirm the sentence. It is, thus, verifiable in principle, though not in practice. The theological sentences which we have been considering are not only unverifiable in practice but also in principle. One cannot imagine any conceivable state of affairs by which to confirm such sentences.

(B) Thus far, we have primarily dealt with the question: What state of affairs would one have to find in order to confirm such sentences as "God exists," etc.? We found that such sentences are incapable of verification (or confirmation). Let us, now, ask the question with respect to falsification. That is: What state of affairs would one have to find which would constitute a falsification of such sentences as "God exists"? In other words, what events would have to occur in order to be a sufficient reason stating "There is no God" or "God does not love us," etc.?

Antony Flew has discussed this problem with respect to the sentence, "God loves us as a father loves his children."[9] Many religious people hold this sentence to be true. But suppose that we see a child dying of cancer. His earthly father is greatly concerned

[9] Flew and Macintyre, *op. cit.*, pp. 98-99.

and expresses his love for the child by attempting every possible method of providing help for him. But God, the "heavenly Father," shows no apparent sign of concern. At this point, religious people often qualify the assertion by adding, "Well, God's love not a merely human love," or "God's ways, including his ways of loving, are inscrutable." Thus, the severe sufferings of the child are held to be compatible with the assertion that "God loves us as a father loves his children"—plus the qualifications. But if the sentence must be qualified—"God's love is different; he has reasons we know not of etc."—why maintain it? What is this affirmation of God's love worth if it must be so qualified as to mean something different from the original sentence? What would have to happen in order to persuade and entitle us to say "God does not love us?" What state of affairs would have to occur in order to constitute a falsification of the assertion that God loves us? Religious people maintain that no conceivable experience could falsify sentences of this sort.

Thus we are left with the peculiar situation whereby all states of affairs are held to be commensurate with an assertion such as "God loves us as a father loves his children," and similar assertions. To a neutral observer, certain states of affairs would seem to show that God loves us, while others would indicate that he does not love us. To the religious person, however, there is no conceivable state of affairs which would be a demonstration that God does not love us. Even innocent children, dying in agony, are held to be no falsification of the sentence "God loves us." But if every state of affairs is compatible with the sentence "God loves us," then no falsification is possible. And if no falsification is possible, then the sentence seems to have no straightforward meaning, and is, hence, cognitively meaningless.

Thus, whether we attempt to verify or falsify a sentence of type (5), we note that there are no criteria which are acceptable. It would seem therefore, that such sentences are cognitively meaningless. One need not thereby deny that such assertions may possess some other status. They may, for example, be expressive of certain emotions, feelings, and attitudes which are felt by the one who utters them, and which, perhaps, evoke similar emotions and attitudes in others.

(C) There have been various attempts to completely escape the predicament in which we find ourselves. These, too, have failed. Some, e.g., have said that sentences of type (5) are known to be true by revelation. They are "revealed truths," rather than natural truths, and, therefore, not subject to verification. But this is a fruitless effort. For sophisticated religious people deny that any propositions are presented in revelation, and naive religious people must posit the notion of inspiration by which to give the revealed propositions the status of truth, forgetting that the notion of inspiration itself is impossible of verification.

Other religious people suggest still another alternative. They maintain that there are "truths of faith" as over against "truths of reason." In this view it is appropriate to seek verification of sentences which fall into the "reason" category, but it is inappropriate to seek verification of those which are in the "faith" group. The meaning of faith, they tell us, is to believe where no proof is possible. Yet beliefs are often notoriously incredible, as well as incompatible at times. Apparently some religious people once believed that Joshua commanded the moon to stand still, or that the bodies of the saints were raised after Jesus' death and appeared to many people. Where is one to draw the line as to what may or may not be believed? How can one know that the belief that God created the world is any more true than the belief that Jesus spoke to demons, and was answered? Furthermore, various religions seem to hold incompatible views with respect to the nature or activity of the deity. What certifies the Christian view, or particular opinions within the Christian view?

In conclusion, it may be affirmed that religious statements of the first four types are meaningful. But religious sentences of type (5) are meaningless.

Thus runs the argument against permitting the status of statements to religious sentences of the fifth type. Can we "save" such sentences from the onslaught? Before answering the question, I would like to turn, briefly, to some interesting insights of R. G. Collingwood, which may reveal a possible path toward an "answer." In Section III, I shall merely state Collingwood's views. In Section IV, I shall apply one of these doctrines toward a possible solution of our problem.

III.

The particular views of Collingwood which are of relevance for the issue at hand are found in *An Essay on Metaphysics*.[10] The opening

---

[10] R. G. Collingwood, *An Essay on Metaphysics* (London: Oxford University Press, 1940).

pages of the work are devoted to a consideration of Aristotle's metaphysics, in which Collingwood finds three definitions of metaphysics: (i) Metaphysics is the science of pure being. (ii) Metaphysics is the science of the highest being. (iii) Metaphysics is the science which deals with the presuppositions underlying ordinary science. Collingwood argues that the first of these definitions cannot be true, as a science of pure being is a contradiction in terms. He dismisses the second definition. He affirms the third as being the proper one, and his book is an effort to explain its meaning.[11] As distinct from metaphysics, the science of pure being—or attempts at it—may be called ontology. It does not designate any actual science. It merely refers to the mistakes which people have made. Thus, by rejecting ontology, Collingwood develops a doctrine of "metaphysics without ontology."[12]

Metaphysics, then, is the science which deals with the presuppositions underlying ordinary science, that is, any science other than metaphysics (and in the broad sense of science, i.e., any organized body of knowledge). However, certain presuppositions are of greater interest to the metaphysician than others. These are absolute, as distinct from relative, presuppositions.

A relative presupposition is one which may stand relatively to one question as its presupposition and relatively to another question as its answer. Collingwood's homely example is that of a man measuring the distance between two points with an old tape. In asking the question, "What is the distance between these two points?" he is making a presupposition, namely, "My tape is accurate (to a certain degree)." This presupposition is also an answer to another question: "Is my tape accurate?" The answer that the tape is accurate was obtained by checking it with some more reliable measure. Thus relative presuppositions may be verified. Since they are answers to questions, they are also propositions, or statements, as well as presuppositions. Therefore, with respect to them it is appropriate to ask: "Are they true (or false)?"[13]

An absolute presupposition, however, is "one which stands, relatively to all questions to which it is related, as a presupposition,

---

11 *Ibid.*, pp. 11–16.

12 *Ibid.*, p. 17.

13 *Ibid.*, pp. 29–30.

never as an answer."[14] Collingwood's illustration (again a commonsensical one) is as follows. Suppose that one were to talk to a pathologist about a certain disease and were to ask him what is the cause of the event, *E*, which occurs in this disease. He would answer that the cause of *E* is C, and he would perhaps recommend some authority on the matter. One finds in the course of the discussion that the pathologist, as well as his authority, assumed that *E* has a cause before it was known what the cause is. If you then asked him: "Why did you assume that it has a cause?" you would probably be told: "Because everything that happens has a cause." If you then asked how, in turn, this is known, you would here encounter one of the pathologist's absolute presuppositions, and you would be told that this is not something which we can prove or verify. We simply have to take it for granted. Thus absolute presuppositions are unverifiable, that is to say, they are not propositions, or statements. The distinction between truth and falsity, or verifiability and unverifiability, does not apply to them at all.[15]

Metaphysics, then, is the attempt to find out what absolute presuppositions have been held by certain persons or groups of persons on certain occasions and in the course of certain "pieces" of thinking. To ask whether or not absolute presuppositions are true, or upon what evidence they may be accepted, is to engage in pseudo-metaphysics.[16]

Metaphysical questions and presuppositions are, thus, historical questions and presuppositions. The metaphysician merely attempts to state what presuppositions were made by various scientists in various periods of history. And he may attempt to compare presuppositions and inquire as to how certain ones grew out of others as the result of internal strain.[17]

In a section entitled "Examples," Collingwood discusses the absolute presupposition "God exists" as an instance (among others) of the kind of presuppositions which have been held in history. He considers the question with reference to the Christian patristic writers, to whom, Collingwood believes, the existence of God was an absolute presupposition of all the thinking done by reflective

---

[14] *Ibid.*, p. 31.

[15] *Ibid.*, pp. 31–32.

[16] *Ibid.*, p. 47.

[17] *Ibid.*, pp. 70 ff.

Christians, especially that which was done in natural science.[18] Since their affirmation, "God exists," is an absolute presupposition, it follows that it is not a proposition or statement. It is, therefore, neither true nor false. And it can neither be proved nor disproved. It can only be presupposed or believed in.[19]

Collingwood then traces the history of this absolute presupposition back to the pre-Christian Greek era and shows how it, along with certain subordinate presuppositions, was held, knowingly or unknowingly, by natural scientists throughout the course of their work.[20] This is an extremely interesting discussion. However, I shall not summarize it because it is, for various reasons, somewhat beside the point for the topic at hand, which is not the relationship of the presupposition of the existence of God to natural science but the significance of this presupposition, and others like it, for theology or philosophy of religion.

So much, then, for Collingwood. I turn, next, to an application of the doctrine of absolute presuppositions to our problem concerning the status of religious sentences of type (5). In so doing, I must make it clear that I am departing from Collingwood's views. This application of the doctrine was apparently never noted by Collingwood. At least he never discussed the matter. Perhaps this is a result of his belief that absolute presuppositions are peculiar to certain historical eras. Thus, he seems to have thought that "God exists" was an absolute presupposition for the few centuries before and after Christ, but not for the present day. My application will also depart from this feature of Collingwood's theory.

IV.

At the end of Section II, we were left with the view of the philosophical analyst, according to which sentences of type (5) are meaningless and, hence, not genuine statements. Nor are they apparent statements or non-statements. Rather, they are, in his opinion, nonsense. Our task was to see whether religious sentences of type (5) could be "saved" from this fate.

The solution of the problem which I should like to suggest may now be stated. I must make it clear that I put it forth only as a

---

[18] *Ibid.*, p. 186.

[19] *Ibid.*, p. 188.

[20] *Ibid.*, pp. 213–27.

possible solution. I do not even imply that I agree with it. It runs as follows:

The philosophical analyst is right in one respect. Sentences of type (5) are not statements. Let us, therefore, remove them from their position as a type under group 3 (statements) and give them a separate classification which above I have called pseudo-statements. I believe that the theologian must "yield" at this point. Why? Because I, for one, find the arguments of the analyst (presented in Section II) to be sound. It was there shown that sentences of type (5) cannot be statements by all the ordinary criteria for statements. Why, then, continue the pretense that they, nevertheless, somehow are statements? Intellectual honesty ought to be the rule in theology as well as in other disciplines.

However, the analyst is wrong in another respect. Pseudo-statements are not meaningless. They merely have different criteria for meaningfulness from those of statements. Let me explain. It is true that sentences such as "God exists," "God loves us," etc., are not statements (or propositions). It is, therefore, inappropriate to ask whether they are true or false. It is also inappropriate to seek verification, or falsification, of them. This, as I said, does not destroy their meaningfulness. Such sentences are meaningful. But they are meaningful (to use Collingwood's term) as absolute presuppositions, and not as statements. This is the important point.

In other words, the existence of God, God's love for man, God's activity in Christ, etc., might be construed as presuppositions (and absolute ones) of all the thinking that is done by Christians not only in natural science but in ethics, theology, and other areas of thought. They are also presuppositions (if one may extend the term) of a certain mode of existence, one which can be characterized and structured by thought. This mode of existence, or way of life, has been called "salvation" or "the new birth."

Now, if we agree with Collingwood that the task of the metaphysician is to discover what absolute presuppositions are, or have been, held and to state them, what is the theologian's task—to explain them, to prove them to be true, to give reasons for them? Obviously not, if it is held that such assertions are absolute presuppositions and not statements. The theologian must, therefore, not yield to the temptation to become apologetic for the absolute presuppositions. He will accept them as sentences which are not to be proved but merely to be supposed or believed in.

Well, then, what is left for the theologian to do? Have we disenfranchised him? On the contrary, he has an important task but from a somewhat different focus. He will expound, not a theology, but an "anthropology."

Perhaps an illustration is in order. Take the sentence, "Jesus is God and man" (or "Jesus is the Son of God," "Jesus is divine," etc.). Even theologians who have denied that this sentence (or some variant) could be "proved" (whatever that would be) have, nevertheless, thought that one could give rational grounds for the belief that Jesus is divine. They did this by the categories of ontology and with the notion of second person of the Trinity, e.g. Thus the language of *Logos, homoousios,* etc. The categories were not only ontological but supernatural. Thus the two natures doctrine of the creedal formulation.

This attempt served a purpose. To continue it in our day is, in my opinion, utterly fruitless. Hence the theologian (or philosopher of religion) who wishes to preserve the meaningfulness of the sentence "Jesus is God" (or some variant) must take another approach. One of the alternatives is: to consider such sentences as being absolute presuppositions, not statements or propositions. But if this path is followed, then the theologian will not ask: Is it true that Jesus is God? How may we find some rational grounds for asserting that sentence to be true? etc. Rather, he will ask: What results from our presupposing that Jesus is God? And have we any means of affirming him as such without the use of supernatural or ontological categories?

It is conceivable that an affirmative answer can be given to the latter question. The task may be achieved if the theologian is content to describe and discuss that which is within experience, rather than beyond it; that which is "natural" rather than "supernatural"; that which is commonsensical rather than ontological; that which may be formulated in statements rather than uttered in perplexing pseudo-statements. He will refrain from asserting problematic sentences of type (5), which, nevertheless, continue to be *held* by him as absolute presuppositions. But his own assertions are not presuppositions. They are, rather, statements. And statements deal with very ordinary and commonsensical matters, such as the mode of existence in which one lives and the concerns and interests of men. Hence no ontological categories are found in the theologian's language. And he will not expound *doctrines* of the Trinity, Incarnation, etc.

This might be put in another way. The theologian will describe the order of possibility and the order of historical being but not the order of ontological objects. Let me elucidate. I find Kierkegaard to be of help at this point.[21] A possible (or possibility), according to Kierkegaard, is that about which one can have meaningful discourse. Such discourse will be in the form of statements which describe or explicate the possible. A possible, hence, is anything which can be reflected about, anything concerning which one can utter significant propositions. Some possibles elicit interest, concern, and passion. These may be called ethical or behavioral possibles. Now behavioral possibles are never exclusive for one's thought. They form a plurality. And one can think and elucidate many possible modes of existence, and all with equal rational plausibility. In thought, one can never reduce the multiplicity to a unity. One can never find only one to be true or right and the others false or wrong. Rather, the greater one's intelligence is, the more possibles one can find, or the more plausibility can be given to those which one has already conceived. However, when one seeks to actualize a possible in one's existence, he finds that they are exclusive. One can maximally actualize only one at a time.[22]

How does this apply to such sentences as "Jesus is God" and to the task of the theologian? Christ can be (and was, by Kierkegaard) construed as a kind of possibility. He can be conceived as one who presents a challenge (an existential challenge, if you please) to all men. Because of his life, death, teaching, etc., he commands attention. And having heard of him, many men are influenced to re-examine their lives and some to shift their interests, concerns, and enthusiasms from themselves to him. Christ, himself, actualized a certain mode of existence. The mode which he realized is present to all men as a possibility. For those who choose to actualize it, Christ

---

[21] S. Kierkegaard, *Concluding Unscientific Postscript*, trans. D. F. Swenson and W. Lowrie (Princeton, NJ.: Princeton University Press, 1944), pp. 267 ff. See also Paul L. Holmer, "Philosophical Criticism and Christology," *Journal of Religion*, XXXIV (1954), 88–100. Professor Holmer arrives at conclusions similar to those presented here. However, he leaves the status of sentences such as "Jesus is divine," etc., in a somewhat vague position. I believe that they can, and ought to, be more adequately characterized, and I suggest that they might be held to be absolute presuppositions.

[22] This paragraph expresses the "heart" of Kierkegaard's doctrine of the Stages.

"becomes" God. I use quotes around "becomes" intentionally. What I mean is: those who actualize the possibility believe him to be God, i.e., believe him to be that which can fully control and captivate one's interests. For those who actualize the possibility, the divinity of Christ is their absolute presupposition. Is he God independently of their supposing him to be so? Who knows? Not only can one not answer the question, but the asking of it is inappropriate. All one can say is that one's supposing him to be God makes him God for one's self. Whether or not he is God ("from all eternity") one cannot know, and does not ask.

Hence the discourse of the theologian will include historical statements. These will be, for example, about a man, Jesus, who lived, taught, etc., nearly 2,000 years ago. These are neutral statements which can be believed by religious and non-religious men alike. And, of course, they are only probable, as are all historical statements. As I already mentioned, the theologian's discourse will not include ontological assertions, such as sentences of type (5). These are merely supposed or believed in. The theologian's discourse will also include testimonies. He will discuss the transformation of personality which resulted when he and/or others exchanged one passionate interest (in his own existence) for another (an interest in Christ's existence). He will elucidate how such transfer of interests has made men into "new creatures," how it resynthesized the factors of men's personalities. And the theologian's discourse may include exhortations. He will, perhaps, invite others to accept the mode of existence which Christ presented, not because of a "proof" that Christ is God, but simply because others have found Christ capable of maintaining their maximum enthusiasm and passion and because such interest has brought about a new synthesis of personality, a revitalized mode of existence.

The theologian, then, has a more limited task than he has heretofore had. It is to delineate Christ as a possible—a conceivable mode of existence, one alternative among others. The task of the religious man is to transform the possible from a possibility to an actuality in his own existence. With respect to both the theologian and the "ordinary" man, the question "Is Jesus *really* divine?" etc., does not arise. For both of them, it is an absolute presupposition which stands at the basis of their thinking and their mode of existence. It is significant both for thought and for life.

I have briefly portrayed what might be considered as an alternative way of dealing with religious sentences of type (5)—sentences which I referred to as "pseudo-statements." To those who insist upon the verification of such sentences as a requirement for their meaningfulness, such sentences will remain pseudo-statements, and no more. But to those who adopt the approach which I have suggested, and which comes largely from some insights of Collingwood, with a few hints from Kierkegaard, these sentences might be considered to be absolute presuppositions. Those who find the latter approach attractive will, I think, see that the notion of absolute presuppositions has significant implications with respect to theological assertions. I cannot expand the point any further at this time. I have tried to indicate how the implications of the doctrine might be construed with respect to one absolute presupposition, namely, the divinity of Christ. A similar treatment might be given to other religious presuppositions.

I repeat: In describing the form in which such a view might be developed, I do not imply that I agree with the position. I merely suggest it as a possible alternative.

3

The Reality of God

Paul Tillich

[Excerpt from *Dynamics of Faith*]

The Meaning of Symbol

Man's ultimate concern must be expressed symbolically, because symbolic language alone is able to express the ultimate. This statement demands explanation in several respects. In spite of the manifold research about the meaning and function of symbols which is going on in contemporary philosophy, every writer who uses the term "symbol" must explain his understanding of it.

Symbols have one characteristic in common with signs; they point beyond themselves to something else. The red sign at the street corner points to the order to stop the movements of cars at certain intervals. A red light and the stopping of cars have essentially no relation to each other, but conventionally they are united as long as the convention lasts. The same is true of letters and numbers and partly even words. They point beyond themselves to sounds and meanings. They are given this special function by convention within a nation or by international conventions, as the mathematical signs. Sometimes such signs are called symbols; but this is unfortunate because it makes the distinction between signs and symbols more difficult. Decisive is the fact that signs do not participate in the reality of that to which they point, while symbols do. Therefore, signs can be replaced for reasons of expediency or convention, while symbols cannot.

This leads to the second characteristic of the symbol: It participates in that to which it points: the flag participates in the power and dignity of the nation for which it stands. Therefore, it cannot be replaced except after an historic catastrophe that changes the reality of the nation which it symbolizes. An attack on the flag is felt as an attack on the majesty of the group in which it is acknowledged. Such an attack is considered blasphemy.

The third characteristic of a symbol is that it opens up levels of reality which otherwise are closed for us. All arts create symbols for a level of reality which cannot be reached in any other way. A picture and a poem reveal elements of reality which cannot be approached scientifically. In the creative work of art we encounter reality in a dimension which is closed for us without such works. The symbol's fourth characteristic not only opens up dimensions and elements of reality which otherwise would remain unapproachable but also unlocks dimensions and elements of our soul which correspond to the dimensions and elements of reality. A great play gives us not only a new vision of the human scene, but it opens up hidden depths of our own being. Thus we are able to receive what the play reveals to us in reality. There are within us dimensions of which we cannot become aware except through symbols, as melodies and rhythms in music.

Symbols cannot be produced intentionally—this is the fifth characteristic. They grow out of the individual or collective unconscious and cannot function without being accepted by the unconscious dimension of our being. Symbols which have an especially social function, as political and religious symbols, are created or at least accepted by the collective unconscious of the group in which they appear.

The sixth and last characteristic of the symbol is a consequence of the fact that symbols cannot be invented. Like living beings, they grow and they die. They grow when the situation is ripe for them, and they die when the situation changes. The symbol of the "king" grew in a special period of history, and it died in most parts of the world in our period. Symbols do not grow because people are longing for them, and they do not die because of scientific or practical criticism. They die because they can no longer produce response in the group where they originally found expression.

These are the main characteristics of every symbol. Genuine symbols are created in several spheres of man's cultural creativity. We have mentioned already the political and the artistic realm. We could add history and, above all, religion, whose symbols will be our particular concern.

Religious Symbols

We have discussed the meaning of symbols generally because, as we said, man's ultimate concern must be expressed symbolically! One may ask: Why can it not be expressed directly and properly? If money, success or the nation is someone's ultimate concern, can this not be said in a direct way without symbolic language? Is it not only in those cases in which the content of the ultimate concern is called "God" that we are in the realm of symbols? The answer is that everything which is a matter of Unconditional concern is made into a god. If the nation is someone's ultimate concern, the name of the nation becomes a sacred name and the nation receives divine qualities which far surpass the reality of the being and functioning of the nation. The nation then stands for and symbolizes the true ultimate, but in an idolatrous way. Success as ultimate concern is not the natural desire of actualizing potentialities, but is readiness to sacrifice all other values of life for the sake of a position of power and social predominance. The anxiety about not being a success is an idolatrous form of the anxiety about divine condemnation. Success is grace; lack of success, ultimate judgment. In this way concepts designating ordinary realities become idolatrous symbols of ultimate concern.

The reason for this transformation of concepts into symbols is the character of ultimacy and the nature of faith. That which is the true ultimate transcends the realm of finite reality infinitely. Therefore, no finite reality can express it directly and properly. Religiously speaking, God transcends his own name. This is why the use of his name easily becomes an abuse or a blasphemy. Whatever we say about that which concerns us ultimately, whether or not we call it God, has a symbolic meaning. It points beyond itself while participating in that to which it points. In no other way can faith express itself adequately. The language of faith is the language of symbols. If faith were what we have shown that it is not, such an assertion could not be made. But faith, understood as the state of being ultimately concerned, has no language other than symbols. When saying this I always expect the question: Only a symbol? He who asks this question shows that he has not understood the difference between signs and symbols nor the power of symbolic language, which surpasses in quality and strength the power of any non-symbolic language. One should never say "only a symbol," but one should say "not less than a symbol." With this in mind we can now describe the different kinds of symbols of faith.

The fundamental symbol of our ultimate concern is God. It is always present in any act of faith, even if the act of faith includes the denial of God. Where there is ultimate concern, God can be denied only in the name of God. One God can deny the other one. Ultimate concern cannot deny its own character as ultimate. Therefore, it affirms what is meant by the word "God." Atheism, consequently, can only mean the attempt to remove any ultimate concern—to remain unconcerned about the meaning of one's existence. Indifference toward the ultimate question is the only imaginable form of atheism. Whether it is possible is a problem which must remain unsolved at this point. In any case, he who denies God as a matter of ultimate concern affirms God, because he affirms ultimacy in his concern. God is the fundamental symbol for what concerns us ultimately. Again it would be completely wrong to ask: So God is nothing but a symbol? Because the next question has to be: A symbol for what? And then the answer would be: For God! God is symbol for God. This means that in the notion of God we must distinguish two elements: the element of ultimacy, which is a matter of immediate experience and not symbolic in itself, and the element of concreteness, which is taken from our ordinary experience and symbolically applied to God. The man whose ultimate concern is a sacred tree has both the ultimacy of concern and the concreteness of the tree which symbolizes his relation to the ultimate. The man who adores Apollo is ultimately concerned, but not in an abstract way. His ultimate concern is symbolized in the divine figure of Apollo. The man who glorifies Jahweh, the God of the Old Testament, has both an ultimate concern and a concrete image of what concerns him ultimately. This is the meaning of the seemingly cryptic statement that God is the symbol of God. In this qualified sense God is the fundamental and universal content of faith.

It is obvious that such an understanding of the meaning of God makes the discussions about the existence or nonexistence of God meaningless. It is meaningless to question the ultimacy of an ultimate concern. This element in the idea of God is in itself certain. The symbolic expression of this element varies endlessly through the whole history of mankind. Here again it would be meaningless to ask whether one or another of the figures in which an ultimate concern is symbolized does "exist." If "existence" refers to something which can be found within the whole of reality, no divine being exists. The question is not this, but: which of the innumerable symbols of faith is most adequate to the meaning of faith? In other words, which symbol of ultimacy expresses the ultimate without idolatrous elements? This is the problem, and not the so-called "existence of God"—which is in itself an impossible combination of words. God as the ultimate in man's ultimate concern is more certain than any other certainty, even that of oneself. God as symbolized in a divine figure is a matter of daring faith, of courage and risk.

God is the basic symbol of faith, but not the only one. All the qualities we attribute to him, power, love, justice, are taken from finite experiences and applied symbolically to that which is beyond finitude and infinity. If faith calls God "almighty," it uses the human experience of power in order to symbolize the content of its infinite concern, but it does not describe a highest being who can do as he pleases. So it is with all the other qualities and with all the actions, past, present and future, which men attribute to God. They are symbols taken from our daily experience, and not information about what God did once upon a time or will do sometime in the future. Faith is not the belief in such stories, but it is the acceptance of symbols that express our ultimate concern in terms of divine actions.

Another group of symbols of faith are manifestations of the divine in things and events, in persons and communities, in words and documents. This whole realm of sacred objects is a treasure of symbols. Holy things are not holy in themselves, but they point beyond themselves to the source of all holiness, that which is of ultimate concern.

Symbols and Myths

The symbols of faith do not appear in isolation. They are united in "stories of the gods," which is the meaning of the Greek word "mythos"—myth. The gods are individualized figures, analogous to human personalities, sexually differentiated, descending from each other, related to each other in love and struggle, producing world and man, acting in time and space. They participate in human greatness and misery, in creative and destructive works. They give to man cultural and religious traditions, and defend those sacred rites. They help and threaten the human race, especially some families, tribes or nations. They appear in epiphanies and incarnations, establish sacred places, rites and persons, and thus create a cult. But they themselves are under the command and threat of a fate which is beyond everything that is. This is mythology as developed most impressively in ancient Greece. But many of these characteristics can be found in every mythology. Usually the mythological gods are not equals. There is a hierarchy, at the top of which is a ruling god, as in Greece; or a trinity of them, as in India; or a duality of them, as in Persia. There are savior-gods who mediate between the highest gods and man, sometimes sharing the suffering and death of man in spite of their essential immortality. This is the world of the myth, great and strange, always changing but fundamentally the same: man's ultimate concern symbolized in divine figures and actions. Myths are symbols of faith combined in stories about divine-human encounters.

Myths are always present in every act of faith, because the language of faith is the symbol. They are also attacked, criticized and transcended in each of the great religions of mankind. The reason for this criticism is the very nature of the myth. It uses material from our ordinary experience. It puts the stories of the gods into the framework of time and space although it belongs to the nature of the ultimate to be beyond time and space. Above all, it divides the divine into several figures, removing ultimacy from each of them without removing their claim to ultimacy. This inescapably leads to conflicts of ultimate claims, able to destroy life, society, and consciousness.

The criticism of the myth first rejects the division of the divine and goes beyond it to one God, although in different ways according to the different types of religion. Even one God is an object of mythological language, and if spoken about is drawn into the framework of time and space. Even he loses his ultimacy if made to be the content of concrete concern. Consequently, the criticism of the myth does not end with the rejection of the polytheistic mythology.

Monotheism also falls under the criticism of the myth. It needs, as one says today, "demythologization." This word has been used in connection with the elaboration of the mythical elements in stories and symbols of the Bible, both of the Old and the New Testaments—stories like those of the Paradise, of the fall of Adam, of the great Flood, of the Exodus from Egypt, of the virgin birth of the Messiah, of many of his miracles, of his resurrection and ascension, of his expected return as the judge of the universe. In short, all the stories in which divine-human interactions are told are considered as mythological in character, and objects of demythologization. What does this negative and artificial term mean? It must be accepted and supported if it points to the necessity of recognizing a symbol as a symbol and a myth as a myth. It must be attacked and rejected if it means the removal of symbols and myths altogether. Such an attempt is the third step in the criticism of the myth. It is an attempt which never can be successful, because symbol and myth are forms of the human consciousness which are always present. One can replace one myth by another, but one cannot remove the myth from man's spiritual life. For the myth is the combination of symbols of our ultimate concern.

A myth which is understood as a myth, but not removed or replaced, can be called a "broken myth." Christianity denies by its very nature any unbroken myth, because its presupposition is the first commandment: the affirmation of the ultimate as ultimate and the rejection of any kind of idolatry. All mythological elements in the Bible, and doctrine and liturgy should be recognized as mythological, but they should be maintained in their symbolic form and not be replaced by scientific substitutes. For there is no substitute for the use of symbols and myths: they are the language of faith.

The radical criticism of the myth is due to the fact that the primitive mythological consciousness resists the attempt to interpret the myth of myth. It is afraid of every act of demythologization. It believes that the broken myth is deprived of its truth and of its convincing power. Those who live in an unbroken mythological world feel safe and certain. They resist, often fanatically, any attempt to introduce an element of uncertainty by "breaking the myth," namely, by making conscious its symbolic character. Such resistance is supported by authoritarian systems, religious or political, in order to give security to the people under their control and unchallenged power to those who exercise the control. The resistance against demythologization expresses itself in "literalism." The symbols and myths are understood in their immediate meaning. The material, taken from nature and history, is used in its proper sense. The character of the symbol to point beyond itself to something else is disregarded. Creation is taken as a magic act which happened once upon a time. The fall of Adam is localized on a special geographical point and attributed to a human individual.

The virgin birth of the Messiah is understood in biological terms, resurrection and ascension as physical events, the second coming of the Christ as a telluric, or cosmic, catastrophe. The presupposition of such literalism is that God is a being, acting in time and space, dwelling in a special place, affecting the course of events and being affected by them like any other being in the universe. Literalism deprives God of his ultimacy and, religiously speaking, of his majesty. It draws him down to the level of that which is not ultimate, the finite and conditional. In the last analysis it is not rational criticism of the myth which is decisive but the inner religious criticism. Faith, if it takes its symbols literally, becomes idolatrous! It calls something ultimate which is less than ultimate. Faith, conscious of the symbolic character of its symbols, gives God the honor which is due him.

One should distinguish two stages of literalism, the natural and the reactive. The natural stage of literalism is that in which the mythical and the literal are indistinguishable. The primitive period of individuals and groups consists in the inability to separate the creations of symbolic imagination from the facts which can be verified through observation and experiment. This stage has a full right of its own and should not be disturbed, either in individuals or in groups, up to the moment when man's questioning mind breaks the natural acceptance of the mythological visions as literal. If, however, this moment has come, two ways are possible. The one is to replace the unbroken by the broken myth. It is the objectively demanded way, although it is impossible for many people who prefer the repression of their questions to the uncertainty which appears with the breaking of the myth. They are forced into the second stage of literalism, the conscious one, which is aware of the questions but represses them, half consciously, half unconsciously. The tool of repression is usually an acknowledged authority with sacred qualities like the Church or the Bible, to which one owes unconditional surrender. This stage is still justifiable, if the questioning power is very weak and can easily be answered. It is unjustifiable if a mature mind is broken in its personal center by political or psychological methods, split in his unity, and hurt in his integrity. The enemy of a critical theology is not natural literalism but conscious literalism with repression of and aggression toward autonomous thought.

Symbols of faith cannot be replaced by other symbols, such as artistic ones, and they cannot be removed by scientific criticism. They have a genuine standing in the human mind, just as science and art have. Their symbolic character is their truth and their power.

Nothing less than symbols and myths can express our ultimate concern.

One more question arises, namely, whether myths are able to express every kind of ultimate concern. For example, Christian theologians argue that the word "myth" should be reserved for natural myths in which repetitive natural processes, such as the seasons, are understood in their ultimate meaning. They believe that if the world is seen as a historical process with beginning, end and center, as in Christianity and Judaism, the term "myth" should not be used. This would radically reduce the realm in which the term would be applicable. Myth could not be understood as the language of our ultimate concern, but only as a discarded idiom of this language. Yet history proves that there are not only natural myths but also historical myths. If the earth is seen as the battleground of two divine powers, as in ancient Persia, this is an historical myth. If the God of creation selects and guides a nation through history toward an end which transcends all history, this is an historical myth. If the Christ—a transcendent, divine being—appears in the fullness of time, lives, dies and is resurrected, this is an historical myth. Christianity is superior to those religions which are bound to a natural myth. But Christianity speaks the mythological language like every other religion. It is a broken myth, but it is a myth; otherwise Christianity would not be an expression of ultimate concern.

[Excerpt from *Systematic Theology,* Volume I, Part I.]

Truth and Verification

Every cognitive act strives for truth. Since theology claims to be true, it must discuss the meaning of the term "truth," the nature of revealed truth, and its relation to other forms of truth. In the absence of such a discussion the theological claim can be dismissed by a simple semantic device, often used by naturalists and positivists. According to them, the use of the term "truth" is restricted to empirically verifiable statements. The predicate "true" should be reserved either for analytic sentences or for experimentally confirmed propositions. Such a terminological limitation of the terms "true" and "truth" is possible and is a matter of convention. But, whenever it is accepted, it means a break with the whole Western tradition and necessitates the creation of another term for what has been called *alethes* or *verum* in classical, ancient, medieval, and modern literature. Is such a break necessary? The answer ultimately depends not on reasons of expediency but on the nature of cognitive reason.

Modern philosophy usually speaks of true and false as qualities of judgments. Judgments can grasp or fail to grasp reality and can, accordingly, be true or false. But reality in itself is what it is, and it can neither be true nor false. This certainly is a possible line of arguing, but it is also possible to go beyond it. If the question is asked, "What makes a judgment true?" something must be said about reality itself. There must be an explanation of the fact that reality can give itself to the cognitive act in such a way that a false judgment can occur and in such a way that many processes of observation and thought are necessary in order to reach true judgments. The reason is that things hide their true being; it must be discovered under the surface of sense impressions, changing appearances, and unfounded opinions. This discovery is made through a process of preliminary affirmations, consequent negations, and final affirmations. It is made through "yes and no" or dialectically. The surface must be penetrated, the appearance undercut, the "depth" must be reached, namely, the *ousia*, the "essence" of things, that which gives them the power of being. This is their truth, the "really real" in difference from the seemingly real. It would not be called "true," however, if it were not true for someone, namely, for the mind which in the power of the rational word, the *logos*, grasps the level of reality in which the really real "dwells." This notion of truth is not bound to its Socratic-Platonic birthplace. In whatever way the terminology may be changed, in whatever way the relation between true and seeming reality may be described, in whatever way the relation of mind and reality may be understood, the problem of the "truly real" cannot be avoided. The seemingly real is not unreal, but it is deceptive if it is taken to be really real.

One could say that the concept of true being is the result of disappointed expectations in our encounter with reality. For instance, we meet a person, and the impressions we receive of him produce expectations in us about his future behavior. Some of these expectations will be deceptive and will provoke the desire for a "deeper" understanding of his personality, in comparison with which the first understanding was "superficial." New expectations arise and prove again to be partially deceptive, driving us to the question of a still deeper level of his personality. Finally we may succeed in discovering his real, true personality structure, the essence and power of his being, and we will not be deceived any longer. We may still be surprised; but such surprises are to be expected if a personality is the object of knowledge. The truth of something is that level of its being the knowledge of which prevents wrong expectations and consequent disappointments. Truth, therefore, is the essence of things as well as the cognitive act in which their essence is grasped. The term "truth" is, like the term "reason," subjective-objective. A judgment is true because it grasps and expresses true being; and the really real becomes truth if it is grasped and expressed in a true judgment.

The resistance of recent philosophy against the ontological use of the term has been aroused by the assumption that truth can be verified only within the realm of empirical science. Statements which cannot be verified by experiment are considered tautologies, emotional self-expressions, or meaningless propositions. There is an important truth in this attitude. Statements which have neither intrinsic evidence nor a way of being verified have no cognitive value. "Verification" means a method of deciding the truth or falsehood of a judgment. Without such a method, judgments are expressions of the subjective state of a person but not acts of cognitive reason. The verifying test belongs to the nature of truth; in this positivism is right. Every cognitive assumption (hypothesis) must be tested. The safest test is the repeatable experiment. A cognitive realm in which it can be used has the advantage of methodological strictness and the possibility of testing an assertion in every moment. But it is not permissible to make the experimental method of verification the exclusive pattern of all verification. Verification can occur within the life process itself. Verification of this type (experiential in contradistinction to experimental) has the advantage that it need not halt and disrupt the totality of a life-process in order to distil calculable elements out of it (which experimental verification must do). The verifying experiences of a non-experimental character are truer to life, though less exact and definite. By far the largest part of all cognitive verification is experiential. In some cases experimental and experiential verification work together. In other cases the experimental element is completely absent.

It is obvious that these two methods of verification correspond to the two cognitive attitudes, the controlling and the receiving.

Controlling knowledge is verified by the success of controlling actions. The technical use of scientific knowledge is its greatest and most impressive verification. Every working machine is a continuously repeated test of the truth of the scientific assumptions on the basis of which it has been constructed.

Receiving knowledge is verified by the creative union of two natures, that of knowing and that of the known. This test, of course, is neither repeatable, precise, nor final at any particular moment. The life-process itself makes the test. Therefore, the test is indefinite and preliminary; there is an element of risk connected with it. Future stages of the same life-process may prove that what seemed to be a bad risk was a good one and vice versa. Nevertheless, the risk must be taken, receiving knowledge must be applied, experiential verification must go on continually, whether it is supported by experimental tests or not.

Life-processes are the object of biological, psychological, and sociological research. A large amount of controlling knowledge and experimental verification is possible and actual in these disciplines; and, in dealing with life-processes, scientists are justified in striving to extend the experimental method as far as possible. But there are limits to those attempts which are imposed not by impotence but by definition. Life processes have the character of totality, spontaneity, and individuality. Experiments presuppose isolation, regularity, generality. Therefore, only separable elements of life-processes are open to experimental verification, while the processes themselves must be received in a creative union in order to be known. Physicians, psychotherapists, educators, social reformers, and political leaders deal with that side of a life-process which is individual, spontaneous, and total. They can work only on the basis of a knowledge which unites controlling and receiving elements. The truth of their knowledge is verified partly by experimental test, partly by a participation in the individual life with which they deal. If this "knowledge by participation" is called "intuition," the cognitive approach to every individual life-process is intuitive. Intuition in this sense is not irrational, and neither does it by-pass a full consciousness of experimentally verified knowledge.

[Excerpt from *Systematic Theology,* Volume I, Part II.]

God as Being

a) God as being and finite being.—The being of God is being-itself. The being of God cannot be understood as the existence of a being alongside others or above others. If God is *a* being, he is subject to the categories of finitude, especially to space and substance. Even if he is called the "highest being" in the sense of the "most perfect" and the "most powerful" being, this situation is not changed. When applied to God, superlatives become diminutives. They place him on the level of other beings while elevating him above all of them. Many theologians who have used the term "highest being" have known better. Actually they have described the highest as the absolute, as that which is on a level qualitatively different from the level of any being—even the highest being. Whenever infinite or unconditional power and meaning are attributed to the highest being, it has ceased to be a being and has become being-itself. Many confusions in the doctrine of God and many apologetic weaknesses could be avoided if God were understood first of all as being-itself or as the ground of being. The power of being is another way of expressing the same thing in a circumscribing phrase. Ever since the time of Plato it has been known—although it often has been disregarded, especially by the nominalists and their modern followers—that the concept of being as being, or being-itself, points to the power inherent in everything, the power of resisting non-being. Therefore, instead of saying that God is first of all being-itself, it is possible to say that he is the power of being in everything and above everything, the infinite power of being. A theology which does not dare to identify God and the power of being as the first step toward a doctrine of God relapses into monarchic monotheism, for if God is not being-itself, he is subordinate to it, just as Zeus is subordinate to fate in Greek religion. The structure of being-itself is his fate, as it is the fate of all other beings. But God is his own fate; he is "by himself"; he possesses "aseity." This can be said of him only if he is the power of being, if he is being-itself.

As being-itself God is beyond the contrast of essential and existential being. We have spoken of the transition of being into existence, which involves the possibility that being will contradict and lose itself. This transition is excluded from being-itself (except in terms of the christological paradox), for being-itself does not participate in non-being. In this it stands in contrast to every being. As classical theology has emphasized, God is beyond essence and existence. Logically, being-itself is "before," "prior to," the split which characterizes finite being.

For this reason it is as wrong to speak of God as the universal essence as it is to speak of him as existing. If God is understood as universal essence, as the form of all forms, he is identified with the unity and totality of finite potentialities; but he has ceased to be the power of the ground in all of them, and therefore he has ceased to transcend them. He has poured all his creative power into a system of forms, and he is bound to these forms. This is what pantheism means.

On the other hand, grave difficulties attend the attempt to speak of God as existing. In order to maintain the truth that God is beyond essence and existence while simultaneously arguing for the existence of God, Thomas Aquinas is forced to distinguish between two kinds of divine existence: that which is identical with essence and that which is not. But an existence of God which is not united with its essence is a contradiction in terms. It makes God a being whose existence does not fulfil his essential potentialities; being and not-yet-being are "mixed" in him, as they are in everything finite. God ceases to be God, the ground of being and meaning. What really has happened is that Thomas has had to unite two different traditions: the Augustinian, in which the divine existence is included in his essence, and the Aristotelian, which derives the existence of God from the existence of the world and which then asserts, in a second step, that his existence is identical with his essence. Thus the question of the existence of God can be neither asked nor answered. If asked, it is a question about that which by its very nature is above existence, and therefore the answer—whether negative or affirmative—implicitly denies the nature of God. It is as atheistic to affirm the existence of God as it is to deny it. God is being-itself, not a being. On this basis a first step can be taken toward the solution of the problem which usually is discussed as the immanence and the transcendence of God. As the power of being, God transcends every being and also the totality of beings—the world. Being-itself is beyond finitude and infinity; otherwise it would be conditioned by something other than itself, and the real power of being would lie beyond both it and that which conditioned it. Being-itself infinitely transcends every finite being. There is no proportion or gradation between the finite and the infinite. There is an absolute break, an infinite "jump." On the other hand, everything finite participates in being-itself and in its infinity. Otherwise it would not have the power of being. It would be swallowed by non-being, or it never would have emerged out of non-being. This double relation of all beings to being-itself gives being-itself a double characteristic. In calling it creative, we point to the fact that everything participates in the infinite power of being. In calling it abysmal, we point to the fact that everything participates in the power of being in a finite way, that all beings are infinitely transcended by their creative ground.

Man is bound to the categories of finitude. He uses the two categories of relation—causality and substance—to express the relation of being itself to finite beings. The "ground" can be interpreted in both ways, as the cause of finite beings and as their substance. The former has been elaborated by Leibniz in the line of the Thomistic tradition, and the latter has been elaborated by Spinoza in the line of the mystical tradition. Both ways are impossible. Spinoza establishes a naturalistic pantheism, in contrast to the idealistic type which identifies God with the universal essence of being, which denies finite freedom and in so doing denies the freedom of God. By necessity God is merged into the finite beings, and their being is his being. Here again it must be emphasized that pantheism does not say that God is everything. It says that God is the substance of everything and that there is no substantial independence and freedom in anything finite.

Therefore, Christianity, which asserts finite freedom in man and spontaneity in the non-human realm, has rejected the category of substance in favor of the category of causality in attempting to express the relation of the power of being to the beings who participate in it. Causality seems to make the world dependent on God, and, at the same time, to separate God from the world in the way a cause is separated from its effect. But the category of causality cannot "fill the bill," for cause and effect are not separate; they include each other and form a series which is endless in both directions. What is cause at one point in this series is effect at another point and conversely. God as cause is drawn into this series, which drives even him beyond himself. In order to disengage the divine cause from the series of causes and effects, it is called the first cause, the absolute beginning. What this means is that the category of causality is being denied while it is being used. In other words, causality is being used not as a category but as a symbol. And if this is done and is understood, the difference between substance and causality disappears, for if God is the cause of the entire series of causes and effects, he is the substance underlying the whole process of becoming. But this "underlying" does not have the character of a substance which underlies its accidents and which is completely expressed by them. It is an underlying in which substance and accidents preserve their freedom. In other words, it is substance not as a category but as a symbol. And, if taken symbolically, there is no difference between *prima causa* and *ultima substantia*. Both mean, what can be called in a more directly symbolic term, "the creative and abysmal ground of being." In this term both naturalistic pantheism, based on the category of substance, and rationalistic theism, based on the category of causality, are overcome.

Since God is the ground of being, he is the ground of the structure of being. He is not subject to this structure; the structure is grounded in him. He *is* this structure, and it is impossible to speak about him except in terms of this structure. God must be approached cognitively through the structural elements of being-itself. Those elements make him a living God, a God who can be man's concrete concern. They enable us to use symbols which we are certain point to the ground of reality.

b) God as being and the knowledge of God.—The statement that God is being-itself is a non-symbolic statement. It does not point beyond itself. It means what it says directly and properly; if we speak of the actuality of God, we first assert that he is not God if he is not being itself. Other assertions about God can be made theologically only on this basis. Of course, religious assertions do not require such a foundation for what they say about God; the foundation is implicit in every religious thought concerning God. Theologians must make explicit what is implicit in religious thought and expression; and, in order to do this, they must begin with the most abstract and completely unsymbolic statement which is possible, namely, that God is being-itself or the absolute.

However, after this has been said, nothing else can be said about God as God which is not symbolic. As we already have seen, God as being itself is the ground of the ontological structure of being without being subject to this structure himself. He *is* the structure; that is, he has the power of determining the structure of everything that has being. Therefore, if anything beyond this bare assertion is said about God, it no longer is a direct and proper statement, no longer a concept. It is indirect, and it points to something beyond itself. In a word, it is symbolic.

The general character of the symbol has been described. Special emphasis must be laid on the insight that symbol and sign are different; that, while the sign bears no necessary relation to that to which it points, the symbol participates in the reality of that for which it stands. The sign can be changed arbitrarily according to the demands of expediency, but the symbol grows and dies according to the correlation between that which is symbolized and the persons who receive it as a symbol. Therefore, the religious symbol, the symbol which points to the divine, can be a true symbol only if it participates in the power of the divine to which it points.

There can be no doubt that any concrete assertion about God must be symbolic, for a concrete assertion is one which uses a segment of finite experience in order to say something about him. It transcends the content of this segment, although it also includes it. The segment of finite reality which becomes the vehicle of a concrete assertion about God is affirmed and negated at the same time. It becomes a symbol, for a symbolic expression is one whose proper meaning is negated by that to which it points. And yet it also is affirmed by it, and this affirmation gives the symbolic expression an adequate basis for pointing beyond itself.

The crucial question must now be faced. Can a segment of finite reality become the basis for an assertion about that which is infinite? The answer is that it can, because that which is infinite is being-itself and because everything participates in being-itself. The *analogia entis* is not the property of a questionable natural theology which attempts to gain knowledge of God by drawing conclusions about the infinite from the finite. The *analogia entis* gives us our only justification of speaking at all about God. It is based on the fact that God must be understood as being-itself.

The truth of a religious symbol has nothing to do with the truth of the empirical assertions involved in it, be they physical, psychological, or historical. A religious symbol possesses some truth if it adequately expresses the correlation of revelation in which some person stands. A religious symbol *is* true if it adequately expresses the correlation of some person with final revelation. A religious symbol can die only if the correlation of which it is an adequate expression dies. This occurs whenever the revelatory situation changes and former symbols become obsolete. The history of religion, right up to our own time, is full of dead symbols which have been killed not by a scientific criticism of assumed superstitions but by a religious criticism of religion. The judgment that a religious symbol *is* true is identical with the judgment that the revelation of which it is the adequate expression is true. This double meaning of the truth of a symbol must be kept in mind. A symbol *has* truth: it is adequate to the revelation it expresses. A symbol *is* true: it is the expression of a true revelation.

Theology as such has neither the duty nor the power to confirm or to negate religious symbols. Its task is to interpret them according to theological principles and methods. In the process of interpretation, however, two things may happen: theology may discover contradictions between symbols within the theological circle and theology may speak not only as theology but also as religion. In the first ease, theology can point out the religious dangers and the theological errors which follow from the use of certain symbols; in the second case, theology can become prophecy, and in this role it may contribute to a change in the revelatory situation.

Religious symbols are double-edged. They are directed toward the infinite which they symbolize *and* toward the finite through which they symbolize it. They force the infinite down to finitude and the finite up to infinity. They open the divine for the human and the human for the divine. For instance, if God is symbolized as "Father," he is brought down to the human relationship of father and child. But at the same time this human relationship is consecrated into a pattern of the divine human relationship. If "Father" is employed as a symbol for God, fatherhood is seen in its theonomous, sacramental depth. One cannot arbitrarily "make" a religious symbol out of a segment of secular reality. Not even the collective unconscious, the great symbol-creating source, can do this. If a segment of reality is used as a symbol for God, the realm of reality from which it is taken is, so to speak, elevated into the realm of the holy. It no longer is secular. It is theonomous. If God is called the "king," something is said not only about God but also about the holy character of kinghood. If God's work is called "making whole" or "healing," this not only says something about God but also emphasizes the theonomous character of all healing. If God's self-manifestation is called "the word," this not only symbolizes God's relation to man but also emphasizes the holiness of all words as an expression of the spirit.

The list could be continued. Therefore, it is not surprising that in a secular culture both the symbols for God and the theonomous character of the material from which the symbols are taken disappear.

A final word of warning must be added in view of the fact that for many people the very term "symbolic" carries the connotation of non-real. This is partially the result of confusion between sign and symbol and partially due to the identification of reality with empirical reality, with the entire realm of objective things and events. Both reasons have been undercut explicitly and implicitly in the foregoing chapters. But one reason remains, namely, the fact that some theological movements, such as Protestant Hegelianism and Catholic modernism, have interpreted religious language symbolically in order to dissolve its realistic meaning and to weaken its seriousness, its power, and its spiritual impact. This was not the purpose of the classical essays on the "divine names," in which the symbolic character of all affirmations about God was strongly emphasized and explained in religious terms, nor was it a consequence of those essays. Their intention and their result was to give to God and to all his relations to man more reality and power than a non-symbolic and therefore easily superstitious interpretation could give them. In this sense symbolic interpretation is proper and necessary; it enhances rather than diminishes the reality and power of religious language, and in so doing it performs an important function.

God as Living

a) God as being and God as living.—Life is the process in which potential being becomes actual being. It is the actualization of the structural elements of being in their unity and in their tension. These elements move divergently and convergently in every life-process; they separate and reunite simultaneously. Life ceases in the moment of separation without union or of union without separation. Both complete identity and complete separation negate life. If we call God the "living God," we deny that he is a pure identity of being as being; and we also deny that there is a definite separation of being from being in him. We assert that he is the eternal process in which separation is posited and is overcome by reunion. In this sense, God lives. Few things about God are more emphasized in the Bible, especially in the Old Testament, than the truth that God is a living

God. Most of the so-called anthropomorphisms of the biblical picture of God are expressions of his character as living. His actions, his passions, his remembrances and anticipations, his suffering and joy, his personal relations and his plans—all these make him a living God and distinguish him from the pure absolute, from being-itself.

Life is the actuality of being, or, more exactly, it is the process in which potential being becomes actual being. But in God as God there is no distinction between potentiality and actuality. Therefore, we cannot speak of God as living in the proper or non-symbolic sense of the word "life." We must speak of God as living in symbolic terms. Yet every true symbol participates in the reality which it symbolizes. God lives in so far as he is the ground of life.[1] Anthropomorphic symbols are adequate for speaking of God religiously. Only in this way can he be the living God for man. But even in the most primitive intuition of the divine a feeling should be, and usually is, present that there is a mystery about divine names which makes them improper, self-transcending, symbolic. Religious instruction should deepen this feeling without depriving the divine names of their reality and power. One of the most surprising qualities of the prophetic utterances in the Old Testament is that, on the one hand, they always appear concrete and anthropomorphic and that, on the other hand, they preserve the mystery of the divine ground. They never deal with being as being or with the absolute as the absolute; nevertheless, they never make God a being alongside others, into something conditioned by something else which also is conditioned. Nothing is more inadequate and disgusting than the attempt to translate the concrete symbols of the Bible into less concrete and less powerful symbols. Theology should not weaken the concrete symbols, but it must analyze them and interpret them in abstract ontological terms. Nothing is more inadequate and confusing than the attempt to restrict theological work to half-abstract, half-concrete terms which do justice neither to existential intuition nor to cognitive analysis.

The ontological structure of being supplies the material for the symbols which point to the divine life. However, this does not mean that a doctrine of God can be derived from an ontological system. The character of the divine life is made manifest in revelation. Theology can only explain and systematize the existential knowledge

---

[1] "He that formed the eye, shall he not see?" (Ps. 94:9).

of revelation in theoretical terms, interpreting the symbolic significance of the ontological elements and categories.

While the symbolic power of the categories appears in the relation of God to the creature, the elements give symbolic expression to the nature of the divine life itself. The polar character of the ontological elements is rooted in the divine life, but the divine life is not subject to this polarity. Within the divine life, every ontological element includes its polar element completely, without tension and without the threat of dissolution, for God is being-itself. However, there is a difference between the first and the second elements in each polarity with regard to their power of symbolizing the divine life. The elements of individualization, dynamics, and freedom represent the self or subject side of the basic ontological structure within the polarity to which they belong. The elements of participation, form, and destiny represent the world or object side of the basic ontological structure within the polarity to which they belong. Both sides are rooted in the divine life. But the first side determines the existential relationship between God and man, which is the source of all symbolization. Man is a self who has a world. As a self he is an individual person who participates universally, he is a dynamic self-transcending agent within a special and a general form, and he is freedom which has a special destiny and which participates in a general destiny. Therefore, man symbolizes that which is his ultimate concern in terms taken from his own being. From the subjective side of the polarities he takes—or more exactly, receives—the material with which he symbolizes the divine life. He sees the divine life as personal, dynamic, and free. He cannot see it in any other way, for God is man's ultimate concern, and therefore he stands in analogy to that which man himself is. But the religious mind—theologically speaking, man in the correlation of revelation—always realizes implicitly, if not explicitly, that the other side of the polarities also is completely present in the side he uses as symbolic material. God is called a person, but he is a person not in finite separation but in an absolute and unconditional participation in everything. God is called dynamic, but he is dynamic not in tension with form but in an absolute and unconditional unity with form, so that his self-transcendence never is in tension with his self-preservation, so that he always remains God. God is called "free," but he is free not in arbitrariness but in an absolute and unconditional identity with his destiny, so that he himself is his destiny, so that the essential structures of being are not strange to his freedom but are the actuality of his freedom. In this way, although the symbols used for the divine life are taken from the concrete situation of man's relationship to God, they imply God's ultimacy, the ultimacy in which the polarities of being disappear in the ground of being, in being-itself.

The basic ontological structure of self and world is transcended in the divine life without providing symbolic material. God cannot be called a self, because the concept "self" implies separation from and contrast to everything which is not self. God cannot be called the world even by implication. Both self and world are rooted in the divine life, but they cannot become symbols for it. But the elements which constitute the basic ontological structure can become symbols because they do not speak of kinds of being (self and world) but of qualities of being which are valid in their proper sense when applied to all beings and which are valid in their symbolic sense when applied to being-itself.

b) The divine life and the ontological elements.—The symbols provided by the ontological elements present a great number of problems for the doctrine of God. In every special case it is necessary to distinguish between the proper sense of the concepts and their symbolic sense. And it is equally necessary to balance one side of the ontological polarity against the other without reducing the symbolic power of either of them. The history of theological thought is a continuous proof of the difficulty, the creativeness, and the danger of this situation. This is obvious if we consider the symbolic power of the polarity of individualization and participation. The symbol "personal God" is absolutely fundamental because an existential relation is a person-to-person relation. Man cannot be ultimately concerned about anything that is less than personal, but since personality (*persona, prosopon*) includes individuality, the question arises in what sense God can be called an individual. Is it meaningful to call him the "absolute individual"? The answer must be that it is meaningful only in the sense that he can be called the "absolute participant." The one term cannot be applied without the other. This can only mean that both individualization and participation are rooted in the ground of the divine life and that God is equally "near" to each of them while transcending them both.

The solution of the difficulties in the phrase "personal God" follows from this. "Personal God" does not mean that God is *a* person. It means that God is the ground of everything personal and that he carries within himself the ontological power of personality. He is not a person, but he is not less than personal. It should not be forgotten that classical theology employed the term *persona* for the trinitarian hypostases but not for God himself. God became "a person" only in the nineteenth century, in connection with the Kantian separation of nature ruled by physical law from personality ruled by moral law. Ordinary theism has made God a heavenly, completely perfect person who resides above the world and mankind. The protest of atheism against such a highest person is correct. There is no evidence for his existence, nor is he a matter of ultimate concern. God is not God without universal participation. "Personal God" is a confusing symbol.

God is the principle of participation as well as the principle of individualization. The divine life participates in every life as its ground and aim. God participates in everything that is; he has community with it; he shares in its destiny. Certainly such statements are highly symbolic. They can have the unfortunate logical implication that there is something alongside God in which he participates from the outside. But the divine participation creates that in which it participates. Plato uses the word *parousia* for the presence of the essences in temporal existence. This word later becomes the name for the preliminary and final presence of the transcendent Christ in the church and in the world. *Parousia* means "being by," "being with"—but on the basis of being absent, of being separated. In the same way God's participation is not a spatial or temporal presence. It is meant not categorically but symbolically. It is the parousia, the "being with" of that which is neither here nor there. If applied to God, participation and community are not less symbolic than individualization and personality. While active religious communication between God and man depends on the symbol of the personal God, the symbol of universal participation expresses the passive experience of the divine parousia in terms of the divine omnipresence.

The polarity of dynamics and form supplies the material basis for a group of symbols which are central for any present-day doctrine of God. Potentiality, vitality, and self-transcendence are indicated in the term "dynamics," while the term "form" embraces actuality, intentionality, and self-preservation.

Potentiality and actuality appear in classical theology in the famous formula that God is *actus purus*, the pure form in which everything potential is actual, and which is the eternal self-intuition of the divine fulness (*pleroma*). In this formula the dynamic side in the dynamics-form polarity is swallowed by the form side. Pure actuality, that is, actuality free from any element of potentiality, is a fixed result; it is not alive. Life includes the separation of potentiality and actuality. The nature of life is actualization, not actuality. The God who is *actus purus* is not the living God. It is interesting that even those theologians who have used the concept of *actus purus* normally speak of God in the dynamic symbols of the Old Testament and of Christian experience. This situation has induced some thinkers—partly under the influence of Luther's dynamic conception of God and partly under the impact of the problem of evil—to emphasize the dynamics in God and to depreciate the stabilization of dynamics in pure actuality. They try to distinguish between two elements in God, and they assert that, in so far as God is a living God, these two elements must remain in tension. Whether the first element is called the *Ungrund* or the "nature in God" (Böhme), or the first potency (Schelling), or the will (Schopenhauer), or the "given" in God (Brightman), or *me-onic* freedom (Berdyaev), or the contingent (Hartshorne)—in all these cases it is an expression of what we have called "dynamics," and it is an attempt to prevent the dynamics in God from being transformed into pure actuality.

Theological criticism of these attempts is easy if the concepts are taken in their proper sense, for then they make God finite, dependent on a fate or an accident which is not himself. The finite God, if taken literally, is a finite god, a polytheistic god. But this is not the way in which these concepts should be interpreted. They point symbolically to a quality of the divine life which is analogous to what appears as dynamic in the ontological structure. The divine creativity, God's participation in history, his outgoing character, are based on this dynamic element. It includes a "not yet" which is, however, always balanced by an "already" within the divine life. It is not an absolute "not yet," which would make it a divine-demonic power, nor is the "already" an absolute already. It also can be expressed as the negative element in the ground of being which is overcome as negative in the process of being itself. As such it is the basis of the negative element in the creature, in which it is not overcome but is effective as a threat and a potential disruption.

These assertions include a rejection of a non-symbolic, ontological doctrine of God as becoming. If we say that being is actual as life, the element of self-transcendence is obviously and emphatically included. But it is included as a symbolic element in balance with form. Being is not in balance with becoming. Being comprises becoming and rest, becoming as an implication of dynamics and rest as an implication of form. If we say that God is being-itself, this includes both rest and becoming, both the static and the dynamic elements. However, to speak of a "becoming" God disrupts the balance between dynamics and form and subjects God to a process which has the character of a fate or which is completely open to the future and has the character of an absolute accident. In both cases the divinity of God is undercut. The basic error of these doctrines is their metaphysical-constructive character. They apply the ontological elements to God in a non-symbolic manner and are driven to religiously offensive and theologically untenable consequences.

If the element of form in the dynamics-form polarity is applied symbolically to the divine life, it expresses the actualization of its potentialities. The divine life inescapably unites possibility with fulfilment. Neither side threatens the other, nor is there a threat of disruption. In terms of self-preservation one could say that God cannot cease to be God. His going-out from himself does not diminish or destroy his divinity. It is united with the eternal "resting in himself."

The divine form must be conceived in analogy with what we have called "intentionality" on the human level. It is balanced with vitality, the dynamic side on the human level. The polarity in this formulation appears in classical theology as the polarity of will and intellect in God. It is consistent that Thomas Aquinas had to subordinate the will in God to the intellect when he accepted the Aristotelian *actus purus* as the basic character of God. And it must be remembered that the line of theological thought which tries to preserve the element of dynamics in God actually begins with Duns Scotus, who elevated the will in God over the intellect. Of course, both will and intellect in their application to God express infinitely more than the mental acts of willing and understanding as these appear in human experience. They are symbols for dynamics in all its ramifications and for form as the meaningful structure of being-itself. Therefore, it is not a question of metaphysical psychology, whether Aquinas or Duns Scotus is right. It is a question of the way in which psychological concepts should be employed as symbols for the divine life. And with respect to this question it is obvious that for more than a century a decision has been made in favor of the dynamic element. The philosophy of life, existential philosophy, and process philosophy agree. Protestantism has contributed strong motives for this decision, but theology must balance the new with the old (predominantly Catholic) emphasis on the form character of the divine life.

If we consider the polarity of freedom and destiny in its symbolic value, we find that there hardly is a word said about God in the Bible which does not point directly or indirectly to his freedom. In freedom he creates, in freedom he deals with the world and man, in freedom he saves and fulfils. His freedom is freedom from anything prior to him or alongside him. Chaos cannot prevent him from speaking the word which makes light out of darkness; the evil deeds of men cannot prevent him from carrying through his plans; the good deeds of men cannot force him to reward them; the structure of being cannot prevent him from revealing himself; etc. Classical theology has spoken in more abstract terms of the aseity of God, of his being *a se*, self-derived. There is no ground prior to him which could condition his freedom; neither chaos nor non-being has power to limit or resist him. But aseity also means that there is nothing given in God which is not at the same time affirmed by his freedom. If taken non-symbolically, this naturally leads to an unanswerable question, whether the structure of freedom, because it constitutes his freedom, is not itself something given in relation to which God has no freedom. The answer can only be that freedom, like the other ontological concepts, must be understood symbolically and in terms of the existential correlation of man and God. If taken in this way, freedom means that that which is man's ultimate concern is in no way dependent on man or on any finite being or on any finite concern. Only that which is unconditional can be the expression of unconditional concern. A conditioned God is no God.

Can the term "destiny" be applied symbolically to the divine life? The gods of polytheism have a destiny—or, more correctly, a fate—because they are not ultimate. But can one say that he who is unconditional and absolute has a destiny in the same manner in which he has freedom? Is it possible to attribute destiny to being-itself? It is possible, provided the connotation of a destiny-determining power above God is avoided and provided one adds that God is his own destiny and that in God freedom and destiny are one. It may be argued that this truth is more adequately expressed if destiny is replaced by necessity, not mechanical necessity, but structural necessity, of course, or if God is spoken of as being his own law. Such phrases are important as interpretations, but they lack two elements of meaning which are present in the word "destiny." They lack the mystery of that which precedes any structure and law, being-itself; and they lack the relation to history which is included in the term "destiny." If we say that God is his own destiny, we point both to the infinite mystery of being and to the participation of God in becoming and in history.

c) God as spirit and the trinitarian principles.—Spirit is the unity of the ontological elements and the *telos* of life. Actualized as life, being itself is fulfilled as spirit. The word *telos* expresses the relation of life and spirit more precisely than the words "aim" or "goal." It expresses the inner directedness of life toward spirit, the urge of life to become spirit, to fulfil itself as spirit. *Telos* stands for an inner, essential, necessary aim, for that in which a being fulfils its own nature. God as living is God fulfilled in himself and therefore spirit. God is spirit. This is the most embracing, direct, and unrestricted symbol for the divine life. It does not need to be balanced with another symbol, because it includes all the ontological elements.

Some anticipatory remarks about spirit must be made at this point, although the doctrine of the spirit is the subject of a separate part of systematic theology. The word "spirit" (with a lower-case *s*) has almost disappeared from the English language as a significant philosophical term, in contrast to German, French, and Italian, in which the words *Geist, esprit,* and *spirito* have preserved their philosophical standing. Probably this is a result of the radical separation of the cognitive function of the mind from emotion and will, as typified in English empiricism. In any case, the word "spirit" appears predominantly in a religious context, and here it is spelled with a capital *S*. But it is impossible to understand the meaning of Spirit unless the meaning of spirit is understood, for Spirit is the symbolic application of spirit to the divine life.

The meaning of spirit is built up through the meaning of the ontological elements and their union. In terms of both sides of the three polarities one can say that spirit is the unity of power and meaning. On the side of power it includes centered personality, self-transcending vitality, and freedom of self-determination. On the side of meaning it includes universal participation, forms and structures of reality, and limiting and directing destiny. Life fulfilled as spirit embraces passion as much as truth, libido as much as surrender, will to power as much as justice. If one of these sides is absorbed by its correlate, either abstract law or chaotic movement remains. Spirit does not stand in contrast to body. Life as spirit transcends the duality of body and mind. It also transcends the triplicity of body, soul, and mind, in which soul is actual life-power and mind and body are its functions. Life as spirit is the life of the soul, which includes mind and body, but not as realities alongside the soul. Spirit is not a "part," nor is it a special function. It is the all embracing function in which all elements of the structure of being participate. Life as spirit can be found by man only in man, for only in him is the structure of being completely realized.

The statement that God is Spirit means that life as spirit is the inclusive symbol for the divine life. It contains all the ontological elements. God is not nearer to one "part" of being or to a special function of being than he is to another. As Spirit he is as near to the creative darkness of the unconscious as he is to the critical light of cognitive reason. Spirit is the power through which meaning lives, and it is the meaning which gives direction to power. God as Spirit is the ultimate unity of both power and meaning. In contrast to Nietzsche, who identified the two assertions that God is Spirit and that God is dead, we must say that God is the living God because he is Spirit.

Any discussion of the *Christian* doctrine of the Trinity must begin with the christological assertion that Jesus is the Christ. The Christian doctrine of the Trinity is a corroboration of the christological dogma. The situation is different if we do not ask the question of the Christian doctrines but rather the question of the *presuppositions* of these doctrines in an idea of God. Then we must speak about the trinitarian principles, and we must begin with the Spirit rather than with the Logos. God is Spirit, and any trinitarian statement must be derived from this basic assertion.

God's life is life as spirit, and the trinitarian principles are moments within the process of the divine life. Human intuition of the divine always has distinguished between the abyss of the divine (the element of power) and the fulness of its content (the element of meaning), between the divine depth and the divine *logos*. The first principle is the basis of Godhead, that which makes God God. It is the root of his majesty, the unapproachable intensity of his being, the inexhaustible ground of being in which everything has its origin. It is the power of being infinitely resisting non-being, giving the power of being to everything that is. During the past centuries theological and philosophical rationalism have deprived the idea of God of this first principle, and by doing so they have robbed God of his divinity. He has become a hypostasized moral ideal or another name for the structural unity of reality. The power of the Godhead has disappeared.

The classical term *logos* is most adequate for the second principle, that of meaning and structure. It unites meaningful structure with creativity. Long before the Christian Era—in a way already in Heraclitus—*logos* received connotations of ultimacy as well as the meaning of being as being. According to Parmenides, being and the logos of being cannot be separated. The *logos* opens the divine ground, its infinity and its darkness, and it makes its fulness distinguishable, definite, finite. The *logos* has been called the mirror of the divine depth, the principle of God's self-objectification. In the *logos* God speaks his "word," both in himself and beyond himself. Without the second principle the first principle would be chaos, burning fire, but it would not be the creative ground. Without the second principle God is demonic, is characterized by absolute seclusion, is the "naked absolute" (Luther).

As the actualization of the other two principles, the Spirit is the third principle. Both power and meaning are contained in it and united in it. It makes them creative. The third principle is in a way the whole (God *is* Spirit), and in a way it is a special principle (God *has* the Spirit as he has the *logos*). It is the Spirit in whom God "goes out from" himself, the Spirit proceeds from the divine ground. He gives actuality to that which is potential in the divine ground and "outspoken" in the divine *logos*. Through the Spirit the divine fulness is posited in the divine life as something definite, and at the same time it is reunited in the divine ground. The finite is posited as finite within the process of the divine life, but it is reunited with the infinite within the same process. It is distinguished from the infinite, but it is not separated from it. The divine life is infinite mystery, but it is not infinite emptiness. It is the ground of all abundance, and it is abundant itself.

The consideration of the trinitarian principles is not the Christian doctrine of the Trinity. It is a preparation for it, nothing more. The dogma of the Trinity can be discussed only after the christological dogma has been elaborated. But the trinitarian principles appear whenever one speaks meaningfully of the living God.

The divine life is infinite, but in such a way that the finite is posited in it in a manner which transcends potentiality and actuality. Therefore, it is not precise to identify God with the infinite. This can be done on some levels of analysis. If man and his world are described as finite, God is infinite in contrast to them. But the analysis must go beyond this level in both directions. Man is aware of his finitude because he has the power of transcending it and of looking at it. Without this awareness he could not call himself mortal. On the other hand, that which is infinite would not be infinite if it wore limited by the finite. God is infinite because he has the finite (and with it that element of non-being which belongs to finitude) within himself united with his infinity. One of the functions of the symbol "divine life" is to point to this situation.

4

Professor Tillich's Confusions

Paul Edwards

1. Anthropomorphic and Metaphysical Conceptions of God

There is a tendency among believers, especially those who are professional philosophers, to make God as unlike human beings as possible. The opposite tendency, of regarding God as very much like a human being, only wiser, kinder, juster, and more powerful, is also, of course, quite common. In Hume's *Dialogues Concerning Natural Religion*, the believers in God, Demea and Cleanthes, are spokesmen for these two positions respectively. "His ways," remarks Demea, "are not our ways. His attributes are perfect, but incomprehensible." "When we mention the supreme Being," it may indeed be "more pious and respectful" to retain various of the terms which we apply to human beings, but in that case we "ought to acknowledge, that their meaning is totally incomprehensible; and that the infirmities of our nature do not permit us to reach any ideas, which in the least correspond to the ineffable sublimity of the divine attributes."[1] Cleanthes denounces Demea and those who share his views as "atheists without knowing it" (*ibid.* p. 159). He maintains that the divine mind must be regarded as a mind in the sense in which we speak of human minds, and when we apply such words as "rational" and "good" and "powerful" to the deity we are using them in one or other of their familiar senses—what we say is by no means incomprehensible.

I shall refer to views like Demea's as "metaphysical" and to those typified by Cleanthes as "anthropomorphic" theology. If this

---

[1] *Dialogues Concerning Natural Religion*, Kemp Smith ed., p. 156.

terminology is adopted then Professor Tillich has to be classified as a metaphysical believer. He is quite emphatic in his rejection of the anthropomorphic position to which he disdainfully applies such labels as "monarchic monotheism." The God of the anthropomorphic believers, Tillich writes, "is a being beside others and as such a part of the whole of reality. He certainly is considered its most important part, but as a part and therefore as subjected to the structure of the whole. He is supposed to be beyond the ontological elements and categories which constitute reality. But every statement subjects him to them. He is seen as a self which has a world, as an ego which is related to a thou, as a cause which is separated from its effect, as having a definite space and an endless time." "He is a being, not being itself."[2] No, God is not "*a* being." "The being of God is being itself.... If God is *a* being, he is subject to the categories of finitude, especially to space and substance. Even if he is called the 'highest being' in the sense of the 'most perfect' and the 'most powerful' being this situation is not changed. When applied to God, superlatives become diminutives.... Whenever infinite or unconditional power and meaning are attributed to the highest being, it has ceased to be a being and has become being-itself."[3] God is that "which transcends the world infinitely." The idea of God is not the idea of "some*thing* or some*one* who might or might not exist" (*ST*, p. 205, Tillich's italics).

Like Demea, Tillich maintains that the words which we apply to human beings cannot be applied to God in their literal senses since God is so very far removed from anything finite. "As the power of being, God transcends every being and also the totality of beings—the world. ... Being-itself infinitely transcends every finite being. There is no proportion or graduation between the finite and infinite. There is an absolute break, an infinite 'jump'" (*ST*, p. 237).

There is only one statement that we can make about God in which we use words "directly and properly," *i.e.* literally, and that is the statement that "God is being-itself." This statement, it is true, can be elaborated to mean that "God as being-itself is the ground of the ontological structure of being without being subject to this structure himself. He *is* the structure; that he has the power of determining the structure of everything that has being.... If anything beyond this bare assertion is true about God, it no longer is a direct and proper

---

[2] *The Courage To Be* (from now on referred to as *CB*), p. 184.

[3] *Systematic Theology*, Vol. 1 (to be referred to as *ST*), p. 235.

statement" (*ST*, p. 239). Tillich does indeed in various places say such things as that God is Love or that God is living. But these, as well as any other statements ascribing characteristics to God, must be treated as "metaphorical or symbolic"[4] utterances. "Any concrete assertion about God," Tillich makes it clear, "must be symbolic, for a concrete assertion is one which uses a segment of finite experience in order to say something about him." (*ST*, p. 239)

God, as Being-itself, so far transcends any separate, conditioned, finite being that we cannot even properly assert his existence. God is indeed "the creative ground of essence and existence," but it is "wrong . . . to speak of him as existing." "God does not exist." God is "above existence" and "it is as atheistic to affirm the existence of God as it is to deny it." (*ST*, pp. 204–205, 236, 237)

It may at first seem pointless for an unbeliever (like myself) to take issue with a philosopher who concedes that "God does not exist." But Tillich does make other remarks which unbelievers would or should oppose. Thus he speaks of the "actuality of God" (*ST*, p. 239) and he also holds that unlike any contingent, finite entity Being-itself possesses necessary being (it is not, as we saw, something or someone who might or might not exist) so that, as Sidney Hook has pointed out, "despite Tillich's denial, Being is endowed with a certain kind of existence—that which cannot not be."[5] But in any event, I do not wish to argue that Being-itself does not exist. To do so would presuppose that Tillich's talk about Being-itself is intelligible and this is what I wish to deny.

When I say, with certain reservations to be explained below, that Tillich's assertions about Being-itself are unintelligible, I am not merely applying the general positivist condemnation of metaphysics to this particular system. The war-cry of the early logical positivists that "metaphysics is nonsense," does seem to be open to serious objections. For one thing, it is notoriously difficult to formulate a criterion of meaning which does not rule out either too much or too

---

[4] *CB*, p. 179. When making admissions of this kind, Tillich seems to use "symbolic," "metaphorical," and "analogous" interchangeably and I shall also follow this practice. It is fair to add that in discussing the history of religious ideas Tillich uses "symbol" in other ways also. For a critical discussion of various uses of this word, see W. Alston's "Tillich's Conception of the Religious Symbol," in S. Hook (ed.), *Religious Experience and Language*, New York University Press, 1961.

[5] "The Quest for 'Being,'" *Journal of Philosophy*, 1953, p. 719.

little and which does not have the appearance of being, in certain respects, arbitrary and question-begging. There can also be no doubt that metaphysical systems are much more complex than some of the enemies of metaphysics believed—frequently they have all kinds of interesting and curious "links" to experience and they are only on the rarest occasions purely "transcendent." Granting this, it seems to me that the logical positivists nevertheless deserve great credit for helping to call attention to certain features of many sentences (and systems) commonly called "metaphysical." The metaphysicians are sometimes obscurely, but never, to my knowledge, clearly aware of these features. On the contrary, they manage by various stratagems to hide these features both from themselves and others. When, in non-philosophical contexts, it is found that a sentence possesses one or more of these characteristics, we do not hesitate to call it meaningless. We do not hesitate to say that it fails to assert anything.

I propose to show now that many of the most important sentences of Tillich's metaphysical system do possess certain of these features. Since they are put forward not merely as expressions of devout feeling or as vehicles of edifying pictures but as truth-claims, it would be interesting to know why, if they really possess the features in question, they should not be rejected as meaningless.

Throughout this article I am using "meaningless," "unintelligible," "devoid of cognitive content," "failing to make an assertion," "saying nothing at all," and "lacking referential meaning" interchangeably. I am aware that, as widely used, not all these expressions have the same meaning or the same force. For example, if I say to a taxi driver, "Go to Amsterdam Avenue and 82nd Street!" this is "intelligible" it is "meaningful," it "says something," but it would not be said to possess "cognitive content" by those who use this expression at all, we would not say that I used the sentence to make an assertion and most of those who used the word "referent" would say that this sentence, like imperatives generally, was without referential meaning. I do not think that this departure from widespread uses is of any consequence for the purposes of this article, but in any event I would be willing to argue that Tillich's theology is all of the things mentioned—meaningless, unintelligible, and all the rest.

2. Tillich's Theology is Compatible with Anything Whatsoever

We normally regard as empty, as devoid of (cognitive) meaning or content a sentence which, while pretending to assert something, is on further examination found to be incompatible with any state of affairs. If, for example, I say "Bomba is going to wear a red tie tonight" and if I do not withdraw my statement even if he shows up wearing a brown or a black or a grey tie, and if it further becomes clear that I will not consider my statement refuted even if Bomba wears no tie at all and in fact that I will consider it "true," no matter what happens anywhere, then it would be generally agreed that I have really said nothing at all. I have in this context deprived the expression "red tie" of any meaning. I have excluded no conceivable state of affairs and this, in the context in which people are attempting to make factual assertions, is generally considered a sufficient ground for condemning the sentence in question as empty or devoid of content.

Now, unless I have misunderstood Tillich, exactly the same is true of *his* belief in God. However, before showing this, it would be well to bring out as forcibly as possible the enormous difference between Tillich's position and the anthropomorphic theology of Cleanthes and of most ordinary believers. Cleanthes at one stage produces what he calls the "illustration" of the "heavenly voice." Suppose, he says, " that an articulate voice were heard in the clouds, much louder and more melodious than any which human art could ever reach: Suppose that this voice were extended in the same instant over all nations and spoke to each nation in its own language and dialect: Suppose, that the words delivered not only contain a just sense and meaning, but convey some instruction altogether worthy of a benevolent Being, superior to mankind." We can make this more definite by supposing that the voice made statements about the cure and prevention of all kinds of illnesses, such as cancer, which are as yet very imperfectly understood, as well as about a large number of other unsolved scientific problems and that upon examination every one of these statements turned out to be true. It is clear that if such a voice were heard, Cleanthes would regard this as confirmation of the existence of God in the sense in which he asserted it. I think it is equally clear that most ordinary believers would be jubilant if such events occurred and that they too would regard their belief confirmed. I do not know how Tillich would in fact react to such events, but I know how he *should* react. The only attitude consistent with his position would be to be (theoretically) wholly indifferent to what happened. The heavenly voice would in no way whatever be a confirmation of *his* theology.

Since heavenly voices do not actually exist, this departure from anthropomorphic theology may not seem to be to Tillich's disadvantage. His position, moreover, may seem to possess a considerable advantage over that of believers in an anthropomorphic God who is declared to be *all*-powerful and *perfectly* good. It has often been shown that the existence of evil falsifies the belief in such a God, and it is generally admitted, even by those who stick to this belief, that the fact of evil presents a ticklish problem. Tillich's theology, however, is immune to any such attack. Since he does not maintain either that God is all-powerful, in the literal sense, or that he is all-good in the literal sense, Tillich's theology does not imply that there is no evil in the world, in any of the ordinary senses of the word. In fact, even if the world were immensely more full of evil than it is, if it were such a frightful place that Nazi concentration camps and cancer hospitals would be regarded, by comparison, as utopian places of health and happiness and justice—even such a state of affairs would in no way falsify Tillich's view. Being-itself, *i.e.* God, would still be "actual."

The same would hold for any other aspect of the world. Whether human beings discover more and more order in the world or not, whether future scientific developments show space to be finite or infinite or neither, whether new observations confirm the steady-state theory of Hoyle and Bondi or the "big-bang" cosmology of Gamow and Lemaitre—it all makes no difference: Being-itself would still be actual. Being-itself, as we noted, is not "something or someone who might or might not be." This may be true of the anthropomorphic deity, but not of Being-itself.

I hope that my point is clear now. Tillich's theology is indeed safe from anti-theological arguments based on the existence of evil, but only at the expense of being *compatible with anything whatever*. All of us normally regard this, as I tried to show, as a reason for calling a sentence meaningless or devoid of cognitive content.

3. Being-itself and Irreducible Metaphors

As we saw, Tillich readily admits that only in the basic statement of his system are all words used in their literal senses. All other statements about Being-itself are symbolic or metaphorical. Tillich not only repeatedly makes general statements to this effect, he also tells us on many, though *not* on all, occasions when he discusses the characteristics of Being-itself that words he uses in characterizing the Ultimate Reality are not be understood literally. Thus he writes, "If one is asked how non-being is related to being-itself, one can only answer metaphorically: being 'embraces' itself and nonbeings. Being has nonbeing 'within' itself as that which is eternally present and eternally overcome in the process of the divine life." (*CB*, p. 34) Again: "In a metaphorical statement (and every assertion about being-itself is either metaphorical or symbolic) one could say that being includes nonbeing but nonbeing does not prevail against it. 'Including' is a spatial metaphor which indicates that being embraces itself and that which is opposed to it, nonbeing. Nonbeing belongs to being, it cannot be separated from it" (*CB*, p. 179). Again: "The divine life participates in every life as its ground and aim. God participates in everything that is; he has community with it; he shares in its destiny. Certainly such statements are highly symbolic. . . . God's participation is not a spatial or temporal presence. It is meant not categorically but symbolically. It is the parousia, the 'being with' of that which is neither here nor there. If applied to God, participation and community are not less symbolic than individualization and personality." (*ST*, p. 245) And again: "But in God as God there is no distinction between potentiality and actuality. Therefore, we cannot speak of God as living in the proper or nonsymbolic sense of the word 'life'." (*ST*, p. 242)

Tillich sees nothing at all wrong in his constant employment of metaphors. On the contrary, he stresses the fact that without employing terms taken from "segments of finite experience," theological sentences would have little or no emotional force. "Anthropomorphic symbols," he writes, "are adequate for speaking of God religiously. Only in this way can he be the living God for man." (*ST*, p. 242) Tillich is indeed aware of the objection of certain philosophers that it is illegitimate to use terms which have a reasonably well-defined meaning in everyday contexts to make assertions about a reality that is infinitely removed from the contexts in which these expressions we originally introduced. He dismisses this objection without much ado. Such "accusations are mistaken," Tillich replies, "they miss the meaning of ontological concepts. . . . It is the function of an ontological concept to use some realm of experience to point to characteristics of being-itself which lie above the split between subjectivity and objectivity and which therefore need not be expressed literally in terms taken from the subjective or the objective side. They must be understood not literally but analogously." This, however, Tillich insists, "does not mean that they have been produced arbitrarily and can easily be replaced by other concepts. Their choice is a matter of experience and thought, and subject to criteria which determine the adequacy or inadequacy of each of them." (*CB*, p. 25)

The rejoinder that "of course" the terms in question are used "analogously," "symbolically" or "merely as metaphors" exercises the same hypnotic spell over Tillich as it has on metaphysicians in the past. He seems to think that it is a solution of the problem. In fact, however, it is nothing of the sort. It is an implicit admission that a problem exists. The concession by an author that he is using a certain word metaphorically is tantamount to admitting that, in a very important sense and a sense relevant to the questions at issue between metaphysicians and their critics, he does not mean what he says. It does not automatically tell us what he does mean or whether in fact he means anything at all. When Bradley, for example, wrote that "the Absolute enters into . . . evolution and progress" it is clear that the word "enter" is used in a metaphorical and not a literal sense. But realizing this does not at once tell us what, if anything, Bradley asserted.

Often indeed when words are used metaphorically, the contest or certain special conventions make it clear what is asserted. Thus, when a certain historian wrote that "the Monroe Doctrine has always rested on the broad back of the British navy," it would have been pedantic and foolish to comment "what on earth does he mean—doesn't he know that navies don't have backs?" Or if a man, who has been involved in a scandal and is advised to flee his country, rejects the advice and says, "No, I think I'll stay and face the music," it would be absurd to object to his statement on the ground that it is not exactly music that he is going to hear. In these cases we know perfectly well what the authors mean although they are using certain words metaphorically. But we know this because we can eliminate the metaphorical expression, because we can specify the content of the assertion in non-metaphorical language, because we can supply the literal equivalent.

The examples just cited are what I shall call "reducible metaphors." I prefer this to the phrase "translatable metaphor" because of certain ambiguities in the use of "translatable." We sometimes say of the English version of a foreign original—*e.g.* of the English version of the *Rosenkavalier*—that it is a bad or inadequate translation although it does in fact reproduce all the truth-claims contained in the original. Conversely we sometimes, as in the case of the Blitzstein version of the *Dreigroschenoper*, speak of a magnificent translation although we know that not all truth-claims of the original have been reproduced. In the present context, however, we are exclusively concerned with reproduction of truth-claims and in calling a metaphor "reducible" all I mean is that the truth-claims made by the sentence in which it occurs can be reproduced by one or more sentences all of whose components are used in literal senses.

Now, Tillich and many other metaphysicians fail to notice the difference between metaphors which are reducible in the sense just explained and those which are not. When a sentence contains an irreducible metaphor, it follows at once that the sentence is devoid of cognitive meaning, that it is unintelligible, that it fails to make a genuine assertion. For what has happened is that the sentence has been deprived of the referent it would have had, assuming that certain other conditions had also been fulfilled, if the expression in question had been used in its literal sense. To say that the metaphor is irreducible is to say in effect that no new referent can be supplied.

It will be instructive to look at an actual case in which a philosopher gave this very reason for his accusation that certain statements by another philosopher were devoid of meaning. I am referring to Berkeley's attack on Locke's claim that the material substratum "supports" the sense-qualities. Berkeley first pointed to the original context in which the word "support" is introduced, as when we say that pillars support a building. He then pointed out that since, according to Locke, the material substratum is a "something, x, I know not what" whose characteristics are unknown and indeed unknowable, and, since, therefore, it is not known to resemble pillars in any way, Locke could not possibly have been using the word "support" in its "usual or literal sense." "In what sense therefore," Berkeley went on, "must it be taken? . . . What that is they (Locke and those who share his view) do not explain." Berkeley then concluded that the sentences in question have "no distinct meaning annexed"[6] to them.

Let us consider some possible answers to Berkeley's criticism without in any way implying that Locke himself would have approved of any of them. Perhaps the most obvious answer would be that Locke should never have spoken of the material substratum as an unknowable entity. It should really be understood as an aggregate of material particles to which certain adjectives like mass-and velocity-predicates can be applied in their literal senses. Locke's statement that the material substratum supports the sense-qualities can then be translated into some such statement as that the particular "gross" sense-qualities perceived at any moment are, in part, causally dependent on the distribution and velocities of the particles in question. On this view there would be no irreducible metaphors in the original sentence.

A second line of defense would begin by admitting that the material substratum *would* be completely unknowable, if sensory observation were the only method of becoming acquainted with objective realities. In fact, however, it would be said, we possess a "super-sensuous" faculty with which we "experience" such realities as material and spiritual substances. We could, if we wanted, introduce a set of terms as the symbols literally referring to the data disclosed by this super-sensuous faculty and we could exchange information about these with all who share in the possession of the faculty. If we call this the "intellectual language," then, so this defense of Locke would run, sentences with metaphors when containing terms from the "sensory level," can be translated into sentences in the intellectual language which will be free from metaphors.

Finally, in view of our later discussion, it is worth looking at a particularly naïve and lame answer to Berkeley. A defender of Locke, when confronted with the question "You do not mean 'support' in its literal sense, what then do you mean?" might say, "I mean that the material substratum holds the sense-qualities together." The answer to this is obvious. "Hold together" is no more used in its literal sense than "support" and hence the difficulty has in no way been removed.

---

[6] *Principles of Human Knowledge*, pp. 16–17.

Turning now to Tillich's metaphysical theology, it seems perfectly clear from numerous of his general observations that Being-itself is, even in principle, inaccessible to anybody's observation. In this respect it is exactly like Locke's material substratum. We do not and cannot have a stock of literally meaningful statements about it at our disposal which would serve as the equivalents of Tillich's "symbolic" statements. The metaphors in Tillich's sentences are, in other words, irreducible and hence, if my general argument has been correct, the sentences are unintelligible. If Tillich's statements are not to become propositions of physics or psychology or history no way out of corresponding to the first of the defenses of Locke is feasible. And unlike certain contemporary writers, Tillich does not avail himself of an appeal to mystical experience which would correspond to the second defense. For, if I understand Tillich correctly, he denies that even the mystic experiences Being-itself. The (true) "idea of God," Tillich writes, "transcends both mysticism and the person-to-person encounter."[7] As I shall show in a moment, Tillich does avail himself of a line of defense corresponding to the third of the defenses of Locke. We already saw, however, that such a defense is altogether futile.

It may be said that I have not been fair to Tillich and other metaphysicians who defend themselves by insisting that they are using certain expressions metaphorically or analogously. It may be said that I have emphasized the negative implications of this admission—that the words in question are not used in their literal senses—without doing justice to its positive implications. For, it may be argued, when it is said that a certain word is used "analogously," it *is* implied that the term has a referent, namely a referent which is in some important respect similar to the referent it has when used literally.

This objection rests on a confusion. We must here distinguish two possible meanings of the assertion that a certain word is used "analogously." This may, firstly, mean no more than that the word in question is *not used literally*. But it may also amount to the much stronger claim that the word *has a referent* and hence that the sentence

---

[7] *CB*, p. 178. I am not sure that I have here correctly understood Tillich. He also seems to be saying the opposite at times—that mystics do have "direct access" to Being-itself. If that is Tillich's position then some of the criticisms which follow would not apply, but it would then be open to a number of other objections.

in which it occurs is, if certain other conditions are fulfilled, cognitively significant. If "analogously" is used in the former sense, then of course I would not for a moment deny that the relevant words are used analogously in Tillich's sentences and in the sentences of other metaphysicians. But this is an innocuous admission. For to say that the words are used analogously in this sense has no tendency whatever to imply that the sentences in which they occur possess cognitive meaning. If "analogously" is used in the second case, then, as just observed, it would automatically follow that the sentences are, if other conditions are also fulfilled, cognitively significant; but in that event I would deny that the terms we have discussed are used analogously in Tillich's sentences or in the sentences of other metaphysicians. To put the matter very simply: merely saying that a sentence, or any part of it, has meaning does not by itself give it meaning. Such a claim does not assure us that the sentence is intelligible. Similarly the claim that a sentence has an "analogous" referent is a claim and no more—it may be false. If I say, to use an example given by Sidney Hook,[8] that the sea is angry, the word "angry" really has a referent which is analogous to its referent when used literally. I can in this case specify the features of the sea to which I am referring when I call it angry and I can also specify the similarities between these features and the anger of human beings. If, however, I say that Being-itself is angry, I could not independently identify the features of Being-itself to which I am supposedly referring. Nor of course could I specify the similarities between the anger of human beings and the putative anger of Being-itself. My claim that "angry" is used analogously in this sentence in a sense in which this implies that it has a referent would be false or at any rate baseless.

The narcotic effect of such phrases as "symbolic language" or "analogous sense" is only a partial explanation of Tillich's failure to be clear about the irreducibility of his metaphors. To tell the whole story one has to take notice of an aspect of Tillich's philosophizing which I have so far ignored. What I have so far brought out may be called Tillich's "modest" side—"modest" because he does not in the passages in question claim any literal knowledge about Being-itself. But there is also what may be called Tillich's "dogmatic" side. He then seems to be jotting down in a matter-of-fact way the characteris-

---

[8] "The Quest for Being," *op. cit.* p. 715.

tics of Being-itself, much as a doctor might jot down descriptions of the symptoms displayed by a patient. He then writes as if he had a completely unobstructed view of the Ultimate Reality. Thus we are told as a plain matter of fact and without the use of any quotation marks that "God is infinite because he has the finite (and with it that element of non-being which belongs to finitude) within himself united with his infinity." The expression "divine life," we are told, points to "this *situation*" (*ST*, p. 252, my italics). "The divine life," Tillich admits, "is infinite mystery," but we can nevertheless say that "it is not infinite emptiness. It is the ground of all abundance, and it is abundant itself" (*ST*, p. 251). Again, we are told, without the use of any quotation marks, and I do not think their absence is a mere oversight, that God "is the eternal process in which separation is posited and is overcome by reunion" (*ST*, p. 242). In one place, to give one more illustration of the dogmatic side of his philosophy, Tillich discusses the question of whether will or intellect are dominant "in God." He quotes the rival views of Aquinas and Duns Scotus and he notes that Protestants have tended to favour the latter position which subordinates the intellect. Tillich easily resolves this dispute as if he were reading off the truth by a quick glance at God. "Theology," he writes, "must balance the new with the old (predominantly Catholic) emphasis on the form character of the divine life" (*ST*, p. 248), i.e. it must assign equal rank to will and intellect in God. The divine life, we are assured, "inescapably unites possibility with fulfillment. Neither side threatens the other nor is there a threat of disruption" (*ST*, p. 247).

Tillich, the dogmatist, does not hesitate to offer translations or what I have called reductions of his "symbolic" statements about God. We can also express literally, for example, what we mean "symbolically" when we say that God is living. "God lives," the reduction runs, "insofar as he is the ground of life" (*ST*, p. 242). Again, our symbolic statement that God is personal "does not mean that God is *a* person. It means that God is the ground of everything personal and that he carries within himself the ontological power of personality" (*ST*, p. 245). And if we symbolically say God is "his own destiny" we thereby "point to . . . the participation of God in becoming and in history" (*ST*, p. 249).

I wish to make two observations concerning all this. Firstly, although Tillich gives the impression that the metaphors have been eliminated in these and similar cases, this is not so. He never seems to have noticed that even in his basic statement, when elaborated in terms of "ground" and "structure," these words are used metaphorically and not literally. When Tillich writes that God or Being-itself "is the ground of the ontological structure of being and has the power of determining the structure of everything that has being," the word "ground," for example, is clearly not used in any of its literal senses. Being-itself is surely not claimed to be the ground of the ontological structure in the sense in which the earth is the ground beneath our feet or in the sense in which the premises of a valid argument may be said to be the ground for accepting the conclusion. Similar remarks apply to the use of "structure," "power," and "determine." Hence when we are told that "God lives insofar as he is the ground of life" or that "God is personal" means "God is the ground of everything personal and . . . carries within himself the ontological power of personality," expressions like "ground" and "carry within himself" and even "power" are not used literally. Tillich is here in no better a position than the supporter of Locke who substituted "hold together" for "support." That Tillich does not succeed in breaking through the circle of expressions lacking literal significance, i.e. lacking referential meaning, is particularly clear in the case of the "translation" of the sentence "God is his own destiny." By this "symbolic" characterization, as we just saw, we "point" among other things to "the participation of God in becoming and in history." But a little earlier, in a passage which I also reproduced, we were informed that "God's participation is not a spatial or temporal presence" and twice in the same paragraph we were given to understand that when "applied to God," participation "is meant not categorically but symbolically." In other words, one metaphorical statement is replaced by another but literal significance is never achieved.

Tillich constantly engages in "circular" translations of this sort. Again and again he "explains" the meaning of one "symbolically" used expression in terms of another which is really no less symbolic. Thus in a passage reproduced at the beginning of section 3 of this article the sentence "being includes nonbeing" which contains the admittedly symbolic word "include" is translated into "nonbeing belongs to being, it cannot be separated from it." "Belong" and "separate" are no longer put inside quotation marks and one is apt to suppose that some progress has been made. Countless other illustrations of the practice could be given.

Secondly, I have the impression that, in spite of his distaste for "monarchic monotheism," Tillich occasionally relapses into something not too different from it. When offering translations such as those just quoted and generally when assessing the adequacy of certain symbols as "pointers" to the "divine life" Tillich seems to think that he has at his disposal a stock of literal truths about God not too different from those asserted by anthropomorphic believers. There is a remarkable passage in which this is strikingly evident:

> Religious symbols are double-edged. They are directed toward the infinite which they symbolize and toward the finite through which they symbolize it. They force the infinite down to finitude and the finite up to infinity. They open the divine for the human and the human for the divine. For instance, if God is symbolized as 'Father,' he is brought down to the human relationship of father and child. But at the same time this human relationship is consecrated into a pattern of the divine-human relationship. If 'Father' is employed as a symbol for God, fatherhood seen in its theonomous, sacramental depth. . . . If God is called the 'king,' something is said not only about God but also about the holy character of kinghood. If God's work is called 'making whole' or 'healing,' this not only says something about God but also emphasizes the theonomous character of all healing. . . . The list could be continued (*ST*, pp. 240-241).

Now, if it were known or believed that God is "majestic" in the same sense in which human beings have sometimes been called that, it would make sense to call God a "king" and it would be right to prefer this symbol to symbols like "slave" or waiter" or "street-cleaner." Similarly, if it were known or believed that God is "concerned with the welfare" of all human beings in the literal sense of this expression, then it would make sense to speak of him as our "father" and it would be right to prefer this symbol to symbols like "daughter" or "soprano" or "carpenter." An anthropomorphic believer has criteria at his disposal in such cases, but Tillich's non-anthropomorphic theology necessarily deprives him of it. Tillich says very correctly that this list of adjectives "could be continued." Since the "comparison" between fathers and kings on the one hand and the infinitely transcending, infinitely mysterious, indescribable Being-itself, on the other, is a bogus comparison, God may no less appropriately be said to be a soprano, a slave, a street-dancer, a daughter, or even a fascist and a hater than a father or a king.

4. Bombastic Redescriptions of Empirical Facts

Readers who were less critical than Berkeley did not realize the meaninglessness of the sentence "the material substance supports the sense-qualities" or its equivalents chiefly because of the presence of words like "support" which automatically call up certain images. Similarly, I have no doubt that the presence of such words as "embrace" and "resist" and the mental pictures connected with them prevents many a reader from realizing the meaningless of Tillich's talk about being and nonbeing and their mutual relations. But there is also another reason why this unintelligibility is not always obvious. The reason is that in a *certain sense,* some of Tillich's sentences are *not* unintelligible.

In this connection I wish to call attention to a technique which is employed by Tillich as well as by many other metaphysicians and certainly by all other existentialists with whose writings I am familiar. I will call it the technique of "bombastic redescription" and I think that one simple illustration will make quite clear what I am referring to. Some well-known chronological facts about Freud may be stated in the following words:

> Freud was born in 1856 and died in 1939 (1)

The very same facts may also be expressed in a much more bombastic fashion:

> In 1856 Freud migrated from nonbeing to being and then in 1939 he returned from being to nonbeing (2). Now, let us assume for a moment that the author of (2) is not a metaphysician and does not in fact claim that (2) asserts anything over and above what is asserted by (1). In that event we cannot accuse him of uttering either a meaningless sentence or a falsehood, since what he says is perfectly intelligible and moreover true, or of performing an illegitimate inference; (2) does follow from (1) no less than for example "some mortal beings are men" follows from "some men are mortal." We can, however, point out that our author is employing needlessly high-sounding language to express a truth which can be stated much more simply and that (2) does not embody any grand new "insight" into anything whatever.

Let us next assume that the author of (2) is a metaphysician who assures us that (2) is not a set of simple biographical statements but belongs to "ontology"—the study of "being" and "non-being." He assures us that (2) asserts a great deal more than (1). In that event we would be entitled to reply, first, that it is not at all clear what, if anything, (2) means now, and secondly, that if it does mean more than (1), the step from (1) to (2) is not warranted. Our ontologist is thus either guilty of making a meaningless pronouncement and of performing an invalid inference or at the very least of the latter.

Let us finally assume that we are dealing with an exceedingly nebulous ontologist whose writings hardly ever contain anything that can be dignified as an "argument" or a "definition." Among his many observations about being and nonbeing he on one occasion includes sentence (2) and somewhere, not too remote in space, there also occurs sentence (1). This nebulous ontologist, unlike the other two people we considered, has not committed himself to any view about the relation between (2) and (1) and, because of this he enjoys the best of two worlds. To certain uncritical readers, (2) will appear to be a profound metaphysical utterance—surely not just a redescription of the familiar facts asserted by (1). At the same time, however, (1) does remain in the background and the pictures aroused by it will tend to be vaguely associated also with (2). It will be felt that it is unfair to accuse the author of "wild speculation" since his ontological statement is "firmly rooted" in experience: after all, Freud was born in 1856 and he did die in 1939.

A more critical reader could, however, confront our nebulous ontologist with the following dilemma: either (2) merely asserts what is already asserted by (1)—in that event it is nothing but a bombastic redescription of familiar facts which hardly needed an ontologist or a metaphysician for their discovery, and in that event, furthermore, it is an *empirical* proposition and its truth is in no way incompatible with empiricism or positivism or any of the doctrines despised by ontologists; or also (2) does assert more—in that event it is not at all clear what, if anything, it does assert and secondly, as already pointed out, in that event it does not follow from (1).

In much of what he is doing, Tillich, no less than other existentialists, closely resembles this nebulous ontologist. Like the ontologist he talks grandiloquently about being and nonbeing and he goes even one better in talking about "not-yet-being." Tillich's observations about being and nonbeing and not-yet-being correspond to sentence (2). Like the ontologist, Tillich also either explicitly mentions certain well-known empirical facts in conjunction with his ontological pronouncements or, when he does not actually mention them, the language chosen nevertheless very strongly tends to call these facts to the reader's mind and, I am pretty certain, to Tillich's mind also. This would correspond to sentence (1). Finally, like our nebulous ontologist, Tillich leaves the relation between his ontological remarks and the background empirical facts suitably vague. In this way what he says simultaneously enjoys the appearance of being profound, of revealing to us special insights into superempirical facts—facts about transcendent realms to which science and ordinary observation have no access but to which "existential analysis" holds the clue—and of being quite intelligible and indeed "firmly rooted" in human experience, in the "existential situation." Tillich is of course open to the same objection as our nebulous ontologist. He cannot, logically, have it both ways: either his ontological talk is merely a bombastic redescription of certain empirical facts which are often trivial and in no instance new; or it is not clear what, if anything, the sentences assert and in any event they are not then warranted by any of the empirical facts presented to the reader.

I will now give a few illustrations of this procedure. In each case, I will first summarize, in bald and untarnished language, the empirical facts of the case whether they are openly mentioned by Tillich or whether they merely hover discreetly in the background. We might refer to this as the cash-value of the doctrine in question. I will then state the corresponding ontological doctrine and whenever possible I will reproduce Tillich's own words. The reader can judge for himself whether one is justified in confronting Tillich with the dilemma mentioned in the last paragraph.

Let us begin with the subject of man's most heroic deeds.

Cash-value: Selfishness and other motives are involved in even the best human actions.

Ontological doctrine: "Even in what he considers his best deed nonbeing is present and prevents it from being perfect.... Nonbeing is mixed with being in his moral self-affirmation as it is in his spiritual and ontic self-affirmation" (*CB*, p. 52).

Let us turn next to man's "creatureliness."

Cash value: Human beings have not always existed; all of them are born and before they were born or rather before they were conceived they did not exist; all of them also eventually die, and after they die they are dead, they are not then alive.

Ontological doctrine: Nonbeing in man has a dialectical character.

Full statement of ontological doctrine: "The doctrine of man's creatureliness is another point in the doctrine of man where nonbeing has a dialectical character.

> Being created out of nothing means having to return to nothing. The stigma of having originated out of nothing is impressed on every creature. . . . Being, limited by nonbeing, is finitude. Nonbeing appears as the 'not yet' of being and as the 'no more' of being . . . everything which participates in the power of being is 'mixed' with nonbeing. It is being in process of coming from and going toward nonbeing. It is finite" (*ST*, pp. 188–189).

Nonbeing, as we just found, appears at times as the "not-yet" of being. Ontologists can therefore hardly neglect the question of man's relation to "not-yet-being" and Tillich promptly addresses himself to this problem.

Cash-value: Human beings frequently fail to have attributes which they may or will possess at a later time—for example, babies sometimes don't have hair, but later on their heads are covered with hair; a person may at one time know only his native language, but several years later he may have mastered other languages as well, etc., etc.

Ontological doctrine: "Being and not-yet-being are 'mixed' in him (man), as they are in everything finite" (*ST*, p. 236).

5. Being, Nonbeing and "Some Logicians"

Tillich is much irked by "some logicians" who "deny that nonbeing has conceptual character and try to remove it from the philosophical scene except in the form of negative judgments" (*CB*, p. 34). As against the logicians, Tillich insists on "the mystery of nonbeing" and he recommends that the "fascinating" and "exasperating" question, "What kind of being must we attribute to non-being?" should be taken seriously. His answer to the logicians is worth reproducing in full:

> There are two possible ways of trying to avoid the question of nonbeing, the one logical. . . . One can assert that nonbeing is a negative judgment devoid of ontological significance. To this we must reply that every logical structure which is more than merely a play with possible relations is rooted in an ontological structure. The very fact of logical denial presupposes a type of being which can transcend the immediate given situation by means of expectations which may be disappointed. An anticipated event does not occur. This means that the judgment concerning the situation has been mistaken, the necessary conditions for the occurrence of the expected event have been non-existent. Thus disappointed, expectation creates the

> distinction between being and nonbeing. But how is such an expectation possible in the first place? What is the structure of this being which is able to transcend the given situation and to fall into error? The answer is that man, who is this being, must be separated from his being in a way which enables him to look at it as something strange and questionable. And such a separation is actual because man participates not only in being but also in nonbeing. Therefore, the very structure which makes negative judgments possible proves the ontological character of nonbeing. Unless man participates in non-being, no negative judgments are possible. The mystery of nonbeing cannot be solved by transforming it into a type of logical judgment (*ST*, p. 187).

Elsewhere, if I understand him correctly, Tillich repeatedly quotes, as support of his view concerning the reality of nonbeing, the existence of such "negativities" as "the transitoriness of everything created and the power of the 'demonic' in the human soul and history" (*CB*, pp. 33–34). I am certain that Tillich would also endorse Heidegger's appeal to such a "negative" phenomena as loathing, refusal, mercilessness, and renunciation[9] and William Barrett's discussion of the effects of blindness[10] as evidence for the same position.

There are so many confusions here that it is difficult to know where to begin. Probably the most serious defect of Tillich's discussion is his failure to be clear about the real point at issue between himself and the "logicians." By the "logicians" Tillich presumably means philosophers like Russell, Carnap and Ayer[11] who deny that

---

[9] *Existence and Being*, p. 373.

[10] *Irrational Man*, pp. 256–257.

[11] Russell discusses the subject of negation in "The Philosophy of Logical Atomism," which is reprinted in *Logic and Knowledge*, in *An Enquiry Meaning and Truth* and in *Human Knowledge—Its Scope and Limits;* Carnap in "The Elimination of Metaphysics through Logical Analysis of Language," which is reprinted in Ayer's *Logical Positivism;* Ayer discusses the subject in "Jean-Paul Sartre," *Horizon*, 1945, in "Some Aspects of Existentialism," *Rationalist Annual*, 1948 and in "Negation," reprinted in his *Philosophical Essays*. It is perhaps worth adding that the "logicians" are divided among themselves on the question of whether, in Russell's words, "there are facts which can only be asserted in sentences containing the word 'not'." William Barrett, who is the most lucid of the existentialist defenders of Nothingness, seems to think that their case would be helped if it could be shown, to use Russell's words once more, that "the world cannot be completely described without the employment of logical words like 'not'." This, however is a confusion. From the admission that "not" or "nothing" are indispensable it in no way follows that these words are names or descriptions

such words as "nothing" and "nobody" and "not" are names or descriptions. Although they deny *this,* there are two other things which the "logicians" do not deny. Firstly, they do not deny the existence of the various phenomena to which Tillich refers as "negatives." They do not deny that human beings quite often behave destructively, that they feel disgust, hatred, or what have you. Nor do they deny that human beings sometimes become blind or crippled in various ways and that the loss of eyes, limbs, or other parts of their bodies produces vast amounts of grief. Not only do the logicians not deny any of these phenomena, but it is difficult to see how anybody could believe or argue that such denials are logically implied by the view that "nothing" is not a name or a description. Yet, unless such denials are implied by this view, references to phenomena like hatred or blindness are completely beside the point.

The logicians, furthermore, do not deny that "not" and "nothing" are words in the "object-language" and that sentences in which they occur are frequently just as "descriptive of reality" as affirmative sentences. I do not know of any "logician" who has ever denied, for example, that the sentence "there is no butter in the refrigerator" is as descriptive of the world as the sentence "there is butter in the refrigerator" or that the sentence "I know nothing about Chinese grammar" is just as descriptive as the sentence "I know a good deal about German grammar." It is again not easy to see how it could be argued that such denials are logically implied in the view that "nothing" is not a description. I for one also see nothing objectionable in saying that while sentences like "there is butter in the refrigerator" refer to "positive" facts, sentences like "there is no butter in the refrigerator" refer to "negative" facts, that the former sentence refers to the *presence,* while the latter refers to the *absence* of butter in the refrigerator. Whatever misgivings I have about this way of talking concern the use of "fact" and not the use of "positive" and "negative" as qualifying adjectives.[12]

Once the ground is cleared in this way and no appeal is made to such totally irrelevant matters as the existence of hatred and blindness or to the fact that "not" and "nothing" occur in descriptive

---

since it is anything but obvious that only names and descriptions are indispensable.

[12] For an innocuous use of "unreality" similar to my use of "negative facts," see R. L. Cartwright, "Negative Existentials," *Journal of Philosophy,* 1960.

sentences it is easily seen that the "logicians" are right and that Tillich and other believers in nothingness are wrong. It becomes plain that Tillich and his fellow existentialists are wrong, not necessarily in believing in some mysterious realm or mode of being which they call "nonbeing" or "nothingness," but in holding that, if there is such a realm, it is named by the word "nothing," *as that word is normally used*. They are wrong, further, in believing that the existence of such "logical structures" as negative judgments implies any transcendent ontological truths. I need not waste much time over showing that words like "nobody" or "nothing" are not names or descriptions. If somebody asks me, "Who is outside?" and I say "Bomba is outside" and on a second occasion I answer "Mrs. Bomba is outside," "Bomba" and "Mrs. Bomba" function as names—they refer to unmysterious human beings. If on a third occasion I answer "Nobody is outside," the word "nobody" is not the name of a mysterious shadowy human being. It functions as a sign of denial. To say that nobody is outside is to say that it is false to maintain that anybody is outside. Similarly, if I say that Germany is separated from Russia by Poland or that New Jersey and New York are separated by the Hudson River, "Poland" and "the Hudson River" are names of certain things or areas. But to say about two objects or areas, the boroughs of Queens and Brooklyn, for example, that they are separated by nothing, is to say, in Ayer's words, "that they are not separated; and that is all that it amounts to."[13] One is not asserting here that the two areas are separated by a mysterious area which is named by the word "nothing." "Nothing," like "nobody," functions as a sign of denial and not as a name—either of something familiar or of something mysterious in a realm to which only specially gifted persons have access.

It is perhaps worth adding that the dispute is not, as Tillich suggests, between himself and existentialists on one side and "some logicians" on the other. It is between the former group and practically the whole of mankind. Ordinary people do *not* believe that "nothing" is a name. I do not suppose that ordinary people hold any explicit view on this subject, but any occasion on which the existentialist theory is presented to them, they regard it as a joke. They simply do not believe that anybody seriously advocates such a position. This surely is the only possible interpretation of the mirth provoked by

---

[13] "Jean-Paul Sartre," *op. cit.* p. 18.

such exchanges as those between the Messenger and the King of *Alice Through the Looking Glass.*

> "Who did you pass on the road?" the King went on, holding out his hand to the Messenger for some more hay.
>
> "Nobody," said the Messenger.
>
> "Quite right," said the King, "this young lady saw him too. So of course Nobody walks slower than you."
>
> "I do my best," said the Messenger in a sullen tone. "I'm sure nobody walks much faster than I do."
>
> "He can't do that," said the King, "or else he'd have been here first."

I have often wondered why existential ontologists pay so little attention to caves, hollow tubes and holes in general. These are clear instances of nonbeing which should silence any sceptic. In certain tablecloths, for example, it is the number and the position of the holes which determines the excellence of the tablecloths. This surely shows that holes are real negativities. I was pleased to come across a discussion of this subject in an essay entitled "On the Social Psychology of Holes" by the unjustly forgotten German writer, Kurt Tucholsky. "When a hole is filled," Tucholsky asks, "where does it go? . . . If an object occupies a place, this place cannot also be occupied by another object but what about holes? If there is a hole in a given place can that place be occupied by other holes as well? And why aren't there halves of holes?" In short: what kind of being must we attribute to holes? I hope that Tillich or some other existentialist will before long address himself to this question.

To my knowledge the only people who have believed that "nothing" is a name are certain metaphysicians (including, it is true, some of the most famous like Hegel) and *some* beginning students of philosophy who in their first gropings tend to assume that all words are names.

Tillich is right in regarding disappointed expectations and the erroneous beliefs connected with them, as one of the motives for the introduction of various negative terms. He is wrong, incidentally, if he thinks that it is only the motive—such phenomena as disagreement, refusal to give information, ignorance, rejection, in a sense in which this is not simply disagreement, have also made it necessary to employ these expressions. His statement that "every logical structure is rooted in an ontological structure" is true in the case of negation if it means no more than, firstly, that negative terms would not have been introduced into our various languages if it were not for disappointed expectations, disagreement, ignorance and other phenomena of the kinds just mentioned and, secondly, that they frequently occur in sentences which are descriptive of reality. His statement is not true if it means that the word "nothing" names a special reality which needs existentialists or some rival group of ontologists for its exploration. Tillich's error becomes very evident when we reflect that words like "or" and "and" also have "existential roots." We would not have introduced them if we never hesitated, if our knowledge in a given field were always complete, if we never felt the need to enumerate our possessions, etc. Again, there is no doubt that sentences containing "or" and "and" are frequently descriptive of reality. Yet not even Tillich has had the heart to add and-being or or-being to his ontological inventory.

Suggested Reading

Achinstein, P. & Barker, S. F. (eds.). 1969. *The Legacy of Logical Positivism*. Baltimore: Johns Hopkins Press. A very good account of the received tradition, and the challenges to it from Kuhn, Feyerabend, Hanson, and others.

Ayer, A. J. (ed.). 1959. *Logical Positivism*. Glencoe, Ill.: Free Press. An excellent overview of the difficulties in forging an acceptable verification principle.

Davidson, D. 1984. What Metaphors Mean & Communication and Convention. In *Inquiries into Truth and Interpretation.* Oxford: Clarendon Press. The semantics of metaphor framed in these essays can be critically applied to post-Tillichean theologies that stress symbol and metaphor as the language of religion. On Davidson's analysis, there is no special content or meaning to metaphor over and above literal meaning.

Quine, W. V. 1963. Two Dogmas of Empiricism. In *From a Logical Point of View.* New York: Harper & Row. By calling into question the meaning of "analytic" statements, this influential essay helped to break the grip that the analytic-synthetic distinction had on empiricism.

For classic representatives of the two-level theory of truth among religious authors, see:

Buber, M. 1970. *I and Thou*. New York: Scribner.

Bultmann, R. 1958. *Jesus Christ and Mythology*. New York: Scribner.

James, W. 1956. The Will to Believe. In *The Will to Believe*. Dover: New York.

Kierkegaard, S. 1992. *Concluding Unscientific Postscript.* New Jersey: Princeton University Press.

Part II

From Logical Positivism to Functionalism

INTRODUCTION TO PART II

When the father of British anthropology, E. B. Tylor, asserted that the religious beliefs and myths of "primitive" peoples were false, he rested his case on an assumption that would become axiomatic by A. J. Ayer's time. Tylor was convinced that not only religious beliefs and myths but also religious rituals were empirically false, because it could be demonstrated that the various gods and spirits did not cause rain, illness, or death. According to Tylor and others, religious beliefs and myths were attempts to explain our experience of the world. Although such beliefs and actions were false, they were not irrational, according to Tylor. The mere fact that someone holds a false belief need not entail irrationality. If that were the case, the history of science could be characterized as one long episode of irrationality. This approach to the study of religion is often called the "intellectualist" or "rationalist" theory of religion and is very much alive in the work of such scholars as Robin Horton and Melford Spiro.

The theory raises many problems. One of them can be framed as follows: how do we explain the fact that throughout history the vast majority of human beings have lived their lives in a network of beliefs that are false? One answer, social evolutionism, has assumed human societies evolved from the simple to the complex, as from childhood to adulthood. "Primitive" societies, like our children, personify or "animate" the world in imaginative ways. Many scholars, such as Freud, assumed the "phylogenetic law" that phylogeny repeats ontogeny, or cultures repeat the development of the individual. The obvious problem with this theory, however, is its full-blown ethnocentrism. We know perfectly well that "primitive" cultures are not at all like our children, for such cultures include adults who are not children either biologically or socially. Few scholars today would be so bold as to equate any particular culture with childhood or to assume that so-called "primitive" cultures consist of a species frozen at the dawn of human existence. Nevertheless, the current notion of "underdeveloped" cultures retains an echo of a bias that does not die quickly or easily.

Aware of the problem, most scholars have dropped the phylogenetic law but held to the principle of empirical verification as fundamental to the question of meaning. Given time and place, so the argument goes, we can well explain why certain cultures have certain beliefs and in the long run we can well imagine that many of our own beliefs will turn out to be false. This theory invites the question as to *why* such beliefs and actions persist in a particular society, especially in those societies that have progressed beyond (false) religious beliefs to more refined scientific explanations.

There is another well known theory that avoids most of these problems. It not only drops the phylogenetic law but also denies that religious beliefs are rational (or intellectual) assertions about the world that are either true or false. Standing firm on the principle of verification as the semantic rule for meaning, this theory asserts that all religious beliefs and practices are nonsense. On this account, religious beliefs and practices are held to be symbolic or expressive. This theory, too, invites the question as to *why* such symbolic or expressive beliefs persist in a society. A variation of the question raised against the "intellectualist" theory appears once again: why is it the case that religious believers do not know that they should not take their beliefs and practices literally, that they are more properly understood as symbolic or expressive and thus in need of interpretation or decoding? Moreover, there seems to be no agreement among scholars as to just what the code is, or which semantic theory of religious symbols to use for a proper understanding of religion.

When we encounter this issue we are usually told that religious symbols are multivalent, that polysemy is the essence of religion. There simply is no single meaning to a religious belief, practice or symbol; the meaning is multiple. In brief, this is as much as to concede that given the nature of religion there can be no unified theory of semantics that adequately explains its meaning. However, it is important to notice that this dismissal of the problem clearly presupposes that the nature of religion is non-rational and also a theory of meaning that entails both reference and the polysemy of symbols.

Intellectualist, emotive, and other symbolic theories of religion find a nearly irresistible auxiliary theory in functionalism. Functionalist theories of religion fit in well with assumptions that religious beliefs and practices are not verifiable. Disarmingly simple, functionalism answers the question of the persistence of religions by arguing that they fulfill certain needs in the person and in the society. Any of a multiplicity of needs may be cited by functionalists, ranging from biological needs (Malinowski), to sociological/ethical needs (Durkheim), to psychological needs (Freud), to political/economic needs (Marx), and extending even to ontological needs (Eliade). Some approaches to religion combine several kinds of needs into "manifest" and "latent" ones, or into a complex set of needs. The underlying principle in all of these theories is that religious beliefs function to provide stability, maintenance, order, reduction of anxiety, survival, or coherence to human life. The meaning of religious beliefs and practices is to be explained by that which they do. The semantic emphasis in all versions of this theory accents *use*.

The popularity of this theory is in part due to the fact that it can be used by scholars who begin with individual experience (methodological individualism) such as Freud, Weber, and Malinowski, or by those who stress the social system, such as Durkheim or Radcliffe-Brown. What must be noticed is that most of the debates between these scholars are not about the basic premises of functionalism but about what the specific needs are; are they individual, social, or both? The long, often bitter, debate between Radcliffe-Brown and Malinowski, or between E. Leach and Spiro, are excellent examples of this.

Functionalism is at work in the most common assumptions ordinary people make about religion. Why do people believe in the gods? Because "it makes them feel good," we hear frequently, or "because it provides stability, and thus maintains equilibrium in the community." It is this explanation of the meaning of religion that led Durkheim to claim that "all religions are true." Indeed, the emphasis on use has led some scholars to assert that we should give up the analysis of "belief" and inquire instead into what people "do" rather than what they "say." It has led others to the odd conclusion that some religions emphasize "orthopraxis" rather than "orthodoxy" (practice rather than belief) as though practice could ever be separated from belief, or action from language, in the explanation of human behavior. In most texts, journals, newspapers, as well as television commentary on religious events, functionalism is the theory *du jour*. In the cultural sciences it has become so widespread that it is virtually the only theory of explanation appealed to even on the part of scholars who are fully aware of the logical problems inherent in it.

The logical problems pertain to two major premises in functionalist theory. First, the theory is clearly causal, a feature that gives it an empirical or scientific appearance. The core of the theory is the notion that individuals or societies, or both, have certain needs that must be satisfied. The second premise asserts that religious beliefs and/or acts function to satisfy those needs. The theory need not be teleological in its claims, retaining the rather odd notion that the cause of religion is some final end which determines its existence. Neither does the theory need to entail a quest for the origins of religion in any diachronic sense of "origin." Proponents of functionalist explanation seek to avoid such metaphysical conjectures. The theory is presented as resting on the sure foundation of all scientific method, a deductive model whose conclusions are empirically verifiable.

Literally thousands of books and articles employ functionalism as a theory for explaining the function, and thus the meaning, of religion. We have selected two essays as examples. The first essay, by Melford Spiro, is a classic simply by virtue of making explicit its use of the theory of functionalism. Spiro also encompasses both Tylor and Freud in his functional explanation of religion, thus providing the theory with greater power as well as complexity. Clifford Geertz's influential essay is included here because it too has become a classic touchstone for scholars of religion in search of a definition of religion as well as a theory of its use. The enduring appeal of Geertz's essay is evidence of how easily a theory can be simply assumed to be true and seldom subjected to further elaboration or critical evaluation. The editors' essay on Geertz attempts to remedy that.

Penner's essay concludes this section with a development of the first important critique of functionalism published by Carl Hempel in 1959. In presenting a detailed argument against the *logic* of functionalism, he shows that this form of reasoning commits the fallacy of affirming the consequent.

By the end of Part II readers will have all the critical tools necessary for making their own critique of the implicit or explicit functionalism that appears in the suggested readings.

5

Religion: Problems of Definition and Explanation

Melford Spiro

Introduction[1]

Before examining various approaches to the explanation of religion, we must first agree about what it is that we hope to be able to explain. In short, we must agree on what we mean by "religion." Anthropology, like other immature sciences—and especially those whose basic vocabulary is derived from natural languages—continues to be plagued by problems of definition. Key terms in our lexicon—"culture," "social system," "needs," "marriage," "function," and the like—continue to evoke wide differences in meaning and to instigate heated controversy among scholars. Frequently the differences and controversies stem from differences in the *types* of definition employed.

Logicians distinguish between two broad types of definition: nominal and real definitions (Hempel, 1952, pp. 2–14). Nominal definitions are those in which a word, whose meaning is unknown or unclear, is defined in terms of some expression whose meaning is already known. We all engage in such an enterprise in the classroom when we attempt to define, i.e. to assign meaning to, the new terms to which we expose our untutored undergraduates. Our concern in this case is to communicate ideas efficiently and unambiguously; and, in general, we encounter few difficulties from our students, who have no ego-involvement in alternative definitions to our own. We do have difficulties with our colleagues, however, because they—unlike us!—are ego-involved in their immortal prose and,

---

[1] Work on this paper is part of a cross-cultural study of religion supported by research grant M-2255 from the National Institutes of Health, U.S. Public Health Service.

intransigently, prefer their nominal definitions to ours. Despite their intransigence, however, the problem of achieving consensus with respect to nominal definitions is, at least in principle, easily resolved. We could, for example, delegate to an international committee of anthropologists the authority to publish a standard dictionary of anthropological concepts, whose definitions would be mandatory for publication in anthropological journals.

The problem is more serious, and its resolution correspondingly more difficult, in the case of real definitions. Unlike nominal definitions which arbitrarily assign meaning to linguistic symbols, real definitions are conceived to be true statements about entities or things. Here, three difficulties are typically encountered in anthropology (and in the other social sciences). The first difficulty arises when a hypothetical construct—such as culture or social structure—is reified and then assigned a real definition. Since that which is to be defined is not an empirically observable entity, controversies in definition admit of no empirical resolution.

A second difficulty is encountered when real definitions are of the kind that stipulate what the definer takes to be the "essential nature" of some entity. Since the notion of "essential nature" is always vague and almost always non-empirical, such definitions are scientifically useless. Kinship studies represent a good case in point, with their—at least so it seems to a non-specialist—interminable controversies concerning the essential nature of marriage, descent, corporality, and the like.

Sometimes, however, real definitions are concerned with analyzing a complex concept—which has an unambiguous empirical referent—by making explicit the constituent concepts which render its meaning. These are known as analytic definitions. Thus, the expression "*X* is a husband" can be defined as "*X* is a male human, and *X* is married to some female human." But the possible objections which such a definition would evoke among some anthropologists, at least, exemplifies the third definitional difficulty in anthropology: what might be called our obsession with universality. Since there are instances in parts of Africa of a phenomenon similar to what is ordinarily termed "marriage," but in which both partners are female, some scholars would rule out this definition on the grounds that it is culturally parochial. This insistence on universality in the interests of a comparative social science is, in my opinion, an obstacle to the comparative method for it leads to continuous changes in definition and, ultimately, to definitions which, because of their vagueness or abstractness, are all but useless. (And of course they commit the fallacy of assuming that certain institutions must, in fact, be universal, rather than recognizing that universality is a creation of definition. I am also at a loss to understand why certain institutions—marriage, for example—must be universal, while others—such as the state—need not be.)

The Problem of Definition in Religion

An examination of the endemic definitional controversies concerning religion leads to the conclusion that they are not so much controversies over the meaning either of the term "religion" or of the concept which it expresses, as they are jurisdictional disputes over the phenomenon or range of phenomena which are considered to constitute legitimately the empirical referent of the term. In short, definitional controversies in religion have generally involved differences in what are technically termed ostensive definitions. To define a word ostensively is to point to the object which that word designates. In any language community, the fiery ball in the sky, for example, evokes a univocal verbal response from all perceivers; and a stranger arriving in an English-speaking community can easily learn the ostensive definition of the word "sun" by asking any native to point to the object for which "sun" is the name. Similarly the empirical referent of "table" can be designated unequivocally, if not efficiently, by pointing to examples of each sub-set of the set of objects to which the word applies.

The community of anthropologists, however, is not a natural language community—more important, perhaps, it does not share a common culture—and although there is little disagreement among anthropologists concerning the class of objects to which such words as "sister," "chief," "string figure"—and many others—properly *do* apply, there is considerable disagreement concerning the phenomena to which the word "religion" *ought* to apply. Hence the interminable (and fruitless) controversies concerning the religious status of coercive ritual or an ethical code or supernatural beings, and so on. From the affect which characterizes many of these discussions one cannot help but suspect that much of this controversy stems, consciously or unconsciously, from extra-scientific considerations—such as the personal attitudes to religion which scholars bring to its study. Since I am concerned with the logic of inquiry, I must resist a tempting excursion into the social psychology of science.

The scientific grounds for disagreement are almost always based on comparative considerations. Thus Durkheim rejects the belief in supernatural beings as a legitimate referent of "religion" on the grounds that this would deny religion to primitive peoples who, allegedly, do not distinguish between the natural and the supernatural. Similarly, he rejects the belief in gods as a distinguishing characteristic of "religion" because Buddhism, as he interprets it, contains no such belief (1954, pp. 24–36). Such objections raise two questions; one factual, the other methodological. I shall return to the factual question in a later section, and confine my present remarks to the methodological question. Even if it were the case that Theravada Buddhism contained no belief in gods or supernatural beings, from what methodological principle does it follow that religion—or, for that matter, anything else—must be universal if it is to be studied comparatively? The fact that hunting economies, unilateral descent groups, or string figures do not have a universal distribution has not prevented us from studying *them* comparatively. Does the study of religion become any the less significant or fascinating—indeed, it would be even more fascinating—if in terms of a consensual ostensive definition it were discovered that one or seven or sixteen societies did not possess religion? If it indeed be the case that Theravada Buddhism is atheistic and that, by a theistic definition of religion, it is not therefore a religion, why can we not face, rather than shrink, from this consequence? Having combatted the notion that "we" have religion (which is "good") and "they" have superstition (which is "bad"), why should we be dismayed if it be discovered that society *x* does not have "religion," as we have defined that term? For the premise "no religion" does not entail the conclusion "therefore superstition"—nor, incidentally, does it entail the conclusion "therefore no social integration," unless of course religion is defined as anything which makes for integration. It may rather entail the conclusion "therefore science" or "therefore philosophy." Or it may entail no conclusion and, instead, stimulate some research. In short, once we free the word "religion" from all value judgments, there is reason neither for dismay nor for elation concerning the empirical distribution of religion attendant upon our definition. With respect to Theravada Buddhism, then, what loss to science would have ensued if Durkheim had decided that, as he interpreted it, it was atheistic, and therefore not a religion? I can see only gain. First, it would have stimulated fieldwork in these apparently anomalous Buddhist societies and, second, we would have been spared the confusion created by the consequent real and functional definitions of religion which were substituted for the earlier substantive or structural definitions.

Real definitions, which stipulate the "essential nature" of some phenomenon are, as I have already argued, necessarily vague and almost always non-empirical. What, for example, does Durkheim's "sacred"—which he stipulates as the essential nature of religion—really mean? How useful is it, not in religious or poetic, but in scientific discourse? It is much too vague to be taken as a primitive term in a definitional chain, and it is useless to define it by equally vague terms such as "holy" or "set apart." But if such real definitions are unsatisfactory when the phenomenal referent of the *definiendum* is universally acknowledged, they are virtually useless when, as in this case, it is the phenomenal referent which is precisely at issue. If there is no agreement about what it is that is being defined, how can we agree on its essential nature? Durkheim, to be sure, circumvented this problem by arguing that the sacred is whatever it is that a society deems to be sacred. But even if it were to be granted that one obscurity can achieve clarity by the substitution of another, real definitions of this type—like functional definitions to which I now wish to turn—escape the trap of overly narrow designate only to fall into the trap of overly broad ones.

Most functional definitions of religion are essentially a subclass of real definitions in which functional variables (the promotion of solidarity, and the like) are stipulated as the essential nature of religion. But whether the essential nature consists of a qualitative variable (such as "the sacred") or a functional variable (such as social solidarity), it is virtually impossible to set any substantive boundary to religion and, thus, to distinguish it from other sociocultural phenomena. Social solidarity, anxiety reduction, confidence in unpredictable situations, and the like, are functions which may be served by any or all cultural phenomena—Communism and Catholicism, monotheism and monogamy, images and imperialism—and unless religion is defined substantively, it would be impossible to delineate its boundaries. Indeed, even when its substantive boundaries are limited, some functional definitions impute to religion some of the functions of a total sociocultural system.

It is obvious, then, that while a definition cannot take the place of inquiry, in the absence of definitions there can be no inquiry—for it is the definition, either ostensive or nominal, which designates the phenomenon to be investigated. Thus when Evans-Pritchard writes that "objectivity" in studies of religion requires that "we build up general conclusions from particular ones" (1954, p. 9), this caution is certainly desirable for discovering empirical generalizations or for testing hypotheses. But when he tells us that "one must not ask 'what is religion?' but what are the main features of, let us say, the religion of one Melanesian people . . ." which, when compared with findings among other Melanesian peoples, will lead to generalizations about Melanesian religion, he is prescribing a strategy which, beginning with the study of that one Melanesian people cannot get started. For unless he knows, ostensively what religion is, how can our anthropologist in his Melanesian society know which, among a possible *n*, observations constitute observations of religious phenomena, rather than of some other phenomenal class, kinship, for example, or politics?

Indeed, when the term "religion" is given no explicit ostensive definition, the observer, perforce, employs an implicit one. Thus, Durkheim warns that in defining religion we must be careful not to proceed from our "prejudices, passions, or habits" (1954, p. 24). Rather, ". . . it is from the reality itself which we are going to define" (ibid.). Since any scientist—or, for that matter, any reasonable man—prefers "reality" to "prejudice," we happily follow his lead and, together with him, ". . . set ourselves before this reality" (ibid.). But since, Durkheim tells us, "religion cannot be defined except by the characteristics which are found wherever religion itself is found," we must ". . . consider the various religions in their concrete reality, and attempt to disengage that which they have in common" (ibid.). Now, the very statement of this strategy raises an obvious question. Unless we already know, by definition, what religion is, how can we know which "concrete reality" we are to "consider"? Only if religion has already been defined can we perform either this initial operation or the subsequent one of disengaging those elements which are shared by all religions.

In sum, any comparative study of religion requires, as an operation antecedent to inquiry, an ostensive or substantive definition that stipulates unambiguously those phenomenal variables which are designated by the term. This ostensive definition will, at the same time, be a nominal definition in that some of its designate will, to other scholars, appear to be arbitrary. This, then, does not remove "religion" from the arena of definitional controversy; but it does remove it from the context of fruitless controversy over what religion "really is" to the context of the formulation of empirically testable hypotheses which, in anthropology, means hypotheses susceptible to cross-cultural testing.

But this criterion of cross-cultural applicability does not entail, as I have argued above, universality. Since "religion" is a term with historically rooted meanings, a definition must satisfy not only the criterion of cross-cultural applicability but also the criterion of intra-cultural intuitivity; at the least, it should not be counter-intuitive. For me, therefore, any definition of "religion" which does not include, as a key variable, the belief in superhuman—I won't muddy the metaphysical waters with "supernatural"—beings who have power to help or harm man is counter-intuitive. Indeed, if anthropological consensus were to exclude such beliefs from the set of variables which is necessarily designated by "religion," an explanation for these beliefs would surely continue to elicit our research energies.

Even if it were the case that Theravada Buddhism postulates no such beings, I find it strange indeed, given their all-but universal distribution at every level of cultural development, that Durkheim—on the basis of this one case—should have excluded such beliefs from a definition of religion, and stranger still that others should have followed his lead. But this anomaly aside, is it the case that Buddhism contains no belief in superhuman beings? (Let us, for the sake of brevity, refer to these beings as "gods.") It is true, of course, that Buddhism contains no belief in a creator god; but creation is but one possible attribute of godhood, one which—I suspect—looms not too large in the minds of believers. If gods are important for their believers because—as I would insist is the case—they possess power greater than man's, including the power to assist man in, or prevent him from, attaining mundane and/or supermundane goals, even Theravada Buddhism—Mahayana is clearly not at issue here—most certainly contains such beliefs. With respect to supermundane goals, the Buddha is certainly a superhuman being. Unlike ordinary humans, he himself acquired the power to attain Enlightenment and, hence Buddhahood. Moreover, he showed others the means for its attainment. Without his teachings, natural man could not, unassisted, have discovered the way to Enlightenment and to final Release.

The soteriological attributes of the Buddha are, to be sure, different from those of the Judaeo-Christian-Islamic God. Whereas the latter is living, the former is dead; whereas the latter is engaged in a continuous and active process of salvation, the former had engaged in only one active ministry of salvation. But—with the exception of Calvinism—the soteriological consequences are the same. For the Buddhist and the Western religionist alike the Way to salvation was revealed by a superhuman being, and salvation can be attained only if one follows this revealed Way. The fact that in one case compliance with the Way leads directly to the ultimate goal because of the very nature of the world; and, in the other case, compliance leads to the goal only after divine intercession, should not obscure the basic similarity: in both cases man is dependent for his salvation upon the revelation of a superhuman being. (Indeed, there is reason to believe—I am now analyzing field data collected in a Burmese village which suggest that this might be the case—that Buddhist worship is not merely an expression of reverence and homage to the One who has revealed the Way, but is also a petition for His saving intercession.)

But superhuman beings generally have the power to assist (or hinder) man's attempts to attain mundane as well as super-mundane goals, and when it is asserted that Buddhism postulates no such beings, we must ask to which Buddhism this assertion has reference. Even the Buddhism of the Pali canon does not deny the existence of a wide range of superhuman beings who intervene, for good and for ill, in human affairs; it merely denies that they can influence one's salvation. More important, in contemporary Theravada countries, the Buddha himself—or, according to more sophisticated believers, his power—is believed to protect people from harm. Thus Burmese peasants recite Buddhist spells and perform rites before certain Buddha images which have the power to protect them from harm, to cure snake bites, and the like. And Buddhist monks chant passages from Scripture in the presence of the congregation which, it is believed, can bring a wide variety of worldly benefits.

There are, to be sure, atheistic Buddhist philosophies—as there are atheistic Hindu philosophies—but it is certainly a strange spectacle when anthropologists, of all people, confuse the teachings of a philosophical school with the beliefs and behavior of a religious community. And if—on some strange methodological grounds—the teachings of the philosophical schools, rather than the beliefs and behavior of the people, were to be designated as the normative religion of a society, then the numerous gods and demons to be found in the Pali canon—and in the world-view of most Theravadists, including the monastic virtuosos—find more parallels in other societies than the beliefs held by the numerically small philosophical schools.

Finally—and what is perhaps even more important from an anthropological point of view—the Pali canon is only one source for the world-view of Buddhist societies. Indeed, I know of no society in which Buddhism represents the exclusive belief system of a people. On the contrary, it is always to be found together with another system with which it maintains an important division of labor. Whereas Buddhism (restricting this term, now, to Canonical Buddhism) is concerned with supermundane goals—rebirth in a better human existence, in a celestial abode of gods, or final Release—the other system is concerned with worldly goals: the growing of crops, protection from illness, guarding of the village, etc., which are the domain of numerous superhuman beings. These are the *nats* of Burma, the *phi* of Laos and Thailand, the *neak ta* of Cambodia, etc. Although the Burmese, for example, distinguish sharply between Buddhism and *nat* worship, and although it is undoubtedly true—as most scholars argue—that these non-Buddhist belief systems represent the pre-Buddhist religions of these Theravada societies, the important consideration for our present discussion is that these beliefs, despite the long history of Buddhism in these countries, persist with undiminished strength, continuing to inform the world-view of these Buddhist societies and to stimulate important and extensive ritual activity. Hence, even if Theravada Buddhism were absolutely atheistic, it cannot be denied that Theravada Buddhists adhere to another belief system which is theistic to its core; and if it were to be argued that atheistic Buddhism—by some other criteria—is a religion and that, therefore, the belief in superhuman beings is not a necessary characteristic of "religion," it would still be the case that the belief in superhuman beings and in their power to aid or harm man is a central feature in the belief systems of all traditional societies.

But Theravada Asia provides only one example of the tenacity of such beliefs. Confucianist China provides what is, perhaps, a better example. If Theravada Buddhism is somewhat ambiguous concerning the existence and behavior of superhuman beings, Confucianism is much less ambiguous. Although the latter does not explicitly deny the existence of such beings, it certainly ignores their role in human affairs. It is more than interesting to note, therefore, that when Mahayana Buddhism was introduced into China, it was precisely its gods (including the Boddhisatvas), demons, heavens, and hells that, according to many scholars, accounted for its dramatic conquest of China. To summarize, I would argue that the belief in superhuman beings and in their power to assist or to harm man approaches universal distribution, and this belief—I would insist—is the core variable which ought to be designated by any definition of religion. Recently Horton (1960) and Goody (1961) have reached the same conclusion.

Although the belief in the existence of superhuman beings is the core religious variable, it does not follow—as some scholars have argued—that religious, in contrast to magical, behavior is necessarily other-worldly in orientation, or that, if it is otherworldly, its orientation is "spiritual." The beliefs in superhuman beings, other-worldliness, and spiritual values vary independently. Thus, ancient Judaism, despite its obsession with God's will, was essentially this-worldly in orientation. Catholicism, with all its other-worldly orientation is, with certain kinds of Hinduism, the most "materialistic" of the higher religions. Confucianism, intensely this-worldly, is yet concerned almost exclusively with such "spiritual" values as filial piety, etc. In short, superhuman beings may be conceived as primarily means or as ends. Where values are worldly, these beings may be viewed as important agents for the attainment and/or frustration of worldly goals, either "material" or "spiritual." Where values are materialistic, superhuman beings may be viewed as important agents for the attainment of material goals, either in this or in an afterlife. Where values are other-worldly, mystical union with superhuman beings may be viewed as an all consuming goal, and so on.

Although the differentiating characteristic of religion is the belief in superhuman beings, it does not follow, moreover, that these beings are necessarily objects of ultimate concern. Again, it depends on whether they are viewed as means or as ends. For those individuals whom Weber has termed "religiously musical" (Gerth &; Mills, 1946, p. 287), or whom Radin (1957, p. 9) has termed "the truly religious," superhuman beings are of ultimate concern. For the rest, however, superhuman beings are rarely of ultimate concern, although the ends for which their assistance is sought may be. Hence, though their benevolent ancestral spirits are not of great concern to the Ifaluk, restoration of health—for which these spirits are instrumental—most certainly is. Similarly, while the Buddha may not be of ultimate concern to a typical Burmese peasant, the escape from suffering—for which He is instrumental—can certainly be so designated.

Conversely, while religious beliefs are not always of ultimate concern, non-religious beliefs sometimes are. This raises a final unwarranted conclusion, viz. that religion uniquely refers to the "sacred," while secular concerns are necessarily "profane." Thus, if "sacred" refers to objects and beliefs of ultimate concern, and "profane" to those of ordinary concern, religious and secular beliefs alike may have reference either to sacred or to profane phenomena. For the members of Kiryat Yedidim, an Israeli *kibbutz,* the triumph of the proletariat, following social revolution, and the ultimate classless society in which universal brotherhood, based on loving kindness, will replace parochial otherhood, based on competitive hostility, constitutes their sacred belief system. But, by definition, it is not a religious belief system, since it has no reference to—indeed, it denies the existence of—superhuman beings.

Similarly, if communism, or baseball, or the stockmarket are of ultimate concern to some society, or to one of its constituent social groups, they are, by definition, sacred. But beliefs concerning communism, baseball, or the stockmarket are not, by definition, religious beliefs, because they have no reference to superhuman beings. They may, of course, serve many of the functions served by religious beliefs; and they are, therefore, members of the same functional class. Since however, they are, substantively dissimilar, it would be as misleading to designate them by the same term as it would be to designate music and sex by the same term because they both provide sensual pleasure. (Modern American society presents an excellent example of the competition of sports, patriotism, sex, and God for the title, perhaps not exclusively, of "the sacred." Indeed, if the dictum of Miss Jane Russell is taken seriously—God, she informs us, is a "livin' doll"—I would guess that, whichever wins, God is bound to lose.)

A Definition of Religion

On the assumption that religion is a cultural institution, and on the further assumption that all institutions—though not all of their features—are instrumental means for the satisfaction of needs, I shall define "religion" as "an institution consisting of culturally patterned interaction with culturally postulated superhuman beings." I should like to examine these variables separately.

Institution. This term implies, of course, that whatever phenomena we might wish to designate by "religion," religion is an attribute of social groups, comprising a component part of their cultural heritage; and that its component features are acquired by means of the same enculturation processes as the other variables of a cultural heritage are acquired. This means that the variables constituting a religious system have the same ontological status as those of other cultural systems: its beliefs are normative, its rituals collective, its values prescriptive. This, I take it, is what Durkheim (1954, p. 44) had in mind in insisting that there can be no religion without a church. (It means, too, as I shall observe in a later section, that religion has the same methodological status as other cultural systems; i.e. religious variables are to be explained by the same explanatory schemata—historical, structural, functional, and causal—as those by which other cultural variables are explained.)

Interaction. This term refers to two distinct, though related, types of activity. First, it refers to activities which are believed to carry out, embody, or to be consistent with the will or desire of superhuman beings or powers. These activities reflect the putative *value system* of these superhuman beings and, presumably, they constitute part—but only part—of the actors' value system. These activities may be viewed as desirable in themselves and/or as means for obtaining the assistance of superhuman beings or for protection against their wrath. Second it refers to activities which are believed to influence superhuman beings to satisfy the needs of the actors. These two types of activity may overlap, but their range is never coterminous. Where they do overlap, the action in the overlapping sphere is, in large measure, symbolic; that is, it consists in behavior whose meaning, cross-culturally viewed, is obscure and/or arbitrary; and whose efficacy, scientifically viewed, is not susceptible of ordinary scientific "proof." These symbolic, but definitely instrumental, activities constitute, of course, a *ritual,* or symbolic *action, system.*

Unlike private rituals, such as those found in an obsessive-compulsive neurosis, religious rituals are culturally patterned; i.e. both the activities and their meaning are shared by the members of a social group by virtue of their acquisition from a shared cultural heritage.

Superhuman beings. These refer to any beings believed to possess power greater than man, who can work good and/or evil on man, and whose relationships with man can, to some degree, be influenced by the two types of activity described in the previous section. The belief of any religious actor in the existence of these beings and his knowledge concerning their attributes are derived from and sanctioned by the cultural heritage of his social group. To that extent—and regardless of the objective existence of these beings, or of personal experiences which are interpreted as encounters with them—their existence is culturally postulated. Beliefs concerning the existence and attributes of these beings, and of the efficacy of certain types of behavior (ritual, for example) in influencing their relations with man, constitute a *belief system.*

This brief explication of our definition of "religion" indicates that, viewed systemically, religion can be differentiated from other culturally constituted institutions by virtue only of its reference to superhuman beings. All institutions consist of *belief systems,* i.e. an enduring organization of cognitions about one or more aspects of the universe; *action systems,* an enduring organization of behavior patterns designed to attain ends for the satisfaction of needs; and *value systems,* an enduring organization of principles by which behavior can be judged on some scale of merit. Religion differs from other institutions in that its three component systems have reference to superhuman beings.

Having defined "religion," our next task is to examine the types of explanation that have been offered to account for its existence. First, however, we must answer some elementary questions concerning the nature of anthropological explanation.

Explanation of Social Anthropology

What do anthropologists attempt to explain? Of what do explanations consist? How do these explanations differ from each other? Once we penetrate beneath our jargon, it appears that always the phenomenon to be explained is *(a)* the *existence* of some social or cultural variable, and *(b)* the *variability* which it exhibits in a cross-cultural distribution. These statements of course are really one, because the variable "exists" in the range of values which it can assume. If a theory purports to explain the existence of religion, but its concepts are so general or so vague that it cannot explain the variability exhibited by its empirical instances, it is disqualified as a *scientific*, i.e. a testable, theory.

"Existence" is an ambiguous term. In asking for an explanation for the existence of religion, we might be asking how it came to exist in the first place—this is the question of religious origins—or how it is that it exists (i.e. has persisted) in some ethnographic present. Since a testable, i.e. scientific, theory of religious origins will probably always elude our explanatory net, this paper will be concerned with the persistence, not the origin, of religion.

In all of our explanations, to answer the second question, we stipulate a condition or a set of conditions in whose absence the variable to be explained would not exist. Now, to say that any sociocultural variable—religion, for example—"exists" is, in the last analysis, to say that in some society—or, in one of its constituent social groups—a proposition is affirmed, a norm complied with, a custom performed, a role practiced, a spirit feared, etc. In short, the "existence" of a sociocultural variable means that in any sense of "behavior"—cognitive, affective, or motor—there occurs some behavior in which, or by which, the variable in question is instanced. Hence, a theory of the "existence" of religion must ultimately be capable of explaining religious "behavior."

In general, theories of the existence—in the sense of persistence—of sociocultural variables are cast in four explanatory modes: historical (in the documentary, not the speculative, sense), structural, causal, and functional. When analyzed, the first two can be reduced to either the third or the fourth. Thus historical explanations are either no explanation at all, or they are causal explanations. Surely, the mere listing of a series of events which are antecedent to the appearance of the variable in question does not constitute explanation—unless it can be shown that one or more of these events was a condition, either necessary or sufficient, for its appearance. If this can be demonstrated, the explanation is based on a causal theory, the fact of its having originated in the past being incidental to the theoretical aim of explaining a certain type of social or cultural innovation.

The key term here is "innovation." Although a causal explanation of the historical type may account for the existence of some sociocultural variable during the period in which it made its appearance, it is not a sufficient explanation for its persistence into a later period—no more than a genetic explanation for the birth of an organism is a sufficient explanation for its persistence. Thus while a historico-genetic explanation is necessary to account for Burma's adoption of Buddhism, it cannot account for its persistence nine hundred years later. Alternatively, historical data explain why it is that the Burmese, if they practice any religion at all, practice Buddhism rather than, for example, Christianity; but they do not explain why they practice any religion at all—and, therefore, they do not explain why they practice Buddhism.

Structural explanations, too, can be reduced either to causal or to functional modes. Those structural accounts which delineate the configuration in, or relationships among, a set of sociocultural variables are essentially descriptive rather than explanatory—unless of course some theory, causal or functional, is offered to explain the configuration. Structural explanations which purport to explain some variable by means of a structural "principle"—such as the principle of the unity of the sibling group—are either verbal labels which at best order a set of data according to a heuristic scheme; or they are phenomenological "principles" of the actors (cognitive maps), in which case they comprise a cognitive sub-set in a set of causal variables. Similarly, structural explanations which stipulate some variable as a "structural requirement" of a system, on the one hand, or as a "structural implication," on the other, can be shown to be either causal or functional respectively.

This brings us, then, to causal and functional explanations. Causal explanations attempt to account for some sociocultural variable by reference to some antecedent conditions—its "cause." Functional explanations account for the variable by reference to some consequent condition—its "function." (For a detailed analysis of the logic of causal and functional explanation, cf. Spiro, 1963.)

How, then, is the existence of religion to be explained, causally or functionally? The answer depends, I believe, on which aspect of a religion is to be explained.

Typically, explanations for the existence of religion have been addressed to one or both of two questions. (*a*) On what grounds are religious propositions believed to be true? That is, what are the grounds for the belief that superhuman beings with such-and-such characteristics exist, and what ritual is efficacious in influencing their behavior? (*b*) What is the explanation for the practice of religion? That is, what is the basis for belief in superhuman beings, and for the performance of religious rituals? These questions, though clearly related—religious practice presupposes religious cognitions —are yet distinct; and they probably require different types of explanation.

The "Truth" of Religious Beliefs

Every religious system consists, in the first instance, of a cognitive system, i.e. it consists of a set of explicit and implicit propositions concerning the superhuman world and of man's relationship to it, which it claims to be true. These include beliefs in superhuman beings of various kinds, of rituals of a wide variety, of existences—both prior and subsequent to the present existence—and the like. To the extent that documentary evidence is available, it is possible to discover a testable explanation for their origin and their variability. Since, for most of man's religions, however, such evidence is lacking, explanations are necessarily speculative. I shall be concerned, therefore, with explanations for their persistence.

This cognitive system, or parts of it, is of course acquired by the members of a group, and, on the individual level, it becomes a "culturally constituted belief system." It is a "belief" system because the propositions are believed to be true; and it is "culturally constituted" because the propositions are acquired from this culturally provided religious system. But the latter fact, surely, is not a sufficient basis for the belief that these propositions are true. Children are taught about many things which, when they grow up—often, before they grow up—they discard as so much nonsense. The fact that my personal belief system is acquired from my society explains why it is that the existence of the Lord Krishna rather than that of the Virgin Mary is one of the propositions I believe to be true; it does not explain the grounds on which I believe in the existence of superhuman beings of any kind, whether Krishna or the Virgin.

The notion of "need" fares no better as an explanation. A need, in the sense of desire, may provide the motivational basis for the acquisition of a taught belief, but it cannot establish its truth. Similarly, a need, in the sense of a functional requirement of society, may explain the necessity for some kind of religious proposition(s), but—even if this need is recognized and its satisfaction is intended—it does not explain why the proposition is believed to be true.

Most theorists seem to agree that religious statements are believed to be true because religious actors have had social experiences which, corresponding to these beliefs, provide them with face validity. Thus Durkheim and Freud, agreeing that the cognitive roots of religious belief are to be found in social experience, disagree only about the structural context of the experience. Durkheim (1954) argues that the two essential attributes of the gods—they are beings more powerful than man, upon whom man can depend—are the essential attributes of society; it is in society that man experiences these attributes. These attributes are personified in superhuman beings, or imputed to extra-social powers, because of highly affective collective experiences in which the physical symbols of the group are taken to be symbolic of the one or the other. Freud (1928), emphasizing man's helplessness in a terrifying world, stresses the importance of personifying these terrifying forces so that, on a human analogy, they can be controlled. These personifications—the gods—reflect the child's experience with an all-powerful human being, his father.

In both Freud and Durkheim, then, society is the cause for the fixation of religious belief. It is ironical to observe, however, that it is Freud rather than Durkheim who anchors this experience within a specified structural unit, the family. In general, I believe that Freud has the better case. To be sure, his ethnocentric conception of patriarchal fathers, and of gods reflecting this conception of "father," is entirely inadequate for comparative analysis: but the general theory which can be generated from this ethnocentric model is both adequate and, I believe, essentially correct. The theory, briefly, is that it is in the context of the family that the child experiences powerful beings, both benevolent and malevolent, who—by various means which are learned in the socialization process—can sometimes be induced to accede to his desires. These experiences provide the basic ingredients for his personal projective system (Kardiner, 1945) which, if it corresponds (structurally, not substantively) to his taught beliefs, constitutes the cognitive and perceptual set for the acceptance of these beliefs. Having had personal experience with "superhuman beings" and with the efficacy of "ritual," the taught beliefs re-enforce, and are re-enforced by, his own projective system (Spiro, 1953).

This theory is superior to Durkheim's, first, in its ability to explain these latter two nuclear religious variables. It is difficult to see how they can be deduced from Durkheim's theory. More important, even if they were deducible, it is difficult to see how Durkheim's theory can explain their cross-cultural variability. Since the antecedent condition—a power greater than man upon which man can rely—is a constant, how can it explain the consequent condition—religious belief—which is a variable? Hence, although the general theory may be true, there is a serious question concerning what empirical operations, if any, would permit us to decide whether it is true or false. The Freudian-derived theory, on the other hand, *is* capable of explaining cross-cultural differences and, therefore, it can be tested empirically. If personal projective systems, which form the basis for religious belief, are developed in early childhood experiences, it can be deduced that differences in religious beliefs will vary systematically with differences in family (including socialization) systems which structure these experiences. A number of anthropological field studies have been able to test—and have confirmed—this conclusion. And one need not go so far astray as personality-and-culture studies to find the evidence. In his illuminating analysis of Tallensi religion, Fortes (1959, p. 78) concludes that, "All the concepts and beliefs we have examined are religious extrapolations of the experiences generated in the relationships between parents and children."

As important as they are, case studies do not constitute rigorous proof of theories. The cross-cultural method, in which large samples can be used for statistical testing of hypotheses, is more rigorous. A fairly large number of hypotheses, predicting religious variables—the character of supernatural beings, the means (performance of rituals or compliance with norms) which are believed to influence them, the conception of ritual (coercive or propitiatory) and the like—from child-training variables have been tested by this method, and many of them have been confirmed. (These studies are summarized in Whiting, 1961.)

Despite the differences between Freud and Durkheim, both propose causal explanations of the credibility of religious cognitions, in which society, as cause, produces a religious (cognitive) effect by means of psychological processes—in one case, in the *feeling* of dependency; in the other, in the feeling of dependency combined with the personal *projection* of nuclear experiences. For both theorists the independent, sociological, variable may be said to "cause" the dependent, religious, variable by means of a set of intervening, psychological, variables.

Before passing to the next section it is necessary to counter one assumption which is often linked to this type of explanation, but which is not entailed by it. From the hypothesis that the antecedent condition for belief in superhuman beings is to be found in specified sociological variables, it does not follow that for the believer these beings are identical with, have reference to, or are symbolic of these variables. To put it bluntly, the fact that conceptions of God have their roots in society does not mean that *for the believer* society is God, or that God is merely a symbol of society, or that society is the true object of religious worship. Freud never said this, nor—despite some claims to the contrary—did Durkheim. Hence, it is no refutation of Durkheim's sociological hypothesis—as Horton (1960, p. 204) believes it to be—that for the Kalabari—and, I would add, for every other people—the statement "I believe in God" does not imply, "I subscribe to the system of structural symbolism of which this belief statement is part."[2]

Similarly it is not only among the Kalabari that a person who uses belief or ritual "merely to make a statement about social relations or about his own structural alignment" is viewed as one who "does not really believe" (ibid., p. 203). Indeed the contrary notion is so absurd that it is difficult to believe that it could be proposed by anyone who has personally observed a Micronesian exorcising a malevolent ghost, a Catholic penitent crawling on hands and knees to worship at the shrine of Our Lady of Guadalupe, an Orthodox Jew beating his breast on Yom Kippur to atone for his sins, a Burmese spirit-medium dancing in a trance before a *nat* image. And yet, Leach, writing of Kachin spirits, insists (1954, p. 189) that "the various nats of Kachin religious ideology are, in the last analysis *nothing more* than ways of describing the formal relationships that exist between real persons and real groups in ordinary Kachin society" (italics mine). For Leach, then, not only are religious beliefs derived from social structure, but the only referent of these beliefs, even for the believer, is social structure. Since Leach has, I am sure,

---

[2] In any case, Durkheim's sociology of religion is unconcerned with structural symbolism. It is concerned with society as a collectivity, not as a configuration of structural units; with collective representations, not with social structure.

observed as many manifestations of religious belief as I have, what are we to make of this extraordinary statement? I should like to suggest that this assertion reflects a confusion between the *practice* of religion and its *manipulation;* and although the former may be of as much interest to the student of religion as the latter, not to recognize this distinction is to sow confusion.

Leach, it will be recalled, interprets Kachin religion as almost exclusively an instrument in the political struggle for power and prestige. That theology, myth, or ritual may be manipulated for prestige and power, and that the latter drives may provide motivational bases for their persistence are documented facts of history and ethnology. But the manipulation of religion for political ends tells us more about politics than about religion. In the former, religion is used *as a means,* in the latter *religious means* are used, for the attainment of certain ends. (Indeed, they may both be instrumental for the same end.) This is an essential distinction. The differential characteristic of religious, compared with other types of instrumental, behavior consists in an attempt to enlist the assistance, or to execute the will, of superhuman beings. Indeed, by what other criterion *could* religious, be distinguished from non-religious, behavior? Surely not in terms of ends: with the exception of mysticism (confined to religious virtuosos) the range of mundane ends for which religion, cross-culturally viewed, is conceived to be instrumental is as broad as the range of all human ends. My argument, then, is not that political power is disqualified as a *religious end,* but that any attempt to achieve this end by means which do not entail a belief in the existence of superhuman beings is disqualified as *religious means.* A Kachin headman may attempt to manipulate myths and *nats* in order to validate his, or his clan's claim to power and authority; but this political behavior is to be distinguished from his religious behavior, which consists in his belief in the existence of the *nats,* and in his propitiation of them, both at local shrines and during *manaus.* Indeed, only because Kachins do believe that the verbal symbol *nat* has reference to an existential being—and is not merely a social structural symbol—is it possible to manipulate this belief for political ends.

The Practice of Religious Belief

The religious actor not only believes in the truth of propositions about superhuman beings, but he also believes in these beings—they are objects of concern: he trusts in God, he fears and hates Satan. Similarly, he not only believes in the efficacy of ritual, but he performs rituals. Explanations for religion, then, are addressed not only to the truth of religious propositions but also—and more frequently—to certain practices. In order to explain the practice of religion, we must be able to explain the practice of any sociocultural variable.[3]

All human behavior, except for reflexive behavior, is purposive; i.e. it is instigated by the intention of satisfying some need. If a given response is in fact instrumental for the satisfaction of the need, this reinforcement of the response ensures its persistence—it becomes an instance of a behavior pattern. The motivational basis for the practice of a behavior pattern, then, is not merely the intention of satisfying a need, but the expectation that its performance will in fact achieve this end. Institutional behavior, including religious behavior, consists in the practice of repeated instances of culturally constituted behavior

---

[3] The notion that religion necessarily eludes the net of naturalistic explanation, though implicit in certain recent anthropological writing, is beginning to find explicit expression. Thus, Turner (1962, p. 92) claims that "one has to consider religious phenomena in terms of religious ideas and doctrines, and not only, or principally, in terms of disciplines which have arisen in connection with the study of secular institutions and processes. . . . Religion is not *determined* by anything other than itself, though the religious find *expression* sensory phenomena. . . . We must be prepared to accept the fruits of simple wisdom with gratitude and not try to reduce them to their chemical constituents, thereby destroying their essential quality as fruits, and their virtue as food."

To say that religion is determined by religion is surely as meaningless as to say that tables are determined by tables, or that social structure is determined by social structure. But even if this statement is an ellipsis for a meaningful one, I would have thought that the determinants of religion are to be established empirically rather than by verbal assertion. I would have thought, too, that to "reduce" religion to its chemical constituents—which, I take it, refers to the discovery of its social and psychological bases—is precisely the task of the student of culture. I would not have thought that for the religionist—and the anthropologist, *qua* anthropologist, is of course neither a religionist nor an anti-religionist—the reduction of religion to its social and psychological "constituents" destroys its "essential quality," any more than the "reduction" of a Brandenburg concerto to its physical "constituents" destroys its "essential quality" for the lover of Bach.

patterns—or customs. Like other behavior patterns they persist as long as they are practiced; and they are practiced because they satisfy, or are believed to satisfy, their instigating needs. If this is so, an explanation for the practice of religion must be sought in the set of needs whose expected satisfaction motivates religious belief and the performance of religious ritual.[4]

Needs

As a concept in the social sciences, need has been borrowed from two sources: biology and psychology. Its ambiguity as a social science concept stems from a confusion in its two possible meanings. In biology "need" refers to what might be termed a "want," i.e. to some requirement which must be satisfied if an organism is to survive. In psychology, on the other hand, it refers to what might be termed a "desire," i.e. a wish to satisfy some felt drive by the attainment of some goal. These two meanings may, of course, overlap. Thus water satisfies an organic want and it may also be the object of desire. Just as frequently, however, they do not overlap. The circulation of the blood is a want, but—for most animals, at any rate—it is not the object of desire. In sociological and, especially, in functionalist discourse, much confusion has resulted from not distinguishing these two meanings of "need" when it is applied to society. In this paper I shall, when clarity does not suffer, use the generic "need" to refer both to sociological wants and to psychological desires. Otherwise, I shall use "sociological want" to refer to any functional requirement of society; and I shall use "desire" in its motivational sense. I hasten to add that desires are not

---

[4] There is, of course, no convincing evidence for the existence of a distinctively "religious need." That the belief in superhuman beings corresponds to and satisfies a "need" for a belief in them is an unfounded instinctivist assumption. Nor is there any evidence for the assumption that the motivational basis for religious action, or the affect which it arouses, are unique. The meager evidence from religious psychology suggests that any drive or affect connected with religious behavior is also found in such activities as science, warfare, sex, art, politics, and others. The "religious thrill" which Lowie (1924) and others have pointed to as a differentiating characteristic of religion is still to be documented. A clinical psychologist, commenting on still another set of data remarks: "Some of our tests seem able to tap fairly deep levels of personality functioning, and yet we rarely encounter a clearly religious response to our Rorschach and Thematic Apperception tests. . . . For the psychology of religion this means that the clinical psychologist will not readily be able to furnish new data" (Pruyser, 1960, p. 122).

necessarily "selfish," oriented to the welfare of the self. The goal, by whose attainment a drive is satisfied, may be—and, obviously, it often is—the welfare of an entire group, or of one or more of its constituent members.

We may now return to our question. If the practice of religion is instigated by the expectation of satisfying needs, by which set of needs—desires or wants—is its practice to be explained? It should be perfectly obvious that although behavior can *satisfy* both wants and desires, it is motivated by desires, not by wants. Wants in themselves have no causal properties. The absorption of moisture, for example, is a functional requirement of plants; but this requirement cannot cause the rains to fall. Human behavior, to be sure, is different from the growth of plants. A social group may recognize the existence of some, at least, of its functional requirements, and these recognized wants may constitute a set of stimulus conditions which evoke responses for their satisfaction. Notice, however, that it is not the functional requirement—even when it is recognized—which evokes the response, but rather the wish to satisfy it. A functional requirement of society becomes a stimulus for a response, i.e. it acquires motivational value if, and only if (*a*) it is recognized, and (*b*) its satisfaction becomes an object of desire. If the functional requirement of social solidarity, for example, is not recognized, or, if recognized, it is not an object of desire, or, although both recognized and desired, it is not the desire whose intended satisfaction motivates the practice of the variable to be explained, it cannot be used to explain behavior, even though need-satisfaction may be one of its consequences. If social solidarity is a consequence—an unintended consequence—of the practice of religion, social solidarity is properly explained by reference to the religious behavior by which it is achieved; but religion, surely, is improperly explained by reference to social solidarity. An unintended consequence of behavior—however important it may be—can hardly be its cause. If religious behavior is to be explained by reference to those functions which it serves—and, indeed, it must be—the functions must be those that are intended, not those that are unintended (and probably unrecognized). We must, therefore, remind ourselves of some elementary distinctions among functions.

Functions

I should like, first, to distinguish between "psychological" and "sociological" functions. The psychological functions of behavior consist in the satisfaction of desires;[5] its sociological functions consist in the satisfaction of functional requirements.

Second, I should like to distinguish between "manifest" and "latent" functions. In his now-classic analysis of functional explanation, Merton (1957) distinguished between intended and recognized functions—which he termed "manifest"—and unintended and unrecognized functions—which he termed "latent." Merton's dichotomous classification can be shown to yield a four-class functional typology. In addition to intended-recognized and unintended-unrecognized functions, we can also distinguish intended-unrecognized and unintended-recognized functions (Spiro, 1961a). The latter is a simple concept to grasp; social solidarity may be a recognized function of religious ritual, for example, although the intention of satisfying this functional requirement may not motivate its performance. An intended-unrecognized function, however, seems paradoxical. Assuming that intentions may be conscious as well as unconscious, this paradox is more apparent than real: if a behavior pattern is unconsciously motivated—or, more realistically, if its motivational set includes both conscious and unconscious intentions—one of its functions, although intended, is unrecognized.

The final distinction I should like to make is between real and apparent functions. "Real functions" are those which, in principle at least, can be discovered by the anthropologist, whether or not they are recognized by the actors. "Apparent functions" are those which the actors attribute to the sociocultural variable in question, but which cannot be confirmed by scientific investigation.

With these distinctions in mind, we may now attempt to answer the question with which we began this section. If institutional behavior in general is motivated by the expectation of satisfying desires, to what extent can religious behavior, specifically, be explained within this framework? That is, what desires are satisfied

[5] That a function is psychological does not mean that the object of desire is psychological. The object of desire may be political, meteorological, economic, nutritional, sexual—and all other goals known to man. These goals are cathected because they satisfy some drive, acquired or innate. The attainment of the goal reduces the drive or, alternatively, satisfies the desire. The satisfaction of the desire—or, more realistically, the set of desires—whose intended (conscious or unconscious) satisfaction instigates behavior is its psychological function.

by religion? Since this question remains one of the unfinished tasks of empirical research, I can only make some tentative suggestions. As I interpret the record, I would suggest that there are at least three sets of desires which are satisfied by religion and which—for lack of better terms—I shall call cognitive, substantive, and expressive. The corresponding functions of religion can be called adjustive, adaptive, and integrative.

Cognitive

I believe that it can be shown that everywhere man has a desire to know, to understand, to find meaning;[6] and I would suggest—although this is a terribly old-fashioned nineteenth-century idea—that religious beliefs are held, and are of "concern," to religious actors because, *in the absence of competitive explanations,* they satisfy this desire. Religious belief systems provide the members of society with meaning and explanation for otherwise meaningless and inexplicable phenomena.

"Meaning," of course, is often used in two senses. It may be used in an exclusively cognitive sense, as when one asks for the meaning of a natural phenomenon, of a historical event, of a sociological fact. In this sense, it has the connotation of "explanation," as that word is typically used. But "meaning" is also used in a semantic-affective sense, as when one asks for the meaning of unequal life-fates, frustration, or death. The phenomena for which religion provides meaning, in this second sense of "meaning," have been classified by Weber under the general rubric of "suffering" (Gerth & Mills, 1946, Ch. 11). The main function of the higher religions, he argues, is to provide meaning for suffering (and some means to escape from or to transcend it).

Although the range of phenomena for which religious beliefs provide meaning in the first, explanatory, sense of "meaning,"

---

[6] The most striking evidence, on the simplest perceptual level, of this need for meaning is provided by the cross-cultural use of the Rorschach test. As Hallowell has observed (1956, pp. 476–488), the most dramatic finding of cross-cultural Rorschach investigations is that at every level of technological and cultural development in which this test has been administered, subjects have attempted to offer meaningful responses to what are, objectively, meaningless ink-blots. The insistence, even on the part of primitive peoples, on finding meaning in what is for them an exotic task—something concerning which many anthropologists had been skeptical—is certainly consistent with the assumption concerning a universal need for meaning.

occupies a broad spectrum, some structuralists hold to the peculiar notion that man's curiosity is so limited that religious explanations, regardless of their ostensible meaning, are concerned almost exclusively with phenomena of social structure. Again I should like to use an example from Leach—although the example concerns magical rather than religious belief—because, with his usual verve, he adopts what I would think to be an extreme position.

In his highly critical evaluation of Frazer, Leach (1961) tells us that Frazer (and Roth, too) is naïve in interpreting Australian explanations for conception as in fact referring to conception—and, therefore, as reflecting ignorance of physiological paternity. According to the "modern interpretation," their notions of conception are to be seen, not as biological, but as sociological, statements. Let us examine the ethnographic facts, as Leach (p. 376) quotes them from Roth. Among the Tully River Blacks,

> A woman begets children because *(a)* she has been sitting over the fire on which she has roasted a particular species of black bream, which must have been given to her by the prospective father, *(b)* she has purposely gone a-hunting and caught a certain kind of bull-frog, (c) some man may have told her to be in an interesting condition, or (d) she may dream of having the child put inside her.

Both Frazer and Roth agree—and, I may add, I agree with them—that these statements are addressed to the problem to which they appear to be addressed—the problem of conception; and they agree that from these statements it may validly be deduced that the aborigines are ignorant of physiological paternity, believing rather that conception is the result of four kinds of "magical" causation. Leach will have none of this. For him (ibid.) it is not

> a legitimate inference to assert that these Australian aborigines were ignorant of the connection between copulation and pregnancy. The modern interpretation of the rituals described would be that in this society the relationship between the woman's child and the clansmen of the woman's husband stems from public recognition of the bonds of marriage, rather than from the fact of cohabitation, which is a very normal state of affairs.

The logic of this "modern interpretation" is certainly not evident to me. Ignoring the fact that only two of the four explanatory beliefs have reference to a male—so that they, at least, are hardly susceptible of this modern interpretation—by what evidence or from what inference can it be concluded that the other two statements mean what Leach claims that they mean? Is this the interpretation which the aborigines place on these beliefs? There is certainly no evidence for this assumption. Perhaps, then, this is the meaning which they intended to convey, even though they did not do so explicitly? But even if we were to grant that, for some strange reason, aborigines prefer to express structural relationships by means of biological symbolism, how do we *know* that this was their intention? Perhaps, then, the symbolism is unconscious, and the structural meaning which Leach claims for these beliefs, although intentional, is latent? This interpretation is certainly congenial to other "modern interpretations." Again, however, we are hung up on the problem of evidence. From what ethnographic data, or from what psychological theory of the unconscious, can this meaning be inferred? If, then, there is no way of *demonstrating* that either the manifest or the latent content of these symbols has reference to the structural relationship between a woman's children and the clansmen of her husband, I am compelled to discard this interpretation as not only implausible but false. I shall insist, instead, that the aborigines are indeed ignorant of physiological paternity, and that the four statements quoted in Roth are in fact proffered explanations for conception.

Substantive

The most obvious basis for religious behavior is the one which any religious actor tells us about when we ask him—and, unlike some anthropologists, I believe him. He believes in superhuman beings and he performs religious ritual in order that he may satisfy, what I am calling, substantive desires: desires for rain, nirvana, crops, heaven, victory in war, recovery from illness, and countless others. Everywhere man's mammalian desires (those which can be satisfied by naturalistic goals) must be satisfied, and *in the absence of competing technologies which confer reasonable confidence,* religious techniques are believed to satisfy these desires. Almost everywhere, moreover, the human awareness of the cessation of existence and/or of the unsatisfactory character of existence, produces anxiety concerning the persistence of existence (in some cases, it is desired; in others, it is not desired), and *in the absence of competing goals for the reduction of anxiety,* belief that one is successfully pursuing these religious goals (heaven-like or nirvana-like states) serves to reduce this anxiety.

Most, if not all, of these substantive desires, then, can be classified as attempts to overcome or transcend suffering. The religious actor wishes to overcome specific suffering—economic, political, physical, and the like; and he wishes to transcend more general suffering induced by some conception of life and the world as being evil, frustrating, sinful, and so on. Religion, as Weber (op. cit.) points out, not only provides an explanation for, but it also promises redemption from, suffering. Religious techniques—performance of ritual, compliance with morality, faith, meditation, etc.—are the means by which this promise is felt to be fulfilled.

For the religious actor, if we can believe him, the expectation of realizing this promise is the most important motivational basis for religious behavior; the realization of this promise is its function. For him, it is an intended and recognized function. Believing in its reality, he clings tenaciously to his religious beliefs and practices—however irrational they may seem, and however dysfunctional with respect to other ends their consequences may be. From the anthropologist's point of view—and this is what presents such a knotty problem to many classical functionalists—these functions are apparent; they are not real. Ritual cannot effect rainfall, prayer cannot cure organic diseases, nirvana is a figment of the imagination, etc. It is this seeming irrationality of religion and, therefore, the apparent—rather than real—nature of its intended functions, that has given rise, I believe, to misplaced emphases on the importance of its sociological functions. Thus, despite Merton's incisive analysis of functional theory, it is highly questionable if the persistence of Hopi rain ceremonies is to be explained by the social integration to which *he* (Merton) thinks their performance is conducive (their real, but latent, functions), rather than by the meteorological events to which *Hopi* think they are conducive (their manifest, but apparent, functions).

The Hopi belief in the efficacy of their rainmaking ritual is not irrational—although it is certainly false—because the conclusion, rain ceremonies cause the rains to fall, follows validly from a world-view whose major premise states that gods exist, and whose minor premise states that the behavior of the gods can be influenced by rituals. That the premises are false does not render them irrational—until or unless they are disconfirmed by evidence. But all available "evidence" confirms their validity: whenever the ceremonies are performed it does, indeed, rain. Hence, given their "behavioral environment" (Hallowell, 1955, pp. 75-110), Hopi beliefs are not irrational; and given their ecological environment, the apparent function of these ceremonies is surely a sufficient explanation for their persistence. (For further argument, see Spiro, 1964.)

If it is not sufficient, however, no appeal to unintended sociological functions will provide us with a better explanation—indeed, as we have already seen, it can provide us with no explanation at all. For how can the function of social solidarity explain the practice of these—or of any other—rituals? Notice that the objection to such an explanation is not that social solidarity may not be an object of desire—there is no reason why it cannot; and it is not that social solidarity is not achieved by the practice of these rituals—it often is. The objection, rather, is that the achievement of this end is *not* the desire which the practice of *these* rituals is intended to satisfy. Surely, not even the proponents of this type of explanation would suggest that Hopi rain ceremonies, sacrifices to Kali, exorcism of demons, celebration of the Mass, and the like are practiced with the conscious intention of achieving social solidarity. Is it suggested, then, that this is their unconscious intention? I would doubt that anyone would make this suggestion, for this suggests that if the efficacy of these rituals for the attainment of their designated ends were to be disbelieved, they would nevertheless be performed so that their solidarious functions might be served. This argument surely cannot be sustained. I can only conclude, then, that the persistence of these rituals is explicable by reference to what, for anthropologists, are their apparent, rather than their real, functions.[7]

Even if it were to be conceded that institutions must have real, rather than apparent, functions, anthropologists must surely be aware of those real functions of ritual which *are* recognized by religious actors and which may, therefore, reenforce their practice. For although religious ritual may not, in fact, be efficacious for the elimination of poverty, the restoration of health, the bringing of rain, and the like, the belief that it does achieve these ends serves the important psychological (real) function of reducing hopelessness—

---

[7] One might, of course, wish to defend the weaker thesis, viz. that if these practices were sociologically dysfunctional, they would eventually disappear. Even this thesis is somewhat doubtful, however, when applied to multi-religious societies in which the practice of religion, however solidarious it may be for each religious group, has important dysfunctional consequences for the total social system. Still these religions persist, and with undiminished vigor, despite—one is tempted to say, because of—these consequences.

and its attendant anxiety—concerning their otherwise impossible attainment.

Expressive

A third set of desires which, I would suggest, constitutes a motivational source of religious behavior consists of painful drives which seek reduction and painful motives which seek satisfaction. By "painful drives" I refer to those fears and anxieties concerning which psychoanalysis has taught us so much: fears of destruction and of one's own destructiveness, castration anxiety, cataclysmic fantasies, and a host of other infantile and primitive fears which threaten to overpower the weak and defenseless ego of the young child and which, if they become too overwhelming, result in schizophrenic and paranoid breakdown. By "painful motives" I refer to those motives which, because culturally forbidden—prohibited forms of aggression, dependency, (Oedipal) sexuality, and the like—arouse feelings of shame, inadequacy, and moral anxiety. These drives and motives are much too painful to remain in consciousness and they are generally rendered unconscious. Although unconscious, they are not extinguished; they continue to seek reduction and satisfaction.

In the absence of other, or of more efficient means, religion is the vehicle—in some societies, perhaps, the most important vehicle—by which, symbolically, they can be handled and expressed. Since religious belief and ritual provide the content for culturally constituted projective, displacement, and sublimative mechanisms by which unconscious fears and anxieties may be reduced and repressed motives may be satisfied, these drives and motives, in turn, constitute an important unconscious source of religious behavior. Because the range of painful drives and motives which find expression in religion remains to be discovered by empirical research, I shall merely comment on two motives which I believe to be universally—but not exclusively—satisfied by religion; and since I have already attempted to deal with this problem elsewhere (Spiro, 1961b), I shall be brief.

Forbidden dependency needs inevitably seek satisfaction in religious behavior, in that the religious actor depends on superhuman beings for the gratification of his desires. Repressing his desire to remain in a state of childlike dependency on powerful adult figures, he can still satisfy this desire, symbolically, by his trust in and reliance upon superhuman beings.

Similarly, since all religions of which I am aware postulate the existence of malevolent, as well as of benevolent, superhuman beings, repressed hostility motives can be displaced and/or projected in beliefs in, and rituals designed for protection against, these malevolent beings. Prevented from expressing his hostility against his fellows, the religious actor can satisfy this desire symbolically through religion (Spiro, 1952).

These, then, are three sets of desires whose satisfaction by, partially explains the persistence of, religion. But though the persistence of religion is to be found in motivation—a psychological variable—the sources of motivation are to be sought, in part, in society. For just as the sociological causes (social structural variables) of the truth of religious beliefs achieve their effects through mediating psychological processes—feelings, projections, perceptions, and the like—so too the psychological causes (desires) of religious behavior may be explained by reference to those sociocultural (and biological) variables by which they are produced. With few exceptions, human drives are acquired rather than learned; and all human goals, it is probably safe to assume, are acquired. Since the crucial context for the learning of human drives and goals is social, and since most religious drives—but not most goals—are acquired in the child's early experiences, it is the family that once again is the nuclear structural variable.

Indeed, because these motivational variables are acquired within specified structural contexts, and because these contexts exhibit a wide range of variability, differences in the kinds and/or intensity of desires which constitute the motivational basis for religious behavior should vary systematically with differences in family systems (including socialization systems), *as well as with the alternative, non-religious means for their satisfaction.* The latter qualification is important. I have stressed, with respect to the three sets of desires which have been discussed, that in the absence of alternative institutional means, it is religion which is the means *par excellence* for their satisfaction. If cognitive desires, for example, are satisfied by science; if substantive desires are satisfied by technology; or if expressive desires are satisfied by politics or art or magic, religion should, by that extent, be less important for their satisfaction. In short, the importance of religion would be expected to vary inversely with the importance of other, projective and realistic, institutions.[8]

Holding other institutions constant, then, the kinds and intensity of drives which are satisfied by religion, the means by which they are believed to be satisfied, and the conceptions of the superhuman beings that are the agents of satisfaction should vary with variations in childhood experiences in which drives (and their intensity) are acquired, the means by which children influenced parents (and surrogates) to satisfy their drives, and the degree to which parents (and surrogates) do, in fact, satisfy them (Spiro & D'Andrade, 1958).

In short, a motivational explanation of religious behavior can, in principle, explain variability in behavior and, hence, can be tested empirically. A great deal of culture-and-personality research, too extensive to cite here, has been devoted to this very problem. Indeed, much of the research concerned with the structural bases for religious cognitions has, simultaneously, been devoted to the motivational bases for religious behavior. Unfortunately, however, cognitive desires have received less attention than expressive and substantive desires, possibly because we know comparatively little about how they are acquired.

Causal and Functional Explanations

We may now return to the question with which we began this paper: is the existence of religion to be explained causally or functionally? I have suggested that the acquisition of religious beliefs is to be explained causally, and that the practice of these beliefs is to be explained in terms of motivation—which means that it is explained both causally and functionally. Religion persists because it has functions—it does, or is believed to, satisfy desires; but religion persists because it has causes—it is caused by the expectation of satisfying these desires. Both are necessary, neither is sufficient, together they are necessary and sufficient. The causes of religious

---

[8] This does not imply, as some nineteenth-century thinkers believed, that as other institutions assume more of the traditional functions of religion, the latter will disappear. So far, at least, there has been no viable alternative to religion in providing a solution to the problem of suffering; and the malaise of modern man, on the one hand, and the persistence of religion among many modern intellectuals, on the other, seem to suggest that a viable functional alternative is yet to be discovered.

behavior are to be found in the desires by which it is motivated, and its functions consist in the satisfaction of those desires which constitute its motivation.

Classical functionalist theory has, of course, tended to dismiss motivation and other psychological variables as being outside the domain of anthropology. Firth, for example (1956, p. 224), writes that in the study of ritual the anthropologist is not concerned with ". . . the inner state as such of the participants," but rather with "the kinds of social relations that are produced or maintained."[9] If "inner states" were irrelevant for an explanation of religion, one might wish to defend the thesis that anthropology, whose central concern is the explanation of social and cultural institutions, should ignore them. But if by ignoring "inner states," and other psychological variables, we cannot adequately explain religion, or, for that matter, the "kinds of social relations" which it produces, we ignore them at our peril. Let me, beginning with the first proposition, take up each in turn.

An explanation of religion, or of any other sociocultural variable, consists in the specification of those conditions without which it could not exist. If religion is what is to be explained, if religion, that is, is the dependent variable, it can be explained only in terms of some independent variable, some condition by which it is maintained or sustained. I have argued that motivation is the independent variable. That religion, like other sociocultural variables, has sociological functions—it produces or maintains certain kinds of "social relations"—is undeniable; and it is one of our tasks to study these sociological functions. Indeed, these sociological functions may be crucial for the maintenance of society. If, for example, social solidarity is a functional requirement of society, and if religion—as it is frequently argued—is one of the institutions that satisfies this requirement, religion is necessary (a cause) for the maintenance of society. Notice, however, that if religion does produce solidarious social relations, solidarity provides us with an explanation of society, not of religion. In this case, in short, social solidarity does not explain religion; religion explains social solidarity. For social solidarity is the dependent, and it is religion that is the independent, variable. In sum, if we are interested in the "kinds of social relations" that are

---

[9] I should hasten to add that, in a later publication (1959, p. 133), Firth changed his view and stressed the importance of the individual for a complete explanation of religion.

produced by religion, we are interested in explaining society; and religion—it is assumed—can supply us with an entire, or a partial, explanation.

But the functionalist argument sometimes assumes a different form. Religion, it is argued, not only satisfies certain functional requirements of society, but it is a necessary condition for their satisfaction. Since society cannot exist unless these requirements are satisfied, and since religion is a necessary condition for their satisfaction, these requirements "cause" the existence of religion. It is not that the desire to satisfy some requirement motivates religious behavior—the latter may be accounted for by numerous other desires of the kind suggested, perhaps, in this paper. Rather, since religion is a necessary condition for the satisfaction of this requirement, the need for its satisfaction can explain the existence of religion. This argument, I think, is implicit in most functionalist interpretations of the Radcliffe-Brown variety. Thus Radcliffe-Brown himself (1948, p. 324) writes that religious ceremonies "are the means by which the society acts upon its individual members and keeps alive in their minds a certain system of sentiments. Without the ceremonial these sentiments would not exist, and without them the social organization in its actual form could not exist."

Notice, before we examine this type of explanation, that it is not a functionalist explanation at all; it is a causal explanation in which the cause happens to be a functional requirement. Notice, too, that despite the present tense of the predicates, this is really an explanation of the origin, not the persistence, of religion: the practice of religion—which is the only means by which religion persists—is not motivated by a desire to keep these sentiments alive, although the persistence of these sentiments is its consequence. But these questions aside, as an explanation of religion, this theory suffers from three defects: technical, methodological, and theoretical. Technically, no mechanism is specified by which the need for solidarity—and, therefore, the need for religion—gives rise to, or "causes," religion. Methodologically, it cannot explain the variability of religion—how is it that the need to sustain social sentiments produces such a bewildering range of religious beliefs and rituals?—and, therefore, there is no way by which it can be tested. Theoretically, it is based on an unwarranted functionalist assumption, which Merton (1957) has aptly termed the assumption of "indispensability." What does this mean?

For some functional requirements any number of variables may be adequate for their satisfaction. Since none is necessary, although each may be sufficient, they are called "functionally equivalent alternatives." These are to be distinguished from a variable which is necessary or indispensable for the satisfaction of a requirement—without it the requirement could not be satisfied. The cross-cultural evidence strongly suggests that there are few, if any, indispensable variables; that, rather, for almost any sociocultural variable there are functional equivalents. Hence, even if it is the case that religion is the means by which Andamanese "sentiments" are kept alive, it does not follow that religion is the only means by which this end could be accomplished, or that in other societies other institutions do not or cannot serve the identical function.[10]

In sum, from the fact that religion is a sufficient condition for the satisfaction of a requirement, it is invalidly deduced that it is a necessary condition. And, if it is not a necessary condition, its existence cannot be explained by arguing that without it society could not survive.

Although it is society, rather than religion, which is explained by the sociological consequences of religion, social anthropology—as the comparative study of social and cultural systems—is most certainly concerned with these functions; and psychological variables are not only necessary for the explanation of religion, but without them certain of its sociological functions would go unrecognized. (The classic example, of course, is Weber's (1930) analysis of the rise of capitalism, but it deals with the change in, rather than the persistence of, a social system.) Thus, the adjustive (real) function of religion, by satisfying the need for explanation, provides a society with a common "behavioral environment" which, as Hallowell (op. cit) observes, satisfies a set of minimal requirements for the existence of any society: the requirement for a common object orientation, spatiotemporal orientation, motivational orientation, and normative

---

[10] To cite but two counter-instances. First, there are the more than 150 atheistic *kibbutzim* in Israel, in which religious ceremonial does not exist (Spiro, 1956). Second, there are societies in which the important social sentiments are supported by secular rather than religious institutions. It would be difficult, for example, to discover even one sentiment important for the maintenance of capitalist democracy which is conveyed by the paramount Christian ceremony, the Eucharist. National celebrations, however, especially as interpreted by Warner (1959), serve this function *par excellence.*

orientation. It would be difficult to conceive of the possibility of social integration without a minimum level of such shared orientations.

The adaptive (apparent) function of religion, in satisfying the desire for the attainment of goals, provides—as Marxism has stressed—a most important basis for social stability. Disbelief in the efficacy of superhuman means for the achievement of this-worldly goals could certainly become a potential basis for social discontent and socioeconomic change. At the same time, the (real) function of religion in reducing anxiety concerning the attainment of goals—especially those for whose attainment available technological skills are ineffective—and, thus, in providing a minimum level of psychological security, serves to release energy for coping with the reality problems of society.

Finally, the integrative (real) function of religion, in allowing the disguised expression of repressed motives, serves a number of sociological functions. By providing a culturally approved means for the resolution of inner conflict (between personal desires and cultural norms), religion (*a*) reduces the probability of psychotic distortion of desires, thereby providing a society with psychologically healthy members,[11] (*b*) protects society from the socially disruptive consequences of direct gratification of these forbidden desires, (*c*) promotes social integration by providing a common goal (superhuman beings) and a common means (ritual) by which the desires may be gratified.

Conclusion

It would appear from the foregoing discussion that an adequate explanation for the persistence of religion requires both psychological and sociological variables. If the cognitive bases for religious belief have their roots in childhood experience, their explanation must be found in social structural and, more specifically, family structure variables. Here religion is the dependent variable, and family structure is the independent sociological variable which effects

[11] Nadel, recognizing the "defensive" function of religion, writes that in providing rituals by which forbidden impulses may be expressed, religion . . . "anticipates as well as canalizes the working of psychological mechanisms, which might otherwise operate in random fashion or beyond the control of society, in the 'private worlds' of neurosis and psychopathic fantasies" (1954, p. 275).

religious belief by means of such intervening psychological variables as fantasies, projections, perceptions, and the like.

If religion persists because of its gratification of desires, explanations for the bases of religious behavior must be found in psychological and, specifically, motivational variables. Here, again, religion is the dependent, and motivation is the independent, variable. Since, however, motivation consists in the intention of gratifying desires, and since desires are rooted either in organic or in acquired drives, the motivational roots of religious behavior can, ultimately, be found in those biological and social structural variables, respectively, by which they are produced and/or canalized. Again, it is the family which emerges as the crucial sociological variable. Religion, then, is to be explained in terms of society and personality.

Many studies of religion, however, are concerned not with the explanation of religion, but with the role of religion in the explanation of society. Here, the explanatory task is to discover the contributions which religion, taken as the independent variable, makes to societal integration, by its satisfaction of sociological wants. This is an important task, central to the main concern of anthropology, as the science of social systems. We seriously err, however, in mistaking an explanation of society for an explanation of religion which, in effect, means confusing the sociological functions of religion with the bases for its performance.

In this paper, I have been concerned almost exclusively with the latter aspect of religion. I have not, except incidentally, dealt with its sociological functions or, what is perhaps more important, with how these are to be measured. I have not dealt, moreover, with the problem of religious origins because—despite the fact that numerous speculations have been proposed (and I have my own, as well)—these are not testable. Nor have I dealt with the problem of the cross-cultural variability in religion, except to suggest some motivational bases for the persistence of different types of belief and ritual. But the crucial problems—to which Max Weber has most importantly contributed—I have not even touched upon. If, for example, religion is centrally concerned with the problem of "suffering" why is it that explanations for suffering run such a wide gamut: violation of ethical norms, sin of ancestors, misconduct in a previous incarnation, etc.? Or, if religion promises redemption from suffering, how are the different types of redemption to be explained?

And, moreover, what is the explanation for the different means by which the redemptive promise is to be achieved? These are but a few of the central problems in the study of religion with which this paper, with its limited focus, has not been concerned.

References

Durkheim, E. 1954. *The Elementary Forms of the Religious Life*. Glencoe, Ill.: Free Press.

Evans-Pritchard, E. E. 1954. *The Institutions of Primitive Society*. Oxford: Blackwell.

Firth, R. 1956. *Elements of Social Organization*. London: Watts; New York: Philosophical Library.

— 1959. Problem and Assumption in an Anthropological Study of Religion. *Journal of the Royal Anthropological Institute* 89.

Fortes, M. 1959. *Oedipus and Job in West African Religion*. Cambridge: Cambridge University Press.

Freud, S. 1928. *The Future of an Illusion*. London: Hogarth Press.

Gerth, H. H. & Mills, C. W. (eds.). 1946. *From Max Weber: Essays in Sociology*. New York: Oxford University Press.

Goody, J. 1961. Religion and Ritual: The Definitional Problem. *British Journal of Sociology* 12.

Hallowell, A. I. 1955. *Culture and Experience*. Philadelphia: University of Pennsylvania Press.

— 1956. The Rorschach Technique in Personality and Culture Studies. In B. Klopfer (ed.), *Developments in the Rorschach Technique*, Vol. 2. Yonkers-on-Hudson, N.Y.: World Books; London: Harrap.

Hempel, C. G. 1952 *Fundamentals of Concept Formation in Empirical Science*. Chicago: University of Chicago Press; London: Cambridge University Press.

Horton, R. 1960. A Definition of Religion and its Uses. *Journal of Royal Anthropological Institute* 90.

Kardiner, A. 1945. *The Psychological Frontiers of Society*. New York: Columbia University Press.

Leach, E. R. 1954. *Political Systems of Highland Burma*. London: Bell.

— 1961. Golden Bough of Gilded Twig? *Daedalus*.

Lowie, R. 1924. *Primitive Religion*. New York: Boni & Liveright.

Merton, R. K. 1957. *Social Theory and Social Structure* (revised edition), Glencoe, Ill.: Free Press.

Nadel, S.F. 1954. *Nupe Religion*. Glencoe, Ill.: Free Press.

Pruyser, P. 1960. Some Trends in the Psychology of Religion, *Journal of Religion* 40.

Radcliffe-Brown, A. R. 1948. *The Andaman Islanders*. Glencoe, Ill.: Free Press.

Radin, P. 1957. *Primitive Religion*. New York: Mayflower & Vision.

Spiro, M. E. 1952. Ghosts, Ifaluk, and Teleological Functionalism. *American Anthropologist* 45.

— 1953. Ghosts: An Anthropological Inquiry into Learning and Perception. *Journal of Abnormal and Social Psychology* 48.

— 1956. *Kibbutz: Venture in Utopia*. Cambridge, Mass.: Harvard University Press.

— 1961a. Social Systems, Personality, and Functional Analysis. In B. Kaplan (ed.), *Studying Personality Cross-Culturally*. Evanston, Ill.: Row, Peterson.

— 1961b. An Overview and a Suggested Reorientation. In F. L. K. Hsu (ed.), *Psychological Anthropology*. Homewood, Ill.: Dorsey.

— 1963. Causes, Functions, and Cross-Cousin Marriage: An Essay in Anthropological Explanation. *Journal of Royal Anthropological Institute* 97.

— 1964. Religion and the Irrational. In *Symposium on New Approaches to the Study of Religion*. (Proceedings of the American Ethnological Society). Seattle.

Spiro, M. E. & D'Andrade, R. G. 1958. A Cross-Cultural Study of Some Supernatural Beliefs. *American Anthropologist* 60.

Turner, V. W. 1962. *Chihamba: The White Spirit*. Manchester: Manchester University Press.

Warner, W. I. 1959. *The Living and the Dead*. New Haven: Yale University Press.

Weber, M. 1930. *The Protestant Ethic and the Spirit of Capitalism*. London: Allen & Unwin; New York: Scribner's.

Whiting, J. W. M. 1961. Socialization Process and Personality. In F. L. K. Hsu (ed.), op. cit.

6

Religion as a Cultural System

Clifford Geertz

> Any attempt to speak without speaking any particular language is not more hopeless than the attempt to have a religion that shall be no religion in particular. . . . Thus every living and healthy religion has a marked idiosyncrasy. Its power consists in its special and surprising message and in the bias which that revelation gives to life. The vistas it opens and the mysteries it propounds are another world to live in; and another world to live in—whether we expect ever to pass wholly over into it or no—is what we mean by having a religion.
>
> Santayana: *Reason in Religion* (1905–6)

I.

Two characteristics of anthropological work on religion accomplished since the second world war strike me as curious when such work is placed against that carried out just before and just after the first. One is that it has made no theoretical advances of major importance. It is living off the conceptual capital of its ancestors, adding very little, save a certain empirical enrichment, to it. The second is that it draws what concepts it does use from a very narrowly defined intellectual tradition. There is Durkheim, Weber, Freud, or Malinowski, and in any particular work the approach of one or two of these transcendent figures is followed, with but a few marginal corrections necessitated by the natural tendency to excess of seminal minds or by the expanded body of reliable descriptive data. But virtually no one even thinks of looking elsewhere—to philosophy, history, law, literature, or the "harder" sciences—as these men themselves looked, for analytical ideas. And it occurs to me, also, that these two curious characteristics are not unrelated.

If the anthropological study of religion is in fact in a state of general stagnation, I doubt it will be set going again by producing more minor variations on classical theoretical themes. Yet one more meticulous case in point for such well-established propositions as that ancestor worship supports the jural authority of elders, that initiation rites are means for the establishment of sexual identity and adult status, that ritual groupings reflect political oppositions, or that myths provide charters for social institutions and rationalizations of social privilege, may well finally convince a great many people, both inside the profession and out, that anthropologists are, like theologians, firmly dedicated to proving the indubitable. In art, this solemn reduplication of the achievements of accepted masters is called academicism; and I think this is the proper name for our malady also. Only if we abandon, in a phrase of Leo Steinberg's (1953), that sweet sense of accomplishment which comes from parading habitual skills and address ourselves to problems sufficiently unclarified as to make discovery possible, can we hope to achieve work which will not just reincarnate that of the great men of the first quarter of this century, but match it.

The way to do this is not to abandon the established traditions of social anthropology in this field, but to widen them. At least four of the contributions of the men who, as I say, dominate our thought to the point of parochializing it—Durkheim's discussion of the nature of the sacred, Weber's *Verstehenden* methodology, Freud's parallel between personal rituals and collective ones, and Malinowski's exploration of the distinction between religion and common sense—seem to me inevitable starting-points for any useful anthropological theory of religion. But they are starting-points only. To move beyond them we must place them in a much broader context of contemporary thought than they, in and of themselves, encompass. The dangers of such a procedure are obvious: arbitrary eclecticism, superficial theory-mongering, and sheer intellectual confusion. But I, at least, can see no other road of escape from what, referring to anthropology more generally, Janowitz (1963, p. 151) has called the dead hand of competence.

In working toward such an expansion of the conceptual envelope in which our studies take place, one can, of course, move in a great number of directions; and perhaps the most important initial problem is to avoid setting out, like Stephen Leacock's mounted policeman, in all of them at once. For my part, I shall confine my effort to developing what, following Parsons and Shils (1951), I refer to as the cultural dimension of religious analysis. The term "culture" has by now acquired a certain aura of ill-repute in social anthropological circles because of the multiplicity of its referents and the studied vagueness with which it has all too often been invoked. (Though why it should suffer more for these reasons than "social structure" or "personality" is something I do not entirely understand.) In any case, the culture concept to which I adhere has neither multiple referents nor, so far as I can see, any unusual ambiguity: it denotes an historically transmitted pattern of meanings embodied in symbols, a system of inherited conceptions expressed in symbolic forms by means of which men communicate, perpetuate, and develop their knowledge about and attitudes toward life. Of course, terms such as "meaning," "symbol," and "conception" cry out for explication. But that is precisely where the widening, the broadening, and the expanding come in. If Langer (1962, p. 55) is right that "the concept of meaning, in all its varieties, is the dominant philosophical concept of our time," that "sign, symbol, denotation, signification, communication . . . are our [intellectual] stock in trade," it is perhaps time that social anthropology, and particularly that part of it concerned with the study of religion, became aware of the fact.

II.

As we are to deal with meaning, let us begin with a paradigm: viz. that sacred symbols function to synthesize a people's ethos—the tone, character, and quality of their life, its moral and aesthetic style and mood—and their world-view—the picture they have of the way things in sheer actuality are, their most comprehensive ideas of order (Geertz, 1958). In religious belief and practice a group's ethos is rendered intellectually reasonable by being shown to represent a way of life ideally adapted to the actual state of affairs the world-view describes, while the world-view is rendered emotionally convincing by being presented as an image of an actual state of affairs peculiarly well arranged to accommodate such a way of life. This confrontation and mutual confirmation has two fundamental effects. On the one hand, it objectivizes moral and aesthetic preferences by depicting them as the imposed conditions of life implicit in a world with a particular structure, as mere common sense given the unalterable shape of reality. On the other, it supports these received beliefs about the world's body by invoking deeply felt moral and aesthetic sentiments as experiential evidence for their truth. Religious symbols formulate a basic congruence between a particular style of life and a specific (if, most often implicit) metaphysic, and in so doing sustain each with the borrowed authority of the other.

Phrasing aside, this much may perhaps be granted. The notion that religion tunes human actions to an envisaged cosmic order and projects images of cosmic order onto the plane of human experience is hardly novel. But it is hardly investigated either, so that we have very little idea of how, in empirical terms this particular miracle is accomplished. We just know that it is done, annually, weekly, daily, for some people almost hourly and we have an enormous ethnographic literature to demonstrate it. But the theoretical framework which would enable us to provide an analytic account of it, an account of the sort we can provide for lineage segmentation, political succession, labor, exchange, or the socialization of the child, does not exist.

Let us, therefore, reduce our paradigm to a definition, for although it is notorious that definitions establish nothing, in themselves they do, if they are carefully enough constructed provide a useful orientation, or reorientation, of thought, such that an extended unpacking of them can be an effective way of developing and controlling a novel line of inquiry. They have the useful virtue of explicitness: they commit themselves in a way discursive prose, which, in this field especially, is always liable to substitute rhetoric for argument, does not. Without further ado, then, a *religion* is:

> (1) a system of symbols which acts to (2) establish powerful, pervasive, and long-lasting moods and motivations in men by (3) formulating conceptions of a general order of existence and (4) clothing these conceptions with such an aura of factuality that (5) the moods and motivations seem uniquely realistic.

1. a system of symbols which acts to . . .

Such a tremendous weight is being put on the term "symbol" here that our first move must be to decide with some precision what we are going to mean by it. This is no easy task, for, rather like "culture," "symbol" has been used to refer to a great variety of things, often a number of them at the same time. In some hands it is used for anything which signifies something else to someone: dark clouds are the symbolic precursors of an oncoming rain. In others it is used only for explicitly conventional signs of one sort or another: a red flag is a symbol of danger, a white of surrender. In others it is confined to something which expresses in an oblique and figurative manner that which cannot be stated in a direct and literal one, so that there are symbols in poetry but not in science, anti-symbolic logic is misnamed. In yet others, however (Langer, 1953, 1960, 1962), it is used for any object, act, event, quality, or relation which serves as a vehicle for a conception—the conception is the symbol's "meaning"—and that is the approach I shall follow here. The number 6, written, imagined, laid out as a row of stones, or even punched into the program tapes of a computer is a symbol. But so also is the Cross, talked about, visualized, shaped worriedly in air or fondly fingered at the neck, the expanse of painted canvas called "Guernica" or the bit of painted stone called a churinga, the word "reality," or even the morpheme "-ing." They are all symbols, or at least symbolic elements, because they are tangible formulations of notions, abstractions from experience fixed in perceptible forms, concrete embodiments of ideas, attitudes, judgments, longings, or beliefs. To undertake the study of cultural activity—activity in which symbolism forms the positive content—is thus not to abandon social analysis for a Platonic cave of shadows, to enter into a mentalistic world of introspective psychology or, worse, speculative philosophy, and wander there forever in a haze of "Cognitions," "Affections," "Conations," and other elusive entities. Cultural acts, the construction, apprehension, and utilization of symbolic forms, are social events like any other; they are as public as marriage and as observable as agriculture.

They are not, however, exactly the same thing; or, more precisely, the symbolic dimension of social events is, like the psychological, itself theoretically abstractable from those events as empirical totalities. There is still, to paraphrase a remark of Kenneth Burke's (1941, p. 9), a difference between building a house and drawing up a plan for building a house, and reading a poem about having children by marriage is not quite the same thing as having children by marriage. Even though the building of the house may proceed under the guidance of the plan or—a less likely occurrence—the having of children may be motivated by a reading of the poem, there is something to be said for not confusing our traffic with symbols with our traffic with objects or human beings, for these latter are not in themselves symbols, however often they may function as such.[1] No matter how deeply interfused the cultural, the social, and the psychological may be in the everyday life of houses, farms, poems, and marriages, it is useful to distinguish them in analysis, and, so doing, to isolate the generic traits of each against the normalized background of the other two (Parsons & Shils, 1951).

So far as culture patterns, i.e. systems or complexes of symbols, are concerned, the generic trait which is of first importance for us here is that they are extrinsic sources of information (Geertz, 1964a). By "extrinsic," I mean only that—unlike genes, for example—they lie outside the boundaries of the individual organism as such in that intersubjective world of common understandings into which all human individuals are born, in which they pursue their separate careers, and which they leave persisting behind them after they die (Schulz, 1962). By "sources of information," I mean only that—like genes—they provide a blueprint or template in terms of which processes external to themselves can be given a definite form (Horowitz, 1956). As the order of bases in a strand of DNA forms a coded program, a set of instructions, or a recipe, for the synthesization of the structurally complex proteins which shape organic functioning, so culture patterns provide such programs for the institution of the social and psychological processes which shape public behavior. Though the sort of information and the mode of its transmission are vastly different in the two cases, this comparison of gene and symbol is more than a strained analogy of the familiar "social heredity" sort. It is actually a substantial relationship, for it is precisely the fact that genetically programmed processes are so highly generalized in men, as compared with lower animals, that culturally programmed ones are so important, only because human behavior is so loosely determined by intrinsic sources of information that extrinsic sources are so vital (Geertz, 1962). To build a dam a beaver needs only an appropriate site and the proper materials—his mode of procedure is shaped by his physiology. But man, whose genes are silent on the building trades, needs also a conception of what it is to build a dam, a conception he can get only from some

---

[1] The reverse mistake, especially common among neo-Kantians such as Cassirer (1953–57), of taking symbols to be identical with, or "constitutive of," their referents is equally pernicious. "One can point to the moon with one's finger," some, probably well-invented, Zen Master is supposed to have said, "but to take one's finger for the moon is to be a fool."

symbolic source—a blueprint, a textbook, or a string of speech by someone who already knows how dams are built, or, of course, from manipulating graphic or linguistic elements in such a way as to attain for himself a conception of what dams are and how they are built.

This point is sometimes put in the form of an argument that cultural patterns are "models," that they are sets of symbols whose relations to one another "model" relations among entities, processes or what-have-you in physical, organic, social, or psychological systems by "paralleling," "imitating," or "simulating" them (Craik, 1952). The term "model" has, however, two senses—an "of" sense and a "for" sense—and though these are but aspects of the same basic concept they are very much worth distinguishing for analytic purposes. In the first, what is stressed is manipulation of symbol structures so as to bring them, more or less closely, into parallel with the pre-established non-symbolic system, as when we grasp how dams work by developing a theory of hydraulics or constructing a flow chart. The theory or chart models physical relationships in such a way—i.e. by expressing their structure in synoptic form—as to render them apprehensible: it is a model *of* "reality." In the second, what is stressed is the manipulation of the non-symbolic systems in terms of the relationships expressed in the symbolic, as when we construct a dam according to the specifications implied in an hydraulic theory or the conclusions drawn from a flow chart. Here, the theory is a model under whose guidance physical relationships are organized: it is a model *for* "reality." For psychological and social systems, and for cultural models that would not ordinarily refer to as "theories," but rather as "doctrines," "melodies," or "rites," the case is in no way different. Unlike genes, and other non-symbolic information sources, which are only models *for*, not models *of*, culture patterns have an intrinsic double aspect: they give meaning, i.e. objective conceptual form, to social and psychological reality both by shaping themselves to it and by shaping it to themselves.

It is, in fact, this double aspect which sets true symbols off from other sorts of significative forms. Models *for* are found, as the gene example suggests, through the whole order of nature, for wherever there is a communication of pattern such programs are, in simple logic, required. Among animals, imprint learning is perhaps the most striking example, because what such learning involves is the automatic presentation of an appropriate sequence of behavior by a model animal in the presence of a learning animal which serves, equally automatically, to call out and stabilize a certain set of responses genetically built into the learning animal (Lorenz, 1952). The communicative dance of two bees, one of which has found nectar and the other of which seeks it, is another, somewhat different, more complexly coded, example (von Frisch, 1962). Craik (1952) has even suggested that the thin trickle of water which first finds its way down from a mountain spring to the sea and smooths a little channel for the greater volume of water that follows after it plays a sort of model *for* function. But models *of*—linguistic, graphic, mechanical, natural, etc. processes which function not to provide sources of information in terms of which other processes can be patterned, but to represent those patterned processes as such, to express their structure in an alternative medium—are much rarer and may perhaps be confined, among living animals, to man. The perception of the structural congruence between one set of processes, activities, relations, entities, etc. and another set for which it acts as a program, so that the program can be taken as a representation, or conception—a symbol—of the programmed, is the essence of human thought. The inter-transposability of models *for* and models *of* which symbolic formulation makes possible is the distinctive characteristic of our mentality.

2. . . . to establish powerful, pervasive, and long-lasting moods and motivations in men by . . .

So far as religious symbols and symbol systems are concerned this inter-transposability is clear. The endurance, courage, independence, perseverance, and passionate willfulness in which the vision quest practices the Plains Indian are the same flamboyant virtues by which he attempts to live: while achieving a sense of revelation he stabilizes a sense of direction (Lowie, 1024). The consciousness of defaulted obligation, secreted guilt, and, when a confession is obtained, public shame in which Manus' seance rehearses him are the same sentiments that underlie the sort of duty ethic by which his property-conscious society is maintained: the gaining of an absolution involves the forging of a conscience (Fortune, 1936). And the same self-discipline which rewards a Javanese mystic staring fixedly into the flame of a lamp with what he takes to be an intimation of divinity drills him in that rigorous control of emotional expression which is necessary to a man who would follow a quietistic style of life (Geertz, 1960). Whether one sees the conception of a personal guardian spirit, a family tutelary or an immanent God as synoptic formulations of the character of reality or as templates for producing reality with such a character seems largely arbitrary, a matter of which aspect, the model *of* or model *for*, one wants for the moment to bring into focus. The concrete symbols involved—one or another mythological figure materializing in the wilderness, the skull of the deceased household head hanging censoriously in the rafters, or a disembodied "voice in the stillness" soundlessly chanting enigmatic classical poetry—point in either direction. They both express the world's climate and shape it.

They shape it by inducing in the worshipper a certain distinctive set of dispositions (tendencies, capacities, propensities, skills, habits, liabilities, pronenesses) which lend a chronic character to the flow of his activity and the quality of his experience. A disposition describes not an activity or an occurrence but a probability of an activity being performed or an occurrence occurring in certain circumstances: "When a cow is said to be a ruminant, or a man is said to be a cigarette-smoker, it is not being said that the cow is ruminating now or that the man is smoking a cigarette now. To be a ruminant is to tend to ruminate from time to time, and to be a cigarette-smoker is to be in the habit of smoking cigarettes" (Ryle, 1949, p. 117). Similarly, to be pious is not to be performing something we would call an act of piety, but to be liable to perform such acts. So, too, with the Plains Indian's bravura, the Manus' compunctiousness, or the Javanese's quietism which, in their texts, form the substance of piety. The virtue of this sort of view of what are usually called "mental traits" or if the Cartesianism is unavowed, "psychological forces" (both unobjectionable enough terms in themselves) is that it gets them out of any dim and inaccessible realm of private sensation into that same well-lit world of observables in which reside the brittleness of glass, the inflammability of paper, and, to return to the metaphor, the dampness of England.

So far as religious activities are concerned (and learning a myth by heart is as much a religious activity as detaching one's finger at the knuckle), two somewhat different sorts of disposition are induced by them: moods and motivations.

A motivation is a persisting tendency, a chronic inclination to perform certain sorts of acts and experience certain sorts of feeling in certain sorts of situation, the "sorts" being commonly very heterogeneous and rather ill-defined classes in all three cases:

> . . . on hearing that a man is vain [i.e. motivated by vanity] we expect him to behave in certain ways, namely to talk a lot about himself, to cleave to the society of the eminent, to reject criticisms, to seek the footlights and to disengage himself from conversations about the merits of others. We expect him to indulge in roseate daydreams about his own successes, to avoid recalling past failures and to plan for his own advancement. To be vain is to tend to act in these and innumerable other kindred ways. Certainly we also expect the vain man to feel certain pangs and flutters in certain situations; we expect him to have an acute sinking feeling when an eminent person forgets his name, and to feel buoyant of heart and light of toe on hearing of the misfortunes of his rival. But feelings of pique and buoyancy are not more directly indicative of vanity than are public acts of boasting or private acts of daydreaming . . . (Ryle, 1949, p. 86).

Similarly for any motivations. As a motive, "flamboyant courage" consists in such enduring propensities as to fast in the wilderness, to conduct solitary raids on enemy camps, and to thrill to the thought of counting coup. "Moral circumspection" consists in such ingrained tendencies as to honor onerous promises, to confess secret sins in the face of severe public disapproval, and to feel guilty when vague and generalized accusations are made at seances. And "dispassionate tranquility" consists in such persistent inclinations as to maintain one's poise come hell or high water, to experience distaste in the presence of even moderate emotional displays, and to indulge in contentless contemplations of featureless objects. Motives are thus neither acts (i.e. intentional behaviors) nor feelings, but liabilities to perform particular classes of act or have particular classes of feeling. And when we say that a man is religious, i.e. motivated by religion, this is at least part—though only part—of what we mean.

Another part of what we mean is that he has, when properly stimulated, a susceptibility to fall into certain moods, moods we sometimes lump together under such covering terms as "reverential," "solemn," or "worshipful." Such generalized rubrics actually conceal, however, the enormous empirical variousness of the dispositions involved, and, in fact, tend to assimilate them to the unusually grave tone of most of our own religious life. The moods that sacred symbols induce, at different times and in different places, range from exultation to melancholy, from self-confidence to self-pity, from an incorrigible playfulness to a bland listlessness—to say nothing of the erogenous power of so many of the world's myths and rituals. No more than there is a single sort of motivation one can call piety is there a single sort of mood one can call worshipful.

The major difference between moods and motivations is that where the latter are, so to speak, vectorial qualities, the former are merely scalar. Motives have a directional cast, they describe a certain overall course, gravitate toward certain, usually temporary, consummations. But moods vary only as to intensity: they go nowhere. They spring from certain circumstances and they are responsive to no ends. Like fogs, they just settle and lift; like scents, suffuse and evaporate. When present they are totalistic: if one is sad everything and everybody seems dreary; if one is gay, everything and everybody seems splendid. Thus, though a man can be vain, brave, willful and independent at the same time, he can't very well be playful and listless, or exultant and melancholy, at the same time (Ryle, 1949, p. 99). Further, where motives persist for more or less extended periods of time, moods merely recur with greater or lesser frequency, coming and going for what are often quite unfathomable reasons. But perhaps the most important difference, so far as we are concerned, between moods and motivations is that motivations are "made meaningful" with reference to the ends toward which they are conceived to conduce, whereas moods are "made meaningful" with reference to the conditions from which they are conceived to conduce. We interpret motives in terms of their consummations, but we interpret moods in terms of their sources. We say that a person is industrious because he wishes to succeed, we say that a person is worried because he is conscious of the hanging threat of nuclear holocaust. And this is no less the case when the interpretations invoked are ultimate. Charity becomes Christian charity when it is enclosed in a conception of God's purposes; optimism is Christian optimism when it is grounded in a particular conception of God's nature. The assiduity of the Navaho finds its rationale in a belief that, since "reality" operates mechanically, it is coercible; their chronic fearfulness finds its rationale in a conviction that, however "reality" operates, it is both enormously powerful and terribly dangerous (Kluckhohn, 1949).

3. . . . by formulating conceptions of a general order of existence and . . .

That the symbols or symbol systems which induce and define dispositions we set off as religious and those which place those dispositions in a cosmic framework are the same symbols ought to occasion no surprise. For what else do we mean by saying that a particular mood of awe is religious and not secular except that it springs from entertaining a conception of all-pervading vitality like mana and not from a visit to the Grand Canyon? Or that a particular case of asceticism is an example of a religious motivation except that it is directed toward the achievement of an unconditioned end like nirvana and not a conditioned one like weight-reduction? If sacred symbols did not at one and the same time induce dispositions in human beings and formulate, however obliquely, inarticulately, or unsystematically, general ideas of order, then the empirical differentia of religious activity or religious experience would not exist. A man can indeed be said to be "religious" about golf, but not merely if he pursues it with passion and plays it on Sundays: he must also see it as symbolic of some transcendent truths. And the pubescent boy gazing soulfully into the eyes of the pubescent girl in a William Steig cartoon and murmuring, "There is something about you, Ethel, which gives me a sort of religious feeling," is, like most adolescents, confused. What any particular religion affirms about the fundamental nature of reality may be obscure, shallow, or, all too often, perverse, but it must, if it is not to consist of the mere collection of received practices and conventional sentiments we usually refer to as moralism, affirm something. If one were to essay a minimal definition of religion today it would perhaps not be Tylor's famous "belief in spiritual beings," to which Goody (1961), wearied of theoretical subtleties, has lately urged us to return, but rather what Salvador de Madariaga has called "the relatively modest dogma that God is not mad."

Usually, of course, religions affirm very much more than this: we believe, as James (1904, Vol. 2, p. 299) remarked, all that we can and would believe everything if we only could. The thing we seem least able to tolerate is a threat to our powers of conception, a suggestion that our ability to create, grasp, and use symbols may fail us, for were this to happen we would be more helpless, as I have already pointed out, than the beavers. The extreme generality, diffuseness, and variability of man's innate (i.e. genetically programmed) response capacities means that without the assistance of cultural patterns he would be functionally incomplete, not merely a talented ape who had, like some under-privileged child, unfortunately been prevented from realizing his full potentialities, but a kind of formless monster with neither sense of direction nor power of self-control, a chaos of spasmodic impulses and vague emotions (Geertz, 1962). Man depends upon symbols and symbol systems with a dependence so great as to be decisive for his creatural viability and, as a result, his sensitivity to even the remotest indication that they may prove unable to cope with one or another aspect of experience raises within him the gravest sort of anxiety:

> [Man] can adapt himself somehow to anything his imagination can cope with; but he cannot deal with Chaos. Because his characteristic function and highest asset is conception, his greatest fright is to meet what he cannot construe—the "uncanny," as it is popularly called. It need not be a new object; we do meet new things, and "understand" them promptly, if tentatively, by the nearest analogy, when our minds are functioning freely; but under mental stress even perfectly familiar things may become suddenly disorganized and give us the horrors. Therefore our most important assets are always the symbols of our general *orientation* in nature, on the earth, in society, and in what we are doing: the symbols of our *Weltanschauung* and *Lebensanschauung*. Consequently, in a primitive society, a daily ritual is incorporated in common activities, in eating, washing, fire-making, etc., as well as in pure ceremonial; because the need of reasserting the tribal morale and recognizing its cosmic conditions is constantly felt. In Christian Europe the Church brought men daily (in some orders even hourly) to their knees, to enact if not to contemplate their assent to the ultimate concepts (Langer, 1960, p. 287, italics original).

There are at least three points where chaos—a tumult of events which lack not just interpretations but *interpretability*—threatens to break in upon man: at the limits of his analytic capacities, at the limits of his powers of endurance, and at the limits of his moral insight. Bafflement, suffering, and a sense of intractable ethical paradox are all, if they become intense enough or are sustained long enough, radical challenges to the proposition that life is comprehensible and that we can, by taking thought, orient ourselves effectively within it—challenges with which any religion, however "primitive," which hopes to persist must attempt somehow to cope.

Of the three issues, it is the first which has been least investigated by modern social anthropologists (though Evans-Pritchard's (1937) classic discussion of why granaries fall on some Azande and not on others, is a notable exception). Even to consider people's religious beliefs as attempts to bring anomalous events or experiences—death, dreams, mental fugues, volcanic eruptions, or marital infidelity—within the circle of the at least potentially explicable seems to smack of Tyloreanism or worse. But it does appear to be a fact that at least some men—in all probability, most men—are unable to leave unclarified problems of analysis merely unclarified, just to look at the stranger features of the world's landscape in dumb astonishment or bland apathy without trying to develop, however fantastic, inconsistent, or simple-minded, some notions as to how such features might be reconciled with the more ordinary deliverances of experience. Any chronic failure of one's explanatory apparatus, the complex of received culture patterns (common sense, science, philosophical speculation, myth) one has for mapping the empirical world, to explain things which cry out for explanation tends to lead to a deep disquiet—a tendency rather more widespread and a disquiet rather deeper than we have sometimes supposed since the pseudo-science view of religious belief was, quite rightfully, deposed. After all, even that high priest of heroic atheism, Lord Russell, once remarked that although the problem of the existence of God had never bothered him, the ambiguity of certain mathematical axioms had threatened to unhinge his mind. And Einstein's profound dissatisfaction with quantum mechanics was based on a—surely religious—inability to believe that, as he put it, God plays dice with the universe.

But this quest for lucidity and the rush of metaphysical anxiety that occurs when empirical phenomena threaten to remain intransigently opaque is found on much humbler intellectual levels. Certainly, I was struck in my own work, much more than I had at all expected to be, by the degree to which my more animistically inclined informants behaved like true Tyloreans. They seemed to be constantly using their beliefs to "explain" phenomena: or, more accurately, to convince themselves that the phenomena were explainable within the accepted scheme of things, for they commonly had only a minimal attachment to the particular soul possession, emotional disequilibrium, taboo infringement, or bewitchment hypothesis they advanced and were all too ready to abandon it for some other, in the same genre, which struck them as more plausible given the facts of the case. What they were not ready to do was abandon it for no other hypothesis at all; to leave events to themselves.

And what is more, they adopted this nervous cognitive stance with respect to phenomena which had no immediate practical bearing on their own lives, or for that matter on anyone's. When a peculiarly shaped, rather large toadstool grew up in a carpenter's house in the short space of a few days (or, some said, a few hours), people came from miles around to see it, and everyone had some sort of explanation—some animist, some animatist, some not quite either—for it. Yet it would be hard to argue that the toadstool had any social value in Radcliffe-Brown's (1952) sense, or was connected in any way with anything which did and for which it could have been standing proxy, like the Andaman cicada. Toadstools play about the same role in Javanese life as they do in ours and in the ordinary course of things Javanese have about as much interest in them as we do. It was just that this one was "odd," "strange," "uncanny"—*aneh.* And the odd, strange, and uncanny simply must be accounted for—or, again, the conviction that it *could be accounted* for sustained. One does not shrug off a toadstool which grows five times as fast as a toadstool has any right to grow. In the broadest sense the "strange" toadstool did have implications, and critical ones, for those who heard about it. It threatened their most general ability to understand the world, raised the uncomfortable question of whether the beliefs which they held about nature were workable, the standards of truth they used valid.

Nor is this to argue that it is only, or even mainly, sudden eruptions of extraordinary events which engender in man the disquieting sense that his cognitive resources may prove unavailing or that this intuition appears only in its acute form. More commonly it is a persistent, constantly re-experienced difficulty in grasping certain aspects of nature, self, and society, in bringing certain elusive phenomena within the sphere of culturally formulatable fact, which renders man chronically uneasy and toward which a more equable flow of diagnostic symbols is consequently directed. It is what lies beyond a relatively fixed frontier of accredited knowledge that, looming as a constant background to the daily round of practical life, sets ordinary human experience in a permanent context of metaphysical concern and raises the dim, back-of-the-mind suspicion that one may be adrift in an absurd world:

> Another subject which is matter for this characteristic intellectual enquiry [among the Iatmul] is the nature of ripples and waves on the surface of water. It is said secretly that men, pigs, trees, grass—all the objects in the world—are only patterns of waves. Indeed there seems to be some agreement about this, although it

> perhaps conflicts with the theory of reincarnation, according to which the ghost of the dead is blown as a mist by the East Wind up the river and into the womb of the deceased's son's wife. Be that as it may—there is still the question of how ripples and waves are caused. The clan which claims the East Wind as a totem is clear enough about this: the Wind with her mosquito fan causes the waves. But other clans have personified the waves and say that they are a person (Kontum-mali) independent of the wind. Other clans, again, have other theories. On one occasion I took some Iatmul natives down to the coast and found one of them sitting by himself gazing with rapt attention at the sea. It was a windless day, but a slow swell was breaking on the beach. Among the totemic ancestors of his clan he counted a personified slit gong who had floated down the river to the sea and who was believed to cause the waves. He was gazing at the waves which were heaving and breaking when no wind was blowing, demonstrating the truth of his clan myth (Bateson, 1958, pp. 130–131).[2]

The second experiential challenge in whose face the meaningfulness of a particular pattern of life threatens to dissolve into a chaos of thingless names and nameless things—the problem of suffering—has been rather more investigated, or at least described, mainly because of the great amount of attention given in works on tribal religion to what are perhaps its two main loci: illness and mourning. Yet for all the fascinated interest in the emotional aura that surrounds these extreme situations, there has been, with a few exceptions such as Lienhardt's recent (1961, pp. 151ff) discussion of Dinka divining, little conceptual advance over the sort of crude confidence-type theory set forth by Malinowski: viz. that religion helps one to endure "situations of emotional stress" by "open[ing] up escapes from such situations and such impasses as offer no empirical way out except by ritual and belief into the domain of the supernatural" (1948, p. 67).

---

[2] That the chronic and acute forms of this sort of cognitive concern are closely interrelated, and that responses to the more unusual occasions of it are patterned on responses established in coping with the more usual is also clear from Bateson's description, however, as he goes on to say: "On another occasion I invited one of my informants to witness the development of photographic plates. I first desensitized the plates and then developed them in an open dish in moderate light, so that my informant was able to see the gradual appearance of the images. He was much interested, and some days later made me promise never to show this process to members of other clans. Kontum-mali was one of his ancestors, and he saw in the process of photographic development the actual embodiment of ripples into images, and regarded this as a demonstration of the clan's secret" (Bateson, 1958).

The inadequacy of this "theology of optimism," as Nadel (1957) rather drily called it, is, of course, radical. Over its career religion has probably disturbed men as much as it has cheered them; forced them into a head-on, unblinking confrontation of the fact that they are born to trouble as often as it has enabled them to avoid such a confrontation by projecting them into sort of infantile fairy-tale world where—Malinowski again (1948, p. 67)—"hope cannot fail nor desire deceive." With the possible exception of Christian Science, there are few if any religious traditions, "great" or "little," in which the proposition that life hurts is not strenuously affirmed and in some it is virtually glorified:

> She was an old [Ba-Ila] woman of a family with a long genealogy. Leza, "the Besetting-One," stretched out his hand against the family. He slew her mother and father while she was yet a child, and in the course of years all connected with her perished. She said to herself, "Surely I shall keep those who sit on my thighs." But no, even they, the children of her children, were taken from her. . . . Then came into her heart a desperate resolution to find God and to ask the meaning of it all. . . . So she began to travel, going through country after country, always with the thought in her mind: "I shall come to where the earth ends and there I shall find a road to God and I shall ask him: "What have I done to thee that thou afflicts me in this manner?" She never found where the earth ends, but though disappointed she did not give up her search, and as she passed through the different countries they asked her, "What have you come for, old woman?" And the answer would be, "I am seeking Leza." "Seeking Leza! For what?" "My brothers, you ask me! Here in the nations is there one who suffers as I have suffered?" And they would ask again, "How have you suffered?" "In this way. I am alone. As you see me, a solitary old woman; that is how I am!" And they answered, "Yes, we see. That is how you are. Bereaved of friends and husband? In what do you differ from others? The Besetting-One sits on the back of every one of us and we cannot shake him off." She never obtained her desire: she died of a broken heart (Smith & Dale, 1920, II, pp. 197ff; quoted in Radin, 1957, pp. 100–101).

As a religious problem, the problem of suffering is, paradoxically, not how to avoid suffering but how to suffer, how to make of physical pain, personal loss, worldly defeat, or the helpless contemplation of others' agony something bearable, supportable—something, as we say, sufferable. It was in this effort that the Ba-Ila woman—perhaps necessarily, perhaps not—failed and, literally not knowing how to feel about what had happened to her, how to suffer, perished in confusion and despair. Where the more intellective aspects of what Weber called the Problem of Meaning are a matter affirming the ultimate explicability of experience, the more affective aspects are a matter of affirming its ultimate sufferableness. As religion on one side anchors the power of our symbolic resources for formulating analytic ideas in an authoritative conception of the overall shape of reality, so on another side it anchors the power of our, also symbolic, resources for expressing emotions—moods, sentiments, passions, affections, feelings—in a similar conception of its pervasive tenor, its inherent tone and temper. For those able to embrace them, and for so long as they are able to embrace them, religious symbols provide a cosmic guarantee not only for their ability to comprehend the world, but also, comprehending it, to give a precision to their feeling, a definition to their emotions which enables them, morosely or joyfully, grimly or cavalierly, to endure it.

Consider in this light the well-known Navaho curing rites usually referred to as "sings" (Kluckhohn & Leighton, 1946; Reichard, 1950). A sing—the Navaho have about sixty different ones for different purposes, but virtually all of them are dedicated to removing some sort of physical or mental illness—is a kind of religious psychodrama in which there are three main actors: the "singer" or curer, the patient, and, as a kind of antiphonal chorus, the patient's family and friends. The structure of all the sings, the drama's plot, is quite similar. There are three main acts: a purification of the patient and audience; a statement, by means of repetitive chants and ritual manipulations, of the wish to restore well-being ("harmony") in the patient; an identification of the patient with the Holy People and his consequent "cure." The purification rites involved forced sweating, induced vomiting, etc. to expel the sickness from the patient physically. The chants, which are numberless, consist mainly of simple optative phrases ("may the patient be well, "I am getting better all over," etc.). And, finally, the identification of the patient with the Holy People, and thus with cosmic order generally, is accomplished through the agency of a sand painting depicting the Holy People in one or another appropriate mythic setting. The singer places the patient on the painting, touching the feet, hands, knees, shoulders, breast, back, and head of the divine figures and then the corresponding parts of the patient, performing thus what is essentially a communion rite between the patient and the Holy People, a bodily identification of the human and the divine

(Reichard, 1950). This is the climax of the sing: the whole curing process may be likened, Reichard says, to a spiritual osmosis in which the illness in man and the power of the deity penetrate the ceremonial membrane in both directions, the former being neutralized by the latter. Sickness seeps out in the sweat, vomit, and other purification rites; health seeps in as the Navaho patient touches, through the medium of the singer, the sacred sand painting. Clearly, the symbolism of the sing focuses upon the problem of human suffering and attempts to cope with it by placing it in a meaningful context, providing a mode of action through which it can be expressed, being expressed understood, and being understood, endured. The sustaining effect of the sing (and since the commonest disease is tuberculosis, it can in most cases be only sustaining), rests ultimately on its ability to give the stricken person a vocabulary in terms of which to grasp the nature of his distress and relate it to the wider world. Like a calvary, a recitation of Buddha's emergence from his father's palace or a performance of *Oedipus Tyrannos* in other religious traditions, a sing is mainly concerned with the presentation of a specific and concrete image of truly human, and so endurable suffering powerful enough to resist the challenge of emotional meaninglessness raised by the existence of intense and unremovable brute pain.

The problem of suffering passes easily into the problem of evil, for if suffering is severe enough it usually, though not always, seems morally undeserved as well, at least to the sufferer. But they are not, however, exactly the same thing—a fact I think Weber, too influenced by the biases of a monotheistic tradition in which, as the various aspects of human experience must be conceived to proceed from a single, voluntaristic source, man's pain reflects directly on God's goodness, did not fully recognize in his generalization of the dilemmas of Christian theodicy Eastward. For where the problem of suffering is concerned with threats to our ability to put our "undisciplined squads of emotion" into some sort of soldierly order the problem of evil is concerned with threats to our ability to make sound moral judgments. What is involved in the problem of evil is not the adequacy of our symbolic resources to govern our affective life, but the adequacy of those resources to provide a workable set of ethical criteria, normative guides to govern our action. The vexation here is the gap between things as they are and as they ought to be if our conceptions of right and wrong make sense, the gap between what we deem various individuals deserve and what we see that they get—a phenomenon summed up in that profound quatrain:

> The rain falls on the just
> And on the unjust fella;
> But mainly upon the just,
> Because the unjust has the just's umbrella.

Or if this seems too flippant an expression of an issue that in somewhat different form, animates the Book of Job and the *Baghavad Gita*, the following classical Javanese poem, known, sung, and repeatedly quoted in Java by virtually everyone over the age of six, puts the point—the discrepancy between moral prescriptions and material rewards, the seeming inconsistency of "is" and "ought"—rather more elegantly:

> We have lived to see a time without order
> In which everyone is confused in his mind.
> One cannot bear to join in the madness,
> But if he does not do so
> He will not share in the spoils,
> And will starve as a result.
> Yes, God; wrong is wrong:
> Happy are those who forget,
> Happier yet those who remember and have deep insight.

Nor is it necessary to be theologically self-conscious to be religiously sophisticated. The concern with intractable ethical paradox, the disquieting sense that one's moral insight is inadequate to one's moral experience, is as alive on the level of so-called "primitive" religion as it is on that of the so-called "civilized." The set of notions about "division in the world that Lienhardt describes (1961, pp. 28–55) for the Dinka is a useful case in point. Like so many peoples, the Dinka believe that the sky, where "Divinity" is located, and earth, where man dwells, were at one time contiguous, the sky lying just above the earth and being connected to it by a rope, so that men could move at will between the two realms. There was no death and the first man and woman were permitted but a single grain of millet a day, which was all that they at that time required. One day, the woman—of course—decided, out of greed, to plant more than the permitted grain of millet and in her avid haste and industry accidentally struck Divinity with the handle of the hoe. Offended, he severed the rope, withdrew into the distant sky of today, and left man to labor for his food, to suffer sickness and death, and to experience separation from the source of his being, his Creator. Yet the meaning of this strangely familiar story to the Dinka is, as indeed is Genesis to Jews and Christians, not homiletic but descriptive:

> Those [Dinka] who have commented on these stories have sometimes made it clear that their sympathies lie with Man in his plight, and draw attention to the smallness of the fault for which Divinity withdrew the benefits of his closeness. The image of striking Divinity with a hoe . . . often evokes a certain amusement, almost as though the story were indulgently being treated as too childish to explain the consequences attributed to the event. But it is clear that the point of the story of Divinity's withdrawal from men is not to suggest an improving moral judgment on human behaviour. It is to represent a total situation known to the Dinka today. Men now are—as the first man and woman then became—active, self-assertive, inquiring, acquisitive. Yet they are also subject to suffering and death, ineffective, ignorant and poor. Life is insecure; human calculations often prove erroneous and men must often learn by experience that the consequences of their acts are quite other than they may have anticipated or consider equitable. Divinity's withdrawal from Man as the result of a comparatively trifling offence, by human standards, presents the contrast between equitable human judgments and the action of the Power which are held ultimately to control what happens in Dinka life. . . . To the Dinka, the moral order is ultimately constituted according to principles which often elude men, which experience and tradition in part reveal, and which human action cannot change. . . . The myth of Divinity's withdrawal then reflects the facts of existence as they are known. The Dinka are in a universe which is largely beyond their control, and where events may contradict the most reasonable human expectations (Lienhardt 1961, p. 53–54).

Thus the problem of evil, or perhaps one should say the problem *about* evil, is in essence the same sort of problem of or about bafflement and the problem of or about suffering. The strange opacity of certain empirical events, the dumb senselessness of intense or inexorable pain, and the enigmatic unaccountability of gross iniquity all raise the uncomfortable suspicion that perhaps the world, and hence man's life in the world, has no genuine order at all—no empirical regularity, no emotional form, no moral coherence. And the religious response to this suspicion is in each case the same: the formulation, by means of symbols, of an image of such a genuine order of the world which will account for, and even celebrate, the perceived ambiguities, puzzles, and paradoxes in human experience. The effort is not to deny the undeniable—that there are unexplained events, that life hurts, or that rain falls upon the just—but to deny that there are inexplicable events, that life is unendurable, and that justice is a mirage. The principles which constitute the moral order may indeed often elude men, as Lienhardt puts it, in the same way as fully satisfactory explanations of anomalous events or effective forma for the expression of feeling often eludes them. What is important, to a religious man at least, is that this elusiveness be accounted for, that it be not the result of the fact that there are no such principles, explanations, or forms, that life is absurd and the attempt to make moral, intellectual or emotional sense out of experience is bootless. The Dinka can admit, in fact insist upon, the moral ambiguities and contradictions of life as they live it because these ambiguities and contradictions are seen not as ultimate, but as the "rational," "natural," "logical" (one may choose one's own adjective here, for none of them is truly adequate) outcome of the moral structure of reality which the myth of the withdrawn "Divinity" depicts, or as Lienhardt says, "images."

The Problem of Meaning in each of its intergrading aspects (how these aspects in fact intergrade in each particular case, what sort of interplay there is between the sense of analytic, emotional, and moral impotence, seems to me one of the outstanding, and except for Weber untouched, problems for comparative research in this whole field) is a matter of affirming, or at least recognizing, the inescapability of ignorance, pain, and injustice on the human plane while simultaneously denying that these irrationalities are characteristic of the world as a whole. And it is in terms of religious symbolism, a symbolism relating man's sphere of existence to a wider sphere within which it is conceived to rest, that both the affirmation and the denial are made.[3]

---

[3] This is *not,* however, to say that everyone in every society does this, for as the immortal Don Marquis once remarked, you don't have to have a soul unless you really want one. The oft-heard generalization (e.g. Kluckhohn, 1953) that religion is a human universal embodies a confusion between the probably true (though on present evidence unprovable) proposition that there is no human society in which cultural patterns that we can, under the present definition or one like it, call religious are totally lacking, and the surely untrue proposition that all men in all societies are, in any meaningful sense of the term, religious. But if the anthropological study of religious commitment is underdeveloped, the anthropological study of religious non-commitment is non-existent. The anthropology of religion will have come of age when some more subtle Malinowski writes a book called "Belief and Unbelief (or even "Faith and Hypocrisy") in a Savage Society."

4. . . . and clothing those conceptions with such an aura of factuality that . . .

There arises here, however, a profounder question: how is it that this denial comes to be believed? how is it that the religious man moves from a troubled perception of experienced disorder to a more or less settled conviction of fundamental order? just what does "belief" mean in a religious context? Of all the problems surrounding attempts to conduct anthropological analysis of religion this is the one that has perhaps been most troublesome and therefore the most often avoided, usually by relegating it to psychology, that raffish outcast discipline to which social anthropologists are forever consigning phenomena they are unable to deal with within the framework of a denatured Durkheimianism. But the problem will not go away, it is not merely psychological (nothing social is), and no anthropological theory of religion which fails to attack it is worthy of the name. We have been trying to stage Hamlet without the Prince quite long enough.

It seems to me that it is best to begin any approach to this issue with frank recognition that religious belief involves not a Baconian induction from everyday experience—for then we should all be agnostics—but rather a prior acceptance of authority which transforms that experience. The existence of bafflement, pain, and moral paradox—of The Problem of Meaning—is one of the things that drive men toward belief in gods, devils, spirits, totemic principles, or the spiritual efficacy of cannibalism (an enfolding sense of beauty or a dazzling perception of power are others), but it is not the basis upon which those beliefs rest, but rather their most important field of application:

> We point to the state of the world as illustrative of doctrine but never as evidence for it. So Belsen illustrates a world of original sin, but original sin is not an hypothesis to account for happenings like Belsen. We justify a particular religious belief by showing its place in the total religious conception; we justify a religious belief as a whole by referring to authority. We accept authority because we discover it at some point in the world at which we worship, at which we accept the lordship of something not ourselves. We do not worship authority, but we accept authority as defining the worshipful. So someone may discover the possibility of worship in the life of the Reformed Churches and accept the Bible as authoritative; or in the Roman Church and accept papal authority (MacIntyre, 1957, pp. 201–202).

This is, of course, a Christian statement of the matter; but it is not to be despised on that account. In tribal religions authority lies in the persuasive power of traditional imagery; in mystical ones in the apodictic force of supersensible experience; in charismatic ones in the hypnotic attraction of an extraordinary personality. But the priority of the acceptance of an authoritative criterion in religious matters over the revelation which is conceived to flow from that acceptance is not less complete than in scriptural or hieratic ones. The basic axiom underlying what we may call "the religious perspective" is everywhere the same: he who would know must first believe.

But to speak of "the religious perspective" is, by implication, to speak of one perspective among others. A perspective is a mode of seeing, in that extended sense of "see" in which it means "discern," "apprehend," "understand," or "grasp." It is a particular way of looking at life, a particular manner of construing the world, as when we speak of an historical perspective, a scientific perspective, an aesthetic perspective, a common-sense perspective, or even the bizarre perspective embodied in dreams and in hallucinations.[4] The question then comes down to, first, what is "the religious perspective" generically considered, as differentiated from other perspectives; and second, how do men come to adopt it.

If we place the religious perspective against the background of three of the other major perspectives in terms of which men construe the world—the common-sensical, the scientific, and the aesthetic—its special character emerges more sharply. What distinguishes common sense as a mode of "seeing" is, as Schutz (1962) has pointed out, a simple acceptance of the world, its objects, and its processes as being just what they seem to be—what is sometimes called naïve

---

[4] The term "attitude" as in "aesthetic attitude" (Bell, 1914) or "natural attitude" (Schutz, 1962; the phrase is originally Husserl's) is another, perhaps more common term for what I have here called "perspective." But I have avoided it because of its strong subjectivist connotations, its tendency to place the stress upon a supposed inner state of an actor rather than on a certain sort of relation—a symbolically mediated one—between an actor and a situation. This is not to say, of course, that a phenomenological analysis of religious experience, if cast in inter-subjective, non-transcendental, genuinely scientific terms (see Percy, 1958) is not essential to a full understanding of religious belief, but merely that that is not the focus of my concern here. "Outlook," "frame of reference," "frame of mind," "orientation," "stance," "mental set," etc. are other terms sometimes employed, depending upon whether the analyst wishes to stress the social, psychological, or cultural aspects of the matter.

realism—and the pragmatic motive, the wish to act upon that world so as to bend it to one's practical purposes, to master it, or so far as that proves impossible, to adjust to it. The world of everyday life, itself, of course, a cultural product, for it is framed in terms of the symbolic conceptions of "stubborn fact" handed down from generation to generation, is the established scene and given object of our actions. Like Mt. Everest it is just there and the thing to do with it, if one feels the need to do anything with it at all is to climb it. In the scientific perspective it is precisely this givenness which disappears (Schulz, 1962). Deliberate doubt and systematic inquiry, the suspension of the pragmatic motive in favor of disinterested observation, the attempt to analyze the world in terms of formal concepts whose relationship to the informal conceptions of common sense become increasingly problematic—there are the hallmarks of the attempt to grasp the world scientifically. And as for the aesthetic perspective, which under the rubric of "the aesthetic attitude" has been perhaps most exquisitely examined, it involves a different sort of suspension of naïve realism and practical interest, in that instead of questioning the credentials of everyday experience that experience is merely ignored in favor of an eager dwelling upon appearances, an engrossment in surfaces, an absorption in things, as we say, "in themselves": "The function of artistic illusion is not 'make-believe" . . . but the very opposite, disengagement from belief—the contemplation of sensory qualities without their usual meanings of 'here's that chair', 'That's my telephone' . . . etc. The knowledge that what is before us has no practical significance in the world is what enables us to give attention to its appearance as such" (Langer, 1957, p. 49). And like the common-sensical and the scientific (or the historical, the philosophical, and the artistic) this perspective, this "way of seeing" is not the product of some mysterious Cartesian chemistry, but is induced, mediated, and in fact created by means of symbols. It is the artist's skill which can produce those curious quasi-objects—poems, dramas, sculptures, symphonies—which, dissociating themselves from the solid world of common sense, take on the special sort of eloquence only sheer appearances can achieve.

The religious perspective differs from the common-sensical in that, as already pointed out, it moves beyond the realities of everyday life to wider ones which correct and complete them, and its defining concern is not action upon those wider realities but acceptance of them, faith in them. It differs from the scientific perspective in that it questions the realities of everyday life not out of an institutionalized skepticism which dissolves the world's givenness into a swirl of probabilistic hypotheses, but in terms of what it takes to be wider, non-hypothetical truths. Rather than detachment, its watchword is commitment; rather than analysis, encounter. And it differs from art in that instead of effecting a disengagement from the whole question of factuality, deliberately manufacturing an air of semblance and illusion, it deepens the concern with fact and seeks to create an aura of utter actuality. It is this sense of the "really real" upon which the religious perspective rests and which the symbolic activities of religion as a cultural system are devoted to producing, intensifying, and, so far as possible, rendering inviolable by the discordant revelations of secular experience. It is, again, the imbuing of a certain specific complex of symbols—of the metaphysic they formulate and the style of life they recommend—with a persuasive authority which, from an analytic point of view is the essence of religious action.

Which brings us, at length, to ritual. For it is in ritual—i.e. consecrated behavior—that this conviction that religious conceptions are veridical and that religious directives are sound is somehow generated. It is in some sort of ceremonial form—even if that form be hardly more than the recitation of a myth, the consultation of an oracle, or the decoration of a grave—that the moods and motivations which sacred symbols induce in men and the general conceptions of the order of existence which they formulate for men meet and reinforce one another. In a ritual, the world as lived and the world as imagined, fused under the agency of a single set of symbolic forms, turn out to be the same world, producing thus that idiosyncratic transformation in one's sense of reality to which Santayana refers in my epigraph. Whatever role divine intervention may or may not play in the creation of faith—and it is not the business of the scientist to pronounce upon such matters one way or the other—it is, primarily at least, out of the context of concrete acts of religious observance that religious conviction emerges on the human plane.

However, though any religious ritual, no matter how apparently automatic or conventional (if it is truly automatic or merely conventional it is not religious), involves this symbolic fusion of ethos and world-view, it is mainly certain more elaborate and usually more public ones, ones in which a broad range of moods and motivations on the one hand and of metaphysical conceptions on the other are caught up, which shape the spiritual consciousness of a people. Employing a useful term introduced by Singer (1955), we may call these full-blown ceremonies "cultural performances" and note that they represent not only the point at which the dispositional and conceptual aspects of religious life converge for the believer, but also the point at which the interaction between them can be most readily examined by the detached observer:

> Whenever Madrasi Brahmans (and non-Brahmans, too, for that matter) wished to exhibit to me some feature of Hinduism, they always referred to, or invited me to see, a particular rite or ceremony in the life cycle, in a temple festival, or in the general sphere of religious and cultural performances. Reflecting on this in the course of my interviews and observations I found that the more abstract generalizations about Hinduism (my own as well as those I heard) could generally be checked, directly or indirectly, against these observable performances (Singer, 1958).

Of course, all cultural performances are not religious performances, and the line between those that are and artistic, or oven political ones is often not so easy to draw in practice, for, like social forms, symbolic forms can serve multiple purposes. But the point is that, paraphrasing slightly, Indians—"and perhaps all peoples"—seem to think of their religion "as encapsulated in these discrete performances which they [can] exhibit to visitors and to themselves" (Singer, 1955). The mode of exhibition is however radically different for the two sorts of witness, a fact seemingly overlooked by those who would argue that "religion is a form of human art" (Firth, 1951, p. 260). Where for "visitors" religious performances can, in the nature of the case only be presentations of a particular religious perspective, and thus aesthetically appreciated or scientifically dissected, for participants they are in addition enactments, materializations, realizations of it—not only models of what they believe, but also models *for* the believing of it. In those plastic dramas men attain their faith as they portray it.

As a case in point, let me take a spectacularly theatrical cultural performance from Bali—that in which a terrible witch called Rangda engages in a ritual combat with an endearing monster called Barong.[5]

---

[5] The Rangda-Barong complex has been extensively described and analyzed by a series of unusually gifted ethnographers (Belo, 1949, 1960; deZoete & Spies, 1938; Bateson & Mead, 1942; Covarrubias, 1937) and I will make no attempt to present it here in more than schematic form. Much of my interpretation of the

Usually, but not inevitably presented on the occasion of a death temple celebration, the drama consists of a masked dance in which the witch—depicted as a wasted old widow, prostitute, and eater of infants—comes to spread plague and death upon the land and is opposed by the monster—depicted as a kind of cross between a clumsy bear, a silly puppy, and a strutting Chinese dragon. Rangda, danced by a single male, is a hideous figure. Her eyes bulge from her forehead like swollen boils. Her teeth become tusks curving up over her cheeks and fangs protruding down over her chin. Her yellowed hair falls down around her in a matted tangle. Her breasts are dry and pendulous dugs edged with hair, between which hang, like so many sausages, strings of colored entrails. Her long red tongue is a stream of fire. And as she dances she splays her dead-white hands, from which protrude ten-inch claw-like fingernails, out in front of her and utters unnerving shrieks of metallic laughter. Barong, danced by two men fore-and-aft in vaudeville horse fashion, is another matter. His shaggy sheepdog coat is hung with gold and mica ornaments that glitter in the half-light. He is adorned with flowers, sashes, feathers, mirrors, and a comical beard made from human hair. And though, a demon too, his eyes also pop and he snaps his fanged jaws with seemly fierceness when faced with Rangda or other affronts to his dignity, the cluster of tinkling bells which hang from his absurdly arching tail somehow contrives to take most of the edge off his fearfulness. If Rangda is a satanic image, Barong is a farcical one, and their clash is a clash (an inconclusive one) between the malignant and the ludicrous.

This odd counterpoint of implacable malice and low comedy pervades the whole performance. Rangda, clutching her magical white cloth, moves around in a slow stagger, now pausing immobile in thought or uncertainty, now lurching suddenly forward. The moment of her entry (one sees those terrible long-nailed hands first as she emerges through the split gateway at the top of a short flight of stone stairs) is one of terrific tension when it seems, to a "visitor" at least, that everyone is about to break and run in panic. She herself seems insane with fear and hated as she screams deprecations at Barong amid the wild clanging of the gamelan. She may in fact go amok. I have myself seen Rangdas hurl themselves headlong into the

---

complex rests on personal observations made in Bali during 1957–1958 (see Geertz, 1964b).

gamelan or run frantically about in total confusion, being subdued and reoriented only by the combined force of a half-dozen spectators; and one hears many tales of amok Rangdas holding a whole village in terror for hours and of impersonators becoming permanently deranged by their experiences. But Barong, though he is charged with the same mana-like sacred power (*sakti* in Balinese) as Rangda, and his impersonators are also entranced, seems to have very great difficulty in being serious. He frolics with his retinue of demons (who add to the gaiety by indelicate pranks of their own), lies down on a metallaphone while it is being played or beats on a drum with his legs, moves in one direction in his front half and another in his rear or bends his segmented body into foolish contortions, brushes flies from his body or sniffs aromas in the air, and generally prances about in paroxysms of narcissistic vanity. The contrast is not absolute, for Rangda is sometimes momentarily comic as when she pretends to polish the mirrors on Barong's coat, and Barong becomes rather more serious after Rangda appears, nervously clacking his jaws at her and ultimately attacking her directly. Nor are the humorous and the horrible always kept rigidly separated, as in that strange scene in one section of the cycle in which several minor witches (disciples of Rangda) toss the corpse of a stillborn child around to the wild amusement of the audience; or another, no less strange, in which the sight of a pregnant woman alternating hysterically between tears and laughter while being knocked about by a group of grave-diggers, seems for some reason excruciatingly funny. The twin themes of horror and hilarity find their purest expression in the two protagonists and their endless, indecisive struggle for dominance, but they are woven with deliberate intricacy through the whole texture of the drama. They—or rather the relations between them—are what it is about.

It is unnecessary to attempt a thoroughgoing description of a Rangda-Barong performance here. Such performances vary widely in detail, consist of several not too closely integrated parts, and in any case are so complex in structure as to defy summary. For our purposes, the main point to be stressed is that the drama is, for the Balinese, not merely a spectacle to be watched but a ritual to be enacted. There is no aesthetic distance here separating actors from audience and placing depicted events in an unenterable world of illusion, and by the time a full-scale Rangda-Barong encounter has been concluded a majority, often nearly all, of the members of the group sponsoring it will have become caught up in it not just imaginatively but bodily. In one of Belo's examples (1960, pp. 159–168) I count upwards of seventy-five people—men, women, and children—taking part in the activity at some point or other, and thirty to forty participants is in no way unusual. As a performance, the drama is like a high mass not like a presentation of *Murder in the Cathedral*: it is a drawing near, not a standing back.

In part, this entry into the body of the ritual takes place through the agency of the various supporting roles contained in it—minor witches, demons, various sorts of legendary and mythical figures—which selected villagers enact. But mostly it takes place through the agency of an extraordinarily developed capacity for psychological dissociation on the part of a very large segment of the population. A Rangda-Barong struggle is inevitably marked by anywhere from three or four to several dozen spectators becoming possessed by one or another demon, falling into violent trances "like firecrackers going off one after the other" (Bela, 1960), and, snatching up krisses, rushing to join the fray. Mass trance, spreading like a panic, projects the individual Balinese out of the commonplace world in which he usually lives into that most uncommonplace one in which Rangda and Barong live. To become entranced is, for the Balinese, to cross a threshold into another order of existence—the word for trance is *nadi*, from *dadi*, often translated "to become" but which might be even more simply rendered as "to be." And even those who, for whatever reasons, do not make this spiritual crossing are caught up in the proceedings, for it is they who must keep the frenzied activities of the entranced from getting out of hand by the application of physical restraint if they are ordinary men, by the sprinkling of holy water and the chanting of spells if they are priests. At its height a Rangda-Barong rite hovers, or at least seems to hover, on the brink of mass amok with the diminishing band of the unentranced striving desperately (and, it seems almost always unsuccessfully) to control the growing band of the entranced.

In its standard form—if it can be said to have a standard form—the performance begins with an appearance of Barong, prancing and preening, as a general prophylactic against what is to follow. Then may come various mythic scenes relating the story—not always precisely the same one—upon which the performance is based—until finally Barong and then Rangda appear. Their battle begins. Barong drives Rangda back toward the gate of the death temple. But he has not the power to expel her completely and he is in turn driven back toward the village. At length, when it seems as though Rangda will finally prevail, a number of entranced men rise, krisses in hand, and rush to support Barong. But as they approach Rangda (who has turned her back in meditation), she wheels upon them and, waving her *sakti* white cloth, leaves them comatose on the ground. Rangda then hastily retires (or is carried) to the temple, where she herself collapses, hidden from the aroused crowd which, my informants said, would kill her were it to see her in a helpless state. The Barong moves among the kris dancers and wakens them by snapping his jaws at them or nuzzling them with his beard. As they return, still entranced, to "consciousness," they are enraged by the disappearance of Rangda, and unable to attack her they turn their krisses (harmlessly because they are entranced) against their own chests in frustration. Usually sheer pandemonium breaks out at this point with members of the crowd, of both sexes, falling into trance all around the courtyard and rushing out to stab themselves, wrestle with one another, devour live chicks or excrement, wallow convulsively in the mud, and so on, while the non-entranced attempt to relieve them of their krisses and keep them at least minimally in order. In time, the trancers sink, one by one, into coma from which they are aroused by the priests' holy water and the great battle is over—once more a complete stand-off. Rangda has not been conquered, but neither has she conquered.

One place to search for the meaning of this ritual is in the collection of myths, tales, and explicit beliefs which it supposedly enacts. However, not only are these various and variable—for some people Rangda is an incarnation of Durga, Siva's malignant consort, for others she is Queen Mahendradatta, a figure from a court legend set in eleventh-century Java, for yet others, the spiritual leader of witches as the Brahmana Priest is the spiritual leader of men; and notions of who (or "what") Barong is are equally diverse and even vaguer—but they seem to play only a secondary role in the Balinese' perception of the drama. It is in the direct encounter with the two figures in the context of the actual performance that the villager comes to know them as, so far as he is concerned, genuine realities. They are, then, not representations of anything, but presences. And when the villagers go into trance they become—*nadi*—themselves part of the realm in which those presences exist. To ask, as I once did, a man who has *been* Rangda whether he thinks she is real is to leave oneself open to the suspicion of idiocy.

The acceptance of authority that underlies the religious perspective that the ritual embodies thus flows from the enactment of the ritual itself. By inducing a set of moods and motivations—an ethos—and defining an image of cosmic order—a world-view—by means of a single set of symbols, the performance makes the model *for* and model *of* aspects of religious belief mere transpositions of one another. Rangda evokes fear (as well as hatred, disgust, cruelty, horror, and, though I have not been able to treat the sexual aspects of the performance here, lust); but she also depicts it:

> The fascination which the figure of the Witch holds for the Balinese imagination can only be explained when it is recognized that the Witch is not only a fear inspiring figure, but that she is Fear. Her hands with their long menacing finger-nails do not clutch and claw at her victims, although children who play at being witches do curl their hands in such gestures. But the Witch herself spreads her arms with palms out and her finger flexed backward, in the gesture the Balinese call *kapar*, a term which they apply to the sudden startled reaction of a man who falls from a tree. . . . Only when we see the Witch as herself afraid, as well as frightening, is it possible to explain her appeal, and the pathos which surrounds her as she dances, hairy, forbidding, tusked and alone, giving her occasional high eerie laugh (Bateson & Mead 1942, p. 36).

And on his side Barong not only induces laughter, he incarnates the Balinese version of the comic spirit—a distinctive combination of playfulness, exhibitionism, and extravagant love of elegance which, along with fear, is perhaps the dominant motive in their life. The constantly recurring struggle of Rangda and Barong to an inevitable draw is thus—for the believing Balinese—both the formulation of a general religious conception and the authoritative experience which justifies, even compels, its acceptance.

5. . . . *that the moods and motivations seem uniquely realistic.*

But no one, not even a saint, lives in the world religious symbols formulate all of the time, and the majority of men live in it only at moments. The everyday world of common-sense objects and practical acts is, as Schutz (1962, pp. 226ff.) says, the paramount reality in human experience—paramount in the sense that it is the world in which we are most solidly rooted, whose inherent actuality we can hardly question (however much we may question certain portions of it), and from whose pressures and requirements we can least escape. A man, even large groups of men, may be aesthetically insensitive, religiously unconcerned, and unequipped to pursue formal scientific analysis, but he cannot be completely lacking in common sense and survive. The dispositions which religious rituals induce thus have their most important impact—from a human point of view—outside the boundaries of the ritual itself as they reflect back to color the individual's conception of the established world of bare fact. The peculiar tone that marks the Plains vision quest, the Manus confession, or the Javanese mystical exercise pervades areas of the life of these peoples far beyond the immediately religious, impressing upon them a distinctive style in the sense both of a dominant mood and a characteristic movement. The interweaving of the malignant and the comic, which the Rangda-Barong combat depicts, animates a very wide range of everyday Balinese behavior, much of which, like the ritual itself, has an air of candid fear narrowly contained by obsessive playfulness. Religion is sociologically interesting not because, as vulgar positivism would have it (Leach, 1954, pp. 10ff.), it describes the social order (which, in so far as it does it does not only very obliquely but very incompletely), but because, like environment, political power, wealth, jural obligation, personal affection, and a sense of beauty, it shapes it.

The movement back and forth between the religious perspective and the common-sense perspective is actually one of the more obvious empirical occurrences on the social scene, though, again, one of the most neglected by social anthropologists, virtually all of whom have seen it happen countless times. Religious belief has usually been presented as an homogeneous characteristic of an individual, like his place of residence, his occupational role, his kinship position, and so on. But religious belief in the midst of ritual, where it engulfs the total person, transporting him, so far as he is concerned, into another mode of existence, and religious belief as the pale, remembered reflection of that experience in the midst of everyday life are not precisely the same thing, and the failure to realize this has led to some confusion, most especially in connection with the so-called "primitive mentality" problem. Much of the difficulty between Lévy-Bruhl (1926) and Malinowski (1948) on the nature of "native thought," for example, arises from a lack of full recognition of this distinction; for where the French philosopher was concerned with the view of reality savages adopted when taking a specifically religious perspective, the Polish-English ethnographer was concerned with that which they adopted when taking a strictly common-sense one. Both perhaps vaguely sensed that they were not talking about exactly the same thing, but where they went astray was in failing to give a specific accounting of the way in which these two forms of "thought"—or, as I would rather say, these two modes of symbolic formulation—interacted, so that where Lévy-Bruhl's savages tended to live, despite his postludial disclaimers, in a world composed entirely of mystical encounters, Malinowski's tended to live, despite his stress on the functional importance of religion, in a world composed entirely of practical actions. They became reductionists (an idealist is as much of a reductionist as a materialist) in spite of themselves because they failed to see man as moving more or less easily, and very frequently, between radically contrasting ways of looking at the world, ways which are not continuous with one another but separated by cultural gaps across which Kierkegaardian leaps must be made in both directions:

> There are as many innumerable kinds of different shock experiences as there are different finite provinces of meaning upon which I may bestow the accent of reality. Some instances are: the shock of falling asleep as the leap into the world of dreams; the inner transformation we endure if the curtain in the theatre rises as the transition to the world of the stageplay; the radical change in our attitude if, before a painting, we permit our visual field to be limited by what is within the frame as the passage into the pictorial world; our quandary relaxing into laughter, if, in listening to a joke, we are for a short time ready to accept the fictitious world of the jest as a reality in relation to which the world of our daily life takes on the character of foolishness; the child's turning toward his toy as the transition into the play-world; and so on. But also the religious experiences in all their varieties—for instance Kierkegaard's experience of the "instant" as the leap into the religious sphere—are examples of such a shock, as well as the decision of the scientist to replace all passionate participation in the affairs of "this world" by a disinterested attitude (Schutz, 1962, p. 231).

The recognition and exploration of the qualitative difference—an empirical, not a transcendental difference—between religion pure and religion applied, between an encounter with the supposedly "really real" and a viewing of ordinary experience in light of what that encounter seems to reveal, will, therefore, take us further toward an understanding of what a Bororo means when he says "I am a parakeet," or a Christian when he says "I am a sinner," than either a theory of primitive mysticism in which the commonplace world disappears into a cloud of curious ideas or of a primitive pragmatism in which religion disintegrates into a collection of useful fictions. The parakeet example, which I take from Percy (1961), is a good one. For as he points out, it is unsatisfactory to say either that the Bororo thinks he is literally a parakeet (for he does not try to mate with other parakeets), that his statement is false or nonsense (for, clearly, he is not offering—or at least not only offering—the sort of class-membership argument which can confirmed or refuted as, say, "I am a Bororo" can be confirmed or refuted), or yet again that it is false scientifically but true mythically (because that leads immediately to the pragmatic fiction notion which, as it denies the accolade of truth to myth in the very act of bestowing it, is internally self-contradictory). More coherently it would seem to be necessary to see the sentence as having a different sense in the context of the "finite province of meaning" which makes up the religious perspective and of that which makes up the common-sensical. In the religious, our Bororo is "really" a "parakeet," and given the proper ritual context might well "mate" with other "parakeets"—with metaphysical ones like himself not commonplace ones such as those which fly bodily about in ordinary trees. In the common-sensical perspective he is a parakeet in the sense—I assume—that he belongs to a clan whose members regard the parakeet as their totem, a membership from which, given the fundamental nature of reality as the religious perspective reveals it, certain moral and practical consequences flow. A man who says he is a parakeet is, if he says it in normal conversation, saying that, as myth and ritual demonstrate, he is shot through with parakeetness and that this religious fact has some crucial social implications—we parakeets must stick together, not marry one another, not eat mundane parakeets, and so on, for to do otherwise is to act against the grain of the whole universe. It is this placing of proximate acts in ultimate contexts that makes religion, frequently at least, socially so powerful. It alters, often radically, the whole landscape presented to common sense, alters it in such a way that the moods and motivations induced by religious practice seem themselves supremely practical, the only sensible ones to adopt given the way things "really" are.

Having ritually "lept" (the image is perhaps a bit too athletic for the actual facts—"slipped" might be more accurate) into the framework of meaning which religious conceptions define and, the ritual ended, returned again to the common-sense world, a man is—unless, as sometimes happens, the experience fails to register—changed. And as he is changed so also is the common-sense world, for it is now seen as but the partial form of a wider reality which corrects and completes it. But this correction and completion is not, as some students of "comparative religion" (e.g. Campbell, 1949, pp. 236–237) would have it, everywhere the same in content. The nature of the bias religion gives to ordinary life varies with the religion involved, with the particular dispositions induced in the believer by the specific conceptions of cosmic order he has come to accept. On the level of the "great" religions, organic distinctiveness is usually recognized, at times insisted upon to the point of zealotry. But even at its simplest folk and tribal levels—where the individuality of religious traditions has so often been dissolved into such desiccated types as "animism," "animalism," "totemism," "shamanism," "ancestor worship," and all the other insipid categories by means of which ethnographers of religion devitalize their data—the idiosyncratic character of how various groups of men behave because of what they believe they have experienced is clear. A tranquil Javanese would be no more at home in guilt-ridden Manus than an activist Crow would be in passionless Java. And for all the witches and ritual clowns in the world, Rangda and Barong are not generalized but thoroughly singular figurations of fear and gaiety. What men believe is as various as what they are—a proposition that holds with equal force when it is inverted.

It is this particularity of the impact of religious systems upon social systems (and upon personality systems) which renders general assessments of the value of religion in either moral or functional terms impossible. The sorts of moods and motivations which characterize a man who has just come from an Aztec human sacrifice are rather different from those of one who has just put off his Kachina mask. Even within the same society, what one "learns" about the essential pattern of life from a sorcery rite and from a commensual meal will have rather diverse effects on social and psychological functioning. One of the main methodological problems in writing about religion scientifically is to put aside at once the tone of the village atheist and that of the village preacher, as well as their more sophisticated equivalents, so that the social and psychological implications of particular religious beliefs can emerge in a clear and neutral light. And when that is done, overall questions about whether religion is "good" or "bad," "functional," "dysfunctional," "ego strengthening," or "anxiety producing"—disappear like the chimeras they are, and one is left with particular evaluations, assessments, and diagnoses in particular cases. There remain, of course, the hardly unimportant questions of whether this or that religious assertion is true, this or that religious experience genuine, or whether true religious assertions and genuine religious experiences are possible at all. But such questions cannot even be asked, much less answered, within the self-imposed limitations of the scientific perspective.

III.

For an anthropologist, the importance of religion lies in its capacity to serve, for an individual or for a group, as a source of general, yet distinctive conceptions of the world, the self, and the relations between them, on the one hand—its model *of* aspect—and of rooted, no less distinctive "mental" dispositions—its model *for* aspect—on the other. From these cultural functions flow, in turn, its social and psychological ones.

Religious concepts spread beyond their specifically metaphysical contexts to provide a framework of general ideas in terms of which a wide range of experience—intellectual, emotional, moral—can be given meaningful form. The Christian sees the Nazi movement against the background of The Fall which, though it does not, in a causal sense, explain it, places it in a moral, a cognitive, even an affective sense. An Azande sees the collapse of a granary upon a friend or relative against the background of a concrete and rather special notion of witchcraft and thus avoids the philosophical dilemmas as well as the psychological stress of indeterminism. A Javanese finds in the borrowed and reworked concept of *rasa* ("sense-taste-feeling-meaning") a means by which to "see" choreographic, gustatory, emotional, and political phenomena in a new light. A synopsis of cosmic order, a set of religious beliefs, is also a gloss upon the mundane world of social relationships and psychological events. It renders them graspable.

But more than gloss, such beliefs are also a template. They do not merely interpret social and psychological processes in cosmic terms—in which case they would be philosophical, not religious—but they shape them. In the doctrine of original sin is embedded also a recommended attitude toward life, a recurring good, and a persisting set of motivations. The Zande learns witchcraft conceptions not just to understand apparent "accidents" as not accidents at all, but to react to those spurious accidents with hatred for the agent who caused them and to proceed against him with appropriate resolution. *Rasa,* in addition to being a concept of truth, beauty, and goodness, is also a preferred mode of experiencing, a kind of affectless detachment, a variety of bland aloofness, an unshakable calm. The moods and motivations a religious orientation produces cast a derivative, lunar light over the solid features of a people's secular life.

The tracing of the social and psychological role of religion is thus not so much a matter of finding correlations between specific ritual acts and specific secular social ties—though these correlations do, of course, exist and are very worth continued investigation, especially if we can contrive something novel to say about them. More, it is a matter of understanding how it is that men's notions, however implicit, of the "really real" and the dispositions these notions induce in them, color their sense of the reasonable, the practical, the humane, and the moral. How far they do so (for in many societies religion's effects seem quite circumscribed, in others completely pervasive); how deeply they do so (for some men, and groups of men, seem to wear their religion lightly so far as the secular world goes, while others seem to apply their faith to each occasion, no matter how trivial); and how effectively they do so (for the width of the gap between what religion recommends and what people actually do is most variable cross-culturally)—all these are crucial issues in the comparative sociology and psychology of religion. Even the degree to which religious systems themselves are developed seems to vary extremely widely, and not merely on a simple evolutionary basis. In one society, the level of elaboration of symbolic formulations of ultimate actuality may reach extraordinary degrees of complexity and systematic articulation; in another, no less developed socially, such formulations may remain primitive in the true sense, hardly more than congeries of fragmentary by-beliefs and isolated images, of sacred reflexes and spiritual pictographs. One need only think of the Australians and the Bushmen, the Toradja and the Alorese, the Hopi and the Apache, the Hindus and the Romans, or even the Italians and the Poles, to see that degree of religious articulateness is not a constant even as between societies of similar complexity. The anthropological study of religion is therefore a two stage operation: first, an analysis of the system of meanings embodied in the symbols which make up the religion proper, and, second, the relating of these systems to social-structural and psychological processes. My dissatisfaction with so much of contemporary social anthropological work in religion is not that it concerns itself with the second stage, but that it neglects the first, and in so doing takes for granted what most needs to be elucidated. To discuss the role of ancestor worship in regulating political succession, of sacrificial feasts in defining kinship obligations, of spirit worship in scheduling agricultural practices of divination in reinforcing social control, or of initiation rites in propelling personality maturation are in no sense unimportant endeavors, and I am not recommending they be abandoned for the kind of jejune cabalism into which symbolic analysis of exotic faiths can so easily fall. But to attempt them with but the most general, commonsense view of what ancestor worship, animal sacrifice, spirit worship, divination, or initiation rites are as religious patterns seems to me not particularly promising. Only when we have a theoretical analysis of symbolic action comparable in sophistication to that we now have for social and psychological action, will we be able to cope effectively with those aspects of social and psychological life in which religion (or art, or science, or ideology) plays a determinant role.

References

Bateson, G. 1958. *Naven*. Stanford: Stanford University Press, 2nd ed.

Bateson, G. & Mead, M. 1942. *Balinese Character*. New York: N.Y. Academy of Sciences.

Bell, C. 1914. *Art*. London: Chatto & Windus.

Belo, J. 1949. *Bali: Rangda and Barong*. New York: J. J. Augustin.

— 1960. *Trance in Bali*. New York: Columbia University Press.

Burke, K. 1941. *The Philosophy of Literary Form*. n.p.: Louisiana State University Press.

Campbell, J. 1949. *The Hero with a Thousand Faces*. New York: Pantheon.

Cassirir, E. 1953–57. *The Philosophy of Symbolic Forms* (trans. R. Mannheim). New Haven: Yale University Press. 3 vols.

Covarrubias, M. 1937. *The Island of Bali*. New York: Knopf.

Craik, K. 1952. *The Nature of Explanation*. Cambridge: Cambridge University Press.

Evans-Pritchard, E. E. 1937. *Witchcraft, Oracles, and Magic Among the Azande*. Oxford: Claredon Press.

Firth, R. 1951. *Elements of Social Organization*. London: Watts; New York: Philosophical Library.

Fortune, R. F. 1935. *Manus Religion*. Philadelphia: American Philosophical Society.

Von Frisch, K. 1962. Dialects in the Language of the Bees. *Scientific American*, August.

Geertz, C. 1958. Ethos, World-View and the Analysis of Sacred Symbols. *Antioch Review*, Winter (1957–58): 421–437.

— 1960. *The Religion of Java*. Glencoe, Ill.: The Free Press.

— 1962. The Growth of Culture and the Evolution of Mind. In J. Scher (ed.), *Theories of the Mind*. New York: The Free Press. 713–740.

— 1964a. Ideology as a Cultural System. In D. Apter (ed.), *Ideology of Discontent*. New York: The Free Press.

— 1964b. "Internal Conversion" in Contemporary Bali. In J. Bastin & R. Roolvink (eds.), *Malayan and Indonesian Studies*, Oxford: Oxford University Press, 282–302.

Goody, J. 1961. Religion and Ritual: The Definition Problem. *British Journal of Sociology* 12: 143–164.

Horowitz, N. H. 1956. The Gene. *Scientific American*, February.

James, William. 1904. *The Principles of Psychology*. New York: Henry Holt, 2 vols.

Janowitz, M. 1963. Anthropology and the Social Sciences. *Current Anthropology* 4: 139, 146–154.

Kluckhohn, C. 1949. The Philosophy of the Navaho Indians. In F. S. C. Northrop (ed,), *Ideological Differences and World Order*. New Haven: Yale University Press, 356–384.

— 1953. Universal Categories of Culture. In A. L. Kroeber (ed.), *Anthropology Today*. Chicago: University of Chicago Press, 507–523.

Kluckhorn, C. & Leighton, D. 1946. *The Navaho*. Cambridge, Mass.: Harvard University Press.

Langer, S. 1953. *Feeling and Form*. New York: Scribner's.

— 1960. *Philosophy in a New Key*. Fourth Edition. Cambridge, Mass.: Harvard University Press.

— 1962. *Philosophical Sketches*. Baltimore: Johns Hopkins.

Leach, E. R. 1954. *Political Systems of Highland Burma*. London: Bell; Cambridge, Mass.: Harvard University Press.

Lévy-Bruhl, L. 1926. *How Natives Think*. New York: Knopf.

Lienhardt, G. 1961. *Divinity and Experience*. Oxford: Claredon Press.

Lorenz, K. 1952. *King Solomon's Ring*. London: Methuen.

Lowie, R. H. 1924. *Primitive Religion*. New York: Boni and Liveright.

MacIntyre, A. 1957. The Logical Status of Religious Belief. In A. MacIntyre (ed.), *Metaphysical Beliefs*. London: SCM Press, 167–211.

Malinowski, B. 1948. *Magic, Science and Religion*. Boston: Beacon Press.

Nadel, S. F. 1957. Malinowski on Magic and Religion. In R. Firth (ed.), *Man and Culture*. London: Routledge & Kegan Paul, 189–208.

Parsons, T. & Shills, E. 1951. *Toward a General Theory of Action*. Cambridge, Mass.: Harvard University Press.

Percy, W. 1958. Symbol, Consciousness and Intersubjectivity. *Journal of Philosophy* 15: 631–641.

— 1961. The Symbolic Structure of Interpersonal Process. *Psychiatry* 24: 39–52.

Radcliffe-Brown, A. R. 1952. *Structure and Function in Primitive Society*. Glencoe, Ill.: Free Press.

Radin, P. 1957. *Primitive Man as a Philosopher*. New York: Dover.

Reichard, G. 1950. *Navaho Religion*. New York: Pantheon, 2 vols.

Ryle, G. 1949. *The Concept of Mind*. London: Hutchinson; New York: Barnes & Noble.

Santayana, G. 1905–1906. *Reason in Religion*. Vol. 2 of *The Life of Reason, or The Phases of Human Progress*. London: Constable; New York: Scribner's.

Schutz, A. 1962. *The Problem of Social Reality* (vol. I of *Collected Papers*). The Hague: Martinus Nijhoff.

Singer, M. 1955. The Cultural Pattern of Indian Civilization. *Far Eastern Quarterly* 15: 23–36.

— 1958. The Great Tradition in a Metropolitan Center: Madras. In M. Singer (ed.), *Traditional India*. Philadelphia: American Folklore Society, 140–82.

Smith, C. W. & Dale, A. M. 1920. *The Ila-Speaking Peoples of Northern Rhodesia*. London: Macmillan.

DeZoete, B. & Spies, W. 1938. *Dance and Drama in Bali*. London: Faber & Faber.

7

Geertz's Longlasting Moods, Motivations, and Metaphysical Conceptions

Nancy K. Frankenberry and Hans H. Penner

In this paper we present a critique of Geertz's classic essay as embodying three of the most "powerful, pervasive, and longlasting moods and motivations" that permeate theories of religion in this century: the symbolic-meaning mood; the functionalist mood; and the relativist mood. Underlying and sustaining these moods are certain philosophical and epistemological dogmas and myths which we identify. To the extent that these pervade the study of religion, they hinder its theoretical development and we argue for their removal.

Some scholars may suppose that Geertz's essay has already received ample critical attention and is, therefore, no longer a "front burner" in theoretical debates in religious studies. We continue to find, to the contrary, that the legacy of the Geertzian approach to religion is indeed very much alive. As Daniel Pals wrote of Geertz in 1996, "his critics are few; his admirers legion."[1] In 1997, Jacob Neusner, the well-known historian of religions and of Judaica, could report that Geertz seemed to write "that wonderful essay 'Religion as a Cultural System' as a personal letter to me," so that it became "the source for my scholarly paradigm."[2]

The frequency with which scholars continue to cite Geertz's 1966 essay and endorse its definition of religion uncritically is surprising. Studying this classic thirty years after its initial publication,

---

[1] Daniel L Pals, *Seven Theories of Religion* (New York: Oxford University Press, 1996), p. 259.

[2] Jacob Neusner, "From History to Religion," in *The Craft of Religious Studies* (Berkeley: University of California, 1997), p. 107.

we surveyed the secondary literature around it and discovered that between 1966 and 1996 "Religion as a Cultural System" was cited at least 500 times in journals of religion or anthropology. With but a few exceptions, Geertz's well-known definition of religion was simply quoted without comment and allowed to serve as a basis for understanding religion or the meaning of religious symbolism. Such popularity can be explained only in part by the fact that Geertz has been such a major figure in constructing a bridge between the social sciences and the humanities, and more specifically between anthropology and theology.[3] At its first appearance in 1966, "Religion as a Cultural System" could represent a fairly rare instance of an eminent anthropologist drawing on the cultural sciences to rescue religion from the ravages of positivism. Since then, however, we suspect that the continued use of this definition of religion has gone hand in hand with a diminution of critical reflection on its central theoretical and methodological assumptions.[4]

---

[3] For but one example of the latter, see John Morgan, "Religion and Culture as Meaning Systems: A Dialogue between Geertz and Tillich," *Journal of Religion* 57 (1977): 363–75. From the side of anthropology, William A. Sewell, Jr. has recently described Geertz as "surely the most influential American anthropologist of his generation" and cited Renata Rosaldo's remark that it is Clifford Geertz who has become "the ambassador from anthropology." See William A. Sewell, Jr., "Geertz, Cultural Systems, and History: From Synchrony to Transformation," *Representations* 59 (1997): 35.

[4] Segal, Munson, and Shankman provide critical analyses of Geertz's approach to religion but they do not focus on his definition of religion or its interpretation. See: Robert A. Segal, *Explaining and Interpreting Religion: Essays on the Issue* (New York: Peter Lang, 1992), Henry Munson, Jr., "Geertz on Religion: The Theory and the Practice," *Religion* 16 (1986): 19–32, and Paul Shankman, "The Thick and the Thin: On the Interpretive Theoretical Perspective of Clifford Geertz," *Current Anthropology* 25 (1984): 261–79. Most of the sources we have surveyed simply cite or mention Geertz's definition as a settled issue, or piously speak of room for improvement: "The doubts do suggest, however, that other and future theorists who see promise in this approach—as indeed there is—would be quite mistaken to suppose that there is no need still to assess, revise, and improve it" (Pals, p. 263). Shankman's conclusion is more critical: "A movement without direction, a program troubled by inconsistency, an approach that claims superiority over conventional social science but is limited by the absence of criteria for evaluating alternative theories, and type cases that do not necessarily support the interpretive theory—can this be the basis for a different anthropology and a major intellectual movement? Granted that the ideas are alluring, exciting, and even glamorous, the assessment of theory is not merely a matter of taste" (Shankman, p. 270). Two recent authors who do deal directly and

The critique offered here is important for several reasons. First, it reveals much about the problems that frame the study of religion. Second, it raises several basic philosophical issues that have received new evaluation in recent years. Third, it allows us to expose for further critique several methodological assumptions that are widely shared by our colleagues in the academy.

I. The Inscrutability of Definition

Geertz reminds us that although it is notorious that definitions establish nothing, they do, if carefully constructed, provide an orientation, an effective way of developing and controlling a novel line of inquiry. The carefully constructed definition of religion Geertz proposes is by now familiar to most students of religion:

> (1) a system of symbols which acts to (2) establish powerful, pervasive, and long-lasting moods and motivations in men by (3) formulating conceptions of a general order of existence and (p. 4) clothing these conceptions with such an aura of factuality that (5) the moods and motivations seem uniquely realistic.[5]

We find all five points in Geertz's definition of religion problematic. First, in defining religion as "a system of symbols," Geertz himself notes the "tremendous weight" (p. 179) that he places on the notion of symbol. Yet this notion remains ambiguous and underdeveloped despite the heavy work it is made to do. Brushing aside the long history of intellectual efforts to construct a coherent theory of symbol, Geertz turns to Suzanne Langer for an articulation of the meaning of symbol. A symbol, he says, is "used for any object, act, event, quality, or relation which serves as a vehicle for a

---

critically with Geertz's definition notice only Foucauldian gaps. See Benson Saler, *Conceptualizing Religion: Immanent Anthropologists, Transcendent Natives, and Unbounded Categories* (Leiden: Brill, 1993) and Talal Asad, "The Construction of Religion as an Anthropological Category," in Asad, *Genealogies of Religion* (Baltimore: The Johns Hopkins Press, 1993), pp. 27–54, originally published in *Man* 18:2 (June 1983): 23–59. Asad's thrust is basically the question, ignored by Geertz, How does power create religion? Saler's focus is largely explicative, with a critical evaluation of Asad's critique. Our investigation differs from both of these in being primarily philosophical and epistemologically oriented.

[5] Clifford Geertz, "Religion as a Cultural System," 184. *Anthropological Approaches to the Study of Religion*, ed. Michael Banton, (London: Tavistock Publications, 1966), reprinted in Geertz, Clifford, *The Interpretation of Cultures: Selected Essays*, (New York: Basic Books, 1973) & this vol. by permission. All page references in our Chap. 7 are to Geertz, Chap. 6 in this volume.

conception—the conception is the symbol's meaning" (p. 180). The sheer commonplaceness of this statement masks two problems. First, the use of "vehicle," made famous by I. A. Richards in 1936, is purely metaphorical. What we want to know but are not told is what semantic rules apply to symbols as vehicles of conception. Second, just what does Geertz mean by "conception?" Clarification of this term is crucial since "conception," given his definition, is the meaning of a symbol. Without clarification we are at a loss from the very beginning to interpret the meaning of the crucial terms "vehicle," "meaning," "symbol" and "conception."

As examples, Geertz uses the number 6, the cross, the churinga, the word "reality," and the morpheme "-ing" as symbols. They are all "vehicles for a conception." In that case, we might suppose they are something like words or "lexemes" in a sentence. But that would not quite do justice to Geertz's emphasis. Symbols, he thinks, are something more complex; these examples are "at least symbolic elements, because they are tangible formulations of notions, abstractions from experience fixed in perceptible forms, concrete embodiments of ideas, attitudes, judgments, longings, or beliefs" (p. 180).

The question posed here is whether there are any constraints on what can count as a "vehicle for conceptions." Without constraints on what can count as a symbol Geertz runs the risk of making symbols completely arbitrary. What sense would it make to say that symbols are "vehicles" of meaning if the arbitrariness of the symbol lacked any of the semantic features we are familiar with? In other words, if symbols are completely arbitrary how would a speaker/hearer or the scholar of religion tell the difference between a good interpretation and a bad one? It would seem that the art of hermeneutics, already somewhat an airy activity, would go into a free fall.

The central problem is that Geertz never explains the basic premise of his definition of religion—the inscrutable relation between symbols and concepts. The claim that symbols are vehicles for conceptions, and that the conception is the meaning of a symbol or a symbolic element, remains opaque. Worse than opaque, Geertz seems confused about the relation between symbols and concepts, a relation of central importance for making sense of the theory. In some passages, symbols are not vehicles for meaning but are said to be the very constitution of meaning itself. That is to say, they do not function as symbols "of" concepts, but as symbols "for" concepts. We consider this difficulty more closely in the next section.

Turning away from the complexity of this issue, Geertz moves to a discussion of intrinsic and extrinsic information systems, coded instructions of DNA, and the recipes of proteins. Detours into the biological sciences in essays on religion and culture usually signal a profound loss of direction. But Geertz quickly finds his way by pointing out that beavers may well be physiologically wired to build dams but that we humans also need a "conception of what it is to build a dam, a conception we can get only from some symbolic source—a blueprint, a textbook, or a string of speech by someone who already knows how dams are built, or, of course, from manipulating [a well worn euphemism in anthropology] graphic or linguistic elements in such a way as to attain for himself a conception of what dams are and how they are built" (pp. 181–82).

No one would disagree with this, of course. The linguistic ability of human beings and the production of blueprints, textbooks, speech and graphics is species-specific. Therefore, Geertz's detour into DNA and the synthesis of proteins does not take us very far in understanding how a symbol or a system of complex symbolism can provide, carry, or express conceptions. If it is the case that symbols and symbolic systems presuppose or entail conceptions, it is also the case that to "manipulate" symbols presupposes language, and language entails propositional attitudes.

Presupposed throughout is precisely what Geertz needs to explain—the relation between a symbol and a concept. More particularly what requires clarification is the notion that the relation between a symbol and a concept signifies meaning. How is it possible, we wonder, to talk about meaning without considering truth conditions? The more the essay unfolds, the more the definition of symbol (and its variants) leads us to suspect that symbolic language is devoid of truth conditions, that it does not make sense on Geertz's terms to talk about whether symbolic statements are true or false, or whether certain symbols contradict each other. We will return to this issue in our conclusion.

We see but two options for interpreting the implications of Geertz's theory, neither of which is very satisfactory for work in religious studies. Either religious symbol systems have their own unique truth conditions, or such systems are non-cognitive, illusory, and beyond "the whole question of factuality." In light of developments within the philosophy of language in the last thirty years we find the first option incoherent and unintelligible and the second simply mistaken.

II. A Nice Derangement of Epithets

In an apparent effort to explicate symbols as cultural patterns, Geertz next shifts to the topic of "model," whose repeated enclosure within quotation marks signals something non-literal. Citing Craik (1952), Geertz presents cultural patterns as models that are "sets of symbols whose relations to one another 'model' relations among entities, processes or what-have-you in physical, organic, social or psychological systems, 'paralleling', 'imitating', or 'simulating' them" (p. 182). As sets of symbols, models have two senses: as "models of" and as "models for." Models *of* reality entail the "manipulation of symbol structures so as to bring them, more or less closely, into parallel with the pre-established non-symbolic system, as when we grasp how dams work by developing a theory of hydraulics or constructing a flow chart" (p. 182). But this simply will not do. The problem is not with the phrase "more or less" although we would all hope that engineers have "manipulating" skills that will produce more rather than less. Rather, the important question concerns the unspecified relation between the "symbolic structures" we manipulate and any "pre-established non-symbolic system." Geertz has made this relation inscrutable, and to our knowledge none of his commentators has succeeded in explicating it either. Yet it is precisely this relation that is crucial for making sense of Geertz's definition of symbol as a genus of the vehicle of meaning and of religion as a species of symbolic systems. The same problem that clouds the conceptualization of "symbol" also attends the use of the term "model." The example from hydraulics backfires, unfortunately, because there are both clear constraints and semantic truth conditions in a theory of hydraulics that are lacking in Geertz's theory of religion.

Perhaps we can best make sense of Geertz's discussion of models *of* by thinking of it as an epithet for a correspondence theory of truth. After all, blueprints, maps, and flow charts are expected to "correspond," in some sense of the word, to "pre-established non-symbolic" reality (p. 182). So when Geertz says that models "are sets of symbols whose relations to one another 'model' relations among entities, processes, or what-have-you in physical, organic, social, or psychological systems, 'paralleling', 'imitating', or 'simulating' them" (p. 182), we can understand him as saying that symbolic systems *correspond* to non-symbolic physical, organic, or social systems in some complex way. But now another complex issue has been introduced, scarcely acknowledged on the surface of the text. Correspondence theories are notoriously difficult to defend, and are elusive at precisely the point where Geertz's account of symbols breaks down—that is, in specifying the nature of the correspondence *relation*.

What correspondence theorists require is an explanation of the presumed correspondence between the symbolic and the non-symbolic. Just how do sets of symbols parallel, simulate or imitate non-symbolic reality? How does one obtain a conception of what a dam is by "manipulating graphic or linguistic" sets of symbols? Is the blueprint or map accurate? Does the flow chart fit the facts? Is the symbolic representation an accurate description of the actual social system? Does the blueprint of the house match the actual house? Questions such as these have been the Achilles heel of all correspondence theories of truth, leading to their demise. Even in the unlikely event that a correspondence theory of meaning could be rescued philosophically, a further question would remain as to whether the symbols and models of various *religions* correspond to anything.

In light of these difficulties, we may well question the very notion of symbolic representation. What are the entities, processes, or facts to which symbols as vehicles can be said to correspond? How could we ever know if the simulation or the imitation is correct? Geertz does not even hint at how to go about answering such questions. Instead, he assigns religious symbolism to a shadowy domain beyond "the whole question of factuality," aligns it, like Plato, with "the really real," and declares that it is concerned with "utter actuality" (p. 201). Any question of whether religious symbolic systems are "right" or "correct," "good" or "bad" models cannot be asked or answered on these grounds.

Oddly, no scholar of religion who has analyzed this essay has, to our knowledge, raised the most crucial question of all: in what sense are symbols "representations?" It may conceivably be the case that the notion that religious symbols or sets of symbols are "models" is simply wrong-headed. Most of the sentences in our language, after all, are not models. Why should religious language be taken as an exception? Although we cannot present a complete argument here, we are claiming that theories that treat symbolic representation as models *of* presume some version of a correspondence theory of truth that cannot in the final analysis be made intelligible.[6]

Representational theories of symbolism begin and end as incomprehensible theories of truth. Their failure can be traced to the desire to include in the entities (the non-symbolic domain) to which a symbolic system corresponds not only the objects the symbols are "about" but also whatever the symbols say about them. However, there is no vantage point from which speakers can transcend the symbolic language in which they are embedded in order to judge that the correspondence is indeed "simulating," "imitating" or in any other way representing some non-symbolic reality. But it is exactly this impossible feat that all correspondence theories of truth and Geertz's notion of model *of* requires, on our analysis.

Turning next to the second sense of models as models *for,* we find additional problems also overlooked by previous commentators. Geertz's examples of models *for* reality pertain to the codes of DNA and the dance of bees. But such examples do little to explicate the problematic relation of non-symbolic systems to symbolic ones. As Geertz himself points out, the difference between the dance of bees and the coded program of DNA, on the one hand, and culture, on the other hand, is due to the fact that cultural patterns "give meaning, i.e. objective conceptual form, to social and psychological reality both by shaping themselves to it and by shaping it to themselves" (p. 182). Thus both senses of model *for* and model *of* entail a conceptualization process entirely lacking in the case of DNA and the dance of bees, making these analogies either highly metaphorical or simply false.

If a model *for* reality "is the manipulation of the non-symbolic systems in terms of the relationships expressed in the symbolic," then construction of a dam according to a hydraulic theory would be an example of "a model under whose guidance physical relationships are organized: it is a model *for* 'reality'" (p. 182). The conceptual process here is reversed. Now it is the symbolic vehicle (theory,

---

[6] See Donald Davidson, "On the Very Idea of a Conceptual Scheme," in *Inquiries Into Truth And Interpretation* (Oxford: Oxford University Press, 1984), pp. 13–51, and also Fredrick Stoutland, "Realism And Antirealism in Davidson's Philosophy of Language," I & II. *Critica* 14/15 (1982/3): 19–47.

doctrines, rites and myths) "under whose guidance physical relationships are organized" that becomes the model *for* reality. In this second kind of model, it appears that symbols become concepts. The non-symbolic domain comprises the engine of the vehicle for meaning. But once again the exact process by which this takes place is never specified by Geertz.

If he were to spell it out in terms of a theoretical concern with truth we suspect that models *for* would conform to what is known as a coherence theory of truth which places heavy emphasis on the internal consistency or coherence of a program, theory, or symbolic system. At stake would be the determination of whether the model *for* offers a reasonable and well-integrated picture, useful fiction, or illuminating paradigm. For Geertz has stipulated that "they [cultural patterns, the domain of the symbolic] give meaning, i.e. objective form, to social and psychological reality both by shaping themselves to it and by shaping it to themselves" (p. 182). Thus, models *for* reality "shape" or "organize" non-symbolic processes or "realities." Such models act as a program, "so that the program can be taken as a representation, or conception—a symbol—of the programmed [in an alternative medium]" (p. 183). The problem posed by this account is that, given a coherence theory of truth, there is no way to stave off skeptical worries that the world could be completely different from what we actually believe it to be, or from what the symbolic vehicles represent it as being—a curious consequence to say the least.

By positing a dialectical interplay between models *of* and models *for,* Geertz presumably aims at coherence, on the assumption that the interplay of symbolic and non-symbolic systems will mirror each other and form a coherent whole with both descriptive and prescriptive operations reinforcing one another. On our interpretation, however, what Geertz presents as "inter-transposable" models *of*/models *for* should be read as implying *alternative* theories of truth. In maintaining them both dialectically, Geertz presupposes two theories that are not only normally in conflict with each other, but, that are each individually flawed.

On the correspondence theory, the objective form that is given in cultural patterns is independent of symbol systems, and the symbols are supposed to be representations of that objective form, yet there is no way of knowing that any symbol system does indeed "correspond" or "represent" the non-symbolic domain. On the coherence theory the religious symbol system is said to organize, shape, or otherwise endow cultural patterns with meaning, but, as we have noted, the symbol system could be just as it is and yet the non-symbolic domain could be very different, for all we know, from the symbolic representations of it.

Geertz appears to want to have it both ways. "The inter-transposablity," he tells us, "of models *for* and models *of* which symbolic formulation makes possible is the distinctive characteristic of our mentality" (p. 183). Against this, we read Geertz's understanding of models as disclosing highly ideological operations. The models *for* reality derive their efficacy only from the illusion that they are models *of* reality.

Therefore, the key element in this claim—the notion of "symbolic formulation"—remains confused if not contradictory in Geertz's account of the two senses of model *of* and model *for*. Precisely how "symbolic formulation" makes "the inter-transposability of models" possible remains unexplained, along with any reason to suppose that the "inter-transposability" of symbolic models really occurs in the case of religion (p. 183). This in turn makes vacuous Geertz's statement that "true symbols" can be distinguished from other significations by their having a double aspect of being both models *of* and models *for* (p. 182). Instead, we would maintain that only sentences can be true or false, and that references to "true symbols" greatly muddles matters. Geertz only reiterates the problem when he states:

> Whether one sees the conception of a personal guardian spirit, a family tutelary or an immanent God as synoptic formulations of the character of reality or as templates for producing reality with such a character seems largely arbitrary, a matter of which aspect, the model *of* or model *for*, one wants for the moment to bring into focus. . . . They both express the world's climate and shape it (pp. 183-84).

This passage reinforces our interpretation of Geertz's definition of religion as tacitly employing two classical theories in a fusion of correspondence and coherence models both of which reduce to models *for* reality because they effect the illusion that they *are* uniquely realistic. Our criticism can now be summarized: to think of symbols as at once providing a kind of "synoptic formulation" of the world and serving "as templates for producing" it is to presuppose two competing theories the first of which is unintelligible and the second of which is untenable.[7] Geertz cannot explain what would be meant by "model of" without recourse to "correspondence" of some sort, and he cannot invoke a notion of correspondence without positing something like "intrinsic features a thing has independent of how it is described," or "reality as it is in itself." Because the presumed distinction between the "in itself" and the "for us" cannot be made intelligible, Geertz would be better off jettisoning it, and along with it, any notion of correspondence. On the other hand, he cannot explain what would be meant by "model for" without recourse to "coherence," and he cannot invoke a notion of coherence without positing a set of beliefs, or of sentences held to be true, whose consistency would be enough to make them true.

Moreover, because many different sets of belief are possible which are not consistent with one another—especially across religious "conceptions of a general order of existence"—the argument for coherence as the criterion of truth often produces the specter of relativism as an easy solution to the problems raised by the theory.

In the end, Geertz leaves the impression that "the distinctive characteristic of our mentality" could be schizophrenic, or a nice derangement of epithets.

III. Religion Is What It Does

For thirty years, one commentator after another, virtually without exception,[8] has characterized Clifford Geertz as an opponent of functionalism who rejects not only a functionalist explanation of religion but also any functionalist account of human cultural systems in general. Instead, it is frequently noted that Geertz pioneered a non-reductionistic, "thick" description of the systems of meanings

---

[7] Those not familiar with this debate may consult Donald Davidson, "The Structure and Content of Truth," *The Journal of Philosophy*, Vol. LXXXVII No. 6, (1990): 279–328, Gareth Evans, *The Varieties of Reference* (New York: Oxford University Press, 1995), and John H. McDowell, *Mind and World*, (Cambridge: Harvard University Press, 1994), in addition to the Davidson (1984) and Stoutland articles.

[8] For an interesting exception, see Stephen Karatheodoris, "From Social to Cultural Systems and Beyond: Twenty Years After 'Religion as a Cultural System," *Soundings: An Interdisciplinary Journal* Vol. LXXXI, No. 1 (1988): 53–94. Not surprisingly, the author is a sociologist; as a rule, most scholars of religion have not recognized, let alone offered a critique of, the outdated functionalist theory ingredient in Geertz's definition of religion.

religions convey, forging a hermeneutical view of the social sciences, a textual view of reality, and a semiotic view of culture. Like most received traditions, this account overlooks inconvenient counter-evidence. "Religion as a Cultural System" abounds with strong evidence of Geertz's retention of a functionalist approach to religion. In the last analysis, and despite their differences, Geertz is not very far at all from Malinowski's reasoning that "since we cannot define cult and creed by their objects, perhaps it will be possible to perceive their function."[9] As Martin Hollis once noted, "sacred anthropology is sceptical theology."[10]

This should come as no surprise. Beginning with the heyday of logical positivism, the history of the study of religion has shown that the Charybdis of positivism is escaped most often by embracing the Scylla of functionalism, and this in turn regularly empties into relativism. When symbols are thought not to have truth-conditions, the criterion of meaning shifts to use, and from there easily becomes relativized to the context of what it *does*. The very notion of symbol as a "vehicle" of meaning leads to the relativizing of concepts (symbols) and a return to Malinowski's question. For these reasons, the notion of a symbol as a *vehicle* of meaning seems just as misleading to us as the related notion that religious language has a special *kind* of meaning.

Although Geertz eschews crude versions of functionalism, and does not appeal to "biological needs" or explicitly to "psychological needs" that serve to explain the presence and persistence of religion, he indeed appeals to a subtle set of *needs*: human beings create religion (and other cultural systems) out of a *need for meaning*. Geertz's functionalist theory of religion is most evident in the middle section of his definition to which the largest part of the essay is devoted, augmenting the claim that sacred symbols "function to synthesize a people's ethos . . . and their worldview. . ." by establishing certain dispositions and formulating conceptions of a general order of existence (p. 179). This thesis comprises the heart of Geertz's essay and the part that, we suspect, has held most interest to many students of religion. With this, Geertz associates religion's persistence with its function of satisfying certain needs, chiefly the

---

[9] Branislaw Malinowski, *Magic, Science, and Religion* (New York: Doubleday, 1954), p. 37.

[10] Martin Hollis, "Reason and Ritual," *Philosophy* XLIII (1967): 247.

need for relief from anxiety, especially from the threat of disorder and chaos. Above all, human nature harbors the need for *meaning*, and so the question of why religion exists or persists is answered in terms of its functioning to provide meaning. Tempting as this thesis remains to many scholars in and outside of religious studies, we are convinced that the thesis is flawed.

The argument involves an erroneous causal claim: "If sacred symbols did not at one and the same time induce dispositions in human beings and formulate, however obliquely, inarticulately, or unsystematically, general ideas of order, then the empirical differentia of religious activity or religious experience would not exist" (p. 187). The slightest hint that this symbolic order might fail in the face of uncertainty "raises within [us] the gravest sort of anxiety." Chaos, Geertz suggests, engenders anxiety, and in three direct challenges: 1) at the limits of our knowledge, 2) at the limits of our powers of endurance, and 3) at the limit of our moral insight (p. 188). Where our analytic capacities, or powers of endurance, or moral insight come up against severe limits, we face the experiential challenges with which religion is designed to cope. Religious symbols endow the world with meaning in the face of "the inescapability of ignorance, pain and injustice . . . while simultaneously denying that these irrationalities are characteristic of the world as a whole" (p. 197).

By claiming that religion is a response to the anxieties that are produced by our experience of cognitive, physical and moral uncertainty, Geertz casts religion in the role of being a response to needs, i.e., the need to reduce uncertainty, to order chaos, to have meaning. It is precisely this kind of attempt to explain religion, or other cultural elements, or symbol systems, as responses to certain needs by means of causal analysis, that is known as functionalism in the social sciences. Although functionalism does not and logically cannot offer an adequate theoretical explanation of religion, it remains intuitively persuasive to many people, as Geertz illustrates in the following passage:

> The strange opacity of certain empirical events, the dumb senselessness of intense pain, and the enigmatic unaccountability of gross iniquity all raise the uncomfortable suspicion that perhaps the world, and hence man's life in the world, has no genuine order at all—no empirical regularity, no emotional form, no moral coherence. And the religious response to this suspicion is in each case the same: the formulation, by means of symbols, of an image

> of such genuine order of the world which will account for, and even celebrate, the perceived ambiguities, puzzles, and paradoxes in human experience (p. 196).

This is classic functionalism in a richly embroidered robe. Religion as a symbolic system responds to our sense of "analytic, emotional, and moral impotence" (p. 197). In brief, religion *is* what religion *does*.

What does religion do? It functions to overcome "the rush of metaphysical anxiety that occurs when empirical phenomena threaten to remain. . . opaque" (p. 189). It functions to resolve the threats to our "most general ability to understand the world" (p. 190), the suspicion "that one may be adrift in an absurd world" (p. 190), as when moral life "threatens to dissolve into a chaos of thingless and nameless things. . ." (p. 191). What does religion do? It functions to deny that there are "inexplicable events, that life is unendurable, and that justice is a mirage" (p. 197). Functionalism has never been more clearly invoked than in Geertz's statement that

> The existence of bafflement, pain and moral paradox is one of the things that drive men [sic] toward belief in gods, devils, spirits, totemic principles, or the spiritual efficacy of cannibalism . . . but it is not the basis upon which those beliefs rest, but rather their most important field of application (p. 198).

The need for meaning *causes* belief in gods but it is not the epistemic *reason* for those beliefs. What must be emphasized here is the assumption that the needs of an individual are separate from the domain of symbols. Needs are treated as independent of symbolic systems as though they were formally prior to the question of meaning. As Geertz says, the needs are not the basis of the beliefs but their field of application. Bafflement, although not the cause (basis) of belief in gods is a need that must be satisfied. The argument is that if the symbol system of belief in gods is present then as an effect the need will be satisfied. The temptation, of course, is to conclude that, therefore, the belief is present and persists. The conclusion is obviously invalid because it commits the fallacy of affirming the consequent.[11] Moreover, the logic of claiming that religion satisfies certain cognitive needs is not any different from the logic of claiming

---

[11] See Carl Hempel, "The Logic of Functional Analysis," in *Aspects of Scientific Explanation* (New York: Free Press, 1965), and Hans H. Penner, *Impasse and Resolution: A Critique of the Study of Religion* (New York: Peter Lang, 1988).

that religion functions to satisfy biological needs or emotional desires. It is precisely the logic of the claim that we cite as constituting the failure of such a theory.[12]

Although revisions have been proposed in the literature, we have yet to discover a version of the theory that salvages functional accounts of religion from the foregoing critique.[13] Nor do we know of a successful account of semantic theory based on functionalism. What Geertz and other closet functionalists have yet to demonstrate is how religious "symbol systems" or "the problem of meaning" can be derived from a response to certain specified needs, that is to say, in more general theoretical terms, how meaning can be adequately dealt with by means of a causal explanation.

There is something sadly ironic in Geertz's lament on the opening page of this essay about "the state of general stagnation" of theoretical development in the anthropological study of religion. For in fact functionalism, the very theory he most relies on in explicating a definition of religion, was bankrupt as a theory before Geertz's essay was even written.

IV. On the Very Idea of a Religious Perspective

An unannounced but crucial shift occurs in "Religion as a Cultural System" when Geertz exchanges the term "religion" for the locution "the religious perspective" in taking up the question of what "belief" means in a religious context. "Of all the problems surrounding attempts to conduct anthropological analysis of

---

[12] For a review, critique, and bibliography on functionalism in the study of religion, see Penner, pp. 103–128. For the original critique of functionalism in the social sciences see Hempel (n. 11 above). Also helpful is John H. McDowell, "Functionalism and Anomalous Monism," in *Actions and Events*, eds. Ernest Lepore and Brian P. McLaughlin (Oxford: Basil Blackwell, 1985), pp. 387–398, including references; and Peter Halfpenny, "A refutation of historical materialism," *Social Science Information* 22 (1983): 61–87.

[13] This applies even to the revised versions found in the following sources: G. A. Cohen, *Karl Marx's Theory of History: A Defense* (Princeton: Princeton University, 1978); Jon Elster, "Marxism, Functionalism and Game Theory," *Theory and Society 11* (1982): 453–82; Herbert Burhenn, "Functionalism and the Explanation of Religion," *Journal for the Scientific Study of Religion* 19 (1980), pp. 350–60; Robert Cummins, "Functional Analysis," *The Journal of Philosophy* Vol. LXXII, (1975), pp. 741–765, reprinted in E. Sober, *Conceptual Issues in Evolutionary Biology* (Boston: MIT, 1984); and Martin Southwold, "Religious Belief," *Man* (1979): 628–44.

religion," he claims, "this is the one that has perhaps been most troublesome and therefore the most often avoided" (p. 203). The best way to approach it, according to Geertz, is "with frank recognition that religious belief involves [not induction from everyday experience] but rather a prior acceptance of authority which transforms that experience" (p. 198), so that it is a "mode of seeing," "a particular manner of construing the world" (p. 199).

The religious perspective contrasts with common-sense, scientific, and aesthetic perspectives. The common-sense perspective, according to Geertz, is simply an acceptance of the way the world is. Its "givenness" is suspended in the scientific perspective of doubt, disinterested observation, and formalized concepts of explanation. The aesthetic perspective shares the scientific "suspension of naive realism" and practical interest, and goes one step further by disengaging from belief itself, attending to the appearance of the world as such (p. 200). In brief, then, the religious perspective differs from common-sense by moving beyond "the realities of everyday life to wider ones which correct and complete them," and it differs from the scientific perspective by questioning everyday life from the perspective of "non-hypothetical truths." "Rather than detachment, its watchword is commitment; rather than analysis, encounter." In contrast to the aesthetic perspective, "instead of effecting a disengagement from the whole question of factuality, . . . [religion] deepens the concern with fact and seeks to create an aura of utter actuality" (p. 201). The essence of religion involves "imbuing" symbols with "persuasive authority." In other words, as Asad glosses this passage, "although the religious perspective is not exactly rational, it is not irrational either."[14]

What most interests us is the idea that religion, now rendered as a "perspective," is not simply a representation of social life, or a projection of it, but that it "creates" it. The religious concern with "fact" is flexible enough, on Geertz's account, to be content with but an "aura of utter actuality" when it comes to "the really real" (p. 201). Consistently avoided in Geertz's definition is the question whether some religious perspectives can be correlated to some metaphysical "really real" or "utter actuality," or not.

Far from being but one among several perspectives, Geertz presents the religious perspective as incommensurable with other

---

[14] Asad (1993), p. 49.

ways of viewing the world. Human beings are portrayed as "moving more or less easily, and very frequently, between *radically contrasting ways of looking* at the world, ways which are *not continuous with one another* but separated by cultural gaps across which Kierkegaardian leaps must be made in both directions" (p. 209, emphasis added). Significantly, and fatally to this picture, Geertz cites the case of the Bororo of Central Brazil who say they are "red parakeets." But this case is really about ethnographical confusion and mis-translation more than it is about an exotic and incommensurable "primitive mentality."[15] Geertz's handling of it only highlights his own problematic adoption of an "as-if" approach to religious belief. That "the religious perspective" is finally a fiction for Geertz becomes obvious when he asserts that in "the religious perspective" the Bororo is "really" a parrot. One might even "mate" with other such parrots, he suggests, if they are, like oneself, "metaphysical ones" (p. 210). If this is an example of the sort of "conception of a general order of existence" which religions urge upon us, it could not be more transparently fictional. Taken as indicative of the "wider sphere" onto which the religious perspective opens, the idea of "metaphysical mating" may offer attractions, but how would one ever know when one has met one's match?

Just when one might suppose that Clifford Geertz's "wider sphere" can be read as akin to William James's "More" or "unseen moral order" in which shipwrecked souls may find or create order out of chaos, Geertz adds a jarring note that would never be found in James. The "wider realities," he tells us, "correct and complete" the common-sense world (p. 200). How can this be? In terms of the example of the Bororo, Geertz's assertion would seem to entail that, after metaphysical mating with parrots, the Bororo find their common-sense world *changed*, corrected, and completed. Presumably, the correct and complete world, from the religious perspective, would be one in which metaphysical mating (whatever that is) can

[15] Sixty years of academic debate on this case have produced a fascinating body of literature, much of it no closer to resolving the puzzle of an apparently contrary-to-fact-religious-assertion than the original narrative given by Karl von den Steinen, *Unter den Naturvolkern Zentral-Brasiliens* (Berlin, 1897). For overviews see J. Z. Smith, "I am a Parrot (Red)," in *Map Is Not Territory*, (Leiden: E. J. Brill, 1978), pp. 265–288, and J. Christopher Crocker, "My Brother the Parrot," in *The Social Use of Metaphor*, eds. J. David Sapir and J. C. Crocker (Pennsylvania: University of Pennsylvania, 1977), pp. 164–192.

and does occur, and in doing so creates meaning, structure, and certainty. In this respect, the religious perspective enjoys a unique privilege; pressure from the perspectives of common-sense or science or aesthetics exert no comparable constraints on what is taken as fact or illusion in the religious world, as Geertz presents it.

Perched on the slippery slope of relativism, Geertz writes, almost as an aside: "There remain, of course, the hardly unimportant questions of whether this or that religious assertion is true, this or that religious experience genuine, or whether true religious assertions and genuine religious experience are possible at all. But such questions cannot even be asked, much less answered, within the self-imposed limitations of the scientific perspective" (p. 212). Why not, we must ask? What exactly are the "self-imposed limitations" that a scientific perspective imposes on us? Or, to put it in other terms, is truth relative to a certain "perspective" such that what is true from a "scientific perspective" is incommensurable with what is true from "religious," "aesthetic" and "political/moral" perspectives? From what perspective, if any, can the question of truth be raised?

Geertz's answer to these questions is clear. The perspective is one in which religion is held to be incommensurable with both common sense and with the empirical principles of science. Here are a few examples from the essay. First, and most important, Geertz posits something distinctive that is a "religious perspective." True, it is one among many perspectives, but it is a "mode of seeing," a way of "apprehending," a "particular way of looking at life" (p. 199). The religious perspective moves "beyond the realities of everyday life," to "wider ones" and simply accepts these on faith (p. 200). The religious perspective stands in contrast to science because it "questions" everyday life in terms of "wider, non-hypothetical truths" (p. 201). Furthermore, the religious perspective rests on the "really real," or "utter actuality," which is reached by "disengagement from the whole question of factuality, deliberately manufacturing an air of semblance and illusion" (p. 201). One enters into this kind of perspective only by ritual "leaps" or else one "slips" into a "framework of meaning which religious conceptions define" (p. 210). In other words, religion as a system of symbols manufactures an illusion and produces moods and motivations that "seem uniquely realistic." It should now be clear that the question regarding the truth of religious symbolism no longer requires "the self-imposed limitations of the scientific perspective."

Together with the association of the religious perspective with a sphere one can only enter by a leap of faith, this claim about the impossibility of even asking the question concerning the truth of religious beliefs links Geertz with a large group of scholars of religion who view religion and science as two different conceptual systems. Conceptual schemers, as we might call them, hold that there are widely different "modes of seeing" the world, different perspectives, such as science, or religion, or common sense, which use different "symbolic vehicles" to signify what the world is all about. Thus different languages or symbolic vehicles cope with, organize, or "see" reality in importantly different ways. Symbol systems serve as colored glasses, or filters, or screens through which one's knowledge of the world, or the resolution of human problems with the world, must pass. Such perspectives are presented as incommensurable where incommensurability means untranslatability. Different models *of* and *for* reality create different worlds that do not share a common syntax and semantics. In Peter Winch's words, "what is real and what is not real shows itself *in* the sense that language has."[16] Geertz's variation amounts to the claim that what is real and what is not real is given in the sense that a specific symbolic system has. Thus truth (ever an elusive notion in Geertz's writings) is relative to the symbolic system or conceptual scheme. Although he stops short of directly saying so, Geertz's position implies that it does not make sense to ask whether what is true in one system is also true in another. Despite his protestations elsewhere against relativism (and anti-relativism), this is relativism with a vengeance.

The incoherence of cognitive or conceptual perspectivism is so well known that we need only summarize the by-now-familiar questions that this position is incapable of answering. If taken as true, from what perspective is conceptual relativism supposed to be true? If not taken as true, why should it be considered seriously? How does anyone know that there is a radical gap between conceptual or symbolic systems? From what perspective, viewpoint, or conceptual scheme is this radical gap known? In brief, what sense does it make to claim a radical gap exists between symbolic forms, systems, or schemes? Does it entail that a language or symbolic system is not translatable? Or that not only societies but individuals live in

---

[16] Peter Winch, "Understanding a Primitive Society," in Bryan R. Wilson, ed., *Rationality* (New York: Blackwell, 1970), p. 82.

radically different worlds, and not only that, they do not even know it?

Finally, the *reductio* argument can be put simply and forcefully: one cannot proclaim relativism without rising above it, and one cannot rise above it without giving it up.[17] Thus, relativism of the sort operative in Geertz's essay is always covert and more implicit than explicit for it cannot proclaim itself, or even recognize itself, without defeating itself. The relativist is surely caught either in a self-contradiction or in a triviality. One can always ask, from which side of the gap between perspectives are any claims made? Or are they made from a perspective which stands above the gap? We cannot help but notice that Geertz has been able to assert a great deal about religious symbol systems, models *of* and models *for* reality, unconditioned aims, a wider context, and the "really real" without using a specific religious model or religious perspective. How is this possible? We take this to be further evidence that the notion of symbols as vehicles for special meanings is simply untenable.

In the last analysis, to say as Geertz does that the questions of religion cannot even be asked, much less answered, within the self-imposed limitations of the scientific perspective implies a specific view of science and truth that is a direct consequence of the doctrines of positivism. All one needs is a brief description of the "self-imposed limitations of science" in order to discover how powerful positivism has been in twentieth century debates about religion, religious language, religious beliefs and science.

Moreover, if we can read Geertz's statement that it is "not the business of the scientist to pronounce upon such matters one way or another" (p. 201) as a vestige of the stand-off bequeathed by logical positivism, we can also hear an echo of the refrain favored by liberal theology. For both, there can be no conflict between religion and science because, as Paul Tillich put it, "scientific truth and the truth of faith do not belong to the same *dimension of meaning*" (emphasis added).[18] Quite to the contrary, we find that most scientists have in fact pronounced verdicts on the matter of religion.[19]

---

[17] W. V. O. Quine, "On Empirically Equivalent Systems of the World," *Erkenntnis* 9 (1975): 327–8.

[18] Paul Tillich, *Dynamics of Faith* (New York: Harper and Row, 1957), p. 82.

[19] To better understand the popularity of "Religion as a Cultural System" one could consider how tempting it was for those already in the Tillichean mode of

V. Metaphysical Scheming

If one thinks of religions as worldviews in accord with Geertz's account, they are neither true nor false but comprise the frameworks within which people construe what is true and what is false. The framework or worldview, with its symbolic modeling of the social order, is what makes it possible to make judgments of truth or falsity at all. Thus, what is true or false is determined by the framework of a particular worldview, lived-world, or form of life. In recent years such a framework theory of religion has become the most prevalent and influential theory in contemporary religious studies. It is also responsible for inviting what is perhaps the most common form of relativism in the study of religion. Both the theory and the relativism that is its outcome can be traced to an underlying philosophical assumption we will examine next: scheme-content dualism.

The major philosophical weakness we find with Geertz's theory of symbolism and religion is its presumption of a dualism between

---

theology and philosophy of religion to appropriate Geertzian symbolic anthropology. Their joint impact at roughly the same time on the generation of scholars in graduate schools in the 60s and 70s created a vocabulary that has cast "longlasting moods and motivations" over several decades of debates about theory and method in religious studies. As Geertz was advancing the idea that religious symbols might be studied in terms of their functions of creating "moods" and supplying "meaning and motivation," Tillich was writing of religion as "ultimate concern," faith as "the courage to be," and symbols as "participating" in that to which they point. Geertzian social anthropology with its attention to the phenomenological-symbolic character and functioning of religion meshed easily with the Tillichean moment in theology and philosophy of religion. Something very similar to Tillich's emphasis on ultimacy and his theological contention that only that which is "unconditioned" can be ultimate is at work in Geertz's analysis of religion as a special kind of symbol system that evokes a sense of ultimate, encompassing meaning. For both Geertz and Tillich, nothing less than religion can make sense of life. Secular culture, or common sense, inevitably fails, according to Geertz, offering only what Tillich termed "existential disapppointment" if taken as ultimate. For Geertz the failure of secular culture to explain, justify, or alleviate life's anxieties and meaninglessness (Tillich's "power of nonbeing") is a serious mark of its deficiency. What is needed is an "all-pervading" vision and "unconditioned end." The problem we find in Geertz is the same trouble we have with Tillich. Concerned with the meaning of "the whole of life," religion is thus beyond the scope of the empirical sciences. Once this move is made, whether by social scientists or by theologians, not only religious symbol systems but "truth" and "meaning" are placed outside the reach of rational or empirical criticism; they then tend to become reified as special kinds of truth and meaning.

symbolic models and a "world" that stands ready to be symbolized. Throughout his account, both models *of* and models *for* have reference to some kind of uninterpreted reality, a "given" that is to be shaped, organized, made apprehensible, or represented. As we have seen, religion asserts and maintains a "worldview," and "the religious perspective" is described as an overarching framework of meaning. In other words, a religion is a scheme and as such it filters or organizes (model *for*) or fits (model *of*) some content. Geertz's definition of religion thus aligns him with a broad based group of philosophers of religion, theologians, and social scientists who embrace the paradigm of "religion as conceptual scheme."[20]

According to this paradigm, religions serve as schemes in one of two ways: either they organize something or they fit it. As worldviews, religions might organize reality, the universe, world, nature, or they might organize experience, described as the passing show, sensory promptings, sense-data, and so on.

Closely examined, the notion of organizing—whether "reality" or "experience"—is puzzling in this paradigm. One does not organize a single object but only the objects which make up some thing or category. The only way to organize a closet, for example, is to organize the shoes and shirts and dresses and contents within it. If religions as conceptual schemes and frameworks of meaning are said to organize reality (the world, the universe, nature) they would surely have to organize an infinite number of objects which comprise "the world." But religious worldviews cannot merely organize the world for that would be like trying to organize the closet or the Pacific Ocean. How would one go about doing that? The metaphor of the huge closet of nature that then gets organized by the use of different schemes only works if the closet is already partitioned into other objects, just as when we set out to organize a closet, we are really arranging the things in it. Now any language, framework,

---

[20] One of the few critics to call attention to the ubiquity of scheme-content dualism in the study of religion is Terry F. Godlove. See his excellent study, *Religion, Interpretation, and Diversity of Belief,* (Cambridge: Cambridge University Press, 1989), reprinted by Mercer University Press 1997. Donald Davidson has inveighed against scheme-content dualism as "the third dogma of empiricism." Our criticism in this section follows closely Davidson's own argument, as will be evident to readers familiar with his influential paper "On the Very Idea of a Conceptual Scheme." The examples of the Pacific Ocean and a closet are Davidson's.

conceptual scheme, or worldview which organizes all the infinite number of objects in the world must be a language or conceptual scheme or worldview comparable to our own. That is, if they are said to organize the world, they must organize everything within the world. And any language that organizes the infinite things within the world must be a language very similar to all the other languages. Therefore, such a language cannot fail of intertranslatability and so must be understood as commensurable with other so-called schemes and thus not constitutive of a different "dimension of meaning."

Examining the second form of the idea, that conceptual schemes organize *experience*, we find it is not intelligible either. How could something that could count as a language organize *only* experience? Would it not also have to organize other things that need organizing, such as silverware, e-mail messages, cabbages and kingdoms?

When the metaphor is one of "fitting" rather than "organizing," a different difficulty occurs. To say that religion as a scheme or worldview fits the evidence, facts, world, or experience seems to say little more than that the sentences of some language are true. In that case, the claim that different conceptual schemes all fit the evidence, facts, world, or experience but in incommensurable ways amounts to the claim that they are all largely true but not intertranslatable. The real problem with the idea of "fitting" then is that it disconnects truth and translation and therefore forfeits its own intelligibility. Or, if it does not, it forfeits the dramatic effect of incommensurability by saying no more than that different theories can be true. In short, we are arguing that the Geertzian method of viewing religions as worldviews (conceptual schemes, epistemes, frameworks, or models *for*) results in either incoherence or hyperbole.

These criticisms of scheme-content dualism bear on a related problem that is at work in Geertz's assumption of the "myth of the given."[21] On the "content" side of the dualism, what does Geertz suppose is given? Our interpretation of the extended passages we have quoted earlier is that Geertz presupposes there is, at a minimum, a given something waiting to be organized by metaphysical conceptions which fill in as a third thing, a medium, between what is represented and how it is represented. Upon this

---

[21] Wilfrid Sellars, "Empiricism and the Philosophy of Mind," in *Science, Perception, and Reality* (London and New York, 1963).

given is founded an untenable form of dualism.[22] Its mythical quality inheres in the presupposition of a scheme-independent "given" which alternative schemes somehow organize, confront, cope with, or systematize. The most problematic ingredient in this presupposition is the requirement of something that, since it lies outside all schemes just waiting to be "organized" or "fitted," must be neutral and common and inchoate. If it is not dubbed "the given," it might be simply called "the stream of experience" or "the world."

In calling attention to the operation of this myth in Geertz's essay, we are disputing the presence of any kind of non-linguistic or pre-linguistic meaning assumed to be present to us without signs. Geertz's Weberian preoccupation with The Problem of Meaning presumes this problematic sense of "meaning," as do many ordinary expressions about "meaning." The "Politics of Meaning" debated in the 1990s or the "meaning of life" pondered in adolescents' diaries partake of this notion of meaning. The myth of the given is also shared by many theorists who are, on the surface, opposed to sense-data received by experience, and to Platonic objects inspected by the mind, but who posit things called "meanings" that are directly present or given in some way. Any theory which posits a domain of unmediated or uninterpreted semantic items to which we are alleged to have direct epistemological access is a theory that sets up the myth of the given. That Geertz courts just such a myth is apparent, for example, in his treatment of the threat of chaos to "not just interpretations but interpretability" (p. 188), in his dualistic depiction of "the empirical world" on the one hand, and, on the other hand, "the complex of received culture patterns (common sense, science, philosophical speculation, myth)"(p. 189), that map it, and in the overall contention of his work, that "culture patterns give meaning (i.e., objective conceptual form) to social and psychological reality" (p. 182).

To posit things called "meanings" that are directly present to the inspecting mind is to land immediately in the ontological version of the myth of the given. On our view, there are no such metaphysical primitives, no absolute, fundamental "real things."

---

[22] There is an innocent version of "scheme" and "content" which can be employed nondualistically as a simple distinction between *what* is represented and *how* it is represented, but we do not read Geertz this innocently. Instead, we find evidence that his construal of "content" commits the myth of the given.

Once one has rejected the myth of the given, the very notion of the way the world is in itself becomes unintelligible. If there is no such thing as the ontological structure of the world as it is in itself, why should we suppose that a specific human activity could lead us to the "truth" about what there "really" is? Therefore, we think it best *not* to maintain with the conceptual schemers that we have no access to reality in itself, only to reality-as-we-conceive-it-through-a-conceptual-scheme. The notion of "reality in itself" makes no sense itself and only tempts us into a futile distinction between "in itself" and "for us." Instead, we would simply maintain that we are "in unmediated touch with the familiar objects whose antics make our sentences and opinions true or false."[23]

Having dissolved the dualisms and demythologized the myths so briefly traced in this paper, we find we can make no sense of Geertz's notion of symbolic meaning, which we might dub the Butterfly Theory of Meaning since it treats meaning as something to be captured in the symbols we use, like butterflies in a net. This view results in the reification of meaning, as though meaning first exists and then the sacred symbols point it out and name it for religious persons. It also leads to the valorization of symbolic action, as though symbols bear meanings as vehicles bear cargo. Freighted with these two assumptions, religious studies, heavy with cartesian cargo, has too long been sinking.

VI. Another World to Live In

For the most part we have been dealing with various critiques of the "worldview" side of Geertz's definition. But his own emphasis leans more to the "ethos" side of culture, to which we now turn. The basic distinction Geertz posits between ethos and worldview is vital to his view of the function of symbols, and the problems we have identified with that view. The former intellectualizes religious belief, while the latter renders it emotionally convincing. "Ethos" designates a people's "underlying attitude toward themselves and their world," that is, the aesthetic and moral aspects of a culture, which Geertz also terms "dispositions." Dispositions, in turn, are of two kinds: moods and motivations. "Worldview," in contrast, designates the cognitive

[23] Davidson (1984), p. 198.

aspects of a culture, a people's sense of the "really real," their most comprehensive "idea of a general order of existence."

If we ask what exactly *is* that general order of existence, we find that religion does not have any specific semantic content in Geertz's analysis. Because he dwells so compellingly on the attitudinal side, the answer to the question "attitude toward *what*?" is allowed to remain blank. Presumably, it could be filled in by many different general orders of existence, just as long as *some*thing fills it in. In this light, Geertz's definition of religion looks like an anthropologist's elevated version of the remark attributed to President Eisenhower in about the same era: "I don't care *what* religion you believe in, as long as you believe in *some*thing." Perhaps just any ontology will do for religious people, as long as it is taken *as if* it is "ultimate actuality" or the "really real." If this is like trying to stage Hamlet without the Prince, Geertz appears not to mind. When the play's the thing, ethos has the last word.

We suspect that this very vagueness has contributed to the widespread appeal that "Religion as a Cultural System" continues to exercise for theologians and social scientists alike. Indeed, the essay has cast its own "aura of factuality" in a way that manages to lull both believers and secularists into uncritical adoption of Geertz's definition of religion. Believers can see in it an affirmation of the intentional reference of their symbolic meanings, and secularists can still understand religion as an "as if" fictional affair whose aura of factuality is largely illusory or self-induced. The definition may be read as neutral between these, and thus potentially supportive of both. The fictional interpretation, however, is incompatible with the functionalist strain in Geertz's description of religion, but that gnat is probably not too hard to swallow after such camels as the myth of the given and scheme/content dualism.

In conclusion, it is worth calling attention to the fictional feature that many commentators on this classic essay simply finesse. The whole drift of Geertz's definition is toward the conclusion that religions urge upon us conceptions of a general order of existence that are *fictional* conceptions. If religious beliefs only supplied a gloss on the commonsense everyday world or a synopsis of cosmic order, they would be philosophical, with nothing particularly religious about them. The distinctive aspect that makes them religious, according to Geertz, is that a set of religious beliefs also supplies a template—recommending an attitude, a recurring mood, a persisting motivation (pp. 212–13). Thus, in religion, "worldview" is related to "ethos" as cause to effect. Ideas of the "really real" (worldview) induce dispositions (moods and motivations) in individuals and all of these color people's sense of "the reasonable, the practical, the humane, and the moral" (p. 213). "The moods and motivations a religious orientation produces," Geertz explains, "cast a derivative, lunar light over the solid features of a people's secular life" (p. 213). Just what is this "lunar light?" Geertz's definition contains the answer: the long-lasting moods and motivations are produced by a system of symbols that formulate "conceptions of a general order of existence, clothing these conceptions with such an aura of factuality that the moods and motivations seem uniquely realistic" (p. 179).

Since this last part of Geertz's definition has received very little critical comment let us look at it closely. Symbols formulate a general order of existence and clothe these conceptions with an aura of factuality. We can take this assertion as a clear example of symbols functioning as models *for* reality. This aura of factuality produces moods and motivations that *seem* uniquely realistic because they *seem* to correspond with secular life. In other words, religious symbols function as a model *for* reality when they are believed to be models *of* reality. But of course, this is a mistake, an illusion, a dream world! Karatheodoris reminds us that illusions and dreams are not deceptions or false descriptions, but are deceptive "because they are mistaken by the dreamer for the reality they depict." It is the lunar light's "aura" of factuality that "deludes the dreamer into mistaking them for reality."[24]

At this junction, all of the critical questions raised by this essay reduce to two: how do we explain why an individual would mistakenly believe a model *for* reality to be a model *of* reality? Given what Geertz has proclaimed to be the limits of science and the boundaries of perspectives, how, and by what process could Geertz ever discover this mistake?

In the end, the power of a symbolic system, on Geertz's own terms, comes through as more subjective than social. It may produce a transformation in an individual's "*sense* of reality" (p. 201, italics added), he says, but this is not a claim that symbolic systems produce any transformation in the public world at all. We find a final irony in the fact that Geertz's opening epigram features George Santayana's

---

[24] Karatheodoris, p. 85.

praise of religion for providing "another world to live in." Santayana understood that "another world" was purely an ideal one, not to be confused with actual powers or postmortem opportunities. Religion was to be celebrated and prized for affording a great "time out," a poetic and imaginative slant on everyday life, an as-if glow to normal routines and contingencies, but not something to be taken realistically, lest it invite superstition and fanaticism. The construction of a universalist definition of religion like Geertz's would never have tempted Santayana who thought that what religion people have is an historical accident, quite as much as what language they speak, and "the attempt to speak without speaking any particular language is not more hopeless than the attempt to have a religion that shall be no religion in particular."[25]

---

[25] Santayana, George, *The Life of Reason* (New York: Charles Scribner's Sons, 1905–6) Vol. 3, p. 198.

8

What's Wrong with Functional Explanations?

Hans H. Penner

In this chapter I want to examine functionalist theories as explanations of religion. This examination is also intended to serve as an example of how to demonstrate what is wrong with a theory rather than simply calling those who use it "reductionists." Most of the time, such accusations are warnings to the "faithful"—they are encyclicals not critiques.

The status of functionalism and the meaning of the term "function" in the history and phenomenology of religion are unclear. Some scholars, for example, seem to be both for and against functionalism. As we have already noticed, functionalist methods are called reductionistic on the one hand, and auxiliary sciences on the other. In fact, we sometimes read that religion "functions" to express The Sacred.

Let us recall Eliade's assertion about the proper study of religious phenomena: "To try to grasp the essence of such phenomena by means of physiology, psychology, sociology, economics, linguistics or any other study is false; it misses the one unique and irreducible element in it—the element of the sacred." We must assume that Eliade is not making a metaphorical statement, that what he is asserting is an important methodological principle. But then, what do we make of the following assertion: "I cannot conclude this chapter better than by quoting the classic passages in which Bronislaw Malinowski undertook to show the nature and function of myth in primitive societies."[1] The quote which follows this assertion

[1] Mircea Eliade, *Myth and Reality*, trans. Willard R. Trask (New York: Harper, 1963) 19.

is indeed the classic paragraph from Malinowski's essay "Myth in Primitive Psychology." Eliade quotes it as follows:

> Studied alive, myth . . . is not an explanation in satisfaction of a scientific interest, but a narrative resurrection of primeval reality, told in satisfaction of deep religious wants, moral cravings, social submissions, assertions, even practical requirements. Myth fulfills in primitive culture an indispensable function; it expresses, enhances, and codifies belief; it safeguards and enforces morality; it vouches for the efficiency of ritual and contains practical rules for the guidance of man. Myth is thus a vital ingredient of human civilization; it is not an idle tale, but a hard-worked active force; it is not an intellectual explanation or an artistic imagery, but a pragmatic charter of primitive faith and moral wisdom. . . . These stories . . . are to the natives a statement of primeval, greater, and more relevant reality, by which the present life, fates and activities of mankind are determined, the knowledge of which supplies man with the motive for ritual and moral actions, as well as with indications as to how to perform them.[2]

Since Malinowski is a well-known social anthropologist, often cited as the father of functionalism, which of the two statements by Eliade is true? Which statements are we to take seriously? Has Malinowski grasped the essence of The Sacred in this quotation, or is he describing the psychology of myth among primitives and explaining religion as a function of biological and social needs? If it is the latter, and I do not doubt that it is, then according to Eliade's first assertion, Malinowski's position is false. Yet, we are to take this false statement about myth as the best description of myth that Eliade can find. This kind of confusion, which is widespread, makes it difficult to evaluate just what is being asserted about the proper study of religion.

Malinowski's statement concerning myth simply does not make sense without knowledge of the theory it entails. It is embedded in a theory regarding social institutions and is consistent with his own functionalist position regarding religion. Thus, if we want to avoid confusion, it must be made clear whether we accept his theory or not. If we reject Malinowski's theory of religion and myth as "reductionistic," then it would seem that we would also want to reject his descriptions of the function of myth and religion. Given the decades of methodological confusion, I am not optimistic at all that pointing

---

[2] Eliade 20. The passage and its context is taken from Bronislaw Malinowski, *Magic, Science and Religion* (New York: Doubleday, 1954) 101 and 108.

this out will change anything. Perhaps the best we can hope for is greater recognition that The Sacred and its theological ramifications cannot be disguised, at least not so easily, with the language of functionalism.

Functional explanations of religion have maintained a powerful hold on most of the human sciences. Over the decades, scholars who committed themselves to functional theories of religion have done so because the theory is empirically testable. Moreover, it is also claimed that the theory is able to explain many of the problems older theories could not explain, as well as do more than older theories in terms of explaining social institutions. All these claims and aims are to be applauded as noteworthy examples of the development of a science.

The effects of this new theory were revolutionary. Instead of explaining a society by religious traits or units, functional theory reversed the procedure by explaining religion as a variable from within the structure or system of a particular society. The famous slogan became "religion is what it does." The test became one of showing why and how religion functions in a society. Anyone familiar with the development of the theory also knows that its complexity increased in proportion to the problems and criticisms it confronted.

The power of the theory bound together a variety of scholars in the human sciences, even though they disagreed on fundamental issues concerning religion. Three examples suffice to illustrate the point. The first is the lifelong feud between A. R. Radcliffe-Brown and Malinowski concerning ritual and anxiety. For Malinowski, the methodological biologist, anxiety arises in circumstances which human beings cannot control, for example, fishing in the ocean. Although rituals are not technological means which actually control the threat of death on the ocean, they do function to reduce anxiety. For Radcliffe-Brown, the methodological sociologist, it is a society's expectations that produce anxiety, and the performance of rituals is an individual's response to those expectations and the anxiety they generate. Notice that although there is disagreement on what generates anxiety, both use functionalism as an explanation for the existence of rituals. The conflict was finally resolved by Homans in

1941. Homans solved the problem by showing that both are right, that it is not a question of either/or.[3]

The second example is the famous debate between Melford Spiro and Edmund Leach on the belief in virgin birth. Spiro argued that belief in the existence of water spirits, and the like, as the cause of pregnancy were to be taken as rational, although false, explanations for pregnancy. Leach argued that there is sufficient evidence to show that most, if not all, societies are well versed in the causes of physiological paternity. Such beliefs, therefore, were not to be taken as mistaken explanations, but as symbolic expressions that reinforce existing social institutions, the marriage bonds for example. The publications of both scholars, however, are excellent examples of functionalism at work in contemporary anthropology.[4] My final example is the well-known debate between J. Beattie and R. Horton on the proper understanding of ritual and belief. For Beattie, as we have seen, rituals and religious beliefs are expressive; for Horton they are to be explained as cognitive, rational attempts at explanation.[5] Once again, we have an example where both scholars are excellent representatives of the functionalist theory at work in the social sciences despite a fundamental disagreement between them about the cognitive status of religious beliefs.

Functionalism can be viewed as *the* theory for explaining things in the social sciences. Most of the time the theory is never described in any detail but simply assumed as a valid model of explanation. This is especially true of scholars who have become popular in the study of religion. Mary Douglas's book, *Purity And Danger,* is a good example. The thesis of the book may be summed up as follows. Anomaly creates disturbances of a high level in undifferentiated societies. Such disturbances must be reduced or removed in order for the society to function adequately. Classification systems, taxono-

---

[3] See George C. Homans, "Anxiety and Ritual: The Theories of Malinowski and Radcliffe-Brown," *American Anthropologist* 43 (1941): 164–171, for the argument and references.

[4] See Edmund Leach, *Genesis as Myth and Other Essays* (London Cape, 1969) 85–112, for the argument and references. The argument is continued on in several issues of *Man.*

[5] See Bryan R. Wilson, ed., *Rationality* (New York: Blackwell, 1971) chaps. 7 and 12, for the relevant arguments and references, and Martin Hollis and Steven Lukes, eds., *Rationality and Relativism* (Cambridge: MIT Press 1982) 201ff., for Horton's return to the issues.

mies, and taboos function to reduce anomalies in a society and thus create solidarity by reducing disturbances created by anomalies. Clifford Geertz's elegant essays are clearly located within functionalism, as is Victor Turner's description of the function of "communitas." Festinger's explanation of religious movements based upon "cognitive dissonance" assumes the same functionalist model. All of these scholars have become popular resources for students interested in the study of religion. This is especially true for those who have recognized that the tradition of Otto, Van der Leeuw and Eliade has reached a dead end. It is also true for many Biblical scholars who have discovered the importance of the "social context" for interpreting texts.

The theory is very persuasive. You need not really bother about why people hold religious belief. All you need do is recognize that the beliefs are relative to a cultural system. As Barnes puts it, "If we ask why an individual believes 'X' the usual answer in all cultures will be that he was told or taught 'X' by a trusted knowledge source. We can then ask why belief 'X' is present in the culture, and that is where *functionalism makes claims to provide explanation*."[6] Indeed it does! The problem is that most scholars who use this model of explanation do not pause to critically reflect on the validity of their claims. Why, then, do they believe it? Well, they were told or taught the theory by a trusted knowledge source! How else do we explain the persistence of such a widespread theory of explanation which is seriously defective.

We can simplify the theory of functionalism as an explanation of religion in the following way: If y (e.g. religion) then z, (e.g. anxiety reduction) where z is a functional requirement of x, (e.g. social maintenance) and y satisfies z. This formula was fully described in 1964 by Melford Spiro. His article, "Causes, Functions, and Cross-Cousin Marriage: An Essay In Anthropological Explanation," makes explicit the claim that functional explanations are causal explanations with an important difference.[7] The difference can be described in the

---

[6] Barry Barnes, "The Comparison of Belief-Systems: Anomaly Versus Falsehood," *Modes of Thought*, eds. Robin Horton and Ruth Finnegan (London: Faber, 1973) 193. Italics mine.

[7] Melford E. Spiro, "Causes, Functions and Cross-Cousin Marriage: An Essay in Anthropological Explanation," *The Journal of the Royal Anthropological Institute of Great Britain and Ireland* 94 (1964): 30–43. Another useful essay which clearly defines functional explanations is Melford E. Spiro, "Religion: Problems of

following way. Functional explanations are like causal explanations in that they also want to account for *y* (religion, for example) in causal terms. The difference, however, is that functional explanations explain *y* by reference to some condition *z*, in which *z* constitutes the contribution of *y* necessary to the maintenance of some social system *x*. Thus, the satisfaction of *z* is the function of *y*. Religion, for example, is not simply explained as functioning to satisfy social maintenance. Religion functions to reduce anxiety which constitutes the contribution of religion for satisfying a necessary need for the maintenance of a social system. The Kula ritual performed by Trobriand society is explained by reference to reduction of social tensions that must be satisfied for the maintenance of the social system.

The shift here is important. We explain a religion by showing how it satisfies a functional requirement of a social system. The functional requirement is usually expressed as some "need" in the social system. The use of functionalism in psychology focuses on "needs" in the personality system.

I shall not reproduce Spiro's functional explanation for the existence of cross-cousin marriage. I shall, instead, present a simpler model using religion as an example. I do not believe that this simplified model distorts the claims made about functionalism as an explanation. The simplified version for an explanation of religion can be described as follows:

1. *x* = a particular social system under a setting of kind *c*.
2. *y* = a particular structural unit, (religion or ritual) which is a sufficient condition for satisfying *z*.
3. *z* = a functional requirement (let us say family confidence and trust) which is a *necessary condition* for *x*, the social system.

In arguing for his model, Spiro makes three things clear. First, functional requirements (*z*) are necessary, but not sufficient, conditions for the maintenance of a social system. Secondly, structural units (*y*) may satisfy different functional requirements, and different structural units may satisfy the same functional requirement; in other words, structural units have functional equivalents. Thirdly, within a system it is a joint set of units which is the sufficient condition for satisfying the functional requirement of a system. In conclusion, Spiro is aware that our knowledge of the functional

---

Definition and Explanation," *Anthropological Approaches to the Study of Religion*, ed. Michael Banton (London: Tavistock, 1966).

requirements of a social system will not allow us to predict which social unit will satisfy the requirements.[8]

It is important to notice that in the above description the explanation is more complex. Instead of *y* representing a particular unity (see premise #2 of the simplified model), *y* represents a set or class of units. As we shall see in a moment, this revision of the model is necessary in order to avoid a conclusion which is invalid.

To complete the description of our model, it is important to point out that a functional explanation must specify the relations between *y*, *z* and *x*. It does this by stating that the relations are either necessary or sufficient or both necessary and sufficient conditions.

Since the criticism of functional explanations will depend on these logical relations, it is best to describe them before entering into an analysis of the model. To focus on these relations, let us simplify the model and assume that *z*, the functional requirement, is social maintenance. Let us also assume that *y*, the explanandum (what we want to explain), is a religious ritual, a particular social unit. We may then write out the following table of necessary and sufficient conditions.

1. Necessary conditions.
   a. The absence of social maintenance (*z*) entails the absence of the ritual (y).
   b. The absence of the ritual does not entail the absence of social maintenance.
   c. The presence of social maintenance does not entail the presence of the ritual, and
   d. The presence of the ritual entails the presence of social maintenance. Social maintenance (*z*) is then a necessary, but not a sufficient, condition for the presence of the ritual (y).

2. Sufficient conditions.
   a. The absence of social maintenance does not entail the absence of ritual.
   b. The absence of the ritual entails the absence of social maintenance.
   c. The presence of social maintenance entails the presence of the ritual.

---

[8] Spiro, "Causes . . ." 34.

d. The presence of the ritual does not entail the presence of social maintenance. The presence of social maintenance (z), then, is a sufficient condition for the presence of ritual (y).

3. *Necessary and sufficient conditions.*

a. The presence of social maintenance entails the presence of the ritual.

b. The presence of the ritual entails the presence of social maintenance.

c. The absence of social maintenance entails the absence of the ritual, and

d. The absence of the ritual entails the absence of social maintenance.

With the above table in hand, we can move to an analysis of the logic of functional explanations. The model I shall use for this analysis is taken from Hempel's now classic essay on the logic of functionalism.[9] I have modified it only slightly, using Spiro's symbols to bring out how religion is explained functionally. I remain convinced that functional theories of religion as presently used in the human sciences can be reduced to this analysis.

Since this assertion has been misunderstood by some of my colleagues, I believe a brief clarification is necessary before the analysis is presented. The first problem arises because of my use of Hempel. Since Hempel is usually identified as a logical positivist, I must also be a logical positivist when I use his analysis of functionalist explanations. This is not bothersome because the accusation is similar to phenomenologists calling scholars they disagree with reductionists.

What is bothersome is a second accusation; that since Hempel's nomological-deductive model for scientific explanations has been devastated along with the logical positivist notions of observational/theoretical language and their relation to correspondence rules, I am

[9] Carl G. Hempel, "The Logic of Functional Analysis," *Symposium on Sociological Theory*, ed. Llewellyn Gross (New York: Harper, 1959) 271–307. Hempel's essay has been reprinted in many anthologies; it is included in May Brodback, ed., *Readings in the Philosophy of the Social Sciences* (New York: Macmillian, 1968) and Carl G. Hempel, *Aspects of Scientific Explanation* (New York: Free Press, 1965).

using a model that is out of date and irrelevant.[10] Let me just say that I am fully aware of the withering attack on logical positivism by contemporary historians and philosophers of science.[11] I am also aware that the analysis I am presenting is controversial. It should be,

---

[10] For a good example of this response see Robert N. McCauley and E. Thomas Lawson, "Functionalism Reconsidered," *History of Religions* 23 (1984): 372–381. It should be made clear that I do not disagree with them about the validity of functional explanations in biology. In such explanations, natural selection provides the mechanism which becomes the basis for arguing that beneficial consequences explain their own causes. McCauley and Lawson do not provide us with a similar mechanism in their "reconsideration" of functionalism in the social sciences. It is therefore impossible to determine just what their argument is all about. Appeal to biological explanations which do succeed based on the mechanism of natural selection simply begs the question. An excellent description of this mechanism in biology can be found in Ernst Mayr, *The Growth of Biological Thought* (Cambridge: Harvard University Press, 1982), esp. chaps. 11, 12 and 13. I do not regard Herbert Burhenn's attempted revisions as an adequate solution to the problems which beset functionalism. He does not make any attempt at defining functional explanations, and his representation of Hempel is incomplete. Hempel's critique is certainly not concerned with the origin of cultural traits. Burhenn's attempt at revising functionalism from answering a "why" question into a "how-possibly" question seems to entail that he agrees with Hempel that functional explanations fail to answer "why" a cultural trait persists. What he seems to have overlooked is the argument that explanations similar to Dray's "how-possibly" presuppose an answer to the "why" question. Burhenn concludes his essay by stating that he has tried to show that functional explanations have "the possibility of being helpful in understanding religious phenomena. . . ." They may indeed be helpful, heuristic devices. I know of no one who would want to argue the contrary. Once this is admitted, however, it seems clear that we have given up the central claims of functionalism as an explanation in the human sciences. And given the logical problems of this kind of explanation, I think it is only proper to ponder just how "helpful" such an approach really is for studying religion. See Herbert Burhenn, "Functionalism and the Explanation of Religion," *Journal for the Scientific Study of Religion* 19 (1980): 350–60. The quote is taken from page 359.

[11] One of the best critiques I have found is Frederick Suppe, ed., *The Structure of Scientific Theories*, 2nd ed. (Urbana: University of Illinois Press, 1977). Scholars in the study of religion who have become fascinated with Kuhn and Feyerabend will also find, to their dismay, a thorough critique of their positions in this volume. I have also found Peter Achinstein, *Concepts of Science* (Baltimore: Johns Hopkins University Press, 1968) helpful in reflecting on the complexity of theoretical construction. See also Peter Achinstein and Stephen F. Barker, eds., *The Legacy of Logical Positivism* (Baltimore: Johns Hopkins University Press, 1969). I think that the question which must be answered by those who are attracted by the notion of heuristic and imaginative devices in scientific discovery is, Where do hypotheses come from?

because if it is an accurate description of the logic of functionalism, then this well-known, almost common sense, explanation is in serious trouble regarding its claims as an explanation of religious phenomena; I would extend this to include explanations of any cultural or social phenomena.

The point which needs to be stressed is that I have not invented functionalism as a model for explaining religion. I have not created titles such as Spiro's for an explanation of cross-cousin marriage. I am not interested at the moment in whether "explanation" must be broadened, or revised. The central issue is this; does the history of functionalism in the human sciences, as we know it, fit Hempel's model? I have yet to find one critic who has demonstrated that it does not. In fact, several functionalists I have read explicitly state that this approach to explaining the element of society and culture is at best a heuristic device and they have reached this conclusion because of Hempel's analysis.[12] Once again, it is what functionalists claim they are doing as cultural scientists that is the issue. What the critics will have to demonstrate is that Hempel did not capture this in his analysis of the logic of functional analysis. With this clarification in mind, let us turn to the analysis.

1. At time t, a society x functions adequately in a setting of kind c.
2. x functions adequately in a setting of kind c only if a necessary functional requirement z is satisfied (let z = social maintenance).

---

[12] See I. C. Jarvie, *Functionalism* (Minneapolis: Burgess, 1973). See also I. C. Jarvie, "Limits to Functionalism and Alternatives to it in Anthropology," *Theory in Anthropology,* eds. Robert A. Manners and David Kaplan (Chicago: Aldine, 1968) 196–203 and Piotr Sztompka, *System and Function: Toward a Theory of Society* (New York: Academic, 1974). Sztompka's book is typical of much that has been written about functional explanations; he mentions Hempel but curiously omits any analysis or criticism of Hempel's description of the logic of functional explanations. This cannot be said about G. A. Cohen's brilliant book *Karl Marx's Theory of History: A Defense* (Princeton: Princeton University Press, 1978) esp. chaps. IX and X. I shall turn to the debate Cohen has generated later in this chapter. His thesis is that historical materialism stands or falls with the validity of functionalism as an explanation of history. His criticism of functional explanations in the social sciences and in Marxist writings is excellent. However, I do not believe that he succeeds in overcoming Hempel's basic arguments against the logic of such explanations. For a refutation of Cohen's thesis that "functional explanations in the social sciences can be successful," see Peter Halfpenny, "A refutation of historical materialism?" *Social Science Information* 22 (1983): 61–87.

3. If unit y were present in x then, as an effect condition z would be satisfied. (let y = a ritual)
4. Hence, at t unit y is present in x.

Both the logical and empirical requirements of functional explanations are clear in the above model. The first premise gives us, in abbreviated form, the empirical observations of a society at a particular time. It also describes the conditions in which the society is found. It describes rather nicely what we find in the first chapter of many texts which are about societies studied by anthropologists and sociologists. The society is usually placed in its geographical setting, and a full description is given of natural resources, social structure and the like.

The second premise states a necessary condition which must be met in order for the society to function adequately. In our example, it is the necessary, requirement of "maintenance" that must be satisfied in order for the society to function adequately. In some explanations this necessary condition is often cited as a "functional prerequisite." Premise three states that if a ritual were present, then, as a consequence, the necessary condition would be satisfied, i.e., the satisfaction of z is the function of y. The existence of the ritual is explained by what it does. The conclusion, however, is invalid. We have not explained why the ritual is present in the society, and this is precisely what it was we wanted to explain. We want to explain why ritual or religion is present in a society. This assertion has often been misunderstood. I am not saying that the conclusion is false. All that has been shown is that the argument is invalid. The conclusion may be true, but the invalid argument does not establish its truth.

The argument is invalid because it commits the fallacy of affirming the consequent. It asserts that "if y then z; z therefore y." It is a simple fallacy which we often commit when we are careless. Here is a clear example of the fallacy: "If John misses his bus he will be late for class; John is late for class. Therefore, he missed the bus." Clearly many other events could have taken place to explain why John was late for class. All we can conclude is that something must have happened to make him late for class and one possibility is his missing the bus. In our table of necessary and sufficient conditions, the conclusion contradicts "*c*" under necessary conditions.

The above conclusion is the same for functional explanations. Instead of explaining why a particular ritual is present in the society, or persists in the society, all we can conclude is that somehow the necessary condition of maintenance is being satisfied in order for the society to function adequately at time *t* under the specified conditions *c*. I believe that most functionalists since Malinowski have seen this problem, and the history of functionalism can be viewed as a history in which revisions were made in an attempt to overcome the problem.

One way of correcting the result is to introduce the notion of "functional equivalents" into the explanation. We may, for example, introduce new terms into the third and fourth premises. Thus, premise one and two would remain the same, but three becomes,

3. If unit *y*, or its functional equivalent, were present in *x*, then, as an effect condition *z* would be satisfied.
4. Hence, at *t*, *y* or its functional equivalent is present in *x*.

The addition of functional equivalents, however, does not help us. In fact, this revision of the model now leaves us with an explanation that is vacuous. It simply asserts that if a society is functioning adequately, then something or other must account for that. Once again, this is not enlightening about what it is we wanted to explain: the existence of ritual in the society. The conclusion tells us that somehow the need for social maintenance is being satisfied given the truth of premises one and two.

The addition of "functional equivalents," moreover, makes the explanation more problematic. First, as Hempel has pointed out, what do we mean by "functional equivalents?" How are we to identify the functional equivalents of a religious ritual? Secondly, the introduction of functional equivalents produces serious complications regarding the empirical status of the explanation. If we are free to substitute equivalent units for a particular unit (say, ritual), then the question arises whether we are still observing the same society at *t*, under the conditions specified.

What is worse, this revision of changing "ritual" to "ritual or its functional equivalent" does not correct the contradiction of requirement "c" in the table of necessary conditions. I find it odd that Hempel did not notice this error in his presentation of the revision. The revised model is invalid on the same basis as the first.

The first model was abbreviated as follows to demonstrate the fallacy: If *y* then *z*; *z*, therefore *y*. The revised model seems to assert the following: If (*y* v A v B v C . . . n) then *z*. *z*, therefore, (*y* v A v B v

C . . . n). Inserting functional equivalents into the argument does not validate the invalid argument.[13]

There is a third way of correcting the validity of the conclusion. This move is the opposite of the solution we have discussed thus far. Instead of attempting to expand premise three, it tightens it by making premise three a necessary condition for social maintenance. Premise one and two remain the same, but three is changed as follows:

3. Only if unit *y* were present in *x*, then, as an effect condition *z* would be satisfied.
4. Hence, at *t*, unit *y* is present in x.

From a logical point of view the change of premise three provides us with a valid conclusion. This is so because when we refer to the tables we find that "d" under "necessary conditions" states that "the presence of the ritual entails the presence of social maintenance."

The problem, however, of turning a cultural unit such as ritual into a necessary condition for the maintenance of a society is a severe one. How are we to maintain that a ritual is indispensable or necessary, to a society? Critics of functionalism, such as Merton, Hempel, Nagel, and Jarvie, have pointed out that the claim of "functional indispensability" for any cultural unit is difficult to sustain on empirical grounds and, in the end reduces functional explanations to a tautology.[14]

Hempel presents one last possible revision which might satisfy the requirements for a valid explanation. Once again the first two premises remain the same. Premise three is changed as follows:

3. *i* is the class of empirically sufficient conditions for *z* in the context determined by *x* and *c*, and *i* is not empty.
4. Hence, some one of the items included in *i* is present in *x* at *t* under conditions *c*.

---

[13] I am indebted to the philosopher Merrie Bergmann for this insight as well as other criticisms and suggestions on an earlier draft of the argument.

[14] See Robert K. Merton, *Social Theory and Social Structure*, rev. and enl. ed. (Glencoe, Ill.: Free Press, 1957); E. Nagel, "A Formalization of Functionalism," *Logic Without Metaphysics* (Glencoe, Ill.: Free, 1957); Hempel, "The Logic of Functional Analysis"; and Jarvie, *Functionalism*. For a critique of the argument that religion is a necessary unit for the satisfaction of a need, see also Spiro, "Religion: Problems of Definition and Explanation" 117–121.

The argument as it stands is trivial; some one item is present, but we are not able to specify which item is functioning to satisfy the requirement of social maintenance. Once again, let us recall that functional explanations have been presented as explanations which account for why ritual, myth, or religion is present in a society and why these cultural units persist in a society. On reflecting on this fourth alternative it seems to me that it is no different in its logical construction then the second revision which includes functional equivalents in premise three. Hempel believes that this last revision is valid, although trivial in its conclusion. This seems odd. What we would need, I think, is an additional premise which could be stated as follows:

3. *i* is the class of empirically sufficient conditions for *z* in the conditions determined by *x* and *c*, and *i* is not empty.
3.1 The class of empirically sufficient conditions for *z* constitutes a disjointly necessary condition for *z*.
4. Hence, some one of the items. . . .

With this revision we are back to a notion of indispensable conditions which are necessary for the presence of ritual in a society. As we have seen, this claim is indeed more plausible since it asserts that some one of a class of items is necessary for *z*—if not ritual, then something else. This seems plausible, but it is simply not informative.

Most, if not all, functional arguments do not take the task of specifying an item or unit (religion) as a necessary condition. How could they? Instead they agree with Spiro who asserts that it is a class of structural units which are the sufficient conditions for satisfying the functional requirements of a society. Thus, most functional explanations assert that "it is highly likely," or "it is highly probable," that religion fulfills the requirement. Such conclusions are not only trivial, they are also impossible to confirm or disconfirm. Moreover, this conclusion seems to be invalid given my correction of Hempel's analysis.

It seems to be almost self-evident that religion is what it does until we actually examine the premises which support such a doctrine. If the above analysis is accurate, functionalism fails as a well-formed methodological procedure for explaining religion. It would seem that we are left with heuristic devices and "scholarly guesses" once again.

In an interesting essay on "Religion and the Irrational," Spiro seems to recognize the problem of explaining a religion as included in a class which is the sufficient condition for satisfying a requirement of society. Although his argument is an attempt to show the rationality of religion, the basic theory is functionalist. In arguing for the rationality of religious beliefs and their persistence in a society, Spiro concludes that "Their tenacity in the face of rival scientific beliefs may be simply explained—scientific beliefs may be functional *alternatives* for religious beliefs, but they are not their functional *equivalents*. *Religious beliefs have no functional equivalents;* being less satisfying, alternative beliefs are rejected as less convincing."[15]

What is of interest to us in the above quotation is the assertion that there are no functional equivalents to religious beliefs. To make this claim is of course to argue for the function of religious beliefs as a necessary condition for satisfying the functional requirements of a society or the maintenance or integration of personality or both.

Spiro argues that religious beliefs have a cognitive basis. If religious beliefs are attempts at explaining the world, this need not in itself lead us to the conclusion that such beliefs are irrational because they are false. All we need to remember is that there are many scientific theories which have turned out to be false and have been discarded. No one would conclude from this history of science that the falsified theories were, therefore, irrational.

The problem with religious beliefs, according to Spiro, is somewhat different. Instead of discarding a religious belief in the face of new discoveries and explanations, it seems that people hold onto their religious beliefs in spite of scientific progress in our knowledge of the world. The question then is not, are religious beliefs irrational, but, why do people continue to persist in holding onto them? This is a problem that most historians and phenomenologists have abandoned long ago. In doing so, we have not solved the problem; in fact, we have left it to be solved by disciplines such as anthropology, clinical psychology and philosophy. Since we claim to be specialists in the study of religion, this is most unfortunate.

Spiro solves the problem by setting both scientific and religious beliefs in the context of systems which satisfy our intellectual needs.

---

[15] Melford E. Spiro, "Religion and the Irrational," *Symposium on New Approaches to the Study of Religion,* Proceedings of the 1964 Annual Meeting of the American Ethnological Society, ed. June Helm (Seattle: University of Washington P, 1964) 112–113.

Where the two sets or systems differ is on the satisfaction of emotional needs. According to Spiro, religious beliefs satisfy both intellectual and emotional needs. The emotional or motivational basis of religious beliefs thus becomes a partial explanation of their persistence. Religious beliefs, however, cannot be explained as a function of motivation. After all, Spiro notes, there are many religious beliefs which are anything but satisfying. Thus, although it is the case that some religious beliefs are both intellectually and emotionally satisfying and that some religious beliefs may indeed involve empirical support, we must add the importance of "perceptual sets," formed in early childhood, as a strong contributor to the quality of religious conviction and the persistence of the belief system.[16]

Let us assume that religious beliefs are indeed necessary conditions for the satisfaction of individual and social needs and that religious beliefs are held not merely from a craving to satisfy intellectual needs, but also from a craving to satisfy emotional needs.[17] The additional argument that there are no functional equivalents for religious beliefs is important here. In contrast to what Spiro has written about social units jointly providing the sufficient condition for a functional requirement, we now have one social unit, a religious belief system, that can be substituted. Scientific beliefs may well take the place of religious beliefs, but they are not to be understood as providing the identical effects of religious beliefs. If this is not what is meant, then it will be exceedingly difficult to understand the meaning of the statement that "religious beliefs have no functional equivalent."

Spiro goes on to say that "neither the truth of the beliefs nor the etiology of the conviction by which they are held is relevant to the question of their rationality."[18] The criteria of their rationality are dependent on the degree to which religious beliefs satisfy our intellectual, motivational, and perceptual needs. Obviously, the quality of conviction alone will not suffice as a criterion for rationality.

Notice, once again, that Spiro's explanation of the function and rationality of religious belief does not reduce the data we are

---

[16] Spiro, "Religion and the Irrational" 113. See also Melford E. Spiro, *Buddhism and Society*, 2nd, expanded ed. (Berkeley: University of California Press, 1982).

[17] Spiro, "Religion and the Irrational" 112.

[18] Spiro, "Religion and the Irrational" 114.

attempting to understand. On the contrary, the theory is offered as a way of solving certain problems that have not been adequately solved by previous theories. The virtue of Spiro's approach is that it attempts to resolve three stubborn problems; the problem of the rationality of religious belief, the problem of the truth of religious beliefs, and an explanation of the persistence of religious beliefs. It should be satisfying to us all if such a theory succeeds on both logical and empirical grounds. It would advance our knowledge about religion, open new problems for analysis which would in turn provide greater explanatory power and methodological procedures for solving the new problems. In brief, it would provide the "science of religion" with a process for growth in knowledge about religion instead of the stagnant and dogmatic accusation that such an explanation is "reductionistic."

Unfortunately, not even the most sophisticated functionalist theories present us with well-formed arguments for explaining religion. Spiro's "revised" explanation does not commit a logical fallacy. Furthermore, the explanation is not to be taken as a strict causal explanation in the sense that religion is to be explained by its antecedent conditions. Religion is explained by its effect on some consequent condition, which in turn is a necessary condition for the maintenance of a society. Spiro's claim that there are no functional equivalents to religious belief systems also seems to evade the trivial conclusion that "somehow" the requirements of a social system are being satisfied. Nevertheless, serious weaknesses remain, and I believe they are weaknesses of the kind which will not allow us to use the theory as an explanation of religion.

There are at least two basic problems with the example we have used. The first problem has been discussed at some length, and we need not repeat it again. It involves the problem of stating that a religious belief system is a necessary condition for satisfying a functional requirement or set of requirements of a social or personal system. The difficulty here is justifying such an explanation empirically without becoming engaged in circular argument. What we would have to show is that all the relations between perceptual, motivational, and intellectual needs of a person and their relation to the structure of a society are sustained *only if* a specific system of religious beliefs is present. No one has succeeded in showing that this is the case. I do not know how it could be shown to be the case without circular argument. The usual option is to argue for functional equivalents or a set of social units taken jointly as a class of sufficient conditions. I have argued that this option does not solve the invalidity of functionalist explanations and the trivial conclusions it ends up with.

There is a second problem with the statement that "religious beliefs have no functional equivalent; being less satisfying, alternative beliefs are rejected as less convincing." At first, such statements may appear to assert the existence of a necessary condition. They are, however, usually qualified in such a way that they become ambiguous as necessary conditions for a functionalist explanation. Just how, for example, are we to interpret the statement that "there are no functional equivalents for religious belief systems because alternative beliefs are *less* satisfying?" Such qualifications surely do not entail, "only the present belief system satisfies. . . ." What has been introduced is the notion of a range or degree of satisfaction. Some beliefs have a greater power of satisfying certain requirements than others. The difficulties now become compounded. For, to sustain the statement that other beliefs are *less* satisfying than a religious belief system present in a society, we will have to specify the range or degree of satisfaction as well as a means for measuring the range. If we fail to provide such a scale and the means for calibrating the scale, our statement will remain vague—not false but simply incapable of being tested or confirmed.

We might also ask whether the statement that "alternative belief systems are *less* satisfying" means that religious beliefs function as providing *maximum* satisfaction of a requirement. Once again, we would need some scale which would permit us to measure and test such a maximum. Moreover, the statement "alternative belief systems are less satisfying" does not entail "only this belief system provides maximum satisfaction." It may imply that the religious belief system is more satisfying than alternative belief systems; but, again, this does not entail that the present religious belief system is a necessary condition for satisfying the social requirements.

My argument leads to the following conclusion. A second inspection of Spiro's "revised" explanation of religious beliefs reveals that it will be difficult to create a scale for measuring beliefs which are "more" or "less" satisfying. Nevertheless, such a scale might be created and tested. The deeper problem is that the qualification "more" or "less" removes the necessary condition of the religious belief system as satisfying a requirement of need in a society. For to say that in the context of a specific social system certain beliefs are "more" satisfying clearly does not exclude the possibility that certain alternative beliefs *may* become more effective than the beliefs presently held. In brief, we have not explained why the religious belief system is a *necessary* condition for satisfying the need, and thus we have not shown that there are no functional equivalents for a particular religious belief system in a society.

I believe these problems illustrate the inherent logical difficulties which functionalist theories must resolve before they can be accepted as adequate explanations of religion. If the critique I have presented is not convincing enough, there is a final methodological move which may clinch my argument. This involves the notion that a social system is a self-regulating system.

Both Ernest Nagel and Robert Brown have examined the problems of this model in their analysis of functionalist explanations. According to Nagel, "functional statements are regarded as appropriate in connection with systems possessing self-maintaining mechanisms for certain of their traits, but seem pointless and even misleading when used with reference to systems lacking such self-regulating devices."[19]

Robert Brown describes a self-maintaining system, a system that has negative feedback, in the following way:

> A self-persisting system is commonly taken to be a system which maintains at least one of its properties in an equilibrium position despite variations in the other properties, either inside or outside the system, to which the presence of the first property is causally related. This ability to maintain a property in a steady state while its causal factors vary within certain limits depends on the system containing certain devices. These must be self-regulators in the sense that they must register any significant variations in the state of the property which is being maintained and must compensate for these variations in such a way as to preserve the property within a range of permissible values. The simplest example and the one most favored by recent authors, is the thermostat which increases or reduces the heat throttle according to whether its thermometer registers above or below a set value.[20]

The model for many contemporary theories of religion is something like the above description of a system having negative

[19] Nagel 251–252. Also quoted in Robert Brown, *Explanation in Social Science* (Chicago: Aldine, 1963) 111; see also Jarvie, *Functionalism* 28–29.

[20] Brown 110–111.

feedback. This model often permits the functionalist to argue that the criticism of functionalism is basically irrelevant because the argument is directed against attempts to explain the origin of religion. By use of a negative feedback model, many functionalists claim that this is not what functionalism is all about, even though some of the fathers of functionalism made this mistake. The aim of functional theories of religion is not to show why a religious unit comes into existence, but how it functions and persists, what role it plays in a self-regulating system. Religious units in a social system are to be understood as variables in a self-maintaining system. This is an important distinction, but the success of the model for explaining religion is negligible.

Self-regulating systems are often assumed in the explanation of religion. A brief example must suffice to illustrate how the model is used. What we wish to explain is how a particular religious ritual works in the self-regulation of a social system. We assume for example, that both social equilibrium and personal stability are being maintained, since according to our observations both are functioning adequately. The religious ritual is explained if we can show how it functions to satisfy the requirements of equilibrium in the society and the stability in the individual. The religious ritual is explained, then, if we can show the relations of the ritual as reinforcing not only the "perceptual sets" formed in early childhood but also how the satisfaction of intellectual and emotional needs, in turn, reinforces the social structure of the society in which the religious ritual is a unit.

The use of this functionalist model has often been misunderstood. The explanation begins with religion present as a variable and then attempts to explain how it works in providing the self-regulation of the system. Failure to see the significance of this kind of explanation has often led to criticisms which are wide of the mark. The common mistake is to accuse functionalists who use self-adjusting models of not explaining why religion occurs, i.e. they fail to explain what causes religion. This often takes the following form. Let us assume that we have just read a functional explanation which makes it explicit that the model being used is a self-regulating one and that what is to be explained is how religion functions as a variable for providing equilibrium or adjustment as an effect; for example, that the belief in the existence of "Nats" among Burmese Buddhists, or in witchcraft among the Azande, functions to maintain social solidarity. The criticism of such an explanation often states that the belief has not really been explained. After all, the believer in "Nats" or witches is certainly not saying that he has acted in a way which will maintain social solidarity by believing in them or by performing a ritual which will protect him from their evil influences. The reason he believes in them, or performs certain rituals which are related to them is because he believes both that they exist and that they affect his life. If I asked a Shaivite why he believes in Shiva, I would certainly be surprised to hear that he believes in Shiva because Shiva is a symbolic representation of "perceptual sets" formed in early childhood and that, furthermore, such a belief reinforces both emotional and intellectual needs and the social structure as an unintended consequence.

The mistake we make in such critical replies is that the criticism is beside the point. We do not usually travel all the way to India, Africa or Burma, or spend our lives reading ancient texts, only to report what is self-evident, that Azande believe in witches, Burmese Buddhists believe that "Nats" exist, and some Hindus who belong to the Shaivite tradition believe in the existence of Shiva.

If a functionalist theory is explicit about the aims of the explanation, it should come as no surprise that an Azande or a Hindu does not make the same kinds of functional statements. Most scholars who are interested in explaining the function of religion are interested in the unintended consequences of the beliefs that are held and the rituals that are performed. What the functionalist is interested in is not primarily a report about these beliefs and rituals (as important as they are for an explanation), but the unintended consequences which these beliefs and rituals have for providing feedback into the regulation of the system. And if the functionalist can discover such unintended consequences, then it is surely odd to criticize the explanation because the believer did not report them when asked about the particular beliefs held. Once again, such an explanation would certainly advance our knowledge of religion.

If, however, we wish to take this approach to explain religion as providing feedback in a system of relations which is self-regulating, then it will become necessary to answer several important questions. Robert Brawn has come up with three questions which require an answer. The first is, what property is being maintained in a steady state? Secondly, what are the internal variables and can they or their effects be measured? Finally, what are the external conditions which are assumed to be constant?[21] No functionalist theory constructed on the model of a feedback system that I know of has come close to meeting the above requirements. In fact, I am not certain about how we could possibly meet them.

Let us imagine, for the moment, that it is conceivable that we could meet the requirements. We could begin by claiming that social solidarity or social equilibrium was the property which was being held in a steady state. We would then have to specify which of the variables or which single variable works to provide the steady state, and we would also have to provide a range of values to determine when the system is in equilibrium. To compound the difficulties, we would also have to specify which external threat of whatever kind could prevent the function of a unit from providing the necessary effects of maintaining the system.

We have discussed the difficulties of establishing whether a religious unit is a sufficient or necessary condition for maintaining a social system. In a self-regulating model, if the unit is a necessary condition for maintaining the system, we will then have to specify the exact relations which it maintains; since it would be most difficult to uphold the notion that a religious belief system, for example, functions to maintain all the relations in a social system. On the other hand, if we state that the unit is a sufficient condition, we then fail to explain exactly how the religious unit functions to satisfy the requirement. If we move to a class of units which jointly function to satisfy the needs of a society, we are reduced to trivial if not invalid conclusions. And no one as far as I know has been able to specify the external conditions which are constant or the degree of variation which will allow a social system to continue to maintain itself. Functionalism is at best a heuristic device, a strategy, for interpreting religion; heuristic devices are neither true nor false, they are in the domain of "your guess is as good as mine."

I believe that this conclusion is fully confirmed by the current debate among Marxists and other social scientists regarding the validity of functionalism in the corpus of publications, ever since Marx, which attempt to "explain" political/economic history.

Jon Elster, for example, offers us the following strong definition of a functional explanation: "On my definition then, *an institution or a*

---

[21] Brown 118–119.

behavioral pattern X *is explained by its function* Y *for group* Z if and only if:

(1) Y is an *effect* of X;
(2) Y is *beneficial* for Z;
(3) Y is *unintended* by the actors producing X;
(4) Y (or at least the causal relationship between X and Y) is *unrecognized* by the actors in Z;
(5) Y maintains X by a causal feedback loop passing through Z."[22]

Elster admits that "a closer analysis of purported functionalist explanations shows that in virtually all cases one or more of the defining features are lacking." He then argues that "it is close to impossible to find any cases of functional analysis in sociology where the presence of all features (1)–(5) is demonstrated."[23] Given the strong definition entailed in the "if and only if" clause, this is not a surprise. We are back to Hempel's argument. How would anyone claim that an institution or behavioral pattern X is explained by its function Y if and only if "Y is beneficial for Z?" Elster goes on to assert that there is a "naive brand of functional analysis . . . that from the presence of features (1), (3) and (4) concludes to the presence of feature (2) and often of feature (5). [Moreover,] there exists a more sophisticated brand of functionalism (represented by Merton) that from the presence of features (1)–(4) fallaciously concludes to the presence of feature (5)."[24] I think that Elster's argument is correct. Feature (5) is precisely the mechanism, often called a "self-regulating system," which is fallaciously inferred from the presence of the other features.

In other words, functional explanations in the social sciences have turned biological explanations upside-down. Elster's quarrel with Cohen and other functionalists rests on this fundamental point. In his review of Cohen's book Elster asserts that "I believe that I have seen no other mechanism that comes closer to being for sociology what natural selection is for biology, even if this is not, to repeat, to say that it comes very close." Cohen, however, does not even attempt

---

22 Jon Elster, *Ulysses and the Sirens: Studies in Rationality and Irrationality* (Cambridge: Cambridge University Press, 1979) 28.

23 Elster 28–29.

24 Elster 29.

to provide such a mechanism, which is why I believe that his enterprise must be judged a failure."[25]

What we must not lose sight of in this particular debate is where we began. We began with the problem of why a particular social institution or behavioral pattern exists or persists in a society! In the complex and often confusing debate, this problem seems to disappear. Nevertheless, it remains the central issue, and as far as I can see it has not been answered or explained. As Anthony Giddens puts it, "I agree with most of the elements of Elster's critique of functionalism, and I take as radical a stance as he does in suggesting that functionalist notions should be excluded altogether from the social sciences."[26] I think this is good advice.

In the discussion of phenomenology of religion, I pointed out that functionalism is often described as an auxiliary science for the study of religion. Although this claim is often held in contradiction with the claim that such an explanation is reductionistic, we often find anthropology, psychology, and sociology linked up with a phenomenology of religion as useful (and sometimes necessary) for a complete understanding of religion. We can abbreviate this claim by saying that for many phenomenologists of religion a complete study of religion must include both the nature (i.e., the essence) and the function of religion.

This partnership is an illusion. It is an illusion because functionalists do not attempt to explain the "essence" or nature of religion as The Sacred because they want to leave this research to other scholars of religion. The slogan "religion is what it does" is a

---

[25] Jon Elster, "Cohen on Marx's Theory of History," *Political Studies* XXVII (1980): 127. For Cohen's response see, G. A. Cohen, "Functional Explanations: Reply to Elster," *Political Studies XXVII* (1980): 129–35. For the current debate see the following articles in *Theory and Society* 11 (1982): Jon Elster, "Marxism, Functionalism and Game Theory" 453–82; G. A. Cohen, "Reply to Elster on 'Marxism, Functionalism and Game Theory'" 483–95; Philippe Van Parijs, "Functionalist Marxism Rehabilitated: A Comment on Elster" 497–511; Johannes Berger and Claus Offe, "Functionalism vs. Rational Choice" 521–26; and Anthony Giddens, "Commentary on the Debate" 527–39. Cohen's 1982 response is a version of G. A. Cohen, "Functional Explanation, Consequence Explanation, and Marxism," *Inquiry* 25 (1982): 27–56. For a revision of Elster's definition, see Russell Hardin, "Rationality, irrationality and functionalist explanation," *Social Science Information* 19 (1980): 755–72. For a critical review of Elster, see Steven Walt, "Rationality and Explanation," *Ethics* 94 (1983–84): 680–700.

[26] Giddens, "Commentary on the Debate" 527.

clear indication that functionalist approaches to religion also involve a rejection of all forms of essentialism.

When biblical scholars, historians and phenomenologists of religion discover the theological roots of their discipline, they are often tempted to become unregenerate or revisionist functionalists. Both Drijvers and Leertouwer, among others, seem to have yielded to this temptation. In their "Epilogue" they offer the following advice: "Van Baaren inquires what cultural function of religion still subsists when a great number of persons in the culture no longer feels any emotional or rational tie with religion. This question is not dependent on theological developments, but on the loss of function of the Christian religion in Western culture. In such a situation it becomes urgent to find the function of religion *tout court*."[27] If my analysis of functionalism is accurate, I believe there are good reasons for not following this kind of methodological advice.

Given the nature of the problems we have described thus far, it would seem that we have reached a theoretical and methodological impasse in the study of religion. I think we have no one to blame but ourselves for this situation. The utter lack of concern about the methodological issues is symptomatic of the present condition in which we find ourselves. It is simply astonishing to discover that an academic discipline, a "science," of religion has little, if any, concern with theory. Perhaps we have been lulled into this slumber because we have become a part of our subject; "we do what we do because in the beginning our ancestors did it that way." If the impasse is of our own making, we can also overcome it. Chapter 17 in this volume is one attempt to describe a way out of theological disguises, the quest for essences, the ideology of neutrality, the bankruptcy of functionalism as a type of causal explanation, and sloppy methodological eclecticism. Please note that I wrote "a way out." There may be other ways that are more adequate—I have not discovered them.

---

[27] Th. P. van Baaren and H. J. W. Drijvers, eds., *Religion, Culture and Methodology* (The Hague: Mouton, 1973) 168.

Suggested Readings

Burhenn, Herbert. 1980. Functionalism and the Explanation of Religion. *Journal for the Scientific Study of Religion* 19: 350–360. A clear misinterpretation of Hempel's critique as a concern with origin theories of cultural traits concluding that functionalism may be helpful in understanding religion. This popular notion transforms functionalism from causal explanation into a heuristic device that is neither true or false.

Cummins, Robert. 1975. Functional Analysis. *The Journal of Philosophy LXXII:* 741–765. An excellent attempt to work out a valid theory of functionalism that fails.

Douglas, Mary. 1966. *Purity and Danger*. New York: Penguin Books. A classic that assumes functionalism as the basis for explaining prohibitions in religions such as the taboo on pork.

Hempel, Carl G. 1965. The Logic of Functional Analysis. In *Aspects of Scientific Explanations.* Glencoe, Ill.: Free Press. The classic critique of the logic of functionalism. Also published in many anthologies.

Homans, George C. 1941. Anxiety and Ritual: The Theories of Malinowski and Radcliffe Brown. *American Anthropologist* 43: 164–171. A classic use of functionalism that resolves the long dispute between two great scholars in anthropology.

Kluckholm, Clyde. 1942. Myth and Ritual: A General Theory. *Harvard Theological Review* 35: 45–79. Reprinted in R. A. Georges (ed.), *Studies On Mythology*, 1968. Homewood, Ill.: The Dorsey Press. A classic example of applied functionalism.

Lawson, E. Thomas & McCauley, Robert N. 1984. Functionalism Reconsidered. *History of Religions* 23: 372–381. An attempt to use biology in the cultural sciences. Unfortunately, the mechanism of "natural selection" is missing.

Leach, Edmund. 1969. Virgin Birth. In *Genesis as Myth and Other Essays.* London: Jonathan Cape. 85–110. This essay should be read in conjunction with Spiro's essay, to which it is a reply. This encounter is an excellent example of disagreement on particulars (symbol vs non-symbol) but fundamental agreement on theory (functionalism).

Rappaport, Roy. 1979. *Ecology, Meaning, and Religion.* Berkeley: North Atlantic Books. A good example of a response to Hempel that misses the the central logical argument of Hempel's critique.

Spickard, James V. 1991. A Revised Functionalism in the Sociology of Religion. *Religion* 21: 141–164. A good example of an attempt to solve the problems in functionalism while employing the flawed logic of the theory.

Part III

From Functionalism to Relativism

Introduction to Part III

Functionalism as a theory of culture need not entail relativism. Melford Spiro and Robin Horton are good examples of well known anthropologists who use functionalist theory but reject relativism. Freud, Durkheim, and Marx represent further examples. Yet, the two approaches are so deeply connected both historically and theoretically that it is fair to say that relativism is a frequent consequence of adopting functionalism. In the cultural sciences, and by extension in the public media, cultural and conceptual relativism remain popular explanations of the existence of a multiplicity of worldviews, ideologies, and ethical and religious beliefs.

On the assumption that different religious systems exist to satisfy social and psychological needs, it is an easy step into conceptual and cultural relativism and the assertion that different religious systems or worldviews express different truth values about the world and human life. In an essay included in Part III, Peter Winch bluntly states: "Reality is not what gives language sense. What is real and what is unreal shows itself *in* the sense that language has." Against Evans-Pritchard, Winch holds that we cannot proclaim that the Azande or any other social group's beliefs "are not in accord with reality." Why? Because what is in accord with reality and what is not in accord with reality is given in the sense that a particular cultural "language" has. The multiplicity of world-views, religious beliefs, and ethical systems leads to the conclusion that truth varies with specific language systems. According to some relativists, people literally live in different worlds. The point of relativism, then, is that we cannot assert that any religious beliefs at all are false, or "not in accord with reality," because truth is relative to a particular language game.

Interestingly, however, this claim does not impinge upon any of the claims of functionalist theory (at least not at first sight, as we shall see). Some students of religion will want to assert with Durkheim that "all religions are true." That is, they are all true in whatever way they function to satisfy the needs of the individual and society. A religion is true, or meaningful, in terms of its use as a satisfaction of needs, on this account. Consistent relativists, however, should not make judgements about the truth of religious beliefs for this would violate the relativist principle that what is true and what is not true is given in the sense that a particular language has.

Most scholars of religion who adhere to the positivist principle of verification will reject the notion that religious beliefs and ritual practices entail any truth conditions whatsoever. They will see religious beliefs and practices as purely expressive or symbolic. Bronislaw Malinowski and John Beattie remain good examples of this approach to religion. In their view, scholars such as Evans-Pritchard, Melford Spiro, and Robin Horton are wrong not because of the relativity of truth conditions in a specific language or worldview, but because religious language does not express or represent truth values at all. Religious beliefs are therefore neither true nor false. In that case, we may ask, why do religious beliefs persist? Functionalism appears at precisely this point and supplies the answer that religious beliefs persist because they function to satisfy non-cognitive needs.

For over forty years a great deal of debate has focused on the intelligibility of cognitive relativism, the claim that truth or knowledge is relative to a specific language. Often identified as "linguistic relativity," the originating expression of this theory is found in the famous "Sapir-Whorf" hypothesis. Anyone who would understand relativism in the study of religion should be familiar with the most famous passages in Whorf:

> [The example] is an illustration of how language produces an organization of experience. We are inclined to think of language simply as a technique of expression, and not to realize that language first of all is a classification and arrangement of the stream of sensory experience which results in a certain world-order. (1956: 55)

> We dissect nature along lines laid down by our native languages. The categories and types that we isolate from the world of phenomena we do not find there because they stare every observer in the face; on the contrary, the world is presented in a kaleidoscopic flux of impressions which has to be organized by our minds—and this means largely by the linguistic systems of our minds. We cut nature up, organize it into concepts, and ascribe significances as we do, largely because we are parties to an agreement to organize it in this way—an agreement that holds throughout our speech community and is codified in the patterns

> of our language. The agreement is, of course, an implicit and unstated one, *but its terms are absolutely obligatory*. . . . (1956: 213, italics original)
>
> From this fact [involuntary grammars] proceeds what I have called the 'linguistic relativity principle' which means, in informal terms, that users of markedly different grammars are pointed by their grammars toward different types of observations and different evaluations of externally similar acts of observation and hence are not equivalent as observers but must arrive at somewhat different views of the world. (1956: 221)

Crucial to the various theories of cultural and linguistic relativity is the notion that truth and the content of truth is relative to a particular language or worldview. Pressed to its logical conclusion, relativism asserts that religions or worldviews are incommensurable, that is to say, not translatable, since there is no universal truth or grammar to provide a bridge between religions, language games, worldviews or ideologies. Thus we cannot conclude that the belief system of one religion rather than another is false, because what is true or false is dependent upon the sense that the language of the particular religion has. Not only are different opinions, interests, life styles and skills relative to different cultures but so too are fundamental concepts, including the very presuppositional attitudes that constitute cognition and culture in the first place. Truth, so the argument goes, is relative to each worldview or grammar. But if all translation is held to be impossible because cultures or languages are incommensurable, then relativism fails to account for the obvious fact that translations are in fact forged and can be deemed better or worse translations. Driven to its logical end, relativism turns into an absurdity.

What sense does it make to say that "all worldviews are relative to some context," or that "what is real and what is unreal is given in the sense that a language has"? Are these statements also relative to some context or language? If not, are they universal? Is relativism relative to a particular language and culture? One statement would appear to escape the claims of relativism and that is the assertion that relativism itself is true. As a theory, relativism is unable to cope with the dilemma that *either* its thesis is exempt from itself, which means that *all* truth is *not* relative, *or* it is not self-exempting and therefore we have no reason for taking any of the statements in the theory seriously. The relativist is forced to choose between these two horns of the dilemma, and neither makes the theory sound.

We can put the criticism in slightly different terms. How might one go about validating the hypothesis that meaning, belief, and truth are culturally determined? If the hypothesis is true isn't its meaning given from a specific cultural context, a particular language? In order to answer such questions the relativist would have to be able to rise above all contexts, including the language in which the hypothesis is stated, to judge whether it is true. This is clearly impossible. No one is able to transcend all languages and contexts in order to demonstrate that the hypothesis is true. Understandably, very few relativists carry the theory to this self-refuting end.

The question of the relation of Wittgensteinian "forms of life" to relativism is complex. On one interpretation favored by some philosophers of religion, Wittgenstein is a thorough-going relativist for whom different "language-games" constitute incommensurable languages (e.g. science and religion). Other commentators interpret Wittgenstein as committed to no such theory. Not all students of Wittgenstein follow Norman Malcolm's lead in interpreting religious beliefs as groundless. The suggested readings below help to clarify some of these questions.

As a brace against Wittgenstein, Malcolm, Winch, and Horton, we have placed two essays by the philosopher Donald Davidson at the beginning of this section. "The Very Idea of a Conceptual Scheme" has become a classic critique of all theories of truth that assume some kind of correspondence between language or belief, on the one hand, and experience, understood as "the given," on the other hand. Davidson calls this a correspondence between a "scheme" and a "content." By content, Davidson means something like Hume's "sense impressions" or Kant's "noumena"—any kind of sense data, uninterpreted sensations, or pure experiences. The overall target of this critique is "subjective experience."

Davidson argues that all theories of relativism fall under this critique. In a similar way, we argue that all theories of language and belief as worldviews or frameworks of meaning also fall under this critique insofar as they are said to serve as schemas for a certain kind of content. In Part II, we showed that Clifford Geertz's notion of a "model of" reality is just such a schema. Most contemporary studies of religious mysticism also employ this misleading "scheme/content" dichotomy.

In "The Myth of the Subjective" Davidson develops additional criticisms and comes to conclusions he says mark a "sea change in contemporary philosophical thought." Taken together, both essays amount to a devastating critique of a great deal of scholarship in the study of religion, religious symbolism, language, and culture.

References:

Whorf, Benjamin Lee. 1956. *Language, Thought and Reality: Selected Writings*. Edited by John B. Carroll. Cambridge, Mass.: M. I. T. Press.

9

On the Very Idea of a Conceptual Scheme

Donald Davidson

Philosophers of many persuasions are prone to talk of conceptual schemes. Conceptual schemes, we are told, are ways of organizing experience; they are systems of categories that give form to the data of sensation; they are points of view from which individuals, cultures, or periods survey the passing scene. There may be no translating from one scheme to another, in which case the beliefs, desires, hopes, and bits of knowledge that characterize one person have no true counterparts for the subscriber to another scheme. Reality itself is relative to a scheme: what counts as real in one system may not in another.

Even those thinkers who are certain there is only one conceptual scheme are in the sway of the scheme concept; even monotheists have religion. And when someone sets out to describe "our conceptual scheme," his homey task assumes, if we take him literally, that there might be rival systems.

Conceptual relativism is a heady and exotic doctrine, or would be if we could make good sense of it. The trouble is, as so often in philosophy, it is hard to improve intelligibility while retaining the excitement. At any rate that is what I shall argue.

We are encouraged to imagine we understand massive conceptual change or profound contrasts by legitimate examples of a familiar sort. Sometimes an idea, like that of simultaneity as defined in relativity theory, is so important that with its addition a whole department of science takes on a new look. Sometimes revisions in the list of sentences held true in a discipline are so central that we may feel that the terms involved have changed their meanings. Languages that have evolved in distant times or places may differ extensively in their resources for dealing with one or another range of phenomena. What comes easily in one language may come hard in another, and this difference may echo significant dissimilarities in style and value.

But examples like these, impressive as they occasionally are, are not so extreme but that the changes and the contrasts can be explained and described using the equipment of a single language. Whorf, wanting to demonstrate that Hopi incorporates a metaphysics so alien to ours that Hopi and English cannot, as he puts it, "be calibrated," uses English to convey the contents of sample Hopi sentences."[1] Kuhn is brilliant at saying what things were like before the revolution using—what else?—our post-revolutionary idiom.[2] Quine gives us a feel for the "pre-individuative phase in the evolution of our conceptual scheme,"[3] while Bergson tells us where we can go to get a view of a mountain undistorted by one or another provincial perspective.

The dominant metaphor of conceptual relativism, that of differing points of view, seems to betray an underlying paradox. Different points of view make sense, but only if there is a common co-ordinate system on which to plot them; yet the existence of a common system belies the claim of dramatic incomparability. What we need, it seems to me, is some idea of the considerations that set the limits to conceptual contrast. There are extreme suppositions that founder on paradox or contradiction; there are modest examples we have no trouble understanding. What determines where we cross from the merely strange or novel to the absurd?

We may accept the doctrine that associates having a language with having a conceptual scheme. The relation may be supposed to be this: where conceptual schemes differ, so do languages. But speakers of different languages may share a conceptual scheme provided there is a way of translating one language into the other. Studying the criteria of translation is therefore a way of focusing on criteria of identity for conceptual schemes. If conceptual schemes aren't associated with languages in this way, the original problem is needlessly doubled, for then we would have to imagine the mind, with its ordinary categories, operating with a language with its

---

1 B. L. Whorf, "The Punctual and Segmentative Aspects of Verbs in Hopi."

2 T. S. Kuhn, *The Structure of Scientific Revolutions.*

3 W. V. Quine, "Speaking of Objects," 24.

organizing structure. Under the circumstances we would certainly want to ask who is to be master.

Alternatively, there is the idea that *any* language distorts reality, which implies that it is only wordlessly if at all that the mind comes to grips with things as they really are. This is to conceive language as an inert (though necessarily distorting) medium independent of the human agencies that employ it; a view of language that surely cannot be maintained. Yet if the mind can grapple without distortion with the real, the mind itself must be without categories and concepts. This featureless self is familiar from theories in quite different parts of the philosophical landscape. There are, for example, theories that make freedom consist in decisions taken apart from all desires, habits, and dispositions of the agent; and theories of knowledge that suggest that the mind can observe the totality of its own perceptions and ideas. In each case, the mind is divorced from the traits that constitute it; an inescapable conclusion from certain lines of reasoning, as I said, but one that should always persuade us to reject the premises.

We may identify conceptual schemes with languages, then, or better, allowing for the possibility that more than one language may express the same scheme, sets of intertranslatable languages. Languages we will not think of as separable from souls; speaking a language is not a trait a man can lose while retaining the power of thought. So there is no chance that someone can take up a vantage point for comparing conceptual schemes by temporarily shedding his own. Can we then say that two people have different conceptual schemes if they speak languages that fail of intertranslatability?

In what follows I consider two kinds of case that might be expected to arise: complete, and partial, failures of translatability. There would be complete failure if no significant range of sentences in one language could be translated into the other; there would be partial failure if some range could be translated and some range could not (I shall neglect possible asymmetries.) My strategy will be to argue that we cannot make sense of total failure, and then to examine more briefly cases of partial failure.

First, then, the purported cases of complete failure. It is tempting to take a very short line indeed: nothing, it may be said, could count as evidence that same form of activity could not be interpreted in our language that was not at the same time evidence that that form of activity was not speech behaviour. If this were right, we probably ought to hold that a form of activity that cannot be interpreted as language in our language is not speech behaviour. Putting matters this way is unsatisfactory, however, for it comes to little more than making translatability into a familiar tongue a criterion of language-hood. As fiat, the thesis lacks the appeal of self-evidence; if it is truth, as I think it is, it should emerge as the conclusion of an argument.

The credibility of the position is improved by reflection on the close relations between language and the attribution of attitudes such as belief, desire, and intention. On the one hand, it is clear that speech requires a multitude of finely discriminated intentions and beliefs. A person who asserts that perseverance keeps honour bright must, for example, represent himself as believing that perseverance keeps honour bright, and he must intend to represent himself as believing it. On the other hand, it seems unlikely that we can intelligibly attribute attitudes as complex as these to a speaker unless we can translate his words into ours. There can be no doubt that the relation between being able to translate someone's language and being able to describe his attitudes is very close. Still, until we can say more about *what* this relation is, the case against untranslatable languages remains obscure.

It is sometimes thought that translatability into a familiar language, say English, cannot be a criterion of languagehood on the grounds that the relation of translatability is not transitive. The idea is that some language, say Saturnian, may be translatable into English, and some further language, like Plutonian, may be translatable into Saturnian, while Plutonian is not translatable into English. Enough translatable differences may add up to an untranslatable one. By imagining a sequence of languages, each close enough to the one before to be acceptably translated into it, we can imagine a language so different from English as to resist totally translation into it. Corresponding to this distant language would be a system of concepts altogether alien to us.

This exercise does not, I think, introduce any new element into the discussion. For we should have to ask how we recognized that what the Saturnian was doing was *translating* Plutonian (or anything else). The Saturnian speaker might tell us that that was what he was doing or rather we might for a moment assume that that was what he was telling us. But then it would occur to us to wonder whether our translations of Saturnian were correct.

According to Kuhn, scientists operating in different scientific traditions (within different "paradigms") "work in different worlds."[4] Strawson's *The Bounds of Sense* begins with the remark that "It is possible to imagine kinds of worlds very different from the world as we know it."[5] Since there is at most one world, these pluralities are metaphorical or merely imagined. The metaphors are, however, not at all the same. Strawson invites us to imagine possible non-actual worlds, worlds that might be described, using our present language, by redistributing truth values over sentences in various systematic ways. The clarity of the contrasts between worlds in this case depends on supposing our scheme of concepts, our descriptive resources, to remain fixed. Kuhn, on the other hand, wants us to think of different observers of the same world who come to it with incommensurable systems of concepts. Strawson's many imagined worlds are seen or heard or described from the same point of view; Kuhn's one world is seen from different points of view. It is the second metaphor we want to work on.

The first metaphor requires a distinction within language of concept and content: using a fixed system of concepts (words with fixed meanings) we describe alternative universes. Some sentences will be true simply because of the concepts or meanings involved, others because of the way of the world. In describing possible worlds, we play with sentences of the second kind only.

The second metaphor suggests instead a dualism of quite a different sort, a dualism of total scheme (or language) and uninterpreted content. Adherence to the second dualism, while not inconsistent with adherence to the first, may be encouraged by attacks on the first. Here is how it may work.

To give up the analytic-synthetic distinction as basic to the understanding of language is to give up the idea that we can clearly distinguish between theory and language. Meaning, as we might loosely use the word, is contaminated by theory, by what is held to be true. Feyerabend puts it this way:

> Our argument against meaning invariance is simple and clear. It proceeds from the fact that usually some of the principles involved in the determinations of the meanings of older theories or points of views are inconsistent with the new . . . theories. It points out that it

[4] T. S. Kuhn, *The Structure of Scientific Revolutions*, 134.

[5] P. Strawson, *The Bounds of Sense*, 15.

> is natural to resolve this contradiction by eliminating the troublesome . . . older principles, and to replace them by principles, or theorems, of a new . . . theory. And it concludes by showing that such a procedure will also lead to the elimination of the old meanings.[6]

We may now seem to have a formula for generating distinct conceptual schemes. We get a new out of an old scheme when the speakers of a language come to accept as true an important range of sentences they previously took to be false (and, of course, vice versa). We must not describe this change simply as a matter of their coming to view old falsehoods as truths, for a truth is a proposition, and what they come to accept, in accepting a sentence as true, is not the same thing that they rejected when formerly they held the sentence to be false. A change has come over the meaning of the sentence because it now belongs to a new language.

This picture of how new (perhaps better) schemes result from new and better science is very much the picture philosophers of science, like Putnam and Feyerabend, and historians of science, like Kuhn, have painted for us. A related idea emerges in the suggestion of same other philosophers, that we could improve our conceptual lot if we were to tune our language to an improved science. Thus both Quine and Smart, in somewhat different ways, regretfully admit that our present ways of talking make a serious science of behaviour impossible. (Wittgenstein and Ryle have said similar things without regret.) The cure, Quine and Smart think, is to change how we talk. Smart advocates (and predicts) the change in order to put us on the scientifically straight path of materialism: Quine is more concerned to clear the way for a purely extensional language. (Perhaps I should add that I think our actual scheme and language are best understood as extensional and materialist.)

If we were to follow this advice, I do not myself think science or understanding would be advanced, though possibly morals would. But the present question is only whether, if such changes were to take place, we should be justified in calling them alterations in the basic conceptual apparatus. The difficulty in so calling them is easy to appreciate. Suppose that in my office of Minister of Scientific Language I want the new man to stop using words that refer, say, to emotions, feelings, thoughts, and intentions, and to talk instead of the

6 P. Feyerabend, "Explanation, Reduction, and Empiricism," 82.

physiological states and happenings that are assumed to be more or less identical with the mental riff and raff. How do I tell whether my advice has been heeded if the new man speaks a new language? For all I know, the shiny new phrases, though stolen from the old language in which they refer to physiological stirrings, may in his mouth play the role of the messy old mental concepts.

The key phrase is: for all I know. What is clear is that retention of some or all of the old vocabulary in itself provides no basis for judging the new scheme to be the same as, or different from, the old. So what sounded at first like a thrilling discovery—that truth is relative to a conceptual scheme—has not so far been shown to be anything more than the pedestrian and familiar fact that the truth of a sentence is relative to (among other things) the language to which it belongs. Instead of living in different worlds, Kuhn's scientists may, like those who need Webster's dictionary, be only words apart.

Giving up the analytic-synthetic distinction has not proven a help in making sense of conceptual relativism. The analytic-synthetic distinction is however explained in terms of something that may serve to buttress conceptual relativism, namely the idea of empirical content. The dualism of the synthetic and the analytic is a dualism of sentences some of which are true (or false) both because of what they mean and because of their empirical content, while others are true (or false) by virtue of meaning alone, having no empirical content. If we give up the dualism, we abandon the conception of meaning that goes with it, but we do not have to abandon the idea of empirical content: we can hold, if we want, that *all* sentences have empirical content. Empirical content is in turn explained by reference to the facts, the world, experience, sensation, the totality of sensory stimuli, or something similar. Meanings gave us a way to talk about categories, the organizing structure of language, and so on; but it is possible, as we have seen, to give up meanings and analyticity while retaining the idea of language as embodying a conceptual scheme. Thus in place of the dualism of the analytic-synthetic we get the dualism of conceptual scheme and empirical content. The new dualism is the foundation of an empiricism shorn of the untenable dogmas of the analytic-synthetic distinction and reductionism—shorn, that is, of the unworkable idea that we can uniquely allocate empirical content sentence by sentence.

I want to urge that this second dualism of scheme and content, of organizing system and something waiting to be organized, cannot be made intelligible and defensible. It is itself a dogma of empiricism, the third dogma. The third, and perhaps the last, for if we give it up it is not clear that there is anything distinctive left to call empiricism.

The scheme-content dualism has been formulated in many ways. Here are same examples. The first comes from Whorf, elaborating on a theme of Sapir's. Whorf says that:

> . . . language produces an organization of experience. We are inclined to think of language simply as a technique of expression, and not to realize that language first of all is a classification and arrangement of the stream of sensory experience which results in a certain world-order. . . . In other words, language does in a cruder but also in a broader and more versatile way the same thing that science does. . . . We are thus introduced to a new principle of relativity, which holds that all observers are not led by the same physical evidence to the same picture of the universe, unless their linguistic backgrounds are similar, or can in some way be calibrated.[7]

Here we have all the required elements: language as the organizing force, not to be distinguished clearly from science; what is organized, referred to variously as "experience," "the stream of sensory experience," and "physical evidence"; and finally, the failure of intertranslatability ("calibration"). The failure of intertranslatability is a necessary condition for difference of conceptual schemes; the common relation to experience or the evidence is what is supposed to help us make sense of the claim that it is languages or schemes that are under consideration when translation fails. It is essential to this idea that there be something neutral and common that lies outside all schemes. This common something cannot, of course, be the *subject matter* of contrasting languages, or translation would be possible. Thus Kuhn has recently written:

> Philosophers have now abandoned hope of finding a pure sense-datum language . . . but many of them continue to assume that theories can be compared by recourse to a basic vocabulary consisting entirely of words which are attached to nature in ways that are unproblematic and to the extent necessary, independent of theory. . . . Feyerabend and I have argued at length that no such vocabulary is available. In the transition from one theory to the next words change their meanings or conditions of applicability in subtle ways. Though most of the same signs are used before and after a revolution—e.g. force, mass, element, compound, cell—the

---

[7] B. L. Whorf, "The Punctual and Segmentative Aspects of Verbs in Hopi," 55.

> way in which some of them attach to nature has somehow changed. Successive theories are thus, we say, incommensurable.[8]

"Incommensurable" is, of course, Kuhn and Feyerabend's word for "not intertranslatable." The neutral content waiting to be organized is supplied by nature.

Feyerabend himself suggests that we may compare contrasting schemes by "choosing a point of view outside the system or the language." He hopes we can do this because "there is still human experience as an actually existing process"[9] independent of all schemes.

The same, or similar, thoughts are expressed by Quine in many passages: "The totality of our so-called knowledge or beliefs . . . is a man-made fabric which impinges on experience only along the edges . . . ,"[10] "total science is like a field of force whose boundary conditions are experience";[11] "As an empiricist I . . . think of the conceptual scheme of science as a tool . . . for predicting future experience in the light of past experience."[12] And again:

> We persist in breaking reality down somehow into a multiplicity of identifiable and discriminable objects. . . . We talk so inveterately of objects that to say we do so seems almost to say nothing at all; for how else is there to talk? It is hard to say how else there is to talk, not because our objectifying pattern is an invariable trait of human nature, but because we are bound to adapt any alien pattern to our own in the very process of understanding or translating the alien sentences.[13]

The test of difference remains failure or difficulty of translation: ". . . to speak of that remote medium as radically different from ours is to say no more than that the translations do not come smoothly."[14] Yet the roughness may be so great that the alien has an "as yet unimagined pattern beyond individuation."[15]

The idea is then that something is a language, and associated with a conceptual scheme, whether we can translate it or not, if it

---

[8] T. S. Kuhn, "Reflections of my Critics," 266, 267.

[9] P. Feyerabend, "Problems of Empiricism," 214.

[10] W. V. Quine, "Two Dogmas of Empiricism," 42.

[11] Ibid.

[12] Ibid., 44.

[13] W. V. Quine, "Speaking of Objects," 1.

[14] Ibid., 25.

[15] Ibid., 24.

stands in a certain relation (predicting, organizing, facing, or fitting) experience (nature, reality, sensory promptings). The problem is to say what the relation is, and to be clearer about the entities related.

The images and metaphors fall into two main groups: conceptual schemes (languages) either *organize* something, or they *fit* it (as in "he warps his scientific heritage to fit his . . . sensory promptings"[16]). The first group contains also *systematize* , *divide up* (the stream of experience); further examples of the second group are *predict, account for, face* (the tribunal of experience). As for the entities that get organized, or which the scheme must fit, I think again we may detect two main ideas: either it is reality (the universe, the world, nature), or it is experience (the passing show, surface irritations, sensory promptings, sense-data, the given).

We cannot attach a clear meaning to the notion of organizing a single object (the world, nature etc.) unless that object is understood to contain or consist in other objects. Someone who sets out to organize a closet arranges the things in it. If you are told not to organize the shoes and shirts, but the closet itself, you would be bewildered. How would you organize the Pacific Ocean? Straighten out its shores, perhaps, or relocate its islands, or destroy its fish.

A language may contain simple predicates whose extensions are matched by no simple predicates, or even by any predicates at all, in some other language. What enables us to make this point in particular cases is an ontology common to the two languages, with concepts that individuate the same objects. We can be clear about breakdowns in translation when they are local enough, for a background of generally successful translation provides what is needed to make the failures intelligible. But we were after larger game: we wanted to make sense of there being a language we could not translate at all. Or, to put the point differently, we were looking for a criterion of languagehood that did not depend on, or entail, translatability into a familiar idiom. I suggest that the image of organizing the closet of nature will not supply such a criterion.

How about the other kind of object, experience? Can we think of a language organizing *it*? Much the same difficulties recur. The notion of organization applies only to pluralities. But whatever plurality we take experience to consist in—events like losing a button or stubbing a toe, having a sensation of warmth or hearing an

[16] W. V. Quine, "Two Dogmas of Empiricism," 46.

oboe—we will have to individuate according to familiar principles. A language that organizes *such* entities must be a language very like our own.

Experience (and its classmates like surface irritations, sensations and sense-data) also makes another and more obvious trouble for the organizing idea. For how could something count as a language that organized only experiences, sensations, surface irritations, or sense-data? Surely knives and forks, railroads and mountains, cabbages and kingdoms also need organizing.

This last remark will no doubt sound inappropriate as a response to the claim that a conceptual scheme is a way of coping with sensory experience; and I agree that it is. But what was under consideration was the idea of *organizing* experience, not the idea of *coping with* (or fitting or facing) experiences. The reply was apropos of the former, not the latter, concept. So now let's see whether we can do better with the second idea.

When we turn from talk of organization to talk of fitting we turn our attention from the referential apparatus of language—predicates, quantifiers, variables, and singular terms—to whole sentences. It is sentences that predict (or are used to predict), sentences that cope or deal with things, that fit our sensory promptings, that can be compared or confronted with the evidence. It is sentences also that face the tribunal of experience, though of course they must face it together.

The proposal is not that experiences, sense-data, surface irritations, or sensory promptings are the sole subject matter of language. There is, it is true, the theory that talk about brick houses on Elm Street is ultimately to be construed as being about sense data or perceptions, but such reductionistic views are only extreme, and implausible, versions of the general position we are considering. The general position is that sensory experience provides all the evidence for the acceptance of sentences (where sentences may include whole theories). A sentence or theory fits our sensory promptings, successfully faces the tribunal of experience, predicts future experience, or copes with the pattern of our surface irritations, provided it is borne out by the evidence.

In the common course of affairs, a theory may be borne out by the available evidence and yet be false. But what is in view here is not just actually available evidence; it is the totality of possible sensory evidence past, present, and future. We do not need to pause to contemplate what this might mean. The point is that for a theory to fit or face up to the totality of possible sensory evidence is for that theory to be true. If a theory quantifies over physical objects, numbers, or sets, what it says about these entities is true provided the theory as a whole fits the sensory evidence. One can see how, from this point of view, such entities might be called posits. It is reasonable to call something a posit if it can be contrasted with something that is not. Here the something that is not is sensory experience—at least that is the idea.

The trouble is that the notion of fitting the totality of experience, like the notion of fitting the facts, or of being true to the facts, adds nothing intelligible to the simple concept of being true. To speak of sensory experience rather than the evidence, or just the facts, expresses a view about the source or nature of evidence, but it does not add a new entity to the universe against which to test conceptual schemes. The totality of sensory evidence is what we want provided it is all the evidence there is; and all the evidence there is is just what it takes to make our sentences or theories true. Nothing, however, no *thing*, makes sentences and theories true: not experience, not surface irritations, not the world, can make a sentence true. *That* experience takes a certain course, that our skin is warmed or punctured, that the universe is finite, these facts, if we like to talk that way, make sentences and theories true. But this point is put better without mention of facts. The sentence "My skin is warm" is true if and only if my skin is warm. Here there is no reference to a fact, a world, an experience, or a piece of evidence.[17]

Our attempt to characterize languages or conceptual schemes in terms of the notion of fitting some entity has come down, then, to the simple thought that something is an acceptable conceptual scheme or theory if it is true. Perhaps we better say *largely* true in order to allow sharers of a scheme to differ on details. And the criterion of a conceptual scheme different from our own now becomes: largely true but not translatable. The question whether this is a useful criterion is just the question how well we understand the notion of truth, as applied to language, independent of the notion of translation. The answer is, I think, that we do not understand it independently at all.

We recognize sentences like "'Snow is white' is true if and only if snow is white" to be trivially true. Yet the totality of such English

[17] See Essay 3.

sentences uniquely determines the extension of the concept of truth for English. Tarski generalized this observation and made it a test of theories of truth: according to Tarski's Convention T, a satisfactory theory of truth for a language L must entail, for every sentence *s* of L, a theorem of the form "*s* is true if and only if *p*" where "*s*" is replaced by a description of *s* and "*p*" by *s* itself if L is English, and by a translation of *s* into English if L is not English.[18] This isn't, of course, a definition of truth, and it doesn't hint that there is a single definition or theory that applies to languages generally. Nevertheless, Convention T suggests, though it cannot state, an important feature common to all the specialized concepts of truth. It succeeds in doing this by making essential use of the notion of translation into a language we know. Since Convention T embodies our best intuition as to how the concept of truth is used, there does not seem to be much hope for a test that a conceptual scheme is radically different from ours if that test depends on the assumption that we can divorce the notion of truth from that of translation.

Neither a fixed stock of meanings, nor a theory-neutral reality, can provide, then, a ground for comparison of conceptual schemes. It would be a mistake to look further for such a ground if by that we mean something conceived as common to incommensurable schemes. In abandoning this search, we abandon the attempt to make sense of the metaphor of a single space within which each scheme has a position and provides a point of view.

I turn now to the more modest approach: the idea of partial rather than total failure of translation. This introduces the possibility of making changes and contrasts in conceptual schemes intelligible by reference to the common part. What we need is a theory of translation or interpretation that makes no assumptions about shared meanings, concepts, or beliefs.

The interdependence of belief and meaning springs from the interdependence of two aspects of the interpretation of speech behaviour: the attribution of beliefs and the interpretation of sentences. We remarked before that we can afford to associate conceptual schemes with languages because of these dependencies. Now we can put the point in a somewhat sharper way. Allow that a man's speech cannot be interpreted except by someone who knows a good deal about what the speaker believes (and intends and wants),

[18] A. Tarski, "The Concept of Truth in Formalized Languages."

and that fine distinctions between beliefs are impossible without understood speech; how then are we to interpret speech or intelligibly to attribute beliefs and other attitudes? Clearly we must have a theory that simultaneously accounts for attitudes and interprets speech, and which assumes neither.

I suggest, following Quine, that we may without circularity or unwarranted assumptions accept certain very general attitudes towards sentences as the basic evidence for a theory of radical interpretation. For the sake of the present discussion at least we may depend on the attitude of accepting as true, directed to sentences, as the crucial notion. (A more full-blooded theory would look to other attitudes towards sentences as well, such as wishing true, wondering whether true, intending to make true, and so on.) Attitudes are indeed involved here, but the fact that the main issue is not begged can be seen from this: if we merely know that someone holds a certain sentence to be true, we know neither what he means by the sentence nor what belief his holding it true represents. His holding the sentence true is thus the vector of two forces: the problem of interpretation is to abstract from the evidence a workable theory of meaning and an acceptable theory of belief.

The way this problem is solved is best appreciated from undramatic examples. If you see a ketch sailing by and your companion says, "Look at that handsome yawl," you may be faced with a problem of interpretation. One natural possibility is that your friend has mistaken a ketch for a yawl, and has formed a false belief. But if his vision is good and his line of sight favourable it is even more plausible that he does not use the word "yawl" quite as you do, and has made no mistake at all about the position of the jigger on the passing yacht. We do this sort of off the cuff interpretation all the time, deciding in favour of reinterpretation of words in order to preserve a reasonable theory of belief. As philosophers we are peculiarly tolerant of systematic malapropism, and practised at interpreting the result. The process is that of constructing a viable theory of belief and meaning from sentences held true.

Such examples emphasize the interpretation of anomalous details against a background of common beliefs and a going method of translation. But the principles involved must be the same in less trivial cases. What matters is this: if all we know is what sentences a speaker holds true, and we cannot assume that his language is our own, then we cannot take even a first step towards interpretation without knowing or assuming a great deal about the speaker's beliefs. Since knowledge of beliefs comes only with the ability to interpret words, the only possibility at the start is to assume general agreement on beliefs. We get a first approximation to a finished theory by assigning to sentences of a speaker conditions of truth that actually obtain (in our own opinion) just when the speaker holds those sentences true. The guiding policy is to do this as far as possible, subject to considerations of simplicity, hunches about the effects of social conditioning, and of course our common-sense, or scientific, knowledge of explicable error.

The method is not designed to eliminate disagreement, nor can it; its purpose is to make meaningful disagreement possible, and this depends entirely on a foundation—*some* foundation—in agreement. The agreement may take the form of widespread sharing of sentences held true by speakers of "the same language," or agreement in the large mediated by a theory of truth contrived by an interpreter for speakers of another language.

Since charity is not an option, but a condition of having a workable theory, it is meaningless to suggest that we might fall into massive error by endorsing it. Until we have successfully established a systematic correlation of sentences held true with sentences held true there are no mistakes to make. Charity is forced on us; whether we like it or not, if we want to understand others, we must count them right in most matters. If we can produce a theory that reconciles charity and the formal conditions for a theory, we have done all that could be done to ensure communication. Nothing more is possible, and nothing more is needed.

We make maximum sense of the words and thoughts of others when we interpret in a way that optimizes agreement (this includes room, as we said, for explicable error, i.e. differences of opinion). Where does this leave the case for conceptual relativism? The answer is, I think, that we must say much the same thing about differences in conceptual scheme as we say about differences in belief: we improve the clarity and bite of declarations of difference, whether of scheme or opinion, by enlarging the basis of shared (translatable) language or of shared opinion. Indeed, no clear line between the cases can be made out. If we choose to translate some alien sentence rejected by its speakers by a sentence to which we are strongly attached on a community basis, we may be tempted to call this a difference in schemes; if we decide to accommodate the evidence in other ways, it may be more natural to speak of a difference of opinion. But when others think differently from us, no general principle, or appeal to evidence, can force us to decide that the difference lies in our beliefs rather than in our concepts.

We must conclude, I think, that the attempt to give a solid meaning to the idea of conceptual relativism, and hence to the idea of a conceptual scheme, fares no better when based on partial failure of translation than when based on total failure. Given the underlying methodology of interpretation, we could not be in a position to judge that others had concepts or beliefs radically different from our own.

It would be wrong to summarize by saying we have shown how communication is possible between people who have different schemes, a way that works without need of what there cannot be, namely a neutral ground, or a common co-ordinate system. For we have found no intelligible basis on which it can be said that schemes are different. It would be equally wrong to announce the glorious news that all mankind—all speakers of language, at least—share a common scheme and ontology. For if we cannot intelligibly say that schemes are different, nether can we intelligibly say that they are one.

In giving up dependence on the concept of an uninterpreted reality, something outside all schemes and science, we do not relinquish the notion of objective truth—quite the contrary. Given the dogma of a dualism of scheme and reality, we get conceptual relativity, and truth relative to a scheme. Without the dogma, this kind of relativity goes by the board. Of course truth of sentences remains relative to language, but that is as objective as can be. In giving up the dualism of scheme and world, we do not give up the world, but re-establish unmediated touch with the familiar objects whose antics make our sentences and opinions true or false.

10

The Myth of the Subjective

Donald Davidson

This is an essay on an old topic, the relation between the human mind and the rest of nature, the subjective and the objective as we have come to think of them. This dualism, though in its way too obvious to question, carries with it in our tradition a large, and not necessarily appropriate, burden of associated ideas. Some of these ideas are now coming under critical scrutiny, and the result promises to mark a sea change in contemporary philosophical thought—a change so profound that we may not recognize that it is occurring.

The present essay, while clearly tendentious, is not designed primarily to convert the skeptic; its chief aim is to describe, from one point of view, a fairly widely recognized development in recent thinking about the contents of the mind, and to suggest some of the consequences that I think follow from this development.

Minds are many; nature is one. Each of us has one's own position in the world, and hence one's own perspective on it. It is easy to slide from this truism to some confused notion of conceptual relativism. The former, harmless, relativism is just the familiar relativism of position in space and time. Because each of us preempts a volume of space-time, two of us cannot be in exactly the same place at the same time. The relations among our positions are intelligible because we can locate each person in a single, common world and a shared time frame.

Conceptual relativism may seem similar, but the analogy is difficult to carry out. For what is the common reference point, or system of coordinates, to which each scheme is relative? Without a good answer to this question the claim that each of us in some sense inhabits his own world loses its intelligibility.

For this reason and others I have long held that there are limits to how much individual or social systems of thought can differ. If by conceptual relativism we mean the idea that conceptual schemes and moral systems, or the languages associated with them, can differ massively—to the extent of being mutually unintelligible or incommensurable, or forever beyond rational resolve—then I reject conceptual relativism.[1] Of course there are contrasts from epoch to epoch, from culture to culture, and person to person of kinds which we all recognize and struggle with; but these are contrasts which, with sympathy and effort, we can explain and understand. Trouble comes when we try to embrace the idea that there might be more comprehensive differences, for this seems (absurdly) to ask us to take up a stance outside our own ways of thought.

In my opinion we do not understand the idea of such a really foreign scheme. We know what states of mind are like, and how they are correctly identified; they are just those states whose contents can be discovered in well-known ways. If other people or creatures are in states not discoverable by these methods, it can be, not because our methods fail us, but because those states are not correctly called states of mind—they are not beliefs, desires, wishes, or intentions. The meaninglessness of the idea of a conceptual scheme forever beyond our grasp is due not to our inability to understand such a scheme or to our other human limitations; it is due simply to what we mean by a system of concepts.

Many philosophers are not satisfied with arguments like these because they think there is another way in which conceptual relativism can be made intelligible. For it seems that we could make sense of such relativism provided we could find an element in the mind untouched by conceptual interpretation. Then various schemes might be seen as relative to, and assigned the role of organizing, this common element. The common element is, of course, some version of Kant's "content," Hume's impressions and ideas, sense data, uninterpreted sensation, the sensuous given. Kant thought only one scheme was possible, but once the dualism of scheme and content was made explicit, the possibility of alternative schemes was apparent. The idea is explicit in the work of C. I. Lewis:

---

[1] I have argued for this in "On the Very Idea of a Conceptual Scheme," reprinted in *Inquiries into Truth and Interpretation* (The Clarendon Press, 1984).

> There are, in our cognitive experience, two elements; the immediate data, such as those of sense, which are presented or given to the mind, and a form, construction, or interpretation, which represents the activity of thought.[2]

If we could conceive of the function of conceptual schemes in this way, relativism would appear to be an abstract possibility despite doubts about how an alien scheme might be deciphered: the idea would be that different schemes or languages constitute different ways in which what is given in experience may be organized. On this account there would be no point of view from which we could survey such schemes, and perhaps no way we could in general compare or evaluate them; still, as long as we thought we understood the scheme-content dichotomy, we could imagine the unsullied stream of experience being variously reworked by various minds or cultures. In this way, it may be held, conceptual relativism can be provided with the element to which alternative schemes are related: that element is the uninterpreted given, the uncategorized contents of experience.

To a large extent this picture of mind and its place in nature has defined the problems modern philosophy has thought it had to solve. Among these problems are many of the basic issues concerning knowledge: how we know about the "external world," how we know about other minds, even how we know the contents of our own mind. But we should also include the problem of the nature of moral knowledge, the analysis of perception, and many troubling issues in the philosophy of psychology and the theory of meaning.

Corresponding to this catalog of problems or problem areas is a long list of ways in which the supposed scheme-content contrast has been formulated. The scheme may be thought of as an ideology, a set of concepts suited to the task of organizing experience into objects, events, states, and complexes of such; or the scheme may be a language, perhaps with predicates and associated apparatus, interpreted to serve an ideology. The contents of the scheme may be objects of a special sort, such as sense-data, precepts, impressions, sensations, or appearances; or the objects may dissolve into adverbial modifications of experience: we may be "appeared to redly."

---

[2] C. I. Lewis, *Mind and the World Order* (Scribner's, 1929), p. 38. Lewis declares that it is the task of philosophy "to reveal those categorical criteria which the mind applies to what is given to it." (p. 36)

Philosophers have shown ingenuity in finding ways of putting into words the contents of the given; there are those strange, verbless sentences like "Red here now" and the various formulations of protocol sentences over which the logical positivists quarreled.

Putting the matter, or content, into words, however, is not necessary, and according to some views, not possible. The scheme-content division can survive even in an environment that shuns the analytic-synthetic distinction, sense-data, or the assumption that there can be thoughts or experiences that are free of theory. If I am right, this is the environment provided by W. V. Quine. According to Quine's "naturalized epistemology" we should ask no more from the philosophy of knowledge than an account of how, given the evidence we have to go on, we are able to form a satisfactory theory of the world. The account draws on the best theory we have: our present science. The evidence on which the meanings of our sentences, and all our knowledge, ultimately depend is provided by stimulations of our sense organs. It is these stimulations that provide a person with his only cues to "what goes on around him." Quine is not, of course, a reductionist: "we cannot strip away the conceptual trappings sentence by sentence." Nevertheless, there is according to Quine a definite distinction to be made between the invariant content and the variant conceptual trappings, between "report and invention, substance and style, cues and conceptualization." For,

> we can investigate the world, and man as a part of it, and thus find out what cues he could have of what goes on around him. Subtracting his cues from his world view, we get man's net contribution as the difference. This difference marks the extent of man's conceptual sovereignty—the domain within which he can revise theory while saving the data.[3]

Worldview and cues, theory and data: these are the scheme and content of which I have been speaking.

What matters, then, is not whether we can describe the data in a neutral, theory-free idiom; what matters is that there should be an ultimate source of evidence whose character can be wholly specified without reference to what it is evidence for. Thus patterns of stimulation, like sense-data, can be identified and described without

---

[3] This passage, and the quotations that precede it, are from W. V. Quine, *Word and Object* (M.I.T. Press, 1960). In fairness it should be noted that Quine has often stated explicitly that he is not a conceptual relativist.

reference to "what goes on around us." If our knowledge of the world derives entirely from evidence of this kind, then not only may our senses sometimes deceive us; it is possible that we are systematically and generally deceived.

It is easy to remember what prompts this view: it is thought necessary to insulate the ultimate sources of evidence from the outside world in order to guarantee the authority of the evidence for the subject. Since we cannot be certain what the world outside the mind is like, the subjective can keep its virtue—its chastity, its certainty for us—only by being protected from contamination by the world. The familiar trouble is, of course, that the disconnection creates a gap no reasoning or construction can plausibly bridge. Once the Cartesian starting point has been chosen, there is no saying what the evidence is evidence for, or so it seems. Idealism, reductionist forms of empiricism, and skepticism loom.

The story is familiar, but let me continue in my breathless way through one more chapter. If the ultimate evidence for our schemes and theories, the raw material on which they are based, is subjective in the way I have described, then so is whatever is directly based on it: our beliefs, desires, intentions, and what we mean by our words. Though these are the progeny of our "view of the world"—indeed, taken together, they constitute our view of the world—nevertheless they too retain the Cartesian independence from what they purport to be about that the evidence on which they are based had: like sensations, they could be just as they are, and the world be very different. Our beliefs purport to represent something objective, but the character of their subjectivity prevents us from taking the first step in determining whether they correspond to what they pretend to represent.

Instead of saying it is the scheme-content dichotomy that has dominated and defined the problems of modern philosophy, then, one could as well say it is how the dualism of the objective and the subjective has been conceived. For these dualisms have a common origin: a concept of the mind with its private states and objects.

I have reached the point to which I have been leading, for it seems to me that the most promising and interesting change that is occurring in philosophy today is that these dualisms are being questioned in new ways or are being radically reworked. There is a good chance they will be abandoned, at least in their present form. The change is just now becoming evident, and its consequences have barely been recognized, even by those who are bringing it about; and of course it is, and will be, strongly resisted by many. What we are about to see is the emergence of a radically revised view of the relation of mind and the world.

Let me describe what I take to be some of the portents of this change.

The action has centered on the concept of subjectivity, what is "in the mind." Let us start with what it is we know or grasp when we know the meaning of a word or sentence. It is a commonplace of the empirical tradition that we learn our first words (which at the start serve the function of sentences)—words like "apple," "man," "dog," "water"—through a conditioning of sounds or verbal behavior to appropriate bits of matter in the public domain. The conditioning works best with objects that interest the learner and are hard to miss by either teacher or pupil. This is not just a story about how we learn to use words: it must also be an essential part of an adequate account of what words refer to and what they mean.

Needless to say, the whole story cannot be this simple. On the other hand, it is hard to believe that this sort of direct interaction between language users and public events and objects is not a basic part of the whole story, the part that, directly or indirectly largely determines how words are related to things. Yet the story entails consequences that seem to have been ignored until very recently. One consequence is that the details of the mechanisms that constitute the causal chains from speaker to speaker, and spoken-of object to speaker to language learner, cannot matter to meaning and reference. The grasp of meanings is determined only by the terminal elements in the conditioning process and is tested only by the end product: use of words geared to appropriate objects and situations. This is perhaps best seen by noticing that two speakers who "mean the same thing" by an expression need have no more in common than their dispositions to appropriate verbal behavior; the neural networks may be very different. The matter may be put the other way around: two speakers may be alike in all relevant physical respects, and yet they may mean quite different things by the same words because of differences in the external situations in which the words were learned. Insofar, then, as the subjective or mental is thought of as supervenient on the physical characteristics of a person, and nothing more, meanings cannot be purely subjective or mental. As Hilary

Putnam put it, "meanings ain't in the head."[4] The point is that the correct interpretation of what a speaker means is not determined solely by what is in his head; it depends also on the natural history of what is in the head. Putnam's argument depends on rather elaborate thought experiments which some philosophers have found unconvincing. But as far as I can see, the case can best be made by appealing directly to obvious facts about language learning and to facts about how we interpret words and languages with which we are unfamiliar.[5] The relevant facts have already been mentioned above; in the simplest and most basic cases words and sentences derive their meaning from the objects and circumstances in which they were learned. A sentence which one has been conditioned by the learning process to be caused to hold true by the presence of fires will be true when there is a fire present; a word one has been conditioned to be caused to hold applicable by the presence of snakes will refer to snakes. Of course very many words and sentences are not learned this way, but it is those that are that anchor language to the world.

If the meanings of sentences are propositions, and propositions are the objects of attitudes like belief, intention, and desire, then what has been said about meanings must hold true of all of the propositional attitudes. The point can be made without recourse to propositions or other supposed objects of the attitudes. For from the fact that speakers are in general capable of expressing their thoughts in language, it follows that to the extent that the subjectivity of meaning is in doubt, so is that of thought generally.

The fallout from these considerations for the theory of knowledge is (or ought to be) nothing less than revolutionary. If words and thoughts are, in the most basic cases, necessarily about the sorts of objects and events that cause them, there is no room for Cartesian doubts about the independent existence of such objects and events. Doubts there can be, or course. But there need be nothing we are indubitably right about for it to be certain that we are mostly right about the nature of the world. Sometimes skepticism seems to rest on a simple fallacy, the fallacy of reasoning from the fact that

---

[4] Hilary Putnam, "The Meaning of 'Meaning'," reprinted in *Philosophical Papers*, vol. 2: *Mind, Language, and Reality* (Cambridge University Press, 1975), p. 227.

[5] Donald Davidson, "Knowing One's Own Mind," *Proceedings and Addresses of the American Philosophical Association*, 1986. (Forthcoming).

there is nothing we might not be wrong about to the conclusion that we might be wrong about everything. The second possibility is ruled out if we accept that our simplest sentences are given their meanings by the situations that generally cause us to hold them true or false, since to hold a sentence we understand to be true or false is to have a belief. Continuing along this line, we see that general skepticism about the deliverances of the senses cannot even be formulated, since the senses and their deliverances play no central *theoretical* role in the account of belief, meaning, and knowledge if the contents of the mind depend on the causal relations, whatever they may be, between the attitudes and the world. This is not to deny the importance of the actual causal role of the senses in knowledge and the acquisition of language, of course.

The reason the senses are of no primary theoretical importance to the philosophical account of knowledge is that it is an empirical accident that our ears, eyes, taste buds, and tactile and olfactory organs play a causal role in the formation of beliefs about the world. The causal connections between thought and objects and events in the world could have been established in entirely different ways without this making any difference to the contents or veridicality of belief. Philosophy has made the mistake of supposing that because it is often natural to terminate the defense of a particular claim to knowledge with "I saw it with my own eyes," all justification of empirical knowledge must trace back to sensory experience. What is true is that certain beliefs directly caused by sensory experience are often veridical and therefore often provide good reasons for further beliefs. But this does not set such beliefs apart in principle or award them epistemological priority.

If this is right, epistemology (as apart, perhaps, from the study of perception, which is now seen to be only distantly related to epistemology) has no basic need for purely private, subjective "objects of the mind," either as uninterpreted sense data or experience on the one hand, or as fully interpreted propositions on the other. Content and scheme, as remarked in the quotation from C. I. Lewis, came as a pair; we can let them go together. Once we take this step, no *objects* will be left with respect to which the problem of representation can be raised. Beliefs are true or false, but they represent nothing. It is good to be rid of representations, and with them the correspondence theory of truth, for it is thinking there are representations that engenders thoughts of relativism.

Representations *are* relative to a scheme; a map represents Mexico, say—but only relative to a mercator, or same other, projection.

There is an abundance of puzzles about sensation and perception, but these puzzles are not, as I said, foundational for epistemology. The question of what is directly experienced in sensation, and how this is related to judgments of perception, while as hard to answer as it ever was, can no longer be assumed to be a central question for the theory of knowledge. The reason has already been given: although sensation plays a crucial role in the causal process that connects beliefs with the world, it is a mistake to think it plays an *epistemological* role in determining the contents of those beliefs. In accepting this conclusion we abandon the key dogma of traditional empiricism, what I have called the third dogma of empiricism. But that is to be expected: empiricism is the view that the subjective is the foundation of objective empirical knowledge. I am suggesting that empirical knowledge has no epistemological foundation and needs none.[6]

There is another familiar problem that is transformed when we recognize that beliefs, desires, and the other so-called propositional attitudes are not subjective in the way we thought they were. The problem is how one person knows the mind of another. Perhaps it is obvious that if the account I have sketched of our understanding of language, and its connection with the contents of thought, is correct, the accessibility of the minds of others is assured from the start. Skepticism about the *possibility* of knowing other minds is thus ruled out. But to recognize this is not to answer the question what conceptual conditions do we place on the pattern of thought that make it possible for an interpreter to progress from observed behavior to knowledge of the intentional attitudes of another. That this question *has* an answer, however, is guaranteed by the fact that the nature of language and thought is such as to make them interpretable.[7]

It should not be assumed that if we cease to be bullied or beguiled by the scheme-content and subjective-objective dichotomies, all the problems of epistemology will evaporate. But the problems that seem salient will change. Answering the global skeptic will no

---

[6] Donald Davidson, "A Coherence Theory of Truth and Knowledge," in *Kant oder Hegel*, ed. D. Henrich (Klett-Cotta, 1983).

[7] Donald Davidson, "First Person Authority," *Dialectica* 38 (1984).

longer be a challenge, the search for epistemological foundations in experience will be seen as pointless, and conceptual relativism will lose its appeal. But plenty of questions of equal or greater interest will remain, or be generated by the new stance. The demise of the subjective as previously conceived leaves us without foundations for knowledge and relieves us of the need for them. New problems then arise, however, that cluster around the nature of error, for error is hard to identify and explain if the holism that goes with a nonfoundational approach is not somehow constrained. It is not problematic whether knowledge of the world and of other minds is possible; it remains as much a question as ever how we attain such knowledge, and the conditions belief must satisfy to count as knowledge. These are not so much questions in traditional epistemology as they are questions about the nature of rationality. They are questions that, like the epistemological questions they replace, have no final answer; but unlike the questions they replace, they are worth trying to answer.

Familiarity with many of the points I have been making is fairly widespread among philosophers today. But only a few among these philosophers, as far as I know, have appreciated the scope of the entailed revolution in our ways of thinking about philosophy. At least part of the reason for this failure may be traced to certain misunderstandings concerning the nature of the new antisubjectivism (as we may try calling it). Here are three of the misunderstandings.

1. People have been persuaded of the dependence of meanings on factors outside the head by examples rather than by general arguments. There is, therefore, a strong tendency to suppose that the dependence is limited to the sorts of expressions that recur in the examples: proper names, natural kind words like "water" and "gold," and indexicals. But in fact, the phenomenon is ubiquitous, since it is inseparable from the social character of language. It is not a local problem to be solved by same clever semantic trick; it is a perfectly general fact about the nature of thought and speech.[8]

2. If mental states like belief, desire, intention, and meaning are not supervenient on the physical states of the agent alone, then, it has been argued, theories that identify mental states and events with

---

[8] Tyler Burge, "Individualism and the Mental," in *Midwest Studies in Philosophy*, vol. 4, ed. Peter French, Theodore Uehling, and Howard Wettstein (University of Minnesota Press, 1979).

physical states of and events in the body must be wrong. This is suggested by Putnam's claim that "Meanings ain't in the head," and it is explicitly claimed by Tyler Burge and Andrew Woodfield.[9] The argument assumes that if a state or event is identified (perhaps necessarily if it is a mental state or event) by reference to things outside of the body, then the state or event itself must be outside the body, or at least not identical with any event in the body. This is simply a mistake: one might as well argue that a sunburned patch of skin is not located on the body of the person who is sunburned (since the state of the skin has been identified by reference to the sun). Similarly mental states are characterized in part by their relations to events and objects outside of the person, but this does not show that mental states are states of anything more than the person or that they are not identical with physical states.

3. A third misunderstanding is closely related to the second. It is thought that if the correct determination of an agent's thoughts depends, at least to some degree, on the causal history of those thoughts, and the agent may be ignorant of that history, then the agent may not know what he thinks (and, mutatis mutandis, what he means, intends, and so on). The "new antisubjectivism" is, thus, seen as a threat to first person authority—to the fact that people generally know without recourse to inference from evidence, and so in a way that others do not, what they themselves think, want, and intend. A natural, if unjustified, reaction is to resort to maneuvers designed to insulate mental states once more from their external determiners.

The maneuvers are not needed, and surely not wanted if knowledge is to be defended, for first person authority is not threatened. I may not know the difference between an echidna and a porcupine; as a result I may call all echidnas I come across porcupines. Yet, because of the environment in which I learned the word "porcupine," my word "porcupine" refers to porcupines and not to echidnas; this is what I think it refers to, and what I believe I see before me when I honestly affirm, "That's a porcupine." My ignorance of the circumstances that determine what I mean and think has no tendency to show that I don't know what I mean and think. To suppose otherwise is to show how strongly we are wed to the idea of

[9] Ibid., p. 111, and Andrew Woodfield, *Thought and Object*, ed. Andrew Woodfield (Claredone Press, 1982), 1979.

subjective mental states that might be just as they are independent of the rest of the world and its history.

Another reaction to the imagined threat to our real inner lives is to concede that beliefs and other mental states as we normally identify them are not truly subjective, but at the same time to hold that there are similar inner mental states that are. The idea might be, for example, that since nothing in my inner state or my behavior distinguishes between porcupines and echidnas, what I really believe when I see an echidna (or a porcupine) is that what is before me is an animal with certain general characteristics—characteristics that are in fact shared by porcupines and echidnas. The trouble is that since my *word* "porcupine" refers only to porcupines, I apparently do not know what I mean when I say, "That's a porcupine." This unattractive solution is unnecessary, for it is based on a confusion about what is inner. Since there is no present *physical* difference between my actual state and the state I would be in if I meant "echidna or porcupine" or "animal with such and such properties" rather than "porcupine" and believed what I would then mean, it does not follow that there is no *psychological* difference. (There may be no physical difference between being sunburned and being burned by a sunlamp, but there is a difference, since one state was, and the other was not, caused by the sun. Psychological states are in this respect like sunburn.) So nothing stands in the way of saying I can know what I mean when I use the word "porcupine" and what I believe when I have thoughts about porcupines, even though I cannot tell an echidna from a porcupine. The psychological difference, which is just the difference between meaning and believing there is a porcupine before me, and meaning and believing there is a creature with certain common features of porcupines and echidnas, is exactly the difference needed to insure that I know what I mean and what I think. All that Putnam and others have shown is that this difference does not have to be reflected in the physical state of the brain.

Inventing a new set of truly "inner," or "narrow," psychological states is not, then, a way of restoring first person authority to the mental; quite the contrary. There remains the claim, however, that a systematic science of psychology requires states of the agent that can be identified without reference to their history or other connections with the outside world. Otherwise, it is said, there would be no accounting for the fact that I, who may refer only to porcupines by my word "porcupine," can no more tell the difference between a porcupine and an echidna than if (physically unchanged) I meant instead "porcupine or echidna."

The prospects for a scientific psychology are not directly relevant to the topic of this paper, and so we may disregard the question whether there are inner states of agents which might explain their behavior better than ordinary beliefs and desires. But it is relevant to consider whether there are states of mind which have a better claim to be called subjective than the propositional attitudes as these are usually conceived and identified.

Two suggestions have been made. The more modest (to be found in the work of Jerry Fodor, for example) is that we might take as the true inner or solipsistic states selected states from among the usual attitudes and modifications of these. Thoughts about porcupines and echidnas would be eliminated, since the contents of such thoughts are identified by relations to the outside world; but admissible would be thoughts about animals satisfying certain general criteria (the very ones we use in deciding whether something is a porcupine, for example).[10]

Such inner states, if they exist, would qualify as subjective by almost any standards: they could be identified and classified without reference to external objects and events; they could be called on to serve as the foundations of empirical knowledge; and the authority of the first person could plausibly apply to them.

It seems clear, however, that there are no such states, at least if they can be expressed in words. The "general features" or "criteria" we use to identify porcupines are such as having four feet, a nose, eyes, and quills. But it is evident that the meanings of the words that refer to these features, and the contents of the concepts the words express, depend as much on the natural history of how the words and concepts were acquired as was the case for "porcupine" and "echidna." There are no words, or concepts tied to words, that are not to be understood and interpreted, directly or indirectly in terms of causal relations between people and the world (and, or course, the relations among words and other words, concepts and other concepts).

At this point one can imagine a proposal to the effect that there are inexpressible phenomenal criteria to which the publicly

---

[10] Jerry Fodor, "Methodological Solipsism Considered as a Research Strategy in Cognitive Psychology," *The Behavioral and Brain Sciences* 3 (1980).

expressible criteria can be reduced; and here it is to be hoped that memories of past failures of such reductionistic fantasies will serve to suppress the thought that the proposal could be carried out. But, even aside from nostalgic musings about phenomenalistic reduction, it is instructive to find the effort to make psychology scientific turning into a search for internal propositional states that can be detected and identified apart from relations to the rest of the world, much as earlier philosophers sought for something "given in experience" which contained no necessary clue to what was going on outside. The motive is similar in the two cases: it is thought that a sound footing, whether for knowledge or for psychology, requires something inner in the sense of being nonrelational.

The second, and more revolutionary, suggestion is that the mental states needed for a scientific psychology, though roughly propositional in character, bear no direct relation to common beliefs, desires, and intentions.[11] These states are, in effect, stipulated to be those that explain behavior, and they are therefore inner or subjective only in the sense of characterizing a person or similar subject and being beneath the skin. There is no reason to suppose that people can tell when they are in such states.

In summary, I have made five connected points about the "contents of the mind."

First, states of mind like doubts, wishes, beliefs, and desires are identified in part by the social and historical context in which they are acquired; in this respect they are like other states that are identified by their causes, such as suffering from snow blindness or favism (a disease caused by contact with the fava bean).

Second, this does not show that states of mind are not physical states of a person; how we describe and identify events and states has nothing directly to do with where those states and events are.

Third, the fact that states of mind, including what is meant by a speaker, are identified by causal relations with external objects and events is essential to the possibility of communication, and it makes one mind accessible in principle to another; but this public and interactive aspect of the mind has no tendency to diminish the importance of first-person authority.

---

[11] This idea has been promoted by Steven Stich, *From Folk Psychology to Cognitive Science: The Case Against Belief* (M. I. T. Press, 1983).

Fourth, the idea that there is a basic division between uninterpreted experience and an organizing conceptual scheme is a deep mistake, born of the essentially incoherent picture of the mind as a passive but critical spectator of an inner show. A naturalistic account of knowledge makes no appeal to such epistemological intermediaries as sense-data, qualia, or raw feels. As a result, global skepticism of the senses is not a position that can be formulated.

Finally, I have argued against the postulation of "objects of thought," whether these are conceived on the model of sense-data or as propositional in character. There are the many states of mind, but their description does not require that there be ghostly entities that the mind somehow contemplates. To dispense with such entities is to eliminate rather than solve a number of vexing problems. For we cannot ask how such objects can represent the world if there are no such objects, nor can we be puzzled by the question of how the mind can directly be acquainted with them.

What remains of the concept of subjectivity? So far as I can see, two features of the subjective as classically conceived remain in place. Thoughts are private, in the obvious but important sense in which property can be private, that is, belong to one person. And knowledge of thoughts is asymmetrical, in that the person who has a thought generally knows he has it in a way in which others cannot. But this is all there is to the subjective. So far from constituting a preserve so insulated that it is a problem how it can yield knowledge of an outside world or be known to others, thought is necessarily part of a common public world. Not only can others learn what we think by noting the causal dependencies that give our thoughts their content, but the very possibility of thought demands shared standards of truth and objectivity.

11

Religious Belief

Ludwig Wittgenstein

I.

An Austrian general said to someone: "I shall think of you after my death, if that should be possible." We can imagine one group who would find this ludicrous, another who wouldn't.

(During the war, Wittgenstein saw consecrated bread being carried in chromium steel. This struck him as ludicrous.)

Suppose that someone believed in the Last Judgement, and I don't, does this mean that I believe the opposite to him, just that there won't be such a thing? I would say: "not at all, or not always."

Suppose I say that the body will rot, and another says "No. Particles will rejoin in a thousand years, and there will be a Resurrection of you."

If some said: "Wittgenstein, do you believe in this?" I'd say: "No." "Do you contradict the man?" I'd say: "No."

If you say this, the contradiction already lies in this.

Would you say: "I believe the opposite," or "There is no reason to suppose such a thing"? I'd say neither.

Suppose someone were a believer and said: "I believe in a Last Judgement," and I said: "Well, I'm not so sure. Possibly." You would say that there is an enormous gulf between us. If he said "There is a German aeroplane overhead," and I said "Possibly I'm not so sure," you'd say we were fairly near.

It isn't a question of my being anywhere near him, but on an entirely different plane, which you could express by saying: "You mean something altogether different, Wittgenstein."

The difference might not show up at all in any explanation of the meaning.

Why is it that in this case I seem to be missing the entire point?

Suppose somebody made this guidance for this life: believing in the Last Judgment. Whenever he does anything, this is before his mind. In a way, how are we to know whether to say he believes this will happen or not?

Asking him is not enough. He will probably say he has proof.

But he has what you might call an unshakeable belief. It will show, not by reasoning or by appeal to ordinary grounds for belief, but rather by regulating for in all his life.

This is a very much stronger fact—foregoing pleasures, always appealing to this picture. This in one sense must be called the firmest of all beliefs, because the man risks things on account of it which he would not do on things which are by far better established for him. Although he distinguishes between things well-established and not well-established.

Lewy: Surely, he would say it is extremely well-established.

First, he may use "well-established" or not use it at all. He will treat this belief as extremely well-established, and in another way as not well-established at all.

If we have a belief, in certain cases we appeal again and again to certain grounds, and at the same time we risk pretty little—if it came to risking our lives on the ground of this belief.

There are instances where you have a faith—where you say "I believe"—and on the other hand this belief does not rest on the fact on which our ordinary everyday beliefs normally do rest.

How should we compare beliefs with each other? What would it mean to compare them?

You might say: "We compare the states of mind."

How do we compare states of mind? This obviously won't do for all occasions. First, what you say won't be taken as the measure for the firmness of a belief? But, for instance, what risks you would take?

The strength of a belief is not comparable with the intensity of a pain.

An entirely different way of comparing beliefs is seeing what sorts of grounds he will give.

A belief isn't like a momentary state of mind. "At 5 o'clock he had very bad toothache."

Suppose you had two people, and one of them, when he had to decide which course to take, thought of retribution, and the other did not. One person might, for instance, be inclined to take everything that happened to him as a reward or punishment, and another person doesn't think of this at all.

If he is ill, he may think: "What have I done to deserve this?" This is one way of thinking of retribution. Another way is, he thinks in a general way whenever he is ashamed of himself: "This will be punished."

Take two people, one of whom talks of his behaviour and of what happens to him in terms of retribution, the other one does not. These people think entirely differently. Yet, so far, you can't say they believe different things.

Suppose someone is ill and he says: "This is a punishment," and I say: "If I'm ill, I don't think of punishment at all." If you say: "Do you believe the opposite?"—you can call it believing the opposite, but it is entirely different from what we would normally call believing the opposite.

I think differently, in a different way. I say different things to myself. I have different pictures.

It is this way: if someone said: "Wittgenstein, you don't take illness as punishment, so what do you believe?"—I'd say: "I don't have any thoughts of punishment."

There are, for instance, these entirely different ways of thinking first of all—which needn't be expressed by one person saying one thing, another person another thing.

What we call believing in a Judgement Day or not believing in a Judgement Day—The expression of belief may play an absolutely minor role.

If you ask me whether or not I believe in a Judgement Day, in the sense in which religious people have belief in it, I wouldn't say: "No. I don't believe there will be such a thing." It would seem to me utterly crazy to say this.

And then I give an explanation: "I don't believe in . . . ," but then the religious person never believes what I describe.

I can't say. I can't contradict that person.

In one sense, I understand all he says—the English words "God," "separate," etc. I understand. I could say: "I don't believe in this," and this would be true, meaning I haven't got these thoughts or anything that hangs together with them. But not that I could contradict the thing.

You might say: "Well, if you can't contradict him, that means you don't understand him. If you did understand him, then you might." That again is Greek to me. My normal technique of language leaves me. I don't know whether to say they understand one another or not.

These controversies look quite different from any normal controversies. Reasons look entirely different from normal reasons.

They are, in a way, quite inconclusive.

The point is that if there were evidence, this would in fact destroy the whole business.

Anything that I normally call evidence wouldn't in the slightest influence me.

Suppose, for instance, we knew people who foresaw the future; make forecasts for years and years ahead; and they described some sort of a Judgement Day. Queerly enough, even if there were such a thing, and even if it were more convincing than I have described . . . belief in this happening wouldn't be at all a religious belief.

Suppose that I would have to forego all pleasures because of such a forecast. If I do so and so, someone will put me in fires in a thousand years, etc. I wouldn't budge. The best scientific evidence is just nothing.

A religious belief might in fact fly in the face of such a forecast, and say "No. There it will break down."

As it were, the belief as formulated on the evidence can only be the last result—in which a number of ways of thinking and acting crystallize and come together.

A man would fight for his life not to be dragged into the fire. No induction. Terror. That is, as it were, part of the substance of the belief.

That is partly why you don't get in religious controversies, the form of controversy where one person is sure of the thing, and the other says: "Well, possibly."

You might be surprised that there hasn't been opposed to those who believe in Resurrection those who say "Well, possibly."

Here believing obviously plays much more this role: suppose we said that a certain picture might play the role of constantly admonishing me, or I always think of it. Here, an enormous difference would be between those people for whom the picture is constantly in the foreground, and the others who just didn't use it at all.

Those who said: "Well, possibly it may happen and possibly not" would be on an entirely different plane.

This is partly why one would be reluctant to say: "These people rigorously hold the opinion (or view) that there is a Last Judgement." "Opinion" sounds queer.

It is for this reason that different words are used: "dogma," "faith."

We don't talk about hypothesis, or about high probability. Nor about knowing.

In a religious discourse we use such expressions as: "I believe that so and so will happen," and use them differently to the way in which we use them in science.

Although, there is a great temptation to think we do. Because we do talk of evidence, and do talk of evidence by experience.

We could even talk of historic events.

It has been said that Christianity rests on an historic basis.

It has been said a thousand times by intelligent people that indubitability is not enough in this case. Even if there is as much evidence as for Napoleon. Because the indubitability wouldn't be enough to make me change my whole life.

It doesn't rest on an historic basis in the sense that the ordinary belief in historic facts could serve as a foundation.

Here we have a belief in historic facts different from a belief in ordinary historic facts. Even, they are not treated as historical, empirical, propositions.

Those people who had faith didn't apply the doubt which would ordinarily apply to *any* historical propositions. Especially propositions of a time long past, etc.

What is the criterion of reliability, dependability? Suppose you give a general description as to when you say a proposition has a reasonable weight of probability. When you call it reasonable, is this *only* to say that for it you have such and such evidence, and for others you haven't?

For instance, we don't trust the account given of an event by a drunk man.

Father O'Hara[1] is one of those people who make it a question of science.

---

[1] Contribution to a Symposium on *Science and Religion* (Lond: Gerald Howe, 1931, pp. 107–116).

Here we have people who treat this evidence in a different way. They base things on evidence which taken in one way would seem exceedingly flimsy. They base enormous things on this evidence. Am I to say they are unreasonable? I wouldn't call them unreasonable.

I would say, they are certainly not *reasonable,* that's obvious.

"Unreasonable" implies, with everyone, rebuke.

I want to say: they don't treat this as a matter of reasonability.

Anyone who reads the Epistles will find it said: not only that it is not reasonable, but that it is folly.

Not only is it not reasonable, but it doesn't pretend to be.

What seems to me ludicrous about O'Hara is his making it appear to be *reasonable.*

Why shouldn't one form of life culminate in an utterance of belief in a Last Judgement? But I couldn't either say "Yes" or "No" to the statement that there will be such a thing. Nor "Perhaps," nor "I'm not sure."

It is a statement which may not allow of any such answer.

If Mr. Lewy is religious and says he believes in a Judgement Day, I won't even know whether to say I understand him or not. I've read the same things as he's read. In a most important sense, I know what he means.

If an atheist says: "There won't be a Judgment Day, and another person says there will," do they mean the same?—Not clear what criterion of meaning the same is. They might describe the same things. You might say, this already shows that they mean the same.

We come to an island and we find beliefs there, and certain beliefs we are inclined to call religious. What I'm driving at is, that religious beliefs will not. . . . They have sentences, and there are also religious statements.

These statements would not just differ in respect to what they are about. Entirely different connections would make them into religious beliefs, and there can easily be imagined transitions where we wouldn't know for our life whether to call them religious beliefs or scientific beliefs.

You may say they reason wrongly.

In certain cases you would say they reason wrongly, meaning they contradict us. In other cases you would say they don't reason at all, or "It is an entirely different kind of reasoning." The first, you would say in the case in which they reason in a similar way to us, and make something corresponding to our blunders.

Whether a thing is a blunder or not—it is a blunder in a particular system. Just as something is a blunder in a particular game and not in another.

You could also say that where we are reasonable, they are not reasonable—meaning they don't use *reason* here.

If they do something very like one of our blunders, I would say, I don't know. It depends on further surroundings of it.

It is difficult to see, in cases in which it has all the appearances of trying to be reasonable.

I would definitely call O'Hara unreasonable. I would say, if this is religious belief, then it's all superstition.

But I would ridicule it, not by saying it is based on insufficient evidence. I would say: here is a man who is cheating himself. You can say: this man is ridiculous because he believes, and bases it on weak reasons.

II.

The word "God" is amongst the earliest learnt—pictures and catechisms, etc. But not the same consequences as with pictures of aunts. I wasn't shown [that which the picture pictured].

The word is used like a word representing a person. God sees, rewards, etc.

"Being shown all these things, did you understand what this word meant?" I'd say: "Yes and no. I did learn what it didn't mean. I made myself understand. I could answer questions, understand questions when they were put in different ways—and in that sense could be said to understand."

If the question arises as to the existence of a god or God, it plays an entirely different role to that of the existence of any person or object I ever heard of. One said, had to say, that one *believed* the existence, and if one did not believe, this was regarded as something bad. Normally if I did not believe in the existence of something no one would think there was anything wrong in this.

Also, there is this extraordinary use of the word "believe." One talks of believing and at the same time one doesn't use "believe" as one does ordinarily. You might say (in the normal use): "You only believe—oh well. . . ." Here it is used entirely differently; on the other hand it is not used as we generally use the word "know."

If I even vaguely remember what I was taught about God, I might say: "Whatever believing in God may be, it can't be believing in something we can test, or find means of testing." You might say: "This is nonsense, because people say they believe on *evidence* or say they believe on religious experiences." I would say: "The mere fact that someone says they believe on evidence doesn't tell me enough for me to be able to say now whether I can say of a sentence 'God exists' that your evidence is unsatisfactory or insufficient."

Suppose I know someone, Smith. I've heard that he has been killed in a battle in this war. One day you come to me and say: "Smith is in Cambridge." I inquire, and find you stood at Guildhall and saw at the other end a man and said: "That was Smith." I'd say: "Listen. This isn't sufficient evidence." If we had a fair amount of evidence he was killed I would try to make you say that you're being credulous. Suppose he was never heard of again. Needless to say, it is quite impossible to make inquiries: "Who at 12.05 passed Market Place into Rose Crescent?" Suppose you say: "He was there." I would be extremely puzzled.

Suppose there is a feast on Mid-Summer Common. A lot of people stand in a ring. Suppose this is done every year and then everyone says he has seen one of his dead relatives on the other side of the ring. In this case, we could ask everyone in the ring. "Who did you hold by the hand?" Nevertheless, we'd all say that on that day we see our dead relatives. You could in this case say: "I had an extraordinary experience. I had the experience I can express by saying: 'I saw my dead cousin'." Would we say you are saying this on insufficient evidence? Under certain circumstances I would say this, under other circumstances I wouldn't. Where what is said sounds a bit absurd I would say: "Yes, in this case insufficient evidence." If altogether absurd, then I wouldn't.

Suppose I went to somewhere like Lourdes in France. Suppose I went with a very credulous person. There we see blood coming out of something. He says: "There you are, Wittgenstein, how can you doubt?" I'd say: "Can it only be explained one way? Can't it be this or that?" I'd try to convince him that he'd seen nothing of any consequence. I wonder whether I would do that under all circumstances. I certainly know that I would under normal circumstances.

"Oughtn't one after all to consider this?" I'd say: "Come on. Come on." I would treat the phenomenon in this case just as I would treat an experiment in a laboratory which I thought badly executed.

"The balance moves when I will it to move." I point out it is not covered up, a draught can move it, etc.

I could imagine that someone showed an extremely passionate belief in such a phenomenon, and I couldn't approach his belief at all by saying: "This could just as well have been brought about by so and so" because he could think this blasphemy on my side. Or he might say: "It is possible that these priests cheat, but nevertheless in a different sense a miraculous phenomenon takes place there."

I have a statue which bleeds on such and such a day in the year. I have red ink, etc. "You are a cheat, but nevertheless the Deity uses you. Red ink in a sense, but not red ink in a sense."

Cf. Flowers at seance with label. People said: "Yes, flowers are materialized with label." What kind of circumstances must there be to make this kind of story not ridiculous?

I have a moderate education, as all of you have, and therefore know what is meant by insufficient evidence for a forecast. Suppose someone dreamt of the Last Judgement, and said he now knew what it would be like. Suppose someone said: "This is poor evidence." I would say: "If you want to compare it with the evidence for it's raining to-morrow it is no evidence at all." He may make it sound as if by stretching the point you may call it evidence. But it may be more than ridiculous as evidence. But now, would I be prepared to say: "You are basing your belief on extremely slender evidence, to put it mildly." Why should I regard this dream as evidence—measuring its validity as though I were measuring the validity of the evidence for meteorological events?

If you compare it with anything in Science which we call evidence, you can't credit that anyone could soberly argue: "Well, I had this dream . . . therefore . . . Last Judgement." You might say: "For a blunder, that's too big." If you suddenly wrote numbers down on the blackboard, and then said: "Now, I'm going to add," and then said: "2 and 21 is 13," etc. I'd say: "This is no blunder."

There are cases where I'd say he's mad, or he's making fun. Then there might be cases where I look for an entirely different interpretation altogether. In order to see what the explanation is I should have to see the sum, to see in what way it is done, what he makes follow from it, what are the different circumstances under which he does it, etc.

I mean, if a man said to me after a dream that he believed in the Last Judgement, I'd try to find what sort of impression it gave him.

One attitude: "It will be in about 2,000 years. It will be bad for so and so and so, etc." Or it may be one of terror. In the case where there is hope, terror, etc., would I say there is insufficient evidence if he says: "I believe . . ."? I can't treat these words as I normally treat "I believe so and so." It would be entirely beside the point, and also if he said his friend so and so and his grandfather had had the dream and believed, it would be entirely beside the point.

I would not say: "If a man said he dreamt it would happen to-morrow," would he take his coat?, etc.

Case where Lewy has visions of his dead friend. Cases where you don't try to locate him. And case where you try to locate him in a business-like way. Another case where I'd say: "We can pre-suppose we have a broad basis on which we agree."

In general, if you say: "He is dead" and I say: "He is not dead" no-one would say: "Do they mean the same thing by 'dead'?" In the case where a man has visions I wouldn't offhand say: "He means something different."

Cf. A person having persecution mania.

What is the criterion for meaning something different? Not only what he takes as evidence for it, but also how he reacts, that he is in terror, etc.

How am I to find out whether this proposition is to be regarded as an empirical proposition—"You'll see your dead friend again?" Would I say: "He is a bit superstitious?" Not a bit.

He might have been apologetic. (The man who stated it categorically was more intelligent than the man who was apologetic about it).

"Seeing a dead friend," again means nothing much to me at all. I don't think in these terms. I don't say to myself: "I shall see so and so again" ever.

He always says it, but he doesn't make any search. He puts on a queer smile. "His story had that dreamlike quality." My answer would be in this case "Yes," and a particular explanation.

Take "God created man." Pictures of Michelangelo showing the creation of the world. In general, there is nothing which explains the meanings of words as well as a picture, and I take it that Michelangelo was as good as anyone can be and did his best, and here is the picture of the Deity creating Adam.

If we ever saw this, we certainly wouldn't think this the Deity. The picture has to be used in an entirely different way if we are to call the man in that queer blanket "God," and so on. You could imagine that religion was taught by means of these pictures. "Of course, we can only express ourselves by means of pictures." This is rather queer . . . . I could show Moore the pictures of a tropical plant. There is a technique of comparison between picture and plant. If I showed him the picture of Michelangelo and said: "Of course, I can't show you the real thing, only the picture.".. The absurdity is, I've never taught him the technique of using this picture.

It is quite clear that the role of pictures of Biblical subjects and role of the picture of God creating Adam are totally different ones. You might ask this question: "Did Michelangelo think that Noah in the ark looked like this, and that God creating Adam looked like this?" He wouldn't have said that God or Adam looked as they look in this picture.

It might seem as though, if we asked such a question as: "Does Lewy *really* mean what so and so means when he says so and so is alive?"—it might seem as though there were two sharply divided cases, one in which he would say he didn't mean it literally. I want to say this is not so. There will be cases where we will differ, and where it won't be a question at all of more or less knowledge, so that we can come together. Sometimes it will be a question of experience, so you can say: "Wait another 10 years." And I would say: "I would disencourage this kind of reasoning" and Moore would say: "I wouldn't disencourage it." That is, one would *do* something. We would take sides, and that goes so far that there would really be great differences between us, which might come out in Mr. Lewy saying: "Wittgenstein is trying to undermine reason," and this wouldn't be false. This is actually where such questions rise.

III.

Today I saw a poster saying: " 'Dead' Undergraduate speaks." The inverted commas mean: "He isn't really dead." "He isn't what people call dead. They call it 'dead' not quite correctly."

We don't speak of "door" in quotes.

It suddenly struck me: "If someone said "He isn't really dead, although by the ordinary criteria he is dead"—couldn't I say "He is not only dead by the ordinary criteria; he is what we all call 'dead'."

If you now call him "alive," you're using language in a queer way, because you're almost deliberately preparing misunderstandings. Why don't you use some other word, and let "dead" have the meaning it already has?

Suppose someone said: "It didn't always have this meaning. He's not dead according to the old meaning" or "He's not dead according to the old idea."

What is it, to have different ideas of death? Suppose you say: "I have the idea of myself being a chair after death" or "I have the idea of myself being a chair in half-an-hour"—you all know under what circumstances we say of something that it has become a chair.

Cf. (1) "This shadow will cease to exist."

(2) "This chair will cease to exist." You say that you know what this chair ceasing to exist is like. But you have to think. You may find that there isn't a use for this sentence. You think of the use.

I imagine myself on the death-bed. I imagine you all looking at the air above me. You say "You have an idea."

Are you clear when you'd say you had ceased to exist?

You have six different ideas [of "ceasing to exist"] at different times.

If you say: "I can imagine myself being a disembodied spirit. Wittgenstein, can you imagine yourself as a disembodied spirit?"—I'd say: "I'm sorry. I [so far] connect nothing with these words."

I connect all sorts of complicated things with these words. I think of what people have said of sufferings after death, etc.

"I have two different ideas, one of ceasing to exist after death, the other of being a disembodied spirit."

What's it like to have two different ideas? What is the criterion for one man having one idea, another man having another idea?

You gave me two phrases, "ceasing to exist," "being a disembodied spirit." "When I say this, I think of myself having a certain set of experiences." What is it like to think of this?

If you think of your brother in America, how do you know that what you think is, that the thought inside you is, of your brother being in America? Is this an experiential business?

Cf. How do you know that what you want is an apple? [Russell].

How do you know that you believe that your brother is in America?

A pear might be what satisfied you. But you wouldn't say: "What I wanted was an apple."

Suppose we say that the thought is some sort of process in his mind, or his saying something, etc. then I could say: "All right, you call this a thought of your brother in America, well, what is the connection between this and your brother in America?"

Lewy: You might say that this is a question of convention.

Why is it that you don't doubt that it is a thought of your brother in America?

One process [the thought] seems to be a shadow or a picture of something else.

How do I know that a picture is a picture of Lewy?—Normally by its likeness to Lewy, or, under certain circumstances, a picture of Lewy may not be like him, but like Smith. If I give up the business of being like [as a criterion], I get into an awful mess, because anything may be his portrait, given a certain method of projection.

If you said that the thought was in some way a picture of his brother in America—Yes, but by what method of projection is it a picture of this? How queer it is that there should be no doubt what it's a picture of.

If you're asked: "How do you know it is a thought of such and such?" the thought that immediately comes to your mind is one of a shadow, a picture. You don't think of a causal relation. The kind of relation you think of is best expressed by "picture," "shadow," etc.

The word "picture" is even quite all right—in many cases it is even in the most ordinary sense, a picture. You might translate my very words into a picture.

But the point is this, suppose you drew this, how do I know it is my brother in America? Who says it is him—unless it is here ordinary similarity?

What is the connection between these words, or anything substitutable for them, with my brother in America?

The first idea [you have] is that you are looking at your own thought, and are absolutely sure that it is a thought that so and so. You are looking at some mental phenomenon, and you say to yourself "obviously this is a thought of my brother being in America." It seems to be a super-picture. It seems, with thought, that there is no doubt whatever. With a picture, it still depends on the method of projection, whereas here it seems that you get rid of the projecting relation, and are absolutely certain that this is thought of that.

Smythies's muddle is based on the idea of a super-picture.

We once talked about how the idea of certain superlatives came about in Logic. The idea of a super-necessity, etc.

"How do I know that this is the thought of my brother in America?"—that *what* is the thought?

Suppose my thought consists of my *saying* "My brother is in America"—how do I know that I *say* my brother is in America?

How is the connection made?—We imagine at first a connection like strings.

Lewy: The connection is a convention. The word designates.

You must explain "designates" by examples. We have learnt a rule, a practice, etc.

Is thinking of something like painting or shooting at something?

It seems like a projection connection, which seems to make it indubitable, although there is not a projection relation at all.

If I said "My brother is in America"—I could imagine there being rays projecting from my words to my brother in America. But what if my brother isn't in America?—then the rays don't hit anything.

[If you say that the words refer to my brother by expressing the proposition that my brother is in America—the proposition being a middle link between the words and what they refer to]—What has the proposition, the mediate link, got to do with America?

The most important point is this—if you talk of painting, etc. your idea is that the connection exists *now*, so that it seem as though as long as I do this thinking, this connection exists.

Whereas, if we said it is a connection of convention, there would be no point in saying it exists while we think. There is a connection by convention—What do we mean?—This connection refers to events happening at various times. Most of all, it refers to a technique.

["Is thinking something going on at a particular time, or is it spread over the words?" "It comes in a flash." "Always?"—it sometimes does come in a flash, although this may be all sorts of different things.]

If it does refer to a technique, then it can't be enough, in certain cases, to explain what you mean in a few words; because there is something which might be thought to be in conflict with the idea going on from 7 to 7.5, namely the practice of using it [the phrase.]

When we talked of: "So and so is an automaton," the strong hold of that view was [due to the idea] that you could say: "Well, I know what I mean" as though you were looking at something happening while you said the thing, entirely independent of what came before and after the application [of the phrase]. It looked as though you could talk of understanding a word, without any reference to the technique of its usage. It looked as though Smythies said he could understand the sentence, and that we then had nothing to say.

What was it like to have different ideas of death?—What I meant was—Is having an idea of death something like having a certain picture, so that you can say "I have an idea of death from 5 to 5.1 etc."? "In whatever way anyone will use this word, I have now a certain idea"—if you call this "having an idea," then it is not what is commonly called "having an idea," because what is commonly called "having an idea," has a reference to the technique of the word, etc.

We are all here using the word "death," which is a public instrument, which has a whole technique [of usage]. Then someone says he has an idea of death. Something queer; because you might say "You are using the word 'death,' which is an instrument functioning in a certain way."

If you treat this [your idea] as something private, with what right are you calling it an idea of death?—I say this, because we, also, have a right to say what is an idea of death.

He might say "I have my own private idea of death"—why call this an "idea of death" unless it is something you connect with death. Although this [your "idea"] might not interest us at all. [In this case,] it does not belong on the game played with "death," which we all know and understand.

If what he calls his "idea of death" is to become relevant, it must become part of our game.

"My idea of death is the separation of the soul from the body" —if we know what to do with these words. He can also say: "I connect with the word 'death' a certain picture—a woman lying in her bed"—that may or may not be of some interest.

If he connects

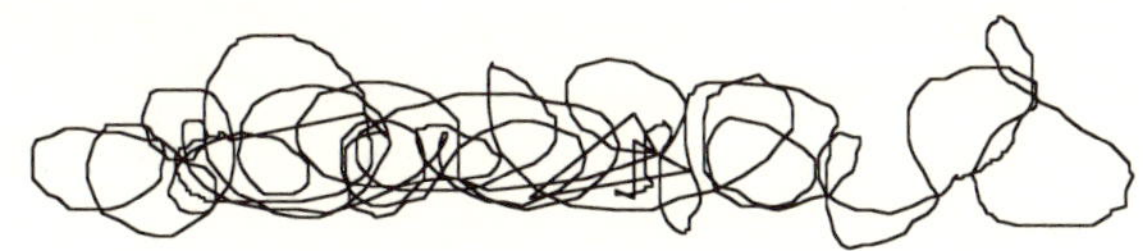

with death, and this was his idea, this might be interesting psychologically.

"The separation of soul from body" [only had a public interest.] This may act like black curtains or it may not act like black curtains. I'd have to find out what the consequences [of your saying it] are. I am not, at least, at present at all clear. [You say this]—"So what?"—I know these words, I have certain pictures. All sorts of things go along with these words.

If he says this, I won't know yet what consequences he will draw. I don't know what he opposes this to.

Lewy: "You oppose it to being extinguished."

If you say to me—"Do you cease to exist?"—I should be bewildered, and would not know what exactly this is to mean.

"If you don't cease to exist, you will suffer after death," there I begin to attach ideas, perhaps ethical ideas of responsibility. The point is, that although these are well-known words, and although I can go from one sentence to another sentence, or to pictures [I don't know what consequences you draw from this statement].

Suppose someone said: "What do you believe, Wittgenstein? Are you a sceptic? Do you know whether you will survive death?" I would really, this is a fact, say "I can't say. I don't know," because I haven't any clear idea what I'm saying when I'm saying "I don't cease to exist," etc.

Spiritualists make one kind of connection.

A Spiritualist says "Apparition" etc. Although he gives me a picture I don't like, I do get a clear idea. I know that much, that some people connect this phrase with a particular kind of verification. I know that some people don't—religious people e.g.—they don't refer to a verification, but have entirely different ideas.

A great writer said that, when he was a boy, his father set him a task, and he suddenly felt that nothing, not even death, could take away the responsibility [in doing this task]; this was his duty to do, and that even death couldn't stop it being his duty. He said that this was, in a way, a proof of the immortality of the soul—because if this lives on [the responsibility won't die.] The idea is given by what we call the proof. Well, if this is the idea, [all right].

If a Spiritualist wishes to give *me* an idea of what he means or doesn't mean by "survival," he can say all sorts of things—

[If I ask what idea he has, I may be given what the Spiritualists say or I may be given what the man I quoted said, etc., etc.]

I would at least [in the case of the Spiritualist] have an idea of what this sentence is connected up with, and get more and more of an idea as I see what he does with it.

As it is, I hardly connect anything with it at all.

Suppose someone, before going to China, when he might never see me again, said to me: "We might see one another after death"—would I necessarily say that I don't understand him? I might say [want to say] simply, "Yes. I *understand* him entirely."

Lewy :"In this case, you might only mean that he expressed a certain attitude."

I would say "No, it isn't the same as saying 'I'm very fond of you'"—and it may not be the same as saying anything else. It says what it says. Why should you be able to substitute anything else?

Suppose I say: "The man used a picture."

"Perhaps now he sees he was wrong." What sort of remark is this?

"God's eye sees everything"—I want to say of this that it uses a picture.

I don't want to belittle him [the person who says it.]

Suppose I said to him "You've been using a picture," and he said "No, this is not all"—mightn't he have misunderstood me? What do I want to do [by saying this]? What would be the real sign of disagreement? What might be the real criterion of his disagreeing with me?

Lewy: "If he said: 'I've been making preparations [for death]."

Yes, this might be a disagreement—if he himself were to use the word in a way in which I did not expect, or were to draw conclusions I did not expect him to draw. I wanted only to draw attention to a particular technique of usage. We should disagree, if he was using a technique I didn't expect.

We associate a particular use with a picture.

Smythies: "This isn't all he does—associate a use with a picture."

Wittgenstein: Rubbish. I meant: what conclusions are you going to draw? etc. Are eyebrows going to be talked of, in connection with the Eye of God?

"He could just as well have said so and so"—this [remark] is foreshadowed by the word "attitude." He couldn't just as well have said something else.

If I say he used a picture I don't want to say anything he himself wouldn't say. I want to say that he draws these conclusions.

Isn't it as important as anything else, what picture he does use?

Of certain pictures we say that they might just as well be replaced by another—e.g. we could, under certain circumstances, have one projection of an ellipse drawn instead of another.

[*He may say*]: "I would have been prepared to use another picture, it would have had the same effect . . . ."

The whole *weight* may be in the picture.

We can say in chess that the exact shape of the chess-men plays no role. Suppose that the main pleasure was, to see people ride; then, playing it in writing wouldn't be playing the same game. Someone might say: "All he's done is change the shape of the head"—what more could he do?

When I say he's using a picture I'm merely making a *grammatical* remark: [What I say] can only be verified by the consequences he does or does not draw.

If Smythies disagrees, I don't take notice of this disagreement.

All I wished to characterize was the conventions he wished to draw. If I wished to say anything more I was merely being philosophically arrogant.

Normally, if you say "He is an automaton" you draw consequences, if you stab him, [he'll feel pain]. On the other hand, you may not wish to draw any such consequences, and this is all there is to it—except further muddles.

12

The Groundlessness of Belief

Norman Malcolm

I.

In his final notebooks Wittgenstein wrote that it is difficult "to realize the groundlessness of our believing."[1] He was thinking of how much mere acceptance, on the basis of no evidence, forms our lives. This is obvious in the case of small children. They are told the names of things. They accept what they are told. They do not ask for grounds. A child does not demand a proof that the person who feeds him is called "Mama." Or are we to suppose that the child reasons to himself as follows: "The others present seem to know this person who is feeding me, and since they call her 'Mama' that probably is her name"? It is obvious on reflection that a child cannot consider evidence or even doubt anything until he has already learned much. As Wittgenstein puts it: "The child learns by believing the adult. Doubt comes *after* belief " (*OC*, 160).

What is more difficult to perceive is that the lives of educated, sophisticated adults are also formed by groundless beliefs. I do not mean eccentric beliefs that are out on the fringes of their lives, but fundamental beliefs. Take the belief that familiar material things (watches, shoes, chairs) do not cease to exist without some physical

---

[1] Ludwig Wittgenstein, *On Certainty*, ed. G.E.M. Anscombe and G.H. von Wright; English translation by D. Paul and G.E.M. Anscombe (Oxford, 1969), paragraph 166. Henceforth I include references to this work in the text, employing the abbreviation "*OC*" followed by a paragraph number. References to Wittgenstein's *The Blue and Brown Books* (Oxford, 1958) are indicated in the text by "*BB*" followed by page number. References to his *Philosophical Investigations*, ed. G.E.M. Anscombe and R. Rhees; English translation by Anscombe (Oxford, 1967) are indicated by "*PI*" followed by a paragraph number. In *OC* and *PI*, I have mainly used translations of Paul and Anscombe but with some departures.

explanation. They don't "vanish in thin air." It is interesting that we do use that very expression: "I know I put the keys right here on this table. They must have vanished in thin air!" But this exclamation is hyperbole; we are not speaking in literal seriousness. I do not know of any adult who would consider, in all gravity, that the keys might have inexplicably ceased to exist.

Yet it is possible to imagine a society in which it was accepted that sometimes material things do go out of existence without having been crushed, melted, eroded, broken into pieces, burned up, eaten, or destroyed in some other way. The difference between those people and ourselves would not consist in their saying something that we don't say ("It vanished in thin air"), since we say it too. I conceive of those people as acting and thinking differently from ourselves in such ways as the following: If one of them could not find his wallet he would give up the search sooner than you or I would; also he would be less inclined to suppose that it was stolen. In general, what we would regard as convincing circumstantial evidence of theft those people would find less convincing. They would take fewer precautions than we would to protect their possessions against loss or theft. They would have less inclination to save money, since it too can just disappear. They would not tend to form strong attachments to material things, animals, or other people. Generally, they would stand in a looser relation to the world than we do. The disappearance of a desired object, which would provoke us to a frantic search, they would be more inclined to accept with a shrug. Of course, their scientific theories would be different; but also their attitude toward experiment, and inference from experimental results, would be more tentative. If the repetition of a familiar chemical experiment did not yield the expected result this could be because one of the chemical substances had vanished.

The outlook I have sketched might be thought to be radically incoherent. I do not see that this is so. Although those people consider it to be possible that a wallet might have inexplicably ceased to exist, it is also true that they regard that as unlikely.

For things that are lost usually do turn up later; or if not, their fate can often be accounted for. Those people use pretty much the same criteria of identity that we do; their reasoning would resemble ours quite a lot. Their thinking would not be incoherent. But it would be different, since they would leave room for some possibilities that we exclude.

If we compare their view that material things do sometimes go out of existence inexplicably, with our own rejection of that view, it does not appear to me that one position is supported by better evidence than is the other. Each position is compatible with ordinary experience. On the one hand it is true that familiar objects (watches, wallets, lawn chairs) occasionally disappear without any adequate explanation. On the other hand it happens, perhaps more frequently, that a satisfying explanation of the disappearance is discovered.

Our attitude in this matter is striking. We would not be willing to consider it as even improbable that a missing lawn chair had "just ceased to exist." We would not entertain such a suggestion. If anyone proposed it we would be sure he was joking. It is no exaggeration to say that this attitude is part of the foundations of our thinking. I do not want to say that this attitude is unreasonable; but rather that it is something that we do not try to support with grounds. It could be said to belong to "the framework" of our thinking about material things.

Wittgenstein asks: "Does anyone ever test whether this table remains in existence when no one is paying attention to it?" (OC, 163). The answer is: Of course not. Is this because we would not call it "a table" if that were to happen? But we do call it "a table" and none of us makes the test. Doesn't this show that we do not regard that occurrence as a possibility? People who did so regard it would seem ludicrous to us. One could imagine that they made ingenious experiments to decide the question; but this research would make us smile. Is this because experiments were conducted by our ancestors that settled the matter once and for all? I don't believe it. The principle that material things do not cease to exist without physical cause is an unreflective part of the framework within which physical investigations are made and physical explanations arrived at. Wittgenstein suggests that the same is true of what might be called "the principle of the continuity of nature":

> Think of chemical investigations. Lavoisier makes experiments with substances in his laboratory and now concludes that this and that takes place when there is burning. He does not say that it might happen otherwise another time. He has got hold of a world-picture—not of course one that he invented: he learned it as a child. I say world-picture and not hypothesis, because it is the matter-of-course (*selbstverständliche)* foundation for his research and as such also goes unmentioned (*OC*, 167).

> But now, what part is played by the presupposition that a substance A always reacts to a substance B in the same way, given the same circumstances? Or is that part of the definition of a substance? (*OC*, 168).

Framework principles such as the continuity of nature or the assumption that material things do not cease to exist without physical cause belong to what Wittgenstein calls a "system." He makes the following observation, which seems to me to be true: "All testing, all confirmation and disconfirmation of a hypothesis takes place already within a system. And this system is not a more or less arbitrary and doubtful point of departure for all our arguments: no, it belongs to the nature of what we call an argument. The system is not so much the point of departure, as the element in which arguments have their life" (*OC*, 105).

A "system" provides the boundaries within which we ask questions, carry out investigations, and make judgments. Hypotheses are put forth, and challenged, *within* a system. Verification, justification, the search for evidence, occur *within* a system. The framework propositions of the system are not put to the test, not backed up by evidence. This is what Wittgenstein means when he says: "Of course there is justification; but justification comes to an end" (*OC*, 192); and when he asks: "Doesn't testing come to an end?" (*OC*, 164); and when he remarks that "whenever we test anything we are already presupposing something that is not tested" (*OC*, 163).

That this is so is not to be attributed to human weakness. It is a conceptual requirement that our inquiries and proofs stay within boundaries. Think, for example, of the activity of calculating a number. Some steps in a calculation we will check for correctness, but others we won't: for example, that 4+4=8. More accurately, some beginners might check it, but grown-ups won't. Similarly, some grown-ups would want to determine by calculation whether 25x 25=625, whereas others would regard that as laughable. Thus the boundaries of the system within which you calculate may not be exactly the same as *mine.* But we do calculate; and, as Wittgenstein remarks, "In certain circumstances . . . we regard a calculation as sufficiently checked. What gives us a right to do so? . . . Somewhere we must be finished with justification, and then there remains the proposition that *this* is how we calculate" (*OC*, 212). If someone did not accept any boundaries for calculating this would mean that he had not learned *that* language-game: "If someone supposed that *all* our calculations were uncertain and that we could rely on none of them (justifying himself by saying that mistakes are always possible) perhaps we would say he was crazy. But can we say he is in error? Does he not just react differently? We rely on calculations, he doesn't; we are sure, he isn't" (*OC*, 217). We are taught, or we absorb, the systems within which we raise doubts, make inquiries, draw conclusions. We grow into a framework. We don't question it. We accept it trustingly. But this acceptance is not a consequence of reflection. We do not decide to accept framework propositions. We do not decide that we live on the earth, any more than we decide to learn our native tongue. We do come to adhere to a framework proposition, in the sense that it forms the way we think. The framework propositions that we accept, grow into, are not idiosyncrasies but common ways of speaking and thinking that are pressed on us by our human community. For our acceptances to have been withheld would have meant that we had not learned how to count, to measure, to use names, to play games, or even *to talk.* Wittgenstein remarks that "a language-game is only possible if one trusts something." Not *can,* but *does* trust something (OC, 509). I think he means by this trust or acceptance what he calls belief "in the sense of religious belief" (*OC*, 459). What does he mean by belief "in the sense of religious belief"? He explicitly distinguishes it from *conjecture* (*Vermutung:* ibid.). I think this means that there is nothing tentative about it; it is not adopted as a hypothesis that might later be withdrawn in the light of new evidence. This also makes explicit an important feature of Wittgenstein's understanding of belief, in the sense of "religious belief," namely, that it does not rise or fall on the basis of evidence or grounds: it is "groundless."

II.

In our Western academic philosophy, religious belief is commonly regarded as unreasonable and is viewed with condescension or even contempt. It is said that religion is a refuge for those who, because of weakness of intellect or character, are unable to confront the stern realities of the world. The objective, mature, *strong* attitude is to hold beliefs solely on the basis of *evidence.*

It appears to me that philosophical thinking is greatly influenced by this veneration of evidence. We have an aversion to statements, reports, declarations, beliefs, that are not based on grounds. There are many illustrations of this philosophical bent.

For example, in regard to a person's report that he has an image of the Eiffel Tower we have an inclination to think that the image must resemble the Eiffel Tower. How else could the person declare so confidently what his image is of? How could he know?

Another example: A memory-report or memory-belief must be based, we think, on some mental datum that is equipped with various features to match the corresponding features of the memory-belief. This datum will include an image that provides the content of the belief, and a peculiar feeling that makes one refer the image to a past happening, and another feeling that makes one believe that the image is an accurate portrayal of the past happening, and still another feeling that informs one that it was oneself who witnessed the past happening. The presence of these various features makes memory-beliefs thoroughly reasonable.

Another illustration: If interrupted in speaking one can usually give a confident account, later on, of what one had been about to say. How is this possible? Must not one remember a feeling of tendency to say just those words? This is one's basis for knowing what one had been about to say. It justifies one's account.

Still another example: After dining at a friend's house you announce your intention to go home. How do you know your intention? One theory proposes that you are presently aware of a particular mental state or bodily feeling which, as you recall from your past experience, has been highly correlated with the behavior of going home; so you infer that that is what you are going to do now. A second theory holds that you must be aware of some definite mental state or event which reveals itself, not by experience but intrinsically, as the intention to go home. Your awareness of that mental item informs you of what action you will take.

Yet another illustration: This is the instructive case of the man who, since birth, has been immune to sensations of bodily pain. On his thirtieth birthday he is kicked in the shins and for the first time he responds by crying out, hopping around on one foot, holding his leg, and exclaiming, "The pain is terrible!" We have an overwhelming inclination to wonder, "How could he tell, this first time, that what he felt was pain?" Of course, the implication is that after the first time there would be no problem. Why not? Because his first experience of pain would provide him with a sample that would be preserved in memory; thereafter he would be equipped to determine whether any sensation he feels is or isn't pain; he would just compare it with the memory-sample to see whether the two match! Thus he will have a justification for believing that what he feels is pain. But the first time he will not have this justification. This is why the case is so puzzling. Could it be that this first time he infers that he is in pain from his own behavior?

A final illustration: Consider the fact that after a comparatively few examples and bits of instruction a person can go on to carry out a task, apply a word correctly in the future, continue a numerical series from an initial segment, distinguish grammatical from ungrammatical constructions, solve arithmetical problems, and so on. These correct performances will be dealing with new and different examples, situations, combinations. The performance output will be far more varied than the instruction input. How is this possible? What carries the person from the meager instruction to his rich performance? The explanation has to be that an effect of his training was that he abstracted the Idea, perceived the Common Nature, "internalized" the Rule, grasped the Structure. What else could bridge the gap between the poverty of instruction and the wealth of performance? Thus we postulate an intervening mental act or state which removes the inequality and restores the balance.

My illustrations belong to what could be called the pathology of philosophy. Wittgenstein speaks of a "general disease of thinking" which attempts to explain occurrences of discernment, recognition, or understanding, by postulating mental states or processes from which those occurrences flow "as from a reservoir" (BB, p. 143). These mental intermediaries are assumed to contribute to the causation of the various cognitive performances. More significantly for my present purpose, they are supposed to justify them; they provide our grounds for saying or doing this rather than that; they explain how we know. The Image, or Cognitive State, or Feeling, or Idea, or Sample, or Rule, or Structure, tells us. It is like a road map or a signpost. It guides our course.

What is "pathological" about these explanatory constructions and pseudoscientific inferences? Two things at least. First, the movement of thought that demands these intermediaries is circular and empty, unless it provides criteria for determining their presence and nature other than the occurrence of the phenomena they are postulated to explain—and, of course, no such criteria are forthcoming. Second, there is the great criticism by Wittgenstein of this movement of philosophical thought: namely, his point that no matter what kind of state, process, paradigm, sample, structure, or rule, is conceived as giving us the necessary guidance, it could be taken, or understood, as indicating a different direction from the one in which we actually did go. The assumed intermediary Idea, Structure, or Rule, does not and cannot reveal that because of it we went in the only direction it was reasonable to go. Thus the internalized intermediary we are tempted to invoke to bridge the gap between training and performance, as being that which shows us what we must do or say if we are to be rational, cannot do the job it was invented to do. It cannot fill the epistemological gap. It cannot provide the bridge of justification. It cannot put to rest the How-do-we-know? question. Why not? Because it cannot tell us how it itself is to be taken, understood, applied. Wittgenstein puts the point briefly and powerfully: "Don't always think that you read off your words from facts; that you portray these in words according to rules. For even so you would have to apply the rule in the particular case without guidance" (PI, 292). Without guidance! Like Wittgenstein's signpost arrow that cannot tell us whether to go in the direction of the arrow tip or in the opposite direction, so too the Images, Ideas, Cognitive Structures, or Rules, that we philosophers imagine as devices for guidance, cannot interpret themselves to us. The signpost does not tell the traveler how to read it. A second signpost might tell him how to read the first one; we can imagine such a case. But this can't go on. If the traveler is to continue his journey he will have to do something on his own, without guidance.

The parable of the traveler speaks for all of the language games we learn and practice; even those in which there is the most disciplined instruction and the most rigorous standards of conformity. Suppose that a pupil has been given thorough training in some procedure, whether it is drawing patterns, building fences, or proving theorems. But then he has to carry on by himself in new situations. How does he know what to do? Wittgenstein presents the following dialogue: "'However you instruct him in the continuation of a pattern—how can he know how he is to continue by himself?'—Well, how do I know?—If that means 'Have I grounds?', the answer is: the grounds will soon give out. And then I shall act, without grounds" (PI, 211). Grounds come to an end. Answers to How-do-we-know? questions come to an end. Evidence comes to an end. We must speak, act, live, without evidence. This is so, not just on the fringes of life and language, but at the center of our most regularized activities. We do learn rules and learn to follow them. But our training was in the past! We had to leave it behind and proceed on our own.

It is an immensely important fact of nature that as people carry on an activity in which they have received a common training, they do largely agree with one another, accepting the same examples and analogies, taking the same steps. We agree in what to say, in how to apply language. We agree in our responses to particular cases.

As Wittgenstein says: "That is not agreement in opinions but in form of life" (PI, 241). We cannot explain this agreement by saying that we are just doing what the rules tell us—for our agreement in applying rules, formulae, and signposts is what gives them their meaning.

One of the primary pathologies of philosophy is the feeling that we must justify our language-games. We want to establish them as well-grounded. But we should consider here Wittgenstein's remark that a language-game "is not based on grounds. It is there—like our life" (OC, 559).

Within a language-game there is justification and lack of justification, evidence and proof, mistakes and groundless opinions, good and bad reasoning, correct measurements and incorrect ones. One cannot properly apply these terms to a language-game itself. It may, however, be said to be "groundless," not in the sense of a groundless opinion, but in the sense that we accept it, we live it. We can say, "This is what we do. This is how we are."

In this sense religion is groundless; and so is chemistry. Within each of these two systems of thought and action there is controversy and argument. Within each there are advances and recessions of insight into the secrets of nature or the spiritual condition of humankind and the demands of the Creator, Savior, Judge, Source. Within the framework of each system there is criticism, explanation, justification. But we should not expect that there might be some sort of rational justification of the framework itself.

A chemist will sometimes employ induction. Does he have evidence for a Law of Induction? Wittgenstein observes that it would strike him as nonsense to say, "I know that the Law of Induction is true." ("Imagine such a statement made in a law court.") It would be more correct to say, "I believe in the Law of Induction" (OC, 500).

This way of putting it is better because it shows that the attitude toward induction is belief in the sense of "religious" belief—that is to say, an acceptance which is not conjecture or surmise and for which there is no reason—it is a groundless acceptance.

It is intellectually troubling for us to conceive that a whole system of thought might be groundless, might have no rational justification. We realize easily enough, however, that grounds soon give out—that we cannot go on giving reasons for our reasons. There arises from this realization the conception of a reason that is self-justifying—something whose credentials as a reason cannot be questioned.

This metaphysical conception makes its presence felt at many points—for example, as an explanation of how a person can tell what his mental image is of. We feel that the following remarks, imagined by Wittgenstein, are exactly right: "The image must be more similar to its object than any picture. For however similar I make the picture to what it is supposed to represent, it can always be the picture of something else. But it is essential to the image that it is the image of this and of nothing else" (PI, 389). A pen and ink drawing represents the Eiffel Tower; but it could represent a mine shaft or a new type of automobile jack. Nothing prevents this drawing from being taken as a representation of something other than the Eiffel Tower. But my mental image of the Eiffel Tower is necessarily an image of the Eiffel Tower. Therefore it must be a "remarkable" kind of picture. As Wittgenstein observes: "Thus one might come to regard the image as a super-picture" (ibid.). Yet we have no intelligible conception of how a super-picture would differ from an ordinary picture. It would seem that it has to be a superlikeness—but what does this mean?

There is a familiar linguistic practice in which one person tells another what his image is of (or what he intends to do, or what he was about to say) and no question is raised of how the first one knows that what he says is true. This question is imposed from outside, artificially, by the philosophical craving for justification. We can see here the significance of these remarks: "It isn't a question of explaining a language-game by means of our experiences, but of noting a language-game" (PI, 655). "Look on the language-game as the primary thing" (PI, 656). Within a system of thinking and acting there occurs, up to a point, investigation and criticism of the reasons and justifications that are employed in that system. This inquiry into whether a reason is good or adequate cannot, as said, go on endlessly. We stop it. We bring it to an end. We come upon something that satisfies us. It is as if we made a decision or issued an edict: "This is an adequate reason!" (or explanation, or justification). Thereby we fix a boundary of our language-game.

There is nothing wrong with this. How else could we have disciplines, systems, games? But our fear of groundlessness makes us conceive that we are under some logical compulsion to terminate at those particular stopping points. We imagine that we have confronted the self-evident reason, the self-justifying explanation, the picture or symbol whose meaning cannot be questioned. This obscures from us the human aspect of our concepts—the fact that what we call "a reason," "evidence," "explanation," "justification," is what appeals to and satisfies us.

III.

The desire to provide a rational foundation for a form of life is especially prominent in the philosophy of religion, where there is an intense preoccupation with purported proofs of the existence of God. In American universities there must be hundreds of courses in which these proofs are the main topic. We can be sure that nearly always the critical verdict is that the proofs are invalid and consequently that, up to the present time at least, religious belief has received no rational justification.

Well, of course not! The obsessive concern with the proofs reveals the assumption that in order for religious belief to be intellectually respectable it *ought* to have a rational justification. *That* is the misunderstanding. It is like the idea that we are not justified in relying on memory until memory has been proved reliable.

Roger Trigg makes the following remark: "To say that someone acts in a certain way because of his belief in God does seem to be more than a redescription of his action. . . . It is to give a *reason* for it. The belief is distinct from the commitment which may follow it, and is the justification for it."[2] It is evident from other remarks that by "belief in God" Trigg means "belief in the existence of God" or "belief that God exists." Presumably by the *acts* and *commitments* of a religious person Trigg refers to such things as prayer, worship,

---

[2] *Reason and Commitment* (Cambridge, 1973), p. 75.

confession, thanksgiving, partaking of sacraments, and participation in the life of a religious group.

For myself I have great difficulty with the notion of belief in *the existence* of God, whereas the idea of belief *in* God is to me intelligible. If a man did not ever pray for help or forgiveness, or have any inclination toward it, nor ever felt that it is "a good and joyful thing" to thank God for the blessings of this life; nor was ever concerned about his failure to comply with divine commandments—then, it seems clear to me, he could not be said to believe in God. Belief in God is not an all or none thing; it can be more or less; it can wax and wane. But belief in God in any degree does require, as I understand the words, some religious action, some commitment, or if not, at least a bad conscience.

According to Trigg, if I take him correctly, a man who was entirely devoid of any inclination toward religious action or conscience, might believe in *the existence* of God. What would be the marks of this? Would it be that the man knows some theology, can recite the Creeds, is well-read in Scripture? Or is his belief in the existence of God something different from this? If so, what? What would be the difference between a man who knows some articles of faith, heresies, scriptural writings, and in addition believes in the existence of God, and one who knows these things but does not believe in the existence of God? I assume that both of them are indifferent to the acts and commitments of religious life.

I do not comprehend this notion of belief in *the existence* of God which is thought to be distinct from belief *in* God. It seems to me to be an artificial construction of philosophy, another illustration of the craving for justification.

Religion is a form of life; it is language embedded in action—what Wittgenstein calls a "language-game." Science is another. Neither stands in need of justification, the one no more than the other.

Present-day academic philosophers are far more prone to challenge the credentials of religion than of science, probably for a number of reasons. One may be the illusion that science can justify its own framework. Another is the fact that science is a vastly greater force in our culture. Still another may be the fact that by and large religion is to university people an alien form of life. They do not participate in it and do not understand what it is all about.

Their nonunderstanding is of an interesting nature. It derives, at least in part, from the inclination of academics to suppose that their employment as scholars demands of them the most severe objectivity and dispassionateness. For an academic philosopher to become a religious believer would be a stain on his professional competence! Here I will quote from Nietzsche, who was commenting on the relation of the German scholar of his day to religious belief; yet his remarks continue to have a nice appropriateness for the American and British scholars of our own day:

> Pious or even merely church-going people seldom realize *how much* good will, one might even say wilfulness, it requires nowadays for a German scholar to take the problem of religion seriously; his whole trade . . . disposes him to a superior, almost good-natured merriment in regard to religion, sometimes mixed with a mild contempt directed at the "uncleanliness" of spirit which he presupposes wherever one still belongs to the church. It is only with the aid of history (thus *not* from his personal experience) that the scholar succeeds in summoning up a reverent seriousness and a certain shy respect towards religion; but if he intensifies his feelings towards it even to the point of feeling grateful to it, he has still in his own person not got so much as a single step closer to that which still exists as church or piety, perhaps the reverse. The practical indifference to religious things in which he was born and raised is as a rule sublimated in him into a caution and cleanliness which avoids contact with religious people and things, . . . Every age has its own divine kind of naïvety for the invention of which other ages may envy it—and how much naïvety, venerable, childlike and boundlessly stupid naïvety there is in the scholar's belief in his superiority, in the good conscience of his tolerance, in the simple unsuspecting certainty with which his instinct treats the religious man as an inferior and lower type which he himself has grown beyond and *above.*[3]

---

[3] Friedrich Nietzsche, *Beyond Good and Evil*, trans. R.J. Hollingdale, para. 58.

13

Understanding a Primitive Society

Peter Winch

This essay[1] will pursue further some questions raised in my book, *The Idea of a Social Science.*[2] That book was a general discussion of what is involved in the understanding of human social life. I shall here be concerned more specifically with certain issues connected with social anthropology. In the first part I raise certain difficulties about Professor E. E. Evans-Pritchard's approach in his classic, *Witchcraft, Oracles, and Magic among the Azande.*[3] In the second part, I attempt to refute some criticisms recently made by Mr. Alasdair McIntyre of Evans-Pritchard and myself, to criticize in their turn MacIntyre's positive remarks, and to offer some further reflections of my own on the concept of learning from the study of a primitive society.

I. The Reality of Magic

Like many other primitive people, the African Azande hold beliefs that we cannot possibly share and engage in practices which it is peculiarly difficult for us to comprehend. They believe that certain of their members are witches, exercising a malignant occult influence on the lives of their fellows. They engage in rites to counteract witchcraft; they consult oracles and use magic medicines to protect themselves from harm. An anthropologist studying such a people wishes to make those beliefs and practices intelligible to himself and his readers. This means presenting an account of them that will

---

[1] This paper was first published in the *American Philosophical Quarterly* I, 1964, pp. 307–24.

[2] London and New York, 1958.

[3] Oxford, 1937.

somehow satisfy the criteria of rationality demanded by the culture to which he and his readers belong: a culture whose conception of rationality is deeply affected by the achievements and methods of the sciences, and one which treats such things as a belief in magic or the practice of consulting oracles as almost a paradigm of the irrational. The strains inherent in this situation are very likely to lead the anthropologist to adopt the following posture: *We* know that Zande beliefs in the influence of witchcraft, the efficacy of magic medicines, the role of oracles in revealing what is going on and what is going to happen, are mistaken, illusory. Scientific methods of investigation have shown conclusively that there are no relations of cause and effect such as are implied by these beliefs and practices. All we can do then is to show how such a system of mistaken beliefs and inefficacious practices can maintain itself in the face of objections that seem to us so obvious.[4]

Now although Evans-Pritchard goes a very great deal further than most of his predecessors in trying to present the sense of the institutions he is discussing as it presents itself to the Azande themselves; still, the last paragraph does, I believe, pretty fairly describe the attitude he himself took at the time of writing this book. There is more than one remark to the effect that "obviously there are no witches," and he writes of the difficulty he found, during his field work with the Azande, in shaking off the "unreason" on which Zande life is based and returning to a clear view of how things really are. This attitude is not an unsophisticated one but is based on a philosophical position ably developed in a series of papers published in the 1930s in the unhappily rather inaccessible *Bulletin of the Faculty of Arts* of the University of Egypt. Arguing against Lévy-Bruhl, Evans-Pritchard here rejects the idea that the scientific understanding of causes and effects which leads us to reject magical ideas is evidence of any superior intelligence on our part. Our scientific approach, he points out, is as much a function of our culture as is the magical approach of the "savage" a function of his:

---

[4] At this point the anthropologist is very likely to start speaking of the "social function" of the institution under examination. There are many important questions that should be raised about functional explanations and their relations to the issues discussed in this essay; but these questions cannot be pursued further here.

> The fact that we attribute rain to meteorological causes alone while savages believe that Gods or ghosts or magic can influence the rainfall is no evidence that our brains function differently from their brains. It does not show that we "think more logically" than savages, at least not if this expression suggests some kind of hereditary psychic superiority. It is no sign of intelligence on my part that I attribute rain to physical causes. I did not come to this conclusion myself by observation and inference and have, in fact, little knowledge of the meteorological process that lead to rain, I merely accept what everybody else in my society accepts, namely that rain is due to natural causes. This particular idea formed part of my culture long before I was born into it and little more was required of me than sufficient linguistic ability to learn it. Likewise a savage who believes that under suitable natural and ritual conditions the rainfall can be influenced by use of appropriate magic is not on account of this belief to be considered of inferior intelligence. He did not build up this belief from his own observations and inferences but adopted it in the same way as he adopted the rest of his cultural heritage, namely, by being born into it. He and I are both thinking in patterns of thought provided for us by the societies in which we live.
>
> It would be absurd to say that the savage is thinking mystically and that we are thinking scientifically about rainfall. In either case like mental processes are involved and, moreover, the content of thought is similarly derived. But we can say that the social content of our thought about rainfall is scientific, is in accord with objective facts, whereas the social content of savage thought about rainfall is unscientific since it is not in accord with reality and may also be mystical where it assumes the existence of supra-sensible forces.[5]

In a subsequent article on Pareto, Evans-Pritchard distinguishes between "logical" and "scientific":

> Scientific notions are those which accord with objective reality both with regard to the validity of their premises and to the inferences drawn from their propositions. . . . Logical notions are those in which according to the rules of thought inferences would be true were the premises true, the truth of the premises being irrelevant. . . .
>
> A pot has broken during firing. This is probably due to grit. Let us examine the pot and see if this is the cause. That is logical and scientific thought. Sickness is due to witchcraft. A man is sick. Let us consult the oracles to discover who is the witch responsible. That is logical and unscientific thought.[6]

---

[5] E. E. Evans-Pritchard, "Lévy-Bruhl's Theory of Primitive Mentality," *Bulletin of the Faculty of Arts*, University of Egypt, 1934.

[6] "Science and Sentiment," *Bulletin of the Faculty of Arts*, ibid., 1935.

I think that Evans-Pritchard is right in a great deal of what he says here, but wrong, and crucially wrong, in his attempt to characterize the scientific in terms of that which is "in accord with objective reality." Despite differences of emphasis and phraseology, Evans-Pritchard is in fact hereby put into the same metaphysical camp as Pareto: for both of them the conception of "reality" must be regarded as intelligible and applicable *outside* the context of scientific reasoning itself, since it is that to which scientific notions do, and unscientific notions do not, have a relation. Evans-Pritchard, although he emphasizes that a member of scientific culture has a different conception of reality from that of a Zande believer in magic, wants to go beyond merely registering this fact and making the differences explicit, and to say, finally, that the scientific conception agrees with what reality actually is like, whereas the magical conception does not.

It would be easy, at this point, to say simply that the difficulty arises from the use of the unwieldy and misleadingly comprehensive expression "agreement with reality"; and in a sense this is true. But we should not lose sight of the fact that the idea that men's ideas and beliefs must be checkable by reference to something independent—some reality—is an important one. To abandon it is to plunge straight into an extreme Protagorean relativism, with all the paradoxes that involves. On the other hand great care is certainly necessary in fixing the precise role that this conception of the independently real does play in men's thought. There are two related points that I should like to make about it at this stage.

In the first place we should notice that the check of the independently real is not peculiar to science. The trouble is that the fascination science has for us makes it easy for us to adopt its scientific form as a paradigm against which to measure the intellectual respectability of other modes of discourse. Consider what God says to Job out of the whirlwind: "Who is this that darkeneth counsel by words without knowledge? . . . Where wast thou when I laid the foundations of the earth? declare, if thou hast understanding. Who hath laid the measures thereof, if thou knowest? or who hath stretched the line upon it. . . . Shall he that contendeth with the Almighty instruct him? he that reproveth God, let him answer it." Job is taken to task for having gone astray by having lost sight of the reality of God; this does not, of course, mean that Job has made any sort of theoretical mistake, which could be put right, perhaps, by means of an experiment.[7] God's reality is certainly independent of what any man may care to think, but what that reality amounts to can only be seen from religious tradition in which the concept of God is used, and this use is very unlike the use of scientific concepts, say of theoretical entities. The point is that it is *within* the religious use of language that the conception of God's reality has its place, though, I repeat, this does not mean that it is at the mercy of what anyone cares to say; if this were so, God would have no reality.

My second point follows from the first. Reality is not what gives language sense. What is real and what is unreal shows itself in the sense that language has. Further, both the distinction between the real and the unreal and the concept of agreement with reality themselves belong to our language. I will not say that they are concepts of the language like any other, since it is clear that they occupy a commanding, and in a sense a limiting, position there. We can imagine a language with no concept, of, say, wetness, but hardly one in which there is no way of distinguishing the real from the unreal. Nevertheless we could not in fact distinguish the real from the unreal without understanding the way this distinction operates in the language. If then we wish to understand the significance of these concepts, we must examine the use they actually do have—*in* the language.

Evans-Pritchard, on the contrary, is trying to work with a conception of reality which is *not* determined by its actual use in language. He wants something against which that use can itself be appraised. But this is not possible; and no more possible in the case of scientific discourse than it is in any other. We may ask whether a particular scientific hypothesis agrees with reality and test this by observation and experiment. Given the experimental methods, and the established use of the theoretical terms entering into the hypothesis, then the question whether it holds or not is settled by reference to something independent of what I, or anybody else, care to think. But the general nature of the data revealed by the experiment can only be specified in terms of criteria built into the methods of experiment employed and these, in turn, make sense only to someone who is conversant with the kind of scientific activity

[7] Indeed, one way of expressing the point of the story of Job is to say that in it Job is shown as going astray by being induced to make the reality and goodness of God contingent on what happens.

within which they are employed. A scientific illiterate, asked to describe the results of an experiment which he "observes" in an advanced physics laboratory, could not do so in terms relevant to the hypothesis being tested; and it is really only in such terms that we can sensibly speak of the "results of the experiment" at all. What Evans-Pritchard wants to be able to say is that the criteria applied in scientific experimentation constitute a true link between our ideas and an independent reality, whereas those characteristic of other systems of thought—in particular, magical methods of thought—do not. It is evident that the expressions "true link" and "independent reality" in the previous sentence cannot themselves be explained by reference to the scientific universe of discourse, as this would beg the question. We have then to ask how, by reference to what established universe of discourse, the use of those expressions *is* to be explained; and it is clear that Evans-Pritchard has not answered this question.

Two questions arise out of what I have been saying. First, is it in fact the case that a primitive system of magic, like that of the Azande, constitutes a coherent universe of discourse like science, in terms of which an intelligible conception of reality and clear ways of deciding what beliefs are and are not in agreement with this reality can be discerned. Second, what are we to make of the possibility of understanding primitive social institutions, like Zande magic, if the situation is as I have outlined? I do not claim to be able to give a satisfactory answer to the second question. It raises some very important and fundamental issues about the nature of human social life, which require conceptions different from, and harder to elucidate than, those I have hitherto introduced. I shall offer some tentative remarks about these issues in the second part of this essay. At present I shall address myself to the first question.

It ought to be remarked here that an affirmative answer to my first question would not commit me to accepting as rational all beliefs couched in magical concepts or all procedures practiced in the name of such beliefs. This is no more necessary than is the corresponding proposition that all procedures "justified" in the name of science are immune from rational criticism. A remark of Collingwood's is apposite here:

> Savages are no more exempt from human folly than civilized men, and are no doubt equally liable to the error of thinking that they, or the persons they regard as their superiors, can do what in fact cannot be done. But this error is not the essence of magic, it is a

perversion of magic. And we should be careful how we attribute it to the people we call savages, who will one day rise up and testify against us.[8]

It is important to distinguish a system of magical beliefs and practices like that of the Azande, which is one of the principal foundations of their whole social life and, on the other hand, magical beliefs that might be held, and magical rites that might be practised, by persons belonging to our own culture. These have to be understood rather differently. Evans-Pritchard is himself alluding to the difference in the following passage: "When a Zande speaks of witchcraft he does not speak of it as we speak of the weird witchcraft of our own history. Witchcraft is to him a commonplace happening and he seldom passes a day without mentioning it. . . . To us witchcraft is something which haunted and disgusted our credulous forefathers. But the Zande expects to come across witchcraft at any time of the day or night. He would be just as surprised if he were not brought into daily contact with it as we would be if confronted by its appearance. To him there is nothing miraculous about it."[9]

The difference is not merely one of degree of familiarity, however, although, perhaps, even this has more importance than might at first appear. Concepts of witchcraft and magic in our culture, at least since the advent of Christianity, have been parasitic on, and a perversion of other orthodox concepts, both religious and, increasingly, scientific. To take an obvious example, you could not understand what was involved in conducting a Black Mass, unless you were familiar with the conduct of a proper Mass and, therefore, with the whole complex of religious ideas from which the Mass draws its sense. Neither would you understand the relation between these without taking account of the fact that the Black practices are rejected as irrational (in the sense proper to religion) in the system of beliefs on which those practices are thus parasitic. Perhaps a similar relation holds between the contemporary practice of astrology and astronomy and technology. It is impossible to keep a discussion of the rationality of Black Magic or of astrology within the bounds of concepts peculiar to them; they have an essential reference to something outside themselves. The position is like that which Socrates, in Plato's *Gorgias*, showed to be true of the Sophists'

---

[8] R. G. Collingwood, *Principles of Art*, Oxford (Galaxy Books), 1958, p. 67.

[9] *Witchcraft, Oracles and Magic Among the Azande*, p. 64.

conception of rhetoric: namely, that it is parasitic on rational discourse in such a way that its irrational character can be shown in terms of this dependence. Hence, when we speak of such practices as "superstitious," "illusory," "irrational," we have the weight of our culture behind us; and this is not just a matter of being on the side of the big battalions, because those beliefs and practices belong to, and derive such sense as they seem to have, from that same culture. This enables us to show that the sense is only apparent, in terms which are culturally relevant.

It is evident that our relation to Zande magic is quite different. If we wish to understand it, we must seek a foothold elsewhere. And while there may well be room for the use of such critical expressions as "superstition" and "irrationality," the kind of rationality with which such terms might he used to point a contrast remains to be elucidated. The remarks I shall make in Part II will have a more positive bearing on this issue. In the rest of this Part, I shall develop in more detail my criticisms of Evans-Pritchard's approach to the Azande.

Early in this book he defines certain categories in terms of which his descriptions of Zande customs are couched.

> MYSTICAL NOTIONS . . . are patterns of thought that attribute to phenomena supra-sensible qualities which, or part of which, are not derived from observation or cannot be logically inferred from it, *and which they do not possess.*[10] C OMMON-SENSE NOTIONS . . . attribute to phenomena only what men observe in them or what can logically be inferred from observation. So long as a notion does not assert something which has not been observed, it is not classed as mystical even though it is mistaken on account of incomplete observation. . . . SCIENTIFIC NOTIONS. Science has developed out of common sense but is far more methodical and has better techniques of observation and reasoning. Common sense uses experience and rules of thumb. Science uses experiment and rules of Logic. . . . Our *body of scientific knowledge and Logic are the sole arbiters of what are mystical, common sense, and scientific notions.* Their judgments are never absolute. RITUAL BEHAVIOUR. Any behaviour that is accounted for by mystical notions. *There is no objective nexus* between the behaviour and the event it is intended to cause. Such behaviour is usually intelligible to us only when we know the mystical notions associated with it. EMPIRICAL BEHAVIOUR. Any behaviour that is accounted for by common-sense notions.[11]

---

10 The Italics are mine throughout this quotation.

11 Op. cit., p. 12.

It will be seen from the phrases which I have italicized that Evans-Pritchard is doing more here than just defining certain terms for his own use. Certain metaphysical claims are embodied in the definitions identical in substance with the claims embodied in Pareto's way of distinguishing between "logical" and "non-logical" conduct.[12] There is a very clear implication that those who use mystical notions and perform ritual behaviour are making some sort of mistake, detectable with the aid of science and logic. I shall now examine more closely some of the institutions described by Evans-Pritchard to determine how far his claims are justified.

Witchcraft is a power possessed by individuals to harm other individuals by "mystical" means. Its basis is an inherited organic condition, "witchcraft-substance" and it does not involve any special magical ritual or medicine. It is constantly appealed to by Azande when they are afflicted by misfortune, not so as to exclude explanation in terms of natural causes, which Azande are perfectly able to offer themselves within the limits of their not inconsiderable natural knowledge, but so as to supplement such explanations. "Witchcraft explains *why*[12] events are harmful to man and not *how*[13] they happen. A Zande perceives how they happen just as we do. He does not see a witch charge a man but an elephant. He does not see a witch push over the granary, but termites gnawing away its supports. He does not see a psychical flame igniting thatch, but an ordinary lighted bundle of straw. His perception of how events occur is as clear as our own."[14]

The most important way of detecting the influence of witchcraft and of identifying witches is by the revelations of oracles, of which in turn the most important is the "poison oracle." This name, though convenient, is significantly misleading in so far as, according to Evans-Pritchard, Azande do not have our concept of a poison and do not think of, or behave towards, *benge*—the substance administered in the consultation of the oracle—as we do of and towards poisons. The gathering, preparation, and administering of *benge* is hedged with ritual and strict taboos. At an oracular consultation *benge* is

---

[12] For further criticism of Pareto see Peter Winch, *The Idea of a Social Science*, pp. 95–111.

[13] Evans-Pritchard's italics.

[14] Op. cit., p. 72.

administered to a fowl, while a question is asked in a form permitting a yes or no answer. The fowl's death or survival is specified beforehand as giving the answer "yes" or "no." The answer is then checked by administering *benge* to another fowl and asking the question the other way round. "Is Prince Ndoruma responsible for placing bad medicines in the roof of my hut? The fowl DIES giving the answer "Yes.".. Did the oracle speak truly when it said that Ndoruma was responsible? The fowl survives giving the answer 'Yes.'" The poison oracle is all-pervasive in Zande life and all steps of any importance in a person's life are settled by reference to it.

A Zande would be utterly lost and bewildered without his oracle. The mainstay of his life would be lacking. It is rather as if an engineer, in our society, were to be asked to build a bridge without mathematical calculation, or a military commander to mount an extensive coordinated attack without the use of clocks. These analogies are mine but a reader may well think that they beg the question at issue. For, he may argue, the Zande practice of consulting the oracle, unlike my technological and military examples, is completely unintelligible and rests on an obvious illusion. I shall now consider this objection.

First I must emphasize that I have so far done little more than note the *fact*, conclusively established by Evans-Pritchard, that the Azande *do* in fact conduct their affairs to their own satisfaction in this way and are at a loss when forced to abandon the practice—when, for instance they fall into the hands of European courts. It is worth remarking too that Evan-Pritchard himself ran his household in the same way during his field researches and says: "I found this as satisfactory a way of running my home and affairs as any other I know of."

Further, I would ask in my turn: *to whom* is the practice alleged to be unintelligible? Certainly it is difficult for us to understand what the Azande are about when they consult their oracles; but it might seem just as incredible to them that the engineer's motions with his slide rule could have any connection with the stability of his bridge. But this riposte of course misses the intention behind the objection, which was not directed to the question whether anyone in fact understands, or claims to understand, what is going on, but rather whether what is going on actually does make sense: i.e., in itself. And it may seem obvious that Zande beliefs in witchcraft and oracles cannot make any sense, however satisfied the Azande may be with them.

What criteria have we for saying that something does, or does not, make sense? A partial answer is that a set of beliefs and practices cannot make sense in so far as they involve contradictions. Now it appears that contradictions are bound to arise in at least two ways in the consultation of the oracle. On the one hand two oracular pronouncements may contradict each other; and on the other hand a self-consistent oracular pronouncement may be contradicted by future experience. I shall examine each of these apparent possibilities in turn.

Of course, it does happen often that the oracle first says "yes" and then "no" to the same question. This does not convince a Zande of the futility of the whole operation of consulting oracles: obviously, it cannot, since otherwise the practice could hardly have developed and maintained itself at all. Various explanations may be offered, whose possibility, it is important to notice, is built into the whole network of Zande beliefs and may, therefore, be regarded as belonging to the concept of an oracle. It may be said, for instance, that bad *benge* is being used; that the operator of the oracle is ritually unclean; that the oracle is being itself influenced by witchcraft or sorcery; or it may be that the oracle is showing that the question cannot be answered straightforwardly in its present form, as with "Have you stopped beating your wife yet?" There are various ways in which the behaviour of the fowl under the influence of *benge* may be ingeniously interpreted by those wise in the ways of the poison oracle. We might compare this situation perhaps with the interpretation of dreams.

In the other type of case: where an internally consistent oracular revelation is apparently contradicted by subsequent experience, the situation may be dealt with in a similar way, by references to the influence of witchcraft, ritual uncleanliness, and so on. But there is another important consideration we must take into account here too. The chief function of oracles is to reveal the presence of "mystical" forces—I use Evans-Pritchard's term without committing myself to his denial that such forces really exist. Now though there are indeed ways of determining whether or not mystical forces are operating, these ways do not correspond to what we understand by "empirical" confirmation or refutation. This indeed is a tautology, since such differences in "confirmatory" procedures are the main criteria for classifying something as a mystical force in the first place. Here we have one reason why the possibilities of "refutation by experience" are very much fewer than might at first sight be supposed.

There is also another closely connected reason. The spirit in which oracles are consulted is very unlike that in which a scientist makes experiments. Oracular revelations are not treated as hypotheses and, since their sense derives from the way they are treated in their context, they therefore *are not* hypotheses. They are not a matter of intellectual interest but the main way in which Azande decide how they should act. If the oracle reveals that a proposed course of action is fraught with mystical dangers from witchcraft or sorcery, that course of action will not be carried out; and then the question of refutation or confirmation just does not arise. We might say that the revelation has the logical status of an unfulfilled hypothetical, were it not that the context in which this logical term is generally used may again suggest a misleadingly close analogy with scientific hypotheses.

I do not think that Evans-Pritchard would have disagreed with what I have said so far. Indeed, the following comment is on very similar lines:

> Azande observe the action of the poison oracle as we observe it, but their observations are always subordinated to their beliefs and are incorporated into their beliefs and made to explain them and justify them. Let the reader consider any argument that would utterly demolish all Zande claims for the power of the oracle. If it were translated into Zande modes of thought it would serve to support their entire structure of belief. For their mystical notions are eminently coherent, being interrelated by a network of logical ties, and are so ordered that they never too crudely contradict sensory experience but, instead, experience seems to justify them. The Zande is immersed in a sea of mystical notions, and if he speaks about his poison oracle he must speak in a mystical idiom.[15]

To locate the point at which the important philosophical issue does arise, I shall offer a parody, composed by changing round one or two expressions in the foregoing quotation.

> Europeans observe the action of the poison oracle just as Azande observe it, but their observations are always subordinated to their beliefs and are incorporated into their beliefs and made to explain

[15] Ibid., p. 319.

them and justify them. Let a Zande consider any argument that would utterly refute all European skepticism about the power of the oracle. If it were translated into European modes of thought it would serve to support their entire structure of belief. For their scientific notions are eminently coherent, being interrelated by a network of logical ties, and are so ordered that they never too crudely contradict mystical experience but, instead, experience seems to justify them. The European is immersed in a sea of scientific notions, and if he speaks about the Zande poison oracle he must speak in a scientific idiom.

Perhaps this too would be acceptable to Evans-Pritchard. But it is clear from other remarks in the book to which I have alluded, that at the time of writing it he would have wished to add: and the European is right and the Zande wrong. This addition I regard as illegitimate and my reasons for so thinking take us to the heart of the matter.

It may be illuminating at this point to compare the disagreement between Evans-Pritchard and me to that between the Wittgenstein of the *Philosophical Investigations* and his earlier *alter ego* of the *Tractatus Logico-Philosophicus.* In the *Tractatus* Wittgenstein sought "the general form of propositions": what made propositions possible. He said that this general form is: "This is how things are;" the proposition was an articulated model, consisting of elements standing in a definite relation to each other. The proposition was true when there existed a corresponding arrangement of elements in reality. The proposition was capable of saying something because of the identity of structure, of logical form, in the proposition and in reality.

By the time Wittgenstein composed the *Investigations* he had come to reject the whole idea that there must be a general form of propositions. He emphasized the indefinite number of different uses that language may have and tried to show that these different uses neither need, nor in fact do, all have something in common, in the sense intended in the *Tractatus.* He also tried to show that what counts as "agreement or disagreement with reality" takes on as many different forms as there are different use of language and cannot, therefore, be taken as given *prior* to the detailed investigation of the use that is in question.

The *Tractatus* contains a remark strikingly like something that Evans-Pritchard says.

> *The limits of my language mean the limits of my world.* Logic fills the world: the limits of the world are also its limits. We cannot therefore say in logic: This and this there is in the world, and that there is not.
>
> For that would apparently presuppose that we exclude certain possibilities, and this cannot be the case since otherwise logic must get outside the limits of the world: that is, if it could consider these limits from the other side also.[16]

Evans-Pritchard discusses the phenomena of belief and skepticism, as they appear in Zande life. There *is* certainly widespread skepticism about certain things, for instance, about some of the powers claimed by witch-doctors or about the efficiency of certain magic medicinal. But, he points out, such skepticism does not begin to overturn the mystical way of thinking, since it is necessarily expressed in terms belonging to that way of thinking.

> In this web of belief every strand depends on every other strand, and a Zande cannot get outside its meshes because this is the only world he knows. The web is not an external structure in which he is enclosed. It is the texture of his thought and he cannot think that his thought is wrong.[17]

Wittgenstein and Evans-Pritchard are concerned here with much the same problem, though the difference in the directions from which they approach it is important too. Wittgenstein, at the time of the *Tractatus,* spoke of "language," as if all language is fundamentally of the same kind and must have the same kind of "relation to reality"; but Evans-Pritchard is confronted by two languages which he recognizes as fundamentally different in kind, such that much of what may be expressed in the one has no possible counterpart in the other. One might, therefore, have expected this to lead to a position closer to that of the *Philosophical Investigations* than to that of the *Tractatus.* Evans-Pritchard is not content with elucidating the differences in the *two* concepts of reality involved; he wants to go further and say: our concept of reality is the correct one, the Azande are mistaken. But the difficulty is to see what "correct" and "mistaken" can mean in this context.

Let me return to the subject of contradictions. I have already noted that many contradictions we might expect to appear in fact do not in the context of Zande thought, where provision is made for

---

16 Wittgenstein, *Tractatus Logico-Philosophicus*, 5. 6–5. 61.

17 Evans-Pritchard, op. cit., p. 194.

avoiding them. But there are some situations of which this does not seem to be true, where what appear to us as obvious contradictions are left where they are, apparently unresolved. Perhaps this may be the foothold we are looking for, from which we can appraise the "correctness" of the Zande system.[18]

Consider Zande notions about the inheritance of witchcraft. I have spoken so far only of the role of oracles in establishing whether or not someone is a witch. But there is a further and, as we might think, more "direct" method of doing this, namely by post-mortem examination of a suspect's intestines for "witchcraft-substance." This may be arranged by his family after his death in an attempt to clear the family name of the imputation of witchcraft. Evans-Pritchard remarks: "To our minds it appears evident that if a man is proven a witch the whole of his clan are *ipso facto* witches, since the Zande clan is a group of persons related biologically to one another through the male line. Azande see the sense of this argument but they do not accept its conclusions, and it would involve the whole notion of witchcraft in contradiction were they to do so."[19] Contradiction would presumably arise because a few positive results of post-mortem examinations, scattered among all the clans, would very soon prove that everybody was a witch, and a few negative results, scattered among the same clans, would prove that nobody was a witch. Though, in particular situations, individual Azande may avoid personal implications arising out of the presence of witchcraft-substance in deceased relatives, by imputations of bastardy and similar devices, this would not be enough to save the generally contradictory situation I have sketched. Evans-Pritchard comments: "Azande do not perceive the contradiction as we perceive it because they have no theoretical interest in the subject, and those situations in which they express their belief in witchcraft do not force the problem upon them."[20]

It might now appear as though we had clear grounds for speaking of the superior rationality of European over Zande thought, in so far as the latter involves a contradiction which it makes no attempt to remove and does not even recognize: one, however, which is recognizable as such in the context of European *ways* of thinking.

---

[18] I shall discuss this point in a more general way in Part II.

[19] Ibid., p. 24.

[20] Ibid., p. 25.

But does Zande thought on this matter really involve a contradiction? It appears from Evans-Pritchard's account that Azande do not press their ways of thinking about witches to a point at which they would be involved in contradictions.

Someone may now want to say that the irrationality of the Azande in relation to witchcraft shows itself in the fact that they do not press their thought about it "to its logical conclusion." To appraise this point we must consider whether the conclusion we are trying to force on them is indeed a logical one; or perhaps better, whether someone who does press this conclusion is being more rational than the Azande, who do not. Some light is thrown on this question by Wittgenstein's discussion of a game,

> such that whoever begins can always win by a particular simple trick. But this has not been realized—so it is a game. Now someone draws our attention to it—and it stops being a game.
>
> What turn can I give this, to make it clear to myself?—For I want to say: 'and it stops being a game'—not: 'and now we see that it wasn't a game.'
>
> That means, I want to say, it can also be taken like this: the other man did not *draw our attention* to anything; he taught us a different game in place of our own. But how can the new game have made the old one obsolete? We now see something different, and can no longer naively go on playing.
>
> On the one hand the game consisted in our actions (our play) on the board; and these actions I could perform as well now as before. But on the other hand it was essential to the game that I blindly tried to win; and now I can no longer do that.[21]

There are obviously considerable analogies between Wittgenstein's example and the situation we are considering. But there is an equally important difference. Both Wittgenstein's games: the old one without the trick that enables the starter to win and the new one with the trick, are in an important sense on the same level. They are both *games,* in the form of a contest where the aim of a player is to beat his opponent by the exercise of skill. The new trick makes this situation impossible and this is why it makes the old game obsolete. To be sure, the situation could be saved in a way by introducing a new rule, forbidding the use by the starter of the trick which would ensure his victory. But our intellectual habits are such

---

[21] L. Wittgenstein, *Remarks on the Foundations of Mathematics,* Pt. II, Para. 77. Wittgenstein's whole discussion of 'contradiction' in mathematics is directly relevant to the point I am discussing.

as to make us unhappy about the artificiality of such a device, rather as logicians have been unhappy about the introduction of a Theory of Types as a device for avoiding Russell's paradoxes. It is noteworthy in my last quotation from Evans-Pritchard however, that the Azande, when the possibility of this contradiction about the inheritance of witchcraft is pointed out to them, do *not* then come to regard their old beliefs about witchcraft as obsolete. "They have no theoretical interest in the subject." This suggests strongly that the context from which the suggestion about the contradiction is made, the context of our scientific culture, is not on the same level as the context in which the beliefs about witchcraft operate. Zande notions of witchcraft do not constitute a theoretical system in terms of which Azande try to gain a quasi-scientific understanding of the world.[22] This in its turn suggests that it is the European, obsessed with pressing Zande thought where it would not naturally go—to a contradiction—who is guilty of misunderstanding, not the Zande. The European is in fact committing a category-mistake.

Something else is also suggested by this discussion: the forms in which rationality expresses itself in the culture of a human society cannot be elucidated *simply* in terms of the logical coherence of the rules according to which activities are carried out in that society. For, as we have seen, there comes a point where we are not even in a position to determine what is and what is not coherent in such a context of rules, without raising questions about the point which following those rules has in the society. No doubt it was a realization of this fact which led Evans-Pritchard to appeal to a residual "correspondence with reality" in distinguishing between "mystical" and "scientific" notions. The conception of reality is indeed indispensable to any understanding of the point of a way of life. But it is not a conception which can be explicated as Evans-Pritchard tries to explicate it, in terms of what science reveals to be the case; for a form of the conception of reality must already be presupposed before we can make any sense of the expression "what science reveals to be the case."

---

[22] Notice that I have *not* said that Azande conceptions of witchcraft have nothing to do with understanding the world at all. The point is that a different form of the concept of understanding is involved here.

II. Our Standards and Theirs

In Part I, I attempted, by analysing a particular case, to criticize by implication a particular view of how we can understand a primitive institution. In this Part I shall have two aims. First, I shall examine in a more formal way a general philosophical argument, which attempts to show that the approach I have been criticizing is in principle the right one. This argument has been advanced by Mr Alasdair MacIntyre in two places: *(a)* in a paper entitled *Is Understanding Religion Compatible with Believing?* read to the Sesquicentennial Seminar of the Princeton Theological Seminar in 1962.[23] *(b)* In a contribution to *Philosophy, Politics and Society (Second Series)*,[24] entitled *A Mistake about Causality in Social Science.* Next, I shall make some slightly more positive suggestions about how to overcome the difficulty from which I started: how to make intelligible in our terms institutions belonging to a primitive culture, whose standards of rationality and intelligibility are apparently quite at odds with our own.

The relation between MacIntyre, Evans-Pritchard, and myself is a complicated one. MacIntyre takes Evans-Pritchard's later book, *Nuer Religion,* as an application of a point of view like mine in *The Idea of a Social Science;* he regards it as an object lesson in the absurd results to which such a position leads, when applied in practice. My own criticisms of Evans-Pritchard, on the other hand, have come from precisely the opposite direction. I have tried to show that Evans-Pritchard did not at the time of writing *The Azande* agree with me *enough;* that he did not take seriously enough the idea that the concepts used by primitive peoples can only be interpreted in the context of the way of life of those peoples. Thus I have in effect argued that Evans-Pritchard's account of the Azande is unsatisfactory precisely to the extent that he agrees with MacIntyre and not me.

The best point at which to start considering MacIntyre's position is that at which he agrees with me—in emphasizing the importance of possibilities of *description* for the concept of human action. An agent's action "is identified fundamentally as what it is by

---

[23] Published along with other papers in *Faith and the Philosophers,* ed. John Hick. See above pp. 62–77.

[24] Edited by Peter Laslett and W. G. Runciman, Oxford: Blackwell, 1962.

the description under which he deems it to fall." Since, further, descriptions must be intelligible to other people, an action "must fall under some description which is socially recognizable as the description of an action."[25] "To identify the limits of social action in a given period," therefore, "is to identify the stock of descriptions current in that age."[26] MacIntyre correctly points out that descriptions do not exist in isolation, but occur "as constituents of beliefs, speculations and projects." As these in turn "are continually criticized, modified, rejected, or improved, the stock of descriptions changes. The changes in human action are thus intimately linked to the thread of rational criticism in human history."

This notion of rational criticism, MacIntyre points out, requires the notion of choice between alternatives, to explain which "is a matter of making clear what the agent's criterion was and why he made use of this criterion rather than another and to explain why the use of this criterion appears rational to those who invoke it."[27] Hence "in explaining the rules and conventions to which action in a given social order conform *[sic]* we cannot omit reference to the rationality or otherwise of those rules and conventions." Further, "the beginning of an explanation of why certain criteria are taken to be rational in some societies is that they *are* rational. And since this has to enter into our explanation we cannot explain social behaviour independently of our own norms of rationality."

I turn now to criticism of this argument. Consider first MacIntyre's account of changes in an existing "stock" of available descriptions of actions. How does a candidate for inclusion *qualify* for admission to the stock? Unless there are limits, all MacIntyre's talk about possibilities of description circumscribing possibilities of action becomes nugatory, for there would be nothing to stop anybody inventing some arbitrary verbal expression, applying to it some arbitrary bodily movement, and thus adding that expression to the stock of available descriptions. But of course the new description must be an *intelligible* one. Certainly, its intelligibility cannot be decided by whether or not it belongs to an *existing* stock of descriptions, since this would rule out precisely what is being discussed: the addition of *new* descriptions to the stock. "What can

---

[25] Ibid., p. 58.
[26] Ibid., p. 60.
[27] Ibid., p. 61.

intelligibly be said" is not equivalent to "what has been intelligibly said," or it would never be possible to say anything new. *Mutatis mutandis* it would never be possible to *do* anything new. Nevertheless the intelligibility of anything new said or done does depend in a certain way on what already has been said or done and understood. The crux of this problem lies in how we are to understand that "in a certain way."

In *Is Understanding Religion Compatible with Believing?* MacIntyre asserts that the development through criticism of the standards of intelligibility current in a society is ruled out by my earlier account (in *The Idea of a Social Science)* of the origin in social institutions themselves of such standards. I shall not now repeat my earlier argument, but simply point out that I did, in various passages,[28] emphasize the *open* character of the "rules" which I spoke of in connection with social institutions: i.e. the fact that in changing social situations, reasoned decisions have to be made about what is to count as "going on in the same way." MacIntyre's failure to come to terms with this point creates difficulties for him precisely analogous to those which he mistakenly attributes to my account.

It is a corollary of his argument up to this point, as well as being intrinsically evident, that a new description of action must be intelligible to the members of the society in which it is introduced. On my view the point is that what determines this is the further development of rules and principles already implicit in the previous ways of acting and talking. To be emphasized are not the actual members of any "stock" of descriptions; but the *grammar* which they express. It is through this that we understand their structure and sense, their mutual relations, and the sense of new ways of talking and acting that may be introduced. These new ways of talking and acting may very well at the same time involve modifications in the grammar, but we can only speak thus if the new grammar is (to its users) intelligibly related to the old.

But what of the intelligibility of such changes to observers from another society with a different culture and different standards of intelligibility? MacIntyre urges that such observers must make clear "what the agent's criterion was and why he made use of this criterion rather than another and why the use of this criterion appears rational to those who invoke it." Since what is at issue is the precise relation

---

[28] Pp. 57–65; 91–94; 121–23.

between the concepts of rationality current in these different societies it is obviously of first importance to be clear about *whose* concept of rationality is being alluded to in this quotation. It seems that it must be that which is current in the society in which the criterion is invoked. Something can appear rational to someone only in terms of *his* understanding of what is and is not rational. If *our* concept of rationality is a different one from his, then it makes no sense to say that anything either does or does not appear rational to *him* in *our* sense.

When MacIntyre goes on to say that the observer "cannot omit reference to the rationality or otherwise of those rules and conventions" followed by the alien agent, whose concept of rationality is now in question: ours or the agent's? Since the observer must be understood now as addressing himself to members of his own society, it seems that the reference must here be to the concept of rationality current in the observer's society. Thus there is a *non sequitur* in the movement from the first to the second of the passages just quoted.

MacIntyre's thought here and in what immediately follows, seems to be this. The explanation of why, in Society *S*, certain actions are taken to be rational, has got to be an explanation for *us*; so it must be in terms of concepts intelligible to us. If then, in the explanation, we say that in fact those criteria *are* rational, we must be using the word *"rational"* in *our* sense. For this explanation would require that we had previously carried out an independent investigation into the actual rationality or otherwise of those criteria, and we could do this only in terms of an understood concept of rationality—*our* understood concept of rationality. The explanation would run: members of Society *S* have seen to be the case something that we know to be the case. If "what is seen to be the case" is common to us and them, it must be referred to under the same concept for each of us.

But obviously this explanation is not open to us. For we start from the position that standards of rationality in different societies do not always coincide; from the possibility, therefore, that the standards of rationality current in *S* are different from our own. So we cannot assume that it will make sense to speak of members of *S* as discovering something which we have also discovered; such discovery presupposes initial conceptual agreement.

Part of the trouble lies in MacIntyre's use of the expression, "the rationality of criteria," which he does not explain. In the present context to speak thus is to cloak the real problem, since what we are concerned with are differences in *criteria of rationality.* MacIntyre seems to be saying that certain standards are taken as criteria of rationality because they *are* criteria of rationality. But whose?

There are similar confusions in MacIntyre's other paper: *Is Understanding Religion Compatible with Believing?* [29] There he argues that when we detect an internal incoherence in the standards of intelligibility current in an alien society and try to show why this does not appear, or is made tolerable to that society's members, "we have already invoked our standards." In what sense is this true? In so far as we "detect" and "show" something, obviously we do so in a sense intelligible to us; so we are limited by what *counts* (for us) as "detecting," "showing" something. Further, it may well be that the interest in showing and detecting such things is peculiar to our society—that we are doing something in which members of the studied society exhibit no interest, because the institutions in which such an interest could develop are lacking. Perhaps too the pursuit of that interest in our society has led to the development of techniques of inquiry and modes of argument which again are not to be found in the life of the studied society. But it cannot be guaranteed in advance that the methods and techniques we have used in the past—e.g., in elucidating the logical structure of arguments in our own language and culture—are going to be equally fruitful in this new context. They will perhaps need to be extended and modified. No doubt, if they are to have a logical relation to our previous forms of investigation, the new techniques will have to be recognizably continuous with previously used ones. But they must also so extend our conception of intelligibility as to make it possible for us to see what intelligibility amounts to in the life of the society we are investigating.

The task MacIntyre says we must undertake is to make intelligible *(a)* (to us) why it is that members of *S* think that certain of their practices are intelligible *(b)* (to them), when in fact they are not. I have introduced differentiating letters into my two uses of "intelligible," to mark the complexity that MacIntyre's way of stating the position does not bring out: the fact that we are dealing with two

---

[29] See above, pp. 62–77.

different senses of the word "intelligible." The relation between these is precisely the question at issue. MacIntyre's task is not like that of making intelligible a natural phenomenon, where we are limited only by what counts as intelligibility for us. We must somehow bring *S*'s conception of intelligibility *(b)* into (intelligible!) relation with our own conception of intelligibility *(a)*. That is, we have to create a new unity for the concept of intelligibility, having a certain relation to our old one and perhaps requiring a considerable realignment of our categories. We are not seeking a state in which things will appear to us just as they do to members of *S*, and perhaps such a state is unattainable anyway. But we *are* seeking a way of looking at things which goes beyond our previous way in that it has in some way taken account of and incorporated the other way that members of *S* have of looking at things. Seriously to study another way of life is necessarily to seek to extend our own—not simply to bring the other way within the already existing boundaries of our own, because the point about the latter in their present form, is that they *ex hypothesi* exclude that other.

There is a dimension to the notions of rationality and intelligibility which may make it easier to grasp the possibility of such an extension. I do not think that MacIntyre takes sufficient account of this dimension and, indeed, the way he talks about "norms of rationality" obscures it. Rationality is not *just* a concept *in* a language like any other; it is this too, for, like any other concept it must be circumscribed by an established use: a use, that is, established in the language. But I think it is not a concept which a language may, as a matter of fact, have and equally well may not have, as is, for instance, the concept of politeness. It is a concept necessary to the existence of any language: to say of a society that it has a language[30] is also to say that it has a concept of rationality. There need not perhaps be any *word* functioning in its language as "rational" does in ours, but at least there must be features of its members' use of languages analogous to those features of our use of language which are connected with our use of the word "rational." Where there is language it must make a difference what is said and this is only possible where the saying of one thing rules out, on pain of failure to communicate, the saying of something else. So in one sense MacIntyre is right in saying that we have already invoked our

[30] I shall not discuss here what justifies us in saying *this* in the first place.

concept of rationality in saying of a collection of people that they constitute a society with a language: in the sense, namely, that we imply formal analogies between their behaviour and that behaviour in our society which we refer to in distinguishing between rationality and irrationality. This, however, is so far to say nothing about what in particular constitutes rational behaviour in that society; that would require more particular knowledge about the norms they appeal to in living their lives. In other words, it is not so much a matter of invoking "our own norms of rationality" as of invoking our notion of rationality in speaking of their behaviour in terms of "conformity to norms." But how precisely this notion is to be applied to them will depend on our reading of their conformity to norms—what counts for them as conformity and what does not.

Earlier I criticized MacIntyre's conception of a "stock of available descriptions." Similar criticisms apply to his talk about "our norms of rationality," if these norms are taken as forming some finite set. Certainly we learn to think, speak, and act rationally *through* being trained to adhere to particular norms. But having learned to speak, etc., rationally does not *consist* in having been trained to follow those norms; to suppose that would be to overlook the importance of the phrase "and so on" in any description of what someone who follows norms does. We must, if you like, be open to new possibilities of what could be invoked and accepted under the rubric of "rationality"—possibilities which are perhaps suggested and limited by what we have hitherto so accepted, but not uniquely determined thereby.

This point can be applied to the possibilities of our grasping forms of rationality different from ours in an alien culture. First, as I have indicated, these possibilities are limited by certain formal requirements centering round the demand for consistency. But these formal requirements tell us nothing about what in particular is to *count* as consistency, just as the rules of the propositional calculus limit, but do not themselves determine what are to be proper values of p, q, etc. We can only determine this by investigating the wider context of the life in which the activities in question are carried on. This investigation will take us beyond merely specifying the rules governing the carrying out of those activities. For, as MacIntyre quite rightly says, to note that certain rules are followed is so far to say nothing about the *point* of the rules, it is not even to decide whether or not they have a point at all.

MacIntyre's recipe for deciding this is that "in bringing out this feature of the case one shows also whether the use of this concept is or is not a possible one for people who have the standards of intelligibility in speech and action which we have."[31] It is important to notice that his argument, contrary to what he supposes, does not in fact show that our own standards of rationality occupy a peculiarly central position. The appearance to the contrary is an optical illusion engendered by the fact that MacIntyre's case has been advanced in the English language and in the context of twentieth century European culture. But a formally similar argument could be advanced in any language containing concepts playing a similar role in that language to those of "intelligibility" and "rationality" in ours. This shows that, so far from overcoming relativism, as he claims, MacIntyre himself falls into an extreme form of it. He disguises this from himself by committing the very error of which, wrongly as I have tried to show, he accuses me: the error overlooking the fact that "criteria and concepts have a history." While he emphasizes this point when he is dealing with the concepts and criteria governing action in particular social contexts, he forgets it when he comes to talk of the *criticism* of such criteria. Do not the criteria appealed to in the criticism of existing institutions equally have a history? And in whose society do they have that history? MacIntyre's implicit answer is that it is in ours; but if we are to speak of difficulties and incoherencies appearing and being detected in the way certain practices have hitherto been carried on in a society, surely this can only be understood in connection with problems arising *in* the carrying on of the activity. Outside that context we could not begin to grasp what was problematical.

Let me return to the Azande and consider something which MacIntyre says about them, intended to support the position I am criticizing:

> The Azande believe that the performance of certain rites in due form affects their common welfare; this belief cannot in fact be refuted. For they also believe that if the rites are ineffective it is because someone present at them had evil thoughts. Since this is always possible, there is never a year when it is unavoidable for them to admit that the rites were duly performed, but they did not thrive. Now the belief of the Azande is not unfalsifiable in principle (we know perfectly well what would falsify it—the conjunction of

---

31 *Is Understanding Religion Compatible with Believing?* Above, p. 69.

> the rite, no evil thoughts and disasters). But in fact it cannot be falsified. Does this belief stand in need of rational criticism? And if so by what standards? It seems to me that one could not hold the belief of the Azande rational *in the absence of* any practice of science and technology in which criteria of effectiveness, ineffectiveness and kindred notions had been built up. But to say this is to recognize the appropriateness of scientific criteria of judgment from our standpoint. The Azande do not intend their belief either as a piece of science or as a piece of non-science. They do not possess those categories. It is only *post eventum,* in the light of later and more sophisticated understanding that their belief and concepts can be classified and evaluated at all.[32]

Now in one sense classification and evaluation of Zande beliefs and concepts does require "a more sophisticated understanding" than is found in Zande culture; for the sort of classification and evaluation that are here in question are sophisticated philosophical activities. But this is not to say that Zande forms of life are to be classified and evaluated in the way MacIntyre asserts: in terms of certain specific forms of life to be found in our culture, according as they do or do not measure up to what is required within these. MacIntyre confuses the sophistication of the interest in classification with the sophistication of the concepts employed in our classificatory work. It is of interest to us to understand how Zande magic is related to science; the concepts of such a comparison is a very sophisticated one; but this does not mean that we have to see the unsophisticated Zande practice in the light of more sophisticated practices in our own culture, like science—as perhaps a more primitive form of it. MacIntyre criticizes, justly, Sir James Frazer for having imposed the image of his own culture on more primitive ones; but that is exactly what MacIntyre himself is doing here. It is extremely difficult for a sophisticated member of a sophisticated society to grasp a very simple and primitive form of life: in a way he must jettison his sophistication, a process which is itself perhaps the ultimate in sophistication. Or, rather, the distinction between sophistication and simplicity becomes unhelpful at this point.

It may be true, as MacIntyre says, that the Azande do not have the categories of science and non-science. But Evans-Pritchard's account shows that they do have a fairly clear working distinction between the technical and the magical. It is neither here nor there that individual Azande may sometimes confuse the categories, for such

---

[32] Ibid., Above, p. 67.

confusions may take place in any culture. A much more important fact to emphasize is that *we* do not initially have a category that looks at all like the Zande category of magic. Since it is we who want to understand the Zande category, it appears that the onus is on us to extend our understanding so as to make room for the Zande category, rather than to insist on seeing it in terms of our own ready-made distinction between science and non-science. Certainly the sort of understanding we seek requires that we see the Zande category in relation to our own already understood categories. But this neither means that it is right to "evaluate" magic in terms of criteria belonging to those other categories; nor does it give any clue as to *which* of our existing categories of thought will provide the best point of reference from which we can understand the point of the Zande practices.

MacIntyre has no difficulty in showing that *if* the rites which the Azande perform in connection with their harvests are "classified and evaluated" by reference to the criteria and standards of science or technology, then they are subject to serious criticism. He thinks that the Zande "belief" is a sort of *hypothesis* like, e.g., an Englishman's belief that all the heavy rain we have been having is due to atomic explosions.[33] MacIntyre believes that he is applying as it were a neutral concept of "*A* affecting *B*," equally applicable to Zande magic and western science. In fact, however, he is applying the concept with which *he* is familiar, one which draws its significance from its use in scientific and technological contexts. There is no reason to suppose that the Zande magical concept of "*A* affecting *B*" has anything like the same significance. On the contrary, since the Azande do, in the course of their practical affairs, apply something very like our technical concept—though perhaps in a more primitive form—and since their attitude to and thought about their magical rites are quite different from those concerning their technological measures, there is every reason to think that their concept of magical "influence" is quite different. This may be easier to accept if it is remembered that, even in our own culture, the concept of causal influence is by no means monolithic: when we

---

[33] In what follows I have been helped indirectly, but greatly, by some unpublished notes made by Wittgenstein on Frazer, which Mr. Rush Rhees was kind enough to show me; and also by various scattered remarks on folklore in *The Notebooks* of Simone Weil, London, 1963.

speak for example, of "what made Jones get married," we are not saying the same kind of thing as when we speak of "what made the aeroplane crash;" I do not mean simply that the events of which we speak are different in kind but that the relation between the events is different also. It should not then be difficult to accept that in a society with quite different institutions and ways of life from our own, there may be concepts of "causal influence" which behave even more differently.

But I do not want to say that we are quite powerless to find ways of thinking in our own society that will help us to see the Zande institution in a clearer light. I only think that the direction in which we should look is quite different from what MacIntyre suggests. Clearly the nature of Zande life is such that it is of very great importance to them that their crops should thrive. Clearly too they take all kinds of practical "technological" steps, within their capabilities, to ensure that they *do* thrive. But that is no reason to see their magical rites as a further, misguided such step. A man's sense of the importance of something to him shows itself in all sorts of ways: not merely in precautions to safeguard that thing. He may want to come to terms with its importance to him in quite a different way: to contemplate it, to gain some sense of his life in relation to it. He may wish thereby, in a certain sense, to *free* himself from dependence on it. I do not mean by making sure that it does not let him down, because the point is that, *whatever* he does, he may still be let down. The important thing is that he should understand that and come to terms with it. Of course, merely to understand that is not to come to terms with it, though perhaps it is a necessary condition for so doing, for a man may equally well be transfixed and terrorized by the contemplation of such a possibility. He must see that he can still go on even if he is let down by what is vitally important to him; and he must so order his life that he still *can* go on in such circumstances. I stress once again that I do not mean this in the sense of becoming "technologically independent," because from the present point of view technological independence is yet another form of dependence. Technology destroys some dependencies but always creates new ones, which may be fiercer—because harder to understand—than the old. This should be particularly apparent to *us*.[34]

In Judaeo-Christian cultures the conception of "If it be Thy Will," as developed in the story of Job, is clearly central to the matter I am discussing. Because this conception is central to Christian prayers of supplication, they may be regarded from one point of view as freeing the believer from dependence on what he is supplicating for.[35] Prayers cannot play this role if they are regarded as a means of influencing the outcome for in that case the one who prays is still dependent on the outcome. He frees himself from this by acknowledging his complete dependence on God; and this is totally unlike any dependence on the outcome precisely because God is eternal and the outcome contingent.

I do not say that Zande magical rites are at all like Christian prayers of supplication in the positive attitude to contingencies which they express. What I do suggest is that they are alike in that they do, or may, express an attitude to contingencies; one, that is, which involves recognition that one's life is subject to contingencies, rather than an attempt to control these. To characterize this attitude more specifically one should note how Zande rites emphasize the importance of certain fundamental features of their life which MacIntyre ignores. MacIntyre concentrates implicitly on the relation of the rites to consumption, but of course they are also fundamental to social relations and this seems to be emphasized in Zande notions of witchcraft. We have a drama of resentments, evil-doing, revenge, expiation, in which there are ways of dealing (symbolically) with misfortunes and their disruptive effect on a man's relations with his fellows, with ways in which life can go on despite such disruptions.

How is my treatment of this example related to the general criticisms I was making of MacIntyre's account of what it is for us to see the point of the rules and conventions followed in an alien form of life? MacIntyre speaks as though our own rules and conventions are somehow a paradigm of what it is for rules and conventions to have a point, so that the only problem that arises is in accounting for

---

[34] The point is beautifully developed by Simone Weil in her essay on "The Analysis of Oppression" in *Oppression and Liberty*, London, Routledge and Kegan Paul, 1958.

[35] I have been helped to see this point by D. Z. Phillips, *The Concept of Prayer*, London and New York, 1965.

the *point* of the rules and conventions in same other society. But in fact, of course, the problem is the same in relation to our own society as it is in relation to any other; no more than anyone else's are *our* rules and conventions immune from the danger of being or becoming pointless. So an account of this matter cannot be given simply in terms of any set of rules and conventions at all: our own or anyone else's; it requires us to consider the relation of a set of rules and conventions to something else. In my discussion of Zande magical rites just now what I tried to relate the magical rites to was a sense of the significance of human life. This notion is, I think, indispensable to any account of what is involved in understanding and learning from an alien culture; I must now try to say more about it.

In a discussion of Wittgenstein's philosophical use of language games[36] Mr. Rush Rhees points out that to try to account for the meaningfulness of language solely in terms of isolated language games is to omit the important fact that ways of speaking are not insulated from each other in mutually exclusive systems of rules. What can be said in one context by the use of a certain expression depends for its sense on the use of that expression in other contexts (different language games). Language games are played by men who have lives to live—lives involving a wide variety of different interests, which have all kinds of different bearings on each other. Because of this, what a man says or does may make a difference not merely to the performance of the activity upon which he is at present engaged, but to his *life* and to the lives of other people. Whether a man sees a point in what he is doing will then depend on whether he is able to see any unity in his multifarious interests, activities, and relations with other men; what sort of sense he sees in his life will depend on the nature of this unity. The ability to see this sort of sense in life depends not merely on the individual concerned, though this is not to say it does not depend on him at all; it depends also on the possibilities for making such sense which the culture in which he lives does, or does not, provide.

What we may learn by studying other cultures are not merely possibilities of different ways of doing things, other techniques. More importantly we may learn different possibilities of making sense of human life, different ideas about the possible importance that the

---

[36] Rush Rhees, "Wittgenstein's Builders," *Proceedings of the Aristotelian Society*, vol. 20, 1960, pp. 171–86.

carrying out of certain activities may take on for a man, trying to contemplate the sense of his life as a whole. This dimension of the matter is precisely what MacIntyre misses in his treatment of Zande magic; he can see in it only a (misguided) technique for producing consumer goods. But a Zande's crops are not just potential objects of consumption: the life he lives, his relations with his fellows, his chances for acting decently or doing evil, may all spring from his relation to his crops. Magical rites constitute a form of expression in which these possibilities and dangers may be contemplated and reflected on—and perhaps also thereby transformed and deepened. The difficulty we find in understanding this is not merely its remoteness from science, but an aspect of the general difficulty we find, illustrated by MacIntyre's procedure, of thinking about such matters at all except in terms of "efficiency of production"—production, that is, for consumption. This again is a symptom of what Marx called the "alienation" characteristic of man in industrial society, though Marx's own confusions about the relations between production and consumption are further symptoms of that same alienation. Our blindness to the point of primitive modes of life is a corollary of the pointlessness of much of our own life.

I have now explicitly linked my discussion of the "point" of a system of conventions with conceptions of good and evil. My aim is not to engage in moralizing, but to suggest that the concept of *learning from* which is involved in the study of other cultures is closely linked with the concept of *wisdom.* We are confronted not just with different techniques, but with new possibilities of good and evil, in relation to which men may come to terms with life. An investigation into this dimension of a society may indeed require a quite detailed inquiry into alternative techniques (e.g. of production), but an inquiry conducted for the light it throws on those possibilities of good and evil. A very good example of the kind of thing I mean is Simone Weil's analysis of the technique of modern factory production in *Oppression and Liberty,* which is not a contribution to business management, but part of an inquiry into the peculiar form which the evil of oppression takes in our culture.

In saying this, however, I may seem merely to have lifted to a new level the difficulty raised by MacIntyre of how to relate our own conceptions of rationality to those of other societies. Here the difficulty concerns the relation between our own conceptions of good and evil and those of other societies. A full investigation would thus require a discussion of ethical relativism at this point. I have tried to show some of the limitations of relativism in an earlier paper.[37] I shall close the present essay with some remarks which are supplementary to that.

I wish to point out that the very conception of human life involves certain fundamental notions—which I shall call "limiting notions"—which have an obvious ethical dimension, and which indeed in a sense determine the "ethical space" within which the possibilities of good and evil in human life can be exercised. The notions which I shall discuss very briefly here correspond closely to those which Vico made the foundation of his idea of natural law, on which he thought the possibility of understanding human history rested: birth, death, sexual relations. Their significance here is that they are inescapably involved in the life of all known human societies in a way which gives us a clue where to look, if we are puzzled about the point of an alien system of institutions. The specific forms which these concepts take, the particular institutions in which they are expressed, vary very considerably from one society to another; but their central position within a society's institutions is and must be a constant factor. In trying to understand the life of an alien society, then, it will be of the utmost importance to be clear about the way in which these notions enter into it. The actual practice of social anthropologists bears this out, although I do not know how many of them would attach the same kind of importance to them as I do.

I speak of a "limit" here because these notions, along no doubt with others, give shape to what we understand by "human life;" and because a concern with questions posed in terms of them seems to me constitutive of what we understand by the "morality" of a society. In saying this, I am of course, disagreeing with those moral philosophers who have made attitudes of approval and disapproval, or something similar, fundamental in ethics, and who have held that the *objects* of such attitudes were conceptually irrelevant to the conception of morality. On that view, there might be a society where the sorts of attitude taken up in *our* society to questions about relations between the sexes were reserved, say, for questions about the length people wear their hair, and *vice versa.* This seems to me incoherent. In the first place, there would be a confusion in *calling* a

---

[37] Peter Winch, "Nature and Convention," *Proceedings of the Aristotelian Society,* vol. 20, 1960, pp. 231–52.

concern of that sort a "moral" concern, however passionately felt. The story of Samson in the Old Testament confirms rather than refutes this point, for the interdict on the cutting of Samson's hair is, of course, connected there with much else: and pre-eminently, it should be noted, with questions about sexual relations. But secondly, if that is thought to be merely verbal quibbling, I will say that it does not seem to me a merely conventional matter that T. S. Eliot's trinity of "birth, copulation and death" happen to be such deep objects of human concern. I do not mean that they are made such by fundamental psychological and sociological forces, though that is no doubt true. But I want to say further that the very notion of human life is limited by these conceptions.

Unlike beasts, men do not merely live but also have a conception of life. This is not something that is simply added to their life; rather, it changes the very sense which the word "life" has, when applied to men. It is no longer equivalent to "animate existence." When we are speaking of the life of man, we can ask questions about what is the right way to live, what things are most important in life, whether life has any significance, and if so, what.

To have a conception of life is also to have a conception of death. But just as the "life" that is here in question is not the same as animate existence, so the "death" that is here in question is not the same as the end of animate existence. My conception of the death of an animal is of an event that will take place in the world; perhaps I shall observe it—and my life will go on. But when I speak of "my death," I am not speaking of a future event in my life;[38] I am not even speaking of an event in anyone else's life. I am speaking of the cessation of my world. That is also a cessation of my ability to do good or evil. It is not just that *as a matter fact* I shall no longer be able to do good or evil after I am dead; the point is that my very *concept* of what it is to be able to do good or evil is deeply bound up with my concept of my life as ending in death. If ethics is a concern with the right way to live, then clearly the nature of this concern must be deeply affected by the concept of life as ending in death. One's attitude to one's life is at the same time an attitude to one's death.

This point is very well illustrated in an anthropological datum which MacIntyre confesses himself unable to make any sense of.

---

[38] Cf. Wittgenstein, *Tractatus Logico-Philosophicus*, 6.431–6.4311.

> According to Spencer and Gillen some aborigines carry about a stick or stone which is treated *as if* it is or embodies the soul of the individual who carries it. If the stick or stone is lost, the individual anoints himself as the dead are anointed. Does the concept of 'carrying one's soul about with one' make sense? Of course we can redescribe what the aborigines are doing and transform it into sense, and perhaps Spencer and Gillen (and Durkheim who follows them) misdescribe what occurs. But if their reports are not erroneous, we confront a blank wall here, so far as meaning is concerned, although it is easy to give the rules for the use of the concept.[39]

MacIntyre does not say why he regards the concept of carrying one's soul about with one in a stick "thoroughly incoherent." He is presumably influenced by the fact that it would be hard to make sense of an action like this if performed by a twentieth-century Englishman or American; and by the fact that the soul is not a material object like a piece of paper and cannot, therefore, be carried about in a stick as a piece of paper might be. But it does not seem to me as hard to see sense in the practice, even from the little we are told about it here. Consider that a lover in our society may carry about a picture or lock of hair of the beloved; that this may symbolize for him his relation to the beloved and may, indeed, change the relation in all sorts of ways: for example strengthening it or perverting it. Suppose that when the lover loses the locket he feels guilty and asks his beloved for her forgiveness: there might be a parallel here to the aboriginal's practice of anointing himself when he "loses his soul." And is there necessarily anything irrational about either of these practices? Why should the lover not regard his carelessness in losing the locket as a sort of betrayal of the beloved? Remember how husbands and wives may feel about the loss of a wedding ring. The aborigine is clearly expressing a concern with his life as a whole in this practice; the anointing shows the close connection between such a concern and contemplation of death. Perhaps it is precisely this practice which makes such a concern possible for him, as religious sacraments make certain sorts of concern possible. The point is that a concern with one's life as a whole, involving as it does the limiting conception of one's death, if it is to be expressed *within* a person's life, can necessarily only be

---

39 *Is Understanding Religion Compatible with Believing?* Above, p. 68.

expressed quasi-sacramentally. The form of the concern shows itself in the form of the sacrament.

The sense in which I spoke also of sex as a "limiting concept" again has to do with the concept of a human life. The life of a man is a man's life and the life of a woman is a woman's life: the masculinity or the femininity are not just *components* in the life, they are its *mode.* Adapting Wittgenstein's remark about death, I might say that my masculinity is not an experience in the world, but my way of experiencing the world. Now the concepts of masculinity and femininity obviously require each other. A man is a man in relation to women; and a woman is a woman in relation to men.[40] Thus the form taken by man's relation to women is of quite fundamental importance for the significance he can attach to his own life. The vulgar identification of morality with sexual morality certainly is vulgar; but it is a vulgarization of an important truth.

The limiting character of the concept of birth is obviously related to the points I have sketched regarding death and sex. On the one hand, my birth is no more an event in my life than is my death; and through my birth ethical limits are set for my life quite independently of my will: I am, from the outset, in specific relations to other people, from which obligations spring which cannot but be ethically fundamental.[41] On the other hand, the concept of birth is fundamentally linked to that of relations between the sexes. This remains true, however much or little may be known in a society about the contribution of males and females to procreation; for it remains true that man is born of woman, not of man. This, then, adds a new dimension to the ethical institutions in which relations between the sexes are expressed.

I have tried to do no more, in these last brief remarks, than to focus attention in a certain direction. I have wanted to indicate that forms of those limiting concepts will necessarily be an important feature of human society and that conceptions of good and evil in human life will necessarily be connected with such concepts. In any attempt to understand the life of another society, therefore, an

---

[40] These relations, however, are not simple converses. See Georg Simmel, "Das Relative und das Absolute im Geschlechter-Problem" in *Philosophische Kultur,* Leipzig, 1911.

[41] For this reason, among others, I think A. I. Melden is wrong to say that present-child obligations and rights have nothing directly to do with physical genealogy. Cf. Melden, *Rights and Right Conduct.* Oxford: Blackwell, 1959.

investigation of the forms taken by such concepts—their role in the life of the society—must always take a central place and provide a basis on which understanding may be built.

> Now since the world of nations has been made by men, let us see in what institutions men agree and always have agreed. For these institutions will be able to give us the universal and eternal principles (such as every science must have) on which all nations were founded and still preserve themselves.
>
> We observe that all nations, barbarous as well as civilized, though separately founded because remote from each other in time and space, keep these three human customs: all have some religion, all contract solemn marriages, all bury their dead. And in no nation, however savage and crude, are any human actions performed with more elaborate ceremonies and more sacred solemnity than the rites of religion, marriage and burial. For by the axiom that 'uniform ideas, born among peoples unknown to each other, must have a common ground of truth,' it must have been dictated to all nations that from these institutions humanity began among them all, and therefore they must be most devoutly guarded by them all, so that the world should not again become a bestial wilderness. For this reason we have taken those three eternal and universal customs as the first principles of this Science.[42]

---

[42] Giambattista Vico, *The New Science*, paras. 332–333.

14

Professor Winch on Safari

Robin Horton

Introduction

One of the most widely cited of recent writings on the borderland of philosophy and anthropology is Peter Winch's "Understanding a Primitive Society" (referred to hereafter as *UPS*).[1] The main reason for the breadth of its appeal would seem to be a blend of general principle and particular application all too seldom found in the writings of philosophers of social science. Thus, on the one hand Winch develops further some of the general principles of cross-cultural understanding which he first enunciated in his *Idea of a Social Science* (referred to hereafter as *ISS*).[2] And, on the other hand, he attempts to show us, in considerable detail, how these principles can be applied to the solution of a particularly vexing anthropological problem: that of interpreting "primitive" mystical thought.

Now many reputable philosophers have produced critical articles on Winch's general principles of intra- and cross-cultural understanding.[3] And I have nothing very startling to add to what

[1] Winch, P., Understanding a Primitive Society, *American Philosophical Quarterly*, I (1964), 307–324. Reprinted in Wilson, B. (ed.), *Rationality* (Oxford 1970). (Page references are to the reprinted version.)

[2] Winch, P., *The Idea of a Social Science* (London 1958).

[3] Amongst the more interesting of these are: Gellner, E., The New Idealism: cause and meaning in the social sciences, in Lakatos, I., and Musgrave, A. (eds.), *Problems in the Philosophy of Science* (Amsterdam 1968); Jarvie, I., *Concepts and Society* (London 1972) (See especially ch. 11: Understanding and explaining in the social sciences); Kekes, J., Towards a Theory of Rationality, *Philosophy of Social Sciences*, III (1973) 275–288; Lukes, S., Some Problems about Rationality, *European Journal of Sociology*, VIII (1967), 247–264; Mounce, H., Understanding a Primitive Society, *Philosophy*, XLVIII (1973), 347–362; MacIntyre, A., A Mistake about

they have said about these principles. So, at this level, I shall simply make a few brief remarks to show where I stand. In the course of their critiques, several of these philosophers have also looked in passing at Winch's purported application of his principles to the particular problem of mystical thinking. It seems to me, however, that by and large they have not looked closely enough, either at the ethnographic sources from which he claims to derive his inspiration, or at the arguments by which he moves from his sources to his conclusions. It is at this level, then, that I wish to deliver the main thrust of my own criticism.

Winch's General Principles

The basic thesis of *UPS* is a simple one. It is that, in order to understand the utterances of members of an alien culture, one must always seek, in the first instance, to discover the point which such utterances have *for them.* To discover this point, we must set these utterances as fully as possible in the context of social life within which they arise.[4] Only when we have done this shall we be in a position to say which utterances associated with our own conceptual system are the appropriate translation instruments. Further, in the search for translation instruments, we must be as open-minded as possible. We must not exclude in advance any of the various universes of discourse available to us.[5] Nor must we exclude the possibility that *none* of them may be suitable.[6]

Given this view of the anthropological enterprise, the great pitfall, ever-present and ever-to-be-avoided, is the temptation to try and project on to an alien culture a point or purpose which looms very large in our own minds, but which may feature peripherally or not at all in the minds of those whose life and thought we are trying to understand. For the twentieth-century Western anthropologist, the

---

Causality in the Social Sciences, in Laslett, P., and Runciman, W., (eds.), *Philosophy, Politics and Society* (Oxford 1963) vol. II; MacIntyre, A., The Idea of a Social Science, *Aristotelian Society Supplement*, XLI (1967), pp. 95–114.

[4] *UPS* pp. 78–95.

[5] *UPS* p. 102.

[6] Although Winch does not explicitly state this extreme possibility, some of his more gnomic remarks, like "our idea of what belongs to the realm of reality is given for us in the language we use" and "logicals between propositions depend on social relations between men," have led to more than one commentator to read him in this sense. See for instance Lukes, *op. cit.* (1976).

temptation, specifically, is to try and project a preoccupation with explanation, prediction and control which is central to the sciences and to technology, but which may have little or no importance in the life of many non-Western peoples.[7]

Most readers will find this argument persuasive. It does, however, create a problem as large as those it solves. Thus, on the one hand, it raises the possibility that members of different cultures may pursue totally disparate goals, and that their utterances may have totally disparate points. On the other hand, however, it stresses that the process of understanding is not complete until the anthropologist has specified the kind of utterance in his own culture that has the same point as the alien utterances he is trying to make sense of. To his credit, Winch sees the problem; and at the end of *UPS* he suggests a solution. He suggests that men in every culture confront the same "limiting situations" of birth, sexual relations and death; and that from this confrontation arise certain universal attitudes emotions and aims. These form a kind of inter-cultural bridge that permit translation and so makes possible the completion of the process of understanding.[8]

There is much shrewd sense in all of this. Winch conveys very vividly the delicate balance required for the successful pursuit of translational understanding: a balance between, on the one hand, the need to avoid projecting one's own aims and purposes into a situation where they have little or no relevance; and, on the other hand, the need to find *some* area of discourse in one's own culture which has the same point as the area of alien discourse one is trying to make sense of. He also conveys the related and equally important message that there are two great prerequisites for this kind of understanding. One is the need for prolonged and sympathetic participant observation conducted through the language of those whose thought one is trying to understand. The other is the need for the scholar involved to have mastery of the greatest possible variety of kinds of discourse in his own culture. Now although the first prerequisite is emphasized by nearly all writers on this topic, the second is all too often neglected. And Winch's exposition has the virtue of reminding us that the two are equally vital.

---

[7] *UPS* pp. 93, 102, 106.

[8] *UPS* pp. 107–111.

These favourable comments must, however, be balanced by some criticism. First of all, it seems clear that there is potentially much more to anthropological understanding than Winch would allow. For although the procedure he recommends seems indeed to constitute the vital first phase of comprehension, we have every reason to think that there are further possible phases. Here, let us look again at one of the problems which he raises in passing: the problem constituted by the fact that certain aims or purposes may provide the point of a vast corpus of utterances in one culture, yet be of purely peripheral importance in another. For Winch, such a situation is significant only as a potential pitfall for the anthropologist in quest of translational understanding. In itself, it does not call for a further and different act of understanding. For many of us, however, it is at precisely this point that the most intriguing questions arise. Of course, it may be possible to answer them within a Winchian framework: as when we discover that apparently disparate patterns of purpose are merely the products of differing environmental circumstances that force people to pursue the same ultimate end by differing means. In other instances, however, we are likely to be confronted with patterns of purpose that are irreducibly different in their emphases. And if we wish to further our understanding in these cases, we shall be unable to avoid bringing in the kind of causal analysis for which Winch leaves no place.

One might be tempted to rest the critique at this point. But to do so would be a mistake. For the difficulty is not just that Winch's idea of translational understanding represents only the first phase of a multiphase interpretative process. The idea itself suffers from serious internal defects and incompletenesses.

To start with, Winch holds an unduly restricted view of the situational and motivational common ground which makes translational understanding possible. In taking birth, sexual relations and death as the locus of universal human strivings and purposes, he will be well received by those who prefer to think of man as poetic and religious rather than coldly pragmatic in his essence; for these are precisely the situations which, in Western culture at least, favour *homo poetico-religiosus* as against *homo scientifico-technologicus*. However, if we discount the warm glow which his writing on these matters produces, and think through the topic more coolly, we shall surely find his view of the range of universal human strivings inadequate. What, for instance, of the strivings to satisfy hunger and thirst? Of the strivings to avoid extremes of heat and cold? Of the striving for power? Geared as they are to biological needs, these and many other unromantic and unremarkable strivings are common to all human beings in all ages and places. For all the persuasive warmth of Winch's writing on these things, scholars such as Malinowski, Piddington and Goldschmidt, with their dull sociological prose and their long shopping-lists of universal strivings, may well be better guides.[9] Once we accept one of these longer inventories, moreover, the translational bridge becomes much wider and more impressive than the one Winch offers.

However, whether we accept Winch's restricted list of situational and motivational universals, or whether we accept one of the longer lists, a major problem still remains. For though we can see, intuitively, that the broader the motivational common ground, the easier it will be to understand the thought and discourse of another culture, we still have to spell out just *how* we can move from what others share with us to what they do not share with us. And it is at the very point where we are led to hope that Winch will give some account of this process, that he signs off.

Here, perhaps, one can come to the rescue by spelling out the implications for this process of certain other things he says. Typically, a universal human striving derives its universality from the fact that it is geared to a biological need. But although this need may well be one which man shares with other, non-human species, the purposive striving to which it gives rise in the human case is something associated with a completely distinctive mode of behaviour. Notably, as Winch points out, man pursues his aims in a cooperation with his fellows which is mediated by language, and which involves planning, foresight and the following of rules.[10] Now, although he has laid considerable stress on this point, he has not followed through to its full implications. As several other philosophers have shown in recent years, cooperative endeavour of this kind would be impossible without something like our everyday Western conception of material objects which exist and persist independently of

---

[9] Malinowski, B., *A Scientific Theory of Culture* (Chapel Hill 1944); Piddington, R., Malinowski's Theory of Needs, in Firth, R., *Man and Culture* (London 1957); Goldschmidt, W., *Comparative Functionalism* (Berkeley 1966).

[10] *ISS* pp. 40–65.

ourselves; without something like our everyday spatial and temporal concepts; without something like our everyday differentiation between persons and non-persons; without something like our everyday notion of causality; without something like our everyday idea of and attitude to contradiction; without something like our everyday concepts of truth, falsity and agreement with reality.[11]

Now in much of Winch's exposition, this whole apparatus of interlinked concepts and attitudes seems to be treated as a purely Western quirk. But if what these other philosophers have said is correct, it provides the crucial infra-structure for all the more specialized "universes of discourse" and "forms of life" in all cultures.

There is one very obvious sense in which this must be so. In so far as this conceptual apparatus is a prerequisite, not only for the very business of staying alive, but also for the sheer possibility of assembling at given times and places, it is clearly crucial to the viability of more specialized "forms of life" such as the religious, the artistic and the scientific. But to say no more than this would be to say nothing further about the possibility of understanding these special forms. For even if one grants that the universal conceptual infra-structure is essential to a live human quorum, and that a live human quorum is essential to any "form of life," however specialized, one still has to accept the possibility that this infra-structure may not help us to understand the special kind of discourse which goes with the "form of life." To give an example, it is certainly the universal infra-structure that ensures a live quorum for periodic church services. But it by no means follows that the infra-structure will help us to understand what people think and say once they are assembled in church.

In fact, however, I think there is a second and more relevant sense in which the universal conceptual apparatus provides an infra-structure for these more specialized "forms of life." It begins to look more and more as though this apparatus provides the raw material from which all the more specialized "universes of discourse" are built up. Thus, as I suggested in a recent essay, a great deal of light can be

---

[11] On this, see: Hampshire, S., *Thought and Action* (London 1959); Joske, W., *Material Objects* (London 1967); Lukes, S., *op. cit.* (1967); Lukes, S., On the Social Determination of Truth, in Horton, R., and Finnegan, R., (eds), *Modes of Thought* (London 1973); Strawson, P., *Individuals* (London 1959); Strawson, P., *The Bounds of Sense* (London 1966); Zinkernagel, P., *Conditions for Description* (London 1962).

thrown on the more esoteric features of *both* modern Western Christianity and modern Western Science (not to speak of traditional African religion), if we accept that the universes of discourse associated with both these special forms of life have been built up very largely by an extension (and in many places an over-extension) of the concepts of everyday material-object language.[12] Now this suggestion, if valid, is clearly relevant to the solution of our problem. For, if all the more specialized universes of discourse in all cultures are in large measure the products of secondary adaptation of the concepts of a universal material-object language, the problem of how to pass from what is shared to what is idiosyncratic largely evaporates.

So much for Winch's general principles of translational understanding. As I hope will be clear, the critique offered above is a limited one. I have accepted Winch's basic thesis, and have concentrated largely on the business of clarification and development.

Now, however, it is time to turn from qualified approval to unqualified disapproval.

The Problem of Mystical Thinking

Winch's particular application of his general principles is to the understanding of what anthropologists commonly call mystical thinking: i.e. thinking which involves unobservable entities of a spiritualistic kind, such as gods and witchcraft emanations. As his test case, he takes the thought and discourse of the Azande of the Southern Sudan. By implication, however, what he has to say about Zande mystical thinking is applicable to African and indeed to "primitive" peoples generally.[13]

The main drift of his argument is that the interpretation of "primitive" mystical thinking by Evans-Pritchard and other Western anthropologists provides a classic example of the projection, on to a vast body of alien utterances, of strivings and purposes which are centrally important in the culture of the interpreters but which have little or no importance in the minds of the utterers. Thus Evans-Pritchard and his colleagues, in interpreting mystical utterances as

---

[12] Horton, R., Paradox and Explanation: a reply to Mr. Skorupski, Parts I and II, *Philosophy of the Social Sciences*, III (1973), 231–256, 289–312.

[13] Winch does not make it very clear what he understands by "primitive." Here, I assume, he means pre-literate, pre-industrial, pre-scientific.

statements of hypotheses whose point lies in the area of explanation, prediction and control of everyday events, are simply projecting their own obsession with the goals of science and technology on to cultures where such goals are of peripheral importance. If they had made a serious effort to discover the point of such utterances for those concerned, they would have proceeded quite differently. In Winch's words:

> But I do not want to say that we are quite powerless to find ways of thinking in our own society that will help us to see the Zande institution in a clearer light. I only think that the direction in which we should look is quite different from what MacIntyre [a follower of Evans-Pritchard in this: writer] suggests. Clearly the nature of Zande life is such that it is of very great importance to them that their crops should thrive. Clearly too they take all kinds of practical "technological" steps, within their capabilities, to ensure that they do thrive. But that is no reason to see their magical rites as a further, misguided such step. A man's sense of the importance of something to him shows itself in all sorts of ways: not merely in precautions to safeguard that thing. He may want to come to terms with its importance to him in a quite different way: to contemplate it, to gain some sense of his life in relation to it. He may wish thereby, in a certain sense, to *free* himself from dependence on it. I do not mean by making sure it does not let him down, because the point is that, *whatever* he does, he may still be let down. The important thing is that he should understand *that* and come to terms with it. Of course merely to understand that is not to come to terms with it, though perhaps it is a necessary condition for so doing, for a man may equally well be transfixed and terrorized by the contemplation of such a possibility. He must see that he *can* still go on even if he is let down by what is vitally important to him; and he must so order his life that he still *can* go on in such circumstances. I stress once again that I do not mean this in the sense of becoming "technologically independent," because from the present point of view technological independence is yet another form of dependence. Technology destroys some dependencies but always creates new ones, which may be fiercer, because harder to understand, than the old. This should be particularly apparent to *us*.
>
> In Judaeo-Christian cultures the conception of "If it be Thy Will," as developed in the story of Job, is clearly central to the matter I am discussing. Because this conception is central to Christian prayers of supplication, they may be regarded from one point of view as freeing the believer from dependence on what he is supplicating for. Prayers cannot play this role if they are regarded as a means of influencing the outcome for in that case the one who prays is still dependent on the outcome. He frees himself from this

> by acknowledging his complete dependence on God; and this is totally unlike any dependence on the outcome precisely because God is eternal and the outcome contingent.
>
> I do not say that Zande magical rites are at all like Christian prayers of supplication in the positive attitude to contingencies which they express. What I do suggest is that they are alike in that they do, or may, express an attitude to contingencies; one, that is, which involves recognition that one's life is subject to contingencies, rather than an attempt to control these . . . .[14]

In short, Evans-Pritchard and his colleagues should have drawn their translation instruments, not from an area of Western discourse geared to explanation, prediction and control of events, but from an area geared to the development of an acceptance of events for better or for worse; not from the language of science and technology, but from a rather special kind of religious language.

Having pushed the line of interpretation of African mystical beliefs suggested by Evans-Pritchard's work a good deal further than Evans-Pritchard himself would have been prepared to go, I have, naturally, come to find myself in strong disagreement with Winch. And in a recent review of a collection of essays in honour of Evans-Pritchard, he in turn has castigated me for perpetuating the latter's mistake.[15]

In particular, Winch objects to the way in which I criticise "orthodox" interpreters of African religious belief for refusing to take statements of such belief at their quasi-scientistic "face value." In a slick extension of my metaphor, he points out that a banknote has a "face value" only in so far as it belongs to a definite system of currency. Hence my attempt to appeal to the "face value" of African beliefs without answering the crucial questions about what currency these beliefs belong to simply prejudges the issue. African mystical beliefs, he urges, can only be understood by someone who is willing to grant that they may belong to a currency quite other than that constituted by scientific-technological discourse.[16]

In point of fact, Winch twists my words. For in appealing to scholars to take African mystical beliefs at their "face value," I was

---

[14] *UPS* pp. 103–105.

[15] Winch, P., Savage and Modern Minds, *Times Higher Education Supplement*, 7 September 1973, p. 13.

[16] These remarks are part of a critique of my essay "Levy-Bruhl, Durkheim and the Scientific Revolution" which was published in Horton and Finnegan, *op. cit.* (1973).

appealing to them precisely to look at such beliefs in their full context of use, and not make interpretations which run counter to all the evidence as to the nature of this context.[17] A very Winchian appeal, in fact! Be this as it may, the differences between Winch and myself on the interpretation of mystical belief are real enough. In what follows, I hope to show that it is Winch, and not Evans-Pritchard, MacIntyre or myself, who is the most appropriate target for the methodological *caveats* of "Understanding a Primitive Society."

To substantiate his critique of the "scientistic" interpretation of African mystical beliefs, Winch makes extensive reference to Evans-Pritchard's classic monograph on Zande thought.[18] Since there is strong suspicion that many of those who have enrolled most enthusiastically under his banner have never in fact given Evans-Pritchard's long and demanding work a careful, cover-to-cover reading, let me start by saying something about its content.

As its title suggests, the book is an explanation of Zande concepts of the mystical influences involved in the operation of witchcraft, oracles and magic. Perhaps more than any other anthropological monograph before or since, it places mystical concepts in their full context of everyday usage. In this respect, it is a model of the kind of conceptual analysis that Winch and his disciples advocate. Yet what emerges from this exercise? Again and again, by means of anecdote and incident, Evans-Pritchard shows us mystical concepts mobilized in connection with the concern to account for and remedy present misfortune, and with the concern to predict and avoid future misfortune. He portrays the Azande as a people who struggle constantly, manfully and cheerfully to overcome their troubles in this world; a people who have little place in their thought for serene or resigned contemplation. The system of mystical belief, serving as a comprehensive apparatus for explanation, prediction and control, is the principal means whereby they are able to maintain this attitude.

In short, the great body of evidence which Evans-Pritchard presents on the social context of Zande mystical belief seems most unfavourable to Winch's interpretation. Indeed, it seems nothing less

---

[17] For my use of the phrase "face value," see Horton *op. cit.* (1973), pp. 294–295. It should be placed in the context of my remarks on pp. 276–283.

[18] Evans-Pritchard, E., *Witchcraft, Oracles and Magic among the Azande* (Oxford 1937).

than perverse of him to have made this, of all books, the evidential base for his thesis.[19]

Someone holding Winch's general view of the nature of African mystical concepts could, of course, simply say that Evans-Pritchard, during his research and writing, was so overcome by his obsession with scientific-technical discourse that it distorted even his reports of individual instances of belief behaviour and social context. If one took this position, however, one could hardly go on to use Evans-Pritchard's own material as the basis of a re-analysis—which is precisely what Winch tries to do. How in fact does he manage?

In the event, he accepts the descriptive material in Evans-Pritchard's monograph to the extent of admitting, albeit unwillingly, a strong *surface appearance* of similarity between Zande mystical beliefs and the beliefs associated with the sciences. This admission emerges at several points in his essay.

Thus, at one point, he cites the following key passage from Evans-Pritchard:

> Azande observe the action of the poison oracle as we observe it, but their observations are always subordinated to their beliefs and are incorporated into their beliefs and made to explain and justify them. Let the reader consider any argument that would utterly demolish all Zande claims for the power of the oracle. If it were translated into Zande modes of thought it would serve to support their entire structure of belief. For their mystical notions are eminently coherent, being interrelated by a network of logical ties, and are so ordered that they never too crudely contradict sensory experience but, instead, experience seems to justify them. The Zande is immersed in a sea of mystical notions, and if he speaks about his poison oracle he must speak in a mystical idiom.[20]

Not only does Winch appear to approve the cogency of this particular comment. He suggests that, by transposing the terms "Zande" and "European," "mystical" and "scientific," it is possible to construct a parody which is also a cogent comment on the nature of scientific thinking:

---

[19] Relevant passages are found virtually throughout the book. I suggest, however, that the reader in a hurry look particularly at the following: top of p. 88 to top of p. 89; top of p. 90 to halfway down p. 91; halfway down p. 148 to top of p. 149; pp. 261–266; p. 341. In using the word perverse to characterise Winch's interpretation of these and other passages, I have unwittingly followed John Skorupski. See: Skorupski, J., What is Magic? *Cambridge Review*, January 1975.

[20] Evans-Pritchard, *op. cit.* p. 319.

> Europeans observe the action of the poison oracle just as Azande observe it, but their observations are always subordinated to their beliefs and are incorporated into their beliefs and made to explain and justify them. Let a Zande consider any argument that would utterly refute all European scepticism about the power of the oracle. If it were translated into European modes of thought it would serve to support their entire structure of belief. For their scientific notions are eminently coherent, being interrelated by a network of logical ties, and are so ordered that they never too crudely contradict mystical experience but, instead, experience seems to justify them. The European is immersed in a sea of scientific notions, and if he speaks about the Zande poison oracle he must speak in a scientific idiom.[21]

Now although Winch uses this parody to criticise an aspect of Evans-Pritchard's position other than the one under discussion here,[22] his use of it constitutes a clear admission of apparent parallels between Zande mystical and European scientific thought.

Again, in trying to direct our minds to appropriate European parallels to the Zande poison oracle considered as a source of revelation about the mystical forces operating in any situation, he says:

> A Zande would be utterly lost and bewildered without his oracle. The mainstay of his life would be lacking. It is rather as if an engineer, in our own society, were asked to build a bridge without mathematical calculation, or a military commander to mount an extensive coordinated attack without the use of clocks. These analogies are mine, *but a reader may well think they beg the question at issue* [italics mine].[23]

And a little further on, in discussing the appropriate logical placing of oracular revelations, he says:

> We might say that the revelation has the logical status of an unfulfilled hypothetical *were it not that the context in which this logical*

---

[21] *UPS* p. 89.

[22] Winch uses this parody in the course of criticizing Evans-Pritchard for evaluating Zande mystical beliefs in terms of their truth or falsity as judged by the criteria of comtemporary Western science. Since my particular interest in the present paper has been in other issues, I have by-passed this one. Suffice it to say here that my own view is (a) that, for obvious reasons, it is unfruitful, as an initial move, for the sociologist of thought to classify particular beliefs in terms of their having truth or falsity; but (b) that having classified such beliefs in terms of other criteria, it is perfectly legitimate to go on and ask whether, as a matter of fact, they are true or false.

[23] *UPS* p. 87.

> *term is used may again suggest a misleadingly close analogy with scientific hypotheses* [Italics mine].[24]

In both these passages, we see him tempted by Evans-Pritchard's descriptions into drawing parallels between Zande mystical discourse and the area of European discourse geared to the ends of explanation, prediction and control. In the italicized portions of both passages, we also see him pulling himself up short, in embarrassed realization that his arguments are on the verge of providing ammunition for his opponents" fire!

Like Evans-Pritchard, MacIntyre and myself, then, Winch certainly thinks that Zande mystical notions *look* in many ways like Western scientific/technical notions. Unlike us, however, he thinks that the appearances are deceptive.

Now if two parties agree on appearances, but one of them maintains that the appearances are deceptive, the burden of argument falls upon the sceptic. In this instance, Winch is the sceptic; so let us see how he copes with the burden. In fact, he produces three arguments designed to show that "things are not what they seem." One apparently plausible argument is to be found in the following passage:

> The chief function of oracles is to reveal the presence of mystical forces—I use Evans-Pritchard's term without committing myself to his denial that such forces really exist. Now although there are indeed many ways of determining whether or not mystical forces are operating, these ways do not correspond to what we call "empirical" confirmation or refutation. This indeed is a tautology, since such differences in confirmatory procedures are the main criteria for classifying something as a mystical force in the first place. Here we have one reason why the possibilities of "refutation by experience" are much fewer than might at first sight be supposed. There is another closely connected reason. The spirit in which oracles are consulted is very unlike that in which a scientist makes experiments. Oracular revelations are not treated as hypotheses and, since their sense derives from the way they are treated in their context, they therefore *are not* hypotheses. They are not a matter of intellectual interest but the main way in which Azande decide how they should act. If the oracle reveals that a proposed course of action is fraught with mystical dangers from witchcraft or sorcery, that action will not be carried out; and then the question of refutation or confirmation just does not arise.[25]

---

[24] *UPS* p. 88.

[25] *UPS* p. 88.

What Winch seems to be getting at here is that Zande beliefs do not take account of experience in anything like the way theoretical beliefs in the sciences do, and that they must therefore belong to an entirely different universe of discourse.

Now it would be silly to deny that, in this respect, there *are* differences between Zande mystical beliefs and Western scientific beliefs. But, as we shall see, the differences are more subtle than dramatic; more of degree than of kind. And, such as they are, they do nothing to help Winch prove his basic point.

Let us proceed by taking successively stronger senses of "taking account of experience," and try to see at what point we can use this criterion to separate one set of beliefs from the other.

If we start with the broadest and weakest sense of the phrase, we find it impossible to separate the two. Thus, as Evans-Pritchard makes clear at so many points in his book, Azande do not waste time in disinterested speculation about what sort of thing witchcraft emanation is in itself. Rather, they are interested in the observable preconditions and the observable consequences of its coming into play. They are interested, not in what it is in itself, but in what it does in the observable world.[26] In this sense, their attitude to witchcraft influence, like that of scientists to their unobservable entities, is highly empirical, indeed highly "operational."[27]

Again, despite what Winch says, there are many occasions when, during the course of their everyday lives, Azande do put the predicted experiential consequences of their mystical beliefs to the test: as for instance when the oracle has told them that measures taken have cleared mystical obstacles from their path, and that they are therefore free to go ahead with projected plans. On such occasions, they are anything but indifferent to the relation between the predictions generated by their beliefs and subsequent experience. If such predictions are confirmed by experience, they point to this fact with satisfaction as evidence for the correctness of the original oracular revelation and for the efficacy of the oracle poison. If the predictions are refuted, they worriedly look for reasons: e.g. sorcerers

---

[26] Evans-Pritchard, *op. cit.* pp. 21–49, 63–84.

[27] "Operationalism" in the sciences is the doctrine that an entity must be defined solely in terms of the human operations associated with assertions about it.

interfering with the revelation or spoiled oracle poison.[28] Here again, we are still in a world not notably different from that of the scientist.

It may even be that Azande, in their mystical beliefs, have taken account of experience in a yet stronger sense. As I have pointed out elsewhere, some of the correlations suggested by these beliefs, especially those between social disturbance and disease, are by no means as fanciful as they may have seemed at the time when Evans-Pritchard was writing his monograph. Indeed, for a relatively non-mobile population faced with a fairly constant stock of diseases and thus having the fortune to acquire over time a moderate resistance to what might otherwise have been killer organisms, the Zande theory of disease may well have highlighted just those correlations which *were* crucial to death or recovery in a significant number of cases. Limited to a similar range of evidence, medical scientists might have come to strikingly similar conclusions.[29]

Winch, however, may well have in mind a stronger and more Popperian sense of "taking account of experience" than any we have yet considered: a sense which carries connotations of thoroughgoing scepticism about established beliefs, and readiness for radical revolution in the face of adverse experience.

Now if we use the phrase in this sense, Azande certainly do not come up to scratch. For instance, where predictions generated by the central core of mystical beliefs are refuted by experience, they do not, under any circumstances, respond by rejection of this core. Rather, they produce *ad hoc* secondary elaborations, which account for the refutation of the predictions whilst leaving the core intact.[30] This lack of tentativeness or scepticism *vis-à-vis* core beliefs is, presumably, what Winch is thinking of when he says that, for Azande, such beliefs are not hypotheses.

Popper, of course, would say that a readiness to reject core beliefs in the face of adverse experience was precisely what distinguished scientists from other kinds of thinkers, Azande included. In recent years, however, this way of distinguishing scientists from others has been seriously called in question. Michael Polanyi, one of the first to challenge it, actually used Zande reactions to refutation of

[28] This point is well made by Mounce, *op. cit.* (1973).

[29] On this, see: Horton, R., African Traditional Thought and Western Science, Part I, *Africa*, XXXVII (1967), pp. 54–58.

[30] Evans-Pritchard, *op. cit. passim.*

their predictions by experience as an illustration of the way in which scientists react to similar challenges.[31] Thomas Kuhn, a more recent and more widely-known challenger, has suggested that, during long periods of "normal science," when people are primarily concerned to follow up the detailed implications of a core of established theory, particular failures of prediction evoke a response which differ little from that of Azande placed in similar circumstances. Only when failures begin to come thick and fast does some sense of unease arise, and a search for alternative theoretical cores begin. And only when a new core has been formulated and has begun to show promise do members of a discipline begin to react to the established core in the tentative, sceptical manner recommended by Popper.[32] Yet more recent commentators, notably Paul Feyerabend and the late Imre Lakatos, have repudiated Kuhn's "one-at-a-time" picture as failing to do justice to the historical facts. In its place, they sketch a scene of institutionalized competition between different theoretical schools, each by its criticisms stimulating the other to greater feats of theoretical development and systematization. Even in this sort of characterization, however, the adherents of a particular school are portrayed as reacting to failures of prediction very much as Azande do.[33]

There are whole books to be written on this debate, of course; and here it is necessary to get on to other things. For the moment, suffice it to say that, in their eagerness to correct what they see as Popper's caricature of the scientific enterprise, these more recent commentators have tended to produce caricature at the opposite extreme. My own feeling is that there will eventually be a synthesis; and that it will be one which keeps in mind the overriding requirement of the scientific enterprise, that one theory only be succeeded by another when the latter has provided overwhelming evidence of greater explanatory potential. If this is indeed the ultimate goal of scientific institutions, it means that they must provide places for two very different types of scholar. On the one hand, they must provide for the Kuhnian conservative who will

---

[31] Polanyi, M., *Personal Knowledge* (Chicago 1958), pp. 286–294.

[32] Kuhn, T., *The Structure of Scientific Revolutions* (Chicago 1962).

[33] On this, see: Lakatos, I., Methodology of Scientific Research Programmes, and Feyerabend, P., Consolations for the Specialist; both in Lakatos, I. and Musgrave, A., (eds.), *Criticism and the Growth of Knowledge* (Cambridge 1970).

make sure that an established theory is not abandoned until the last drop of explanatory potential is squeezed out of it. On the other hand, they must provide for the Popperian iconoclastic innovator who will make sure, not only that the established theory is subjected to constant destructive criticism, but also that there will always be an embryo new theory around ready for development in its place. As to how the balance is to be struck between these different intellectual types perhaps there can be no single answer. But struck it surely must be.

One implication of this recent work in the philosophy, history and sociology of science is that it is much more difficult than Winch would have us believe to differentiate the Zande mystical thinker from the Western scientific thinker on the grounds that the former is not at all concerned with empirical confirmation and refutation, whilst the latter is centrally concerned with such things. Having said this, however, let us go some of the way with Winch. Let us grant that a certain overriding willingness to make radical revisions of core beliefs in the face of adverse experience is largely absent from the Zande scene but is a pervasive feature of the Western scientific scene, and that this does represent a very significant difference between the two types of thought we are trying to compare.

Having gone so far with him, however one still has to ask, what does this finding do to help him prove his basic point? To which the answer, I fear, is: nothing! Remember that, in this essay, he is concerned above all to show that the whole complex of Zande mystical thinking is geared, not to the ends of explanation, prediction and control, but to the entirely different end of achieving resigned contemplation of the vicissitudes of life. But the essence of his first argument is nothing more than an inference, from the premise that the Zande mystical thinker is unwilling to make radical revisions of his core beliefs in the face of adverse experience, to the conclusion that the point of such beliefs cannot be explanation, prediction and control. And this inference, of course, is a *non sequitur.*

This last remark brings me to my final objection to Winch's first argument. It is that, even if we accept his differentiation between the Zande mystical thinker and the Western scientific thinker on the grounds that the former is not "open" to experience whilst the latter is, we can still only accept it as applicable to the Zande mystical thinker and the Western *research scientist.* For, as Winch himself would be the first to admit, the world of modern science comprises not only the research man who is concerned with the testing and development of theory, but also the scientific technologist who puts well-established theory into practice. And the latter is trained above all to accept established theory in an unquestioning spirit, the better to ensure that he will act decisively when he comes to more oractical use of it. In consequence, all of Winch's remarks about the Zande mystical thinker's attitude to experience are equally applicable to the scientific technologist. He too treats his theory as an article of faith, not as a hypotheses. He too avoids trying out any course of action which his theory says would be practically disastrous. He too greets any disappointment of theory-based prediction with *ad hoc* excuses which account for the disappointment whilst leaving the core of the theory intact—excuses about probable carelessness of operators, faults in instruments and impurities in materials. In short, the scientific technologist, "closed" to adverse experience yet plainly dedicated to the linked ends of explanation, prediction and control, is a living pointer to the spuriousness of the inference on which the first argument of UPS depends.

Let us turn now to Winch's second argument. This one is based on the presence, at the heart of Zande mystical belief, of what looks to the Western observer like unresolved inconsistencies and even outright contradictions. In particular, Winch points to the fact that, whilst certain aspects of Zande doctrine about witchcraft influence stress its hereditary character, others deny any such character. Winch quotes with approval Evans-Pritchard's own comment on this situation:

> Azande do not perceive the contradiction as we perceive it because they have no theoretical interest in the subject, and those situations in which they express their belief in witchcraft do not force the problem upon them.[34]

And he concludes:

> This suggests strongly that the context from which the suggestion about the contradiction is made, the context of our scientific culture, is not on the same level as the context in which the beliefs about witchcraft operate. Zande notions of witchcraft do not constitute a theoretical system in terms of which Azande try to gain a quasi-scientific understanding of the world. This in its turn suggests that it is the European, obsessed with pressing Zande thought where it would not naturally go—to a contradiction—who

[34] Evans-Pritchard, *op. cit.* p. 25.

> is guilty of misunderstanding, not the Zande. The European is in fact committing a category-mistake.[35]

There are several things seriously wrong with this argument.

To start with, it is not entirely clear from the text that Azande *are* completely indifferent to this apparent contradiction within their corpus of mystical belief. It is true that Evans-Pritchard implies this in someplaces. In others, however, he suggests that Azande are sometimes brought face-to-face with the contradiction, and that, when this happens, they use various intellectual devices to help themselves escape from it. For example, he says relatives of a proven witch may accept the thesis of the hereditary nature of witchcraft, yet vigorously deny that they themselves are witches. He also says that, in such situations, they attempt to escape from the contradiction by suggesting that the witch in question was a bastard rather than true relative.[36]

Again, Winch makes a tendentious use of Evans-Pritchard's comment that Azande do not perceive the contradiction "because they have no theoretical interest in it." For although he uses this comment in an attempt to persuade us that Zande mystical notions "do not constitute a theoretical system in terms of which Azande try to gain a quasi-scientific understanding of the world" it is clear that Evans-Pritchard himself neither intends such a conclusion nor makes the comment in a sense that would justify it. Thus, earlier in his monograph, he says:

> The concept of witchcraft nevertheless provides them [the Azande] with a *natural philosophy* by which the relations between men and unfortunate events are *explained* and a ready and stereotyped means of reacting to such events [Italics mine].[37]

And the immediate context of his comment on "no theoretical interest" makes it clear that what he is trying to say at this juncture is simply that Azande have an "applied" rather than a "pure" interest in the subject of witchcraft.

In any case, whatever Evans-Pritchard says or does not say, just what is the inference involved here? It is an inference from the premise that people are not bothered by apparent contradictions in their beliefs to the conclusion that these beliefs cannot be connected

---

[35] *UPS* p. 93.

[36] Evans-Pritchard, *op. cit.* p. 25.

[37] Evans-Pritchard, *op. cit.* p. 63.

with the ends of explanation, prediction and control. And this seems as much of a *non sequitur* as the inference which was at the bottom of Winch's first argument.

Once again, this point gains additional weight when we turn to look at attitudes in the sciences. For we find that the body of theoretical propositions accepted by members of a particular scientific discipline at a given time is seldom free from patches of contradiction and inconsistency. However, even the research scientist tends to tolerate these patches, albeit uneasily so long as current theory still seems to be generating interesting predictions and so long as no more promising theoretical alternative is in sight. One might even suggest that, the more the overall promise of a theory in the realm of explanation and prediction, the more tolerant the scientist is of apparent contradictions within it. Strong support for this thesis could be derived from the history of quantum physics.[38] Here again, then, the scientist provides a living pointer to the spuriousness of Winch's inference.

Winch's third argument is based on the alleged difference between the Zande mystical concept of influence and the Western scientific concept of causality. On this, he says:

> There is no reason to suppose that the Zande magical concept of "*A* affecting *B*" has anything like the same significance [as the Western scientific/technological concept]. On the contrary, since the Azande do, in the course of their practical affairs, apply something very like our technical concept—though perhaps in a more primitive form—and since their attitude to and thought about their magical rites are quite different from those concerning their technological measures, there is every reason to think that their concept of magical "influences" is quite different[. . .].[39]

This argument is as flimsy as its predecessors. In the first place, Evans-Pritchard makes it abundantly clear that there is nothing "different" about Zande attitudes in situations where mystical forces are thought to be at work. Where a Zande discovers such an influence at work, he shows no special feeling of supernaturally-inspired awe. Indeed, where his aims are thwarted by such an

---

[38] On this, see the essays and discussions in Toulmin, S., (ed.), *Quanta and Reality* (London 1962); especially postscript by N. R. Hanson, pp. 85–93. See also Lakatos, I., *op. cit.* especially pp. 142–154, where he characterizes Bohr's development of early quantum theory as "progress on inconsistent foundations."

[39] *UPS* p. 103.

influence, he reacts just as he would if thwarted by some ordinary, everyday occurrence: i.e. he gets very angry.[40]

Secondly, in trying to formulate their concept of mystical influence, Azande make great play with analogies drawn from the sphere of everyday causation. Thus they compare the projection of witchcraft with the shooting of guns and bows. And they refer to witchcraft emanation itself as "the second spear." Here, clearly, they are drawing attention to the similarities between mystical influence and everyday causation.[41]

Thirdly, although Azande do in some contexts draw attention to the peculiarities of mystical influence, they do so in a manner which can bring no comfort to Winch. For they do it by comparing witchcraft with hidden goings-on like adultery.[42] And this of course is strongly reminiscent of the scientist's attempt to elucidate the peculiarities of causation at the level of unobservable entities by using the image of a "hidden mechanism."[43]

Finally, in trying to characterize the kind of situation in which mystical influence is commonly thought by Azande to come into play, Evans-Pritchard makes another point which can only be an embarrassment to Winch. As he says, it is not only in the case of witchcraft that concepts of mystical force and influence are brought into use. Such concepts are also invoked when a man makes a herbal potion with the idea of influencing some faraway person or state of affairs. Yet again, they are invoked to explain the connection between the planting of a seed and its germination some time later. What is common to these apparently diverse situations? It is the fact that, in all of them, there is a spatial and/or temporal gap between an action and its result. The idea of a mystical force, it would seem, is used to bridge this gap.[44] Once more, here is an observation which brings to mind features of Western scientific/technological thought. Amongst Western adults, as the work of Michotte has shown, there is, built into everyday thought processes, a mechanism for direct perception

---

[40] Evans-Pritchard, *op. cit.* p. 64.

[41] Evans-Pritchard, *op. cit.* pp. 37, 74.

[42] Evans-Pritchard, *op. cit.* p. 269.

[43] For the importance of this image, not only in the elucidation of theoretical activity, but perhaps even in its genesis, see my "Paradox and Explanation," esp. pp. 248–250, 303–308.

[44] Evans-Pritchard, *op. cit.* p. 25.

of causality which is at once very sensitive and very limited. Thus it picks up causal connections almost infallibly when the events involved are contiguous in space and time, but loses efficacy rapidly with the emergence of a spatial and/or temporal gap.[45] Now, as I have suggested before, the most fruitful way of looking at the role of ideas about theoretical entities in the life of Western man is to look at them as intellectual devices which supplement his ordinary mechanism of causal perception and make up for its limitations. This they do in two ways. First, they help their users to transcend the limited causal sensitivity of everyday thought, and to spotlight causal connections which such thought could never otherwise have apprehended. Secondly, they help eliminate the sense of anomaly associated with those causal connections which have been registered by everyday perception *despite* a spatial and/or temporal gap between cause and effect. This they do by asserting that the gap is only apparent, and that, at the level of unobservables, there is contiguity.[46] Just like ideas about mystical forces in Zande thought, then, ideas about unobservable entities in Western thought seem important above all in relation to those causal connexions where there is a spatial and/or temporal gap. *Pace* Winch, both sets of ideas are, in a very real sense, "stop-gaps."[47]

So much for the three arguments by means of which Winch seeks to persuade us that superficial resemblances between Zande mystical thought and Western scientific/technological thought are merely a cloak for profound differences. We have found all three to be without substance. Since Winch's interpretation of Zande mystical thought rests on these arguments and these alone, it too is equally devoid of substance.

It is clear from Winch's essay that he sees his remarks as applicable, not only to the mystical thinking of Azande, but also to

---

45 Michotte, A., *The Perception of Causality* (London 1963).

46 On this, see Toulmin, S., and Goodfield, J., *The Architecture of Matter* (London 1962), pp. 194–197; Born, M., *Natural Philosophy of Cause and Chance* (Oxford 1951), pp. 8–9, 16–17, 25–30; Born, M., *Physics in My Generation* (London 1965), pp. 21–22, 96–98.

47 Winch, *op. cit.* (1973): "But one of the points which Evans-Pritchard was at pains to emphasize in his work on the Zande was precisely that the appeal to notions of witchcraft was not used as a stop-gap or underpinning of commonsense explanations, but occurred in the context of answering *different kinds of questions.*"

that of African peoples and of "primitives" generally. It is possible, of course, that, in the Azande Winch has accidentally stumbled upon a particularly bad case for treatment; that mystical thinking amongst most African peoples, and indeed amongst most "primitives," lends itself rather better to his interpretation. This is a possibility we should at least consider before dismissing his essay altogether. Here, let me content myself with a few comments on the applicability of his thesis in other African cultures. Broadly, it would seem, in the light of the monographic material now available, that the same verdict is in order. For what comes out of this material is that mystical thinking is everywhere associated with the same dogged determination to gain control over the contingencies of life. True, there are in most African cultures sectors of life where Winch's beloved transcendence of contingency through contemplation comes to the fore: such for instance are the various arts, especially those of narrative and dance. But although there is often a good deal of overlap between those sectors of life ruled by mystical thinking and those sectors ruled by thought and purpose of a more Winchian kind, the overlap is never more than partial.[48]

In a series of articles written over the past few years, I think I have been able to show that, by accepting explanation, prediction and control as the principal end governing the development and persistence of African mystical thought, we are able to provide a coherent interpretation of a whole congeries of cultural phenomena which would otherwise have remained puzzlingly disparate.[49] Until Winch and those who think like him can produce coherent interpretations of greater explanatory power, rather than just throwing out dark hints about what might be done, they do not deserve to be taken very seriously.

I do not wish to bore readers by going over this well-worn ground again. Those unfamiliar with the literature can refer to it and judge for themselves. Instead, I shall turn now to a particular feature

---

[48] Both Evans-Pritchard and I have emphasized the need to treat various African arts *as Art*. See for instance Evans-Pritchard, E., *The Zande Trickster* (Oxford 1967); Horton, R., The Kalabari Ekine Society: a borderland of religion and art, *Africa*, XXXIII (1963), 94–114. I think Winch would find some of the methodological attitudes in the latter very close to his own.

[49] See for instance Horton, R., African Traditional Thought and Western Science; Paradox and Explanation; African Conversion, *Africa* XLI (1971), 85–108; On the Rationality of Conversion, *Africa* XLV (1975), 219–235, 373–399.

of African religious history which I believe constitutes a clear test case for the validity of our respective views.

The feature I refer to is the reaction of African peoples to Christian missionary activity. This reaction has been the subject of a mass of studies over the last few decades; and the authors of nearly all of these studies have come to the same broad conclusions. By and large, they have found a positive response to Christian teaching, and in particular to the Christian idea of the supreme being. At the same time, the most lively branches of the Christian church are those in which certain decisive forms of "Africanisation" have taken place: forms so decisively different from anything countenanced by the older churches that their creators had to found new institutions in order to perpetuate them.

In defining this "Africanisation," our authors have shown a consensus which is remarkable given the variety of theoretical, religious, cultural and moral perspectives from which they write. By and large, they agree that the key feature of the situation is the central preoccupation of African Christians with the active control of sickness and health, fortune and misfortune. It is in this respect, they suggest, that African Christian ideas show maximum continuity with the pagan religious heritage and minimum continuity with the missionary world-view.[50]

All this is crucially relevant to the debate between Winch and myself. For what has happened here is simply that African peoples have been offered a Winchian conception of religion, and have rejected it. Let me elaborate. As I said earlier, Winch is in no doubt about the area of Western discourse that will provide the most appropriate tools for the translation of African mystical beliefs. He points firmly to that strand of Western religious discourse which features God, not as a being who might help one control the vicissitudes of everyday life, but rather as a being through whom one learns to transcend any care about such vicissitudes. Defined in such terms, religion is naturally seen as having ends quite different from those associated with science and technology, and as removed from any competition with the latter.

---

[50] Amongst the more relevant studies of this phenomenon are Sundkler, B., *Bantu Prophets in South Africa* (London 1961); Pauw, B., *Religion in a Tswana Chiefdom* (London 1960); Barta, C., *Prophetism in Ghana* (London 1962); Turner, H., *African Independent Church* (Oxford 1967). 2 vols.; Peel, J., *Aladura* (London 1968).

As Winch points out, there are traces of this kind of religious thinking as far back in the Western tradition as the Book of Job. And in more recent times, it has found highly articulate exponents in such figures as Kierkegaard, Simone Weil, Bonhoeffer, Wittgenstein, D. Z. Phillips and Winch himself. But it is a kind of thinking by no means confined to theologians and philosophers. Indeed, one might say that it is central to the life of many modern Western Protestants. I for one imbibed it, if not with my mother's milk, at least all through school and university chapel.

Now it was this strand of religious thinking that was brought to Africa at the turn of the century by Christian missionaries in general and by Protestant missionaries in particular. For reasons I have discussed elsewhere,[51] the newcomers' emphasis on an active, morally-concerned supreme being was in most places thoroughly acceptable; and it was this aspect of the Christian message that drew thousands of people to churches all over the continent. Once inside, however, they found they had been misled. For they were used to a cosmos of spiritual forces whose powers could be tapped to improve man's lot in the here and now; and it soon became clear that nothing of the kind was on offer in the churches. So, before long, many of the thousands who had poured into the churches began to pour out of them again, taking away the new message of an active, morally-concerned supreme being, but using it as the basis of a comprehensive scheme for the explanation, prediction and control of events in the space-time world. Hundreds of new "spiritual" churches were founded provide the institutional framework for the resulting world-view. Today, it is these churches rather than the missionary foundations that constitute a growing-point in African religious life.

The comments of those involved show beyond all doubt what the issues at stake have been. In the Eastern Niger Delta, where I have been doing fieldwork for a number of years, puzzled enquirers assailed the early evangelists with the question: "Does your God wish us to climb up to the top of a tall palm tree, open our hands, and drop off?"[52] Many years later, when dozens of "prayer-houses" (spiritual churches) were established alongside the three missionary-

[51] Horton, *op. cit.* (1971).

[52] Rev. Wariboko Amakiri, a pioneer Kalabari evangelist, recalled this reaction vividly in a conversation I had with him not long before his death.

derived churches in the area, people summed up the differences between the two sets of institutions by saying: "The prayer-houses heal our sicknesses; the churches give safe passage to our spirits." Similar comments are reported from nearby Yorubaland. An early spiritualist, criticizing European Christians, said: "They have no definite teaching as to how to meet the circumstances of life;" and "The Englishman does not know much about the power working behind God's word."[53] Present-day members comment on the new churches in such terms as: "since I joined Cherubim and Seraphim I have always seen good things, if there is any difficulty, once you pray, it will go away. Since I have joined, I have enjoyed life;" or "If someone joins the Christ Apostolic Church, he will have rest of mind. There is no need to use medicine if you join; if you ask something from God immediately you will get the result," or again (from a timber-dealer): "Prayer relieves difficulties; whenever there is a glut in the market, I pray to relieve it; other people make medicine to help them; Christ Apostolic Church people just pray and receive God's grace."[54] The same themes recur in comments from the Ghanaian spiritual churches. Defining the differences between his own church and the missionary foundations, the leader of the Musama Disco Christo Church says: "Christ is not only a God of salvation of the soul but also a father that is prepared to meet all our needs."[55] And a catechist in the same church was heard to begin his address with: "We are all in this church because we have found healing here. But for this church the great majority of us here assembled would not be alive today."[56] In South Africa, a prophet of one of the spiritual churches told his congregation: "This is not a church, it is a hospital."[57] And again in this area, the usual answer as to why someone has joined one of the new churches is "I was ill. They prayed for me. Now I am well."[58]

These reactions to the Christian message are beautifully relevant to the present controversy. In the first place, they are the reactions of holders of mystical beliefs, not the interpretations of axe-

---

[53] Peel, *op. cit.* p. 110.

[54] Peel, *op. cit.* p. 212.

[55] Baeta, *op. cit.* pp. 4, 137.

[56] Baeta, *op. cit.* p. 54.

[57] Sundkler, *op. cit.* p. 220.

[58] Sundkler, *op. cit.* p. 220.

grinding scholars. Secondly, they are reactions, not to questions about the nature of mystical beliefs posed in some unrealistic interview situation but to options posed in the course of ongoing daily life. Thirdly and crucially, they are reactions to a concept of religious life which, though it was brought to African peoples by the missionaries, is more or less identical with the concept urged on us by Winch. Hence the rejection of this concept in Africa is a rejection not only of the views of the missionaries but also of the views of Winch. Since Winch makes so much of the need to accept other people's views of their own situation, this is one verdict he is bound to accept.

I think I have now shown clearly enough that Winch is wildly off course in his programme for the interpretation of African mystical concepts. It remains to try and discover what led him astray. One quick answer is that he never got out of his armchair to go and participate in the thought and life he was concerned to interpret. This, however, is unconvincing. For many scholars with years of African fieldwork to their credit have come up with interpretations just as wildly at variance with the facts—even when they themselves have helped to gather those facts.

A more penetrating answer would seem to be that Winch has fallen victim to the very error for which he castigates Evans-Pritchard and myself. Thus he insists that our attempts to understand "primitive" thought-patterns are vitiated by an obsession with the dominant thought-patterns of our own time and place. The principal manifestation of this obsession is our determination to force African mystical thinking into the conceptual moulds associated with Western science and technology. Along the same lines, however, one can argue that it is he who has signally failed to escape from the tyranny of currently-dominant thought patterns. Thus his conception of the religious life is nothing if not parochially modern Western. For whilst it is true that there have always been traces of the Jobian attitude to God in the Western Christian heritage, it is equally true that, up to four hundred years ago, a majority of Western Christians would have found this attitude as alien as most African Christians find it today. For them too, beliefs about God were first and foremost the constituents of a theory in terms of which they explained, predicted and attempted to control the events of the world around them.[59] Four hundred years ago, moreover, the theories of the scientists were still essentially works of religious thinking. In chemistry, a great deal of important research was still guided by notions of "spirit" that bore clear marks of their animistic origin.[60] And in physics, God was an integral feature of the theoretical schemes of Newton himself. Indeed, it seems doubtful if his concepts of absolute space and time (which have been crucial for modern physics down to Einstein) could ever have emerged except as correlatives of his concept of God.[61]

In short, up till this late date in Western history, there was little or no sense of contrast between religious discourse and scientific discourse, religious activity and scientific activity. It was later, when post-Newtonian paradigms in the physical sciences began to dispense with the theistic component, and when the achievements of these sciences in the sphere of explanation, prediction and control became increasingly difficult to challenge, that religious leaders began to grope for definitions of their calling which emphasized its distinctiveness from the sciences. It was then that the theologians began to emphasize that the ends of religion were quite different from the ends of science, and to deny that they were in any sort of competition with the scientists. The sort of definition propounded by Wittgenstein, Phillips and Winch is simply the culmination of this trend.

Now one could say, with these modern theologians and philosophers, that such changes have been a movement toward religious truth; a progressive casting off of superstitious dross. But whether one regards these changes as progress or retrogress, one can hardly deny that the stimulus for them was the need to work out some means of coexisting with the sciences; the need to limit claims of competence to those which scientists were unlikely to contest. And if one grants that the success of the sciences with non-theistic paradigms was the stimulus for these changes in the definition of religious life, must one not also grant that the re-adoption of theistic

---

[59] The transition from a religious life of this kind to a religious life of the kind espoused by Winch is one of the themes of Thomas, K., *Religion and the Decline of Magic* (London 1971).

[60] On this, see Toulmin and Goodfield, *op. cit.* pp. 51–52, 61, 101–105, 148–156, 194–195.

[61] On this, see Burtt, E., *The Metaphysical Foundations of Modern Science* (London 1967), pp. 202–299.

paradigms in the sciences would in all probability trigger off a reversal of these changes? If this sounds like a piece of half-baked speculation, the reader should remember that the history of science to date is by no means a story of the irrevocable replacement of one paradigm by another. Rather, it is a story in which one paradigm comes into the ascendant whilst its predecessor goes dormant. The dormant paradigm, moreover, does not die. Instead, it is kept just alive, perhaps by a few people often labeled as cranks, only to re-emerge into the limelight decades or centuries later totally refurbished but nonetheless recognizable as a reincarnation. Within the general category of impersonal paradigms, this has happened to the wave paradigm, the atomic paradigm and the field paradigm. Going outside this category, there is no reason to believe that the same thing could not happen to the theistic paradigm. Anyone muttering about such a paradigm not lending itself to mathematization, and therefore to exact treatment, should remember the Theory of Games!

Now I am not saying that anything like this is even in the wind. The efforts of Teilhard de Chardin[62] and Alister Hardy[63] to re-import a theistic paradigm into biology have so far failed to convince most serious scholars. And the claim that such a paradigm will have to be re-imported into psychology, in order to do justice to the increasingly accepted phenomena of ESP and pre-cognition, has so far fallen on equally deaf ears.[64] However, there is no reason to suppose that our present theoretical schemes represent anything like a close approach to some final set of truths. And there is no reason why, at some further stage in the struggle to attain such a set of truths, a theistic paradigm should not reappear.

If such a thing were to happen, what would be the attitude of the religious heirs of Kierkegaard, Wittgenstein and Winch? Would they still keep their noses in the air, and continue to maintain that questions of empirical confirmation and refutation were quite alien to religious discourse? Or would they jump on to the bandwagon, and declare themselves the guardians, in its time of adversity, of a paradigm now restored to respectability in the eyes of those supreme arbiters of reality, the scientists? I think there can be little doubt as to

---

[62] Teilhard de Chardin, P., *The Future of Man* (London 1964).

[63] Hardy, A., *The Living Stream* (London 1966).

[64] Arthur Koestler is a typical figure in this context. See his *The Roots of Coincidence* (London 1972).

what would happen. As abandonment of the theistic paradigms by scientists was the stimulus for renunciation of the ends of explanation/prediction/control by religious experts, so re-admission of theistic paradigms by scientists would be the signal for a renewed interest in explanation/prediction/control on the part of the divines.

The aim of this brief exercise in science-fiction is to bring home to the reader, as vividly as possible, the point that the definition of religious discourse which strongly contrasts it with scientific discourse is not just very recent in Western culture, but may also be downright ephemeral. In adopting such a definition, and in insisting on its value in the interpretation of African mystical beliefs, Winch is succumbing to the error of which be so loudly accuses his opponents. He is allowing himself to be blinded by a conceptual pattern peculiar to the culture of his own time and place.

Now to say this is to say that Winch is suffering from a lack of awareness. But a diagnosis in purely cognitive terms would be only half the truth. For what is also clear is that his writings on cultural matters are fired by powerful antipathies and passions. They are a crusade, against the allegedly overweening claims of science, and in favour of all those modes of thought whose aims are incommensurable with those of science. Winch does much to make us feel the unworthiness of the struggle for explanation, prediction and control, and the nobility of the struggle to achieve a resigned contemplation of life's contingencies. Seen in this light, his portrayal of "primitive" societies as dominated by these non-scientistic modes of thought appears, above all, as the product of his desire for a fantasy haven where he can flee from the horrors of science.

Summary and Conclusion

Winch's work on the general principles of anthropological/sociological enquiry is one of the major achievements of the field. Right or wrong, he has done more than any other recent writer to make us look again at the assumptions so many of us make about the continuity between the social and other sciences. Again, in the crucial field of understanding alien belief-systems, he has put his finger on what all thinking scholars must agree to be some of the key principles.

However, much of the popularity of the essay under consideration derives, not from the general principles Winch enunciates, but from the particular interpretation of "primitive" mystical thinking which he would have us believe follows from the application of these principles. And it is precisely at this point that his work is weakest. For, in the course of his interpretation, he flouts his own principles so dramatically as to make one wonder if he is not giving us a tongue-in-cheek example of how not to set about "understanding a primitive society." Thus although one of his important general contributions is an analysis of the roots of ethnocentrism in anthropological enquiry, his interpretation of African mystical beliefs is vitiated by an outsize pair of ethnic blinkers. Again, whereas he repeatedly insists on a reverential readiness to learn *from* other peoples, his interpretation of mystical beliefs involves the projection *on to* these peoples of his own anti-scientistic fantasies.[65]

Our closing verdict on Winch must therefore be a mixed one. As a methodologist of the social sciences, he is clearly a figure who cannot be ignored. As a practitioner in the field of cross-cultural understanding, he seems to be just one more victim of the Leavis-Roszak Syndrome, one more mouthpiece for the siren song of the Counter Culture.

---

[65] It was this aspect of his interpretation which suggested to me the somewhat waspish title of this paper: safari being notoriously the type of expedition on which one learns nothing *from* either the locals or the locale!

SUGGESTED READINGS

Barnes, Barry & Bloor, David. 1982. Relativism, Rationalism and the Sociology of Knowledge. In M. Hollis and S. Lukes (eds.), *Rationality and Relativism*. Cambridge, Mass.: M.I.T. Press: 21–47. A fine paper in defence of relativism.

Berlin, Brent & Kay, Paul. 1991. *Basic Color Terms*. Berkeley: University of California Press. Paper Edition. The original experiment which proved that the perception of color is not in the eye of the beholder.

Gomperz, John H. & Levinson, Stephen C. (eds.). 1996. *Rethinking Linguistic Relativity*. Cambridge, Mass.: Cambridge University Press. The most up-to-date set of essays on the question of linguistic relativity, cognition, and community.

Kay, Peter & Kempton, W. 1984. What is the Sapir-Whorf Hypothesis? *American Anthropologist* 86: 65–79. An excellent summary of the hypothesis with a good bibliography for further research.

Lear, Jonathan. 1982. Leaving the World Alone. *Journal of Philosophy* LXXIX: 382–403. Black, Max. 1978. Lebensform and Sprachspiel in Wittgenstein's Later Work. In *Wittgenstein and His Impact on Contemporary Thought*. Wien: Holder-Pichler-Tempsky. Hinman, Lawrence. Can a Form of Life Be Wrong? *Philosophy* 58: 339–351. These commentators argue against a Wittgensteinian framework relativism.

Penner, Hans. 1989. *Impasse and Resolution: A Critique of the Study of Religion*. New York: Peter Lang Publishers. See Chapter III, which consists of a critique of Sapir-Whorf, Horton, and relativism, and a use of Berlin/Kay.

Putnam, Hilary. 1992. *Renewing Philosophy*. Cambridge, Mass.: Harvard University Press. Excellent critique of relativism as well as an interpretation of Wittgenstein's "Religious Belief."

Sellars, Wilfred. 1997. *Empiricism & The Philosophy Of Mind.* Cambridge, Mass.: Harvard University Press. The classic essay on "The Myth of the Given." Seldom quoted in religious studies but very influential in other areas, with a fine study guide by Robert Brandom.

Spiro, Melford E. 1986. Cultural Relativism and the Future of Anthropology. *Cultural Anthropology* 1: 259–286. An excellent critique of relativism from a well known functionalist.

Wittgenstein, Ludwig. 1967. *Philosophical Investigations,* Sections 293, 258, 265. Here the "later" Wittgenstein criticizes the idea of a private language.

Part IV

New Theories for the Study of Religion

INTRODUCTION TO PART IV

What is the meaning of meaning? The term *meaning* looms large in the study of religion, just as it is ubiquitous in informal conversation about human action and experience. Yet the meaning of *meaning* is theoretically opaque. It is one of those words that, as Humpty Dumpty remarked, ought to be paid overtime because it does so much work. In this volume, very different theories of meaning compete with one another. Authors in the preceding chapters have employed one or another of the following dubious assumptions: (1) meaning is verification: a sentence's meaning is the set of possible experiences that would confirm it or provide evidence for its truth; (2) meaning is reference: words mean by standing for things; a sentence means what it does because its parts correspond referentially to the elements of an actual or possible state of affairs in the world; (3) meaning is use: a linguistic expression has a conventionally assigned role as a game-piece-like token used in various social practices; (4) meaning is function: to determine the meaning, find the function that is fulfilled in social or psychological terms; (5) meaning is existential: "ultimate meaning" is had only in connecting human subjectivity to the absolutely transcendent, without which existence is meaningless; (6) meaning is relative to a framework, conceptual scheme, culture, or worldview: anything goes.

In contrast to these and other theories that have been found to be problematic, Davidsonian semantics advances the idea that the meaning of a sentence is explained by a truth-conditional theory. In this theory, a sentence's meaning is the distinctive conditions under which it *is* true. Davidson's holism rejects the idea that it is possible to separate questions about the truth of propositions from questions about their meaning. That is because the characterization of the meaning of a linguistic expression refers us back necessarily to the totality of the language, where the meaning of an expression depends upon the meanings of its components and vice versa.

We think that the interpretation of the meaning of a sentence as equivalent to its truth conditions has far-reaching implications for understanding the relations among language, truth, and religious belief. Unlike platonic truth that is transcendent and essentialistic, this interpretation leads to a conception of truth as linguistic and holistic. Unlike empiricist truth that is either analytic or synthetic, this theory holds that nothing *makes* our beliefs true except other beliefs. Rather than being anything "out there" waiting to be discovered, or "in here" having only to be recollected, truth lies ready at hand all the time. As Richard Rorty puts it, truth is simply what happens to sentences when their truth-conditions are fulfilled.

For all those who have taken the linguistic turn in twentieth century philosophy, and for whom meaning is defined in terms of truth conditions rather than in terms of "existential significance," the existentializing of *religious* meaning, truth, and belief represents a dead end. Employed as a protectionist strategy for religious thought, it is the last stronghold of twentieth century positivism whose theory of knowledge it accepts. The holistic alternative is to see that meaning is what brings truth and knowledge together coherently. Coherence, rather than being a theory of truth, is at best a *test* of truth, not its definition. The world, on this account, stands in a causal relation to language, but that relation cannot be described in language. We are indeed in touch with "familiar objects whose antics make our sentences and opinions true or false," as Davidson says, but the word "antics" suggests the sheer contingency of the causal relationship of the world to language. Nonsentences and nonbeliefs have no "making true" relationships to sentences and beliefs.

Summarized in its most general terms, holism is the philosophical doctrine that asserts three principles: first, that apparently distinct elements are integrally related in a system, must be analyzed as a whole, and cannot be understood as separable atomic bits; second, that rationality is understood as the coherence of relations in a system of events or beliefs, such that single beliefs or events are neither rational nor irrational in themselves; third, that mental events or propositional attitudes involved with beliefs and desires are irreducible. Holism with regard to meaning claims that words and sentences can only mean in relation to other words and sentences.

Not only meaning, but belief is holistic in nature. In order to differ with another person over religious beliefs, one must first agree in many respects about very many things. All believers necessarily share with non-believers a massive background of belief, a common ground that enables divergences of belief to stand out more clearly. Furthermore, according to neopragmatists like Rorty and Frankenberry in this section, beliefs and other propositional attitudes can be understood to have their meaning through the causal interrelations by which they contribute to the ongoing creation of adaptive or nonadaptive bodily interactions with the environment, rather than through the way they are *about* the world. This understanding unites holism with the tradition of American pragmatism.

By adopting a form of holism, best represented by the writings of Donald Davidson, we believe that the study of religion can begin to identify, explain, and refute persistent problems within its dominant discourses. More than that, holism as presented in Part IV provides a new starting point for the academic study of religion free of such traditional dualisms as fact/value, scheme/content, and appearance/reality. In the last analysis, we are convinced that the academic study of religion has not arrived at such an impasse that its best hope in the twenty-first century is to embrace incompatible theories or to embed a fundamental relativism at the heart of its inquiry. We argue in favor of an alternative approach to religious belief that can avoid the failures of positivism, functionalism, and relativism. All the essays in Part IV can be read as explorations of ways in which we might now overcome the dualisms, dogmatisms, and logical fallacies identified in the first three parts.

Hans Penner's essay lays out the major elements of Davidson's revolution in semantics, introducing the truth conditional theory of meaning, the principle of charity, and the principle of holism. He then takes Davidsonian semantics to entail a radical consequence for an understanding of *religious* language: its content is patently *false,* according to Penner. Readers should be alert to the passages in which Penner blocks the resort to symbolic meaning favored by other authors, and refutes the ruse of relativism.

Terry Godlove's essay develops a Davidsonian criticism of the widespread use of "the framework model" in the study of religion. Showing the dependence of this model on the discredited scheme-content dualism, Godlove's argument indicts such well-known conceptual schemers as Walter Stace, Robin Horton, E. E. Evans-Pritchard, John Hick, Ninian Smart, Peter Winch, Gordon Kaufman, and Peter Berger. In his extension of Davidson's argument to religious frameworks, Godlove makes the distinction between interpretive and epistemic priority and argues that religion is best understood as having interpretive priority (relatively limited and largely theoretical) but not epistemic priority. This proposal coheres well with Penner's reminder that truth is not an epistemic notion. Godlove's effort preserves from the framework model the recognition of diversity of belief but without lapsing into relativism.

Richard Rorty's essay on "Pragmatism, Davidson and Truth" interprets both Davidson and William James as pragmatists who adhere to four theses which lead one to be content to have no "theory of truth." Pragmatists in the American tradition are also content to have, with Davidson, a theory of meaning without having to conjure things called "meanings" or—what is worse—Meaning with a capital M. Rorty's reading of Davidson as a pragmatist tells us much about the evolution of the pragmatic method and theory as it has progressed from Peirce, James, and Dewey to Quine, Davidson, and Rorty. Holism is here depicted chiefly as a way to stop wondering about whether our beliefs shadow, display, mirror, fit, or represent something.

In agreement with Rorty, Nancy Frankenberry's essay reads Davidson as belonging to the American pragmatist tradition and as the first pragmatist to have a satisfactory account of truth. She argues for a better understanding of the nature of pragmatism opened up by Davidsonian methods, and clarifies what pragmatism does and does not offer philosophy of religion. One outcome of the new pragmatism, she suggests, is the disenchantment of subjectivity, which has exhausted itself in modernity's pendulum swing between the metaphysical sense that we are meaningful only because we are created in the image of the divine, and the anti-metaphysical sense that we are meaningless unless we create a world in our own image.

15

Pragmatism, Davidson, and Truth

Richard Rorty

I. Less Is More

Davidson has said that his theory of truth "provides no entities with which to compare sentences," and thus is a "correspondence" theory only in "an unassuming sense."[1] His paper "A Coherence Theory of Truth and Knowledge" takes as its slogan "correspondence without confrontation."[2] This slogan chimes with his repudiation of what he calls the "dualism of scheme and content"—the idea that something like "mind" or "language" can bear some relation such as "fitting" or "organizing" to the world. Such doctrines are reminiscent of pragmatism, a movement which has specialized in debunking dualisms and in dissolving traditional problems created by those dualisms. The close affiliations of Davidson's work to Quine's and of Quine's to Dewey's make it tempting to see Davidson as belonging to the American pragmatist tradition.

Davidson, however, has explicitly denied that his break with the empiricist tradition makes him a pragmatist.[3] He thinks of pragmatism as an identification of truth with assertibility, or with assertibility under ideal conditions. If such an identification is essential to pragmatism, then indeed Davidson is as anti-pragmatist as he is anti-empiricist. For such an identification would merely be an emphasis on the 'scheme" side of an unacceptable dualism, replacing the emphasis on the "content" side represented by traditional

---

[1] Donald Davidson, *Inquiries into Truth and Interpretation* (Oxford University Press, Oxford, 1984), p. xviii.

[2] This article appears in *Kant oder Hegel?*, ed. Dieter Heinrich (Klett-Cotta, Stuttgart, 1983). The quoted slogan is on p. 423 of the original publication.

[3] *Inquiries*, p. xviii.

empiricism. Davidson does not want to see truth identified with anything. He also does not want to view sentences as "made true" by anything—neither knowers or speakers on the one hand nor "the world" on the other. For him, any "theory of truth" which analyses a relation between bits of language and bits of non-language is already on the wrong track.

On this last, negative, point, Davidson agrees with William James. James thought that no traditional theory of truth had come close to explaining "the particular go"[4] of such a special relation, and that it was a hopeless quest. On his view, there was no point in trying to give sense to a notion of "correspondence" which was neutral between, e.g., perceptual, theoretical, moral and mathematical truths. He suggested that we settle for "the true" as being "only the expedient in our way of thinking."[5] When his critics chorused that "truths aren't true because they work; they work because they are true," James thought they had missed his point, viz., that "true" was a term of praise used for endorsing, rather than one referring to a state of affairs the existence of which explained, e.g., the success of those who held true beliefs. He thought that the moral of philosophers" failures to discover, as it were, the micro-structure of the correspondence relation was that there was nothing there to find, that one could not use truth as an explanatory notion.

James, unfortunately, did not confine himself to making this negative point. He also had moments in which he inferred from the false premise that

> If we have the notion of "justified," we don't need that of "truth"

to

> "True" must mean something like "justifiable."

This was a form of the idealist error of inferring from

> We can make no sense of the notion of truth as correspondence

to

> Truth must consist in ideal coherence.

The error is to assume that "true" needs a definition, and then to infer from the fact that it cannot be defined in terms of a relation

---

[4] William James, *Pragmatism* (Hackett, Indianapolis, 1981), p. 92.

[5] Ibid., p. 100.

between beliefs and non-beliefs to the view that it must be defined in terms of a relation among beliefs. But, as Hilary Putnam has pointed out in his "naturalistic fallacy" argument, "it might be true but not *X*" is always sensible, no matter what one substitutes for *X* (the same point G. E. Moore made about "good").[6]

Suppose that we prescind from the moments in which James fell into this error, as well as from Peirce's unfortunate attempt (of which more later) to define truth in terms of "the end of inquiry." Suppose that we follow up James's negative point—his polemic against the notion of "correspondence"—and forget his occasional attempts to say something constructive about truth. We can then, I think, isolate a sense for the term "pragmatism" which will consist simply in the dissolution of the traditional problematic about truth, as opposed to a constructive "pragmatist theory of truth." This dissolution would start from the claim that "true" has no explanatory use, but merely the following uses:

> (a) an endorsing use
> (b) a cautionary use, in such remarks as "Your belief that S is perfectly justified, but perhaps not true"—reminding ourselves that justification is relative to, and no better than, the beliefs cited as grounds for S, and that such justification is no guarantee that things will go well if we take S as a "rule for action" (Peirce's definition of belief)
> (c) A disquotational use: to say metalinguistic things of the form 's" is true iff—[7]

---

[6] Hilary Putnam, *Meaning and the Moral Sciences* (Cambridge University Press, Cambridge, 1978), p. 108.

[7] There is much to be said about the relations between these three uses, but I shall not try to say it here. The best attempt to do so which I have seen is found in an unpublished paper by Robert Brandom called "Truth Talk." Brandom shows how the "primitive pragmatism" which tries to define truth as assertibility is defeated by the use of "true" in such contexts as the antecedents of conditionals. But he then suggests a way of developing a sophisticated pragmatism which, invoking Frege and the Grover-Camp-Belknap prosentential theory of truth, saves Dewey's intentions. Brandom not only shows how "anaphoric or prosentential theories" can, as he says "retain the fundamental anti-descriptive thrust of the pragmatist position, while broadening it to account also for the embedded uses on which primitive pragmatism founders," but suggests ways of reconciling these theories with Davidsonian disquotationalism.

The cautionary use of the term was neglected by James, as was the disquotational use. The neglect of the former led to the association of pragmatism with relativism. The misleading association of the latter (by Tarski) with the notion of "correspondence" has led people to think that there must have been more to this notion than James realized. Davidson, on my view, has given us an account of truth which has a place for each of these uses while eschewing the idea that the expediency of a belief can be explained by its truth.

In the sense of "pragmatism" in which Davidson and James are both pragmatists, the term signifies adherence to the following theses:

> (1) "True" has no explanatory uses.
> (2) We understand all there is to know about the relation of beliefs to the world when we understand their causal relations with the world; our knowledge of how to apply terms such as "about" and "true of" is fallout from a "naturalistic" account of linguistic behavior.[8]
> (3) There are no relations of "being made true" which hold between beliefs and the world.
> (4) There is no point to debates between realism and anti-realism, for such debates presuppose the empty and misleading idea of beliefs "being made true."[9]

Notice that, so defined, pragmatism offers no "theory of truth." All it gives us is an explanation of why, in this area, less is more—of why therapy is better than system-building.

---

[8] This thesis does not, of course, entail that you can define intentional terms in non-intentional terms, nor that a semantical metalanguage can somehow be "reduced" to Behaviorese. It is one thing to say "you learn which sentences using the term 'X' are true by finding out which sentences using the term 'Y' are true" and another to say "You can explain the meaning of 'X' in terms 'Y'" or "You can reduce 'X's to 'Y's." Our intentional concepts are not fall-out from our observation of causal relationships, but our knowledge of how to apply them is. See Section IV below for a discussion of Davidson's non-reductive brand of physicalism.

[9] Jamesian pragmatists heartily agree with Dummett's claim that lots and lots of the traditional "problems of philosophy" (including the problems which Peirce thought to solve with his 'Scotistic realism") are best seen as issues between realists and anti-realists over whether there are "matters of fact" in, e.g., physics, ethics, or logic. But whereas Dummett sees himself as having rehabilitated these fine old problems by semanticizing them, the pragmatist sees him as having conveniently bagged them for disposal.

Both James and Davidson would urge that the only reason philosophers thought they needed an "explanation of what truth consists in" was that they were held captive by a certain picture—the picture which Davidson calls "the dualism of scheme and content" and which Dewey thought of as "the dualism of Subject and Object." Both pictures are of disparate ontological realms, one containing beliefs and the other non-beliefs. The picture of two such realms permits us to imagine truth as a relation between particular beliefs and particular non-beliefs which (a) is non-causal in nature, and (b) must be "correctly analysed" before one can rebut (or concede victory to) the epistemological skeptic. To adopt (1)–(4) above is to erase this picture, and thereby to erase most of the traditional philosophical dualisms which Dewey thought ought to be erased. It is also to drop the picture which the epistemological skeptic needs to make his skepticism interesting and arguable—to make it more than the philosopher's pursuit of *Unheimlichkeit*, of a sense of the strangeness of the world.

II. Peirce's Half-way Measure

Before turning to the question of whether Davidson in fact adheres to (1)–(4), it may be helpful to say something about Peirce's "end of inquiry" pragmatism. This is the version of the so-called "pragmatist theory of truth" (a misleading textbook label for a farrago of inconsistent doctrines) which has received most attention in recent years. It represents, on my view, a half-way house between idealist and physicalist theories of truth on the one hand, and (1)–(4) on the other.

Idealism and physicalism have in common the hope that

(A) "There are rocks" is true

is true if and only if

(B) At the ideal end of inquiry, we shall be justified in asserting that there are rocks.

This suggestion requires them, however, to say that

(C) There are rocks

is implied by (B) as well as by (A). This seems paradoxical, since they also wish to assert

> (D) "There are rocks" is linked by a relation of correspondence—accurate representation—to the way the world is

and there seems no obvious reason why the progress of the language-game we are playing should have anything in particular to do with the way the rest of the world is.

Idealism and physicalism are attempts to supply such a reason. The idealists suggest that

> (E) The world consists of representations arranged in an ideally coherent system

thus permitting them to analyse (C) as

> (F) "There are rocks" is a member of the ideally coherent system of representations.

Idealists support this move by saying that the correspondence relation of (D) cannot be a relation whose existence could be established by confronting an assertion with an object to see if a relation called "corresponding" holds. Nobody knows what such a confrontation would look like. (The relation of "customary response to" which holds between tables and assertions of the presence of tables is clearly not what is wanted.) Since the only criterion of truth is coherence among representations, they say, the only way of saving (D) while avoiding skepticism is (E).

The physicalists, on the other hand, analyse (A) as (D) and then argue that playing the language-games we play will eventually lead us to correspond with reality. It will do so because, so to speak, the world takes a hand in the game. This is the view of philosophers like Friedrich Engels, Jerry Fodor, Michael Devitt, Jay Rosenberg and Hartry Field. They reject the possibility of a priori discovery of the nature of reality, illustrated by the idealists' (E), but they think that one or another empirical science (or the "unified" ensemble of them all) will provide an answer to the skeptic. These philosophers think that, although there are no entailments, there are deeply buried connections between the conditions of the truth of (B) and(C). These connections will not be discovered by an analysis of meanings but by empirical scientific work which will pry out the causal connections between, e.g., rocks and representations of rocks.

Peirce, in his earlier period, wanted to avoid both the revisionary metaphysics of idealism and the promissory notes of physicalism. He tried for a quick fix by analysing (D) as (B). He shared with the idealist and the physicalist the motive of refuting the skeptic, but he thought it enough to say that "reality" means something like "whatever we shall still be asserting the existence of at the end of inquiry." This definition of reality bridges the gap the skeptic sees between coherence and correspondence. It reduces coherence to correspondence without the necessity either for metaphysical system-building or for further empirical inquiry. A simple reanalysis of the term "reality" does the trick.

I do not think (though I once did)[10] that Peircian pragmatism is defensible, but before transcending it I want to remark that Peirce was moving in the right direction. The Peircian pragmatist is right in thinking that the idealist and the physicalist share a common fallacy—namely that "correspondence" is the name of a relation between pieces of thought (or language) and pieces of the world, a relation such that the relata must be ontologically homogenous. The idealist generalizes Berkeley's point by saying: nothing can correspond to a representation except a representation. So he saves us from skepticism by redescribing reality as consisting of representations. The physicalist thinks that nothing can correspond to a bit of spatio-temporal reality except by being another bit linked to the first by appropriate causal relationships. So he saves us from skepticism by offering a physicalistic account of the nature of our representations—one which shows that, as Fodor once said, the correspondence theory of truth corresponds to reality. The Peircian rises above this debate by saying that the "about" and "true of" relations can link utterly disparate relata, and that problems of

---

[10] As, for instance, when I said, falsely, that "we can make no sense of the notion that the view which can survive all objections might be false" (*Consequences of Pragmatism* (University of Minnesota Press, Minneapolis, 1982), p. 165—passage written in 1979). I started retracting this Peircianism in the Introduction to that book (e.g., p. xiv, written in 1981) and am still at it. I was persuaded of the untenability of Peircian view by Michael Williams' "Coherence, Justification and Truth" (*Review of Metaphysics* XXXIV (1980), pp. 243–72), in particular by his claim (p. 269) that "we have no idea what it would be for a theory to be ideally complete and comprehensive . . . or of what it would be good for inquiry to have an end." Cf. his suggestion that we drop the attempt to think of truth as "in some sense an epistemic notion" (p. 269). Davidson spells out what happens when the attempt is dropped.

ontological homogeneity need not arise.[11] All that is necessary is to redefine "reality" as what the winners of the game talk about, thus insuring that the conditions laid down by (B) and (D) coincide.

The Peircian redefinition, however, uses a term—"ideal"—which is just as fishy as "corresponds." To make it less fishy Peirce would have to answer the question "How would we know that we were at the end of inquiry, as opposed to merely having gotten tired or unimaginative?" This is as awkward as "How do we know we are corresponding to reality, rather than merely making conventionally correct responses to stimuli?" Peirce's idea of "the end of inquiry" might make sense if we could detect an asymptotic convergence in inquiry, but such convergence seems a local and short-term phenomenon.[12] Without such a clarification of "ideal" or "end," the Peircian is merely telling that the conditions laid down by (B) and (D) coincide without giving us any reason for thinking they do. Nor is it clear what such a reason could consist in.

Peirce went half-way towards destroying the epistemological problematic which motivated the metaphysical quarrels between idealists and physicalists. He did so by leaving out "mind" and sticking to "signs." But he went only half-way because he still thought that (D) was an intuition which any philosophy had to assimilate. James went the rest of the way by saying that not only was "true of" not a relation between ontologically homogenous relata, but was not an analyzable relation at all, not a relation which could be clarified by a scientific or metaphysical description of the relation

---

[11] Peircian pragmatism is often criticized on the ground that, like idealism, it raises problems about ontological homogeneity and heterogeneity through a counter-intuitive Kantian claim that "objects in the world owe their fundamental structure—and, if they couldn't exist without displaying that structure, their existence—to our creative activity" (Alvin Plantinga, "How To Be An Anti-Realist," *Proceedings of the American Philosophical Association*, 56 (1982), p. 52). But this confuses a criterial claim with a causal one: the Peircian claim that "If there are rocks, they will display their structure at the end of inquiry" and the idealist claim that "If there were no inquiry, there would be no rocks."

[12] See Mary Hesse's distinction between "instrumental progress"—increase in predictive ability—and "convergence of concepts" (*Revolutions and Reconstructions in the Philosophy of Science* (Indiana University Press, Bloomington, 1980), pp. x-xi). The possibility of scientific revolutions endangers conceptual convergence, which is the only sort of convergence which will do the Peircian any good. To insure against the indefinite proliferation of such revolutions in the future one would need something like Peirce's "metaphysics of evolutionary love," or Putnam's attempt to certify contemporary physics as "mature."

between beliefs and non-beliefs. Deciding that no reason could be given for saying that the constraints laid down by (B) and (D) would coincide, he simply dropped (D), and with it the problematic of epistemological skepticism. He thereby set the stage for Dewey's argument that it is only the attempt to supplement a naturalist account of our interaction with our environment with a non-naturalist account (involving some third thing, intermediate between the organism and its environment—such as "mind" or "language") which makes that problematic seem interesting.

III. Davidson and the Field Linguist

What justification is there for attributing (1)–(4) to Davidson? He has asserted (3) on various occasions. But it may seem odd to attribute (4) to him, since he has often been treated as a prototypical "realist." (2) may also sound unDavidsonian, since he has had no truck with recent "causal theories" in semantics. Further, his association with Tarski, and Tarski's with the notion of "correspondence," may seem to make him an unlikely recruit for the pragmatist ranks—for pragmatism, as I have defined it, consists very largely in the claim that only if we drop the whole idea of "correspondence with reality" can we avoid pseudo-problems.

Nevertheless, I propose to argue that all four pragmatist theses should be ascribed to Davidson. To defend this claim, I shall begin by offering an account of what I shall call "the philosophy of language of the field linguist." I shall claim that this is all the philosophy of language (and, in particular, all the doctrine about truth) which Davidson has, and all that he thinks anybody needs.

Davidson, like the traditional philosopher who wants an answer to the epistemological skeptic, wants us to step out of our language-game and look at it from a distance. But his outside standpoint is not the metaphysical standpoint of the idealist, looking for an unsuspected ontological homogeneity between beliefs and non-beliefs invisible to science, nor the hopeful standpoint of the physicalist, looking to future science to discover such a homogeneity. Rather, it is the mundane standpoint of the field linguist trying to make sense of our linguistic behavior. Whereas traditional theories of truth asked "what feature of the world is referred to by 'true'?," Davidson asks "how is 'true' used by the outside observer of the language- game?"

Davidson is surely right that Quine "saved philosophy of language as a serious subject" by getting rid of the analytic-synthetic distinction.[13] Quine's best argument for doing so was that the distinction is of no use to the field linguist. Davidson follows upon this argument by pointing out that, *pace* Dummett and Quine himself,[14] the distinction between the physical objects the natives react to and their neural stimulations is of no use either. The linguist cannot start with knowledge of native meanings acquired prior to knowledge of native beliefs, nor with translations of native observation sentences which have been certified by matching them with stimulations. He must be purely coherentist in his approach, going round and round the hermeneutic circle until he begins to feel at home.

All the linguist has to go on is his observation of the way in which linguistic is aligned with non-linguistic behavior in the course of the native's interaction with his environment, an interaction which he takes to be guided by rules for action (Peirce's definition of "belief"). He approaches this data armed with the regulative principle that most of the native's rules are the same as ours, which is to say that most of them are true. The latter formulation of the principle is an extension of Quine's remark that any anthropologist who claims to have translated a native utterance as "*p* and not-*p*" just shows that she has not yet put together a good translation manual. Davidson generalizes this: any translation which portrays the natives as denying most of the evident facts about their environment is automatically a bad one.

The most vivid example of this point is Davidson's claim that the best way to translate the discourse of a brain which has always lived in a vat will be as referring to the vat-cum-computer environment the brain is actually in.[15] This will be the analogue of

---

13 "A Coherence Theory . . . ," p. 313.

14 See "A Coherence Theory . . . ," p. 430: "Quine and Dummett agree on a basic principle, which is that whatever there is to meaning must be traced back somehow to experience, the given, or patterns of sensory stimulation, something intermediate between belief and the usual objects our beliefs are about. Once we take this step, we open the door to skepticism. . . . When meaning goes epistemological in this way, truth and meaning are necessarily divorced."

15 As far as I know, Davidson has not used this example in print. I am drawing upon unpublished remarks at a colloquium with Quine and Putnam, Heidelberg, 1981.

construing most native remarks as about, e.g., rocks and diseases rather than about trolls and demons. In Davidson's words:

> What stands in the way of global skepticism of the senses is, in my view, the fact that we must, in the plainest and methodologically most basic cases, take the objects of a belief to be the causes of that belief. And what we, as interpreters, must take them to be is what they in fact are. Communication begins where causes converge: your utterance means what mine does if belief in its truth is systematically caused by the same events and objects.[16]

In this passage, Davidson weds the Kripkean claim that causation must have *something* to do with reference to the Strawsonian claim that you figure out what somebody is talking about by figuring out what object most of his beliefs are true of. The wedding is accomplished by saying that Strawson is right if construed holistically—if one prefaces his claim with Aristotle's phrase "on the whole and for the most part." You cannot, however, use Strawson's criterion for individual cases and be sure of being right. But if *most* of the results of your translation scheme, and consequent assignment of reference, do not conform to Strawson's criterion, then that scheme must have something terribly wrong with it. The mediating element between Strawson and Kripke is the Quinean insight that knowledge *both* of causation *and* of reference is (equally) a matter of coherence with the field linguist's own beliefs.

Thesis (2) above can be construed in either a Kripkean or a Davidsonian way. On the former, building-block, approach to reference, we want to trace causal pathways from objects to individual speech-acts. This approach leaves open the possibility that speakers may get these pathways all wrong (e.g., by being largely wrong about what there is) and thus that they may never know to what they are referring. This allows the possibility of a wholesale divorce between referents and intentional objects—just the kind of scheme-content gap which Davidson warns us against. By contrast, Davidson is suggesting that we maximize coherence and truth first, and then let reference fall out as it may.

This guarantees that the intentional objects of lots of beliefs—what Davidson calls "the plainest cases"—will be their causes. Kripkean slippage (e.g., the Godel-Schmidt case) must be the

---

[16] "A Coherence Theory . . . ," p. 436. This line of argument—together with Davidson's account of reference as fallout from translation (as at *Inquiries*, pp. 219ff., 236ff.)—is my chief textual evidence for imputing (2) to Davidson.

exception. For if we try to imagine that a split between entities referred to and intentional objects is the rule we shall have drained the notion of "reference" of any content. That is: we shall have made it, like "analytic," a notion which the field linguist has no use for. The linguist can communicate with the natives if he knows most of their intentional objects (i.e., which objects most of their rules for action are good for dealing with, which objects most of their beliefs are true of). But he can make as little sense of the skeptical claim that this is not "really" communication (but just accidentally felicitous cross-talk) as of the suggestion that the "intended interpretation" of some platitudinous native utterance is "There are no rocks."

Davidson's application of this view of the job of the field linguist to epistemological skepticism is as follows. Unless one is willing to postulate some intermediary between the organism and its environment (e.g., "determinate-meanings," "intended-interpretations," "what is before the speaker's mind," etc.) then radical interpretation begins at home. So, like all other natives, we turn out to have mostly true beliefs. The argument is neat, but does it answer the skeptic, as the idealist and the physicalist want to do? Or does it simply tell the skeptic that his question, "Do we ever represent reality as it is in itself?" was a bad one, as the Jamesian pragmatist does?

A skeptic is likely to reply to Davidson that it would take a lot more than an account of the needs of the field linguist to show that belief is, as Davidson says, "in its nature veridical."[17] He will think that Davidson has shown no more than that the field linguist must assume that the natives believe mostly what we do, and that the question of whether most of our beliefs are true is still wide open. Davidson can only reply, once again, that radical interpretation begins at home—that if we want an outside view of our own language-game, the only one available is that of the field linguist. But that is just what the skeptic will not grant. He thinks that Davidson has missed the philosophical point. He thinks that Davidson's outside standpoint is not, so to speak, far enough outside to count as philosophical.

As far as I can see, the only rejoinder readily available to Davidson at this point is to remark on the intuitive appeal of (2): the naturalistic thesis, which he shares with Kripke, that there is nothing more to be known about the relation between beliefs and the rest of

---

17 "A Coherence Theory . . . ," p. 432.

reality than what we learn from an empirical study of causal transactions between organisms and their environment. The relevant result of this study is the field linguist's translation-manual-cum-ethnographic-report.[18] Since we already have (in dictionaries) a translation manual for ourselves, as well as (in encyclopedias) an auto-ethnography, there is nothing more for us to know *about our relation to reality* than we already know. There is no further job for philosophy to do. This is just what the pragmatist has been telling the skeptic all the time. Both the pragmatist and Davidson are saying that if "correspondence" denotes a relation between beliefs and the world which can vary though nothing else varies—even if all the causal relations remain the same—then "corresponds" cannot be an explanatory term. So if truth is to be thought of as "correspondence," then "true" cannot be an explanatory term. Pressing (2) to the limit, and freeing it from the atomistic presuppositions which Kripkean "building-block" theories of reference add to it, results in (1).

Thus Davidson's strategy with the skeptic would seem to give him reason to subscribe to (1) as well as to (2). Whereas the physicalist invokes (2) with an eye to finding something for "correspondence" to refer to, Davidson takes the absence of such a thing in the field linguist's results as a reason for thinking that there is nothing to look for. Like Dewey's (and unlike Skinner's) his is a non-reductive naturalism, one which does not assume that every important semantical term must describe a physical relationship.[19] He thinks that there will be lots of terms used by theorists who study causal relations (e.g., field linguists, particle physicists) which do not themselves denote causal relations.

On my interpretation, then, Davidson joins the pragmatist in saying that "true" has no explanatory use.[20] His contribution to

---

18 That such a manual cannot be separated from such a report is entailed by the Quine-Davidson argument that you cannot figure out beliefs and meanings independently of one another.

19 Davidson's "Mental Events" illustrates his strategy of combining identity-with-the-physical with irreducibility-to-the-physical.

20 One might object, as Alan Donagan has suggested to me, that the fact that both the linguist's and the native's beliefs are mostly true is an explanation of the fact that they are able to communicate with one another. But this sort of explanation does not invoke a causally efficacious property. It is like explaining the fact of communication by saying that the two inhabit the same space-time continuum. We do not know what it would be like for them not to, any more than we know what it would be like for one or the other to have mostly false

pragmatism consists in pointing out that it has a disquotational use in addition to the normative uses seized upon by James. The traditional philosophical attempt to conflate these two kinds of use, and to view them both as explained by the use of "true" to denote a non-causal relation called "correspondence," is, on this account, a confused attempt to be inside and outside the language-game at the same time.

My interpretation, however, must deal with the fact that Davidson, unlike the pragmatist, does not present himself as repudiating the skeptic's question, but as answering it. He says that "even a mild coherence theory like mine must provide a skeptic with a reason for supposing coherent beliefs are true."[21] Again, he says "the theory I defend is not in competition with a correspondence theory, but depends for its defense on an argument that purports to show that coherence yields correspondence."[22] This sounds as if Davidson were not only adopting something like (D) above, but claiming to deduce (D) from (B), in the manner of idealism and Peircean pragmatism. In wanting "correspondence without confrontation," he shows that he shares with these latter "isms" the view that we cannot compare a belief with a non-belief to see if they match. But what does Davidson suppose is left of correspondence after confrontation is taken away? What is it that he thinks the skeptic wants? What is it that he proposes to give the skeptic by making coherence yield it?

Davidson says that the skeptical question he wishes to answer is: "how, given that we 'cannot get outside our beliefs and our language so as to find some test other than coherence' we nevertheless can have knowledge and talk about an objective public world which is not of our making?"[23] But this does not help us much. Only if one held some view which made it mysterious that there could be such knowledge and such talk (e.g., one which required ontological homogeneity between beliefs and non-beliefs, or one which thought that there was an intermediary "scheme" which

---

beliefs. The only candidates for causally efficacious properties are properties which we can imagine away.

21 "A Coherence Theory . . . ," p. 426.

22 "A Coherence Theory . . . ," p. 423.

23 "A Coherence Theory . . . ," pp. 426–7. Davidson correctly says, in this passage, that I do not think this is a good question. I am here trying to explain what is wrong with it, and why I think Davidson too should regard it as a bad question.

"shaped" the non-beliefs before they became talkable-about), would this be a challenging question. If there is to be a problem here, it must be because the skeptic has been allowed to construe "objective" in such a way that the connection between coherence and objectivity has become unperspicuous.[24] What sense of "correspondence" will both preserve this lack of perspicuity and yet be such that Davidson can argue that coherence will yield it?

To make a start, we can note that Davidson thinks "correspondence" is not, as correspondence-to-fact theorists believe, a relation between a sentence and a chunk of reality which is somehow isomorphic to that sentence. In "True to the Facts," he agrees with Strawson that facts—sentence-shaped chunks of the world—are *ad hoc* contrivances which do not answer to the skeptic's needs. What does, he thinks, is the more complex notion of correspondence made intelligible by Tarski's notion of satisfaction. Rather than thinking of the correspondence of language to reality as symbolized by the relation between two sides of a T-sentence, Davidson says, we should attend to word-world rather than sentence-world mappings, and in particular to the constraints on such mappings required for "the elaboration of a nontrivial theory capable of meeting the test of entailing all those neutral snowbound trivialities"(viz., the T-sentences).[25]

These constraints are what guide the field linguist who tries to guess the causes of the native's behavior, and then goes around the hermeneutic circle long enough to come up with T-sentences which maximize the truth of the native's beliefs. The eventual theory will link native words with bits of the world by the satisfaction-relation, but these links will not be the basis for the translations. Rather, they will be fallout from the translations. Going around this circle means not attempting (in the manner of building-block theories of reference) to start with some "secure" links, but rather going back and forth between guesses at translations of occasion-sentences and of standing

---

[24] I think that Davidson may be worrying, in this passage, about the sort of identification of criterial and causal relations for which I criticized Plantinga in note 11 above. This is the sort of identification which is characteristic of idealism, and which generates fear that coherence theories will result in human beings having "constituted the world." On my interpretation, he has already disposed of that identification, and thus of the need for worry.

[25] *Inquiries*, p. 51.

sentences until something like Rawlsian "reflective equilibrium" emerges.

The correspondence between words and objects provided by the satisfaction-relations incorporated in a T-theory are thus irrelevant to the sort of correspondence which was supposed to be described by "true of," and which is supposed to be revealed by "philosophical analysis," culminating in a "theory of truth." So whatever the skeptic's desired correspondence may be, it is not something which is captured in Tarski's account of satisfaction. For "true" does not offer material for analysis. As Davidson says,

> Truth is beautifully transparent compared to belief and coherence and I take it as primitive. Truth, as applied to utterances of sentences, shows the disquotational feature enshrined in Tarski's Convention T, and that is enough to fix its domain of application.[26]

So we cannot define "true" in terms of satisfaction, nor of anything else. We can only explain our sense that, as Davidson says, "the truth of an utterance depends on just two things, what the words mean and how the world is arranged" by explaining how we go about finding out these two things, and by pointing out that these two inquiries cannot be conducted independently.

I think Davidson should be interpreted as saying that the plausibility of the thesis just cited—that there is no third thing relevant to truth besides meanings of words and the way the world is—is the best explanation we are going to get of the intuitive force of (D): the idea that "truth is correspondence with reality." This thesis is all there is to the "realistic" intuition which idealists, physicalists, and Peirceans have been so concerned to preserve. But, so construed, (D) makes the merely *negative* point that we need not worry about such *tertia* as, in Davidson's words, "a conceptual scheme, a way of viewing things, a perspective" (or a transcendental constitution of consciousness, or a language, or a cultural tradition). So I think that Davidson is telling us, once again, that less is more: we should not ask for more detail about the correspondence relation, but rather realize that the *tertia* which have made us have skeptical doubts about whether most of our beliefs are true are just not there.

To say that they are not there is to say, once again, that the field linguist does not need them—and that therefore philosophy does not need them either. Once we understand how radical interpretation

---

[26] "A Coherence Theory . . . ," p. 425.

works, and that the interpreter can make no good use of notions like "determinate meaning," "intended interpretation," "constitutive act of the transcendental imagination," "conceptual scheme," and the like, then we can take the notion of "correspondence to reality" as trivial, and not in need of analysis. For this term has now been reduced to a stylistic variant of "true."

If this is indeed what Davidson is saying, then his answer to the skeptic comes down to: you are only a skeptic because you have these intentionalistic notions floating around in your head, inserting imaginary barriers between you and the world. Once you purify yourself of the "idea idea" in all its various forms, skepticism will never cross your enlightened mind. If this *is* his response to the skeptic, then I think he is making exactly the right move, the same move which James and Dewey were trying, somewhat more awkwardly, to make. But I also think Davidson was a bit misleading in suggesting that he was going to show us how coherence yields correspondence. It would have been better to have said that he was going to offer the skeptic a way of speaking which would prevent him from asking his question, than to say that he was going to answer that question. It would have been better to tell him that when confrontation goes, so does representation, and thus the picture which made possible both the fears of the skeptic and the hopes of the physicalist, the idealist and the Peircean.

Davidson's favorite characterization of the picture which the skeptic should abjure is "the dualism of scheme and content." A common feature of all the forms of this dualism which Davidson lists is that the relations between the two sides of the dualism are non-causal. Such *tertia* as a "conceptual framework" or an "intended interpretation" are non-causally related to the things which they organize or intend. They vary independently of the rest of the universe, just as do the skeptic's relations of "correspondence" or "representation." The moral is that if we have no such *tertia,* then we have no suitable items to serve as representations, and thus no need to ask whether our beliefs represent the world accurately. We still have beliefs, but they will be seen from the outside as the field linguist sees them (as causal interactions with the environment) or from the inside as the pre-epistemological native sees them (as rules for action). To abjure *tertia* is to abjure the possibility of a third way of seeing them—one which somehow combines the outside view and the inside view, the descriptive and the normative attitudes. To see language in the same way as we see beliefs—not as a "conceptual framework" but as the causal interaction with the environment described by the field linguist, makes it impossible to think of language as something which may or may not (how could we ever tell?) "fit the world." So once we give up *tertia*, we give up (or trivialize) the notions of representation and correspondence, and thereby give up the possibility of formulating epistemological skepticism.

If my understanding of Davidson is right, then—apart from his appeal to physicalistic unified science, the appeal formulated in the pragmatist's (2)—his only arguments for the claim that the philosophy of language of the field linguist is all we need will be the arguments offered in "On the Very Idea of a Conceptual Scheme" to the effect that various "confrontationalist" metaphors are more trouble than they are worth. All that we might add would be further arguments to the same point drawn from the history of philosophy—illustrations of the impasses into which the attempts to develop those metaphors drew various great dead philosophers. It will not be an empirical or a metaphysical discovery that there is no *tertium quid* relevant to the truth of assertions, nor a result of "analysis of the meaning" of "true" or "belief" or any other term. So, like James (though unlike Peirce) Davidson is not giving us a new "theory of truth." Rather, he is giving us reasons for thinking that we can safely get along with less philosophizing about truth than we had thought we needed. On my interpretation, his argument that "coherence yields correspondence" comes down to

> From the field linguist's point of view, none of the notions which might suggest that there was more to truth than the meaning of words and the way the world is are needed. So if you are willing to assume this point of view you will have no more skeptical doubts about the intrinsic veridicality of belief.

IV. Davidson As Non-reductive Physicalist

Before turning to a well-known set of objections to the claim that the philosophy of the field linguist is all the philosophy of language we need—those of Michael Dummett—it will be useful to compare Davidson with a philosopher to whom he is, beneath a few superficial differences in rhetoric, very close: Hilary Putnam. Putnam is a proponent of many familiar pragmatist doctrines. He makes fun, as James and Dewey did, of the attempt to get an outside view—a "God's-eye-view" of the sort which the traditional epistemologist, and the skeptic, have tried for. But when he confronts disquotationalist theories of truth he is troubled. They smell reductionist to him, and he sees them as symptoms of a lingering positivism, a "transcendental Skinnerianism." Putnam says:

> If a philosopher says that *truth* is different from electricity in precisely this way: that there is room for a theory of electricity but *no room* for a theory of truth, that knowing the assertibility conditions is *all there is to know* about truth, then, in so far as I understand him at all, he is denying that there is a *property* of truth (or a property of rightness or correctness), not just in the realist sense, but in *any* sense. But this is to deny that our thoughts and assertions are *thoughts* and *assertions*.[27]

Putnam is here assuming that the only reason why one might disclaim the need for a theory of the nature of *X* is that one has discovered that *Xs* are "nothing but" *Ys*, in good reductivist fashion. So he thinks that Davidson's abjuration of "an account of what it is for an assertion to be correct and what it is for it to be incorrect" must be made on the basis of a reduction of true assertions to conventionally accepted noises.[28] On this view, to assume the point of view of the field linguist is to reduce actions to movements. But Davidson is not saying that assertions are nothing but noises. Rather he is saying that truth, unlike electricity, is not an explanation of anything.

The idea that the property of truth can serve as an explanation is a product of the misleading picture which engenders the idea that its presence requires an explanation. To see this, notice that it would be a mistake to think of "true" as having an explanatory use on the basis of such examples as "He found the correct house because his belief about its location was true" and "Priestley failed to understand the nature of oxygen because his beliefs about the nature of combustion were false." The quoted sentences are not explanations but promissory notes for explanations. To get them cashed, to get real explanations, we need to say things like "He found the correct house because he believed that it was located at . . ." or "Priestley failed because he thought that phlogiston . . . ." The explanation of success

---

[27] Hilary Putnam, *Realism and Reason* (Cambridge University Press, Cambridge, 1983), p. xv.

[28] Ibid., p. xiv.

and failure is given by the details about what was true or what was false, not by the truth or falsity itself—just as the explanation of the praiseworthiness of an action is not "it was the right thing to do" but the details of the circumstances in which it was done.[29]

If truth *itself* is to be an explanation of something, that explanandum must be of something which can be caused by truth, but not caused by the content of true beliefs. The function of the *tertia* which Davidson wishes to banish was precisely to provide a mechanism outside the causal order of the physical world, a mechanism which could have or lack a quasi-causal property with which one might identify truth. Thus to say that our conceptual scheme is "adequate to the world," is to suggest that some cogs and gears are meshing nicely—cogs and gears which are either non-physical or which, though physical, are not mentioned in the rest of our causal story. To suggest, with the skeptic, that our language-game may have nothing to do with the way the world is, is to call up a picture of a gearwheel so out of touch with the rest of the mechanism as to be spinning idly.[30]

Given his distaste for intentionalist notions, Putnam should have no relish for such pictures, and thus no inclination to regard truth as an explanatory notion. But because he still retains the idea that one should give an "account of what it is for an assertion to be correct," he demands more than Davidson is in a position to give. He retains this idea, I think, because he is afraid that the inside point of view on our language-game, the point of view where we use "true" as a term of praise, will somehow be weakened if it receives no support from "a philosophical account." Consider the following passage:

> If the cause-effect-description [of our linguistic behavior qua production of noises] is complete from a philosophical as well as

---

[29] The line of argument I have been employing in this paragraph may also be found in Michael Levin, "What Kind of Explanation is Truth?," (in *Scientific Realism*, ed. Jarrett Leplin (Berkeley, University of California Press, 1984), pp. 124–39) and in Michael Williams, "Do We Need a Theory Of Truth for Epistemological Purposes?" forthcoming in an issue of *Philosophical Topics* devoted to epistemology.

[30] Davidson's position, as Alan Donagan has pointed out to me, is the same as Wittgenstein's: no gears are necessary, for the sentences in which our beliefs are expressed touch the world directly. See *Tractatus Logico-Philosophicus*. 2.1511–2.1515. "What Is a Theory of Meaning?" (II), p. 116.

> from a behavioral-scientific point of view; if all there is to say about language is that it consists in the production of noises (and subvocalizations) according to a certain causal pattern; *if the causal story is not to be and need not be supplemented by a normative story* . . . then there is no way in which the noises we utter . . . are more than mere "expressions of our subjectivity."..[31]

The line I have italicized suggests that disquotationalist theorists of truth think that there is only one story to be told about people: a behavioristic one. But why on earth should such theorists not allow for, and indeed insist upon, supplementing such stories with "a normative story?" Why should we take the existence of the outside point of view of the field linguist as a recommendation never to assume the inside point of view of the earnest seeker after truth? Putnam, I think, still takes a "philosophical account of *X*" to be a synoptic vision which will somehow synthesize every other possible view, will somehow bring the outside and the inside points of view together.

It seems to me precisely the virtue of James and of Dewey to insist that we cannot have such a synoptic vision—that we cannot back up our norms by "grounding" them in a metaphysical or scientific account of the world. Pragmatism, especially in the form developed by Dewey, urges that we not repeat Plato's mistake of taking terms of praise as the names of esoteric things—of assuming, e.g., we would do a better job of being good if we could get more theoretical knowledge of The Good. Dewey was constantly criticized, from the Platonist right, for being reductionist and scientistic, inattentive to our needs for "objective values." This is the kind of criticism Davidson is currently getting from Putnam. He was also constantly criticized, from the positivist left, for a light-minded relativistic instrumentalism which paid too little attention to "hard facts," and for trivializing the notion of "truth" by this neglect.[32] This is the kind of criticism Davidson gets from physicalists such as Field.

Attack from both sides is the usual reward of philosophers who, like Dewey and Davidson, try to stop the pendulum of philosophical fashion from swinging endlessly back and forth between a tough-minded reductionism and a high-minded anti-

---

[31] Hilary Putnam, "On Truth," in *How Many Questions*, ed. Leigh S. Caulman et al. (Indianapolis, Hackett, 1983), p. 44.

[32] So, simultaneously, was Neurath—who is beginning to get a better press these days.

reductionism. Such philosophers do so by patiently explaining that norms are one thing and descriptions another. In Davidson's case, this comes down to saying that the understanding you get of how the word "true" works by contemplating the possibility of a Tarskian truth-theory for your language is utterly irrelevant to the satisfaction you get by saying that you know more truths today than you did yesterday, or that truth is great, and will prevail. Putnam's insistence that there is more to truth than disquotationalism can offer is not based on having looked at "true," or at the language-games we play, and having seen more than Davidson saw. Rather, it is based on a hope that there is more to the notion of a "philosophical account" than Dewey or Davidson think there can be.

This parallel between Dewey and Davidson seems to me reinforced by Stephen Leeds' formulation of what he calls "Naturalistic Instrumentalism": the Quine-like combination of the view that "the only goal relative to which our methods of theory construction and revision fall into place as a rational procedure is the goal of prediction observations"[33] with the claim that the world is, really and truly is, made up of the entities of current science. As Leeds says, this new "ism" may sound like an oxymoron (as a similar "ism" did to Dewey's critics). But it only sounds that way if, as Leeds says, one thinks that "a theory of truth is needed to explain why our theories work"[34]—if one thinks that "truth" can be an explanatory notion. Leeds and Arthur Fine[35] have pointed out the circularity of attempts to use semantics to explain our predictive successes. Such circularity is the natural consequence of trying to be both outside our inquiries and inside them at the same time—to describe them both as motions and as actions. As Davidson has reiterated in his writings on the theory of action, there is no need to choose between these two descriptions: there is only a need to keep them distinct, so that one does not try to use both at once.

---

[33] Stephen Leeds, "Theories of Reference and Truth," *Erkenntnis*, 13 (1978), p. 117.

[34] Dewey would not have restricted theory construction and revision to the sciences which aim at prediction and control, but this difference between Dewey and Leeds is not relevant to the point at hand.

[35] In his "The Natural Ontological Attitude," in *Essays on Scientific Realism*, ed. J. Leplin.

V. Davidson and Dummett

The question of whether "truth" is an explanatory property encapsulates the question of whether the philosophy of the field linguist is philosophy of language enough or whether (as Michael Dummett thinks) we need a philosophy of language which links up with epistemology, and with traditional metaphysical issues. Dummett says that a theory of meaning should tell us how:

> an implicit grasp of the theory of meaning, which is attributed to a speaker, issues in his employment of the language and hence . . . in the content of the theory. Holism in respect of how one might, starting from scratch, arrive at a theory of meaning for a language, on the other hand, has no such implications, and is, as far as I can see, unobjectionable and almost banal. It is certain that Davidson intends his holism as a doctrine with more bite than this.[36]

Dummett thinks that what you get out of Davidsonian radical interpretation does not include "the content" of a theory of meaning—"the specific senses speakers attach to the words of the language." But on the interpretation of Davidson I have been offering, what Dummett calls a "sense" is just the sort of *tertium quid* which Davidson wants us to forget about. So the bite of Davidson's theory is not the sort Dummett wants. Dummett wants a theory that bites down on the problems which he thinks can only be formulated when one has a theory of "sense"—e.g., epistemological and metaphysical issues. Davidson wants a theory of meaning which will serve the field linguists' purposes and to which such problems are irrelevant.

Dummett's argument that more is needed than Davidson gives us is that somebody could know the ensemble of truth-conditions produced by a Davidsonian interpreter without knowing the content of the right-hand, metalinguistic, portions of the T-sentences. He thinks that "a T-sentence for which the metalanguage contains the object-language is obviously unexplanatory" and that if this is so then "a T-sentence for an object-language disjoint from the metalanguage is equally unexplanatory."[37] Davidson will reply that

[36] Michael Dummett, "What Is a Theory of Meaning?" in *Mind and Language*, ed. Samuel Guttenplan (Oxford University Press, Oxford, 1975), p. 127.

[37] Ibid., p. 108. Dummett actually says "M-sentence" (i.e., a sentence of the form "'——' means ——") rather than "T-sentence." I have changed the

no single T-sentence—no single "neutral snowbound triviality"—will tell you what it is to understand any of the words occurring on the left-hand sides, but that the whole body of such sentences tells you *all* there is to know about this. Dummett regards that reply as an admission of defeat. He says:

> On such an account, there can be no answer to the question what constitutes a speaker's understanding of any one word or sentence: one can say only that the knowledge of the entire theory of truth issues in an ability to speak the language, and, in particular, in a propensity to recognize sentences of it as true under conditions corresponding, by and large, to the T-sentences.[38]

And again:

> no way is provided, even in principle, of segmenting his ability to use the language as a whole into distinct component abilities.[39]

Now it is of the essence of Davidson's position, as of the positions of Wittgenstein and Sellars, that there are no such distinct component abilities.[40] For when you get rid of such *tertia* as "determinate meanings," "intended interpretations," "responses to stimuli," and the like, you are left with nothing to split up the overall know-how into component bits—nothing to reply to "How do you know that that's called 'red'?" save Wittgenstein's: "I know English." Davidson has to insist that the individual T-sentences do not replicate any inner structures, and that any attempt to provide such structures will pay the price of reintroducing *tertia*, entities which will get between our words and the world.

Dummett notes that Davidson tries "to make a virtue of necessity," but insists that doing so "is an abnegation of what we are entitled to expect from a theory of meaning."[41] For Dummett thinks

---

quotation for the sake of perspicacity. As Dummett rightly says, for Davidson's purposes the two sorts of sentence are interchangeable.

[38] Ibid., p. 115.

[39] Ibid., p. 116.

[40] A similar position is adopted by Ernest Tugendhat in his *Traditional and Analytical Philosophy* (Cambridge University Press, Cambridge, 1983). Tugendhat thinks of this position as the only alternative to the "objectualist" account of the understanding of language which has dominated the philosophical tradition up through Husserl and Russell.

[41] Ibid., p. 117. Some of the complaints about Davidson I have been citing from Dummett are modified in the appendix to "What is a Theory of Meaning?" (ibid., pp. 123ff.) But the insistence on the point that Davidson "can make no sense of

that we are entitled to a theory of meaning which will preserve the traditional notions of empiricist epistemology. He thinks that any such theory must grant that "an ability to use a given sentence in order to give a report of observation may reasonably be taken, as a knowledge of what has to be the case for that sentence to be true."[42]

Dummett's paradigm case of grasping the content of an expression is what you do when you observe that something is red. He thinks that the contrast between "That's red!" and cases like "Caesar crossed the Rubicon," "Love is better than hate," and "There are transfinite cardinals" is something which any adequate philosophy of language must preserve. But for Davidson's and Wittgenstein's holism there simply is no contrast. On their view, to grasp the content is, in *all* these cases, to grasp the inferential relationships between these sentences and the other sentences of the language.[43]

The same point can be made in reference to Dummett's presentation of the issue about realism and anti-realism in terms of bivalence. Dummett seems to think that the question of bivalence, of whether statements are "determinately true or false, independently of our knowledge or our means of knowing"[44] arises only for statements made by means of sentences "belonging to the less

---

knowing part of the language" (p. 138) and the unargued-for presumption that philosophy of language must preserve an unQuinean language-fact distinction (p. 137) remain.

[42] Dummett, "What Is a Theory of Meaning? (II)" in Gareth Evans and John McDowell (eds), *Truth and Meaning* (Oxford University Press, Oxford, 1976), p. 95.

[43] Dummett thinks that Wittgenstein's view that "acceptance of any principle of inference contributes to determining the meaning of words"—a view which Davidson shares—is unacceptably holistic. (See "What Is A Theory of Meaning? (II)," p. 105). Elsewhere Dummett has said that this sort of holism leads to the view that "a systematic theory of meaning for a language is an impossibility" and thus to the view that philosophy "seeks to remove, not ignorance or false beliefs, but conceptual confusion, and therefore has nothing positive to set in place of what it removes" (*Truth and Other Enigmas* (Harvard University Press, Cambridge, Mass., 1978), p. 453). By "a systematic theory of meaning for a language" Dummett means one which gives him "what we are entitled to expect," viz., a handle on traditional philosophical problems. But he begs the question against Davidson when he rebuts the holism shared by Davidson and Wittgenstein on the ground that it leads to the therapeutic approach to traditional problems shared by Dewey and Wittgenstein.

[44] "What Is a Theory of Meaning?" (II), p. 101.

primitive strata of our language."[45] He has no doubt that for the "lower storeys"—e.g., for statements like "That's red!"—bivalence obtains. Our inarticulable knowledge of what it is for such a statement to be true, presumably, is enough to make us realists about redness. For these types of statements we can have a strong sense of "correspondence to reality"—"strong" in that we are confident that what makes the statement true is "reality" rather than merely ourselves. Here we have the empiricist picture, shared by Quine and Dummett, according to which language stands as a veil between us and reality, with reality punching its way through (or being known to punch its way through) only at the tips of a few sensory receptors. The farther into the upper storeys we get, on the other hand, the more doubt there is that we are in touch with the world, and the more temptation to be an "anti-realist" in regard to certain entities—that is, to adopt a theory of meaning which explains the truth of such statements "in terms of our capacity to recognize statements as true, and not in terms of a condition which transcends human capacities."[46]

By contrast, if one follows Davidson, one will not know what to make of the issue between realist and anti-realist. For one will feel in touch with reality *all the time*. Our language—conceived as the web of inferential relationships between our uses of vocables—is not, on this view, something "merely human" which may hide something which "transcends human capacities." Nor can it deceive us into thinking ourselves in correspondence with something like that when we really are not. On the contrary, using those vocables is as direct as contact with reality can get (as direct as kicking rocks, e.g.). The fallacy comes in thinking that the relationship between vocable and reality has to be piecemeal (like the relation between individual kicks and individual rocks), a matter of discrete component capacities to get in touch with discrete hunks of reality.

If one thinks that, one will, for example, agree with Plato and Dummett that there is an important philosophical question about whether there really are moral values "out there." For Davidson, on the other hand, there is goodness out there in exactly the same trivial sense in which there is redness out there. The relevant sense is explicated by saying that the field linguist will come up with a T-

[45] Ibid., p. 100.

[46] "What Is a Theory of Meaning? (II)," p. 116.

sentence whose right-hand side is "that's morally right" in just the same manner as he comes up with one whose right-hand side is "that's red." He will assume that insofar as the natives fail to find the same things red, or morally right, as we do, our disagreements with them will be explicable by various differences in our respective environments (or the environments of our respective ancestors).

I conclude that for Dummett no philosophy of language is adequate which does not permit the perspicuous reformulation of the epistemological and metaphysical issues discussed by the philosophical tradition. For Davidson this ability is not a desideratum. For James and Dewey, the *in*ability to formulate such issues was a desideratum. I should like to attribute this latter, stronger, view to Davidson, but I have no good evidence for doing so. I commend it to him, because I think that his only recourse in arguing with those who think they have a right to expect more philosophy of language than he offers is to adopt this therapeutic stance. More specifically, all he can do is point out that Dummett's expectations stem from the habit of construing correspondence as confrontation, and then exhibit the unhappy history of this construal, a history which stretches from Plato through Locke to Quine. In the end, the issue is going to be decided on a high metaphilosophical plane—one from which we look down upon the philosopical tradition and judge its worth.

VI. Davidson, Realism and Anti-realism

If the argument of the preceding section is right, then Davidson has been put in a false position by Dummett's attempts to place him on the "realist" side of a distinction between realism and anti-realism. That distinction, stated in terms of a distinction between truth-conditions and assertibility-conditions, will seem a plausible way of classifying philosophical doctrines only if one accepts what Michael Devitt has called Dummett's "propositional assumption:" the assumption that "an L-speaker's understanding of a sentence of L consists in his knowing that the sentence is true-in-L in such and such circumstances."[47] Davidson, however, thinks it hopeless to isolate such circumstances. His holism makes him reject the idea of such knowledge. Yet Dummett gives an account of Davidsonian "truth-

---

[47] Michael Devitt, "Dummett's Anti-Realism," *Journal of Philosophy*, 80 (1983), p. 84.

conditions" which is radically non-holistic. As Devitt rightly says, Dummett tries to infer from "*X* knows the meaning of *S*" and "The meaning of *S* = the truth-conditions of *X*" to "s knows that the truth-conditions of *X* are TC," an inference which only goes through if we construe "*X* knows the meaning of *S*" as "there exists an entity which is the meaning of *S* and *X* is acquainted with it."[48] The latter construal will be made only by someone who accepts the propositional assumption.

Davidson would not accept it,[49] and therefore cannot be seen as a theorist of "truth-conditions" in Dummett's sense. Davidson thinks that one great advantage of his view is that it gives you a theory of meaning without countenancing such things as "meanings." Since he agrees with Quine that a theory of meaning for a language is what comes out of empirical research into linguistic behavior, Davidson would be the first to agree with Devitt, against Dummett, that "any propositional knowledge of a language that a person has is something over and above his competence, something gained from theorizing about the language."[50] If we bear Davidson's holism and behaviorism in mind, he will seem the last philosopher to believe that users of *S* are typically able to envisage acquaintance with sets of circumstances which would conclusively verify *S*.

Dummett misconstrues Davidson because he himself believes that (in Devitt's words), "The only sort of behavior that could manifest the speaker's understanding of *S* is that behavior which brings him into the position in which, if the condition obtains that

---

[48] Ibid., p. 86.

[49] Devitt disagrees. He says "Davidson is open to [Dummett's] argument because he accepts the propositional assumption" (ibid., p. 90). This willingness to accept Dummett's description of Davidson seems to me a blemish in Devitt's incisive criticism of Dummett's attempt to semanticize metaphysics. (Though, as I say below, I also disagree with Devitt's claim that desemanticizing metaphysics restores the purity of that discipline. I think that doing so merely exposes its barrenness.) I suspect the reason why Devitt thinks of Davidson as accepting the propositional assumption is that Davidson, in his earlier articles, identified a theory of meaning for L with what a speaker of L understands, an identification which suggests that the speaker *does* have "distinct component abilities" corresponding to the various T-sentences. But this identification is, as far as I can see, either incompatible with the holism I have described in the previous section or as misleading a metaphor as that billiard balls have "internalized" the laws of mechanics.

[50] Ibid., pp. 89–90.

conclusively justifies the assertion of *S*, he recognizes it as so doing."[51] As Devitt says, this expresses Dummett's commitment to "anti-holist epistemology."[52] Dummett thinks that there are some familiar cases (e.g., so-called "observation sentences") where there are indeed such conditions, and such acts of recognition. But for Davidson there are never any of either. So the contrast which Dummett draws between, e.g., realism about tables and anti-realism about values makes no sense for Davidson. For holists, so to speak, truth is *always* evidence-transcendent. But that is to say that *X's* understanding of *S* is *never* manifested in the kind of recognitional abilities which Dummett envisages.[53]

Dummett takes the upshot of Frege's linguistification of philosophy to be that the only way to make sense of a metaphysical disagreement is by semantic ascent—jacking up the old metaphysical issue into a new semantical issue. Davidson, on my interpretation, thinks that the benefit of going linguistic is that getting rid of the Cartesian mind is a first step toward eliminating the *tertia* which, by seeming to intrude between us and the world, created the old metaphysical issues in the first place. We can take the final step, and dissolve those issues for good, by not letting philosophy of language recreate the factitious contrasts in terms of which those issues were formulated, e.g., the contrast between "objective realities" and "useful fictions," or that between the "ontological status" of the objects of, respectively, physics, ethics and logic. For Davidson, Quine's idea of "ontological commitment" and Dummett's idea of "matter of fact" are both unfortunate relics of metaphysical thought;

---

[51] Ibid., p. 91.

[52] Ibid., p. 92.

[53] See Paul Horwich, "Three Forms of Realism," *Synthese*, 51 (1982), p. 199: "[Dummett's] inference from not being able to establish when *p* is true to not being able to manifest knowledge of its truth-conditions is not at all compelling. All it takes to know *p's* truth-conditions is to understand it; and all it takes to understand *p* is the ability to use it in accordance with community norms, implicit in linguistic practice, for judging in various circumstances, the degree of confidence it should be given." Horwich's own suggestion that we combine what he calls "semantic realism" (the claim that truth may extend beyond our capacity to recognize it) with a "use theory of meaning and a redundancy account of truth" (p. 186) seems to me a succinct description of Davidson's strategy. (For an earlier statement of Horwich's anti-Dummett point, see P. F. Strawson's criticism of Crispin Wright: "Scruton and Wright on Anti-Realism," *Proceedings of the Aristotelian Society*, 1977, p. 16.)

they are among the ideas which metaphysics wove together to form the scheme-content dualism.

These ideas form such a large, mutually reinforcing, network that it is hard to pick one out as crucial. But the best candidate for being at the center of this network may be the idea repudiated in the pragmatists' thesis (3): the idea that sentences can be "made true." Davidson says that "all the evidence there is is just what it takes to make our sentences or theories true. Nothing, however, no thing makes sentences or theories true: not experience, not surface irritations, not the world, can make a sentence true."[54] I interpret this passage as saying that the inferential relations between our belief that *S* and our other beliefs have nothing in particular to do with the aboutness relation which ties *S* to its objects. The lines of evidential force, so to speak, do not parallel the lines of referential direction. This lack of parallelism is the burden of epistemological holism. To know about the former lines is to know the language in which the beliefs are expressed. To know about the latter is to have an empirical theory about what the people who use that language mean by what they say—which is also the story about the causal roles played by their linguistic behavior in their interaction with their environment.

The urge to coalesce the justificatory story and the causal story is the old metaphysical urge which Wittgenstein helped us overcome when he told us to beware of entities called "meanings"—or, more generally, of items relevant to the fixation of belief which are, in Davidson's words, "intermediate between belief and the usual objects which beliefs are about."[55] For such entities are supposed to be *both* causes *and* justifications: entities (like sense-data or surface irritations or clear and distinct ideas) which belong both to the story which justifies me in believing that *S* and to the story which the observer of my linguistic behavior tells us about the causes of my belief that *S*. Devitt succumbs to this pre-Wittgensteinian urge when he follows Field in suggesting that we can explicate the "intuitive idea of correspondence to a 'world out there'" by making truth dependent on "genuine reference relations between words and objective reality."[56] Dummett succumbs to it when he thinks of a given state of the world as capable of "conclusively verifying" a belief. The latter

---

[54] *Inquiries*, p. 194.

[55] "A Coherence Theory . . . ," p. 430.

[56] Devitt, p. 77.

notion embodies just the idea of bits of the world making a belief true which Davidson rejects.

Devitt is, I think, right in saying that, once we drop Dummett's anti-holism, the issue about "realism" is de-semanticized. But it is also trivialized. For there is now nothing for "realism" to name save the banal anti-idealist thesis which Devitt formulates as "Commonsense physical entities objectively exist independently of the mental."[57] Devitt thinks this an interesting and controversial thesis. It is an embarrassment for my interpretation of Davidson as a pragmatist that he apparently does too: witness his pledge of allegiance, cited above, to the idea of "an objective public world which is not of our making."[58] This formula strikes me as no more than out-dated rhetoric. For on my view the futile metaphysical struggle between idealism and physicalism was superseded, in the early years of this century, by a metaphilosophical struggle between the pragmatists (who wanted to dissolve the old metaphysical questions) and the anti-pragmatists (who still thought there was something first-order to fight about).[59] The latter struggle is beyond realism and anti-realism.[60]

---

[57] Devitt, p. 76.

[58] See also *Inquiries into Truth and Interpretation,* p. 198: "In giving up the dualism of scheme and world, we do not give up the world, but re-establish unmediated touch with the familiar objects whose antics make our sentences and opinions true or false." Yet surely these familiar objects are simply not the world which anti-idealist philosophers have tried to underwrite. The idealists had these objects too. The world which their opponents were concerned about was one which could vary independently of the antics of the familiar objects; it was something rather like the thing-in-itself (I developed this distinction between two senses of "world," the familiar objects on the one hand and the contrived philosophical counterpart of "scheme" on the other, in an earlier (1972), and rather awkward, attempt to latch on to Davidson's arguments; see "The World Well Lost," reprinted in *Consequences of Pragmatism.*)

[59] I should try to account for this change by reference to (a) Hegel's demonstration that idealism eventually eats itself up (like the Worm Ourouboros) by deconstructing the mind-matter distinction which it started out with and (b) the disenchantment with that distinction brought about by the theory of evolution. Dewey's importance, I think, lies in having brought Hegel and Darwin together. But this is a long and controversial story.

[60] Current debates about Heidegger's "destruction of the Western metaphysical tradition" and Derrida's "deconstruction of the metaphysics of presence" form another wing of the same struggle. For some connections between Davidson and Derrida, see the essay by Samuel Wheeler in the present volume, and also his "The Extension of Deconstruction," forthcoming in *The*

So, despite his occasional pledges of realist faith, is Davidson.[61] On my version of the history of twentieth-century philosophy, logical empiricism was a reactionary development, one which took one step forward and two steps back. Davidson, by subverting the scheme-content dualism which logical empiricism took for granted, has, so to speak, kept the logic and dropped the empiricism (or better, kept the attention to language and dropped the epistemology). He has thus enabled us to use Frege's insights to confirm the holistic and pragmatist doctrines of Dewey. His work makes possible the kind of synthesis of pragmatism and positivism which Morton White

---

Monist. For parallels between Heidegger's attempt to get beyond both Plato and Nietzsche and Fine's and Davidson's attempts to get beyond realism and anti-realism see my "Beyond Realism and Anti-Realism," forthcoming in the first volume ("Wo steht die sprachanalytische Philosophie heute?") of *Weiner Riehe: Themen der Philosophie*, ed. Herta Nagl-Docekal, Richard Heinrich, Ludwig Nagl and Helmet Vetter.

[61] Arthur Fine has offered the best recent account of why we ought to get beyond this struggle. See the anti-realist polemic of his "The Natural Ontological Attitude" (cited in note 35 above) and the anti-anti-realist polemic of "And Not Anti-Realism Either," *Nous*, 18 (1984), pp. 51–65. The latter paper (p. 54) makes the point that "The anti-realism expressed in the idea of truth-as-acceptance is just as metaphysical and idle as the realism expressed by a correspondence theory." On my interpretation of Davidson, his position pretty well coincides with Fine's "Natural Ontological Attitude."

Frederick Stoutland ("Realism and Anti-Realism in Davidson's Philosophy of Language," Part I in *Critica* XIV (August, 1982) and Part II in *Critica* XIV (December, 1982) has given excellent reasons for resisting attempts (by, e.g., John McDowell and Mark Platts) to construe Davidson as a realist. However, I think that he is wrong in construing him as an anti-realist who holds that "sentences are not true in virtue of their extra-linguistic objects: they are true in virtue of their role in human practise" (Part I, p. 21). To repeat, Davidson thinks that we should drop the question "In virtue of what are sentences true?" Therefore, as I said earlier, he does not wish to be associated with pragmatism, for too many people calling themselves "pragmatists" (including myself) have said things like "a sentence is true in virtue of its helping people achieve goals and realize intentions" (Stoutland, Part II, p. 36). Despite my disagreement with Stoutland, however, I am much indebted to his discussion. In particular, his remark (Part II, p. 22) that Davidson opposes the idea that it is the "intentionality of *thoughts*—their being directed to objects, independently of whether they are true or false—which accounts for the relation of language to reality" seems to me an admirably clear and succinct expression of the difference between Davidson's holism and the "building-block" approach common to Russell, Husserl, Kripke and Searle.

foresaw as a possible "reunion in philosophy."[62] From the point of view of such a synthesis, the Peirce-Frege turn from consciousness to language (and from transcendental to formal logic) was a stage in the dissolution of such traditional problems as "realism vs. anti-realism," rather than a step towards a clearer formulation of those problems.[63]

---

[62] See Morton White, *Toward Reunion in Philosophy* (Harvard University Press, Cambridge, Massachusetts, 1956).

[63] I am very grateful to Robert Brandom, Alan Donagan and Arthur Fine for comments on the penultimate version of this paper. I made substantial changes as a result of their comments, but have not tried to acknowledge my indebtedness in every case.

16

In What Sense Are Religions Conceptual Frameworks?

Terry Godlove

According to one scholarly tradition, as old at least as Durkheim's *Elementary Forms of the Religious Life*, religions confer an indispensable unity onto their practitioner's cognitive stock. Most of us would agree that "individuals and groups don't just 'have' randomly collected bundles of beliefs, attitudes, lifegoals, forms of artistic activity, etc. The bundles generally have some coherency—although it is very hard to say in general in what this coherency consists—the elements in the bundle are complexly related to each other, they all somehow 'fit,' and the whole bundle has a characteristic structure which is often discernible even to an outside observer" (Geuss: 10). Religions have often been held to supply this coherency and structure, serving as "conceptual frameworks" or "schemes" upon which a wide variety of intellectual, emotional, and moral experience finds systematic arrangement. My general concern in this paper is with the validity of this metaphor of religions as conceptual frameworks, with the help it has been, and with the confusions it has perpetuated.

On the debit side, I shall argue that adoption of the metaphor has encouraged an all too familiar conceptual relativism. Religious frameworks are said to organize widespread and deepgoing conceptual differences among their adherents. They are, we are told, categorial schemes through which the world may be viewed; reality for one scheme may be illusion for another. Buddhist and Baptist, not unlike Kuhnian scientists devoted to disparate traditions, may even live in "different worlds." Contributing to the impression of profound conceptual difference are ethnographic reports describing seemingly bizarre episodes—episodes which come enmeshed in religious "forms of life." There are the ubiquitous Brazilian Bororo, claiming to be parrots (Smith), Evans-Pritchard's Nuer, conceiving hippopotami (84), and, closer to home, there are literalist understandings of the Eucharist. Doubts about adjudication *between* frameworks follow naturally from the attribution of dramatic conceptual divergence. We would surely judge the Bororo's assertion flat out wrong were it not for the suspicion that their conceptual framework might not be truly comparable with our own. Taking relativism, then, to be a thesis about possible variation in belief—roughly, that one person's picture of the world may be thoroughly different from someone else's—my aim will be to document and dispute allegations of radical conceptual otherness as they have appeared in the comparative study of religion, letting truth fall where it may.

Still, its relativistic thrust aside, the framework metaphor is apt. Religions do provide alternative holistic, global interpretations of the universe and our place in it, welding everything from the meaning of death to proper food preparation into a unified interpretive whole. It is undeniable that avowal of one religion or another can shape the content of long lists of interconnected beliefs and attitudes. The problem is how to affirm the holistic and systematic features of alternative religious conceptual frameworks without falling into an incoherent relativism.

I shall begin in section 1 by giving some evidence for my contention that relativistic views are common in the comparative study of religion. In section 2, I review an influential antirelativistic argument offered by Donald Davidson. It undermines the ascription of radical conceptual diversity by showing that any language user must find himself in substantial agreement with anyone else whom he takes to be a language user. Suitably redirected, it shows that Taoists and Druids, as well as primitives and Presbyterians, must agree on most matters, though not, perhaps, on most religious matters. Part of what is interesting about this result is its modal packaging: agreement will dwarf disagreement, and necessarily so. In section 3, I come back to my title, and suggest a distinction between "interpretive" and "conceptual priority" which preserves holistic religious diversity precisely against this background of shared truths outside the specifically religious.

I.

It is commonly said of religions as conceptual frameworks that they "organize" something: many times either the practitioner's "experience" or "world." In this section I give some illustrations of each and point out how adoption of the framework metaphor leads to the embracing of relativist theses.

The idea that religions are cognitive forms into which otherwise unstructured "experience" gets poured was perhaps given its first systematic and influential statement by Emile Durkheim. For him the point was explicitly epistemological: "It is . . . the function of the categories to dominate and envelop all other concepts; they are permanent moulds for the mental life" (488). And of course for Durkheim, "the principle categories . . . are born in religion and of religion; they are a product of religious thought" (22). Clifford Geertz expresses the idea that religious conceptual frameworks organize experience in his well-known essay "Religion as a Cultural System": "Religious concepts spread beyond their specifically metaphysical contexts to provide a framework of general ideas in terms of which a wide range of experience—intellectual, emotional, moral—can be given meaningful form" (120). Religious "symbol systems" perform an invaluable service on this account in rendering the believer's presumably un-formed and meaning-less experience "graspable" (124). To take a final example, when Robin Horton contrasts traditional African religious thought with modern Western science, he takes them both as "theoretical schemes in terms of which [their adherents] can grasp and comprehend most of the many vicissitudes of their daily lives" (146). Those under the sway of the traditional African scheme are "victims of a closed [cognitive] predicament." Medicinal divination is the example—the belief that a spiritual agency may be responsible for one's illness, and that the tormentor can be found out and dealt with. Horton makes the striking claim that, "In these traditional cultures, questioning the beliefs on which divining is based and weighing up of successes against failures *are just not among the paths that thought can take*" (163, my emphasis).

Whether under the guise of "conceptual systems" (Durkheim), "systems of symbols" (Geertz), or "theoretical schemes" (Horton), religions are made to do similar organizational work. They are interpretive grids, fitted onto the raw, chaotic stuff of experience, directly so for Durkheim and Geertz, indirectly for Horton, in dictating the scope of the thinkable.[1] The distinction between neutral "content" and active, synthesizing "forms" of thought had been common in epistemology ever since Hegel's historicist reading of Kant, but Durkheim was—to my knowledge—the first major theorist to transplant it into the comparative study of religion. He preserves, in this representative passage, the familiar epistemological formulation: "Sensual representations are in a perpetual flux; they come after each other like the waves of a river, and even during the time that they last, they do not remain the same thing. . . . On the contrary, [our conceptual system] is, as it were, outside of time and change; it is in the depths below all this agitation; it might be said that it is in a different portion of the mind, which is serener and calmer" (481). Religions, functioning as alternative conceptual frameworks, provide alternative sets of concepts necessary for the "constitution of experience."[2]

The ways in which relativist conclusions have been drawn from this picture are, I hope, familiar enough so as not to need much elaborating. Since experience can be constituted or organized in diverse ways (by diverse systems of categories), the project of applying justificatory notions like objectivity, rationality, truth and falsity across frameworks may appear naive, misguided, even imperialistic.

Besides organizing experience, religious frameworks are often said to organize the "world" of the believer. In employing Kuhnian language to talk about religious conversion, Basil Mitchell writes that, "[w]hen a man is converted (whether this process is dramatically sudden or not), he begins to 'see everything in a fresh light.' This is not to be thought of as his having simply (or even at all) some specific 'inner experience,' but as his coming to organize his entire 'world' in a different way" (66). And again, in moving from atheism to theism, "a comparatively large-scale transformation of the individual's 'world' takes place" (70). The quotation marks are meant

---

[1] Several of the themes taken up in this paper, including the relativistic elements in Horton's account, are discussed in Levinson. He there mentions and endorses, but chooses not to develop, an antirelativistic strategy very much like the one adopted here (38).

[2] Rorty (1979) and Gardiner have given good analytical and historical accounts of the scheme/content distinction and the central role it has played in promoting relativistic views in both philosophy and the social sciences. For Durkheim's relation to the epistemological tradition, see LaCapra.

to indicate, evidently, that the convert does not really rocket off to another planet; Mitchell, following Kuhn, is making a point about interpretation. For purposes of interpretation, Mitchell is saying, the theist and atheist might as well inhabit different worlds. The vastness of the conceptual space separating the two can be measured, not in light years, but by the absence of shared subject-matters. They can neither agree nor disagree about enough things to make their "worlds" comparable.

The view that agreement and disagreement are scheme-bound concepts comes out in a passage from Ninian Smart: "We only would be able to say the Mount Fuji is neither sacred nor non-sacred in itself if we are already dispensing with the conceptual scheme in which the concept of sacredness occurs. That is, to put it simply, we are implicitly rejecting the conceptual scheme of religion" (80–81). That the world does not come ready-made with either sacred or nonsacred features is an important (and generalizable) epistemic truth. But Smart goes several steps further in implying that the Buddhist and I cannot disagree over the question, Is Mount Fuji sacred?, until I have exchanged my conceptual scheme for his—until, in the imagery now before us, I step into his sacred "world."

Though the more common picture is of a single world organized in diverse ways, the call of unbridled ontological pluralism has not gone unanswered. Thus, Peter Berger dispenses with the quotation marks: "The Community of faith is . . . understandable as a *constructed entity*—it has been constructed in a specific human history by human beings. . . . [This principle] is applicable to Catholics, Protestants, Theravada Buddhists, Communists, vegetarians, and believers in flying saucers. In other words, the theologian's world has become *one world among many*—a generalization of the problem of relativity that goes considerably beyond the dimensions of the problem as previously posed by historical scholarship" (38, his emphasis). Our intuition that there is at most one world notwithstanding, Berger's unsettling message appears to be that there are many—and that we have made them all.

After such heady stuff Geertz offers at least some stability. He returns us to one world, although we can only "see" it through one of a variety of "perspectives" at a time—the "religious" or the "common-sensical," to take his examples. Geertz remarks, in this connection, that "[m]an [moves] more or less easily, and very frequently, between radically contrasting ways of looking at the world, ways which are not continuous with one another but are separated by cultural gaps across which Kierkegaardian leaps must be made in both directions" (120). Geertz invokes, in this passage, the two central relativist themes with which we have been concerned: the ascription of profound conceptual otherness and—the one we are now tracing—the notion of the world as unknowable (neutral, inert, noumenal) except as viewed through or organized by some conceptual framework, religious or otherwise.

An early version of this second idea is found, once again, in Durkheim. Since the categories comprising our conceptual system are translations of (religious) "social states," they give us knowledge of the "social realm." Durkheim proceeds to ask the natural question, "If the categories originally merely translate social states, does it not follow that they can be applied to the rest of nature only metaphorically?" No, he answers, for "[t]he social realm is a natural realm which differs from the others only by a greater complexity. Now it is impossible that nature should differ radically from itself in the one case and the other in regard to that which is most essential. The fundamental relations that exist between things—just that which it is the function of the categories to express—cannot be essentially dissimilar in the different realms" (31).

But one cannot solve Kant's *quaestio juris* by shouting at it. Puzzles stemming from this dualism of "social world" and "nature" have hounded the sociology of knowledge ever since. If we must allow for a multiplicity of social worlds (a consequence of categorial evolution or cultural diversity), how shall we characterize the relation between all of them and nature? We could have no grounds for saying that one "represents" nature better than the rest, or even that they "approximate" it to varying degrees (this seems to have been Durkheim's view), for such pronouncements presuppose something which, even by hypothesis, we cannot have—direct, unmediated access to "nature itself," necessary in order to judge the degree to which alternative social worlds measure up. One comes in this way to appreciate Berger's bluntness. Why not face up to it and jettison this purely formal appendage called nature, and let each cleave to all he really has, his social constructions?

To sum up: in their conceptual capacity, religions do proffer "seamless webs" of interpretation, encompassing such diverse things as the meaning of sexuality, the need for work, even why the oven blew up. But this systematic, holistic feature of religious belief has encouraged the identification of religions with conceptual frameworks, with relativistic consequences. Alternative religious frameworks are said to organize sometimes radically different kinds of experience, and/or to provide inescapable filters which inevitably mold, distort, or otherwise relativize the world to themselves. These are relativist accounts, first, in imputing massive conceptual difference, and second, in (minimally) calling into question whether justificatory claims (to truth, validity, objectivity, and the like) are applicable except as confined to a particular framework.

Having painted this impressionistic picture of the form which conceptual relativism has taken in the comparative study of religions, I turn now to a criticism of relativism itself, and from it develop my constructive suggestions for how holistic religious diversity might be better conceptualized.

II.

Davidson has offered a brace of antirelativist arguments in which he urges that its motivating idea, "the very idea of a conceptual scheme," is incoherent. His first argument is directed against the possibility of profound or global conceptual disparity, and the second, more germane for my purposes, is directed against the seemingly more plausible possibility of even a preponderance of disagreement.

The first argument can be read as asking the relativist what could count as evidence for the existence of an alien conceptual framework. If we begin by associating the putative alien scheme with a language seemingly unavoidable and so unobjectionable—then this question has to be answered by giving "criteria for language-hood that does not depend on, or entail, translatability into a familiar idiom" (Davidson, 1974: 14). Alternatively, the relativist could admit that difference in scheme simply means "a set of beliefs so different from ours as to leave no common room for debate"—but he needs more than that to stay afloat.

He must show how we could recognize something to be a language without at the same time knowing a lot about how to translate it. Davidson notes that this is usually done by appealing to alternative ways that language might "organize" or "fit" experience, and goes on to argue that the trouble with metaphors such as these is that, "like the notions of fitting the facts, or being true to the facts, [they add] nothing intelligible to the simple concept of being true" (1974:16). So that anyone who imputes an alien conceptual framework is in turn committed to the existence of a language that expresses a set of beliefs that are "largely true but not translatable." Richard Rorty has accurately glossed Davidson's strategy by suggesting that "[t]he point is to substitute the unexciting notion 'true' for the philosophically fascinating notions of 'organizing experience' or 'fitting' the facts to the world" (1979:97). These, remember, were the metaphors which seemed to give relativism its bite. Finally, the question whether "largely true but not translatable" is a useful criterion for identifying alternative conceptual schemes "is just the question how well we understand the notion of truth, as applied to a language, independent of the notion of translation. The answer is . . . that we do not understand it at all" (Davidson, 1974:16). Without translation, meaning and belief must remain opaque to us, because on Davidson's semantics, the meaning of a sentence is given by a statement of the conditions which, if actual, would make the sentence true—and this means giving a Tarski-style translation of the sentence. No translation no truth; no truth, no meaning; no meaning, no belief.[3] But without any of this, on what grounds are we alleging an alien *conceptual* scheme?

We can read Davidson as suggesting that, since we could never know it even if we were in the presence of an alien scheme, the idea is hermeneutically impotent. We cannot dissociate the notion of understanding or identifying a conceptual scheme from that of translation into a language already understood. If it is objected that

---

[3] Though I cannot explicate—much less defend—the view here, such translations take the form of so-called "T sentences," an example of which would be the seemingly trivial "'Il pleut' is true if and only if it is raining," where the conditions (in the world) which we would accept as making the left half of the biconditional true are given by the right half. Tarski took an exhaustive list of such sentences for a given language to yield the extension of the predicate "is true" for that language. Davidson's innovation was to see the form of a theory of meaning in Tarski's theory of truth. I excuse myself from a fuller treatment of Tarski's "Convention T" and Davidson's use of it in his theory of meaning on the ground that the thrust of Davidson's argument against strong relativism is understandable without it. The point to be emphasized is the inseparability of truth and translation: our pre-analytic, common-sense understanding of the concept of truth is unintelligible apart from the notion of translation into a language we already understand. Besides Tarski (1952, 1956) and Davidson (1967, 1969, 1973), see the recent, excellent survey by George Romanos (1983).

different conceptual schemes may exist even though we can have no way of picking them out, the reply will be that such a bare possibility is empty, that for the claim to have any persuasive force, some reason must be given for thinking it so. But it was the possibility of doing just that which was ruled out. Besides this verificationist argument against radical otherness, Davidson also gives a constructive, and logically independent line, pre-empting even widespread disagreement.

It was important to the success of the preceding argument that the ordinary sense of truth—what you get when you *say* it's raining and it *is* (near you)—"embody our best intuition as to how the concept of truth is actually used." But by making the possibility of interscheme interpretation lean so heavily on this intuitive sense of truth, we may arguably be begging a final relativist question. If it should turn out that even most of an agent's or culture's beliefs are false (by our lights, of course), wouldn't that be sufficient to render that agent or culture impervious to our interpretive efforts?

Such a verdict would be forced upon us, were such a scenario a serious possibility. Davidson has argued that it is not: "[w]hat makes interpretation possible . . . is the fact that we can dismiss *a priori* the chance of massive error. A theory of interpretation cannot be correct which makes a man assent to very many false sentences: it must generally be the case that a sentence is true when a speaker holds it to be. . . . [In] the end what must be counted in favor of a method of interpretation is that it puts the interpreter in general agreement with the speaker" (1975:20). A great preponderance of agreement will be found because "[w]e can . . . take it as given that most beliefs are correct. The reason for this is that a belief is identified by its location in a pattern of beliefs; it is this pattern that determines the subject matter of the belief, what the belief is about. Before some object in, or object of, the world can become part of the subject-matter of the belief (true or false) there must be endless true beliefs about the subject matter" (1975:21). The point is not that there cannot be disagreement, even extensive disagreement, between agents and cultures. Rather, the holistic point urged by Davidson is that disagreement, no matter the scope, is intelligible as disagreement only when placed against a background of even more pervasive agreement and shared truths.

Familiarity, Gadamer has said, precedes strangeness. In much the same way, Davidson is pointing out that agreement must be the basis of interpretation. The business of making sense of speakers requires us to attribute to them a substantial number of true beliefs and reasonable desires. If, as interpreters, we attribute to someone a belief as ridiculous as that the earth is flat—to take an example of Davidson's—we thereby take him to be saying that our earth, the one that is part of the solar system, "a system partly identified by the fact that it is a gaggle of large, cool bodies circling around a very large, hot star," is flat. Such a fund of true beliefs is under ordinary circumstances trivial and otiose. But to see that it is a necessary condition for successful interpretation, we need only ask ourselves how, in its absence, we could be sure that it was our earth that was thought to be flat? As Davidson has it, "[it] isn't that any false belief necessarily destroys our ability to identify further beliefs, but that the intelligibility of such identification must depend on a background of largely unmentioned and unquestioned true beliefs. To put it another way: the more things a believer is right about, the sharper his errors are. Too much mistake simply blurs the focus" (1975:21).

Against the conceptual relativist, Davidson is pointing out that his very ability to identify an "alien" concept or belief necessitates his having already marked out areas of wider agreement, since what that concept or belief is about can only be fixed by other true beliefs. An elegant feature of this argument is the way in which its grip tightens as the conceptual schemer squirms harder; as more allegedly alien concepts are discovered, the areas of known agreement will continue to outstrip areas of known difference by an ever-increasing proportion, making the ascription of even a preponderance of otherness a self-defeating activity. It has been shown, in other words, that talk of alternative conceptual schemes must collapse into talk of difference of opinion.[4]

Agreement, then, is the basis of interpretation. This methodological maxim can be refined in such a way as to bring it to bear on the theoretical questions in the comparative study of religion with which we are concerned. As Davidson has elsewhere noted, disagreement will be more tolerable in some subject-matters than in others. We need, roughly, more unanimity in the everyday than in the theoretical. It would be true to say both that unimpeded bodies fall to the ground and that gravitational attraction is responsible, but disagreement is far more tolerable in the one case than in the other.

---

[4] This argument has not persuaded everyone. For varied criticisms, see Glymour, McGinn, Rescher, and Vermazen.

Our theory of interpretation for a particular agent or people will weight agreement on the question whether persons are parrots more heavily than on whether they are mammals. The reason for this has to do with the amount of revision the theory will require in each case: sets of beliefs about something as far-reaching as the difference between humans and birds, versus comparatively localized allowances for ignorance of vertebrate biology.[5]

The avian example is not unpremeditated. Jonathan Z. Smith has recently produced a résumé and analysis of the scholarly controversy—nearing its centennial celebration—over how we are to understand the Brazilian Bororo tribesman's assertion that "I am a parrot." According to Smith, the history of the Bororo brouhaha reflects one of the thorniest methodological questions in his discipline: "How should the historian of religion interpret a religious statement which is apparently contrary to fact?"[6] As Smith's question subsumes the Bororo example, so it in turn falls under the present discussion of the underlying methodology of interpretation. It will be instructive, then, to look briefly at the record of this controversy from the point of view being developed here.

As is well known, Lucien Levy-Bruhl held that the reason the Bororo could honestly maintain something we find so absurd is that their minds operated with a different kind of logic than ours—one in which contradictories do not seem contradictory. Levy-Bruhl is thereby seen to be an early, full-fledged conceptual schemer in the sense in which I am using the term. (In fairness, it should be added that he came, in time, to be bothered by verificationist considerations not unlike those presented above, namely, how could *we* ever have evidence for *their* alternative logic?) Though not in so coarse a way, Geertz too runs afoul of the argument against alternative conceptual

---

[5] Davidson (1975:21) has pointed out that extent of disagreement cannot be measured by a ratio of rejected belief to accepted belief, since there could be an infinite number of both. The interpreter must, then, "optimize" agreement rather than "maximize" it, and optimizing will involve the weighting procedure to which I just alluded. Disagreement is, in general, least tolerable over those beliefs which are most destructive of further understanding, that is, over those beliefs which, if judged false, would make us doubt the accuracy of *other* of our attributions of belief. Thus, quantitative expressions used in this paper, e.g. "most," "largely," "preponderance," "massive," "profound," are to be understood as measures of optimization and not as numbers of belief. Vermazen (1983:71) has made essentially these points.

[6] The following discussion is drawn from Smith: 276–287.

schemes. For him, the statement, "I am a parrot" is true in the "religious" but false in the "common sensical . . . finite province of meaning" (read, scheme). How could this be so? Geertz seems committed to saying that when the Bororo are in their religious mode, there is a sense in which parrots really are people and vice versa. E. E. Evans-Pritchard offers a variation of the Geertzian strategy, which Smith has summarized: "A statement which appears at first glance to be irrational or untrue can be shown to be true or rational by the depth analyses of the criterion for truth or rationality held by a particular culture." But if "I am a parrot" is the correct translation (and if it isn't, of course all bets are off), then criteria which purport to pick out an "alternative truth"—one on which it would be *right* to identify birds with people—are no better off than Levy-Bruhl's alternative logic. We cannot put ourselves in a position to make good sense of either idea. (What would it *be* for a person to be a parrot?)

E. B. Tylor and J. G. Fraser's verdict that the assertion is simply false, "an error or misinterpretation of our normal, rational procedures," is at least plausible, still assuming accuracy in translation. But it is time to bring in our previous results. Though it is not impossible for us and the Bororo to disagree over the question, Are persons parrots?, our theory of interpretation for the Bororo cannot weather very much disagreement over matters as humdrum as this. It is prima facie evidence, in other words, against a theory of interpretation that it has someone—anyone—believing that he is a parrot, though, of course, maybe he really does. At issue are not our ideas of rationality or reasonableness, but rather, as with Davidson's flat earth example, the logically prior task of identification. Without a fund of true beliefs about persons and parrots, neither one can become part of the subject matter of a belief that we could identify as being *about* persons or parrots. But someone who honestly thinks he is a parrot cannot have such a fund. The focus, in this case, seems hopelessly blurred.

A more plausible explanation for such apparent ground-level disagreement as we find in the Bororo example has recently been suggested by J. Christopher Crocker. Though the translation of the offending utterance is correct, making it literally and trivially false, it is being used toward symbolic ends. We have been in the presence of metaphor all along. Separating meaning from use absolves us from having to postulate alternative logics and truths, and from having to fragment the continuity of our lives and language into "finite provinces of meaning."

The Bororo example is an especially good one for my purposes as it illustrates not only the kind of case which has seemed to demand explanation in terms of alternative conceptual schemes (or truths or logics)—namely, those in which another's belief contradicts a belief of our own so basic that we will not give it up (here, the belief that persons are *not* parrots)—but also the a priori truth that the beliefs of anyone we can successfully interpret cannot differ globally from our own. The combined import of Davidson's argument against the very idea of a conceptual scheme and the theory of weighted agreement has been nicely expressed by Hilary Putnam: "The conclusion [to be drawn] from all this is that an interpreted conceptual scheme will necessarily turn out to be for the most part like our own, however violently it may turn out to contradict our own in its higher reaches" (1982b:9).

It is in the context of these "higher reaches" that the question posed in my title can best be answered.

III.

I have been trading on the claim that disagreement over concrete matters is, in general, more destructive of understanding than is disagreement over more theoretical topics. But why should this be so? And what exactly distinguishes the concrete from the theoretical? We might try to rest the distinction on the lesser extent to which increasing theoreticity blocks further interpretation. But we then seem forced to say, with obvious circularity, that a topic's interpretive importance depends on its relative theoreticity. Clearly, we need an independent, general characterization of either theoreticity or interpretive importance. I will try to bring one out through a more detailed discussion of the nature of and reasons for charity in interpretation.

We have seen that, in order to understand a speaker we ordinarily want to know at least what the speaker believes and what his or her utterances mean. The trouble—what has become known as the "meaning-belief cycle"—is that each holds the interpretive key to the other. Without knowing the belief we cannot understand the meaning, but unless we know the meaning we cannot understand the belief. As a practical matter, we ordinarily assume that someone who sounds like a member of our speech community is a member, that his or her use of the familiar words matches ours. That this is our unthinking, time-tested strategy shows that the problem of interpretation is domestic as well as foreign. Yet the assumption is more easily made than justified. Shorn of our unreflective (if successful) assumptions, we face the central problem of radical interpretation: how, given the interdependence of meaning and belief, to learn both at once? Davidson's own proposal relies crucially on our ability to at times discover what sentences a speaker holds true even though we do not know what he means by the sentence, or what he believes about its (to us as yet) unknown subject matter. He writes:

> The principle is as simple and obvious as this: a sentence someone is inspired (caused) to hold true by and only by sightings of the moon is apt to mean something like "there's the moon"; the thought expressed is apt to be that the moon is there. Apt to be, allowing for intelligible error, second hand reports, and so on. Not that all words and sentences are this directly conditioned to what they are about; we can perfectly well learn to use the word "moon" without ever seeing it. The claim is that all thought and language must have a foundation in such direct historical connections, and these connections constrain the interpretation of thought and speech. (1987:450)

The indirect causal conditioning to which Davidson alludes will figure in the interpretation of religious discourse, and I will return to it shortly. The point at hand, however, is that our knowledge of what cause inspires a speaker to assent to a sentence allows us to break out of the meaning-belief cycle. "If I am right," Davidson says, "we can't in general first identify beliefs and meanings and then ask what caused them. The causality plays an indispensable role in determining the content of what we say and believe." And again, "we must in the plainest and methodologically most basic cases, take the objects of a belief to be the causes of that belief. . . . Communication begins where causes converge: your utterance means what mine does if belief in its truth is systematically caused by the same events and objects" (1986:317, 318).

Thus, interpretive success rests fundamentally on those "methodologically most basic cases"—those utterances assent to which depends systematically on observable change in the environment: "according to the method, the speaker holds a sentence true under specified conditions, and these conditions obtain, in the opinion of the interpreter, just when the speaker holds the sentence to be true" (1975:20). At least with respect to such "occasion" sentences we can hope to tell when a speaker holds a sentence true without knowing what the speaker means by the sentence; hence their interpretive primitiveness.

Now to the extent that we grant occasion sentences this interpretive priority, we will have to find a great many of the speaker's beliefs about the world right and reasonable. Davidson puts the point this way: "nor, from the interpreter's point of view, is there any way he can discover the speaker to be largely wrong about the world. For he interprets sentences held true (which is not to be distinguished from attributing beliefs) according to the events and objects in the outside world that cause the sentences to be held true" (1986:317). That is, if we take assent to a sentence inspired by and only by what we know to be sightings of the moon to mean, "there's the moon," we thereby attribute to the speaker a true belief, and so on and on for other of the speaker's utterances which display systematic, direct conditioning to alteration in the world.

In a sense, then, our initial charity is forced. If we want to get interpretation going—if we want to see the animal we confront as having beliefs at all—we must decide to find him or her largely right and reasonable about those objects and events that we appear to confront together.

It may seem that this initial act of interpretive charity guarantees agreement only over a very limited range of basic beliefs, hardly broad enough to preclude our finding the speaker "largely wrong about the world." But this is to overlook the holistic nature of the mental; it is to underestimate the amount of true belief required for the identification of any one belief, true or false. It is to overlook the fact that I cannot reasonably interpret your utterance to mean, "There's the moon"—though I see that you are caused to assent to it by and only by sightings of the moon—unless I also take you to believe many true things about the moon: that it is generally not visible during the day, that it appears to traverse the night sky, that it seems to gradually take on a crescent shape and then to fill out again, and so forth. Without some such broad agreement, I cannot be sure of my original interpretation. The point, as before, is not that there need be a fixed fund of true belief, but that we identify thoughts, distinguish between them, describe them for what they are, only as they can be located within a dense network of related beliefs.

To review this sketch of radical interpretation: Motivated by the vicious meaning-belief cycle, we turn for relief to occasion sentences, and, in virtue of the holistic nature of the mental, must find broad agreement between interpreter and speaker.

We can now draw a noncircular distinction between theoretical and concrete discourse, one that rests on the notion of observationality. As assent to its constituent utterances becomes more difficult to correlate with observable change in the environment, a domain of discourse becomes more theoretical and less concrete. It is also now apparent why increasing theoreticity tends to license the ascription of a broader scope of divergence and error. Strictly speaking, charity is *forced* (again, as the only way out of the meaning-belief cycle) only over observational subject matters. Thus, with increasing theoreticity, the *necessity* (if not the rationale, which continues to be understanding) for charity weakens. If, then, religious discourse were highly theoretical, we would know how—in spite of the dictates of charity—systematic diversity of religious belief is yet possible. For to be free to impute systematic disagreement and error is to be free to encounter systematically divergent yet intelligible belief.

Where, then, does religious discourse fall on the scale of observationality? This is of course an empirical question, one that cannot be settled by purely conceptual argument. But it seems obvious to me—and I hope it will be agreed that—religious discourse is highly theoretical, and that what tempts us to see the contrast, even incommensurability, between alternative religious conceptual frameworks falls within Putnam's "higher reaches." Not that religious discourse is typically unconnected to more concrete, observational subject matters; rather, the connections are typically, in Lukes's words, "complex and intricate." With Geertz, I think that religions show their theoretical purport in supplying "conceptions of a general order of existence." Indeed, at least three commonplace features of religious discourse well reflect its relative independence from observable change. First, religious discourse typically makes no or very little use of ostension; the divine as such cannot be pointed out. Dagfinn Føllesdal notes that it is a basic rule of interpretation that, "when a speaker points in a certain direction, then he should normally be taken to refer to an object which is situated in that direction or to some object related to one of the objects in that direction . . ." (1975:42). Føllesdal goes so far as to say that ostensive evidence should outweigh even considerations of charity, and perhaps this is so. But in any case, the point remains that, with the interpretation of much religious discourse, this agreement-producing interpretive stricture tends to lapse.

Second, religious doctrine, dogma, and belief typically attain a high degree of abstractness and complexity. Third, religious discourse is typically about how things are, and not about how they appear (Wisdom's gardener). If so, we will be unable, or at least will find it hard, to correlate utterance with environmental change. But if a domain of discourse tends to resist such correlation it is, by definition, theoretical in nature. If, as I think, these are three characteristics of religious discourse, they strongly suggest, though they cannot prove, its extreme theoreticity.

How, then, is systematic diversity of religious belief possible? If we grant that religious discourse is, on the whole, highly theoretical, the required argument is now at hand: Speakers can be allowed to differ more often and more radically as the correlation diminishes between apparent assertions and changing events and objects. Religious discourse can be so correlated, at best, to only a limited extent. So, systems of religious belief may be interpretable, incompatible, and incorrect.

But instead of taking this diversity to betray widespread and deep-going conceptual contrast—the thesis motivating relativism and the framework model—we need to recognize that such religious divergence as there is must, by a kind of interpretive necessity, be both largely theoretical in nature and dwarfed by the amount of agreement over more concrete, observational topics. In locating religious conceptual diversity primarily in the theoretical, higher reaches, we make more than an empirical observation about this or that religious belief system—though *as* an empirical observation it is, as I see it, true enough. However, on a deeper level, our "discovery" has been conditioned by the unavoidable truth that only in the context of these higher reaches is systematic conceptual diversity even possible.

That we do find vast community of belief at the more observational level is perhaps best appreciated through the very examples which best illustrate theoretical divergence. Thus, in *Tangu Traditions,* Kenelm Burridge reports that the Tangu people of New Guinea, who practice a form of ancestor worship, "consider it possible that all the particulars in their environment . . . may be possessed of, or inhabited by, inner identities or guardian beings described as *puoker,"* and that if one stubs a toe on a rock, the mishap can likely be traced to some *puoker*-mischief (1969:162). But before we account for this odd-sounding explanation by assigning the Tangu an alien conceptual framework—one which includes *puoker*-causality as a load-bearing member—we should recall that our assignment depends on our quietly holding agreement steady over such otherwise mundane subject matters as the apparent nature of toes, rocks, and pain, to expose just the tip of the conceptual iceberg. Similarly, if (some) Christians and Buddhists believe radically different things about whether persons have souls, they must share a multitude of more commonplace beliefs about what it is to be a person, at all. As before, the holism of the mental dictates that the amount of divergent belief must be relatively limited.

Greater precision seems neither possible nor desirable; indeed, the vagueness comes with the territory. With respect to that held in common, divergence over religious matters must be "relatively" limited because of the difficulties in counting beliefs discussed earlier; and this divergence will be "largely" theoretical because *some* religious beliefs are evidently quite concrete. It may be objected that religious persons often resist what they see as the unnatural division of their lives into religious and nonreligious domains. But in weighing my claim that religious beliefs must be relatively limited and largely theoretical, it is important to distinguish believing something on religious grounds from believing something religious. Take, for example, persons who believe that abortion is the killing of a human being because they believe that a fetus is made in God's image. I am concerned only with the second belief, since the first could as well be affirmed by the heathen. Thus, the objection appeals to something I grant, namely, that statements affirmable on religious grounds may be virtually limitless and thoroughly concrete.

Given the largely theoretical and relatively limited nature of alternative systems of religious belief we can now do justice to our originating intuition that they are—still and all—holistic and systematic. The general strategy is dictated by the holistic approach to interpretation: We must preserve the encompassing nature of religious belief by making it interpretively parasitic upon a world of shared objects and events. This dependency will be conceptual rather than causal. For my purposes, it is an open question whether varieties of religious belief are causally parasitic upon varieties of religious experience, or upon varieties or social organization, or, perhaps, upon the unconscious—if, indeed, the direction of dependence runs that way at all. My point is that the intelligibility of religious belief, as largely theoretical, depends upon the prior intelligibility of more concrete, shared, extra-religious beliefs and subject matters. The direction of *this* dependence is irreversible.

We want to capture the holistic and systematic nature of religious belief, and to do so in a nonrelativistic way. It would, I think, be helpful to distinguish between an *interpretive* and an *epistemic* priority. With the first, we can preserve all that wants saving from the framework model, while relegating the remainder to the second. Granting epistemic priority—the idea that a religious conceptual scheme can organize a believer's otherwise formless experience or world—it is easy to understand the appeal of the framework model and relativism. Certainly religious belief can offer some appraisal, analysis, criticism, or commentary about a wealth of ordinary subject matters from food preparation to burial rites. But the objectivity of such things as the preparation of food or the fact of human burial—their ability to serve as shared objects of belief—stands independently of any religious conception. The encompassing character of religious belief provides, not for the objectivity of such ordinary topics as these, but rather, as with toe-stubbings, for one's assessment of them. In this sense, religious belief can hold an interpretive priority. I am not suggesting that there are no specifically religious subject matters; surely there are. But religious belief—as relatively limited and largely theoretical—must depend on a world of public objects and events whose outlines have already been agreed upon; and because it must depend upon a (comparatively) massive fund of already accepted truths, religious belief cannot hold the epistemic priority accorded it by the framework model.

Rather, to say that religion can come to bear on so many facets of life is just to say that the devout may interpret many (it is hard to imagine *all*) of the world's goings-on with their religious views in mind. In this interpretive sense, a sense which leaves behind the metaphor of organizing neutral content, and preempts the possibility of radical or *even preponderant* diversity of belief, we may, if we wish, speak of religions as alternative conceptual frameworks.

We need to think of religions as holding this interpretive priority while denying them the epistemic variety. Though we must accord religious belief its rightful place of dominance insofar as it can pervasively influence our assessments of other, (often more observational) subject matters, we must also invert the image, remembering that since Muslim and Methodist must agree on most matters, conflicting religious conceptions are, in turn, dwarfed quantitatively by and identifiable only in virtue of areas of wider, less abstract harmony. We are able to recognize thoroughgoing incompatibility among sets of religious beliefs drawn from disparate traditions—that which, at least in part, makes them genuine alternatives—because of their largely theoretical status and relatively limited number. It is natural to say that these two are empirical, contingent features of religious belief systems, but in truth both must be exhibited by any religion that could be identified as such; that is, by any religion at all. The necessity derives not merely from definition or convention, but from the unavoidable nature of our interpretive practice. In this methodological sense, the nature of interpretation makes possible the diversity of religious belief.

This line of thought also has implications for how we might think of variations among religious conceptual frameworks. I would like to close by commenting briefly on three of them.

First, considerations very like the ones which ruled out radical conceptual diversity in the concrete will also work to limit the scope of possible disagreement within the specifically religious. The point can be put as follows: it is inconceivable that two persons could be found who held wholly incompatible sets of religious beliefs, for we should shortly decide that one set is not *religious* at all. A dispute is recognizably a religious dispute—to recast the earlier formulation—only as it stands out from a background of mutually acknowledged religious truth. Witness the long-standing scholarly hesitation over early Buddhism. It is primarily because the amount of belief shared with other unquestioned religions is, for purposes of classification, precariously small that we are unsure whether to count it as a religion or as a pure moral philosophy. I say primarily, because, to an even greater extent than in the mundane or everyday, *amount* of shared belief will not be the only consideration; as before, agreement and disagreement over some subject-matters will be weighted more heavily than others. It may be that adoption of a distinction between the sacred and the profane should be sufficient to certify the religious—but that is a matter for legislation, not proof. Only what might be called the "formal" features of religious belief systems—their limited number and theoretical status—can be deduced from the armchair. Those "material" characteristics in virtue of which we recognize a given belief system to be religious (adoption of a sacred/profane dichotomy, belief in a god or gods, and so on) await empirical inquiry and scholarly consensus.

Second, the fact that alternative religious conceptual frameworks must be largely theoretical in composition means that, unlike the believer who must see at least some truth in all religions, the areligious interpreter stands under no such *a priori* stricture. As his believing counterpart cannot, the heathen hermeneuticist can register his categorical disagreement without fear of thereby misrepresenting himself or misconstruing the other. This would be true of any circumscribed, theoretical subject-matter, since, as we have seen, the attribution of wholesale error in the theoretical "higher reaches" does comparatively little to blur the focus of further interpretation.

Giving religions what I have called interpretive priority lends support, finally, to a common-sense view about the relations between them. Minus conceptual priority neither the world nor truth can be relative to any particular framework, for to say that we share innumerable subject-matters is to say no more or less than that we share an objective, public world. The Buddhist's experience is "organized" no differently from the Christian's; talk of an Islamic conceptual framework boils down to talk about beliefs and attitudes which we may or may not share. Does God hear our prayers or not? I have been urging that the believer and nonbeliever can address this question head-on, so to speak; that the answer floats free of any prior acceptance or rejection of either's conceptual framework. Ordinary agreement and disagreement will do fine.[7]

References

Berger, Peter. 1970. *A Rumor of Angels*. New York: Doubleday.

Burridge, Kenelm. 1969. *Tangu Traditions*. Oxford: The Claredon Press.

---

[7] I wish to thank the editors of this volume and the editor of the *Journal of the American Academy of Religion* for affording me the opportunity to rework much of the material in Part III.

Cooper, David. 1978. Moral Relativism. In Peter A. French et al (ed.), *Midwest Studies in Philosophy* III. 97–108. Minneapolis: The University of Minnesota Press.

Davidson, Donald. 1967. Truth and Meaning. *Synthese* 7:304–23.

— 1969. True to the Facts. *The Journal of Philosophy* 66:748–64.

— 1973. In Defense of Convention T. In Hughes Leblanc (ed.), *Truth, Syntax, and Modality*. Amsterdam: North-Holland.

— 1974. On the Very Idea of a Conceptual Scheme. *Proceedings and Addresses of the American Philosophical Society* 47:5–20.

— 1975. Thought and Talk. In Samuel Guttenplan (ed.), *Mind and Language*. 7–25. Oxford: The Claredon Press.

— 1986. A Coherence Theory of Truth and Knowledge. In Ernest LePore (ed.), *Truth and Interpretation: Perspectives on the Philosophy of Donald Davidson*. Oxford: Blackwell.

— 1987. Knowing One's Own Mind. *Proceedings and Addresses of the American Philosophical Association* 60:443-54.

Durkheim, Emile. 1965. *The Elementary Forms of the Religious Life*. New York: Humanities Press.

Evans-Pritchard, E.E. 1956. *Nuer Religion*. Oxford: The Claredon Press.

Evens, T.M.S. 1982. On the Social Anthropology of Religion. *The Journal of Religion* 62/4:376–91.

Føllesdall, Dagfinn. 1975. Meaning and Experience. In Samuel Guttenplan (ed.), *Mind and Language*. 32-48. Oxford: Oxford University Press.

Gardiner, Patrick. 1981. German Philosophy and the Rise of Relativism. *The Monist* 64:138–54.

Geertz, Clifford. 1973.*The Interpretation of Cultures*. New York: Basic Books, 1973.

Geuss, Raymond. 1981. *The Idea of a Critical Theory*. Cambridge: Cambridge University Press.

Glymour, Clark. 1982. Conceptual Scheming. *Synthese* 51:169–80.

Horton, Robin. 1970. African Traditional Thought and Western Science. In Bryan Wilson (ed.), *Rationality*. 131–71. New York: Basil Blackwell.

Kant, Immanuel. 1965. *Critique of Pure Reason*. New York: St. Martin's Press.

La Capra, Dominick. 1972. *Emile Durkheim; Sociologist and Philosopher*. Ithaca: Cornell University Press.

Levinson, Henry S. 1981. Traditional Religion, Modernity, and Unthinkable Thoughts. *The Journal of Religion* 61/1:37–58.

McGinn, Colin. 1977. Charity, Interpretation and Belief. *The Journal of Philosophy* 74:521–35, 1977.

Mitchell, Basil. *The Justification of Religious Belief*. Oxford: Oxford University Press.

Ortner, Sherry. 1973. On Key Symbols. *American Anthropologist* 75:1338–46.

Putnam, Hilary. 1982a. *Reason, Truth and History*. Cambridge: Cambridge University Press.

— 1982b. The Craving for Objectivity (Unpublished at this time.)

Rescher, Nicholas. 1980. Conceptual Schemes. In Peter A. French et al (ed.), *Midwest Studies in Philosophy V*. 323–46. Minneapolis: The University of Minnesota Press.

Rorty, Richard. 1972. The World Well Lost. *The Journal of Philosophy* 69: 649–65.

— 1979. Transcendental Arguments, Self-Reference, and Pragmatism. In Peter Bieri et al. (ed.), *Transcendental Arguments and Science*. 77–104. Boston: D. Reidel.

Smart, Ninian. The Science of Religion and the Sociology of Knowledge. Princeton: Princeton University Press, 1973.

Smith, Jonathan Z. 1978. "I am a Parrot Red." *Map is not the Territory*. Leiden: E. J. Brill.

Tarski, Alfred. 1952. The Semantic Conception of Truth. In Leonard Linsky (ed.), *Semantics and the Philosophy of Language*. 13–49. Chicago: University of Chicago Press.

— 1956. *Logic, Semantics, Metamathmatics*. Oxford: Oxford University Press.

Vermazen, Bruce. 1982. General Beliefs and the Principle of Charity. *Philosophical Studies* 42:111–18.

— 1983. The Intelligibility of Massive Error. *The Philosophical Quarterly* 33/130:69–74.

Worsley, P. M. 1956. Emile Durkheim's Theory of Knowledge. *The Sociological Review* 4:47–62.

17

Why Does Semantics Matter?

Hans H. Penner

Abstract

Beware of meaning! Meaning is not an entity. It does not refer to anything. This essay is an attempt to describe Donald Davidson's theory of semantics. It took Davidson some time to realize that his truth conditional theory of meaning entailed a radical repudiation of traditional correspondence and coherence theories of meaning. We now have a third theoretical alternative in semantics. In this theory "truth" is left undefined. It is essential that you grasp firmly the fact that truth does not refer, or "connect-up" anything that makes a sentence true. That is the work of epistemology, or perhaps psycho-neurology. The first theoretical task, therefore, is to describe truth, or meaning, as "convention-T." The second principle, the principle of charity, provides an explanation for testing the theory. The third principle, the principle of holism, provides the theoretical framework for truth-conditions and charity. The theory provides new and powerful refutations of relativism and the notion that semantics must be reduced to the function of the brain, sensations, specific stimuli, and the like. It also provides warrants for denying that religion is "symbolic" of experience of the numinous, the sacred, or other "given" foundations of what might be described as "religious experience." Davidson's theory has important, if not radical, consequences for the study of religion. The essay briefly describes a few of these.

I. A Truth-Conditional Theory of Semantics

Much has been written about the meaning of religion. Many scholars think that the meaning of religion is symbolic, idiogramatic, while others think the meaning is hidden, or a code that we need to decipher. Claude Lévi-Strauss thinks that the binary structure of a myth is the meaning of the myth. Stanley Tambiah thinks that rituals are "performative acts," that is to say, they do not entail propositional content, they are neither true or false. Dan Sperber, on the other hand, thinks that symbolism is meaningless and Frits Staal, although for different reasons, thinks the same goes for ritual as well. In between these contradictory views are the many papers and books on religion that use the term "meaning" as "use." Thus religion means what it does. Most publications in the academic study of religion, however, simply use the word without further clarification. We obviously need some help in the domain of semantics.

The help we receive when we look for it comes in two forms. The first tells us, roughly speaking, to look for a reference. Words refer to things—you name it: sensations, certain stimuli, psycho-neurological states, needs, the numinous, the given, and so on. Thus if I can demonstrate what religion refers to I can tell you what it means. This is the famous correspondence theory of meaning, now also labeled as the "realist" theory. It is the implicit theory in most studies of religion from Emile Durkheim to Victor Turner. This theory is critically wounded but has not yet been laid to eternal rest. For example, not all words refer, and if they did, then "The Morning Star," and "The Evening Star," would be synonyms. The theory entails this curious consequence: the world could be completely different from what we actually believe it to be. The sceptics among us are smiling!

The second traditional theory is, of course, the coherence theory of meaning, now also known as the "anti-realist" theory. Roughly and briefly, this theory rejects the principle of reference and emphasizes consistency and coherence of ideas, symbols, archetypes, and the like. The flight into idealism is not the only problem here. The theory entails the shuddering thought that your beliefs could be completely consistent/coherent and be totally wrong. The sceptics are now beginning to laugh.

Until about the beginning of the 1970s it did not do much good to call for help. Most of us found it difficult but we swallowed hard to get some version of the correspondence theory down. At times it was best not to mention the "m" word. In fact, many linguists gave up on the task of trying to come up with a proper theory of meaning. At one point in his early career, Noam Chomsky did not think that semantics was a part of linguistics! However, things have changed. Semantic theory has become an exciting field of study and Donald Davidson's truth conditional theory of meaning is at the centre of the discussion because, among other important things, he has offered us a third alternative. It is, I believe, a theory that deserves attention, especially from those of us who study the religions of the world.

This article is a programmatic essay on the subject of semantics and religion. It has its theoretical foundation in the contemporary cognitive sciences, especially the work of the philosopher of language and mind, Donald Davidson. The paper is divided into four sections. The first section will present an argument for a particular semantic theory. Since it is highly likely that most readers are not familiar with this theory I will attempt to provide a brief description of Davidson's "truth conditional" theory of semantics using a generous amount of quotations from his publications. My use of lengthy quotations from Davidson is necessary simply because of the wide variety of interpretations in the secondary literature. It is important that you read just how Davidson describes his theory. The second section will use this theory to provide an argument against relativism and the notion of languages as "conceptual schemes" or "worldviews." Given a truth theory of semantics, the third section will demonstrate that attempts to reduce language, belief, desire, and the like, i.e., "folk psychology," to neurological or physical states is at best misguided, if not false. I will attempt to show that the theory called "eliminative materialism" is a hangover from the popular positivist party that lasted almost a century. The fourth section will describe what I believe are some of the implications of a truth conditional semantics for the study of religion.

1.1. Davidson's convention-T

Over the last twenty years, Donald Davidson has been developing and refining a semantic theory that is based on truth conditions. Roughly speaking, to say that an utterance has meaning is to say that it is true. As we shall see, to say that something "corresponds to the facts," is to say that this something is true. Before describing the theory it might be best to attempt to present a brief description of what Davidson's theory denies or opposes. There is a great deal of confusion about just where Davidson sits with regard to the debate on truth as correspondence or coherence. Many scholars interpret Davidson as holding a correspondence theory of truth. Yet Davidson himself has written a very influential essay with the title, "A coherence theory of truth and knowledge," which begins: "In this paper I defend what may as well be called a coherence theory of truth and knowledge" (Davidson 1986: 307). In 1969 he wrote: "In this paper I defend a version of the correspondence theory" (Davidson 1984: 37). His essay, "The structure and content of truth," should go a long way toward clarifying his position (Davidson 1990). In his most recent response to this issue he agrees that he "once argued that Tarski's definitions could be said to implement the correspondence theory of truth, and I even called my own theory both a coherence and a correspondence theory. I no longer speak that way . . . when I announced the change I made clear that all I was changing was the terminology, feeling that there were commonly held ideas associated with the terms which I wanted to avoid" (Davidson 1993: 37).[1] He then briefly explains why he has always rejected what he now calls coherence and correspondence theories. His explanation is a summary of "The structure and content of truth."

The issue is as follows. When we attempt to construct a theory of truth, one of the things we must do is specify, at least in part, the content of the concept of truth. How is this to be done? Davidson believes that there are two broad positions on this question. The first, he says, attempts to "humanize truth by making it basically epistemic," while the second promotes "some form of correspondence theory." Coherence theories of truth are "usually driven by an epistemic engine, as are pragmatic characterizations of truth. . . . Relativism about truth is perhaps always a symptom of infection by the epistemological virus." Correspondence theories view truth as "entirely independent of our beliefs; as it is sometimes put, our beliefs might be just as they are and yet reality—and so the truth about reality—very different" (Davidson 1990: 298). Davidson suggests that we tag the coherence theories as "epistemic" theories of truth, and call correspondence theories "realist" theories of truth.

After an analysis of both kinds of theories of truth, Davidson makes his own position clear. He finds the correspondence or realist theory of truth "incomprehensible" and concludes that epistemic theories are "merely false." He then concludes:

> We should not say that truth is correspondence, coherence, warranted assertability, ideally justified assertability, what is accepted in the conversation of the right people, which science will

[1] This book contains some excellent essays on Davidson's truth conditional theory of semantics, and his response to each essay is of great help in understanding his theory. The bibliography, more than fifty pages, covers Davidson's publications, secondary books, articles, and reviews. It is the best I have come across.

> end up maintaining, what explains the convergence on single theories in science, or the success of our ordinary beliefs. To the extent that realism and antirealism [correspondence/epistemic theories] depend on one or another of these views of truth we should refuse to endorse either. Realism, with its insistence on radically nonepistemic correspondence, asks more of truth than we can understand; antirealism, with its limitation of truth to what can be ascertained, deprives truth of its role as an intersubjective standard. We must find another way of viewing the matter. (Davidson, 1990: 308–309)

Davidson has described his theory in many of his essays. I shall follow what I think is the latest version. Tarski, says Davidson, wanted to devise a theory whose concepts would apply to all and only the true sentences of a language. This theory should be explicitly related to our intuitive concept of truth. He did this by devising what is now known as "convention-T."

> Convention-T requires that the truth predicate *'s* is trueL' for a language L be so characterized as to entail, for every sentence *s* of L, a theorem of the form *'s* is trueL if and only if *p'*, when *'s'* is replaced by a systematic description of *s* and *p* is replaced by a translation of *s* into the language of the theory. Let us call these theorems T-sentences. (Davidson 1990: 289)

In an earlier version, T-sentences were described as follows:

> What characterizes a theory of truth in Tarski's style is that it entails, for every sentence *s* of the object language, a sentence of the form: *s* is true (in the object language) if and only if *p*. Instances of the form (which we shall call T-sentences) are obtained by replacing *'s'* by a canonical description of *s*, and *'p'* by a translation of *s*. (Davidson 1984: 130)

For example, "'snow is white' is true if and only if snow is white," or, "'der Schnee ist weiß' is true if and only if snow is white"—*'s'* is the canonical description of a sentence in the object language, *'p'* stands for the sentence itself or its translation into the metalanguage, and 'is true' is the place holder of the truth predicate.

Now, if this is the first time you have come across this example as the basis for a formal theory of truth you might well be thinking, "What is this!" or, words to that effect. I know I did. Perhaps a slightly different interpretation will be of help.

The formulation, "'snow is white' is true if and only if snow is white," is based upon Tarski's distinction between what he called the metalanguage and the object-language. The predicate "true" belongs to the metalanguage. The proposition of which it is predicated, "snow is white" belongs to the object-language. Lyons puts it this way:

> The example thus represents a complex metalanguage proposition, $p \equiv q$ in which p contains an expression referring to an object-language proposition, "Snow is white," and $p \equiv q$ says of this proposition that it is true if and only if a certain state of affairs obtains. It embodies a purely formal notion of truth, in that it abstracts from the empirical or epistemological question of determining whether snow is or is not white. (Lyons 1977: 168)

There are two important consequences we can immediately draw from this illustration of a truth conditional theory of semantics. First, it informs us that our natural language embraces most (all?) of the major conceptual tools we need for explaining the meaning of sentences. That is to say, we are able to explain a particular language by using the same language. Second, if this turns out to be true, then we will not be able to make sense of the notion that the logic of the object-language is different from the logic of the metalanguage. Moreover, we can now see more clearly that the fact that "snow is white" is linguistically identical with the metalanguage is irrelevant. The following example should help make this clear: "'Schnee ist weiß' is true if and only if snow is white."

It is important that we constantly remind ourselves that this theory does not define truth, nor does it tell us what makes a sentence true. What the theory does tell us is that truth and meaning are not independent of each other. As Davidson puts it:

> There is no need to suppress, of course, the obvious connection between a definition of truth of the kind Tarski has shown how to construct, and the concept of meaning. It is this: the definition works by giving the necessary and sufficient conditions for the truth of every sentence, and to give truth conditions is a way of giving the meaning of a sentence. To know the semantic concept of truth for a language is to know what it is for a sentence—any sentence—to be true and this amounts . . . to understanding the language." (1984: 24)

In brief, never confuse a semantic theory with epistemological theories that attempt to explain the conditions for what makes a sentence true.

Davidson believes, and I think he is right, that his theory of semantics helps us clarify an old problem. The question, "what is it for a sentence to be true?," has caused tremendous trouble. A truth conditional theory of semantics highlights just where the problem lies. When we ask, "What is it for a sentence to be true?," we often assume that truth is tested by discovering what a sentence relates to (e.g., some entity, fact, or perhaps some nonlinguistic state of affairs). The recursive theory of T-sentences shows us that this is a dead end and also provides us with a new path.

Except for other sentences it is unclear just what a sentence is supposed to relate to. In fact, Davidson argues that there is nothing in the world that makes a sentence true. He says, for example, that we may want to speak of the totality of experience, rather than facts, as that which makes a sentence true. But this adds nothing of significance to the concept of being true. According to Davidson:

> Nothing, however, no *thing* makes sentences and theories true: not experience, not surface irritations, not the world, can make a sentence true. *That* experience takes a certain course, that our skin is warmed or punctured, that the universe is finite, these facts, if we like to talk that way, make sentences and theories true. But this point is put better without mention of facts. The sentence "My skin is warm," is true if and only if my skin is warm. Here there is no reference to a fact, a world, an experience, or a piece of evidence. (1984: 194)

If this paragraph hits you as hard as it did me the first time I read it, it is because of our addiction to some version of the "realist" or correspondence theory of truth. When we think about "truth" we have an urge to seek and find entities, meanings, or certain items, clear and distinct ideas, that justify or fixate our belief about the world. These items, meanings, and ideas mediate, refer, or are intermediate between, our belief and whatever the object is that our beliefs are about. Davidson is asserting that this quest is mistaken. The truth (meaning) of a sentence has nothing to do with reference, intermediary entities, or ideas, or bits of the world that make a sentence true. Let us pause, briefly, to see why this is the case. Recall that according to Davidson, Tarski's definition of truth works because it gives the necessary and sufficient conditions for the truth of every sentence, that is to say, the meaning of a sentence. Thus, "to know the semantic concept of truth for a language is to know what it is for a sentence—any sentence—to be true, and this amounts, in one good sense we can give the phrase, to understanding the language" (1984: 24).

Stoutland puts it this way:

> If we understand T-sentences as Davidson does, they *cannot* give an extra-linguistic explanation of why sentences are true or false. Davidson disavows such an explanation when he argues that "the failure of correspondence theories based on the notion of fact traces back to a common source: the desire to include in the entity to which a true sentence corresponds not only the objects the sentence is 'about' (another idea full of trouble) but also whatever it is the sentence says about them." What "a sentence says about objects" is presumably the meaning of the sentence, i.e., its truth conditions. In denying that what a sentence "says about an object" should be included "in the entity to which a true sentence corresponds," I take it that Davidson is denying that the truth conditions of a sentence—that in virtue of which it is true (if it is)—should be construed as features of the objects to which a true sentence corresponds. But this is to deny that extra-linguistic objects are that in virtue of which a sentence is true or false. (Stoutland 1982: 49)

(I find both parts of this essay to be an excellent interpretation of Davidson's theory.)

To put this in Davidson's terms, T-sentences do indeed fix the truth value relative to certain conditions, "but it does not say the object language sentence ["'snow is white"'] is true because the conditions hold" (1984: 138).

But, you may ask, if T-sentences do not offer any extra-linguistic explanations regarding truth, then just what does the theory tell us about how language relates to the world? The answer is that the theory tells us nothing whatsoever about the relation of language to extra-linguistic reality. As Stoutland says, "Davidson's theory of meaning is a theory about the structure of language; the relation of language to extra-linguistic reality is not explained within that theory. To explain the relation of language to reality is to explain, not the truth structure of sentences, but the role of discourse in human life, above all the role played by the sentences we accept as true" (Stoutland 1982: 49).

1.2. Summary of Davidson's truth conditional theory of semantics

Using one of Davidson's recent essays we can provide the following summary of his theory of a truth conditional semantics.

(1) "A theory of truth . . . is an empirical theory about the truth conditions of every sentence in some corpus of sentences." Since sentences are "abstract objects" it is "the utterances and writings of language users with which a theory of truth must deal." Nevertheless, the primacy of sentences prevails because of the fact

that it is "sentences, as uttered on particular occasions by particular speakers, for which the theory supplies truth conditions and of which truth is predicated." Davidson is well aware of the important distinction linguists make between "utterance" and "sentence." He introduces the latter term here for two reasons. First, introducing "sentences" in a theory "is merely to make it possible to deal with *types* of utterances and inscriptions, whether or not particular types are realized." Second, it "allows us to speak of all actual utterances of the same type in one breath; and it allows us to stipulate what the truth conditions of an utterance or inscription of a given type would be if it were uttered" (1990: 309).

(2) "A theory of truth does more than describe an aspect of the speech behaviour of an agent, for it not only gives the truth conditions of the actual utterance of the agent; it also specifies the conditions under which the utterance would be true if it would be uttered."

(3) "A theory of truth links speaker with interpreter: it at once describes the linguistic abilities and practices of the speaker and gives the substance of what a knowledgeable interpreter knows which enables him to grasp the meaning of the speaker's utterances. This is not to say that either speaker or interpreter is aware of or has propositional knowledge of the contents of such a theory. The theory describes the conditions under which an utterance of a speaker is true, and so says nothing directly about what the speaker knows [about the contents of the theory]."

(4) "A theory of truth for a speaker is a theory of meaning in this sense, that explicit knowledge of the theory would suffice for understanding the utterances of that speaker."

(5) "A theory of truth, viewed as an empirical theory, is tested by its relevant consequences, and these are the T-sentences entailed by the theory. A T-sentence says of a particular speaker that, every time he utters a given sentence, the utterance will be true if and only if certain conditions are satisfied. T-sentences thus have the form and function of natural laws: they are universally quantified bi-conditionals, and as such are understood to apply counterfactually and to be confirmed by their instances" (1990: 309–313).

It should be clear at this point why it is the case that Davidson thinks that it is best to drop the question, "in virtue of what are sentences true?"

1.3. The principle of charity

A theory of truth for a language is an interpretation of a language. The question we must now ask is, how do we know that the theorems, the truth conditions, are true? That is to say, how can we go about testing our theorems without already knowing the meaning of the sentences in the language we want to interpret? Davidson has consistently replied with an appeal to "the principle of charity." He writes:

> If we suppose, as the principle of charity says we unavoidably must, that the pattern of sentences to which a speaker assents reflects the semantics of the logical constants, it is possible to detect and interpret those constants. . . . [A]n interpreter cannot accept great or obvious deviations from his own standards of rationality without destroying the foundation of intelligibility on which all interpretation rests. The possibility of understanding the speech or actions of an agent depends on the existence of a fundamentally rational pattern, a pattern that must, in general outline, be shared by all rational creatures. We have no choice, then, but to project our own logic on the language and beliefs of another. This means it is a constraint on possible interpretations of sentences held true that they are (within reason) logically consistent with one another. (1990: 319–320)

It is important to note that the principle of charity is not a guideline for tolerance or a liberal attitude toward others who are strangers. It is a "domestic" as well as "foreign" principle. Davidson puts it this way:

> Because I find I cannot use Quine's notion of stimulus meaning as a basis for interpreting certain sentences, I apply the Principle of Charity across the board. So applied, it counsels us quite generally to prefer theories of interpretation that minimize disagreement. . . . But minimizing disagreement or maximizing agreement is a confused ideal. The aim of interpretation is not agreement but understanding. My point has always been that understanding can be secured only by interpreting in a way that makes for the right sort of agreement. The 'right sort,' however, is no easier to specify than to say what constitutes a good reason for holding a particular belief. (1984: xvii)

And again in the famous essay, "Radical interpretation," Davidson writes:

> The methodological advice to interpret in a way that optimizes agreement should not be conceived as resting on a charitable assumption about human intelligence that might turn out to be false. If we cannot find a way to interpret the utterances and other

> behaviour of a creature as revealing a set of beliefs largely consistent and true by our own standards, we have no reason to count that creature as rational, as having beliefs, or as saying anything. (1984: 137)

Some scholars, such as Steven Lukes, have mistakenly interpreted the principle of charity as advice to interpreters or common sense guidelines; "count them right in most matters." Lukes counsels us to use the "Principle of Humanity" that tells us to "count them intelligible." "It has the singular virtue of being the principle we do in practice apply on the interpretation and translations of beliefs" (Hollis 1982: 262). But, Bjørn Ramberg is surely correct in warning against this interpretation of the principle of charity. "For semantics," he writes, "the confusion between interpretation and principles of actual interpretation is fatal. . . . The principle of charity . . . offers no advice to us as interpreters, it yields no interpretational strategy. It is not a heuristic device, nor is it, accordingly, something we could get by without; it is a *condition of the possibility* of interpretation" (Ramberg 1989: 74). Let us follow Ramberg's argument rather closely.

First, the interpretation from one language into another is possible only because an interpreter knows how to apply the truth-predicates of the interpreter's language. Second, Davidson's theory of semantics presupposes that our epistemic knowledge is basically sound. That is to say, it would be unintelligible to assert that either my beliefs or some other person's beliefs are massively mistaken. This is the case because of the principle of holism described in the next section.

An interpreter knows how to apply the truth-predicates of the language because the interpreter has the required pre-theoretical knowledge that some T-sentences are appropriate while others are not. Davidson stresses the point that the interpreter has the knowledge even though the interpreter may not have the "propositional knowledge of the content of the theory." For example, a person understands that the statement "'snow is white' is true if and only if snow is white" is an appropriate statement at a particular time in a way that "'snow is white' is true if and only if grass is green" is not appropriate. (Note that both T-sentences are true.)

Recall convention-T: (T) *s* is T if and only if *p*. Mary knows that the belief expressed by the sentence "snow is white" is caused by the fact that snow is white and not by the fact that "grass is green." Ramberg reminds us that "this understanding is semantic not epistemic. It is this understanding that allows the interpreter to formulate the right side of the biconditional theorems, the *p* of the T-sentences. But it is not sufficient to know what it is for *p*, a sentence of TL [the metalanguage], to be true. She must also know that it is true, that it indeed is true on the occasions of utterance *s*" (Ramberg 1989: 76). Thus, "the assumptions we must make about *p* and *s* [are] that their truth conditions are a product of the structural function of their parts, and that both are true on the occasions that provide empirical evidence for the T-sentence" (1989: 77).

Once again it is important to remember that the "empirical evidence" mentioned here does not entail extra-linguistic evidence by virtue of which a sentence is made true. The truth-conditions mentioned here are not to be understood as extra-linguistic reality or properties. "The intent of a theory of truth . . . is not that it tells us what truth is in general, but that it reveals how the truth of every sentence of a particular *L* depends on its structure and constituents" (Davidson 1984: 218). Or, to put it in other words, "[b]efore some object in, or aspect of, the world can become part of the subject matter of a belief (true or false), there must be endless true beliefs about the subject matter" (Davidson 1984: 168).

As Ramberg notes, the principle of charity is "a precondition for interpretation." We need no further constraints on interpretation of speakers than that they are indeed speakers of a language and that they speak the truth. But we must not be deceived by this apparent simplicity. The principle of charity is complex. Evnine puts it this way:

> The Principle of Charity, it seems, is not a single principle which governs interpretation, namely, interpret so that the objects of interpretation are generally true believers, but rather a collection of all those principles which together regulate the way in which beliefs, desires, and actions rationally connect with each other. . . . In its unreflected state the Principle of Charity also applies plainly and simply to all of us, as rational people. It says: do not act contrary to your best judgment; draw inductive inferences on the basis of all available evidence; believe only things you take to be true, and so on. It is the sum of all those things the rational person will accept just in virtue of being rational. (Evnine 1991: 110–111)

The principle of charity provides us with the necessary constraints of coherence and consistency that operate in interpretation and intentionality. It should be viewed, says Evnine, as "the skeleton of the theory of folk psychology" that includes such primary theoretical terms as "belief," "desire," "action," "intentionality," and "linguistic meaning." Evnine goes on to assert that in relation to such concepts the principle of charity is true by definition, that is, it is analytic. Quoting Lewis, he says that, "a person might have no beliefs, desires, or meanings at all, but it is analytic that if he does have them then they more or less conform to the constraining principles by which the concepts of belief, desire, and meaning are defined" (Evnine 1991: 112).

That this is an accurate reading of the principle of charity can be verified by Davidson's own response to J. J. C. Smart.

> Smart asks "whether people might not actually be approximately rational and consistent in their patterns of belief and desire." In my view this cannot be a factual question: if a creature has propositional attitudes then that creature is approximately rational. Rationality is, however, a normative notion which by its very nature resists regimentation in accord with a single public standard. (Davidson 1985a: 245; also Davidson 1985b)

Or, as he writes in another essay:

> Since charity is not an option but a condition of having a workable theory, it is meaningless to suggest that we might fall into massive error by endorsing it. . . . Charity is forced on us; whether we like it or not, if we want to understand others, we must count them right in most matters. (1984: 197)

Davidson comes back to a description of the principle once again in one of his latest essays. In commenting on Quine's attempt to separate belief and meaning in the process of interpreting a speaker, Davidson asserts that the success of such a separation invokes two key principles: the principle of coherence and the principle of correspondence.

> The Principle of Coherence prompts the interpreter to discover a degree of logical consistency in the thought of the speaker; the Principle of Correspondence prompts the interpreter to take the speaker to be responding to the same features of the world that he (the interpreter) would be responding to under similar circumstances. Both principles can be (and have been) called the principle of charity: one principle endows the speaker with a modicum of logical truth, the other endows him with a degree of true belief about the world. (Davidson 1991: 158)

The principle of charity informs us of an important point that cannot be over-emphasized: meaning and belief are inseparable and interdependent.

1.4. The principle of holism

The principle of holism is common to many disciplines in the social and natural sciences. It is a fundamental principle in all structuralist theories of culture and religion, as well as in the linguistic revolution caused by Saussure. The principle states that the value or significance of elements or units in a system are not given or explained because of some intrinsic value that the element or unit has in itself but because of their relationships or connectedness within the system. Thus a language, for Saussure, is a system "in which all the elements fit together, and in which the value of any one element depends on the simultaneous coexistence of all the others" (Saussure 1986: 113). Thus the elements of a system are constituted by the relations between them.

The system we are interested in as scholars of religion might be called the system of "propositional attitudes." Although they receive the most attention, propositional attitudes include more than beliefs and desires. Propositional attitudes encompass all of our beliefs, desires, hopes, fears, and memories. Propositional attitudes are logically related to perception, learning, and language. What is essential about propositional attitudes is that they are relational, connected, a network. This is what is meant by holism. Thus, what a person says or does is not only dependent on what she believes, but also on what she desires or hopes for; and what a person desires entails belief. For example, suppose that I have decided to drive to Whitefield tomorrow. This decision presupposes certain beliefs and desires. It presupposes that I believe that Whitefield is a town in northern New Hampshire, that New Hampshire is part of New England and that New England is part of the United States, and so forth. Perhaps I want some peace and quiet at a small lake near Whitefield. This presupposes that I desire solitude and that I can actually achieve this end. Moreover, my decision to drive to Whitefield presupposes that I have a vehicle that I believe will get me there. Beliefs, desires, and hopes are holistically constituted.

Malpas provides us with further support for holism by giving an example of what happens when the connections between propositional attitudes break down. Suppose we meet a speaker by the name of Smith whom we cannot interpret in any consistent way. Our best efforts at interpretation tell us that Smith believes that the South Pole is covered in green, that there is nothing but snow at the

South Pole, that the South Pole is north of Australia, that Australia is the capital city of the South Pole, that the South Pole is an imaginary place, and so forth. Malpas now asks, "Are we to attribute all these beliefs to Smith? And if we are not to attribute all of them then just which beliefs are we to attribute?" (Malpas 1992: 58).

We may, following Malpas, interpret Smith as playing a joke on us, or simply pretending. But, suppose that this interpretation will not work. In that case, "it would be hard to work out just what Smith did believe." In fact,

> too much ineradicable inconsistency . . . may lead us to decide that . . . there are no beliefs we can attribute to Smith. The same will apply if it is Smith's attitudes in general which lack consistency. Indeed, such universal failure in the coherence of beliefs will almost certainly imply a failure in the coherence of attitudes. It is hard to see how Smith could have an inconsistent set of beliefs, and yet possess a consistent set of desires, wishes, etc. This is not just because some of Smith's beliefs will be beliefs about her own attitudes, but also because many of the objects of desire will be identical with the objects of belief. . . . Thus any inconsistency in belief will likely be mirrored in an inconsistency amongst Smith's other attitudes. (Malpas 1992: 58–59)

Holism places constraints on our interpretive tasks. It tells us that we cannot ascribe beliefs to other speakers independently of other beliefs and propositional attitudes. This inter-connectedness of propositional attitudes, which entails logical coherence and consistency, constitutes the rationality of the psychological. As Malpas puts it: "It is not that beliefs are held together by the rational connections that hold between them, but beliefs are themselves largely constituted by those connections" (1992: 74). Thus, "[i]f rationality is a matter of coherence between attitudes, behavior and so forth, then this will mean that, while we sometimes treat actions or beliefs as rational or not, no such action or belief will be irrational *per se*. Of course, one reason for this is that there are no such entities as beliefs or actions except insofar as they figure in connection with other beliefs and actions. There are, we might say, no beliefs which are irrational *per se*, because there are no beliefs *per se*" (Malpas 1992: 75). Thus no single belief is in itself rational or irrational. Therefore, rationality from a holistic point of view is not an intrinsic property of a single propositional attitude such as a belief.

However, the principle of holism does not, of course, say that all of our beliefs are true. As Davidson says, "any particular belief or set of beliefs about the world around us may be false. What cannot be the case is that our general picture of the world and our place in it is mistaken, for it is this picture which informs the rest of our beliefs, whether they be true or false, and makes them intelligible." He goes on to say:

> The assumption that the truth about what we believe is logically independent of the truth of what we believe is revealed as ambiguous. Any particular belief may indeed be false; but enough in the framework and fabric of our beliefs must be true to give content to the rest. The conceptual connections between our knowledge of our own minds and our knowledge of the world of nature including the behaviour and knowledge of other minds are not definitional but holistic. (Davidson 1991: 160)[2]

II. Relativism As Untranslatability

I believe it is fair to say that Davidson's essay "On the very idea of a conceptual scheme" has become a classic. He begins the essay by pointing out that it has become quite popular to talk about "conceptual schemes." Conceptual schemes are thought of as ways of organizing life or experience. They are held to be points of view, worldviews, by which we survey and know about "the passing scene." Some scholars would even claim that "[r]eality itself is relative to a scheme: what counts as real in one system may not in another" (Davidson 1984: 183).[3]

In analyzing this claim, Davidson defines a language as something that is translatable. We can identify something as being a language if we can translate it into our own language. He points out, quite correctly, that a language is often thought of as a conceptual scheme. For some scholars, conceptual schemes (languages) may be so radically different that translation is thought to be impossible. It is this supposed untranslatability that provides some scholars with the notion that "people live in different worlds." Thus truth, on this view, is relative to a conceptual scheme—this is the heart of

---

[2] It is only fair to point out, and this should not come as a surprise, that not all scholars think that holism makes sense. In fact, Jerry Fodor thinks that it is "really a crazy theory" (Fodor—Lepore 1992: xii, 59–104; Fodor 1987: 55–95). What someone needs to do is show him that he is right; holism is crazy alright, "crazy like a fox!"

[3] This essay was given on the occasion of his presidential address to the Eastern Division of the American Philosophical Association in 1973.

conceptual relativism. Davidson shows that the notion of alternate conceptual schemes is incoherent. The argument can be summed up in the following way.

Let us assume that translatability is the criterion for being a language. Let us also assume that languages are conceptual schemes. If we are able to translate a language into our language then both languages share the same conceptual scheme. The notion of an alternate conceptual scheme is thus a contradiction because it would have to be both a conceptual scheme and thus translatable and untranslatable as an alternate conceptual scheme. Moreover, as Davidson says, "[w]e have found no intelligible basis on which it can be said that schemes are different. It would be equally wrong to announce the glorious news that all mankind—all speakers of language, at least—share a common scheme and ontology. For if we cannot intelligibly say that schemes are different, neither can we intelligibly say that they are one" (1984: 198).

The argument has been set out most clearly in an interesting essay by Gordon C. F. Bearn (1989). He outlines the Davidsonian argument against relativism as conceptual schemes as follows:

> (1) Conceptual schemes are not odd platonic entities; they are languages.
> (2) Intertranslatability establishes sameness of conceptual scheme.
> (3) Translatability into *our* language is the criterion for something's *being* a language. So,
> (4) An "alternative conceptual scheme" would have to be *both:*
> (4a) a conceptual scheme, hence, (by 1) a language, and hence (by 3) translatable into our own language; *and*
> (4b) an alternative to our conceptual scheme, hence (by 2) not translatable into our own language. So,
> (5) the idea of an alternative conceptual scheme is in contradiction with itself. But,
> (6) "If we cannot intelligibly say that schemes are different, neither can we . . . say that they are one." So,
> (7) the very idea of a conceptual scheme is unintelligible. (Bearn 1989: 210)

Convinced that his argument is a valid one, Davidson moves on to counter any attempt to refute the premise that translatability is the criterion for identifying something as being a language.

Davidson believes that the first alternative, roughly speaking, argues that it is not translatability that is the criterion for identifying a language, but its capacity to "organize," "systematize," or "divide-up," something. The "something" is usually thought of as "reality (the universe, the world, nature), or as experience (the passing show, surface irritations, sensory promptings, sense-data, the given)" (Davidson 1984: 192). The problem with this alternative is its lack of clarity. Can we make sense of organizing a single object? Davidson gives the following example. Suppose you set about arranging the things in your closet and someone came along and told you that it was not shirts, shoes, and suits you were to organize but the closet itself. Davidson thinks you would be rather bewildered. How would you go about organizing the Pacific Ocean?

Davidson then asks, how about experience? Does it make sense to think of a language as "organizing" experience? "Much the same difficulties recur. The notion of organization applies only to pluralities" (1984: 192). The difficulty of thinking of experience, sense-data, or the given makes the organizing problem more severe. "For how could something count as a language that organized only sensations, surface irritations, or sense-data? Surely knives and forks, railroads and mountains, cabbages and kingdoms also need organizing" (1984: 192).

What about another theory according to which language is a conceptual scheme that fits, accounts for, or predicts reality or experience? "The trouble is that the notion of fitting the totality of experience, like the notion of fitting the facts, or of being true to the facts, adds nothing intelligible to the simple concept of being true" (1984: 194). We are now back to a truth conditional semantics—the criterion for identifying something we might want to call a conceptual scheme entails its truth conditions. The issue now becomes, can we have a conceptual scheme that is true but not translatable? Is the notion of truth independent of translation? "The answer is, I think, that we do not understand it independently at all" (1984: 194).[4]

Bearn issues a useful reminder that the notion of a language that is completely untranslatable cannot even be the sort of thing that can be true or false. He says, "[w]e forget this when we consider the language-like activity as the speech of strangers we have yet to translate, we should rather think of it as sounds—whether made by humans or waterfalls—which have completely resisted every attempt

[4] See also, "True to the Facts" (Davidson 1984) for additional arguments for concluding that "fitting the facts" or "corresponds to the facts" tells us no more than "is true."

at translation. There is no temptation to call those noises untranslatable languages" (Bearn 1989: 212).

Davidson, I believe, has convincingly demonstrated that conceptual relativism is based upon the dualism of conceptual scheme and empirical content. He has also provided powerful arguments for concluding that the notion of an "organizing system and something waiting to be organized, cannot be made intelligible and defensible. It is itself a dogma of empiricism, the third dogma. The third, and perhaps the last, for if we give it up it is not clear that there is anything distinctive left to call empiricism" (Davidson 1984: 189).[5]

In a more recent essay, Davidson traces this dualism to its end. "Instead of saying," he writes, "it is the scheme-content dichotomy that has dominated and defined the problems of modern philosophy, then, one could as well say it is how the dualism of the objective and the subjective has been conceived. For these dualisms have a common origin: a concept of the mind with its private states and objects" (Davidson 1989: 163). And again:

> Content and scheme . . . come as a pair; we can let them go together. Once we take this step, no *objects* will be left with respect to which the problem of representation can be raised. Beliefs are true or false, but they represent nothing. It is good to be rid of representations, and with them the correspondence theory of truth, for it is thinking there are representations that engenders thoughts of relativism. Representations *are* relative to a scheme; a map represents Mexico, say—but only relative to a mercator, or some other, projection. (Davidson 1989: 165–166)

III. Reductionism and Eliminative Materialism

I will not enter the long debate concerning reductionism here. I continue to believe that what is often called "ontological reduction" is the most interesting concept of reduction for theoretical discussion. This form of reduction takes the form of "nothing but." Chairs are nothing but collections of molecules. Genes are nothing but DNA. Red is nothing but photon emissions of 600 nanometres. The mental, intentionality, is nothing but . . . ?

---

[5] The first two dogmas of empiricism are, of course, those described by Quine—the analytic/synthetic distinction and verificationism (Quine 1963).

One of the primary aims of modern psychology and philosophy is to provide an answer to this last question. In fact some scholars have proposed that the mental, i.e., intentions, beliefs, desires, and propositional attitudes, etc., are "folk psychology." What we need to do, they say, is come up with an adequate theory that will show that the content of folk psychology is like phlogiston or ghosts. This position has become known as "eliminative materialism." It differs from ontological reductionism in that it argues that since physics cannot accommodate such things as propositional attitudes, they do not exist. Folk psychology is viewed as primitive theory that we need to eliminate. What will take its place is neurophysiology, or psychophysiological laws that will explain human behaviour without an appeal to the propositional attitudes found in folk psychology. (For different versions see Stich [1983]; Paul Churchland [1984]; and Patricia Churchland [1986].)

Davidson has consistently denied that reduction of the psychological, propositional attitudes is possible. In reflecting on Tarski's recursive theory of truth he asserts that "the threat that truth might not turn out to be reducible to physical concepts is a threat that, in my opinion, we neither can nor should want to escape" (Davidson 1990: 297, n. 34). Or, again:

> What lies behind our inability to discover deterministic psychophysical laws is this. When we attribute a belief, a desire, a goal, an intention, or a meaning to an agent, we necessarily operate within a system of concepts in part determined by the structure of beliefs and desires of the agent himself. *Short of changing the subject,* we cannot escape this feature of the psychological; but this feature has no counterpart in the world of physics. (Davidson 1980: 230)

In his reply to J. J. C. Smart, Davidson asserts that "[m]onistic my view is, since it holds that mental events are physical events, but a form of materialist chauvinism it is not, since it holds that being mental is not an eliminable or derivative property." Thus, "[a]n intentional action is an action caused by states and events that rationalize it; it is a basic aspect of belief or desire that it will cause certain sorts of action under appropriate conditions. These are, I think, irreducible aspects of reason-explanations; a science that tries to eliminate the causal element from these concepts will succeed only by *changing the subject,* for here causality is connected with the normative demands of rationality" (Davidson 1985a: 245, 246).

Davidson returns to the subject once again in 'Three varieties of knowledge." He raises the following question: "How does the normative element in mental concepts prevent their reduction to physical concepts?" In other words, since definitional reduction seems out of the question, why cannot there be strict laws that connect mental events or states with theories of physics? Davidson replies with an answer he gave some twenty years ago: "One can hope for strict connecting laws only when the concepts connected by the laws are based on criteria of the same sort, and so a strict law could not combine normative with non-normative concepts." Davidson thinks that this answer still seems to be the correct one. He then adds further considerations.

For example, although strict laws do not use causal concepts, most of our everyday explanations do. Thus the car accident was caused by slippery conditions on the road. We explain why the wing of an airplane does not break when it bends by the fact that the wing is made of elastic materials that cause the wing, under certain conditions, to return to its original shape when it bends. Davidson then makes the point that

> we would not *be changing the subject* if we were to drop the concept of elasticity in favour of a specification of the microstructure of the materials in the airplane wing that cause it to return to its original shape when exposed to certain forces. Mental concepts are not like this. . . . When we want to explain an action, for example, we want to know the agent's reasons, so we can see for ourselves what it was about the action that appealed to the agent. But it would be foolish to suppose that there are strict laws that stipulate that whenever an agent has certain reasons he will perform a given action. (Davidson 1991: 162–163)

(Davidson is fully aware of the fact that these considerations do not add up to a proof.)

Nevertheless, the argument in its totality seems incontestable. If Davidson is right that there are no psychophysical laws, then a very important consequence follows: functionalist reductions, functionalist explanations, are impossible!

The bankruptcy of functionalism is apparent even if we assume that Davidson's argument turns out to be wrong. If so, this would not solve the problems surrounding functionalism as an adequate theory for explaining sociological and psychological structures. Besides the logical problems found in the actual premises of functional explanations there is also a flaw to be found in those versions that argue that there must be one-to-one correlations (identities?) between propositional attitudes and, let us say, neurophysiological states. This surely must be a mistake. As Loar puts it, "it seems highly unlikely that one neural state is in all of us reserved for being, say, the belief that rhubarb is nourishing" (Loar 1981: 21; see also Wilkes 1982). Moreover, if strict identity or correlations are necessary to explain propositional attitudes as caused by neural states, then it would seem to be the case that at the exact time that it was announced that Neil Armstrong had walked on the moon all those millions who heard the announcement and believed it were in the same, identical, neural state. If this is not absurd it would at least seem to defy one of the central axioms of modern physics.[6]

Davidson has called his theoretical position *anomalous monism.* It contains three premises. The first states that propositional attitudes, memories, the acquisition and loss of knowledge, and intentional actions "are directly and indirectly caused by, and the causes of, physical events." The second premise asserts that "when events are related as cause and effect, then there exists a closed and deterministic system of laws into which these events, when appropriately described, fit." The third premise states that "there are no precise psychophysical laws" (Davidson 1980: 231; see also, 207–224; 245–259). Thus it is monistic in that the theory states that all psychological events are physical events, but, anomalous "because it insists that events do not fall under strict laws when described in psychological terms" (Davidson 1980: 231).

In order fully to understand Davidson's insistence on the irreducibility of propositional attitudes, including intentionality, memory, and learning, we must return to the beginning of this essay. The basic premise that supports the argument is to be found in the holistic description of the psychological. The more we strive for accuracy in constructing a theory of the cognitive field, the more persistent the demands for including more and more of a person's propositional attitudes. As you will recall, the holistic character of

---

[6] The attempt to explain propositional attitudes as caused by, for example, a neural slate, or under some hyper-modular description of the brain, is, of course, a brand of functionalism. Functionalism dies very slowly. Ruth Milikan notes that, Cummins, "one of the most clear-headed champions [of functionalism]," describes five unsuccessful functionalist "recipes" for explaining intentionality. She then says: "Surely it would be indelicate for an unbeliever to interrupt this preparation for a last supper" (Milikan 1986: 73).

our propositional attitudes entails rationality. The constraints of consistency, coherence, and rationality are imposed upon our interpretations of a person's beliefs and desires. In other words, the construction of a theory of human behaviour is constrained by the principle of charity. As Davidson puts it: "But in inferring this system [of an agent's beliefs and motives] from the evidence, we necessarily impose conditions of coherence, rationality, and consistency. *These conditions have no echo in physical theory*" (Davidson 1980: 231). In brief, physical theory has nothing to say about truth conditions. (For further elaborations, see "Mental Events," where "changing the subject" is described as "deciding not to accept the criterion of the mental in terms of the vocabulary of the propositional attitudes" [Davidson 1980: 216].)

Anomalous monism describes a theory that moves beyond the materialist/dualist debate just as the rejection of conceptual schemes entails the conclusion that we cannot therefore posit that there is just one conceptual scheme. The materialism of logical positivism is undoubtedly fired by Cartesian dualism. The fear of dualism is the fear of being subjective, unscientific, mystical. Thus physics replaces theology as the queen of the sciences. Do not misunderstand me, I have no doubt about the successes of advanced theoretical physics. What I doubt is that physics is *the* theoretical standard by which all other theories must be measured, or that the only successful notion of explanation entails subsumption under strict laws. In other words I seriously doubt that we ever did need a Queen.

As Davidson puts it, anomalous monism does not inspire the "nothing-but reflex." Although it resembles materialism in its claim that all events are physical events, anomalous monism "rejects the thesis, usually considered essential to materialism, that mental phenomena can be given purely physical explanations," by means of reducibility through law or definition. If this were possible, says Davidson, "we could reduce moral properties to descriptive, and this there is good reason to *believe* cannot be done; and we might be able to reduce truth in a formal system to syntactical properties, and this we *know* cannot in general be done" (Davidson 1980: 214).

In other words,

> [t]heories of belief and meaning . . . use concepts which set such theories apart from the physical and other non-psychological sciences: concepts of meaning and belief are, in a fundamental way, not reducible to physical, neurological, or even behavioristic

> concepts. . . . Each interpretation and attribution of attitude is a move within a holistic theory, a theory necessarily governed by a concern for consistency and general coherence with the truth, and it is this that sets these theories forever apart from those that describe mindless objects, or describe objects as mindless. (Davidson 1984: 154)[7]

I believe that a case can be made for an argument that would demonstrate that attempts to construct reductionist theories of the mental, or propositional attitudes, assume the three dogmas. Malpas is surely correct in seeing that "reductionism thus presupposes something like the analytic-synthetic distinction, as it also presupposes some version of the distinction between scheme and content" (Malpas 1992: 193). Reductionism and eliminative materialism are dependent upon the three dogmas in which the distinctions between the conceptual and the experiential, the linguistic and extra-linguistic, the subjective and the objective, are forever threatening each other. The argument against eliminative materialism does not concern objectivity. That is surely preserved in a truth-conditional theory of semantics such as Davidson's. The issue is the threat of subjectivity, the mental, as the enemy of objectivity. It is the old battle of quantity versus quality, fact versus value, explanation versus understanding, realism versus anti-realism. What we must overcome is the threat that these dualisms create. It should be clear from this argument that those who argue for "eliminative materialism" have not escaped this threat, but are motivated by it.[8]

What I find exciting and fruitful in Davidson's writings is an increasing awareness that we are at a threshold that will indeed take us beyond the dualisms of logical positivism, the dominant form of empiricism in the twentieth century. Quine began this revolutionary journey with his critique of the two dogmas of empiricism. The first dogma, with its distinction between analytic and synthetic meaning, held that some statements are true by definition of the meaning of the terms alone, while synthetic statements are true because of extra-linguistic facts. The second dogma is the dogma of reductionism—that all statements can be redefined, redescribed, confirmed, or

---

[7] For further clarification of Davidson's notions of "cause," "law," "event" and an argument for "anomalous monism," see the fine essay by Brian P. McLaughlin, "Anomalous monism and the irreductibility of the mental" (1985).

[8] See Searle (1992) for a searing criticism of "eliminative materialism"; see also Horgan-Woodward (1985).

disconfirmed in the language of sensory experience. What Quine saw was that these two dogmas are in fact identical at their root. Thus the truth of a statement was assumed to depend upon language and extra-linguistic fact. For the logical positivist this in turn led to the notion that statements could be analyzed into linguistic and factual components, with the factual component referring to confirmatory experience (Quine 1963: 20–46). Davidson's dismissal of the third dogma of empiricism completes the critique. As we have seen, the very idea of a conceptual scheme assumes the dualism of scheme and content. Davidson finds this unintelligible and so do I.

IV. Some Implications for the Study of Religion

If Davidson's theory of a truth conditional semantics is correct, I think we can extract important consequences for the study of religion. Here in very brief form are several implications.

4.1. Holism and religion

I doubt that anyone would want to deny that religion is constituted, or encompassed, by language. Language is a necessary condition for the existence of religion. Now if we use a truth conditional theory of semantics as our entrance into the meaning of religious utterances, sentences, or texts, we will find certain constraints on our translation or interpretation of those utterances, sentences, and texts. Here are a few that I think are of great importance.

First, we will have to acknowledge that religion is not an "autonomous" domain. Contrary to Rudolf Otto or to Mircea Eliade, religion is not *sui generis*. Religion will have to be studied as a part of what I have called "the psychological" or cognitive domain. When we speak of religious beliefs, desires, hopes, fears, acts, and so forth, it should be clear that these mental phenomena are to be identified as propositional attitudes. As such they will be interpreted from within the constraints of the truth conditional theory. There is nothing unique, or special, about religious propositional attitudes except that the utterances and related actions of such attitudes contain the content of superhuman beings. There is, in other words, no special truth that is distinctively a religious truth. Religious language is natural language.

What then gives the study of religion a specific feature or characteristic that sets it apart from other psychological or cognitive studies depends upon our definition of religion. I would suggest, once again, the definition that I and other scholars of religion have used over several years: "Religion is a system of beliefs (more widely, propositional attitudes) and actions that are related to superhuman beings." Superhuman beings, you may recall, are beings that can do things we cannot do, and include such beings as a god, goddess, or a pantheon, ancestors, spirits and the like—just those beings that anyone familiar with religion thinks about when talking about religion.

Second, recall that the theoretical constraints are created from within a theory that is holistic. Thus religious beliefs and actions are to be studied as a system, a semantic structure. It makes no sense, for example, to speak of the meaning of *a* religious belief or action in isolation from the whole system of beliefs, rituals, etc., of a religious tradition. Beliefs make sense only in their relation with other propositional attitudes. Beliefs are holistically structured. Thus studies that focus primarily on "the belief in karma," or "the belief in nirvana," are distortions, if not mistakes, in semantic analysis. The same constraint would apply to the study of *a* ritual or *a* myth, *a* god, or *a* goddess. We should be suspicious of any analysis of a single element or unit taken from a religious system. Structuralist studies of myth and religion have stressed this warning for decades. I am afraid that it has yet to be taken seriously by most scholars who are full-time students of religion.

Having said this, I must emphasize that there is nothing wrong with the study of religion, or, a religious system *qua* religious system. After all, we also study legal systems, political systems, and moral systems. What must be remembered, however, is that we are engaged in an abstract, theoretical enterprise. To forget this is to reject theoretical analysis as such. To think there is an alternative is, I believe, a serious error. Nevertheless, it is true that when the analysis is complete, we must acknowledge that there is always a wider context in which religious systems exist. Religious beliefs and practices are holistically related to a wider web of beliefs and practices which, if Davidson is correct, we cannot correctly believe we are mistaken about in any massive way. It is trivial but important to emphasize that religion, as language, is public and communal. And once again, this public and communal aspect of language and religion has "no echo" in the physical world.

A third implication for the study of religion would obviously entail a holistic analysis of the meaning of religious propositional attitudes and acts. It seems undeniable that rituals entail desires, beliefs, and other propositional attitudes. Thus on the basis of this theory it is simply unintelligible to assert that "ritual is meaningless." Rituals entail and are caused by beliefs and desires. Thus holism instructs us not to view rites of passage as "things in themselves." Belief and action, for example, cannot be separated. Furthermore, we must resist the temptation to come up with a list of beliefs that are essential to a particular religion. From a holistic standpoint there simply is no such list, just as there is no list, or set of beliefs, that make interpretation possible between two persons. And yet, it is the case that interpretation is only possible because we share a vast set of beliefs that we agree are true. This is just another way of stating the principle of charity—without massive agreement, disagreement would not make sense.

Knowledge of the principle of charity and holism might have prevented scholars from thinking that certain religions, Hinduism for example, place less emphasis on belief and more on practice. Thus we often read that Hinduism is a religion of *orthopraxis* rather than *orthodoxis.* From a holistic point of view, this is incomprehensible. Action without belief, without propositional attitudes, does not make sense. Our propositional attitudes cause action. To put this in other terms, reason causes action. We *act* because of reasons, because of the propositional attitudes we have. Reasons are causes, but it is not the case that causes are reasons. This is one more example of why beliefs and actions cannot be reduced to physical or neurological causes.

It would also seem that the creative work done in the analysis of ritual as a type of Austinian "performative" action that is empty of propositional content must also be set aside. All ritual acts, all rituals, are performed in the context of beliefs, hopes, desires, and expectations. Ritual as symbolic, as re-presentation of something, will need serious rethinking, as will the very notion of religion as a "symbol" system.

Finally, there are many reports based on field work that imply that religious thought, belief, or religious language is unique in its opacity, inconsistency, or vagueness. This has often led to the conclusion that religion is beyond the rational domain. When you ask a Hindu, for example, what karma means, you often get very vague replies. People do not seem to have answers for the questions we ask. Why do you perform this ritual? What is nirvana?

There is nothing unique to religion about all this. Ask yourself what you mean by "liberty," "time," "family values," or "blue." Holism teaches us that we should not expect a simple answer, and that perhaps the best outcome will always be vague. I believe that the central lesson to be learned from this brief probe is this: we need to "naturalize" religion, bring it back into language where it belongs. If Davidson's total theory about rationality, truth, and language is correct then there simply is no need for a special theory of semantics for religion, since there are no hidden symbolic meanings or codes that we need to decipher. In brief, there are no "religious" hopes, "religious" fears, "religious" reasons; there are only propositional attitudes that we all share in our competence and performance of a language that is public. What gives religion its identity is not unique or special propositional attitudes, and feelings, but the domain, the language, of superhuman beings.

4.2. Primitive religion

Davidson's truth-conditional theory of semantics surely leads to the conclusion that the notion that there are "primitive" religions that are radically different from our own is incomprehensible. Lucien Lévy-Bruhl was simply mistaken when he thought that "primitive mentality" could be explained as entailing a logic that differed from ours, or that primitive logic, for example, tolerated contradiction, or that it contained no logic at all. The principle of charity places a constraint upon our interpretations; it is a condition for having a workable theory of translation at all. Thus, we should be suspicious of any theory of religion that interprets a particular religion as irrational or as a radically different mode of thinking. In fact, from a Davidsonian perspective it really does not make sense to talk about "primitive religion" at all, just as it makes no sense to talk about a "primitive language."

From a holistic point of view the Eliadian separation of "archaic" religion or sacred thought and "modern" profane thought or life does not make sense. Moreover, when we ascribe to others the belief that they are red parrots we have undoubtedly misunderstood what they said, the result of a bad translation. We should think twice before we report that there are human beings who believe that they are "red parrots," or who believe that their twins are birds. Recall that Davidson thinks that "an interpreter cannot accept great or obvious deviations from his own standards of rationality without destroying the foundations of intelligibility on which all interpretation rests."

Furthermore, Davidson's semantic theory leads to the conclusion that Tylorian and neo-Tylorian theories of religion are, at best, far too simplistic. The notion that religious beliefs are like scientific, theoretical beliefs is a good example. It may turn out that from a Davidsonian point of view some religious beliefs are uttered as explanations, but it is far from intelligible to think that all religious beliefs, as all beliefs as such, are "scientific" or "theoretical" in their truth values. Once we "naturalize" religion we will find, I think, that the difference between "scientific" beliefs and "religious" beliefs is that "religious" beliefs are beliefs that entail superhuman beings. Thus Davidson's truth-conditional theory of semantics would seem to target such beliefs for careful analysis. And we must not forget that given the principle of holism, "religious" beliefs must always be viewed in the context of other propositional attitudes. In a sense, then, there is no such thing, semantically, as a religious belief that could be analyzed as such.

4.3. Religion as a conceptual scheme

I believe that Davidson's essay, "The very idea of a conceptual scheme" (1984, see this volume), has immense significance for the study of religion. First of all, I think it is fair to assert that most scholarship on religion assumes a scheme and content dualism, also variously termed "framework," "episteme," "paradigm," or "world-view." If Davidson is right, then this dualism must be wrong.

We can begin to understand the significance of this "third dogma of empiricism" once we scan the vast bibliography on the religions of the world. Most of that bibliography involves variations on the dualism scheme/content. Scholars have first postulated a given—religions experience, the transcendent, the sacred, faith, the numinous, needs, feelings—and then postulated the history of religion, or the various religions as so many conceptual schemes that interpret, symbolize, represent, or organize the given content. All theories of religion that describe religions as worldviews, as a symbolic representation of the sacred, as ideograms of the numinous, as symbolisms of a transcendent reality, as models of and for reality, assume the scheme/content dualism, a given that needs to be conceptualized, rationalized, symbolized, or "endowed" with meaning.

The criticism of the scheme/content theory of meaning in the history of the study of religion can be easily confirmed by turning to texts that all scholars would agree are, or were, standards for the study of religion. (The work of Otto, Eliade, Durkheim, Feuerbach, Freud, Geertz, and Turner come to mind immediately.) The persistent critic of the contemporary study of religion will note once again that the problem here is not whether we have the right symbolic, worldview, or ideographic theory. The problem, from the very beginning, has to do with the scheme/content dualism.

If there is any agreement about what religions are all about it is this—religions are alternative conceptual schemes, representations, of something. Davidson's truth-conditional semantic theory not only places this notion into question but dismantles the very idea of "conceptual scheme." This is a serious challenge to the Kantian principle of constituting schemes and the content of sensory experience. The dissolution of the scheme/content dualism places the mainstream neo-Kantian approach to the study of religion into serious question. It has become almost commonplace to read that different religious traditions are different ways of organizing, symbolizing, or interpreting experience. We are then told that it is, therefore, impossible to examine religions, including our own, from the outside, to check whether the scheme, the symbol system, or worldview is a good "fit," whether one scheme is "better" or "worse" at interpreting the given of experience. From here it becomes an easy step to conclude that we cannot, therefore, make a rational choice between these incommensurable schemes of religion. How the sceptic must rejoice in all of this.

I have attempted to show in my presentation of Davidson's semantic theory that the doctrine of scheme/content inevitably leads us into scepticism and relativism. Moreover, as I have noted, Davidson argues that this dualism is finally incomprehensible since we simply cannot make sense of a "neutral" or "unorganized" reality that is in need of "fit" or "organization."

4.4. Religious language and semantics

For many years I have been puzzled by the widespread notion that religious language, belief, myth, and ritual are codes or symbols that must be deciphered. Or, on another interpretation of this theme, that religious language is a communication system that contains a hidden meaning. Part of the puzzle is that in many cases we are never told just what the hidden meaning is, or, when we are told the meaning, we discover that the message is banal. Why do people use such bizarre and complicated language to communicate what seem to be simple beliefs and attitudes? When we read the decoded message we are often left with the impression that the gods do not have much to say.

What has led scholars of religion to assert that religious language contains a hidden meaning? Why do some scholars think that rituals, for example, are performative acts that are empty of propositional content, that is, they do not contain truth values, they are neither true or false? Why do other scholars think, for example, that rituals are purely expressive and therefore contain nothing of cognitive significance? Why do scholars think that religious language is symbolic, or bears a special meaning that can be deciphered only on its "own plane," or be interpreted only by those who are themselves religious or have experienced the given, be it numinous or otherwise? Finally, after all these years, why have we failed to come to agreement on just what the code, the symbolism, or the hidden message means? After reading Davidson, especially "What metaphors mean," I think I have an answer to this puzzle (Davidson 1984: 243–264; see also Crosthwaite 1985).

The answer to all these questions, and many more, seems quite simple. We are led to those kinds of questions because we know, and then perhaps forget, that the literal or ordinary surface meaning of religious language is false. As Davidson says of metaphor, "[g]enerally it is only when a sentence is taken to be false that we accept it as metaphor and start to hunt out the hidden implication. It is probably for this reason that most metaphorical sentences are *patently* false, just as all similes are trivially true" (Davidson 1984: 258). The problem here, of course, is that although we can locate the use of religious metaphor ("the Spirit of God moved upon the face of the waters"), religious language as such is not metaphor. Religious language (the language about superhuman beings) often uses metaphor but it would simply be false to say that religious language, in any sense of the term, *is* metaphor.

What I would want to argue is that the content of religious language is *patently* false. This does not mean that people who make mention of superhuman beings in their language from time to time are irrational. Nor does it entail that they are massively mistaken about the world they live in. The mistake is to think or imagine that some people are submerged or enveloped in religious propositional attitudes and actions twenty-four hours a day! The mistake entails thinking that the most profound or "ultimate" moments in life are always "religious," whether we live among the Trobriands or among the citizens of Hanover, New Hampshire. A truth conditional theory of meaning leads to the conclusion that there is no such thing as religious language, as a *sui generis* language, that is distinct from natural language as such. There simply is no "special theory of semantics" for religion.

Faced with the fact that the literal interpretation of religious language is patently false, most "theories" then insist that there must be a second meaning that is special to religion, a symbolic, or a hidden meaning. The extreme conclusion can be found among scholars who conclude that religious language has no meaning at all. At some future time I will develop the thesis that there is no such secondary meaning. The quest for secondary or special, symbolic meaning is illusory. We must give up the idea that the meaning of religious language carries a special message. We must give up the idea that the semantics of religious language has a content or a meaning other than literal meaning, simply because there is none. It should be obvious that this argument does not deny the existence of codes or artificial languages—they are parasitic on natural language.

Functionalists who study religion have known all of this for a long time. They turned to a different kind of question. Given the fact that religious beliefs are false, why then does religion persist? Their answer: it satisfies certain needs. We are now back to the scheme/content problem once again. Demythologizers have also confronted this truth and then supplied a new translation. Such translations also assume the scheme/content dualism and all the problems involved. But, there are no exits from the failure of this particular theoretical box.[9]

---

[9] I wish to express my profound gratitude to my colleague Nancy Frankenberry for a careful reading of the manuscript and a response that improved the argument and grammatical style of the final revision. Whatever confusions or weakness of argument remain are obviously my own responsibility.

References

Bearn, Gordon, C. F. 1989. The Horizon of Reason. In Michael Krause (ed.), *Relativism: Interpretation And Confrontation.* Notre Dame, Ind.: University of Notre Dame Press.

Churchland, Patricia. 1986. *Neurophilosphy*. Cambridge, Mass.: M.I.T. Press.

Churchland, Paul. 1984. *Matter and Consciousness*. Cambridge, Mass.: M.I.T. Press.

Crosthwaite, Jan. 1985. The Meaning of Metaphor. *Australasian Journal Of Philosophy* 63: 320–335.

Davidson, Donald. 1980. *Essays On Actions And Events*. Oxford University Press.

— 1984. *Inquiries Into Truth And Interpretation*. Oxford University Press.

— 1985a. Bruce Vermazen and Merrill B. Hintikka (eds.), *Essays on Davidson*. Oxford: Clarendon Press.

— 1985b. Rational Animals. In Ernest LePore and Brian McLaughlin (eds.), *Actions and Events*. Oxford: Basil Blackwell.

— 1986. A Coherence Theory Of Truth. In Ernest LePore (ed.), *Truth And Interpretation,* 307–319. Oxford: Basil Blackwell.

— 1989. The Myth of Subjectivity. Michael Krause (ed.), *Relativism: Interpretation and Confrontation,* 159–172. University of Notre Dame Press.

— 1990. The Structure And Content Of Truth. *Journal Of Philosophy* LXXXVII (6): 279–328.

— 1991. Three Varieties Of Knowledge. In A. Phillips Griffiths (ed.), *A. J. Ayer Memorial Essays,* 153–166. Cambridge: Cambridge University Press.

— 1993. Ralf Stoecker (ed.), *Reflecting Davidson: Donald Davidson Responding to an International Forum of Philosophers.* Berlin/New York: W. de Gruyter.

Evnine, Donald. 1991. *Donald Davidson*. Stanford University Press.

Horgan Terence, and James Woodward. 1985. Folk Psychology Is Here to Stay. *The Philosophical Review* XCIV: 197–226.

Hollis, M. 1982. Relativism in its Place. In M. Hollis and S. Lukes (eds.), *Rationality and Relativism,* 261–305. Cambridge, Mass.: M.I.T. Press.

Loar, Brian. 1981. *Mind And Meaning.* Cambridge University Press.

Lyons, John. 1977. *Semantics,* Vol. I. Cambridge University Press.

Malpas, J. E. 1992. *Donald Davidson and the Mirror of Meaning.* Cambridge: Cambridge University Press.

Milikan, Ruth. 1986. Thought Without Laws: Cognitive Science With Content. *Philosophical Review,* 95: 64–87.

Penner, Hans H. 1975. The Problem of Semantics in the Study of Religion. In Robert D.Baird, (ed.), *Methodological Issues In The Study of Religion.* Chico, CA.: New Horizons Press. 79–93.

Quine, Willard. 1963. Two Dogmas Of Empiricism. *From A Logical Point Of View.* New York: Harper & Row Publishers, 20–46.

Ramberg, Bjørn T. 1989. *Donald Davidson's Philosophy of Language.* Oxford: Basil Blackwell.

Saussure, Ferdinand de. 1983. *Course in General Linguistics,* translated by Roy Harris. La Salle, Illinois: Open Court.

Searle, John. 1992. *The Rediscovery Of The Mind.* Cambridge, Mass.: M.I.T. Press.

Stich, Steven. 1983. *From Folk Psychology to Cognitive Science.* Cambridge, Mass.: M.I.T. Press.

Stoutland, Frederick. 1982. Realism and Antirealism in Davidson's Philosophy of Language I & II: *Critica,* XIV: 13–51; 19–47.

Wilkes, K. V. 1982. *Mind, Brain and Function* 147–167. Norman: University of Oklahoma Press.

18

Pragmatism, Truth, and the Disenchantment of Subjectivity

Nancy K. Frankenberry

In 1908 Arthur Lovejoy could list thirteen pragmatisms, all standing for different doctrines. Today that list can be expanded by including the versions of pragmatism associated with the work of Williard V. O. Quine, Nelson Goodman, Hilary Putnam, Donald Davidson, and Richard Rorty in philosophy, and of Cornel West, Henry Levinson, Jeffrey Stout, Sheila Davaney, and others in religious studies. This proliferation is a development that William James and John Dewey would applaud but that Charles Sanders Peirce might deplore, complaining as he did in 1905 that the word pragmatism had already begun "to be met with occasionally in the literary journals, where it gets abused in the merciless way that words have to expect when they fall into literary clutches."[1]

In addition to literary clutches, pragmatism has fallen into the hands of positivists, functionalists, and relativists who throughout much of the twentieth century confused its theory of truth with their own. Despite a history of tangled relations with the three most flawed "isms" of our time, pragmatism's evolution has been in the direction of holism. My contention is that the new pragmatism, only apparent by century's end, is for the first time clearly a thorough-going holism, distinguishable from the empiricist assumptions of positivism, the utilitarian aspects of functionalism, and the relativism of scheme-content dualism. This places it in a unique position to offer

---

[1] Charles Sanders Peirce, "What Pragmatism Is," *Collected Papers* (Cambridge, Mass.: Harvard University Press, 1934), 5: 276.

methodological and theoretical directions for overcoming some of philosophy of religion's worst myths, dualisms, and dogmatisms.

In recent decades the old epistemological toils over language, truth, and meaning have come to look very different, due to important shifts that have occurred in epistemology and philosophy of science, in philosophy of language, and in semantics. Perhaps most profound has been the shift from foundationalism as a basic theory of knowledge to holism. In the American pragmatic tradition, the shift away from foundationalism and the evolution toward holism was begun by Peirce, James, and Dewey in the first decades of the twentieth century. It was completed in the second half of the century by the combined work of Quine, Davidson, and Rorty. Quine's pragmatism is what remains when modern empiricism is purified of its two dogmas of reductionism and the analytic-synthetic distinction. Davidson's pragmatism is what remains when empiricism is further purified of the third dogma of scheme-content dualism. In Rorty's convincing narrative, the same dialectic that led Dewey away from a spectator theory of knowledge also led the later Wittgenstein and Davidson away from the picture theory of language.[2] A radically anti-representationalist philosophy of language is the common thematic in neopragmatic writings.

We contemporary pragmatists do not think that language is the expression of thought, for example, or that subjects and subjectivity can exist apart from the signs of subjectivity in the intersubjective exchange of speech and reply. We do not see anything as having an intrinsic, ineluctable nature. From Quine, we learned to give up the myth of the museum: the image of some object (which is the

---

[2] For the best expressions of Quine's pragmatism, in contrast to positivistic empiricism, see W. V. Quine, "The Pragmatists' Place in Empiricism" (1981) in *Pragmatism: Its Sources and Prospects*, ed. Robert J. Mulvaney and Philip M. Zeltner (Columbia: University of South Carolina Press, 1981), pp. 21–39; and W. V. Quine, "Two Dogmas of Empiricism" (1951), in *From a Logical Point of View*, 2nd. ed., rev. (New York: Harper Torchbooks, 1963), pp. 20–46. For Davidson's critique of scheme-content dualism, see the two essays reprinted in the present volume. For Rorty's narrative, see *Philosophy and the Mirror of Nature* (Princeton, N.J.: Princeton University Press, 1979), chapter 6. On the Davidson-Wittgenstein comparison, see Richard Rorty, "Heidegger, Wittgenstein and the Reification of Language," in *The Cambridge Companion to Heidegger*, ed. Charles B. Guignon (Cambridge: Cambridge University Press, 1993), pp. 337–357.

meaning) and next to it some label (the word). From Davidson, we learned to give up the scheme-content dualism: the dogma that our beliefs are formed when we use a contentless scheme to organize a schemeless content. From Rorty, we learned that by following Davidson's truth-conditional semantics, we could even give up a pragmatic theory of truth, and, with it, a set of semantic problems that the older pragmatisms never overcame.

Positively characterized, the new pragmatism is a holism in which all entities are nodes in a network of relations. Knowledge or belief is more like a "raft" (Neurath) than a "pyramid." All the planks of the raft can be pulled up and repaired or scrapped, but not all at once, and only while standing on some provisionally. Or knowledge and belief is more like a "web" (Quine) than a building. Every belief is supported by its ties to its environing beliefs, and ultimately, to the whole web, but nothing serves as a ground or architectonic foundation. In the philosophy of language, holist theories of meaning are the parallel to antifoundationalism in epistemology first seen in the rejection by Peirce, James, and Dewey of both sense experience and rational ideas as privileged, authoritative bases of knowing, or as foundations for the truth of a philosophical system. These American pragmatists also criticized the definition of truth as an isolated correspondence between self and world and affirmed instead an understanding of truth as a social context of meaning shaped by the practical implications of ideas.

Having deconstructed all forms of foundationalism, pragmatists argue for the contingency of language, self, and community. Truth is no more a property of statements than sentences are a representation of reality. For those who have been convinced by Quine, Davidson, and Rorty, all that pragmatism needs is Tarski's semantic conception of truth according to which to say "X is true" is equivalent to *assenting* to the statement. Truth, then, is a notion that allows us to talk about sentences instead of about "facts," but it has no normative or epistemological import. This introduces an important revision to efforts by James, Dewey, Peirce, and others down to Putnam to defend a pragmatic theory of truth. In the new pragmatism, no theory of truth is generated at all, the whole idea of "correspondence with reality" is considered hopeless to assess, and the holistic character of belief and meaning is accented. The new pragmatism is neither realism nor anti-realism, still less is it a form of linguistic idealism.

Pragmatism and Truth

Pontius Pilate's vexing question "What is truth?" concerns what truth consists in, not our ways of finding out what is true. Pragmatic theories of truth were once mistakenly thought to form a third type of answer to this question, along with correspondence and coherence theories. In this section, I argue that all three, as *theories of* truth, are flawed and that pragmatism means *never having to offer a full-fledged theory of truth* at all. I agree with John P. Murphy and Richard Rorty in characterizing Davidson as the first pragmatist to give a satisfactory account of truth.[3]

Correspondence theories depend upon an agreement between a proposition and a state of affairs. They have faltered over what "facts" are, and what it means to "correspond." The existence of a correspondence relation cannot be established by confronting an assertion with an object and then noticing that a relation called "corresponding" holds or fails to hold. What would such a confrontation look like? How can we compare a belief with a non-belief to see if they match? We have no way to pair off sentences or beliefs with things in the world in order to answer such questions as, Which objects made that sentence true? or, Which objects does that sentence accurately represent? This is because there is no way to divide language from world in such a way as to resolve the question that is at issue between correspondence theories and coherence

---

[3] See Rorty's essay reprinted in this volume, "Pragmatism, Davidson, and Truth," as well as John P. Murphy, *Pragmatism From Peirce to Davidson* (Boulder: Westview Press, 1990). Although he has since wobbled, Davidson could describe himself in 1987 as a "pragmatist" about truth. Cf. his "Afterthoughts, 1987" in *Reading Rorty*, ed. Alan Malachowski (Oxford: Blackwell, 1990), p. 134. Cf. also Davidson, "The Structure and Content of Truth," *Journal of Philosophy* 87 (1990): 279–328 where Davidson repudiates correspondence and coherence theories alike. For his regret that he ever called his own theory a coherence theory, see "Afterthoughts, 1987," p. 136–8. Davidson has been explicit about the relationship of his own views to Rorty's: "Where we differ, if we do, is on whether there remains a question how, given that we cannot 'get outside our beliefs and our language so as to find some test other than coherence,' we nevertheless can have knowledge of, and talk about, an objective public world which is not of our own making. I think this question does remain, while I suspect that Rorty doesn't think so." ("Afterthoughts, 1987," p. 137.)

theories: is it the world itself, or other beliefs, which is the truth-maker? Nor is there any way to answer the question, Is it the object in itself, or the object under a description, which is represented?

Coherence theories define truth in terms of a relation among beliefs that fit together in an ideally coherent system of representations. This cannot mean, however, that all the sentences in a consistent set of sentences are true. Rather, proponents of coherence theories of truth are concerned with sets of beliefs, or of sentences held to be true, whose consistency is supposed to be enough to make them true. But the objection to this is that many different sets of belief are possible which are not consistent with one another.[4] Worse still, the argument for coherence as constitutive of the *nature* of truth depends upon raising the specter of radical relativism. Having raised this specter once, what is to prevent us from raising it again to ask what makes even an ideally coherent system of propositions true? The best answers to this question, according to Davidson, have the defect of inviting back an idealist metaphysics which makes ideas or mental data the source and criterion of knowledge. But if we have to embrace idealism in order to evade skepticism, coherentism is not a happy account.

Pragmatic theories of truth have often been presented as an alternative to correspondence and coherence theories, but from the beginning, critics have found fault with pragmatism's conception of truth. In Bertrand Russell's caricature of pragmatism, there is no need "to trouble our heads about what really is true; what is *thought* to be true is all that need concern us." Russell thought that William James believed that "although there is no evidence in favor of religion, we ought nevertheless to believe it if we find satisfaction in so doing."[5] James, for his part, called this kind of interpretation of his pragmatism "the usual slander" and adamantly complained of critics who, he wrote, "accuse me of summoning people to say 'God exists,' even when he doesn't exist, because forsooth in my philosophy the 'truth' of the saying doesn't really mean that he exists in any shape

[4] Cf. Davidson, "The Structure and Content of Truth," p. 305.

[5] Bertrand Russell, *A History of Western Philosophy* (NY: Simon & Schuster, [1945] 1967), p. 818; cf. "William James's Conception of Truth" [1908], in *Philosophical Essays*, p. 124.

whatever, but only that to say so feels good."[6] Indeed, careful readers of James understand that the notion that a proposition could be factually false but emotionally useful and consequently true never entered into James's formulation, not even in the controversial "Will to Believe" writings which *do* call for satisfaction of an emotional, moral, or aesthetic sort, but only when a hypothesis is factually or logically *in*determinate *and* when "reality is led to." With regard to the religious hypothesis, James insisted that "the truth of 'God' has to run the gauntlet of all our other beliefs."[7]

In the logical positivist caricature of pragmatism, A. J. Ayer understood James to be saying that the statement that God exists means no more than that people have spiritual requirements which religious belief may be found to satisfy and that the pragmatic content of the belief in God's existence consists merely in the feeling of optimism it induces.[8] Not surprisingly, Ayer himself regarded religious beliefs as "purely subjective" cases in which "no discernible" facts are available.

While it is not possible to make everything James said on the subject of truth totally consistent, the best understanding of his version of pragmatic truth aligns it with statements about open possibilities rather than statements about settled facts. That is to say, James's remarks about truth fall into one of two classes of propositions: either about settled facts or about open possibilities. The first class is factually and logically determinate, but the second class concerns indeterminate matters where "faith in a fact can help create the fact." Religious fundamentalists, realists, and literalists all locate the question of the truth or falsity of religious beliefs in the first class of settled facts, as though a definite fact of the matter obtains, whether we know it or not. By contrast, religious pragmatists throughout the twentieth century have made a different, more interesting move, placing religious hypotheses in the second class as open possibilities or ideals, *not* already actual truths antecedently given. This opens up the reinterpretation of the doctrinal and creedal

[6] William James, *Pragmatism and the Meaning of Truth* (Cambridge and London: Harvard University Press, 1978), p. 172.

[7] *Pragmatism and the Meaning of Truth*, p. 272, 56; cf. *The Varieties of Religious Experience*, p. 341–42.

[8] A. J. Ayer, *Philosophy in the Twentieth Century* (NY: Random House, 1982), p. 82; and *Pragmatism and the Meaning of Truth*. xx–xxi.

side of religious life as dealing not with matters of fact but with matters of aspiration, not with matters of *faith*, but with matters of *hope*. The most common pragmatist critique of all forms of traditional religious thought, therefore, is that they transpose matters of aspiration too solidly into matters of fact, converting ideal aims into actual powers.

Consistent with this interpretation, we would have to dismiss James's confusing use of "truer" and "truest" to mean, roughly, "better" and "best" and concede that overall James simply failed to produce a satisfactory definition or theory of truth. Charles Sanders Peirce and John Dewey also failed. Peirce proposed that "the opinion which is fated to be ultimately agreed to by all who investigate is what we mean by the truth, and the object represented in this opinion is the real."[9] Peirce could assume there *is* some true opinion to be found, but this assumption is challenged by many contemporary neopragmatists. Why should we posit convergence to a single result? The idea that truth is a *goal* of inquiry seems odd, insofar as it refers to something we could not recognize when we had found it, and from which we shall never be able to measure our distance. Furthermore, as Hilary Putnam has pointed out in his "naturalistic fallacy" argument, it is always possible to say "yada, yada, yada —but maybe not true," no matter what is put in the blank. The argument applies also to Putnam's own definition of truth as idealized rational acceptability.

Turning to Dewey, we find a pragmatic definition of truth as warranted assertibility (of our sentences). This confuses "truth" with a property that accrues to an idea when it is confirmed by inquiry. Wanting to reject the notion of truth as an immutable property, Dewey made it a mutable property, but the mistake, from the standpoint of later pragmatists like Davidson, was in making truth any kind of property at all. Saying a statement is true is not a way of describing the statement but of endorsing it. The common error made by the early pragmatists was in treating truth as a property rather

[9] *Collected Papers*, 5:407; cf. 5:384, 5:494, 5:553. Peirce's definition can be taken in two strikingly different ways: either (i) that truth cannot be known until the end of time (notoriously long in coming) or (ii) that the current best opinion of the community of inquirers generates fallible truth claims. In the first, eschatological foundations bolster conjectures. In the second, consensus replaces foundations of any kind. For the sake of simplicity I am taking account only of (i) here.

than as a redundant expression, similar to "ditto." To say "It is true that this paper is forty pages," means no more than this paper is forty pages, and to say "It is false that this paper is forty pages" means this paper is not forty pages. On this alternative account, "truth" has no normative or epistemological import. If that is thought to be a weakness, i.e., nothing is said about what it is to *be* true, this is also its merit, for it allows us to talk about sentences instead of about objects and to avoid the futility involved in trying to compare language and reality as two distinct realms.

Neopragmatism and Holism

One of the principal advances of the new pragmatism has been a formulation of pragmatism that does not saddle it with correspondence, coherence, or even with pragmatic theories of truth. Thus freed, pragmatism can be usefully described in terms of the three-part characterization offered by Richard Rorty.[10] First, it is *anti-essentialism applied to notions like "truth," "knowledge," "language," "morality," and similar objects of philosophical theorizing.* Anti-essentialism by any other name is holism, the attempt to replace a distinction between schemes and content with a seamless, indefinitely extensible web of relations. That holism's espousal of relationalism is not an assertion of relativism is evident in the second characterization of pragmatism as making the claim that *there is no epistemological difference between truth about what ought to be and truth about what is, nor any metaphysical difference between morality and science.* In other words, for the pragmatist, ethics and physics are equally objective. No anti-relativist could want more. Third, according to Rorty, *there are no constraints on inquiry save conversational ones.* This, too, should be interpreted in a non-relativistic manner to mean that in the wake of the death of all the former underwriters (God, The Forms, the Absolute, Being) there are still constraints that obtain this side of "anything goes" and they are all socially evolved and consensually decided for pragmatic purposes. As Davidson shows perhaps better than Rorty, the very condition for our knowing any language for conversation or inquiry of any kind is the ascription to it of truth-conditions without which we could not even get started on translation, let alone succeed.

---

10 Richard Rorty, "Pragmatism, Relativism, and Irrationalism" in *Consequences of Pragmatism* (Minneapolis: University of Minnesota Press, 1982): 160–175.

Davidson's answer to Pontius Pilate's question utilizes a device called Convention T, summarized in Penner's essay in this section. Taken from the logician Alfred Tarski, Convention T consists of rendering any declarative sentence in the form of a tautology, i.e., "'snow is white' is true if and only if snow is white.'" In this way, the proposition satisfies its own truth-conditions simply by virtue of its logical structures. According to Davidson, Convention T requires that a satisfactory theory of truth for a language L "must entail, for every sentence s of L, a theorem of the form 's is true if and only if p' where 's' is replaced by a description of s and 'p' by s itself if L is English, and by a translation of s into English if L is not English."[11] Obviously, this is neither a definition of truth, pragmatic or otherwise, nor a way of testing for truth in any given instance. It is something altogether more pragmatically useful: it shows us, contrary to relativist confusions, that the attitude of *holding-true* is a primitive concept that logically precedes questions of semantic interpretation. To relativize "true" to a language, conceptual scheme, paradigm, or framework is to forget this priority and incoherently try to reverse it. What is new and improved in Davidson's version of truth-conditional semantics, therefore, is the starting-point: instead of assuming that meaning determines truth, one starts with truth, so that the attitude of holding-true is the basis of all understanding and translation. This explains how it is that we do, in fact, translate from one "conceptual scheme" to another.

Like James and Dewey, Davidsonian pragmatists reject the subject-object dualism that creates the need in the first place to explain the nature of truth as consisting in some relation such as "fitting" or "organizing" of the world to "mind" or "language." Instead of referring to a state of affairs the existence of which explains the practical successes of those who hold true beliefs, the term "true" is more like a term of praise or endorsement. In addition to this endorsing use, Rorty thinks that pragmatists may also add two other things—a cautionary use, and a disquotational use.[12] The cautionary use of "true" occurs in such remarks as "I agree that your belief that Mary is the mother of God is perfectly justified on the basis of

---

11 Donald Davidson, *Inquiries into Truth and Interpretation* (Oxford: Clarendon Press, 1984), p. 194.

12 See Rorty's "Pragmatism, Davidson, and Truth," reprinted as Chapter 15 in this volume.

scripture; still, it may not be true." The disquotational use of "true" is captured by the principle, 'p' is true if and only if 'p'. It occurs in such remarks as "If the testimony of the last witness is true, then at least one of the parties is lying."

Pragmatists thus have an account of truth which has a place for each of these uses while avoiding the early Jamesian idea that the expediency of a belief can be explained by its truth. Saying this much tallies with the characterization of pragmatism as antiessentialism with respect to truth. In other words, "true" has no explanatory uses; it is not the name of a distinct norm.

Furthermore, pragmatists think we understand all there is to know about the relation of beliefs to the world when we understand their causal relations with the world. Our knowledge of how to apply terms like "about" and "true of" to sentences is fallout from a naturalistic account of linguistic behavior. On this account, no relations of "being made true" are needed between beliefs and the world. Therefore, pragmatists can safely abjure all epistemological and metaphysical differences between facts and values.

Finally, if the idea of "being made true" is empty and misleading, then to pragmatists there is no point to the debates between realism and anti-realism, that is, debates between professional philosophers who claim that an objective world (one that exists independent of our thought and language) makes our true statements true (the realists) and those who take issue with that claim (the anti-realists). Accordingly, pragmatists are committed to renouncing all constraints on inquiry save "conversational" ones, just as Rorty has recommended.

Both Davidson and Rorty, on my reading, regard the question "What *makes* sentence S true?" as nothing more than a confused version of the question "What is it for sentence S to be true?" It is confused because it suggests "that truth must be explained in terms of a relation between a sentence as a whole and some entity, perhaps a fact, or state of affairs."[13] In the history of philosophy this is the very move that has spawned what have been termed "representations," and that has always returned us to a correspondence theory. "It is good to be rid of representations," according to Davidson, "and with them the correspondence theory of truth, for it is thinking that

---

[13] *Inquiries into Truth and Interpretation*, p. 70.

there are representations which engenders thoughts of relativism."[14] Even more explicitly, in a passage that deserves repeated attention, Davidson writes: "Nothing, . . . no *thing*, makes sentences and theories true: not experience, not surface irritations, not the world, can make a sentence true. *That* experience takes a certain course, that our skin is warmed or punctured, that the universe is finite, these facts, if we like to talk that way, make sentences and theories true. But this point is put better without mention of facts. The sentence 'My skin is warm' is true if and only if my skin is warm. Here there is no reference to a fact, a world, an experience, or a piece of evidence."[15] In other words, by attending to the holistic character of language, belief, and meaning, something all pragmatists have urged, we can drop the idea of states-of-the-world serving as truth-makers.

Pragmatic Justifications of Religious Belief

If pragmatism is no longer taken as a theory of meaning or of truth, for reasons that Davidson has supplied, it is still frequently taken as a mode of justification. The application of pragmatic norms to the evaluation and justification of religious beliefs is advocated by many recent Anglo-American theologians and philosophers of religion who have given up on capital-T Truth but who still care about reasons and warrants. Justified belief is said to be what passes as true. My argument in this section is that the appeal to pragmatic norms in the justification of religious belief either warps pragmatism into functionalism or winds up so inconclusively as to be useless.

Pragmatic justifications of religious beliefs have usually been specified as a matter of the practical effects, fruitfulness, interest, or value of the beliefs held by individuals. The final recourse is said to be to the idea that a religious belief is true because we find that we must act as if it were true, or because it is most consistent with certain practical purposes, or because it is most beneficial in helping us cope, or because when coherent with other beliefs about matters it makes of our vision of reality a satisfying whole. All such utilitarian or consequentialist arguments turn pragmatism into a version of functionalism, whose flaws we have already explored in this volume.

---

[14] Donald Davidson, "The Myth of the Subjective," reprinted as Chapter 10 in this volume.

[15] *Inquiries into Truth and Interpretation*, p. 194.

Even when the functionalist fallacy is not explicitly committed in the course of formal reasoning, informal appeals of a vulgar pragmatic type fail to explain religious beliefs. At best, the appeal to presumed benefits, consequences, or fruits of beliefs as implicitly justificatory of those beliefs is frustratingly vague and wholesale. Many people no doubt make some rough, overall judgment about the relative benefits and deficits of "religion" as one cultural interest among others. The problem is that these impressionistic, anecdotal generalities cancel each other out. It proves impossible to assess overall interpretations of life or "visions of reality," especially in terms of their pragmatic utility. This is because pragmatic consequences—such as human flourishing, orientation in life, peace of mind—may occur, if and when they do occur, independently of the religious beliefs in question, or in spite of them. In the absence of any way to rule out alternative explanations of the very same beliefs, pragmatic justifications as typically employed in philosophy of religion do not carry any explanatory power. In the end, they overstate the connection between truth and utility. Granted that true beliefs are a good basis for action, why take this to be the very nature of truth? True beliefs may foster success, but actions based on false beliefs may produce beneficial consequences also.

Historicist and pragmatist philosophers of religion usually recommend pragmatic adjudication of what sort of life one religious vision entails in comparison with others, allowing for the ongoing testing and revising of beliefs and practices in light of the forms of life they make possible. This sort of appeal, however, becomes so latitudinous as to admit everything and to exclude nothing and therefore to become indistinguishable from life itself. The criterion, or the norm, or the standard of evaluation cannot be what "works" or what has "practical effects" for a form of life. Everything works, everything impacts a form of life. To be anything at all, a thing (pragma) must work; yet this cannot supply us with a criterion of choice among or between religious systems. Further specification of the pragmatic norm in terms of "human flourishing" or "life-enhancing rather than death-dealing" may introduce some restrictiveness but only at the price of moving the metaphilosophical question up a notch. What counts as "flourishing"? What counts as "life-enhancing"? In the wake of the culture wars, widespread disagreement in ethics, philosophy, the law, and politics, we have no agreement over how to define "flourishing," much less "life-enhancing" or even "the common good." *Nor should we.* My point is not that everything must conduce toward agreement, but that as long as disagreement over these matters is endemic it will be hard for philosophy of religion to command public and critical acceptance. Its validity is likely to be decided more and more in that private realm to which Richard Rorty relegates religion.

The very idea that practical tests can validate religious beliefs (or theological claims) is itself problematic. Even when religious beliefs are understood as fallible, historically-situated, and non-foundational, requiring or permitting nothing other than pragmatic validation, there is still a need to decide at what point to call off inquiry and conclude, provisionally and pragmatically, one way or another. How would one know that point? And how would one justify one's claim to knowledge of it?

Finally, if religious beliefs are to be judged on the basis of an empirical claim about the pragmatic benefits they produce, rather than on the grounds that such propositional attitudes are *true,* they are vulnerable to being outweighed by harmful consequences if the scales happen to tip the other way. Ramakrishna is said to have compared religion to a cow that kicks, but gives milk too. Religious beliefs, theological systems, and religious traditions present very mixed and ambiguous historical records. Trying to assess them for their pragmatic benefits is hardly a very practical undertaking and, when indulged in by theologians, often amounts to special pleading: the positive and purifying aspects of a religion are selectively attended to but not equally its paltry and pulverizing side. The ways in which a particular religion may be shown to function in the benign and salutary manner approved by its adherents helps to obscure the fact that it may also function to express and reinforce superstition, irrationality, fanaticism, sexism, infantilism, and eschatological abstentions from real moral and political tasks. Among scholars of religion, debates over the functional or dysfunctional place of religion in human culture continue to end in a stalemate, with no methodological or theoretical way of determining whether the preponderance of empirical evidence favors Freudian and Marxian reductions, for example, or theological interpretations. The case can be argued either way, with overabundant and inconclusive evidence and counterexamples in support of both. In light of this impasse, no assessment of the practical effects of a religion, or of a theology, can ever be conclusive because the "practical effects" of any particular religious test case are impossible to correlate in a cause-effect manner. At a more theoretical level, the same difficulty besets the pragmatic justifications of theologies called for by a variety of recent historicist theologians.

At the existential level of analyzing one's own beliefs, it is often tempting to take "pragmatic difference" to mean "personal benefit" or "consequences for an individual." Unlike Peirce and Dewey, William James leaned unfortunately in this direction, giving rise to vulgar interpretations of his pragmatism and risking the conflation of pragmatism with existentialism. The problem with the existentialized version of pragmatic justification is that *any* beliefs whatsoever make a pragmatic difference to some degree in the lives of the individuals holding them, but this is a difference that is compatible, for all we know, with their being illusory or false. What we want to show by way of the "pragmatic difference" of a belief system or a theology is what difference its *truth* would make in a public way. A recommendation that we test them in light of the forms of life they make possible does not provide a workable norm either at the existential or the communal level, for the reason that Michel Foucault, a keen observer of human practices, once articulated: "People know what they do; they frequently know why they do what they do; but what they don't know is what what they do does."[16]

Conceptual Scheming and a Common System

If pragmatism is not functionalism, logical empiricism, or existentialism, neither is it relativism. Pursuing the implications of holism further, we can better understand the incoherence involved in relativism concerning the truth of religious beliefs. Davidson's influential paper "On the Very Idea of a Conceptual Scheme," reprinted in Part III of this volume, argues against all those conceptual schemers who hold that truth is relative to conceptual schemes of one kind or another, whether they are termed epistemes, paradigms, frameworks, or symbol systems. The notion of conceptual relativism, according to Davidson, depends on a third dogma of empiricism—the dualism of scheme and content, or of organizing system and something waiting to be organized. It is, in fact, this fundamental dichotomy that tempts many philosophers of religion to

[16] Quoted in H. Dreyfus and P. Rabinow, *Michel Foucault: Beyond Structuralism and Hermeneutics* (Chicago: University of Chicago Press, 1982), p. 187.

think of different religious systems as incommensurable worldviews, and also lends plausibility not only to the idea of the world as a *view*, but to the possibility of *alternative* views. If the dualism of scheme and content is purged from its widespread employment in the philosophy of religion, relativism will be eliminated as well. What will remain, as Terry Godlove's article in this volume shows, is diversity of belief, but that is as non-relativistic as can be.

Contrary to the claims of those who hold that experience, belief, or even reality is relative to conceptual schemes, *Weltanschauungen*, or Wittgensteinian forms of life, all viewed as incommensurable, holism entails that we could not even be in a position to judge that there are systems of beliefs radically different from our own. For the coherence of the idea of a conceptual scheme requires the coherence of the idea of an alternative conceptual scheme. But this idea is incoherent. If an alternative conceptual scheme is translatable into the first conceptual scheme, it is not alternative, and if it is not translatable, nothing intelligible can be said about it to distinguish it from the first conceptual scheme. In the absence of grounds for distinguishing a conceptual scheme from an alternative conceptual scheme, the distinction collapses, and with it the coherence of the very idea of a conceptual scheme, and with that the coherence of most forms of relativism.

The proposal that something might be true in one religious system but false in another is like the claim that a sentence or proposition *p* is true in A but false in B. But to suppose this is nonsense. If the meaning of a sentence is given by its truth conditions, then one could only suppose that *p* was true in A and false in B by assuming that what was false in B was not really a translation of what was true in A—for if there is a difference in truth value there must be a difference in truth conditions, and for there to be a difference in truth conditions is just what we take as evidence of a difference in meaning.

The key notion is that language is translatability, which should be taken not as a criterion of identity for conceptual schemes, but as a condition of language. Failure of translatability would not tell us that members of another culture or religious tradition have a different conceptual scheme, but only that they have not got language at all. Interpretability, in other words, can be taken as a condition of rational mental life. If it is mistaken to suppose that uninterpretable forms of life express intentions, beliefs, desires at all, then conceptual relativism is impossible. All there is is just THE conceptual scheme, so to speak, within which mental life exists. But even this is misleading, for the term "scheme" summons up "content" and it is the very dualism of scheme and content that we need to reject. Rejecting that dualism, we can have a view of mind and world as constitutively interdependent, inextricably engaged with one another. No intermediary such as "language" or "experience" is needed between "subject and object." Without the distinctness of conceptual scheme and what it organizes, that is, without a formulatable independence of mind and world, truth cannot be relative to conceptual scheme. No duality between scheme and reality can be sustained. Interpretation of other tribes and other scribes than our own is possible because of constitutive constraints which provide the background of agreement that makes disagreement about a common subject matter possible. Other humans must share with us various specific beliefs about the world with which we are in causal contact, various specific conceptual contents, standards of formal rationality, and values, if they are to be regarded as rational agents about some of these matters.

The upshot of this argument is the perhaps initially surprising idea that we must consider the bulk of another culture's beliefs as true, or as Davidson says, "we can take it as given that *most* beliefs are correct."[17] The reason for this is that a belief is identified by its location in a holistic pattern of beliefs, and it is this pattern that determines the subject matter of the belief. On Davidson's analysis, before some object in, or aspect of, the world can become part of the subject matter of belief (true or false), there must be endless true beliefs about the subject matter. "False belief," Davidson says, "tends to undermine the identification of the subject matter; to undermine, therefore, the validity of a description of the belief as being about the subject; and so, in turn, false beliefs undermine the claim that a connected belief is false."[18] What makes interpretation possible, then, is that we can dismiss a priori the chance of massive error. A theory of interpretation cannot be correct that makes a person assent to very many false sentences.

---

[17] Donald Davidson, "Thought and Talk," in *Mind and Language*, ed. Samuel Guttenplan (Oxford: Clarendon Press, 1975), p. 149.

[18] Ibid.

Upon reflection, the disconcerting quality of this argument gives way to a better recognition of what a system of belief is, an appreciation of the way the truth of a *particular* belief must figure in a whole pattern of true beliefs, and an understanding of the fact that even in the clash between theories or cultures or historical epochs, there is no threat of a massive, global collision of belief systems. This is because the vast majority of common truths go unchallenged and unchanged; they can be treated as context-invariant while others are seen to be variable. "Different points of view make sense," Davidson points out, "but only if there is a common coordinate system on which to plot them; yet the existence of a common system belies the claim of dramatic incomparability."[19] Furthermore, "if we cannot find a way to interpret the utterances and other behavior of a creature as revealing a set of beliefs largely consistent and true by our standards, we have no reason to count that creature as rational, as having beliefs, or as saying anything."[20]

Pragmatists will avoid the temptation of thinking that this Davidsonian strategy results in the vindication of our own beliefs and values (whoever "we" are) against others, or of the realist conviction that ultimately there will be a single conceptual scheme secure against conceptual relativism. As Davidson cautions, it is "wrong to announce the glorious news that all mankind—all speakers of language, at least—share a common scheme and ontology. For if we cannot intelligibly say that schemes are different, neither can we intelligibly say that they are one."[21] In the clash and clamor of conflicting religious beliefs, relativism will not be rendered implausible by vindicating the view that there is only one rational framework, or a single correct religious representation of reality. Not only do those who declare rationality or truth relative employ the scheme-content duality in order to make plausible the possibility of alternative schemes, but those who think relativism can be defeated only by a defense of objective truth and realism also presume the same dualism, since they require that at the end of inquiry we will be in possession of the *one true* scheme.

Does this argument suffice against relativism in all forms? Has Davidson provided reasons to reject cases that fall short of asserting

---

[19] *Inquiries into Truth and Interpretation*, p. 67.

[20] *Inquiries into Truth and Interpretation*, p. 137.

[21] *Inquiries into Truth and Interpretation*, p. 20.

complete incommensurability, defined as untranslatability? I think not. In a seldom-noted aside in his essay "The Myth of the Subjective," Davidson comments that we can still have what he terms a "harmless relativism" described as "just the familiar relativism of position in space and time." This is philosophically unexciting, he thinks. "Minds are many; nature is one," he tells us. "Each of us has one's own position in the world, and hence one's own perspective on it. It is easy to slide from this truism to some confused notion of conceptual relativism."[22] One cannot help but notice, however, all that is suppressed in this statement and glossed over in the highly formal terms of the argumentation. *Who* is it who occupies different relative positions in space and time? Not *minds*, but human *persons*. *Embodied* persons who are always and everywhere specified in terms of race, class, and gender. Embodied persons whose distances from each other in space constitute cultural differences, and whose distances from each other in time constitute differences in historical consciousness. Reflection on the insistent particularities incorporated in these differences is precisely what has made us postmoderns so hyperconscious and contextualist in our thinking, to the point where Davidsonian reminders of more massive background agreements and taken-for-granted sameness of belief seem dwarfed most of the time. Were Davidson himself to trace out in a less formal and more particular mode all that is entailed by the "harmless relativism" he himself acknowledges, he could, I suggest, complete the historicist turn that he has been making, travelling the same route as the great historicist philosophers from Hegel to Dewey, all of them challenging the distinction between the sensory content of experience and any constituting scheme. His historicist and pragmatist turn remains incomplete without further explication of the "harmless relativism" that attends positionality in all its aspects.

Further Implications for Philosophy of Religion

Rather than pursue that explication here, I would like to draw several implications from these Davidsonian reflections for the philosophy of religion.

An obvious implication of Davidson's principle of charity, but one frequently overlooked in philosophy of religion, is that the real

[22] "The Myth of the Subjective," p. 159.

issues we face have to do not with overcoming Relativism, which offers greatly exaggerated accounts of our cognitive predicament, but with adjudicating Disagreement. This issue—of disagreement, of diversity of conviction, of pluralism of practice—is, of course, not identical with relativism. The interesting feature of cases of evaluative disagreement is that they do not necessarily arise from skepticism about the lack of an independent and neutral standard for judging between theories or beliefs. Indeed, the most critical cases of apparent incommensurability arise not from our inability to make sense of other people's bizarre beliefs, but, as David Wong has shown, precisely from those situations in which we *are* able to understand and see how different their beliefs are from our own. We can see, for example, that their beliefs arise in the context of a life that people would want to live and, as Wong concludes, we can understand this because we can relate features of our own traditions to theirs in such a way that we become aware of what is gained from that sort of life and what we have lost.[23] A principle of charity is *forced* upon us; if we are to maximize the intelligibility of other speakers, we need to assume that most of their beliefs are in agreement with our own.

Some will object that agreement, even massive agreement, does not guarantee truth, and disagreement does not by itself spell error. This last observation, however, misses the point. The basic claim is simply that much community of belief is needed to provide a basis for communication or understanding. The extended claim is that objective error can occur only in a setting of largely true belief. Agreement may not make for truth, but much of what is agreed must be true if some of what is agreed is false. Pragmatists can describe the pattern truth must make among sentences, but without telling us where the pattern falls.

To other philosophers of religion it may seem that this principle gives us merely a formal context for seeing that communication between language users is possible only if they share massive agreement on many more things than those over which they diverge, but that it does nothing to affect the most worrisome cases of intense and interminable *dis*agreement in human culture, cases that are

[23] See David B. Wong, "Three Kinds of Incommensurability," in *Relativism: Interpretation and Confrontation*, ed. Michael Krausz (University of Notre Dame Press, 1989), 140–158.

nowhere more evident than in the area of religion. If Davidsonian arguments serve to show that most of our beliefs must be true, how can this reassurance about the limits of disagreement be reconciled with our knowledge about the many bizarre beliefs and puzzling practices found throughout the religions of the world? Does it bring us any closer to determining questions of truth in the worldwide conflict and collision of religious beliefs?

Having disposed with Terry Godlove of anything as dramatic as the idea that Methodists and Muslims, Taoists and doubters live in different worlds, and having dropped any representation of other cultures, religions, or moralities as self-contained, incommensurate, ideological schemes which can only be understood from inside and not judged from outside, we still face the unexceptional fact of human convictional diversity. The diversity of religious outlooks which command our respect or tolerance is plural. Disagreements among them are profound, genuine, and seemingly intractable. Focusing on the fact of disagreement rather than the ruse of relativism helps in formulating a new set of questions not normally raised by philosophers of religion. Why should agreement be valued over disagreement, or sameness over difference? Why suppose that something like consensus and agreement is as important in religion as it is in, for instance, government? Why is the existence of a pluralistic spectrum of religious beliefs across the cultures of the world cause for philosophical adjudication, as though agreement is the royal road to rationality and alone will produce a shield against irrationalist resentment, hatred, and violence? These assumptions tell us something about the centripetal forces at work in our increasingly global world.

At the same time, however, philosophy of religion has yet to theorize diversity of belief in any way that does not lead either to the absolutizing of some one convictional set above all others or to the relativizing of the notion of truth altogether in light of the mutually conflicting claims of different religions. No one has a good account of this. The most popular approach in World Religions textbooks constructs a simplistic narrative according to which all peoples relate to some "ultimate reality" which each group sees partially—the story of the blind men and the elephant is meant to illustrate this. But the elephant begs all the important questions. In addition to criticizing the conservative and protectionist strategies to which this animal is put (epitomized in its use as that slow-moving symbol of the

Republican Party), pragmatists will point out that no one can stand, or even conceive of what it *would* be to stand, at the point where these perspectives all join. And if we *could* imagine the full syncretistic elephant, it would be one in which all the colorful particularities of the living traditions are bleached out.

Relativizing the elephant to different perspectives has become a practice so rampant among philosophers of religion that I have no confidence that this model will be consigned to the Humean flames for its "sophistry and illusion" very soon. Nonetheless, on the assumption that Davidson has demolished the scheme-content distinction, I suggest two important methodological points that follow for philosophy of religion. First, "religion" should not be treated as *a* scheme, alongside science, for example, or in contrast to secular culture. The particularities of religious belief cannot be separated in an exclusivist way from the secular meanings of the culture in general. Claims conflicting with or challenging those espoused by partisan, sectarian, and ecclesial groups are holistically related to those groups simply by virtue of that fact that they dwell in a larger culture within which discourse inevitably occurs. If the very idea of a conceptual scheme is incoherent, then "church" or "cult" cannot form a conceptual scheme utterly incommensurable with "culture" or "society."

Second, if "religion" (in the singular) should not be treated as a "scheme" vis-a-vis "science" or "secular culture" as another scheme, neither should diverse religions (in the plural) be thought of as alternative schemes which filter different modes of religious experience. In recent years, a growing number of studies of mysticism and religious experience have depicted different religious traditions and their doctrines as though they are epistemological molds into which the raw, volcanic, unstructured lava of experience rushes to be shaped and organized and served up in the distinctive form of a particular tradition. Different religious traditions are treated as different ways of organizing or interpreting either experience or the world. One is asked to notice the impossibility of ever inspecting from the outside a connection or "fit" between the conceptual scheme and experience (or the world), whether in the case of our own conceptual scheme or of diverse religions. Therefore, it is frequently said, we cannot make any rational choice between profoundly divergent conceptual schemes. Each religious system provides its own incommensurable framework for interpretation according to which it relativizes the world to itself.

The flaw in this model and its use in religious epistemology should now be evident. Not only can we not attach a clear meaning to the notion of neutral or unorganized reality waiting to be organized, so that humans might find orientation and Meaning, but any theory of the nature of experience that interposes an ordering mechanism, a mediating category, between the experiencing subject and the environing world will regularly induce the spectre of skepticism, by inviting doubt as to whether the schematizing mediation is a distortion rather than a distillation of the so-called "content" presumed to be "out there." Far better to eliminate such dubious middlemen and do without any "third" device intruding between ourselves as subjects and the world as object.

If philosophers of religion were to agree with Davidson that talk of alternative conceptual frameworks or incommensurable beliefs is incoherent, and accept also the more radical thesis that the very idea of a conceptual scheme is unintelligible, then we could simply give up the very distinction between conceptual scheme and uninterpreted "given" as this has been employed in the study of religion. And to give *that* up would amount to giving up all transcendental arguments as well as all foundationalist philosophical efforts, exactly the move that pragmatists in a variety of disciplines are currently making. In religious studies, pragmatists can cheerfully bypass all the ongoing disputes about how best to *ground* various basic valuational judgments. We can agree with Rorty that the only thing these foundational efforts accomplish is to take the finished first-level product, jack it up a few levels of abstraction, invent a metaphysical or epistemological or semantical vocabulary into which to translate it, and then announce that it has been *grounded.*[24] As William James said, "These are but names for the facts, taken from the facts, and then treated as previous and explanatory."[25]

Nothing grounds or guarantees convergence to agreement, pragmatists say. In religion as in everything else, the old Socratic virtues are *simply* moral virtues—willingness to talk, to listen to other people, to weigh the consequences of our actions upon other sentient beings. The notion of conversation which Richard Rorty commends

---

[24] Cf. Rorty, *Consequences of Pragmatism*, p. 168.

[25] *Pragmatism and the Meaning of Truth*, p. 126.

as a practical substitute for that of reason is, in the end, ungrounded by appeal to the Platonic and Kantian notions of truth as correspondence, knowledge as discovery of essence, morality as obedience to principle. Can we keep the Socratic virtues without the Platonic defense of them? Can we conduct conversation and inquiry without the conviction that there is something atemporal and binding that lies in the background of all possible conversations? Can we, in short, work without a net, and with full awareness of the sheer contingency of our human beliefs and practices? In philosophy of religion, this is currently the question that divides the pragmatists from the platonists.

The Disenchantment of Subjectivity

The most far-reaching implications of holism for method and theory in philosophy of religion have to do with a new understanding of the public dimension to truth and a critique of the putatively private, subjective, dimension to experience. Modernity's long and difficult enchantment with subjectivity, the outgrowth of a misapprehension of the relation the mind has to the world, may finally be coming to an end. Platonic capital T-Truth, already in dire trouble before Nietzsche and James, is disappearing in our time, but its replacement by a non-epistemic conception of truth is not widely understood. Disappearing also is the human subject, characterized as an autonomous entity, a rational soul, prior to and independent of history, language, and the body. Here too the final vestiges of Aristotelian notions of substance, essence, and intrinsicality still linger.

The holistic assault on the notion that there are subjective states of mind begins by questioning what the content of such a state would be. Positivism argues that the mind imposes a mental "scheme" upon the "content" supplied by the senses. Functionalism argues that a subject, one that is already in possession of a particular need, imposes its "given" antecedent need for satisfaction or orientation on a cultural or historical context in which it is subsequently satisfied or oriented. Existentialism, like relativism, makes subjectivity the deep touchstone of truth and authenticity ("true for me") and language but a medium, either of representation or of expression.

The problem with these familiar methodological starting points is their common difficulty in establishing that any such scheme could account for the relationship which subjects have to the world. They all assume that the mind itself imposes its schemes upon what Davidson calls "an ultimate source of evidence whose character can be wholly satisfied without reference to what it is evidence for."[26] Whenever sensory data, psychological or biological needs, and existential interests and desires have been assumed as the basis of the subject's access to the world, and regarded as independent of the schemes imposed upon the world, we have had no way of ascertaining the adequacy of the schemes themselves. Haunting doubts have accompanied these efforts. How could I ever be sure that the thoughts and feelings that I expressed in language were faithfully reproduced in the thoughts and feelings of another subject? What about the possibility of systematic misunderstanding? In the end, the evidence cannot be kept uncontaminated from the subject, because the disjunction between scheme and evidence locates the scheme itself within a subjective realm standing apart from all evidence. The subject, detached from the world, defined in the first place as standing outside the world it experiences and as having access to that world only by virtue of an imposition of its own organizing schemes, can hardly answer for the connection of its beliefs with the world it experiences. "Our beliefs purport to represent something objective," Davidson points out, "but the character of their subjectivity prevents us from taking the first step in determining whether they correspond to what they pretend to represent."[27]

The next step in the disenchantment of subjectivity consists in seeing that the received account of the subject simply cannot explain the communication of beliefs. Alternatively, holism understands that this is possible only because beliefs themselves have as their objects a world which is shared by speakers of language. The relation between beliefs and their objects is causal, rather than representational or expressive. If beliefs are caused by their objects, no place appears for uninterpreted data upon which the subject is presumed to impose itself, and thus there is no coherent account of the realm of the subjective itself. In light of the impossibility of using language to describe states of mind which are presumed to be independent of the public objects which are their causes, no such distinction between the subjective and a public world can be established. Any attempt to

---

[26] "The Myth of the Subjective," p. 162.

[27] "The Myth of the Subjective," p. 163.

communicate a realm of subjectivity is obliged to evoke the very world which the subjective is presumed to stand outside, and over against which it has been privileged.

What are these states of mind possessed by a subject and known only by their causal relations to the world? According to the holism of the mental, they are relationships which the mind has to the world, and no distinction can be made between those mental states which have as their object the causal relations among the objects of the world and those mental states which instead display an affective attitude toward objects in the world. Interests or values are no more subjective and no less caused than are other causal relations in the world. Doubts, wishes, beliefs, and desires are identified in part "by the social and historical context in which they are acquired" and are in this respect "like other states that are identified by their causes."[28] The social and historical context defines a public space in relation to which a subject's states of mind are publicly accessible and therefore knowable. No demarcation, dichotomy, or dualism intrudes between publicly available forms of knowledge and the "private" desires, values, or interests upon which the received tradition has based its enchantment with subjectivity's special inscrutibility, ineffability, and autonomy. From a holist perspective, however, desire, value, and interest are as public, scrutable, effable, and relational as anything else. And that is because relations are constitutive of the mental, not merely a consequence of having a mental state. Thus Davidson can conclude that "the very possibility of thought demands shared standards of truth and objectivity."[29]

Holism requires us to start thinking about religion and the human sciences in quite new ways now that human subjectivity is not "inside" us and there is no "outside" either, now that the myth of the given has been replaced by the world's causal sway over our entire belief structure, and now that we can see the inwardness or subjectivity once celebrated by religious existentialists like Kierkegaard and extolled by romantic poets like Wordsworth to have been a literary effect, produced by prolonged prominence accorded to indexical pronouns. Meaning is social before it is individual.

In the heyday of theology, the conception of subjectivity as a free-standing and self-mastering spiritual entity was transparently

---

[28] "The Myth of the Subjective," p. 170.

[29] "The Myth of the Subjective," p. 171.

only a reflection of the idea of *imago dei*. Holism has spelled the end of the long fallout in Western philosophy of that self-image. The disenchantment of subjectivity means that the godlike subject, as an individual center of autonomous consciousness and will, is no longer the source of the world's meaning, its self-identity no longer a simple given, its privacy ("only I know exactly what I mean") no longer self-transparent. In our time, a more edifying and bracing self-image is emerging in which the sharp contrast between subject and object, mind and world is blurred or erased. Giving a semantic twist to Jesus' admonishment, we might say we have lost our soul but have gained the whole world.

Suggested Readings

Davidson, Donald. 1980. *Essays on Action and Events.* Oxford: Clarendon Press.

—— 1984. *Inquiries into Truth and Interpretation.* Cambridge: Clarendon Press. These collections contain Davidson's principal philosophical papers.

—— 1990. The Structure and Content of Truth. *The Journal of Philosophy* 87, no. 6: 279–328.

—— 1996. The Folly of Trying to Define Truth. *The Journal of Philosophy* 93, no. 6: 263–278. These articles are Davidson's most recent to date on the subject of truth.

Evans, Gareth, and McDowell, John (eds.). 1976. *Truth and Meaning.* Oxford: Clarendon Press. Good background to a variety of views.

Godlove Jr., Terry F. 1997. *Religion, Interpretation, and Diversity of Belief.* Macon, GA: Mercer University Press. An important study of Davidson and holism in light of Kant, Durkheim, and the problem of religious belief.

LePore, Ernest (ed.). 1986. *Truth and Interpretation: Perspectives on the Philosophy of Donald Davidson.* Oxford: Basil Blackwell. Valuable essays of criticism and explication.

Malpas, J. E. 1992. *Donald Davidson and the Mirror of Meaning.* Cambridge: Cambridge University Press. Chapter II gives a particularly good account of holism.

Murphy, John P. 1990. *Pragmatism: From Peirce to Davidson.* Boulder: Westview Press. Demonstrates how Quine, Putnam, Rorty, and Davidson carry on and develop the American pragmatic tradition.

Rorty, Richard. 1996. Religious Faith, Intellectual Responsibility, and Romance. *American Journal of Theology and Philosophy*, vol. 17, No. 2, May: 121–140. One of the few writings to date from a neopragmatist philosopher that deals with religious belief.